2014

DESKBOOK ENCYCLOPEDIA OF
AMERICAN SCHOOL LAW

Electronic Communications

Threats and Bullying

Freedom of Speech

School Athletics

Student Search and Seizure

Students with Disabilities

Center for
Education & Employment Law

Center for Education & Employment Law
P.O. Box 3008
Malvern, Pennsylvania 19355

> "This publication is designed to provide accurate and authoritative information in regard to
> the subject matter covered. It is sold with the understanding that the publisher is not engaged
> in rendering legal, accounting or other professional service. If legal advice or other expert
> assistance is required, the services of a competent professional person should be sought."—
> *from a Declaration of Principles jointly adopted by a Committee of the American Bar
> Association and a Committee of Publishers and Associations.*

ISBN 978-1-933043-72-2
ISSN 1058-4919

The Library of Congress has cataloged this serial title as follows:
Deskbook Encyclopedia of American School Law.—1980/81—Rosemount, Minn.:
Informational Research Systems, 1981-

v.; 23 cm.

Annual.
Published 2013   by: Center for Education & Employment Law
Prepared by the editors of: Legal Notes for Education,
1980/81-
1. Educational law and legislation—United States—Digests. 2. Educational law and legislation—
United States—Periodicals. I. Informational Research Systems (Washington, D.C.) II. Oakstone Legal
& Business Publishing III. Center for Education & Employment Law IV. Legal Notes for Education.
V. Title: Encyclopedia of American School Law.
KF4114.D46   92-054912
                                    344.73'07'02638—dc19
                                    [347.304702638]
                                                    AACR 2#M#MARC-S

Library of Congress   [8704r86]rev

Cover Design by Patricia Jacoby

Other Titles Published By
Center for Education & Employment Law:

Deskbook Encyclopedia of Employment Law
Deskbook Encyclopedia of Public Employment Law
Higher Education Law in America
Keeping Your School Safe & Secure: A Practical Guide
Legal Update for Teachers: The Complete Principal's Guide
Private School Law in America
Students with Disabilities and Special Education

TABLE OF CONTENTS

CHAPTER ONE
Student Rights

CHAPTER TWO
Student Discipline

CHAPTER THREE
Freedom of Speech and Association

CHAPTER FOUR
Religion and the Public Schools

CHAPTER FIVE
Academic Practices

CHAPTER SIX
Students with Disabilities

CHAPTER SEVEN
Employment Practices

CHAPTER EIGHT
Employment Discrimination

CHAPTER NINE
Employment Termination, Resignation and Retirement

CHAPTER TEN
Tenure and Due Process

CHAPTER ELEVEN
Labor Relations

TABLE OF CONTENTS

CHAPTER TWELVE
School Liability and Safety

TABLE OF CONTENTS

CHAPTER THIRTEEN
Interscholastic Athletics

CHAPTER FOURTEEN
School Operations

CHAPTER FIFTEEN
Private Schools

TABLE OF CONTENTS

REFERENCE SECTION

INTRODUCTION

The *2014 Deskbook Encyclopedia of American School Law* is a completely updated encyclopedic compilation of state and federal appellate court decisions that affect education. These decisions have been selected and edited by the editorial staff of Center for Education & Employment Law, publishers of *Legal Notes for Education*. Topical classifications have been revised and edited to reflect rapid changes in education law, and many cases reported in previous editions have been re-edited or reclassified.

This edition contains a brief introductory note on the American judicial system and an updated appendix of recent U.S. Supreme Court cases. Also included are portions of the U.S. Constitution that are most frequently cited in education cases. This publication is intended to provide educators and lawyers with access to the most current available cases in education. We believe that you will find this edition even more readable and easier to use than previous editions.

ABOUT THE EDITORS

James A. Roth is the editor of *Legal Notes for Education* and *Special Education Law Update*. He is a co-author of *Students with Disabilities and Special Education Law* and an adjunct program assistant professor at St. Mary's University in Minnesota. Mr. Roth is a graduate of the University of Minnesota and William Mitchell College of Law. He is admitted to the Minnesota Bar.

Thomas D'Agostino is a managing editor at the Center for Education & Employment Law and is the editor of *Higher Education Legal Alert*. He graduated from the Duquesne University School of Law and received his undergraduate degree from Ramapo College of New Jersey. He is a past member of the American Bar Association's Section of Individual Rights and Responsibilities as well as the Pennsylvania Bar Association's Legal Services to Persons with Disabilities Committee. Mr. D'Agostino is admitted to the Pennsylvania bar.

Curt J. Brown is the Group Publisher of the Center for Education & Employment Law. Prior to assuming his present position, he gained extensive experience in business-to-business publishing, including management of well-known publications such as *What's Working in Human Resources, What's New in Benefits & Compensation, Keep Up to Date with Payroll, Supervisors Legal Update,* and *Facility Manager's Alert.* Mr. Brown graduated from Villanova School of Law and graduated magna cum laude from Bloomsburg University with a B.S. in Business Administration. He is admitted to the Pennsylvania Bar.

HOW TO USE YOUR DESKBOOK

We have designed the *2014 Deskbook Encyclopedia of American School Law* in an accessible format for both attorneys and non-attorneys to use as a research and reference tool toward prevention of legal problems.

Research Tool

As a research tool, our deskbook allows you to conduct your research on two different levels – by topics or cases.

Topic Research

♦ If you have a general interest in a particular **topic** area, our **table of contents** provides descriptive chapter headings containing detailed subheadings from each chapter.

➤ For your convenience, we also include the chapter table of contents at the beginning of each chapter.

Example:
For more information on alternative placements, the table of contents indicates that a discussion of this topic begins in Chapter Two on page 49:

CHAPTER TWO
Student Discipline

♦ If you have a specific interest in a particular **issue**, our comprehensive **index** collects all of the relevant page references to particular issues.

Example:

For more information on defamation and coaches, the index provides references to all of the cases dealing with coaches instead of only those cases dealing with defamation:

Coaching-related issues, 508-516
➤ defamation, 511-513
employment, 508-511
liability, 513-516

Case Research

♦ If you know the **name** of a particular case, our **table of cases** will allow you to quickly reference the location of the case.

Example:

If someone mentioned a case named *Zelman v. Simmons-Harris*, looking in the table of cases, which has been arranged alphabetically, the case would be located under the "Z" section.

Z

Zager v. Chester Community Charter School, 201
Zamecnik v. Indian Prairie School Dist. #204, 110
Zandi v. Fort Wayne Community Schools, 262
Zellner v. Herrick, 357
➤ Zelman v. Simmons-Harris, 172, 173, 174
Zeno v. Pine Plains Cent. School Dist., 19
Zepeda v. Boerne Independent School Dist., 27

✓ Each of the cases summarized in the deskbook also contains the case citation, which will allow you to access the full text of the case if you would like to learn more about it. *See How to Read a Case Citation, p. 619.*

◆ If your interest lies in cases from a **particular state**, our **table of cases by state** will identify the cases from your state and direct you to their page numbers.

Example:

> If cases from Texas were of interest, the table of cases by state, arranged alphabetically, would list all of the case summaries contained in the deskbook from Texas.

➡ TEXAS

A.M. v. Cash, 104
Abbott v. North East Independent School Dist., 282
Academy of Skills & Knowledge v. Charter Schools, 210
Alvin Independent School Dist. v. Patricia F., 233
Barrow v. Greenville Independent School Dist., 294

✓ Remember, the judicial system has two court systems – state and federal court – which generally function independently from each other. *See The Judicial System, p. 615.* We have included the federal court cases in the table of cases by state according to the state in which the court resides. However, federal court decisions often impact other federal courts within that particular circuit. Therefore, it may be helpful to review cases from all of the states contained in a particular circuit.

Reference Tool

As a reference tool, we have highlighted important resources that provide the framework for many legal issues.

◆ If you would like to see specific wording of the **U.S. Constitution**, refer to **Appendix A**, which includes relevant provisions of the U.S. Constitution such as the First Amendment (freedom of speech and religion).

◆ If you would like to review **U.S. Supreme Court decisions** in a particular subject matter area, our topical list of U.S. Supreme Court case citations located in **Appendix B** will be helpful.

We hope you benefit from the use of the *2014 Deskbook Encyclopedia of American School Law*. If you have any questions about how to use the deskbook, please contact Jim Roth at jroth@pbp.com.

TABLE OF CASES

TABLE OF CASES

TABLE OF CASES

TABLE OF CASES

TABLE OF CASES

TABLE OF CASES

TABLE OF CASES

TABLE OF CASES

TABLE OF CASES

TABLE OF CASES

TABLE OF CASES

TABLE OF CASES

TABLE OF CASES BY STATE

TABLE OF CASES BY STATE

TABLE OF CASES BY STATE

TABLE OF CASES BY STATE

TABLE OF CASES BY STATE

TEXAS

TABLE OF CASES BY STATE

WYOMING

CHAPTER ONE

Student Rights

I. BULLYING AND HARASSMENT

A. Bullying

Although almost all states have anti-bullying laws and school districts have implemented anti-bullying policies in recent years, school bullying cases are typically decided under principles of negligence and constitutional law.

In Straiton v. New Milford Board of Educ., *below, a Connecticut court held a vice principal who knew of reported bullying and harassment by a student had a duty to be alert to and to protect a classmate from misconduct. It also held the board of education had a duty to supervise high school students. A general rule in negligence cases is that a school is liable for student-on-student violence only if it had "specific, prior knowledge of the danger that caused the injury." See* Mirand v. City of New York, *84 N.Y. 44, 637 N.E.2d 263 (1994).*

Constitutional claims are limited by the U.S. Supreme Court's decision in DeShaney v. Winnebago County Dep't of Social Services, *489 U.S. 189 (1989). In* Deshaney, *the Court held there must be a "special relationship" between a state agency and a victim of private violence for a constitutional duty to exist. Since public school students do not typically have a special relationship with school officials, schools are rarely liable for the violent acts of private actors.*

A 2012 Michigan law requires school boards and public school academies to adopt and implement policies to prohibit bullying. A policy adopted under the law must include a statement prohibiting student bullying and a statement prohibiting retaliation or false accusations against a target of bullying, a witness or other reliable informant. "Bullying" means a written, verbal, or physical act, or an electronic communication, intended or likely to harm a student either directly or indirectly. To be "bullying," a communication must 1) substantially interfere with educational opportunities, benefits, or programs; 2) adversely affect a student's ability to participate in or benefit from educational programs or activities by placing him or her in reasonable fear of physical harm or by causing substantial emotional distress; or 3) have an actual and substantial detrimental effect on a student's physical or mental health.

The federal government has targeted peer bullying by holding annual bullying prevention summits and joining other federal agencies in the Federal Partners in Bullying Prevention Steering Committee. A "Dear Colleague" letter from the U.S. Department of Education's Office for Civil Rights, dated October 26, 2010 details federal expectations for confronting school bullies. The letter is posted at http://www2.ed.gov/about/offices/list/ocr/letters/colleague-201010.html.

◆   A Connecticut student reported frequent bullying and harassment by a classmate, including physical contact. According to the student, the harassment would stop when a male vice principal "clamped down on them." But he said the classmate continued using anti-gay epithets when he complained to a female vice principal. Some time after the classmate was suspended for two days, he followed the student out of the cafeteria and assaulted him in a school hallway.

In a state court negligence action against the classmate, vice principals, board of education and town, the student asserted that the school officials and government entities had a duty to protect him from known bullying. In the court's view, both vice principals were responsible for monitoring the student body. The female vice principal could not claim she had no duty to protect the student due to her "very limited involvement with the bullying situation." A school policy required staff to "be particularly alert to possible situations, circumstances or events which might include bullying." **The court held a legal duty may be found if it is foreseeable that harm might result if reasonable care is not exercised.** While the court agreed with the board of education and vice principals that the actions alleged in this case were discretionary, it denied their claim to immunity. It found genuine issues of fact involving the question of whether the student was an "identifiable victim" and whether he faced imminent harm. A further defense asserted by the town, board and vice principals was that they could not be the legal cause of harm because of the classmate's misconduct. As the court held this question involved facts that were in dispute, it held the determination of the legal cause of the student's injuries would have to be determined in further proceedings. It denied the board's motion for pretrial judgment. *Straiton v. New Milford Board of Educ.*, No. DBD CV 10 6003255S, 2012 WL 1218160 (Conn. Super. Ct. 3/13/12).

◆   After a Texas middle school student committed suicide, his mother claimed he was the victim of constant bullying by other students at school. She sued the school district in a federal court, asserting that no one protected him from harm at his school. In pretrial activity, the court refused to dismiss claims filed under Title IX of the Education Amendments of 1972 and the Due Process Clause of the Fourteenth Amendment. A few weeks later, the U.S. Court of Appeals, Fifth Circuit, decided *Doe v. Covington County School Dist.*, 675 F.3d 849 (5th Cir. 2012), Chapter Twelve, VII.C.2. In *Doe*, the Fifth Circuit held a Mississippi school district had no constitutional duty to protect a student from molestation by an adult who repeatedly signed her out of school under false pretenses because there was no "special relationship" between the student and district. Upon reviewing *Doe*, the court agreed with the school district that this was one of the unusual circumstances in which reconsideration of a judgment was appropriate.

As a general matter, a state's failure to protect an individual against private violence does not constitute a due process violation. A "special relationship" exists only when the state has taken the person into its custody and held her there against her will. The relationship exists in three situations, none of which involve public schools. While the mother argued that the school district's failure to enforce its anti-bullying policies violated her son's due process rights, the court held *Doe* barred such a ruling in the absence of a special relationship. An alternative argument, based on the school's "culture that condoned bullying" which increased the danger posed to the child during the school day, also failed. *Estate of Brown v. Cypress Fairbanks Independent School Dist.*, 863. F.Supp.2d 632 (S.D. Tex. 2012).

◆   An Oklahoma student who was often ill and absent from school said others ridiculed and threatened her. A psychotherapist diagnosed her with depression, and her mother homeschooled her for several weeks. The student finished the school year at a private school. When she returned to public school, her mother gave the school nurse ibuprofen and Aleve to administer for headaches. During the school year, the mother claimed that nurses denied her child medication or delayed giving it when it was needed. Incidents of bullying by peers increased, and the family's house was vandalized. Some Internet postings were claimed to be cyberbullying. The school issued detentions and counseled students about some misconduct. But the mother felt they should have been suspended, and she eventually removed her child from school due to depression and a suicide attempt. The family moved so the student could attend a new school.

The parent sued the district and officials – including the superintendent and principal – in a federal court. In pretrial activity, the court dismissed the claims against the district and state tort claims against the school employees. According to the parent, school staff members had a constitutional duty to protect the student based on a "special relationship." She claimed the actions by school staff to deny or delay her access to medication prevented her from caring for herself, rendering her vulnerable. **The court found no legal authority for**

a claim that public school students have a special relationship with their teachers or other school employees. Staff members did not create a danger or increase the student's vulnerability, so no constitutional claims could be made against them. State actors are liable only for their own acts, not those of third parties. In any event, qualified immunity protected the staff members. *Reyna v. Independent School Dist. No. 1, Oklahoma County, Oklahoma*, Nos. CIV–09–1223–D, CJ–2009–9583, 2012 WL 1023526 (W.D. Okla. 3/27/12).

◆   A federal district court dismissed an action by a deceased student's family against a Utah school district. The family sought to hold school officials liable for his suicide death based on their alleged failure to address harassment and bullying at school. Although the family claimed school administrators knew of the harassment and bullying and failed to act, **the court found the family did not file an action until more than a year after his death**. A state-law notice of claim requirement thus barred the action. *Hancock v. North Sanpete School Dist.*, No. 2:12-cv-00072, 2012 WL 3060118 (D. Utah 7/25/12).

◆   A Tennessee student claimed a classmate began threatening and harassing him. He complained about the bullying to an assistant school principal and the principal, and his father also reported it to teachers and school officials. But the next school year, the bully paid a friend $5 to hurt the student. The attack was carried out at school, and the student was severely beaten. In a state court action against the bully, friend, their parents and the board of education, the court found the board 25% at fault for the student's injuries. It found the bully, his friend and their parents jointly and severally liable for the remaining 75% of fault. But the court held the board had state law immunity. As a result, the board was dismissed from the case and the judgment was modified to hold the bully, his friend and their parents liable for a damage award in excess of $50,000.

On appeal, the Court of Appeals of Tennessee explained that state law immunized the conduct of government employees who performed discretionary functions. Policy-making and planning-level acts were discretionary and thus entitled to immunity. The court agreed with the student that school officials did not follow the board's disciplinary procedures and policies. **It held the relevant policy arose from a state law against school bullying.** Implementing a policy was operational, not discretionary, so immunity was removed. **Administrators did not follow the board policy on bullying and harassment.** No complaint manager was assigned to investigate, and school disciplinary guidelines were not followed. As the trial court had found, the school was on notice of possible injury to the student. All the defending parties played a role in the harm, so the court held them equally liable. *Moore v. Houston County Board of Educ.*, 358 S.W.3d 612 (Tenn. Ct. App. 2011).

◆   Ohio parents claimed their son was regularly bullied and harassed at school as a 17-year-old senior. They claimed the school and a particular teacher did nothing to intervene, and that the son committed suicide because of the bullying at his school. A federal district court agreed with the school board that the action was untimely and meritless. **The school district had no constitutional duty to take affirmative action to protect the student from bullying or to prevent**

his suicide. Any lack of a policy against bullying and failure to train employees created no liability. *Mohat v. Mentor Exempted Village School Dist. Board of Educ.*, No. 1:09 CV 688, 2011 WL 2174671 (N.D. Ohio 6/1/11).

◆ An Arizona parent called school administrators to report that a classmate was threatening her seventh-grade daughter. But the bullying and threats by the classmate escalated. A teacher called the mother to report rumors that the classmate was planning to attack the daughter. That afternoon, the classmate assaulted the daughter at school. Her family sued the school district and school and law enforcement officers in a federal court for civil rights violations. One of the claims alleged a deprivation of federal due process rights, while others asserted state law negligence and failure to train employees under Arizona's Anti-Bullying law. The court noted that under *DeShaney v. Winnebago County Dep't of Social Services*, 489 U.S. 189 (1989), the Fourteenth Amendment does not generally require the government to prevent private citizens from harming each other. **No special relationship existed in this case that imposed an affirmative duty on school officials to protect the daughter from the classmate.** As Arizona courts had yet to interpret the anti-bullying statute, that claim was sent to a state court. *O'Dell v. Casa Grande Elementary School Dist. No. 4*, No. CV-08-0240-PHX-GMS, 2008 WL 5215329 (D. Ariz. 12/12/08).

B. Texting, Sexting and Electronic Harassment

Electronic communication creates new concerns for inappropriate contacts among students, and between school employees and students. Attorney/author Frederick Lane says that while "sexting" currently has no legal definition, nude or suggestive images of minor children may fall within state and federal definitions of child pornography. Educators who handle images confiscated from students thus risk prosecution for possessing child pornography. For this reason, officials should turn over such evidence to the police and refrain from viewing or forwarding it. For more information, see www.fredericklane.com.

New York's "Cybercrime Youth Rescue Act" created an education reform program for persons charged in family or criminal court with cyberbullying or the sending or receipt of obscenity or nudity, when the sender and receiver were both under the age of 20 and not over five years apart in age.

In J.F.K. v. Troup County School Dist., 678 F.3d 1254 (11th Cir. 2012), this chapter, a Georgia teacher's constant texting to students and other misconduct did not place her principal on notice that she was sexually harassing a student.

◆ Jessica Logan committed suicide in 2008, shortly after graduating from an Ohio high school. Her family attributed her suicide to her anguish over the "sexting" of a nude photo of her among other high school students. In a federal action, it was asserted that high school students were circulating the nude photo with their cell phones. When the student reported the activity to a counselor, the counselor referred her to the high school resource officer. The resource officer agreed to speak to the other students, and he asked them to delete the photo from their cell phones. Later, Jessica appeared on a television broadcast about sexting. She claimed the harassment increased after the broadcast. She committed suicide. Her parents sued her school district, school officials, the resource officer and his municipal employer in a federal court. The school district argued that it could not be held liable because neither the student nor anyone acting on her behalf made a sexual harassment report. The court explained that **there is no constitutional duty of government actors to protect individuals against private parties such as the harassing students in this case.** As there was no evidence that the resource officer acted unreasonably, he was entitled to qualified immunity. There was also no viable claim against his municipal employer for failing to train or supervise him. *Logan v. Sycamore Community School Board of Educ.*, 780 F.Supp.2d 594 (S.D. Ohio 2011).

In a later order, the court found other courts have held appropriate persons for reporting under Title IX of the Education Amendments of 1972 "do not need to be aware of the exact details of a plaintiff's experience to have notice, as long as they 'reasonably could have responded with remedial measures.'" **Since evidence indicated that school officials knew of the harassment, the mother could proceed with her Title IX claim.** *Logan v. Sycamore Community School Board of Educ.*, No. 1:09-CV-00885 (S.D. Ohio 6/5/12).

◆   A West Virginia high school student created a MySpace.com web page that ridiculed a classmate. She opened the page to about 100 MySpace "friends," and some of them added vulgar criticisms of the classmate. The classmate filed a harassment complaint with the school, which found the student had created a "hate website" in violation of a school policy against harassment, bullying and intimidation. She was suspended for five days and excluded from school social activities for 90 days. In a federal court, the student sued the school district for speech rights and due process violations. After the court held for the district, the student appealed. The U.S. Court of Appeals, Fourth Circuit, held *Tinker v. Des Moines Independent Community School Dist.*, 393 U.S. 503 (1969), recognized a need to regulate speech that interfered with school work or discipline.

In upholding the discipline, the court found that bullying is a major concern in schools, leading to student depression and even thoughts of suicide. **The court held "schools have a duty to protect their students from harassment and bullying in the school environment." It was foreseeable that the student's conduct would reach the school via computers, phones or other devices.** The nexus between the speech and school pedagogical interests justified discipline. The court found the speech was materially and substantially disruptive and held that speech originating outside of school "but directed at persons in school and received by and acted on by them was in fact in-school speech." *Kowalski v. Berkeley County Schools*, 652 F.3d 565 (4th Cir. 2011).

◆   Indiana students were excluded from extracurricular activities after they posted suggestive but non-nude pictures of themselves on Internet pages. The images were created at a student's home during the summer. A federal court refused to apply child pornography and obscenity definitions, finding they did not apply to the images. While juvenile and silly, the images were an attempt at humor. Entertainment, even of a questionable nature, communicates ideas and has First Amendment protection. To be deemed obscene or child pornography, the court held there had to be a depiction of the sex organ, mouth or anus of two people. No images depicted this. *Tinker v. Des Moines Independent Community School Dist.*, 393 U.S. 503 (1969), requires material and substantial disruption at school in order to impose school discipline. Complaints by parents do not meet this standard; nor did a claim that the images were divisive to the school volleyball team. The court held the suspensions violated the students' rights.

A school code of conduct provision on out-of-school conduct was held unconstitutional. Language regarding the bringing of "discredit or dishonor upon the student or the school" reached "a substantial amount of protected conduct" and was too broad and subjective to pass constitutional standards. **But the principal was entitled to qualified immunity, as the developing law on off-campus student Internet speech remained very unclear.** *T.V. v. Smith-Green Community School Corp.*, 807 F.Supp.2d 767 (N.D. Ind. 2011).

◆　An Arkansas coach texted frequently with female students. He agreed to stop it after parents complained, but continued making suggestive comments. A student told the superintendent that her ninth-grade cousin "might have a crush" on the coach, and often left classes to visit him in the gym. The student told the ninth-grader's mother of these suspicions, and she approached the principal to discuss it. The cousin offered more information and identified staff members who allegedly knew of inappropriate conduct. According to the mother, the principal promised to investigate. Soon the coach was accused of texting "OMG you look good today" to a student. Due to this report and other concerns, the district made preparations to nonrenew the coach's contract. When students reported details of sexual contact between the coach and ninth-grader, the coach was arrested. He was eventually prosecuted and sentenced to 10 years in prison.

In a federal district court case against the school district, principal and other school officials, the parent asserted claims under 42 U.S.C. § 1983 and Title IX. The court dismissed claims against the district and most of the officials, but the principal was denied immunity. On appeal, the U.S. Court of Appeals, Eighth Circuit, found the principal could be liable for constitutional violations if she knew of the coach's conduct but failed to take remedial action in a manner that caused injury. **The court held the coach's texts did not provide the principal with "actual notice of sexual abuse." Inappropriate comments alone did not alert her to a possible sexual relationship.** "OMG you look good today" did not indicate sexual conduct or abuse. School administrators investigated each report they received, and at the relevant time they lacked any evidence of improper contact. The court held "a student's familiar behavior with a teacher or even an 'excessive amount of time' spent with a teacher, without more, does not automatically give rise to a reasonable inference of sexual abuse." It reversed the order denying immunity to the principal, and held the district was not liable under Title IX. *Doe v. Flaherty*, 623 F.3d 577 (8th Cir. 2010).

◆　A New York student received three emails from a male classmate's school email account. One was profane and disparaged her appearance, and the others sought sexual relations. Although the student promptly reported the emails to the school administration, the classmate denied sending them and claimed other students had his email password. Believing that the school's investigation was inadequate, the student sued the school district in a federal district court for violating Title IX and other federal laws. Appeal reached the U.S. Court of Appeals, Second Circuit, which held that **to prevail on her Title IX claim, the student had to show the district acted with deliberate indifference that was so severe, pervasive, and objectively offensive that it barred her access to an educational opportunity or benefit**. As the district court held, the student did not meet these requirements. While the emails were offensive, they fell well short of the conduct necessary to create Title IX liability. Three offensive emails in a 10-day time period did not demonstrate "severe and pervasive harassment," in the court's view. Neither the Title IX claim nor an equal protection claim based on the district's allegedly more aggressive investigation and pursuit of a prior incident of race-based misconduct persuaded the court, and it affirmed the judgment for the school district. *R.S. v. Board of Educ. of the Hastings-on-Hudson Union Free School Dist.*, 371 Fed.Appx. 231 (2d Cir. 2010).

C. Sexual Harassment by Students

Title IX of the Education Amendments of 1972 prohibits sex discrimination by all recipients of federal funding. In Davis v. Monroe County Board of Educ., *this chapter, the Supreme Court held school districts may be held liable under Title IX for student-on-student harassment, where officials actually know of the harassment, but their response is clearly unreasonable. To establish liability under* Davis, *students must show 1) sexual harassment by peers; 2) deliberate indifference by school officials with actual knowledge of harassment; and 3) harassment so severe, pervasive and objectively offensive it deprived the student of access to educational opportunities. A teacher's knowledge of peer harassment may create "actual knowledge" that triggers Title IX liability.*

Federal courts have applied the Davis *analysis to other forms of harassment by peers, including race, disability and religious harassment. In* Logan v. Sycamore Community School Board of Educ., *this chapter, a federal court explained that school liability under Title IX does not require school officials to know the exact details of a student's experience, if they could have reasonably responded to the harassment being reported.*

In Fitzgerald v. Barnstable School Committee, *the U.S. Supreme Court held Title IX does not bar Equal Protection claims under 42 U.S.C. § 1983. Section 1983 is a federal statute that creates no rights itself, but enforces rights created by federal laws and the Constitution. Section 1983 imposes liability on a school district that has a policy or custom of violating constitutional rights, and also creates individual liability for school officials who violate constitutional rights.*

◆   Michigan basketball teammates often roughhoused in their locker room. Eighth-graders began to play "games" that victimized two seventh-graders. One seventh-grader was subjected to "blind-folded sit-up," in which an eighth-grader "placed his naked buttocks" in his face, resulting in physical contact. Eighth-graders grabbed another seventh-grader, forced him down, "pulled his pants down and anally penetrated him with a marker." When the coach learned of this incident, he did not report it. The student told his mother of the incident, and she met with the principal. After the director of schools returned from out of town two days later, it was found that sufficient evidence supported the report. The perpetrators were suspended from school for 10 days, placed in an alternative school and suspended from the team. Other students learned about the marker incident and harassed the victim to the point that his mother removed him from school. After the perpetrators were assigned an additional day of suspension for the marker incident, they were both reinstated to the basketball team. After this decision, the other parent removed her child from school. Both parents then sued the school board in a federal district court.

After a trial, the jury awarded the students $100,000 each. Appeal reached the U.S. Court of Appeals, Sixth Circuit. It found a jury could have reasonably viewed the marker incident as "not just horseplay gone awry, but rather as a serious incident of sexual assault." Jurors could have expected the perpetrators to receive more severe punishment. As the lower court held, the jury was entitled to find **the decision to allow the perpetrators back on the basketball team was unreasonable since they would be interacting with the victimized students every day**. Testimony suggested the board took little immediate action to stop the harassment. Since the jury could have reasonably found the board's response was "too little to late," the court held for the students. *Mathis v. Wayne County Board of Educ.*, 496 Fed.Appx. 513 (6th Cir. 2012).

◆ A Florida parent claimed her child was inappropriately touched by a male student on a school bus. An administrator met with the male student and prohibited all males from sitting with females on buses. A report was made to the state child protection agency. The parent sued the school board in a federal district court. After the case was dismissed, she appealed to the U.S. Court of Appeals, Eleventh Circuit. It found the complaint overly vague and ambiguous, asserting numerous claims against the board and staff in lengthy paragraphs and accusing officials of lying, harassment and discrimination. While parents have a general due process right to direct the education of their children without unreasonable state interference, **there is no parental right of access to school property**. The parent contradicted her claim that officials failed to address her report that a male student had improperly touched her daughter by admitting they took action after her report. **Schools do not generally have the required level of control over students to have a duty to protect them from third parties.** As the parent identified no district policy or custom that deprived her daughter of her federal rights, the court affirmed the judgment for the board. *Porter v. Duval County School Board*, 406 Fed.Appx. 460 (11th Cir. 2010).

◆ An Illinois student told her mother that a Junior Reserve Officer Training Corps (JROTC) instructor improperly touched her. After the instructor admitted wrongdoing, he was charged criminally and he resigned. In a federal district court sexual harassment action, the student included an equal protection claim under 42 U.S.C. § 1983. She also brought a claim under Title IX against the district. Judgment was entered for the school district, and the student appealed.

The U.S. Court of Appeals, Seventh Circuit, found the dismissal of the Section 1983 claim for equal protection violations was based on a theory of supervisory liability. It noted the U.S. Supreme Court held Title IX did not bar concurrent Section 1983 claims against school officials in *Fitzgerald v. Barnstable School Committee*, below. But as the Section 1983 claim was based on supervisory liability, the court held **the lack of any knowledge of the instructor's misconduct by either the school district or the JROTC supervisor was fatal to the claim**. No school official knew of any sexual abuse of the student until the day she reported it. The court found remarks attributed to the JROTC supervisor were insufficient to pursue Section 1983 claims. As a result, they had been properly dismissed. As there was no legal support for the student's Title IX theory, the judgment for the district and supervisor was affirmed. *Trentadue v. Redmon*, 619 F.3d 648 (7th Cir. 2010).

◆ A Massachusetts kindergarten student told her parents that a third-grader on her school bus bullied her into lifting her skirt. The parents reported this to the principal, but the third-grader repeatedly denied the report, and the school could not corroborate the student's account. After she said the boy made her pull down her underpants and spread her legs, the school called the police, who found insufficient evidence for criminal charges. Finding insufficient evidence for school discipline, the principal suggested transferring the kindergartner to a different bus or leaving rows of empty seats between students of different ages.

The parents suggested moving the third-grader or placing a monitor on the bus. The superintendent denied the requests. After the parents reported that the student had experienced more encounters with the third-grader at school, she began staying home. The family sued the school committee under 42 U.S.C. § 1983, claiming a violation of Title IX. A federal court and the First Circuit held that Title IX's private remedy precluded using 42 U.S.C. § 1983 to advance Title IX claims. The U.S. Supreme Court reversed. It held that Title IX was not meant to be the exclusive mechanism for addressing gender bias in schools. Nor was it meant to be a substitute for parallel Section 1983 lawsuits. **Section 1983 is available as a remedy to enforce Equal Protection claims for gender discrimination in schools.** *Fitzgerald v. Barnstable School Committee*, 555 U.S. 246, 129 S.Ct. 788, 172 L.Ed.2d 582 (2009).

◆ A Georgia fifth-grader complained to her teacher of sexual harassment by a male student. The teacher did not immediately notify the principal. The harasser was eventually charged with sexual battery, but school officials took no action against him. The fifth-grader sued the school board for Title IX violations. A federal district court and federal appeals court ruled against her. The U.S. Supreme Court reversed the judgment, holding that **school districts may be held liable under Title IX for deliberate indifference to known acts of peer sexual harassment, where the school's response is clearly unreasonable under the circumstances**. A recipient of federal funds may be liable for student-on-student sexual harassment, where the recipient is deliberately indifferent to known sexual harassment and the harasser is under the recipient's disciplinary authority. To create Title IX liability, the harassment must be so severe, pervasive and objectively offensive that it deprives the victim of access to educational opportunities or benefits. The Court held the harassment alleged by the student was sufficiently severe to avoid pretrial dismissal. The case was returned to the lower courts. *Davis v. Monroe County Board of Educ.*, 526 U.S. 629, 119 S.Ct. 1661, 143 L.Ed.2d 839 (1999).

D. Sexual Harassment by School Employees

In Gebser v. Lago Vista Independent School Dist., *524 U.S. 274, the U.S. Supreme Court examined the liability of school districts for sexual harassment of students by teachers and other staff under Title IX. The case involved a Texas student who had a sexual relationship with a teacher. The Court rejected the liability standard advocated by the student and by the U.S. government, which resembled* respondeat superior *(vicarious) liability under Title VII. Title IX contains an administrative enforcement mechanism that assumes actual notice has been provided to officials prior to the imposition of enforcement remedies.*

According to the Court, damages would be inappropriate in a Title IX case unless an official with the authority to address the discrimination failed to act despite actual knowledge of it, in a manner amounting to deliberate indifference *to discrimination. In this case, there was insufficient evidence that a school official should have known about the relationship to impose Title IX liability. So the district was not liable for the teacher's misconduct.*

◆ A Georgia teacher called, emailed and wrote to an eighth-grade student. His parents met with the school principal at least twice and reported the continuing communications. But they told the principal they "did not think anything was going on" between the two. It was later learned that the teacher had performed oral sex on the student at least five times during the summer before his eighth-grade year. She pled guilty to criminal child molestation charges and was sentenced to prison. The parents sued the school district in a federal court for violating Title IX. The court found no evidence that the principal knew of sexual harassment by the teacher. It awarded pretrial judgment to the district.

On appeal, the U.S. Court of Appeals, Eleventh Circuit, stated that **the principal was a person with authority to take corrective measure in response to actual notice of sexual harassment under Title IX**. In a previous case, the court had found that lesser forms of harassment may provide actual notice of sexually violent conduct. But in this case, the court found it clear that the principal was never put on notice of a single act of sexual harassment by the teacher. **The court rejected the parents' claim that reports of repeated texting and other contacts put school officials on notice of harassment.** It appeared to the court that the principal knew the teacher's conduct was "inappropriate, devoid of professionalism, and reeked of immaturity." But in the court's estimation, her known conduct was not of a sexual nature and could not have put the principal on notice of sexual harassment, defeating the Title IX claim. *J.F.K. v. Troup County School Dist.*, 678 F.3d 1254 (11th Cir. 2012).

◆ A 26-year-old Wisconsin teacher brought a 14-year-old student to her apartment. She later admitted kissing him for 15 to 20 minutes, while he asserted there was also some other touching. When the student's mother discovered text messages they had sent, she transferred him to a private school. The teacher was fired and pleaded guilty to fourth-degree sexual assault charges. The mother then sued the school district in a federal district court under Title IX. The court held for the district, and the family appealed to the U.S. Court of Appeals, Seventh Circuit. It explained the liability standard for sexual harassment by school staff members was announced in *Gebser v. Lago Vista Independent School Dist.*, this chapter. **Seventh Circuit case law required proof of "actual knowledge of misconduct, not just actual knowledge of the risk of misconduct" in order to impose Title IX liability.** In this case, the teacher had denied the encounter with the student when the principal questioned her. Later, the district superintendent continued investigating. As soon as the mother made a report, the school took prompt action. Suspicions of an improper relationship between the student and teacher did not make the true nature of the relationship "obvious" or a "known risk." In holding for the board, the court noted "judges must be sensitive to the effect on education of heavy-handed judicial intrusion into school disciplinary issues." It dismissed the federal claims and a state court claim as well. *Doe v. St. Francis School Dist.*, 694 F.3d 869 (7th Cir. 2012).

◆   A California student claimed a school counselor engaged him in sexual conduct. He sued the district, counselor and others for negligence. The state's highest court held that although districts and their employees are not "insurers of the physical safety of students, California law has long required school authorities to supervise the conduct of students on school grounds and to enforce the rules and regulations necessary to their protection." Lack of supervision or ineffective supervision may constitute a "lack of ordinary care" in cases alleging lack of student supervision, and a school district is liable for injuries caused by such negligence. **Previous California decisions had found that a school district and its employees have a "special relationship" with students.** Rejecting the district's arguments, the court held administrators must take reasonable measures to guard students against harassment or abuse from foreseeable sources, including teachers or counselors.

Administrators could be held liable for an employee's misconduct based on the "special relationship" theory. The complaint in this case did not identify the administrators who allegedly did not properly hire, train and supervise the counselor. But there were enough facts to preclude pretrial judgment. With respect to duty, the student would have to show that an individual employee's proposal, recommendation or failure to act was a substantial factor in causing the counselor to be hired or retained. Unless an administrator knew (or should have known) that she was a danger, little or no blame could be attached to that action or inaction. Even if an administrator was liable, the court found the greater share of fault would likely lie with the counselor herself. The case was returned to the lower courts for further consideration. *C.A. v. William S. Hart Union High School Dist.*, 138 Cal.Rptr.3d 1, 270 P.3d 699 (Cal. 2012).

◆   A Kentucky teacher sexually harassed a student and then began texting him and making inappropriate remarks. The student did not report the misconduct, even after the teacher exposed himself in a locker room. He complied with the teacher's request to text him nude photos. The student's girlfriend found the photos on the student's phone, and he attempted suicide. After learning of this, the school principal called the police and then suspended the teacher, who was soon fired. The student sued the teacher, principal, board of education and district superintendent in a federal court for negligence. He argued school officials negligently hired the teacher because they knew he had resigned from another school system after being accused of sodomy. But the court noted he was acquitted of these charges. State law immunity protected officials who exercised discretionary functions, such as hiring decisions and supervision of employees.

A background check relied upon by the board did not reveal the teacher had a criminal record. **The court noted the student had taken care to conceal events and made no complaints to anyone.** His negligent hiring claim failed for several reasons, including lack of any breach of duty by the principal and superintendent to further investigate the teacher, and qualified immunity for performing discretionary functions. There was no notice of harm to the school until the suicide attempt. **No school official was aware of the teacher's texts or the requests for nude photos.** As the student did not show it was reasonably foreseeable that he would be victimized or would attempt suicide, the court held for the school officials. *Cole v. Shadoan*, 782 F.Supp.2d 428 (E.D. Ky. 2011).

◆ An Alabama school administrator investigated a teacher's misconduct three times. Each time the teacher denied the charge. After the third incident, the school board transferred him from a high school to an elementary school. There, a female student complained that he made an inappropriate comment. The principal told him that additional reports would result in discharge. Later in the same school year, female students complained about the way the teacher told them to do push-ups. An 11-year-old disabled student sought to transfer from his class, stating that classmates teased her about her disabilities. Over a year later, she told a school counselor that the teacher had raped her. The teacher was placed on administrative leave, and he soon retired. The parents sued the school board and administrator in a state court, asserting the district was deliberately indifferent to the risk of harm to the child. The case reached the Supreme Court of Alabama, which held that the board was not an arm of the state for purposes of Eleventh Amendment immunity. However, the administrator was entitled to qualified immunity. **His failure to recommend the teacher's termination did not amount to deliberate indifference to the student's constitutional rights.** *Madison County Board of Educ. v. Reaves*, 1 So.3d 980 (Ala. 2008).

◆ An Idaho teacher had sexual relations with an 18-year-old student. When this was revealed, the teacher resigned. The student sued the teacher, school district and school officials, including claims for negligent supervision and violation of Title IX. She presented evidence of post-traumatic stress disorder (PTSD), but offered no medical records or damage estimates. The school district offered testimony from a psychologist who stated that her emotional problems were triggered by the lawsuit itself, not the sexual relationship. The jury found the district liable for negligent supervision. However, it found that the student did not prove any damages, and it awarded her none. On appeal, the Supreme Court of Idaho held a reasonable jury could have found the student proved no damages. **Her own experts disagreed as to her condition, with one finding she did not have PTSD.** The district's expert had found the student had no significant psychological difficulties until after the lawsuit was filed. The court upheld the jury's findings. *Hei v. Holzer*, 181 P.3d 489 (Idaho 2008).

E. Sexual Orientation

According to the U.S. Court of Appeals, Eighth Circuit, bullying or harassment that is not based on a student's gender does not create liability under Title IX. In Wolfe v. Fayetteville, Arkansas School Dist., *below, it held that under Title IX, the "acts of discrimination" must be "on the basis of sex."*

In Donovan v. Poway Unified School Dist., *below, a California court observed that school administrators are better situated than courts to address peer sexual harassment. Administrators can take affirmative steps to combat racism, sexism and other forms of bias which courts cannot. And administrative actions are typically resolved far more quickly than private lawsuits.*

◆ An Arkansas student was widely ridiculed by classmates. He reported pushing, shoving, name-calling, and being falsely called a homosexual. He withdrew from school in tenth grade and sued the school district in a federal court for sexual harassment in violation of Title IX. At trial, school officials and classmates claimed the misconduct could not violate Title IX as it was not gender-based. A jury was told that to win, the student had to show he was harassed "on the basis of sex" in a manner so severe, pervasive, and objectively offensive that it deprived him of access to educational benefits or opportunities. He further had to show that the district knew of the harassment but was deliberately indifferent to it. The jury held for the officials, and the student appealed.

On appeal, the Eighth Circuit Court of Appeals held the jury instructions reflected Title IX's "on the basis of sex" requirement and correctly summarized Supreme Court precedents. **The court rejected the student's argument that it would be enough under Title IX that peers called him names and spread rumors in order to "debase his masculinity."** In *Davis v. Monroe County Board of Educ.*, this chapter, the Supreme Court held that **to be actionable, harassment must be gender-oriented conduct amounting to more than "simple acts of teasing and name-calling."** There was no authority supporting the student's claim that the use of sex-based language in rumors or name-calling proved sex-based discrimination. As a result, the court affirmed the judgment. *Wolfe v. Fayetteville, Arkansas School Dist.*, 648 F.3d 860 (8th Cir. 2011).

◆ Two California students claimed they were subjected to severe anti-gay peer harassment. They gave logs of the harassment to the school. After getting little response, the students completed high school in home study programs. They later sued the school district, principal, assistant principal and district superintendent in a federal court. A jury found that the district violated the Education Code and that the principal and assistant principal violated the male student's rights under the Equal Protection Clause. And the principal violated the female student's equal protection rights. The verdict awarded the male student $175,000 in damages and the female student $125,000. They also received attorneys' fees of over $427,000. The Court of Appeal of California found the students had made out a successful claim for "deliberate indifference" to known anti-gay harassment. This satisfied the stringent Title IX standard. In finding for the students on their equal protection claims, the jury had found the **administrators had actual notice of harassment but were deliberately**

indifferent to it. As the principal was an appropriate person to act on behalf of the school district to address peer sexual orientation harassment, and there was evidence that the administrators took no meaningful action to stop the harassment, the judgment was upheld. *Donovan v. Poway Unified School Dist.*, 167 Cal.App.4th 567, 84 Cal.Rptr.3d 285 (Cal. Ct. App. 2008).

◆   A New Jersey student claimed he was repeatedly and severely taunted by classmates who directed homosexual epithets at him beginning in grade four. He endured slurs in the halls and was struck while in the school cafeteria, when 10 to 15 students surrounded and taunted him. The assistant principal did not punish or reprimand the students. During the student's eighth-grade year, his mother claimed a school guidance counselor simply urged her son to "toughen up and turn the other cheek." The principal later agreed to let the student leave classes to report problems directly to him. The school began to discipline perpetrators, and the verbal abuse declined. When the student entered high school, the harassment resurfaced. To avoid derision on school buses, he decided to walk home from school. He reported being followed by others as he walked home. Other students punched him and knocked him down, and he had to miss school.

The student's mother filed a harassment complaint with the state Division on Civil Rights. The student won $50,000 in emotional distress damages, and his mother won $10,000 for emotional distress. The district was fined $10,000 and ordered to pay attorneys' fees. A state appellate division court affirmed the $50,000 award for the student, but it reversed the award for his mother. On appeal, the Supreme Court of New Jersey **recognized a cause of action against school districts for student-on-student harassment based on perceived sexual orientation**. Liability would be imposed for peer harassment only if a district failed to reasonably address harassment and the district knew or should have known about it. The case was returned to the lower courts. *L.W. v. Toms River Regional Schools Board of Educ.*, 189 N.J. 381, 915 A.2d 535 (N.J. 2007).

F. Students with Disabilities

In T.K. and S.K. v. Dep't of Educ. of City of New York, *this chapter, a federal district court held that "Title IX, IDEA and Section 504 of the Rehabilitation Act place upon schools the affirmative duty to address bullying and harassment."*

The U.S. Department of Education has recommended that schools: 1) publish a notice of non-discrimination that identifies laws which prohibit discrimination and harassment; 2) explain what the laws prohibit and the penalties for violations; 3) assure the school community that the laws will be enforced; 4) have a Title IX coordinator and inform the school community that this is the person who will receive harassment complaints; and 5) train the Title IX coordinator to fully understand the job's responsibilities.

◆   A Michigan special education student believed a classmate was his girlfriend. He shoved her into a locker because he saw her talking to another boy, and he later demanded that she perform oral sex on him. At a school basketball game, the student made obscene gestures at the classmate, and her stepfather told him to stay away from her. The stepfather wrote to administrators about the incident and the prior attempt to solicit sex. In response, the school formed a 30-day plan to constantly supervise the student. Seven weeks after the supervisory period passed, the student sexually assaulted the classmate at school. Later, the school board voted to expel him. In a federal court action, the classmate said the student's history of misconduct put school officials on notice of a risk of harm. But she did not assert that any prior misconduct included sexual harassment, and the court held for the school district and officials. On appeal, the U.S. Court of Appeals, Sixth Circuit, held harassment must take place in a context subject to a school's control in order to impose liability. Victims of peer harassment lack rights to make particular remedial demands. The court held the incidents in this case did not amount to severe, pervasive and objectively offensive conduct.

The classmate could not rely on incidents involving other victims to meet the "severe and pervasive" part of the Title IX liability analysis. When the school district learned of the harassment, it imposed a supervision plan. The district's response to the assault was "prompt, reasonable, and not deliberately indifferent." Constant supervision of the student was not required. **No authority supported the argument that activity at other schools or off campus was relevant to a Title IX claim, as the district had no control over it.** As the district was not deliberately indifferent to peer harassment, the court held in its favor. *Pahssen v. Merrill Community School Dist.*, 668 F.3d 356 (6th Cir. 2012).

◆ New York parents claimed teachers and school administrators did not intervene when classmates subjected their autistic child to daily name-calling, abusive language and violent conduct. A teacher was alleged to be present during some of the incidents. In a federal court complaint against the school district and several teachers, administrators and staff members, the student claimed peers called him a "fucking retard," "asshole," "faggot" and "bitch."

According to the parents, nobody took effective measures to deter the harassment or discipline the harassers. In pretrial activity, the court refused to dismiss the disability harassment claims. It used the standard of liability from sexual harassment cases under Title IX and *Davis v. Monroe County Board of Educ.*, this chapter. **Since the student claimed he was regularly harassed and bullied and that officials took no meaningful action, the court held he could pursue the harassment-based Section 504 claims.** Although he cited many incidents in which sexual questions and terms were involved, the court found no evidence of anti-male bias, and it dismissed claims for gender-based harassment under Title IX and the Equal Protection Clause. But the student could pursue claims against the district for negligent hiring and negligent supervision, violation of the state civil rights act, and discrimination under Section 504. *Preston v. Hilton Cent. School Dist.*, 876 F.Supp.2d 235 (W.D.N.Y. 2012).

◆ Parents of a New York student with a learning disability complained to her school that bullying of the child occurred almost every day of the 2007-08 school year. When the committee on special education (CSE) met to discuss her placement for the 2008-09 school year, the parents claimed the principal said a CSE meeting was an inappropriate place to discuss bullying. The parents later challenged the CSE's placement proposal at a hearing. An impartial officer (IHO) heard testimony by school aides and a substitute regarding significant classroom ostracism and teasing of the student. One aide said teachers got upset with the student instead of addressing peer misconduct. An aide claimed she told teachers and the principal about the bullying, but "it was ignored." Despite this evidence, the IHO found bullying was not relevant to the review of an individualized education program. On appeal, a federal court discussed bullying in schools at length. It noted 45 states have laws on bullying in schools.

The court held schools were required to investigate promptly and respond appropriately when they learned that disability harassment may have occurred. There was support for finding that free appropriate public education protections apply to bullying cases. The court applied the "deliberate indifference" approach from *Davis v. Monroe County Board of Educ.*, this chapter. It held "a school must take prompt and appropriate action" in response to bullying incidents, and take appropriate steps to prevent future incidents. This duty existed regardless of whether the conduct was covered in an anti-bullying policy, and regardless of whether a student had complained. *T.K. and S.K. v. Dep't of Educ. of City of New York*, 779 F.Supp.2d 289 (E.D.N.Y. 2011).

◆ Parents of a Michigan student with disabilities asked her school district in writing to keep her safe due to her vulnerability. A special education teacher later allowed her to accompany a male classmate to an unsupervised room. There, the male exposed himself and engaged the student in sexual contact. The parents sued the district in a state court, asserting claims under Title IX and state law. After the Title IX claim was dismissed, a jury found the student was not entitled to protection under a state disability protection act. On appeal, the Court of Appeals of Michigan held the state disabilities civil rights act prohibits schools from discriminating against an individual "because of a disability that is unrelated to the individual's ability to utilize and benefit from the institution or its service." **The court held the student's cognitive impairment prevented her from utilizing or benefiting from educational opportunities** offered in the district. This meant she could not claim state disability law protection. As the trial court did not abuse its discretion, the court affirmed the judgment. It rejected a claim that the jury had been forced to deliberate at a time when jurors wanted to end the case and avoid a fifth day of trial. In a brief memorandum, the Supreme Court of Michigan denied the family's appeal. *Tyler v. Fowlerville Community School Dist.*, 490 Mich. 860, 802 N.W. 43 (Mich. 2011).

◆ A Philadelphia student with mental retardation was vulnerable to peers. Her mother met with a school administrator and a teacher to discuss protecting her. According to the mother, the school promised the student one-on-one adult supervision. But a few weeks later, a male student led her from the cafeteria to the school auditorium. There, the male and four others forced her into having oral sex. In a federal court action against the school district and principal, the student argued the assault would not have occurred if the school had provided the promised protection. The case reached the U.S. Court of Appeals, Third Circuit. It explained that **the Constitution does not impose an affirmative duty on the government to protect citizens from private violence.** Liability for a constitutional violation could not be imposed unless there was official knowledge and acquiescence in the violation. To find the school district liable, it had to be shown that it inflicted injury through a policy or custom. The court held that even if the student was promised one-on-one supervision, this was not an "affirmative act" that created school liability. As there was no affirmative duty to protect her from the assailants, the court affirmed the judgment. *Brown v. School Dist. of Philadelphia*, 456 Fed.Appx. 88 (3d Cir. 2011).

◆ A Michigan student endured many years of peer harassment and bullying. Harassment escalated in his seventh-grade year, when a teacher teased him in front of a class. His grades fell, and he hid during lunch to avoid taunting. In grade eight, the student was found eligible for special education. He was placed in a resource room where the teacher helped him cope with peers. But when the student entered grade nine, the principal refused to let him use the same resource room. When the student was a high school junior, a baseball team member sexually assaulted him in the locker room. The student refused to return to school, and his family sued the school district in a federal district court. Appeal reached the U.S. Court of Appeals, Sixth Circuit, which noted that each time the family reported an incident and the perpetrators were known, the district responded. This was not "deliberate indifference" that would trigger Title IX liability. **But refusing to let the student return to his resource room might be evidence of deliberate indifference, opening the door for Title IX liability.** *Patterson v. Hudson Area Schools*, 551 F.3d 438 (9th Cir. 2008).

The case was returned to the district court, which held the case arose under Title IX, not disability protection laws. **Title IX was intended to protect students from sex discrimination, not general bullying.** While damages are available in a Title IX action for sexual harassment that is so severe, pervasive and objectively offensive that it denied equal access to education, damages are unavailable for teasing and name-calling. Some evidence that the district sought to exclude had sexual overtones and might be more than just teasing or bullying. But the court held materials relating to any time after the student stopped going to school could be excluded from evidence, as the district sought. *Patterson v. Hudson Area Schools,* No. 05-74439, 2010 WL 455410 (E.D. Mich. 2/3/10).

◆ A 16-year-old Texas special education student functioned at a level that was near second grade. Her family reported that she was sexually assaulted at her school by a male special needs student with a record of violence and displaying pornography. Although an aide separated the two when she saw inappropriate contact, she did not report the incident until the next day. The principal called the school district police, and police officers questioned the male student and a teacher. No police action was taken against the male student, but the school separated the students and assigned an escort to the female student. The student sued the school district for sexual harassment under Title IX. A federal district court dismissed the case, and the U.S. Court of Appeals, Fifth Circuit, affirmed the judgment. It held that to establish Title IX liability, there must be sexual harassment so severe, pervasive and objectively offensive that it deprives a victim of access to educational opportunities or benefits. In addition, **a school district must have actual knowledge of harassment, yet act with deliberate indifference to it**. The court held the student did not prove the requirements for Title IX liability, because the actions in this case were not "so severe, pervasive and objectively offensive" as to deprive her of access to education. And the district took remedial action to prevent future incidents. *Watkins v. La Marque Independent School Dist.*, 308 Fed.Appx. 781 (5th Cir. 2009).

II. RACE AND NATIONAL ORIGIN DISCRIMINATION

*Title VI of the Civil Rights Act of 1964 prohibits discrimination based on race, color or national origin in any program that receives federal funds. Title VI is based on equal protection principles, and many discrimination complaints allege violations of Title VI, the Equal Protection Clause, and analogous state laws. **Courts require proof of intentional discrimination in Title VI cases.***

In Plyler v. Doe, *457 U.S. 202 (1982), the U.S. Supreme Court held the states may not deny access to public education to any child residing in the state, whether present in the U.S. legally or otherwise.*

◆ A part-white, part-Latino student moved to an overwhelmingly white New York school district. Students began threatening him and repeatedly calling him "nigger." During the rest of the student's high school career, he continued to report incidents of racial harassment and taunting, some of which involved physical contact, death threats and a reference to lynching. The family attorney, and later the local human rights commission and the local NAACP affiliate, suggested a "shadow" to accompany the student while he was at school. These entities also sought to implement racial sensitivity programs in the district. Although these services were offered for free, the district declined them. A district compliance officer, who was supposed to investigate Title IX violations, did not respond to complaints. The student's mother made the choice to allow him to accept a special education diploma rather than to attend school further.

The student sued the school district for race discrimination. A jury found the district violated Title VI and awarded the student $1.25 million. After the court reduced the damages to $1 million, appeal went to the U.S. Court of Appeals, Second Circuit. Applying *Davis v. Monroe County Board of Educ.*, this chapter, the court held **official action was "deliberately indifferent" under either Title IX or Title VI if it was "clearly unreasonable in light of the known circumstances."** A reasonable juror could find the harassment met Title VI liability standards, as it was "severe, pervasive, and objectively offensive." Peers "taunted, harassed, menaced and physically assaulted" the student, called him "nigger" nearly every day, and threatened him with death. Staff members reported numerous incidents to the principal, and the mother contacted school administrators between 30 and 50 times. Other reports were lodged by the human rights commission, the NAACP, and the police. While the district was not required to eliminate all the harassment, the court held it ignored many signals that more action was necessary, and the decision for the student was affirmed. *Zeno v. Pine Plains Cent. School Dist.*, 702 F.3d 655 (2d Cir. 2012).

◆ Students from different New York school systems filed complaints against their school districts with the State Division of Human Rights (SDHR), claiming the districts permitted race and disability harassment in violation of the state human rights law. The case reached the New York Court of Appeals, which held the SDHR lacked power to investigate human rights law complaints against school districts. But it noted that public school students had other remedies under state and federal laws, and could file complaints with the state commissioner of education. **State legislators enacted the Dignity for All Students Act in 2010 to provide public school students an environment free of any harassment that substantially interfered with education.** The court held for the school districts. *North Syracuse Cent. School Dist. v. New York State Division of Human Rights*, 19 N.Y.3d 481, 973 N.E.2d 162 (N.Y. 2012).

◆   A Mississippi high school assistant principal arrived at the scene of a fight between two students, one African-American and the other white. Police and emergency medical technicians arrived. The African-American student had only minor injuries, and police officers handcuffed him and placed him in a police car. Technicians deemed the white student's injuries serious enough to require hospitalization, and he was not handcuffed. Both students were charged with disorderly conduct, suspended from school for 10 days and denied class credit. The next school year, the African-American student took an auto-body class offered through a community college. There, a student complained he was sexually harassing her during a class. College officials tried to search him.

The student refused to be searched and was suspended for two days. As a condition to returning to class, the college required him to get counseling. In response, the student's family sued the school district, community college and law enforcement officers in a federal district court. The court rejected claims for false arrest and violations of the student's religious free exercise, due process and equal protection rights. On appeal, the U.S. Court of Appeals, Fifth Circuit, held the officers were entitled to qualified immunity. Probable cause existed to arrest the student after the fight. **There was no equal protection violation, as any different treatment was based on the white student's need for medical attention.** An administrator took the student to the office to discuss the suspension. As this was all the process due for a short-term suspension, the judgment was affirmed. A religious objection to the counseling requirement failed, as the student had "no constitutional right to choose his own curriculum." *C.H., II v. Rankin County School Dist.*, 415 Fed.Appx. 541 (5th Cir. 2011).

◆   A Minnesota high school student council encouraged students to dress according to various themes during homecoming week. Some students wore oversized jerseys, sagging pants, "doo-rags" and other items that an African-American student found racially offensive. According to the student, officials did not respond when a similar display was staged the next year, until state and federal government officials intervened. She sued school officials in a federal court for negligence and race discrimination under state and federal laws. School officials moved to dismiss the claims, including one filed under Title VI. The court noted that in Title IX cases, courts have found schools may be held liable for peer sexual harassment. **Since Congress had modeled Title IX after Title VI, the court found it appropriate to look to Title IX for guidance.** Several federal circuit courts have recognized Title VI claims based on a school district's intentional failure to address a racially hostile environment. Since Title

VI supported a lawsuit against a school district for intentional discrimination, the court allowed the student's case to proceed. *Pruitt v. Anderson,* Civil No. 11-2143 (DSD/JJK), 2011 WL 6141084 (D. Minn. 12/29/11).

◆ Nine North Carolina students sued the Durham Public School System, asserting a "wholesale challenge" to its disciplinary process. They claimed that they were disciplined more severely than white students for less serious offenses. In addition, the students claimed that the board's anti-gang policy was unconstitutionally vague. A state trial court dismissed the action, and the students appealed. The Court of Appeals of North Carolina held that most of the claims had been properly dismissed, as each individual student failed to allege a claim for relief against each individual official. But the lower court would have to reconsider a due process claim brought on behalf of a now-deceased student who had been suspended for 13 days. His mother claimed that the superintendent of schools misled her and backdated correspondence to make a long-term suspension appear to be a short-term suspension. The trial court was also to reconsider a challenge to the school board's anti-gang policy. On appeal, the Supreme Court of North Carolina held the student had an adequate remedy under state law. So he could not sue the board for due process violations. Here, **two North Carolina statutes allowed any student who was suspended in excess of 10 school days to appeal to the education board, and then to a state court**. The court did not consider the gang policy issue, which was to return to the trial court. *Copper v. Denlinger,* 688 S.E.2d 426 (N.C. 2010).

◆ A Minnesota school district opened an alternative school for immigrant students with limited English skills and little or no formal education. Thirteen students claimed the school had no coherent curriculum, warehoused them and guaranteed academic failure. Several failed to pass a state test required for high school graduation. A report by the state education department found the school improperly refused to test students for special education eligibility until they had at least three years of English Language Learner (ELL) instruction. The students sued the school and district for violating the Equal Educational Opportunities Act (EEOA), Title VI, and the Minnesota Human Rights Act (MHRA).

A federal district court held for the school and district. On appeal, the U.S. Court of Appeals, Eighth Circuit, held **Title VI prohibits only intentional discrimination**. There was no strong evidence of discrimination based on the statements by staff. Significantly, **the students did not identify students who were treated more favorably by the school district to whom they could be compared.** Eleven of the students presented no evidence of injury from the policy of not testing ELL students for special education needs until they took three years of ELL classes. As for the remaining two, the district stated it did not believe they could be reliably assessed for special services until they had been in the country long enough to learn English. No school or district policy singled out foreign-born students. The testing policy applied to all ELL students, not just those born outside the U.S. Neither the EEOA nor the MHRA authorized monetary damages, and the judgment was affirmed. *Mumid v. Abraham Lincoln High School,* 618 F.3d 789 (8th Cir. 2010).

◆   A Kansas student claimed that the principal and teachers at his alternative school repeatedly forbade students of Hispanic origin from speaking Spanish. According to the student, the principal suspended him after telling him "he was not in Mexico" and that "he should speak only English on school premises." The student's father brought the suspension notice to the superintendent, who overturned the suspension. The family sued the superintendent, principal, teachers, school board and district, and members of the school board. The complaint alleged race and national origin discrimination in violation of Title VI and the Equal Protection Clause. The court noted that the EEOC has stated that rigid English-only workplace rules may violate Title VII of the Civil Rights Act. **By claiming that school officials singled out students of Hispanic origin and targeted them for attributes based upon race or national origin, the student made out a valid equal protection claim.** But the principal and teacher were entitled to qualified immunity from liability because no case had established a right to speak a foreign language at a public school. However, the school district could still be held liable for the principal's acts, because she had authority to take corrective action to end the discrimination. *Rubio v. Turner Unified School Dist.*, 453 F.Supp.2d 1295 (D. Kan. 2006).

III. ADMISSIONS AND ATTENDANCE

The Equal Protection Clause of the Fourteenth Amendment requires government agencies to apply the law equally to all persons. Due to the history of official segregation before Brown v. Board of Educ., *347 U.S. 483 (1954), all government classifications based on race are subject to strict judicial scrutiny.*

A. Race, Admission and School Assignment

◆   Until 2000, Jefferson County Public Schools (JCPS) was under federal court supervision in a desegregation case. Upon being released from federal oversight, JCPS voluntarily adopted an elementary student assignment plan that considered race when making school assignments and some transfers. A federal court challenge to that plan reached the U.S. Supreme Court. In the federal case, the Supreme Court found that enrolling students without regard to race would yield "a substantially diverse student body without any definition of diversity." See *Parents Involved in Community Schools v. Seattle School Dist. No. 1*, this chapter.

Following the Supreme Court's decision, JCPS approved a managed choice attendance plan for 2009-10, under which some JCPS school assignments were based on family income rather than neighborhood. Parents claimed Section 159.070 of Kentucky Revised Statutes permitted them to "enroll" their children in the public school nearest their home, as well as to "attend" classes there. A state circuit court held Section 159.070 allowed children to "enroll" in the public school nearest their homes but did not permit them to also "attend" such schools. On appeal, the Supreme Court of Kentucky found "enroll" was not synonymous with "attend." "Enrollment" meant "registration" and did not automatically permit attendance at a particular school. **The interpretation urged by the parents conflicted with the legislative history of Section**

159.070, as well as court cases regarding the role of local education boards in student assignments. In other education laws, the General Assembly had distinguished between "enroll" and "attend." A predecessor of Section 159.070 granted parents a right to "enroll for attendance." A 1990 amendment deleted this language as part of an overhaul of the state public education system, and this convinced the court that JCPS was correct. *Jefferson County Board of Educ. v. Fell*, 391 S.W.3d 713 (Ky. 2012).

◆ In 1970, a federal court ordered two North Carolina districts to desegregate their schools. In 1986, the districts merged. In 2006, parents complained to the federal Office for Civil Rights (OCR) that the merged board was relying on race in its student assignment plan. To settle the OCR complaint, the board filed a motion to approve a revised assignment plan that would replace explicit racial balancing with a definition of "student diversity." This definition balanced factors such as student achievement, socio-economic status and racial, ethnic and educational sub-groups. In 2009, the court issued a consent order that required the parties to work toward attaining unitary status of the merged district. The board proposed three scenarios for consideration, and it eventually selected a plan emphasizing achievement and prioritizing school proximity. The parents objected to the plan because it only considered 14 of the district's 36 schools. They argued the plan increased racially identifiable schools with lower student achievement levels and moved the district away from unitary status.

The parents sought a court order that would declare the assignment plan in violation of existing desegregation orders. The court denied relief to the parents, who appealed to the U.S. Court of Appeals, Fourth Circuit. It said the law is well-established that once a court has identified an unlawful dual system of segregated schools, **students and parents are entitled to a presumption that current racial disparities in schools were related to a prior segregated system**. In prior activity, the lower court had not found the district in constitutional compliance and had found the 1970 court orders still in effect. Since the board had a heavy burden of showing that its actions were moving the district toward unitary status, the case was returned to the lower court so it could decide if the 2011-12 student assignment plan was having this effect. *Everett v. Pitt County Board of Educ.*, 678 F.3d 281 (4th Cir. 2012).

◆ Nine African-American students claimed a Pennsylvania school board discriminated against them when it assigned them to a smaller high school. The action was part of a reassignment plan devised to equalize the student population at two high schools. After a nine-day trial, a federal district court found the board had a race-neutral goal of equalizing the enrollments of two district high schools. According to the court, the district had legitimate reasons for its actions and had specific concern for African-American students. While some board members considered diversity in adopting the reassignment plan, the court held for the district, finding "race was not the basis of their votes." On appeal to the Third Circuit, the students claimed the district "targeted" them for the smaller high school and imposed an undue burden on African-Americans.

The court held discriminatory intent must be proven to show an equal protection violation. As the district court found, the student reassignments

were race neutral and based on geography. For this reason, the court held the case was distinct from the Supreme Court cases the students cited. While a number of communications by board members, school administrators and advisors stated an awareness of race, this was not the same as making racial classifications or acting with a discriminatory purpose. **Race consciousness in the redistricting process did not prove discrimination.** The court held the school district had legitimate reasons for adopting the plan, such as attempting to equalize the high school enrollments, avoiding excessive busing, minimizing student travel time and ensuring comfortable learning environments. It held the school assignments were based on race-neutral factors. As the court found no evidence of discriminatory intent, and references to "diversity" did not imply a discriminatory purpose, the court held for the district. *Doe 1 v. Lower Merion School Dist.*, 665 F.3d 524 (3d Cir. 2011).

◆ A Louisiana school district was the subject of a longstanding federal court desegregation case. In 2004, the district was found "unitary" in that vestiges of the prior dual school system had been eliminated to the extent practicable. By 2006, one district middle school had become severely overcrowded, and the district adopted an option that changed one primary school to a different feeder zone and assigned two new primary schools to high school feeder zones. Shortly after the board adopted the assignment plan, the parent of two African-American students filed a lawsuit asserting equal protection violations. A federal magistrate judge found the assignment plan race-neutral and nondiscriminatory.

On appeal, the U.S. Court of Appeals, Fifth Circuit, stated that **racial classifications are presumptively invalid and can be upheld based only on "an extraordinary justification," even if they are motivated by a "benign" reason.** Evidence indicated that school officials believed the assignment plan could not upset the unitary status of district high schools. The court questioned the lower court's finding that the board could not have discriminated because it had a "benign" purpose of maintaining post-unitary racial balance in its schools. This assumption was in tension with *Parents Involved in Community Schools v. Seattle School Dist. No. 1*, this chapter. A wealth of evidence indicated school officials were motivated by the desire to preserve the district's unitary status. In addition to statements by school officials indicating their reliance on student race, the parent presented statistics supporting his argument that the assignment plan would increase the racial segregation in district schools, not decrease it. As there was a question about the board's motive in selecting an assignment plan, the court reversed the judgment and returned the case to the district court. *Lewis v. Ascension Parish School Board*, 662 F.3d 343 (5th Cir. 2011).

◆ Seattle never operated a dual system of racially segregated schools, but it used race as a tiebreaker in allocating ninth-grade slots for oversubscribed high schools. Jefferson County, Kentucky formerly operated a dual school system, but a federal court declared the system unitary in 2000 and freed it from federal court supervision. Both school districts voluntarily adopted student assignment plans that relied in part upon race. Jefferson County considered race when making some elementary school assignments and in ruling on transfer requests. It tried to assure that a school's racial balance was within a range reflecting the district's racial composition. Parents of students who were denied the school assignment of their choice sued the school systems. Federal circuit courts later upheld the student assignment plans used in both of the school systems. On appeal, the U.S. Supreme Court noted the plans did not allow meaningful individual review of applicants but instead relied on racial classifications in a "non-individualized, mechanical way." The classifications would only shift a small number of students. By contrast, consideration of race was critical in tripling minority representation at Michigan Law School in *Grutter v. Bollinger*.

The diversity interest approved in *Grutter* "was not focused on race alone but encompassed 'all factors that may contribute to student body diversity.'" The plans in this case "employ only a limited notion of diversity, viewing race exclusively in white/nonwhite terms in Seattle and black/'other' terms in Jefferson County." Enrolling students without regard to race would yield "a substantially diverse student body without any definition of diversity." **Allowing racial balancing was unconstitutional, and using it as a compelling end in itself would assure that race would always be relevant.** This could justify permanent racial classifications, promote notions of racial inferiority and lead to racial hostility. The Court reversed the judgments. *Parents Involved in Community Schools v. Seattle School Dist. No. 1*, 551 U.S. 701 (2007).

◆ Parents of students attending school in Berkeley Unified School District (BUSD) had to rank the school program they preferred for their children. While BUSD attempted to assign students on the basis of parental preference, it made assignments in priority categories. BUSD used neighborhood demographics when assigning students to elementary schools and high school programs. Instead of considering individual student race, BUSD used neighborhood data based on 445 "planning areas" of four-to-eight city blocks. Students in these areas were assigned a score based on their area's demographics. Areas were evaluated by average neighborhood household income, average education level of adults residing in the neighborhood, and neighborhood racial composition.

A parent group charged BUSD with violating Proposition 209, which prohibits state and local government units (including school districts) from discriminating against, or granting preferential treatment to, any individual or group based on race, sex, color, ethnicity or national origin in public employment, education or contracting. The Court of Appeal of California held that the plan did not violate the state constitution, as it did "not show partiality, prejudice, or preference to any student on the basis of that student's race." **All students in an area were treated equally, regardless of individual race or personal characteristics.** To the extent that any preference was given, it was on the basis of the collective composition of a student's neighborhood. *American Civil Rights Foundation v. Berkeley Unified School Dist.*, 172 Cal.App.4th 207, 90 Cal.Rptr.3d 789 (Cal. Ct. App. 2009).

◆ Los Angeles Unified School District (LAUSD) operated magnet programs under a desegregation order which ended 18 years of state court litigation. A state court entered an order in 1981 that approved an integration plan relying in part on magnet schools and a Permit With Transportation (PWT) program. Both programs took student race or ethnicity into account in school applications and admissions. The case ended when the U.S. Supreme Court let stand LAUSD's magnet and PWT programs in *Crawford v. Board of Educ.*, 458 U.S. 527 (1982). In 1996, California voters approved Proposition 209 to amend the state constitution to prohibit public education programs from discriminating against or giving preferential treatment based on race, ethnicity or national origin.

LAUSD continued to assign students to magnet schools on a priority point system that relied in part on racial and ethnic designations. An organization sued LAUSD, claiming it relied on racial classifications in violation of Proposition 209. The case reached the California Court of Appeal, which agreed with LAUSD that desegregation orders do not terminate simply because court supervision of plan implementation has ended. Desegregation efforts were still under way in LAUSD schools in 1996. The 1981 court order had never been reversed, overruled, vacated, revoked, modified or withdrawn. **The Supreme Court has held that school districts may rely on the ongoing validity of a desegregation order.** LAUSD was to take reasonably feasible steps to desegregate its schools. As the 1981 *Crawford* order was in existence when Proposition 209 took effect in 1996, the magnet and PWT programs were upheld. *American Civil Rights Foundation v. Los Angeles Unified School Dist.*, 169 Cal.App.4th 436, 86 Cal.Rptr.3d 754 (Cal. Ct. App. 2008).

◆   In two cases involving the University of Michigan, the Supreme Court considered the use of race in higher education admissions. In the first case, the U.S. Court of Appeals, Sixth Circuit, upheld the University of Michigan Law School's admissions policy. The appeals court found that the law school had a compelling interest in achieving a diverse student body. The Supreme Court noted that any governmental distinction based on race must be examined under the strict scrutiny standard. Under this standard, the classification must be "narrowly tailored to further compelling governmental interests." The Court held, based on *Regents of the Univ. of California v. Bakke*, 438 U.S. 265 (1978), that the goal of a diverse student body is a compelling governmental interest.

The law school admissions policy utilized a narrowly tailored method of achieving that interest through its consideration of race as a "plus" factor. The Court held the policy was flexible, and it did not create an impermissible quota system. One of the most important factors supporting the decision was the individualized review of applicants that considered several race-neutral factors. *Grutter v. Bollinger,* 539 U.S. 306 (2003).

An undergraduate admissions policy for the University of Michigan's College of Literature, Science and the Arts awarded applicants points for a variety of factors, and they needed at least 100 points for admission. Applicants from underrepresented minority groups were automatically awarded 20 points. The Court applied the strict scrutiny analysis to the policy and held that it was not narrowly tailored to achieve the compelling state interest in diversity declared by the university. **The policy impermissibly gave underrepresented minority students an advantage or preference** by automatically awarding them 20 points. The policy was also deficient because it failed to require an individualized review of each applicant, which is essential when race is a consideration. *Gratz v. Bollinger,* 539 U.S. 244, 123 S.Ct. 2411, 156 L.Ed.2d 257 (2003).

◆ A Wisconsin school district had no formal policy for elementary school class assignments, but a principal issued a memo to staff, urging the balancing of classes according to student gender, ethnicity, academic ability, special needs and parental input. A teacher divided her class into five small groups and put two African-American students in each group, so that they sat together in pairs. She said "African-American students need a buddy, and sometimes it works well if they have someone else working with them because they view things in a global manner." An African-American family sued the school district and school officials in a federal court, alleging Equal Protection Clause violations. The court held for the district, teacher and officials, finding the decision to place the student was the result of race-neutral factors. The U.S. Court of Appeals, Seventh Circuit, affirmed the decision concerning the school's policy. But it held the lower court should not have awarded judgment to the teacher. **Even if she believed she was acting in the best interests of minority students by seating them in pairs, her action was based purely on race.** Because the law in this area was well established, the teacher was not entitled to qualified immunity on the equal protection claim arising from the seating policy. *Billings v. Madison Metropolitan School Dist.*, 259 F.3d 807 (7th Cir. 2001).

B. Age and Residency Requirements

In Martinez v. Bynum *(this chapter), the U.S. Supreme Court upheld a Texas law conditioning public school enrollment on residency within a school district or proof that enrollment was not being sought for the sole purpose of attending school within the district. States may restrict eligibility for tuition-free education to residents, and a bona fide residence requirement is constitutional.*

◆ A five-year-old Texas student went to live with his aunt. His birth mother lived outside the school district. The aunt sought to pre-enroll the student in a kindergarten class, but the school registrar informed her that she could not enroll him without proof that she had the legal right to act as his guardian or parent. Later in the day, the registrar rejected a power of attorney document signed by the student's mother. The aunt obtained a legal aid attorney, who asserted that a power of attorney was sufficient to establish residency under a section of the Texas Education Code. The section requires non-resident persons under 18 years of age to establish that their presence in a school district is not for the primary purpose of participation in extracurricular activities. The school district maintained that the section did not create a basis for school enrollment. Instead of pursuing the board's grievance procedure, the aunt filed a lawsuit.

The district superintendent then decided to admit the student on the basis of the power of attorney. When the aunt tried to continue the lawsuit anyway, claiming that the district might again exclude the student, a federal district **court dismissed the case, finding the district had never denied the student admission**. The U.S. Court of Appeals, Fifth Circuit, affirmed. Had the aunt awaited a decision by the superintendent or filed a proper grievance, she would have forced the district's initial decision-maker to take a definitive position. *Zepeda v. Boerne Independent School Dist.*, 294 Fed.Appx. 834 (5th Cir. 2008).

◆ A disabled Colorado student and her family moved out of her school district when she was in second grade. The district permitted her to stay in her school for the rest of the year. It readmitted her to the school for third and fourth grade under the state's school choice law. However, the district denied her application to re-enroll for grade five, stating that its special education program had exceeded its capacity. A special education due process hearing officer held for the district, and an administrative law judge affirmed. The parents moved back into the school district and re-enrolled their daughter in the school she had formerly attended. They sued the district for violating the state school choice law, among others. The court awarded pretrial judgment to the district.

On appeal, the state court of appeals held that the school choice law allowed elementary students who became district "nonresidents" during a school year or between school years to remain in their schools. This right extended only to the next school year and did not entitle a nonresident student to return for subsequent school years, as the parents argued. The district's special education programs exceeded nonresident enrollment limits. **The school choice statute authorized the district to deny re-enrollment based on nonresident status.** The district had a "potentially limitless" obligation to provide special education to disabled resident students, but this was distinct from any obligation to accept nonresidents under the school choice law. The court affirmed the judgment. *Bradshaw v. Cherry Creek School Dist. No. 5*, 98 P.3d 886 (Colo. Ct. App. 2003).

◆ A parent who lived in Chicago sent her daughter to North Carolina after the girl was threatened with assault. The student's uncle attempted to enroll her in a local school, but the district superintendent denied admission because she was not domiciled in a county school administrative unit. The family filed a state court action that reached the North Carolina Court of Appeals.

The court observed that **a child who is not domiciled in a local administrative unit may attend its schools without paying tuition if the child resides with an adult in the unit as the result of a parent or guardian's death, serious illness, incapacity or incarceration**. A non-domiciliary student may also enroll in school in another administrative unit in cases of abandonment, child abuse or natural disaster. In these cases, the student must present an affidavit including a statement that the claim to residency is not primarily related to attendance at a particular school and that an adult with whom the child resides accepts responsibility for the child's educational decisions. The court rejected the family's argument that the law violated due process and equal protection rights. In *Martinez v. Bynum* (this chapter), the U.S. Supreme Court upheld a Texas law conditioning public school enrollment on residency within a school district or proof that enrollment was not being sought for the sole purpose of attending school within the district. The North Carolina statute, like the Texas law, was a reasonable standard for determining the residential status of public school students. *Graham v. Mock*, 545 S.E.2d 263 (N.C. Ct. App. 2001).

◆ Texas law permitted school districts to deny free admission to minors who lived apart from a "parent, guardian, or the person having lawful control of him" if the minor's primary purpose in being in the district was to attend local public schools. A minor left his parent's home in Mexico to live with his sister in a

Texas town for the purpose of attending school there. When the school district denied his application for tuition-free admission, his sister sued, alleging that the law was unconstitutional. A federal court held for the state, and the Fifth Circuit Court of Appeals affirmed. The U.S. Supreme Court upheld the residency requirement. **A bona fide residence requirement, appropriately defined and uniformly applied, furthered a substantial state interest** in assuring that services provided for residents were enjoyed only by residents. Such a requirement with respect to attendance in public free schools did not violate the Equal Protection Clause. Residence generally requires both physical presence and intention to remain. As long as the child was not living in the district for the sole purpose of attending school, he satisfied the statutory test. The Court held that this was a bona fide residency requirement and that the Constitution permits a state to restrict eligibility for tuition-free education to its bona fide residents. *Martinez v. Bynum*, 461 U.S. 321 (1983).

C. Undocumented Students

In 2011, the U.S. Department of Education's Office for Civil Rights (OCR) and the U.S. Department of Justice issued a joint "Dear Colleague" letter advising school officials not to take actions to discourage the enrollment of undocumented students. An OCR question and answer sheet for school districts and parents declares that districts should not inquire into the immigration or citizenship status of a student or parent as a means of establishing residency.

The letter explains that Plyler v. Doe, below, prohibits states from denying access to public education to any child residing in the state, without regard to whether they are present in the U.S. legally. The undocumented status of a student or a parent is irrelevant to the entitlement to public education.

According to the OCR, districts may require students or parents to provide copies of phone and water bills or lease agreements to establish residency. But districts cannot seek information with a "purpose or result of denying access" to public schools on the basis of race, color or national origin.

School districts may restrict attendance to district residents, but the OCR letter states that inquiring into citizenship or immigration status is not relevant to residency status. While schools may require a birth certificate to ensure that a student is within age requirements, "a district may not bar a student from enrolling in its schools based on a foreign birth certificate." Districts cannot deny enrollment to a student if a parent refuses to provide a social security number upon the district's request. The OCR letter states that "it is essential that any request be uniformly applied to all students and not applied in a selective manner." U.S. Dep't of Educ., Office for Civil Rights, U.S. Justice Department Joint Dear Colleague Letter: May 6, 2011, available at http://www2.ed.gov/about/offices/list/ocr/letters/colleague-201101.html.

◆   Alabama legislators enacted H.B. 56 in 2011. Section 8 of H.B. 56 made unlawfully present aliens ineligible for any postsecondary education benefit, including scholarships, grants or financial aid. Section 28 of the same act required public schools to determine if an enrolling child was born outside the U.S. or was the child of an unlawfully present alien on the basis of the student's birth certificate. If no birth certificate was available, or if a birth certificate reflected that a student was born outside the U.S. or was a child of an unlawfully present alien, then the student's parent or guardian had to notify the school of the student's actual citizenship or immigration status under federal law. If parents failed to notify the school of their official citizenship or immigration documentation, along with a sworn attestation that the document identified the child, then the child was presumed to be "an alien unlawfully present in the United States." A federal court held the state could not enforce Section 8. But it found the group which advanced the case did not have standing to challenge Section 28. On appeal, the Eleventh Circuit Court of Appeals noted that by the time of the appeal, state legislators had removed Section 8's prohibition on a wide array of aliens from attending Alabama public postsecondary institutions.

As a result, the lower court's preliminary order was dismissed. Unlike the lower court, the Eleventh Circuit held one of the organizations challenging Section 28 had standing to pursue the case. It held **Section 28 significantly interfered with the exercise of the right to an elementary public education under** *Plyler v. Doe.* The court held the goal of deterring illegal immigration did not justify the law. Finding the increased likelihood of deportation or harassment significantly deterred undocumented children from enrolling in or attending school, the court held Section 28 violated the Equal Protection Clause. Other challenged sections of H.B. 56 were held preempted by federal law in *U.S. v. Alabama,* below. *Hispanic Interest Coalition of Alabama v. Governor of Alabama,* 691 F.3d 1236 (11th Cir. 2012).

◆   A companion case to *Hispanic Interest Coalition of Alabama v. Governor of Alabama,* above, resolved other contested provisions of Alabama's H.B. 56. In it, the Eleventh Circuit held **the state could enforce provisions related to traffic stops by law officers**. But other provisions were preempted by federal law. In a brief opinion, the court held the U.S. government was entitled to an order enjoining enforcement of Section 28 and an unrelated section of the law. The court denied orders sought for other sections of the law pending appeal. *U.S. v. Alabama,* 443 Fed.Appx. 411 (11th Cir. 2011).

In a more recent order, the court held federal law preempted parts of H.B. 56 requiring alien registration, criminalizing certain workplace practices and barring undocumented aliens from contracts. But the court again refused to enjoin provisions for law officers to investigate immigration status of persons in their custody. *U.S. v. Alabama,* 691 F.3d 1269 (11th Cir. 2012).

◆   In May 1975, the Texas legislature revised its education laws to withhold from school districts any state funds for the education of children who were not legally admitted into the U.S. It authorized school districts to deny enrollment to these children. A group filed a class action on behalf of school-age children of Mexican origin who could not establish they had been legally admitted into the U.S. The action complained of the exclusion of the children from public school. A federal court prevented the school district from denying a free education to the children, and the U.S. Court of Appeals, Fifth Circuit, upheld the decision. The legislation was also challenged by numerous other plaintiffs. The court held that the law violated the Equal Protection Clause, and the Fifth Circuit affirmed.

The Supreme Court granted review. The state claimed that undocumented aliens were not "persons" within the jurisdiction of Texas, and so were not entitled to equal protection of its laws. The Court rejected this argument, stating that **whatever an alien's status under the immigration laws, an alien is a "person" in any sense of the term**. The term "within its jurisdiction" was meant as a term of geographic location, and the Equal Protection Clause extended its protection to all persons within a state, whether citizen or stranger. The statute could not be upheld because it did not advance any substantial state interest. The Texas statute imposed a lifetime hardship on a discrete class of children not accountable for their disabling status. There was no evidence to show the exclusion of the children would improve the overall quality of education in the state. *Plyler v. Doe*, 457 U.S. 202 (1982).

D. Homeless Students

Federal law requires schools to provide homeless students access to the same public education as other children receive. This includes transportation, special education, English learner, gifted and talented programs and school lunch programs for which students meet eligibility requirements. Under the McKinney-Vento Homeless Assistance Act, homeless children cannot be stigmatized or segregated from a "mainstream school environment on the basis of their being homeless." ***If a homeless student's school enrollment is disputed, the Act requires school districts to immediately admit a student to the school in which enrollment is sought, pending resolution of the dispute.***

Schools must notify the parents of homeless children about the NCLB Act's school choice provisions. ***Schools must continue the education of a homeless student in the student's "school of origin,"*** *or enroll the student in a public school that non-homeless students in the same attendance area are eligible to attend. NCLB section 722(g), codified at 42 U.S.C. § 11432, defines "school of origin" as the school a child attended when permanently housed or "the school in which the child or youth was last enrolled."*

◆ Fire destroyed the house of two New York students, and they were forced to move. They continued to attend school in the same district. But after a residency investigation, the district decided they were no longer residents and advised their mother they would be "disenrolled" from their schools. Although she applied to the state education department for temporary relief, the department denied her request, and the district notified her that the children could not attend their school as of the end of the next school day. The mother filed a federal court case against the district and the education department. As the court explained, state law incorporated federal McKinney-Vento Act requirements and required school districts to immediately admit homeless students. On the other hand, state law did not create an absolute right to attend any public school.

In addition to preserving a homeless student's school placement pending appeal, the McKinney-Vento Act required each district to establish procedures for the prompt resolution of enrollment disputes. In this case, the court noted the students had lived in an apartment in the school district immediately after they had to leave their house due to a fire. **State law violated the federal act**

because it gave school officials discretion to allow disenrollment of a child pending an enrollment dispute. While the district argued that the students were not "homeless," the court found federal law did not condition its pendency provision on such status. Disenrolling the students could cause great harm, and there was no corresponding harm to the district in the event that they remained. Finding the family likely to succeed in further proceedings, the court issued the requested relief. *N.J. v. State of New York*, 872 F.Supp.2d 204 (E.D.N.Y. 2011).

◆   In an enrollment dispute between two school districts, the New York Court of Appeals noted that the school district in which a child resided at the time of a social services placement had to bear the child's instructional costs. The court held a family's last permanent residence was what counted, not a brief stay in a shelter. **Residence was established by physical presence as an inhabitant within the district, combined with an intent to remain.** Districts were required to provide tuition-free education only to students whose parents or guardians resided in the district. "Temporary stayovers" following an eviction, including time in the homeless shelter, did not change the family residence. *Longwood Cent. School Dist. v. Springs Union Free School Dist.*, 1 N.Y.3d 385, 774 N.Y.S.2d 857, 806 N.E.2d 970 (N.Y. 2004).

IV. COMPULSORY ATTENDANCE

A. Compulsory Attendance and Truancy

States have a compelling interest in providing public education and may establish and enforce reasonable school attendance laws. In 2012, California amended state law to allow school administrators discretion in determining a valid excuse for which a student may be absent from school. When an initial truancy report is issued, a student and his or her parents may be requested to meet with a school counselor to discuss root causes of attendance issues and develop a joint plan to improve attendance. If a second truancy report is issued in the same school year, the student may be given a written warning by a peace officer. If a fourth truancy report is issued in the same year, the student is classified a "truant" and may come under the jurisdiction of a juvenile court. If a truant is found a ward of the court, the court may impose sanctions including community services; a fine of no more than $50 (for which the parent or guardian may be jointly liable); suspension or revocation of driving privileges; and attendance at a court-approved truancy prevention program.

Washington legislators amended state truancy laws in 2012 to specify that truancy petitions will include information about a student's academic status at initial truancy status hearings. Mandatory truancy filing petition provisions are applicable to students under the age of 17. School districts shall periodically update courts regarding actions taken by the district and the child's academic status. Under the amended law, courts may not issue bench warrants against children who fail to appear at an initial truancy petition hearing.

◆ A Washington father learned his child would be reported to a truancy court due to poor school attendance. The father participated in county court truancy review proceedings. At a hearing, the court ordered the child to attend school. In a separate action in federal court, the father asserted civil rights violations as a result of the state truancy proceeding. The family sought an order clearing the child's record of truancy and contempt findings, over $3 million in damages and other relief. In the court's opinion, there was an insufficient factual basis for any liability. **A single action by a municipal employee did not meet the liability standard for constitutional rights violations under 42 U.S.C. § 1983.** Simple dissatisfaction with the truancy hearings and the "sentiment that constitutional violations occurred" did not support the claim. *Blevins v. County of Mason*, No. 3:12-cv-05451 RBL, 2012 WL 3815568 (W.D. Wash. 9/4/12).

◆ A group of Pennsylvania students who claimed a school district unlawfully sought and retained truancy fines could proceed with a federal class action lawsuit against the district. According to the students, the district issued at least 1,489 truancy citations to about 700 parents and students. State law limited fines for truancy violations to $300 against the parents of a child violating the state compulsory attendance law. The students claimed the district sought and retained at least $107,000 in illegal fines. These included 340 fines greater than the statutory maximum, some of which exceeded $900. A federal court found **the students satisfied all the requirements for representing all those in the school district whose rights might have been similarly violated.** *Rivera v. Lebanon School Dist.*, No. 1:11-cv-147, 2012 WL 2504926 (M.D. Pa. 6/28/12).

◆ A Washington juvenile court found a middle school student truant. At her hearing, she was not represented by a lawyer. She kept missing school. At a contempt hearing held three weeks later, a court commissioner found her in contempt and ordered her to perform 10 hours of volunteer work. Over the next year, the student remained in contempt and appeared in juvenile court several times. Various orders were made requiring her to write papers, try an alternative school, spend time in detention at home with a monitor, or obtain therapy.

Each of the orders failed to obtain the student's compliance. More than a year after the initial truancy hearing, her lawyer moved to set aside the finding of truancy, claiming she should have had an attorney at the hearing. The case reached the Supreme Court of Washington, which found state law permitted initial truancy hearings without requiring the parties to be represented by legal counsel. It was significant that a contempt sanction could not be imposed at an initial truancy hearing. **As the truancy order issued at an initial hearing did not deprive the student of physical liberty, the court held she had no due process right to be represented by counsel at that point.** The purpose of the compulsory school attendance and admission statute was to protect a child's right to an education. No interest was affected by the initial truancy hearing that would trigger due process protection. While a child should be afforded an appointed counsel at a contempt hearing, the court held there was no such right at initial truancy hearings. The court held the state law was not unconstitutional. *Bellevue School Dist. v. E.S.*, 171 Wash.2d 695, 257 P.3d 570 (Wash. 2011).

◆   A Maryland student was absent 74 days during the 2006-07 school year. State prosecutors filed an adult truancy petition against her parent for violating the state compulsory attendance act. The parent claimed that the student usually arrived at school on a regular basis. But the student admitted that once at school, she often cut her classes and was "hanging out" in school hallways. The parent asserted that after her child was at school, she was in the care and custody of school officials. The trial judge expressed disbelief at the parent for failing to ask her child about missing classes and found her "involved in" the child's truancy. After the court upheld the petition and placed the parent on probation, she appealed to the Court of Appeals of Maryland, the state's highest court.

The lower court had found the parent's testimony both "incomprehensible" and incredible. As it was error for the trial court judge to make an inference that the opposite of her testimony must be true, the parent was entitled to a new trial. Once the daughter entered the school building, her custody shifted to the school. The compulsory attendance law did not make clear that criminal liability would be imposed on a parent whose child cut classes. **While children were at school, their parents transferred power to act as their guardians to school officials.** In order to find that the parent violated the compulsory attendance law at a new trial, there had to be "proof beyond a reasonable doubt" that her child did not attend school. Evidence that the student was not in her homeroom when attendance was taken would be sufficient to establish that she did not attend school on that day. *In re Gloria H.*, 410 Md. 562, 979 A.2d 710 (Md. 2009).

◆   A Kentucky middle school student had 21 unexcused absences in two months, leading to a family court truancy complaint. He argued that his school district should have determined if his truancy was a manifestation of a disability prior to filing the action. A school attendance coordinator testified that she made a home visit, mailed numerous letters and made many phone calls to gain compliance. Her intervention did not help and the student only complained that "he did not like school." After a hearing, the court found the student habitually truant. While he could remain at home, he was required to attend counseling and school, and cooperate with a state family services agency. On appeal, the Court of Appeals of Kentucky found that **prior to filing a truancy complaint, a school director of pupil personnel must determine the causes of a student's truancy, assess home conditions and conduct home visits.** All these requirements were met and ample evidence supported the finding of habitual truancy. And nothing in the Individuals with Disabilities Education Act (IDEA) required a manifestation determination to see if his truancy related to a disability. The court affirmed the judgment. *R.B.J. v. Commw. of Kentucky*, No. 2008-CA-001349-ME, 2009 WL 1349219 (Ky. Ct. App. 5/15/09).

◆   A New Mexico student of African-American and Hispanic heritage had a specific learning disability. In eighth grade, she stopped coming to school, due in part to family problems. After serving time in juvenile facilities for aggravated battery and assault of her mother and brother, the student was placed in a residential treatment center. Upon returning to school, the student used drugs and alcohol at school and received numerous disciplinary referrals for truancy. She skipped school to provoke her mother's boyfriend into leaving their home. The student became pregnant and was sent to a day shelter. She was then suspended for fighting at school. Her mother claimed the school district denied her access to a Wilson Reading System program and filed a special education due process action. The student transferred to another school district, where she enrolled in a Wilson class. She earned a 4.0 grade average for grade nine, then dropped out due to more family turmoil and drug use. The parent sued the residence school district for equal protection and Title VI violations. A court found no merit to the student's claim that she did not benefit from her education.

On appeal, the U.S. Court of Appeals, Tenth Circuit, affirmed the judgment. It held **the student was seeking the very services she would have received by simply returning to school.** For more details about the student's special education claims, see Chapter Six, Section II.C. of this volume. *Garcia v. Board of Educ. of Albuquerque Public Schools*, 520 F.3d 1116 (10th Cir. 2008).

B. Home Study Programs

◆ Pennsylvania Act 169 specified a number of record-keeping requirements and a portfolio review of home education programs in the state. School districts reviewed home education programs for compliance with minimum hours of instruction, course requirements and student progress. A group of parents who homeschooled their children sought exemptions from Act 169, and claimed the law substantially burdened their free exercise of religion. After their school districts denied exemptions and commenced truancy prosecutions, the parents filed separate actions against the districts. These were eventually consolidated before a federal district court. The cases reached the U.S. Court of Appeals, Third Circuit. It found that **in practice, school districts exercised a "limited level of oversight" over home education programs**. The court held the Free Exercise Clause does not relieve persons from a valid and neutral law of general applicability. A law was "neutral" if it did not target religiously motivated conduct. In this case, Act 169 was a neutral law of general applicability. It did not target religious practices or selectively burden religiously motivated conduct. Nothing suggested school officials discriminated against religiously based home education programs. The act was rationally related to legitimate government objectives. As the right of parents to control the education of their children was "neither absolute nor unqualified," the court held for the school districts. *Combs v. Homer-Center School Dist.*, 540 F.3d 231 (3d Cir. 2008).

◆ A California family had a 20-year history of intervention by children and family services. The parents were subject to a dependency court proceeding for charges of physical abuse, neglect and failure to prevent sexual abuse. They were uncooperative with authorities, and the mother once attempted to hide the children from them. After two children were declared dependent due to the abuse and neglect of their siblings, their attorney sought an order requiring that they be sent to a public or private school so they could remain in regular contact with mandatory reporters. A state superior court refused the request, finding "parents have an absolute constitutional right to home school their children."

On appeal, the state court of appeal explained that homeschooling arose as an issue because one of the children wanted to attend public school. The children and families agency claimed the child was dependent on the additional basis that her parents' refusal to send her to public school placed her at risk of serious emotional damage. The superior court had incorrectly found there was an absolute parental right to homeschool children. Instead, **the constitutional liberty interest of parents to direct the education of their children had to yield to the state interest in child protection and safety**. The court noted this was a dependency case in which the children had been found dependent and the parents were judicially determined not to be fit. Without contact with mandated reporters at school, the court found child safety might not be guaranteed. By allowing the children to attend school, they could remain in their home, while educators would provide them "an extra layer of protection." The court returned the case to the superior court for reconsideration. *Jonathan L. v. Superior Court*, 165 Cal.App.4th 1074, 81 Cal.Rptr.3d 517 (Cal. Ct. App. 2008).

◆   The Court of Appeals of Michigan upheld an order by a family court to exercise jurisdiction over a student with disabilities whose mother claimed she was homeschooling him. Evidence indicated she was not even at home during most of the school day. The family court found that the student had missed 111 days of the current school year. It noted the mother's reluctance to use negative consequences for improper conduct by the student. The court found that it was not in the student's best interests to be homeschooled, especially where this required him to be unsupervised for most of the day. **The court found the mother's homeschooling plan "painfully neglectful" of his educational needs.** Although this was not a severe case of educational neglect, it was proper for the trial court to assume jurisdiction over the student. *Manchester Public Schools v. Flint*, No. 240251, 2003 WL 22244692 (Mich. Ct. App. 2003).

◆   Two Massachusetts children were not enrolled in any school and lacked approved homeschooling plans. The parents contended that school committee approval of their homeschooling activities would conflict with their learner-led approach to education, and that the Constitution prohibited infringement on their privacy and family rights. The school committee initiated a state district court proceeding for the care and protection of the children. The parents did not comply with a court order to file educational plans, resulting in adjudication of the children as in need of care and protection. The case reached a state appellate court. It noted that the state district court had required the parents to submit a detailed homeschooling plan to the school committee to allow assessment of the program and the children's progress. **This was a legitimate educational condition that a school committee could impose on a homeschool proposal without infringing on the constitutional rights of a family.**

The U.S. Supreme Court has recognized a degree of parental autonomy to direct the education of children, but state laws incorporated this requirement by allowing for flexibility in the evaluation of private instruction. The parents rejected accommodations proposed by the school committee, and the custody order was entered only after they had a final opportunity to comply with the committee's requests. The court affirmed the order for temporary care and protection. *In re Ivan*, 717 N.E.2d 1020 (Mass. App. Ct. 1999).

C. Attendance Policies

◆   The Court of Appeal of Louisiana denied relief to a student who was expelled in her eighth-grade year and sought to return the next year as a ninth-grader. She based her claim on her progress as a homeschooled student and her passing score on the state's LEAP test with mastery achievement levels. The parents had sought to have the school board evaluate the student since August 2006, but a state trial court denied their request and the case became mired in appeal procedures. The court of appeal chastised the board and trial court for allowing the student to go without an evaluation until February 2007. Both the court of appeal and state supreme court had ordered such an evaluation. **The school board's decision to return the student to grade eight appeared to be arbitrary.** However, only 65 days remained in the school year, and it was now too late for her to meet the relevant attendance and lesson requirements. *B.W.S., Jr. v. Livingston Parish School Board*, 960 So.2d 997 (La. Ct. App. 2007).

◆   After an Alabama student's tenth tardy in one semester, the school principal reported her to the school truant officer. The principal did not refer her to an early warning program or contact her parents, as specified in the school handbook. The truant officer filed a child in need of supervision petition in the juvenile court. After a trial, the court adjudicated the student a child in need of supervision and placed her on probation for the rest of the school year. On appeal, the student asserted that the principal violated the state Compulsory School Attendance Law and the school policy by failing to investigate the causes of her tardiness before referring her to the truant officer. **The Alabama Court of Civil Appeals found nothing in state law requiring the principal to investigate the causes of a student's tardiness.** The principal did not violate the student's due process rights by failing to follow the student handbook's progressive discipline policies before submitting her name to the truant officer. The handbook placed a duty on students to provide a timely excuse for their absences. The student was unable to show that the school selectively enforced the prosecution of truancy cases. The court affirmed the judgment. *S.H. v. State of Alabama*, 868 So.2d 1110 (Ala. Civ. App. 2003).

◆   An Ohio student was absent without excuse approximately 20 days during a four-month period. On some occasions the parents explained there was a medical problem. The school accepted these explanations until the parents applied to the county educational service center for permission to homeschool the student. But the school did not send them any notices concerning truancy proceedings as required by a school policy. The student's homeschool application was denied, and the principal filed a complaint against the parents in an Ohio county court on charges of contributing to the delinquency of a minor. The court conducted a jury trial and sentenced the parents to seven days in jail and fines of $250. They appealed to a state appeals court, which reversed the judgment. The state failed to meet its burden of proof to show that under local standards, the student was habitually truant. **Because truancy involved more than absenteeism, the court held the state was required to show a lack of excuse or permission as established by school policy.** In this case, the state failed to prove that it had sent the parents written notices that their daughter was absent without an excuse for three or more days. Without this proof, the state could not prove habitual truancy. *State v. Smrekar*, No. 99 CO 35, 2000 Ohio App. Lexis 5381, 2000 WL 1726518 (Ohio Ct. App. 2000).

V. CORPORAL PUNISHMENT

The U.S. Supreme Court held in Ingraham v. Wright, *below, that the infliction of corporal punishment implicates student liberty interests under the Due Process Clause of the Fourteenth Amendment. However, as corporal punishment was authorized by common law, the Court refused to create any procedural safeguards for students beyond those offered by state law. Corporal punishment is distinguishable from "reasonable physical force" to restrain unruly students, maintain order and prevent injury, as permitted by state law.*

In 2009, Florida legislators amended state law to limit the use of zero-tolerance policies and require school boards that permit corporal punishment as a form of discipline to review such policies every three years.

◆   The U.S. Supreme Court held that the use of corporal punishment is a matter of state law. Two Florida students were paddled by school administrators. One was beaten so severely he missed 11 days of school. The other suffered a hematoma and lost the use of his arm for a week. The parents sued school authorities, alleging cruel and unusual punishment and due process violations. **The Supreme Court held that the Eighth Amendment prohibition against cruel and unusual punishment did not apply to corporal punishment in schools.** The Court's reasoning for this decision lay in the relative openness of the school system and its surveillance by the community. The Eighth Amendment was intended to protect the rights of incarcerated persons, not students. State civil and criminal penalties restrained school employees from issuing unreasonable punishment. While corporal punishment implicated the Due Process Clause, state law vested the decision to issue it with school officials. The Court found corporal punishment served important educational interests. There was no requirement for notice and a hearing prior to imposing corporal punishment as the practice was authorized and limited by state law. *Ingraham v. Wright*, 430 U.S. 651 (1977).

A. Student Due Process Rights

◆   A Florida student with autism became aggressive and had trouble obeying rules and completing schoolwork. He pushed and bit others, growled, cursed, scratched himself and threatened to blow up his school. His teacher was placed on leave after two aides reported she had held down another child in the student's class until his eyes swelled and his lips turned blue. Reports were made to the state child abuse hotline, and the teacher was suspended and barred from school grounds. She was eventually convicted of one out of four counts of child abuse. A federal district court action was filed against the teacher on behalf of the student. In pretrial activity, two teaching aides stated that the teacher, who weighed almost 300 pounds, had straddled the student or pinned him against an object and pulled his arms behind his back. One aide testified that the teacher had used restraints in a way that could cause asphyxiation.

The court dismissed claims under the Due Process Clause and the Rehabilitation Act. On appeal, the Eleventh Circuit affirmed the judgment. It held only the most egregious official conduct violates the Constitution. **Corporal punishment has been held actionable by courts only when it is arbitrary, egregious and shocks the conscience.** A tripping incident was not corporal punishment. As for the other incidents, it appeared to the court that the teacher was attempting to restore order, maintain discipline or protect the student from harming himself. In each case, the student refused to go to his "cool down room," called the teacher names or threatened her. The court found no evidence that the teacher provoked the student into misbehaving. Evidence established that the teacher used restraints only until the student calmed down or agreed to comply with her instructions. Each incident lasted only a few minutes. There was also no evidence that the punishment of the student was based on his disability, defeating any discrimination claim. *T.W. v. School Board of Seminole County, Florida*, 610 F.3d 588 (11th Cir. 2010).

◆   A Tennessee student claimed basketball coaches routinely paddled him for missing basketball practice, being late or other misconduct. He claimed a coach punched him in the chest and paddled him for missing a car wash. The student transferred schools and sued the coaches, school principal, the school system and its superintendent in a federal court. After dismissing some of the claims, the court held a jury trial. A jury returned a verdict for the school system and officials on the remaining claims, and the student appealed. The U.S. Court of Appeals, Sixth Circuit, found that neither the student nor his parent ever complained about the paddlings to the principal or other officials. He never sought medical treatment and admitted he was not seriously harmed.

Tennessee law permits teachers and principals to use corporal punishment "in a reasonable manner against any pupil for good cause in order to maintain discipline and order within the public schools." The state supreme court has held **"if corporal punishment is moderate and is inflicted with a proper instrument the teacher is as a rule, not liable civilly for assault and battery."** As only excessive punishment will subject a teacher to civil liability, the state law assault and battery claims failed. As for the constitutional claims, the court explained that to prevail, the student had to show force so severe and "so inspired by malice or sadism" as to be "shocking to the conscience." As he admitted he was not seriously injured, the judgment against him was affirmed. *Nolan v. Memphis City Schools*, 589 F.3d 257 (6th Cir. 2009).

◆   A Georgia eighth-grade student was assigned to a remedial reading class. He arrived late to class, then talked to a classmate. The teacher told the classmate to leave the room, and the student tried to leave with him, refusing to return to his seat when she instructed him to do so. The teacher yelled and shook her finger at him. As the student moved to the door, she blocked it, and he initiated some physical contact with her. The teacher then grabbed the student by the neck. He claimed she squeezed his neck until he could not breathe. The teacher said she was afraid the student was preparing to hit her and put her hands on him to protect herself. The district placed her on administrative leave, and she soon resigned. The student sued the teacher, principal, district superintendent and school district. A federal court awarded pretrial judgment to the school officials, and the student appealed.

The U.S. Court of Appeals, Eleventh Circuit, held that regardless of whether the teacher acted in self-defense or imposed corporal punishment, there was no constitutional violation. **School officials violate substantive due process rights under the Fourteenth Amendment only when their conduct is considered arbitrary or "shocking to the conscience."** Neither party disputed that the teacher was acting within the scope of her discretionary authority. The force she used was not "obviously excessive," and she acted only after he repeatedly disobeyed her. She was entitled to official immunity. *Peterson v. Baker*, 504 F.3d 1331(11th Cir. 2007).

◆ An 18-year-old Texas student attended a public charter school during the 2003-04 school year. The principal disciplined her for leaving campus during a school day. He attempted to administer corporal punishment with a wooden paddle. The student resisted and received temporary, minor injuries to her hand by trying to block the paddle. She sued the school and principal. The case reached the U.S. Court of Appeals, Fifth Circuit, which held that **corporal punishment of public school students deprives them of substantive due process rights only when "arbitrary, capricious or wholly unrelated to the legitimate state goal of maintaining an atmosphere conducive to learning."** Corporal punishment is not arbitrary so long as the state affords local remedies. Texas law afforded adequate remedies for excessive corporal punishment claims. For this reason, the student's due process claims failed. There was no merit to her claim that adult status increased her rights. While the student did not have to attend school past the age of 18, she had voluntarily chosen to do so. Having agreed to attend school, she was not free to disregard school rules. *Serafin v. School of Excellence in Educ.*, 252 Fed.Appx. 684 (5th Cir. 2007).

◆ The U.S. Court of Appeals, Eleventh Circuit, upheld a federal court order denying qualified immunity to an Alabama principal accused of beating a student. The student claimed the principal called him into his office for disciplinary reasons and hit him in the head, ribs and back with a metal cane. His mother sued the district and principal for violating his federal civil rights. The principal sought qualified immunity. He alleged that the student had previously been disciplined for bringing a weapon to school, justifying his use of force. The court denied the request for immunity, and the principal appealed to the Eleventh Circuit. The court held that repeatedly striking a 13-year-old with a metal cane was an obvious constitutional violation. It rejected the principal's assertion that any prior incident involving weapons possession allowed him to beat the student. *Ingraham v. Wright* held that the deliberate infliction of physical pain by school authorities as punishment implicated student due process rights. The Alabama Supreme Court has held that **corporal punishment deprives students of their substantive due process rights when it is arbitrary, capricious or unrelated to the legitimate goal of maintaining**

an atmosphere conducive to learning. The principal was not entitled to qualified immunity. The case required a trial. *Kirkland v. Greene County Board of Educ.*, 347 F.3d 903 (11th Cir. 2003).

B. Teacher Liability Protection

Subpart Five of the No Child Left Behind (NCLB) Act (20 U.S.C. §§ 6731-38) is the Paul D. Coverdell Teacher Protection Act. This NCLB Act provision protects school staff from liability if they act on behalf of the school, within the scope of their employment, in conformity with law and "in furtherance of efforts to control, discipline, expel, or suspend a student or maintain order or control in the classroom or school.;" ... and there is no willful or criminal misconduct, gross negligence or reckless misconduct or flagrant disregard for rights. The Coverdell Act provision parallels state law provisions protecting school employees from liability when they restrain students to preserve order in the school.

◆ A Nevada teacher was accused of grabbing and choking a student who was trying to push open a door where entry was not allowed. After the incident, the student visited a doctor and an uncertified counselor for "emotional and psychological treatments." In an arbitration proceeding, the student won past medical expenses for his family practitioner and a physical therapist. However, the arbitrator did not award costs for the counselor due to his inadequate credentials. The student then sued the teacher and school district in a state court for negligence. On the first day of trial, the teacher and district moved for immunity. They cited the Paul D. Coverdell Teacher Protection Act. The court found the teacher's conduct was unreasonable and outside the act's protections.

The court awarded general damages and expenses of $27,270, an amount that was slightly lower than the arbitration award. This included the $5,700 charged by the counselor that had not been allowed in arbitration. Appeal reached the Supreme Court of Nevada, where the student claimed a Coverdell Act defense could not be raised at the beginning of a trial. He argued the act created an "affirmative defense" that had to be raised at the time of the initial response to a complaint. The court agreed that **the Coverdell Act defense was an affirmative defense which had to be asserted in the response to the complaint**. It then found the counselor's fees were excessive and unreasonable. When the state legislature enacted laws regulating psychologists, it intended to prevent laypersons from practicing the profession. As a result, the award of $5,700 for the counselor's services was found "illegal and not recoverable." *Webb v. Clark County School Dist.*, 145 Nev. 47, 218 P.3d 1239 (Nev. 2009).

◆ An Ohio student's mother claimed that a teacher grabbed, choked and shoved her son in front of the rest of his first-grade class, causing serious physical injury. She sued the school system, its board, and the teacher for negligence and intentional conduct. A court awarded pretrial judgment to the school board but denied it to the teacher. The Court of

Appeals of Ohio explained that the trial court had properly held for the school system. It then considered the teacher's claim to state law immunity and noted the family's assertion that she willfully, wantonly and recklessly grabbed, choked and shoved the student. **As this was sufficient to deny immunity, the case against her would proceed.** *Rogers v. Akron City School System*, No. CV 2006-05-2869, 2008 WL 2439674 (Ohio Ct. App. 6/18/08).

◆   An Ohio school district banned corporal punishment in its schools in 1987. Substitute teachers had to undergo training on the subject before becoming eligible for hire. During orientation, they were informed of the district policy prohibiting corporal punishment and told how to handle student misconduct. Substitutes had to seek assistance from the principal or assistant principal if a disciplinary situation occurred. A third grader claimed a substitute "slammed her into a chalkboard, threw her on the ground, and choked her" for a minute because she did not have a pencil with her. Her parent sued the school district in a federal court. The case reached the U.S. Court of Appeals, Sixth Circuit, which rejected the parent's claim that the state Tort Liability Act violated the Ohio Constitution. To show corporal punishment violates the Constitution, a student must show the force applied caused injury so severe, was so disproportionate to the need presented, and was so inspired by malice or sadism that it amounted to a brutal and inhumane abuse of official power that was shocking to the conscience. In this case, **the student did not show the district was deliberately indifferent to student abuse by substitute teachers**. There had been only two incidents in a two-year period in a school district with 127 schools serving over 69,000 students. This did not create "notice" of constitutional problems. The court affirmed the judgment for the school district. *Ellis v. Cleveland Municipal School Dist.*, 455 F.3d 690 (6th Cir. 2006).

◆   **A Colorado school custodian broke up a fight between two students in a school hallway. He "head-butted" the student he perceived to be the aggressor** and told him "there's always someone bigger than you. Now get out of here." The district investigated the incident and proposed discharging the custodian for inappropriate contact with a student. After a hearing before the superintendent under the collective bargaining agreement, discharge for deliberate or inappropriate conduct was recommended, and the school board approved this. In a state court action, the court held the discharge was unlawful, and it ordered the district to reinstate the custodian to his job with back wages. In doing so, the court conducted a new hearing, described by courts as "*de novo* review." But the Supreme Court of Colorado held the trial court should not have conducted a separate review. Instead, it should have relied on the school board hearing. The district provided the custodian a hearing as required by the collective bargaining agreement. School boards, not courts, retained discretion over employees and the enforcement of their own conduct and discipline codes. *Widder v. Durango School Dist. No. 9-R*, 85 P.3d 518 (Colo. 2004).

CHAPTER TWO

Student Discipline

I. EXPULSIONS AND SUSPENSIONS

A. Due Process

The Due Process Clause of the Fourteenth Amendment prohibits the states from depriving any person of life, liberty or property without due process of law. "Due process" requires school districts to provide students all the notices and procedural protections to which they are entitled under state law or school policies when they are faced with school discipline.

The U.S. Supreme Court first recognized due process rights in a student disciplinary case in Goss v. Lopez, *below. Students facing short-term suspensions and other minor school discipline have minimal due process rights. An informal discussion between the student and administrator typically satisfies due process for suspensions of up to 10 days. The student must be advised of the charges supporting the suspension and receive an opportunity to tell his or her side of the story. When a suspension is for a longer term, greater procedural protections apply, which may include a formal hearing.*

The Supreme Court's decision in Mathews v. Eldridge, *424 U.S. 319 (1976), indicated that* Goss *is merely a starting point for a due process analysis in longer-term suspension and expulsion cases.* Mathews *explained that "due process is flexible, and calls for such procedural protections as the particular situation demands." State laws typically explain the specific procedures that are required and afford greater protections in cases involving long-term discipline.*

◆ In *Goss v. Lopez*, Ohio students were suspended from school for up to 10 days for participating in demonstrations and other school disturbances. Their suspensions were handed down without a hearing either before or after the school board's ruling. The Supreme Court held that students facing temporary suspensions from a public school have property and liberty interests in their education that are protected by the Due Process Clause of the Fourteenth Amendment. **Students facing suspension or expulsion must be given oral or written notice of the charges against them and an opportunity to present their version of what happened.** Recognizing that some situations do not allow time to follow adequate procedures prior to the suspensions, such as cases where there is a danger to students or property, the Court stated that, at the very least, **proper notice and a hearing should be given as soon after the suspension as is practicable.** The Court also stated that if a student is threatened with a suspension of more than 10 days, more elaborate procedural safeguards may be required. *Goss v. Lopez*, 419 U.S. 565 (1975).

1. Notice and Procedural Protections

◆ A Wisconsin student who was expelled for bringing a knife to school continued to use a weight room at the school and pick up friends in his car. A teacher saw him in the weight room and told him to leave. The student became confrontational, swore and punched a locker. School officials notified him that he could no longer enter school property. When the student later drove onto school grounds, a police officer cited him for trespassing. In a federal court, he asserted constitutional rights violations, including interference with his right to travel. The court held the student had no right to enter school property. On appeal to the U.S. Court of Appeals, Seventh Circuit, the student claimed the district violated his due process rights by banning him from school property without notice and an opportunity to be heard. But the court noted that when the ban was enacted, he was attending a private school. **A former student could be constitutionally banned from school property as a "non-student" without notice or a hearing.** The ban was indefinite but not permanent. In the court's view, **a school district has discretion to bar members of the public from school property**. The student was only a member of the general public without constitutional rights to access school property. As there was no violation of his right to intrastate travel, the court held for the district and officials. *Hannemann v. Southern Door County School Dist.*, 673 F.3d 746 (7th Cir. 2012).

◆   A white Tennessee high school senior co-captained his varsity football team. While driving from campus, he swerved his vehicle toward two freshmen, forcing them to jump away. Two days later, the senior again drove toward a group of freshmen. An African-American freshman did not avoid the car. As the senior stopped, a tire pinned the freshman's foot, causing him to fall and suffer minor injuries. The senior got out of the car, and the freshman threatened him. He drove off and ran over the freshman's backpack. The freshman's parents filed a police report and complained to the school principal. The senior's school parking privileges were suspended, and he was later suspended from school for 10 days. A hearing board upheld the suspension after a hearing. A district discipline coordinator held another hearing, at which the senior's attorney argued the first hearing was influenced by the freshman's parents. The discipline coordinator and later the board of education upheld the suspension.

The family filed a state court action and obtained an order setting aside the discipline. The board removed the case to a federal court, but the family filed an emergency motion to keep the case in state court. The state court then heard evidence from the senior's family which challenged the hearing coordinator's impartiality. It held the school had violated his rights by allowing the hearing coordinator to impermissibly serve as both a prosecutor and a decision-maker. In ruling for the family, the court awarded attorneys' fees and costs of almost $400,000. The state court of appeals reversed the decision. On appeal, the state supreme court held the senior received all the due process he deserved before being suspended. In the court's view, had the disciplinary proceeding ended with the principal's action, any due process claim would have been foreclosed by *Goss v. Lopez*. But when the principal offered a hearing, his notice triggered additional state-law protections. In the court's view, the hearing coordinator's "dual role" was not a due process violation. Circumstantial evidence cited by the family did not establish racial bias. The court found that **the trial court did not apply the presumption of good faith accorded to school officials**. The fact that the freshman's family initiated a criminal charge was irrelevant. In ruling for the board, the court reversed the attorneys' fees award. *Heyne v. Metropolitan Nashville Board of Public Educ.*, 380 S.W.3d 715 (Tenn. 2012).

◆   While the state proceedings in *Heyne v. Metropolitan Nashville Board of Public Educ.*, above, were before the state supreme court, the federal claims reached the U.S. Court of Appeals, Sixth Circuit. It held **due process did not require trial-type procedures for suspensions of 10 days or fewer. In such cases, students must have a chance to explain their version of the facts and be told the basis of accusations against them.** The court refused to require the school to provide more than what *Goss v. Lopez* demanded for a 10-day suspension. But there was evidence that the principal and two disciplinary officers were not impartial. And there was evidence that the principal had disciplined the senior to "cover" himself and the school from possible liability in a lawsuit by the freshman. Since the senior made plausible assertions of a biased decision-making process, his due process and equal protection claims against the principal and two disciplinary officials were not dismissed. *Heyne v. Metropolitan Nashville Public Schools*, 655 F.3d 556 (6th Cir. 2011).

◆   Illinois high school administrators received a bomb threat note. After an investigation, a student admitted that a friend had asked him to write the note. Administrators suspended him for 10 days. At an expulsion hearing, the school relied on statements from other students that were obtained by the principal during her investigation. She admitted she had no personal knowledge of any involvement by the student in writing the note, and as a result, the only testimony supporting the expulsion was hearsay. Over objection by the student's attorney, the board admitted the statements and expelled the student from school and school activities for two calendar years.

The student's parent sued the school district and several officials, asserting due process violations. A federal court held that to satisfy the Due Process Clause of the Fourteenth Amendment, "the expulsion procedure must provide the student with a meaningful opportunity to be heard." **Expulsion procedures need not resemble a trial, as students need only receive notice of the charges and the time of hearing, and a full opportunity to be heard.** In fact, the U.S. Court of Appeals, Seventh Circuit, has never held students have a right to cross-examine adverse witnesses at expulsion hearings. In this case, the student was notified of the charges and informed of the time of his hearing. He did not present any witnesses and did not ask that any students attend. Under the circumstances, there was no violation of due process rights. *Werner v. Board of Educ. of Pope County Community Unit School Dist. No. 1*, No. 11-cv-1095-JPG, 2012 WL 3562619 (S.D. Ill. 8/16/12).

◆   A whiskey bottle fell out of a Louisiana student's backpack and broke on the floor of his classroom. He told a disciplinary administrator he did not know the bottle was in his backpack and later gave the same account to a police officer. After the student was arrested for under-age alcohol possession, the school's student council president reported to the school that the whiskey bottle belonged to him and that he had put it in the student's backpack without telling him. The disciplinary administrator did not share this information with other school officials. After the student met informally with administrators, an expulsion and alternative placement for some five months was recommended.

At a board hearing, the student called the student council president to give his account. A board member doubted this account, and the board voted 9-2 to expel the student. Instead of going to the alternative school assignment, he elected to obtain a GED. He sued the board in a state court for tort liability. The court found the disciplinary administrator's failure to tell other school officials the student council president's story tainted the disciplinary process. It held the board had a duty to ensure the correct application of its own policies, and it awarded the student $50,000. On appeal to the Supreme Court of Louisiana, the board argued that, regardless of what the administration did, the board never deprived the student of due process. He received a hearing and was allowed to present evidence and argue on his own behalf. **While administrators did not properly review the evidence, the court found the student was not denied due process at the board hearing,** where his version of the facts was rejected. As the court held he did not show the board violated his due process rights, the judgment was reversed. *Christy v. McCalla*, 79 So.3d 293 (5th Cir. 2011).

◆   After being expelled for fighting, two South Carolina high school students appealed to the district superintendent and the school board. When the decisions were upheld, they did not appeal to a court. Nearly two years later, the family sued the school district in the state court system for due process violations. The court held for the district, finding the students' decision not to appeal their expulsions to a court was a failure to exhaust administrative remedies. The state court of appeals reversed the decision. On appeal, the Supreme Court of South Carolina explained that the type of hearing required to satisfy due process depends on the nature of the case. The right to notice and an opportunity to be heard applies to even short-term disciplinary cases. But in this case, the court found the students received all the process they were due. Under *Goss v. Lopez*, this chapter, a student facing a short-term suspension only needs to receive notice of the charges and an opportunity to explain his or her side of the story. **An accused student should receive greater procedures and protections when facing expulsion.** State Code Section 59-63-240 specifies that parents must be notified in writing of the time and place for a hearing in expulsion cases. At a hearing, parents have statutory rights to have legal counsel present and to present evidence and question witnesses. In this case, the family chose not to have counsel at the initial hearing and did not exercise the right to present evidence or question witnesses. Finding the state law protections were constitutionally sufficient, the court reinstated the trial court's decision. *Stinney v. Sumter School Dist. 17*, 391 S.C. 547, 707 S.E.2d 397 (S.C. 2011).

◆   A Texas kindergartner missed his school bus twice during the first week of school. School officials later required him to a sign a disciplinary form due to bus misbehavior, even though he could not read and his parent was not present. Dissatisfied with the handling of his complaint, the parent sent a grievance to the district's central administration. After an investigation by the district and subsequent hearings, the district's board denied his grievance. On further appeal to the state commissioner of education, an administrative law judge held the commissioner had no authority to hear federal law questions. A state court affirmed the commissioner's order, and appeal reached the Court of Appeals of Texas. It held **the commissioner's power to review school board actions was limited to actions or decisions by a school board that violated the school laws of the state, or a provision of a written employment contract**. It also found the parent did not show a violation of his state law rights. The court found that at most, he showed an inaccurate investigation of his son's bus incidents and failure to accurately follow its local grievance policy. The court held the case had been properly dismissed, and it found no merit to claims regarding the extent of the commissioner's authority. *Maiden v. Texas Educ. Agency*, No. 03-09-00681-CV, 2011 WL 1744963 (Tex. Ct. App. 5/6/11).

◆   A Nevada student took a knife on a school-sponsored choir trip. He was suspended for 10 days pending expulsion. The next school day, a vice principal drafted a letter explaining the district's weapons policy and detailing the violation. A school disciplinary panel held a hearing at which the charges against the student were read, and a police liaison officer testified. The student claimed he had brought the knife to school accidentally, and his parents verified this. After the hearing, the panel recommended expulsion for the remaining weeks of the school year. The school board met with the assistant superintendent in a closed session, and accepted his expulsion recommendation. The family was excluded from the session, and a federal district court action followed. The court noted that **some form of hearing is required before a student can be deprived of a property interest in public school attendance**.

In long-term disciplinary cases, the Ninth Circuit has required procedural protections such as representation by counsel, the opportunity to present witnesses and the ability to cross-examine adverse witnesses. In this case, the disciplinary panel hearing met the heightened requirements for expulsions. The student was provided with the relevant regulations before a hearing where he could present evidence, call and cross-examine witnesses and be represented by counsel. The court found nothing improper about the assistant superintendent's presence at the board meeting. An administrator involved with initiating disciplinary charges may participate in decisions. *Hardie v. Churchill County School Dist.*, No. 3:07-CV-310-RAM, 2009 WL 875486 (D. Nev. 3/30/09).

◆   The Supreme Court of Colorado affirmed a lower court decision vacating a student expulsion order, because **the student's school board refused to allow her to call witnesses to provide evidence of her good character at her expulsion hearing**. The district expelled the student for fighting, but it denied her request to present statements from her teachers at her hearing. The supreme court agreed with the trial court that the school district violated her due process rights and made it "as difficult as possible" to present evidence in her favor. *Nichols v. DeStefano*, 84 P.3d 496 (Colo. 2004).

◆   The Wyoming Supreme Court held that a school board's appeal from a lower court decision reversing a student suspension was moot, as the student had already graduated. The board had expelled the student for violating a state law prohibiting the possession, use, transfer, carrying or selling of a deadly weapon on school property or grounds. The expulsion was modified to a 10-day in-school suspension and the student was required to abide by a behavior contract. **The student appealed to a state court, which held that the board violated the notice and hearing requirements of Wyoming law.** The court also found insufficient evidence to support the discipline. The appeal to the supreme court was moot, as the student had already served his suspension and graduated. *Board of Trustees of Fremont County School Dist. #25 v. BM*, 129 P.3d 317 (Wyo. 2006).

◆   Several South Carolina seniors vandalized a high school they did not attend. After they were suspended, a state trial court granted their request for a temporary injunction, but the South Carolina Court of Appeals held that the trial court had no jurisdiction to hear any case involving a short-term student suspension. The students appealed to the state supreme court, which noted that **state law did not permit judicial review of student suspensions of 10 days or less**. Otherwise, students and parents might burden the court system and strain school resources with a flood of appeals from short-term suspensions. The students received notice, an explanation and an opportunity to respond, which was all the process they were due under *Goss v. Lopez.* The court affirmed the appellate court's decision. *Floyd v. Horry County School Dist.*, 569 S.E.2d 343 (S.C. 2002).

2. Alternative Placements

Many state and federal courts have held that a transfer to an alternative education program does not deny a student's access to public education, and so does not implicate the Fourteenth Amendment. In King v. Beaufort County Board of Educ.*, below, the Supreme Court of North Carolina held school administrators had to articulate a reason for denying a student access to an alternative education, based on her state constitutional right to an education. But in* Flour Bluff Independent School Dist. v. R.S.*, No. 13-05-623-CV, 2006 WL 949968 (Tex. Ct. App. 2006), the Court of Appeals of Texas upheld an education board's decision to assign a cheerleader an alternative education program for drug possession. **The board's decision was final and unappealable.**

◆ A Mississippi student admitted having a key logger program demonstration disk, and after an investigation, he was suspended for possessing software that damaged the school computer system. The student's mother was a school employee. After the superintendent recommended placing the student in an alternative school for 45 days, he learned that personal data on teachers might have been compromised when the student used his mother's computer. She was reassigned and soon discharged. The student and his mother sued the school district for speech and due process violations, and related claims. After a federal court held for the district, the family appealed. The U.S. Court of Appeals, Fifth Circuit, stated that a state's extension of the right to an education is protected by the Fourteenth Amendment and cannot be withheld absent fair procedures.

In *Nevares v. San Marcos Consolidated Independent School Dist.*, 111 F.3d 25 (5th Cir. 1997), the Fifth Circuit held **a student's transfer to an alternative education program does not deny access to public education, and such an assignment does not violate the Fourteenth Amendment**. The student and his parents had opportunities to meet with school officials, and he had "multiple opportunities" to tell his side of the story. As the court found he received notice of the charges and a chance to explain himself, there was no due process violation. And there was no merit to the mother's First Amendment claims. Public employee speech is protected only if it addresses a public concern, and she had expressed only personal concerns. As her contract claim duplicated her speech rights claim, the court affirmed the judgment for the school district. *Harris v. Pontotoc County School Dist.*, 635 F.3d 685 (5th Cir. 2011).

◆ An Alabama student fought with a classmate, and both were suspended for three days. As the school year was nearly over, an assistant principal assigned them to an alternative school for the first 15 days of the following school year. Although the student's parent appeared before the board of education, it took no action to reverse the alternative placement. In a state court action, the student asserted state and federal claims against the board and its members and sought an order to block the alternative school placement. A hearing on the board's request for immunity was postponed until after the court considered temporary relief, which was granted to the student. On appeal, the Supreme Court of Alabama explained that the state constitution confers immunity from damages upon the state, its arms and its agencies. **In prior cases, the court had described this immunity as an "almost invincible wall of immunity."** County boards of education are considered agencies of the state, and for that reason, the board had immunity from state law claims for monetary damages. As the state could not be sued indirectly by suing an officer, the constitution also immunized the board members from state law claims for money damages. But the court held the constitutional immunity provision did not apply to federal claims. As for the request for preliminary relief, the court held the lower court had no evidence to consider it. There was no transcript in the hearing record, and the preliminary order had to be vacated. *Colbert County Board of Educ. v. James*, 83 So.3d 473 (Ala. 2011).

◆   A North Carolina student was suspended for the second semester of her sophomore year for fighting. She was not offered alternative education. After a hearing, a school panel upheld the superintendent's decision to suspend her without services. In a state court lawsuit, the student asserted violation of her right to a sound basic education under the North Carolina constitution. A state trial court dismissed the case, and appeal reached the Supreme Court of North Carolina. It held state laws created a comprehensive scheme granting students a right to an alternative education "when feasible and appropriate" during long-term suspensions. **There was no constitutional right to an alternative education, but there was a constitutional right for a suspended student to know the reason for exclusion from school.** In reaching this conclusion, the court accepted the student's claim that prior cases on state educational funding applied to her case. While students had a right to a sound basic education under the state constitution, the court held school administrators had to articulate an important or significant reason for denying a student access to an alternative education. In this case, administrators did not articulate a reason for denying the student access to alternative education. Since she had a state constitutional right to education, the court reversed the judgment and returned the case to the lower courts so the education board could have an opportunity to explain its decision. *King v. Beaufort County Board of Educ.*, 364 S.E.2d 368 (N.C. 2010).

◆   A North Carolina school decided a ninth-grader should attend an alternative school pending a risk assessment based on threats to harm himself and others. A school counselor recommended a psychological evaluation of the student, but the parents resisted. An in-school suspension (ISS) was imposed after classmates said the student tried to cut or stab himself and threatened violence. He remained in ISS for the rest of the school year and was assigned to an alternative learning center (ALC) pending completion of a risk assessment.

A panel found the assignment to the ALC was not disciplinary in nature. It found a reasonable basis to believe the student was a danger to himself or others and upheld the decision to place him in the ALC until he underwent a risk assessment. He sued the board in a state court for constitutional violations, but the court affirmed the ALC assignment. On appeal, the state court of appeals held **students who were recommended for alternative or ALC placements as an alternative to suspension were entitled to a hearing before the district superintendent**. The student had been suspended for refusal to submit to a risk assessment, and the court found the ALC assignment for the same behavior was an "alternative to suspension" as described in a district policy. Since an ALC assignment would be reflected in the student's cumulative record, the court held he was entitled to a hearing. It reversed the judgment. *Rone v. Winston-Salem/Forsyth County Board of Educ.*, 701 S.E.2d 284 (N.C. Ct. App. 2010).

◆ A Texas student was assigned to an alternative school for being involved in a brawl in a school hallway. An assistant principal allegedly reported that the student was arrested after striking an officer. Part of the fight was videotaped, and the assistant principal observed the student's behavior. At an informal hearing attended by the assistant principal, student and parents, the family was notified of a three-day suspension followed by a 45-day assignment to an alternative education program. In response, the student sued the school district and several officials in a federal court for civil rights violations. **The court held placement in alternative education programs did not implicate due process rights.** Instead, they were considered transfers from one school program to another "with stricter discipline." Since the student had an opportunity to tell his story in the meeting with the assistant principal, due process was satisfied. Many courts, including the Supreme Court in *Goss v. Lopez*, this chapter, have recognized that **sometimes a school disciplinarian may be a witness to the conduct forming the basis for discipline**. *Salas v. United Independent School Dist.*, Civ. No. L-08-22, 2009 WL 1035068 (S.D. Tex. 4/17/09).

◆ A Wyoming school district expelled three students for marijuana violations. One was enrolled in special education programs and continued receiving the educational services described in his individualized education program. The others were adjudicated delinquent in juvenile court proceedings. The Supreme Court of Wyoming held that while education is a fundamental right under the state constitution, the state interest in student safety and welfare was compelling enough to temporarily interfere with this right. It noted with approval *Fowler v. Williamson*, 39 N.C. App. 715, 251 S.E.2d 889 (N.C. Ct. App. 1979), a North Carolina case recognizing that educational services are contingent upon appropriate conduct. The school district had offered students an education system that conformed to its constitutional obligation to provide an equal opportunity for a quality education.

Reasonable suspension rules did not deny the right to an education; they only denied students an opportunity to misbehave. Students could be temporarily denied educational services if their conduct threatened the safety and welfare of others. School districts were in the best position to judge student actions, and the district was not required to provide lawfully expelled students with an alternate education in this case. The court rejected the claim that the expulsions violated the non-disabled students' equal protection rights. Special education students must receive services under federal law, even if discipline is imposed. *In re R.M.*, 102 P.3d 868 (Wyo. 2004).

3. Zero-Tolerance Policies

◆   Texas school officials found a small amount of alcohol in a vehicle parked on school property. Under the school district's zero-tolerance policy, the student who had driven the vehicle to school had to be placed in an alternative school. After several hearings, an alternative school assignment was upheld. According to the district superintendent, the student would have been allowed to avoid the placement had he presented evidence to support his claim that he did not know there was any alcohol in his vehicle. The student sued the school district and officials in a state court for due process violations. The case reached the Court of Appeals of Texas. It held the student did not show the zero-tolerance policy was unconstitutional as it was applied to him. It noted that zero-tolerance policies "have promoted consistency over rationality." **Strict adherence to a zero-tolerance policy, without consideration of a student's state of mind, "would appear to run afoul of substantive due process notions."** But there was no due process violation in this case, because the superintendent offered the student a chance to show he did not know about the alcohol. As the district provided him "an escape mechanism in lieu of strict application of the zero-tolerance policy," his challenge failed. *Hinterlong v. Arlington Independent School Dist.*, No. 2-09-050-CV, 2010 WL 522641 (Tex. Ct. App. 2/11/10).

◆   The Fifth Circuit affirmed the assignment of a Mississippi honor student to an alternative school after a cup of beer was found in a car she had parked in a school lot. Her parent had left the beer in the car, and she said she did not know about it. She appealed the transfer decision to the school board and a federal court, without success. She withdrew from school and obtained a GED. The Fifth Circuit held that however misguided the school district might have been for applying its zero-tolerance policy, the case had to be dismissed. The Supreme Court has observed that public education relies upon the discretion and judgment of school administrators and board members. **An alternative school assignment implicated no constitutional rights.** *Langley v. Monroe County School Dist.*, 264 Fed.Appx. 366 (5th Cir. 2008).

◆   A Florida student who was suspended for violating a school's zero-tolerance policy against weapons possession had no right to appeal the school board decision to the state court system. The Court of Appeal of Florida held the case was properly dismissed because **the Florida Administrative Procedure Act does not permit court review of a suspension order**. The court rejected the student's assertion that he could appeal his suspension because he faced a possible expulsion. Instead, only a hearing that results in an actual expulsion is available for court review. *D.K. v. Dist. School Board of Indian River County*, 981 So.2d 667 (Fla. Dist. Ct. App. 2008).

◆   A drug dog alerted on a Texas honor student's truck during a routine check. School board policy held students responsible for the contents of their vehicles. A hearing officer ruled that the Texas Education Code required expulsion. The board voted to expel the student for one day and to assign him to an alternative school for the rest of the school year. After a state court granted the student's request for a preliminary order halting the expulsion, the school board appealed. The Court of Appeals of Texas found the Texas Education Code required school districts to specify whether they considered intent or lack of intent as a factor in student expulsions. **School districts could choose between zero-tolerance policies or alternatives for involuntary possession of prohibited weapons.** In this case, the district policy allowed it to consider intent, and it could decline to expel the student if possession of a weapon was involuntary. The hearing officer incorrectly interpreted the Education Code as requiring expulsion, even if possession of a prohibited weapon was unknowing. The trial court did not abuse its discretion in issuing a temporary injunction to halt the expulsion. *Tarkington Independent School Dist. v. Ellis*, 200 S.W.3d 794 (Tex. Ct. App. 2006).

◆ A California school district regulation required an immediate suspension with a recommended expulsion for three or more fighting incidents in a year. A 12-year-old student was involved in three fights in one school year. A hearing panel upheld the principal's recommendation for expulsion, and the student was placed in an alternative program. The student was suspended there for physically confronting a staff member. The school district placed her in a community school, where she claimed older male students sexually harassed and physically assaulted her. She sued the district in a state court, which dismissed her personal injury claim. But the court held the district's policy requiring the principal to recommend expulsion violated state law and the Due Process Clause. On appeal, **the Court of Appeal of California found the district's zero-tolerance provision consistent with the education code.** The policy did not require expulsion for specified offenses. It only put these cases before an impartial hearing panel. The elimination of a principal's discretion to refrain from referring a case to a hearing did not deprive students of due process. The court reversed the judgment. *T.H. v. San Diego Unified School Dist.*, 122 Cal.App.4th 1267, 19 Cal.Rptr.3d 532 (Cal. Ct. App. 2004).

B. Misconduct

1. Sexual Harassment

◆ An Indiana school official advised a student that a classmate had accused her of inappropriate sexual conduct. An informal hearing was held between the student's parents and an administrator. Next, the school wrote to the parents that expulsion would be sought. The parents' attorney unsuccessfully sought to delay a hearing. At the hearing, several witnesses testified about multiple incidents of exposure or unwanted sexual advances by the student. The mother was permitted to question each witness and also called a witness who spoke favorably about the student. But her attorney was not allowed into the hearing room. A hearing officer ruled for expulsion, and a state superior court rejected the student's claim for trial-type protections such as a right to be represented by counsel and to confront witnesses. On appeal, the state court of appeals held that in expulsion proceedings, notice and an opportunity for a hearing must be appropriate to the nature of the case. **A full panoply of due process protections did not apply to an expulsion hearing under state law.** A "fair proceeding" meant the student had "the opportunity to respond, explain, and defend." Due process is intended only to protect substantial rights and does not guarantee particular procedures. Due process required only "an informal give-and-take between student and disciplinarian" to hear the student's story. State law defined the notice requirements for an expulsion hearing, and they had been provided in this case. State and federal constitutional provisions did not confer rights to have counsel attend expulsion meetings. Rejecting the student's other arguments, the court affirmed the judgment. *D.L. v. Pioneer School Corp.*, 958 N.E.2d 1151 (Ind. Ct. App. 2011).

◆   South Carolina school officials charged a 14-year-old girl with a "sexual offense" for entering a boys' lavatory. A video camera recorded her following a male student into the lavatory, where she remained for about a minute. The student claimed she went into the lavatory to retrieve a comb that the male had taken from her. But the school suspended her for 10 days and recommended an expulsion for the rest of the year, based on a sexual offense. Earlier in the school year, she had been suspended for two days for a verbal altercation with a classmate. Prior to an expulsion hearing, a school administrator and a hearing officer watched the videotape of the student entering the lavatory. But the tape was recorded over before the student was allowed to view it. The hearing officer found the student committed a sexual offense and expelled her for the rest of the school year. A state court reversed the decision, finding no substantial evidence of a sexual offense. It also found a violation of due process rights.

On appeal, the Court of Appeals of South Carolina noted that the school district did not present any additional evidence to support the charge of sexual offense beyond the videotape. Any prior acts of disruption by the student had no bearing on the case. The school district had chosen not to expel her for her prior conduct. **The only evidence of a sexual offense was the student's voluntary entry into the boys' lavatory for about one minute in pursuit of another student.** Since there was no evidence of sexual activity by the student or the male, and no male student indicated that anything sexual had occurred, the judgment for the student was affirmed. *Doe v. Richland County School Dist. Two*, 382 S.C. 656, 677 S.E.2d 610 (S.C. Ct. App. 2009).

◆   A Michigan school counselor made a presentation to a language arts class. She saw a student place his fingers in his mouth and believed he was making a sexual gesture about her. The school suspended the student, and he appealed to the district superintendent, who interviewed the counselor, student and a classmate who saw the gesture. The students asserted that the gesture simply indicated boredom. The superintendent found the counselor more reliable and upheld the suspension for "indecency," as defined in the high school's student handbook. A trial court affirmed the discipline, and the student appealed.

The Court of Appeals of Michigan held that courts are bound by school administrators' findings when there is any evidence in the record to support them. **A student must be guilty of some willful or malicious act of detriment to a school before being suspended or expelled.** This is "something more than a petty or trivial offense" against school rules. The court found the student's gesture qualified as "gross misbehavior and misconduct," as it was both willful and malicious. The school complied with due process requirements for a short-term suspension by giving him oral notice of the general nature of the charges and a chance to be heard. Allowing him to go unpunished for embarrassing a school employee would welcome more disrespect. *Kloberdanz v. Swan Valley School Dist.*, No. 256208, 2006 WL 234880 (Mich. Ct. App. 2006).

◆ A California student was accused of sexually related misconduct, including grabbing and groping others, making inappropriate comments or gestures, and simulating masturbation and other sexual acts. He denied most of the allegations, explaining that he had accidentally touched one girl. The student's father, an attorney, attended a meeting to consider discipline. The school principal said that he had interviewed several credible witnesses. He issued a five-day suspension. The student served his suspension and graduated. He sued the school district under 42 U.S.C. § 1983. A court held that the district violated his due process rights and awarded him general damages of $45,000, punitive damages of $50,000 and attorneys' fees of $72,268. The school district appealed to the California Court of Appeal, which found **the principal had complied with the "notice and opportunity to respond" requirements of** *Goss v. Lopez* (this chapter). He explained the reasons for the suspension and was not required to give the student any further procedural protections. The student was not entitled to learn the identities of his accusers, and had the principal done so, the school district might be exposed to further lawsuits. The district had issued a proper suspension, and the court reversed the judgment. *Granowitz v. Redlands Unified School Dist.*, 129 Cal.Rptr.2d 410 (Cal. Ct. App. 2003).

2. Drugs, Alcohol and Weapons Possession

In a case involving off-campus alcohol consumption by an Arkansas student, the U.S. Supreme Court limited the role of federal courts to construe school regulations differently than a school board. An Arkansas school board rule required mandatory suspension of students who were "under the influence of" or in possession of narcotics, hallucinogenics, drugs or controlled substances. The Supreme Court held the board could expel a student for drinking alcohol off campus and returning to school. Board of Educ. v. McCluskey, *458 U.S. 966 (1982). But in* Monroe County Board of Educ. v. K.B.*, an Alabama school board improperly disciplined a student for being under the influence of alcohol at a school prom under a rule that only addressed the "use" of alcohol while on school property or at a school function.*

◆ A Massachusetts high school principal claimed a student "was somehow involved" in an on-campus marijuana sale but did not disclose his informants to the student's parent. Claiming he had "direct evidence," the principal advised the father he "had no choice" but immediate expulsion. At a hearing, the student did not answer questions, and the superintendent did not present any witnesses or other evidence. She later upheld the expulsion. In a state court action against the superintendent, a judge asked the student when he had last used marijuana.

The student responded that it had been four to five months earlier, and the judge ordered him to take a urine test. The test returned a positive result for marijuana use, and the student admitted using marijuana a week before the hearing. The judge proposed allowing the student to return to school conditionally, with random drug testing at the family's expense and other conditions including completion of homework. He also required that the student eat together with his family at least three times per week. On appeal, the Supreme Judicial Court of Massachusetts held the trial judge did not consider the proper standards for preliminary relief. He also failed to evaluate the facts and did not analyze the student's likelihood of success on his constitutional challenge. **As the judge did not evaluate the superintendent's decision and fashioned his own remedy to address the case, the preliminary order was vacated**, and the case was returned to the trial court for reconsideration before a different judge. *Doe v. Superintendent of Schools of Weston*, 461 Mass. 159, 959 N.E.2d 403 (Mass. 2011).

◆   A Wisconsin student was arrested and charged with marijuana possession with an intent to distribute it at his school. A hearing officer ordered him expelled, and county authorities filed a juvenile delinquency petition against him. The county human services department recommended that the student attend school regularly, and it noted that the school district had refused to provide him any educational programming. After a hearing, the court ordered the district to provide the student with educational resources and held the district's refusal to consider educational opportunity for the student contributed to the delinquency of a juvenile. After the state court of appeals vacated the juvenile court order, appeal reached the Supreme Court of Wisconsin. It found the state department of public instruction has long held that **school districts are not responsible for providing education to expelled students**. State education officials encouraged districts to provide expelled students alternative education, but this was not required. **Parents were responsible for finding an educational program for an expelled child.** If a court adjudicated a juvenile delinquent, it was to enter a disposition order under Wisconsin law.

For a court to require a student to attend a program, the program had to be "already provided by the school district." When a school expelled a student and ordered that no educational services be provided, there were no programs provided by the district available during that expulsion period. For this reason, the district could deny the student educational services. No state law required the provision of specific educational services to an expelled delinquent juvenile. While a district's participation in providing educational programming would nearly always be in order, the court held this did not imply a duty to deliver direct educational services to an expelled student. As a school district was not a "person," it could not be guilty of contributing to a juvenile's delinquency as the trial court had held. *Madison Metropolitan School Dist. v. Circuit Court for Dane County*, 800 N.W.2d 442 (Wis. 2011).

◆   Alabama high school staff members noticed a student smelled of alcohol at a school prom. A Breathalyzer test showed his blood-alcohol level was between .001 and .006. A disciplinary committee held a hearing and found no evidence of alcohol possession at the prom. The student was also not "under the influence of alcohol to the extent that he would have been guilty of ... criminal offenses."

Based on findings that he drank alcohol on the day of the prom, the board suspended him and sent him to an alternative school. The reason stated was being under the influence of alcohol at the prom in violation of a school handbook provision. In a juvenile court hearing, the court found the term "use" from the school policy meant "to ingest alcohol while on school property or at any other school function." As there was no evidence that the student had "used" alcohol on school property or at a school function, the court held he did not violate the policy. Appeal reached the Court of Civil Appeals of Alabama. A 1985 state supreme court case held "a board of education must comply with the policies it adopts." Rules governing student conduct had to be sufficiently definite to provide them reasonable notice that they must conform their conduct to the expected requirements. In this case, the school had applied a student handbook provision to students who used alcohol shortly before going to the prom. **A policy that did not notify the student of possible consequences for arriving at the prom after drinking alcohol deprived him of due process.** The court affirmed the juvenile court's decision reinstating him to school. *Monroe County Board of Educ. v. K.B.*, 62 So.3d 513 (Ala. Civ. Ct. App. 2010).

◆ A Wisconsin high school student admitted writing a note that a bomb was in a school locker, resulting in the school being evacuated. The school lost over four hours of instructional time. A state court placed the student on probation after he pled no contest to making a bomb scare under a state criminal statute. In addition to ordering him to perform 100 hours of community service, the court ordered him to pay the school district restitution of over $18,000. The student appealed the order to pay restitution. The state court of appeals noted that most of the amount represented salaries and benefits of teachers and staff who had been working but had to evacuate the school due to his note. According to the student, the district did not suffer a true financial loss. But the court held an order for restitution is within a court's discretion. **Pay for teachers and staff who vacated the building amounted to "special damages" that could form the basis of an order for restitution.** As deprivation of employee productivity was a "loss in itself," restitution was reasonable. *State of Wisconsin v. Vanbeek*, 316 Wis.2d 527, 765 N.W.2d 834 (Wis. Ct. App. 2009).

◆ After a Mississippi student reportedly sold drugs on campus, the school principal searched his backpack and found an item described as either a nail file or a knife. A school district appeals committee voted to expel the student after a hearing, and the school board met to review the case. At his hearing, the student was permitted to argue that the item was a nail file. But since the item was unavailable for inspection, the board assigned to the superintendent the decision of determining whether it was a prohibited item. He decided it was a knife. The board upheld the expulsion, and the student was placed in an alternative school. Within weeks, he was accused of possessing marijuana.

Another appeals committee hearing was scheduled to review a new expulsion recommendation. A notice to the student described his offense and the charges. In addition, the notice offered the student a right to have counsel present and to cross-examine witnesses. After the student spoke at the hearing, the committee accepted the expulsion recommendation. The student appealed, and the Supreme Court of Mississippi found **a reasonable basis for the board to find that the item was a knife and not a nail file**. The Mississippi Code did not require the school board to physically examine the weapon. As the student was permitted to speak on his own behalf before the appeals committee, due process was satisfied. The court reinstated the board's decision. *Hinds County School Dist. Board of Trustees v. D.L.B.*, 10 So.3d 387 (Miss. 2008).

◆   A Missouri high school student brought toy guns to school twice. The toys shot small pieces of plastic. On the first occasion, the student shot at another student who was standing outside their school. On the second, two toy guns were found locked in his car on school property. The school superintendent issued an immediate 10-day suspension for the incidents, finding the student in possession of a "weapon" which he had used on school property. The school board voted in a closed session to exclude the student from school for one year.

The student appealed, arguing that the school handbook definition of "weapon" did not include toys and other look-alike items. The Court of Appeals of Missouri **found that superintendents may modify expulsion requirements on a case-by-case basis to comply with requirements of federal law**. The school board had adopted a weapons guide with a definition of "weapon" that included any object designed to look like or imitate a dangerous weapon. While the guidelines were not personally handed to each student or parent, they were accessible through a district website and upon request. The guidelines were properly applied to the student. Finding the toy guns were "dangerous instruments" that could cause an eye injury, the court upheld the suspension. *Moore v. Appleton City R-II School Dist.*, 232 S.W.3d 642 (Mo. Ct. App. 2007).

◆   **A Mississippi school board did not deprive a student of due process by failing to provide him with a list of witnesses in advance of his expulsion hearing** for selling drugs at school. The state court of appeals rejected his claim that he was not informed of the charges against him because a key witness had changed his story. The witness had only changed the date of one alleged drug purchase. As the charges were based on continuous incidents, this change was insignificant. *T.B. v. Board of Trustees of Vicksburg Warren School Dist.*, 931 So.2d 634 (Miss. Ct. App. 2006).

◆   A Pennsylvania court held that **a school district had no power to expel an honor student for using drugs on a school playground after school hours, when no school activity was taking place**. A trial court properly found that the student was not under school supervision at the time of the incident and that the district exceeded its powers by expelling him. The school board had voluntarily reinstated the student to school prior to the trial court decision, and the court's order required it to expunge the expulsion from his record. *D.O.F. v. Lewisburg Area School Dist.*, 868 A.2d 28 (Pa. Commw. Ct. 2004).

◆   A New Mexico school security guard noticed a car parked in a faculty lot without a permit. He called a law enforcement agency to check its registration, then observed a knife in plain view between the passenger seat and console. The guard called the student who had driven the car and had him open the car. A hunting knife, handgun, ammunition and drug paraphernalia were found inside. The student was suspended pending a hearing, and a hearing officer recommended a one-year suspension. After the school board upheld the decision, the student sued for civil rights violations. A federal court found that the board could not suspend a student who unknowingly brought drugs or weapons to school. Appeal reached the U.S. Court of Appeals, Tenth Circuit, which held that a school suspension decision is to be upheld unless it is arbitrary, lacking a rational basis or shocking to the conscience. Here, the board did not suspend the student for "unknowingly" bringing a knife to school. Instead, it found that he should have known he was in possession of a knife, since it was in plain view to persons standing outside the car. **The possession of weapons on school property threatened the board's interest in school safety, and there was a rational basis for the one-year suspension.** *Butler v. Rio Rancho Public Schools Board of Educ.*, 341 F.3d 1197 (10th Cir. 2003).

3. Extracurricular and Co-Curricular Events

◆ A New Jersey board of education approved a rule permitting revocation of student extracurricular participation rights based on off-campus misconduct. The rule encouraged students to maintain good grades and abide by all school rules. Extracurricular-activities participants were required to refrain from using, possessing or distributing any alcoholic beverage or drugs both on and off school grounds during the season or activity in which the students participated.

A student objected to the rule and later filed a petition with the state commissioner of education to invalidate it. Appeal eventually reached the New Jersey Superior Court, Appellate Division, which found **a board's authority to regulate off-campus student conduct is carefully circumscribed by state regulations**. Section 6:A:16-7.6 of the state code permitted the discipline of students for off-campus conduct only when it was reasonably necessary for the safety, security and well-being of students and staff. To be subject to regulation, the off-campus conduct at issue had to materially and substantially interfere with the requirements of appropriate discipline in the operation of the school. The board's regulation exceeded its authority by encompassing too many potential conduct violations that did not meet the requirements of Section 6A:16-7.6. While the board cited the state's recently enacted Anti-Bullying Bill of Rights Act as evidence of a legislative intent to allow school districts to regulate off-campus conduct, the court disagreed. In defining harassment, intimidation or bullying, the act reaffirmed the requirement that there be a connection between the misconduct and school activities. The court held for the student. *G.D.M. v. Board of Educ. of Ramapo Indian Hills Regional High School Dist.*, 427 N.J.Super. 246, 48 A.3d 378 (N.J. Super. Ct. App. Div. 2012).

◆ A group of Ohio students attended a school-sponsored student exchange program in Germany. Before the trip, a teacher explained to students that they would stay with a "host family" for two weeks. While in Germany, a number of students consumed alcoholic beverages at biergartens with their "host parents." They were of legal drinking age in Germany and believed they were permitted to drink without supervision. Upon returning home, the school suspended the students for violating student code prohibitions on consuming or possessing alcohol while in the school's control and custody. The students asked for a hearing before the school board, arguing that the teacher had "verbally created an exception to the school's code of conduct regarding the consumption of alcohol." The board overturned the suspensions but required the students to perform community service. An Ohio trial court vacated the discipline, and the Court of Appeals of Ohio held **the teacher had "engrafted an exception on the disciplinary code's provisions concerning alcohol consumption."** The students and their parents had all stated that their understanding of the policy allowed parents and host parents to determine the circumstances for alcohol consumption by students. *Brosch v. Mariemont City School Dist. Board of Educ.*, No. C-050283, 2006 WL 250947 (Ohio Ct. App. 2006).

◆   Missouri cheerleading squad members reported that two cheerleaders were drinking alcohol before a school football jamboree. An investigation by the squad's faculty advisor was inconclusive. The principal later began a new investigation, but the parents of the cheerleaders did not cooperate. The parents then sued the school district and school officials. The principal continued his investigation and obtained statements from several students who said they had seen the two cheerleaders drinking alcohol. The principal suspended both cheerleaders for 10 days for being under the influence of alcohol at a school event. He advised the parents, and the district sent them written confirmations of the suspensions, informing them of the reason for the action and their right to school board review. The parents did not respond. Meanwhile, the court held for the district and officials, and the parents appealed. The U.S. Court of Appeals, Eighth Circuit, noted evidence that the cheerleaders knew drinking alcohol before a school event violated the disciplinary code. The court rejected the parents' claim that the district "patently failed to train" its employees.

The district provided coaches with training for responding to student misconduct. **To establish school liability for failing to train staff, the parents would have to prove that the district showed deliberate indifference to student rights.** The court found no deliberate indifference by the district in this case. The cheerleaders received proper notice that they were being charged with a violation of the school code. Although the parents complained that the district had deprived their daughters of due process, they themselves had terminated contact with the principal. The students had the opportunity to present their side of the story, satisfying due process requirements. As the suspensions were based on violations of a longstanding, published policy, the judgment was affirmed. *Jennings v. Wentzville R-IV School Dist.*, 397 F.3d 1118 (8th Cir. 2005).

◆   An Indiana wrestling coach confiscated some negatives from a student who was a member of the school wrestling team. A school administrator instructed the coach to develop the negatives, which revealed the student and three other wrestlers naked in the boys' shower room. The school principal recommended expelling the student for "possessing or distributing pornographic material." The student's attorney argued at an expulsion hearing that the district code did not specify this offense. The hearing officer upheld the recommendation for expulsion, but the decision was reversed after a school administrative review.

The student returned to school after six weeks and made up his work. A federal district court reviewed his complaint and held that the principal and hearing officer were entitled to qualified immunity in the case. The student appealed to the U.S. Court of Appeals, Seventh Circuit, which held that the conduct of the principal and hearing officer did not meet the high threshold for proving a substantive due process violation. **School officials are entitled to qualified immunity for federal civil rights violations, unless the unlawfulness of their conduct is apparent in light of preexisting law.** While the school administrators had "exercised questionable judgment," they were entitled to qualified immunity. *Tun v. Whitticker*, 398 F.3d 899 (7th Cir. 2005).

4. Fighting and Violence

◆ An Ohio student with a history of threats against a classmate accused the classmate of talking about her. According to the classmate, the girl had to be restrained while threatening to "kick [her] ass." The classmate responded "I'm sick and tired of you threatening me. If you're going to beat me up, then just do it already ... ." Later, the school suspended both girls for three days. An administrator said the suspensions were based on an "inappropriate verbal confrontation" in violation of a school handbook provision prohibiting assault or battery. "Assault" was defined in the handbook as an "unlawful threat to injure another person" under circumstances calculated to produce fear and when one might reasonably expect that the threat might be carried out. An Ohio court found the classmate did not threaten physical harm or commit an "assault" and reduced her penalty to a Saturday detention. On appeal, the Court of Appeals of Ohio agreed the classmate did not commit an "assault" as defined in the handbook. Despite the board's position that the classmate committed an assault by "offering to fight with somebody," the court found she had only told the other girl to stop threatening her. **As none of the classmate's statements was an "assault" under the student handbook, the lower court was entitled to modify the discipline.** *Cisek v. Nordonia Hills Board of Educ.*, Case No. CV 2009 10 7363, 2011 WL 806518 (Ohio Ct. App. 3/9/11).

◆ A Minnesota student hit another student over the head with a hard plastic tray, disrupting the school cafeteria. The student believed she would be expelled for violating a disciplinary policy against assault and fighting, and she waived her right to a board hearing. The board then expelled her for a full calendar year. Her case reached the Court of Appeals of Minnesota, which found the board did not explain its decision as required by state law. When the case returned to the board, it made a new resolution finding the student had committed "assault with the lunch tray (used as a weapon)," and had tried to break away when being escorted from the cafeteria in order to harm the other student. The case came before the court of appeals a second time. It noted the board did not refer to the weapons policy until after the student had waived her right to a hearing. While the board removed references to the weapons policy after the court's prior decision, it failed to explain in sufficient detail why the student's conduct warranted a full calendar year expulsion. At no time prior to the hearing did the school board indicate that it viewed the use of a lunch tray as a weapons policy violation. **Education is a fundamental right under the state constitution and is protected by the Due Process Clause of the Fourteenth Amendment.** As the board reached its decision in violation of the student's due process rights, the court held in her favor. *Matter of Expulsion of N.Y.B.*, No. A09-670, 2010 WL 1541260 (Minn. Ct. App. 4/20/10).

◆   North Carolina school staff members tried to break up a fight between two students in the cafeteria. One of the students admitted hitting a teacher about 20 seconds after being separated from the other student. After an investigation by police, the student was charged as a juvenile with assault on a school employee and disorderly conduct. The other student was charged as an adult with a misdemeanor. The school board suspended the student for 10 days for violating four school board policies, including one providing for a long-term suspension for assaulting a school employee. After the suspension was imposed, the student received a hearing where he was represented by an attorney and had the opportunity to present evidence, call witnesses and make arguments. A hearing panel voted to affirm a recommendation to place him in an alternative setting.

Appeal reached the Court of Appeals of North Carolina. It appeared to the court that the student had an opportunity to learn the nature of his offense and respond to the charges. He received two hearings, including an "exhaustive fact-finding inquiry" by the school board. **While the student asserted self-defense, he had admitted a delay of 20 seconds from the end of the fight to the time he hit the teacher.** No witnesses supported his claim of self-defense. **State law required imposing a long-term suspension for violating the policy against assaulting school employees.** Protecting school employees is a goal of school discipline, so the court upheld the suspension. There was no showing that an alternative placement was inadequate, and the judgment was affirmed. *Watson-Green v. Wake County Board of Educ.*, 700 S.E.2d 249 (N.C. Ct. App. 2010).

◆   A Michigan law requires the permanent expulsion of a student in grade six or above for a physical assault at school against a school employee, volunteer or contractor. If an assault is reported to the school, the school board is required by law to "expel the pupil from the school district permanently." Four teachers claimed that pupils in grade six or higher physically assaulted them in their classrooms and that the assaults were reported to a school administrator. Instead of expelling the students, the school district only suspended them. The teachers and their association filed a state court action against the school board.

The court held it had no authority to supervise a school district's exercise of discretion. Appeal reached the Supreme Court of Michigan, which held the teachers were likely to suffer an injury that other members of the public did not face. Lower court decisions denying them standing would "slam the courthouse door" on numerous controversies, and the court reversed the judgment. **The intent of the law was to create a safe school environment and a more effective workplace for teachers.** *Lansing Schools Educ. Ass'n MEA/NEA v. Lansing Board of Educ.*, 487 Mich. 387, 792 N.W.2d 686 (Mich. 2010).

The case returned to the state court of appeals. It found the school board had already found the conduct of the students was not "physical assault" under the law. As the court could not grant the requested relief without simultaneously depriving the students of their right to receive an education, it held the teachers and their association failed to present an actual controversy that a court could resolve. As the board had found no physical assaults had occurred, recovery by the teachers was precluded. *Lansing Schools Educ. Ass'n, MEA/NEA v. Lansing School Dist. Board of Educ.*, 293 Mich. App. 506 (Mich. Ct. App. 2011).

5. Cell Phones and Electronic Devices

Off-campus student electronic communications often have a negative impact on school grounds, forcing educators to consider discipline for events that take place off-campus. In such cases, schools may seek the involvement of law enforcement officials and look to criminal laws to justify school discipline.

◆ A New Hampshire principal and a teacher received sexually explicit emails and reported them to the police. The messages were traced to a student who admitted sending them from her house. After a hearing, the school board voted to suspend the student for 34 days for violating several student handbook rules. These included the board's computer use policy, the behavior and discipline code, and the anti-harassment policy. Appeal reached a state education board, and a hearing officer found the student violated the acceptable use policy. It was also held that her misconduct went "well beyond the misuse of a computer," and qualified as "an act of neglect or refusal to conform to reasonable school rules."

Appeal reached the Supreme Court of New Hampshire, where the parents argued the 34-day suspension violated state law, state board rules and the district's own rules. The court rejected the parents' claims regarding state law and state board rules violations. State law authorized expulsion for a variety of reasons. State and local boards had authority to create rules and policies regarding student conduct and discipline. Since the school board had statutory authority to suspend the student in excess of 10 school days for neglect or refusal to conform to reasonable school rules, the court rejected the parents' claim that the suspension was improper under state law or state board rules. But **the family correctly argued that the suspension of 34 days was improper due to the school board's failure to comply with the limits of its own school policy**. As the policy limited long-term suspensions to between 11 and 20 school days, the court held that 20 days was the maximum suspension it could impose. *Appeal of Keelin B.*, 162 N.H. 38, 27 A.3d 689 (N.H. 2011).

◆ An Arkansas teacher confiscated a student's cell phone as he was using it in violation of a school rule. Although his parents demanded the return of the phone, it remained in the school office for two weeks, as required by a district policy. It was then returned, but the family sued the teacher and principal in a state court for trespass and taking property without due process of law. The court held for the district, and appeal reached the Supreme Court of Arkansas.

On appeal, the parents claimed Section 6-18-502 of the Arkansas Code did not authorize the confiscation. They argued that Americans have Fourth Amendment rights to be secure in their persons and property and to be free from unreasonable searches and seizures without due process. The court explained that Section 6-18-502 pertained only to the suspension or dismissal of students from public schools. It was insufficient to simply claim that no law authorized the confiscation. In prior decisions, the court made clear that a party's argument will not be considered unless it is convincing or supported by authority. **Section 6-18-502 declared that school policies were to "prescribe minimum and maximum penalties, including students' suspension or dismissal from school."** Arkansas school boards have broad discretion to direct school operations, and "courts have no power to interfere with such boards in the exercise of that discretion unless there is a clear abuse of it." The court refused to interfere with the board's decision about the best way to enforce its policy. The family did not cite any authority defining a property right to have a cell phone at school. As a result, the judgment for school officials was affirmed. *Koch v. Adams*, 361 S.W.3d 817 (Ark. 2010).

◆   Pennsylvania school officials found photos of nude and semi-nude female students on cell phones. Officials learned that male students traded the images over their cell phones. The district attorney investigated and made a public statement to the media that possession of inappropriate images of minors could justify criminal prosecution for possession or distribution of child pornography. The district attorney presented teens suspected of sexting with a choice of either attending an education program or facing child pornography charges. As part of the education program, female students would have to write a report detailing "why you are here," "what you did," and "why it was wrong." Three parents brought a federal court action to halt the proceeding, arguing the threatened prosecution came in retaliation for refusal to attend the education program.

The court granted them preliminary relief. An appeal was made to the U.S. Court of Appeals, Third Circuit. It found the parent objected to the lessons in morality, and held **the government cannot coerce parents to accept official ideas of morality and gender roles**. While the district attorney could offer a voluntary education program, he could not coerce attendance by threatening prosecution. The parent showed a reasonable likelihood of prevailing on both her claim that the district attorney violated her right to parental autonomy and her daughter's right to be free from compelled speech. As it appeared the district attorney made a retaliatory threat of prosecution, the court upheld the preliminary order. *Miller v. Mitchell*, 598 F.3d 139 (3d Cir. 2010).

◆   A Mississippi school faculty member confiscated a student's cell phone in his class. Pictures on the phone showed the student dancing at home and a classmate holding a BB gun at the student's house. Deeming the items "gang pictures," the principal suspended the student under a school rule prohibiting clothing, accessories, drawings or messages associated with gangs or crime. At a school disciplinary hearing, a municipal police sergeant said he recognized gang signs in the pictures, and the principal said the student "was a threat to school safety." The hearing officer recommended expelling the student for the rest of the school year, and the board of education affirmed the order.

A federal district court held the search of the cell phone did not violate the Fourth Amendment. The city was entitled to dismissal of the claim. A crucial factor was that the student was using his phone in violation of a school rule. The court said that once the staff member saw the student improperly using the phone, it was reasonable for him to find out why he was using it. But the court found no explanation for finding the student was a threat. The sergeant did not state a basis for believing the pictures had gang signs. The court was "troubled" that the student "somehow found himself expelled for an entire school year when the only offense he committed was the minor offense of bringing a phone on school grounds." It was clear to the court that he did not violate the anti-gang policy. The pictures were taken at the student's home, and it appeared that the district misapplied its anti-gang policy. As the most likely reason for expulsion was the principal's testimony that the student was "a threat to school safety," the court found it possible that the expulsion was based on subjective beliefs. *J.W. v. Desoto County School Dist.*, Civil Action No. 2:09-cv-00155-MPM-DAS, 2010 WL 4394059 (N.D. Miss. 11/1/10).

◆ At a school event called Class Day, an Arkansas student played an audio clip from his cell phone of a female student saying "oh my gosh, I'm horny!" A school official confiscated the phone, suspended him for three days and barred him from graduation ceremonies. The family sued the school district and officials in a state court for violating the state Civil Rights Act and the student's speech and due process rights. It was asserted that the discipline was retaliatory because the female in the clip was the stepdaughter of a school board member who happened to be in attendance at the assembly. A state circuit court held for the district, since the student was immediately advised of his improper conduct, and his parents received written notification of the discipline and an opportunity to meet with the superintendent. As the district provided the due process required by *Goss v. Lopez*, 419 U.S. 565 (1975), the court found no violation. Regarding the speech rights claim, the court held schools may determine what constitutes lewd, indecent or offensive speech. Since the court found no speech rights violation and no violation of the Arkansas Civil Rights Act, it held for the school district. On appeal, the Supreme Court of Arkansas found the student had to assert a deprivation of a right, privilege or immunity secured by the Arkansas Constitution to prevail. **Since the family did not show why federal decisions should be applied to find a violation of the state Civil Rights Act, the court refused to develop an argument on his behalf.** Instead, it held the circuit court judgment for the district and officials should be affirmed. *Walters v. Dobbins,* 370 S.W.3d 209 (Ark. 2010).

◆ A Tennessee eighth-grade teacher seized a student's cell phone when it began to ring in a classroom. A student code provision prohibited cell phones and other devices on school property during school hours. Violations were to be reported to the principal, and the phone or device was to be confiscated for 30 days. The code of conduct imposed a one-day, in-school suspension for first offenses and required minimal due process. The student's parent went to the school to retrieve the phone, but the principal refused to return it. The vice principal then assigned the student a day of in-school suspension. The parents sued the school board, principal and vice principal in a federal district court.

The court dismissed the father's due process claim for retention of the phone, but not the student's due process claim. The school board appealed to the U.S. Court of Appeals, Sixth Circuit, which held an in-school suspension could deprive a student of educational opportunities in the same way an out-of-school suspension would. But in this case, the student had been allowed to do her schoolwork. Her attendance was recorded in the same manner as if she had attended regular classes by state law. The court found other courts have held **in-school suspensions do not implicate a student's property interest in public education.** The court held that **"in-school suspension does not exclude the student from school and consequently a student's property interest in public education is not implicated."** A one-day in-school suspension, during which the student was recorded as in attendance and was allowed to do her schoolwork did not deprive her of any due process rights, and the court reversed the judgment. *Laney v. Farley*, 501 F.3d 577 (6th Cir. 2007).

◆   New York City school rules forbade students from bringing cell phones into public schools without authorization from principals. A state court held that any enforcement system focusing on the use, rather than possession, of cell phones would require teachers to observe and enforce the ban. For that reason, the board had a rational basis for a complete ban. The involvement of teachers in enforcing the cell phone ban would take time from their teaching mission and increase the perception of teachers as adversaries to students. Each principal could address specific situations by allowing students to carry cell phones when there was a special need for it. The court refused to recognize a "constitutional right to bear cell phones," and it rejected claims by parents who asserted a right to be able to communicate with their children at school. On appeal, the New York Supreme Court, Appellate Division, upheld the cell phone policy, finding it beyond court review. It was not unreasonable for the school system to ban cell phones, which by their nature could be used surreptitiously and in violation of school rules. Significantly, the court held that "the department has a rational interest in having its teachers and staff devote their time to educating students and not waging a 'war' against cell phones." **The use of cell phones for cheating, sexual harassment, prank calls and intimidation was a threat to order in the schools.** The judgment was affirmed. *Price v. New York City Board of Educ.*, 51 A.D.3d 277, 855 N.Y.S.2d 530 (N.Y. App. Div. 2008).

◆   A Delaware student used his cell phone at a school assembly, in violation of the school code. He refused to surrender his phone to a staff member, and the principal asked him four times to hand it over. The principal tried to escort the student from the assembly. The student struggled, pushed the principal and stepped on his foot. After being removed, he continued to use his cell phone. The student remained disruptive in the school office and told the principal "you can't touch me," and "just wait till I call my mom. She'll sue you." The police arrived at the school and took the student into custody. The school board expelled the student and assigned him to an alternative school. The state board of education affirmed the action, and the student appealed to a state court.

The court held the state board could overturn a local board decision only if it was contrary to state law or state regulations, was not supported by substantial evidence, or was arbitrary and capricious. The court found sufficient evidence that the student had pushed the principal and stepped on his foot. **The student had intentionally and offensively touched the principal in violation of the**

school code. Expulsion with referral to an alternative program was not disproportionate to the misconduct. *Jordan v. Smyrna School Dist. Board of Educ.*, No. 05A-02-004, 2006 WL 1149149 (Del. Super. Ct. 2006).

C. Academic Expulsions or Suspensions

◆ An Ohio student and his parents were Chinese citizens in the U.S. on visas. In addition to earning straight As, the student was a master violinist. After being questioned about a recent high grade on a biology test, the student admitted obtaining a biology test bank via the Internet by guessing the teacher's password and accessing a school computer. The assistant principal completed a notice of removal and/or intended suspension form that indicated a five-day suspension. It also stated that expulsion was possible. The assistant principal notified the family he was recommending expulsion for violating Ohio laws against computer break-ins. Due to the student's visa status and pending criminal charges, he faced possible deportation. A board hearing officer limited the hearing's duration to one hour because "it was a busy day." After the hearing, the hearing officer notified the family that the suspension should be upheld.

However, no conclusions of fact were sent to the family as required by Ohio statute. A state court affirmed the suspension. On appeal, the Court of Appeals of Ohio agreed with the family that there should have been a hearing in the trial court under the statute to supplement the deficient administrative record. As the hearing transcript did not record all the statements, and the hearing officer did not file any conclusions of law, the parents were entitled to submit additional evidence at another hearing. In the absence of a record, the court was unable to tell what rules the student may have violated, or the evidence upon which the board relied. **While the student's behavior was not to be condoned, he deserved an opportunity to present additional evidence under the circumstances.** *Huang v. Kent City School Dist. Board of Educ.*, No. 2008-P-0038, 2008 WL 4901779 (Ohio Ct. App. 11/14/08).

◆ An Oregon student had Attention Deficit Hyperactivity Disorder. With the help of the school football team's quarterback, he created counterfeit money. Both students were caught passing counterfeit bills at the student store. The student was charged with forgery and suspended for ongoing disciplinary issues, including a minor-in-possession charge, two harassment and misconduct complaints, and at least one athletic code violation. The school informed the student that since he intended to finish his course load outside of the classroom, the district was recommending expulsion for the rest of the year. The actual proceedings would be stayed if certain conditions were met. The quarterback received an in-school suspension for four days, and a three-week suspension from athletic activity and community service/grounds work at the high school.

In a federal lawsuit, the student asserted the greater punishment assigned to him was based on his learning disabilities. The court noted that **as long as there was a rational basis for the difference in the way the students were treated, the district was entitled to judgment**. This was because disabled students are not a "protected class" under the Equal Protection Clause. The court noted the student's prior disciplinary record and the fact that the quarterback had no disciplinary history. This distinction permitted disciplining the learning disabled student differently. *Schneider v. Corvallis School Dist. 509J*, No. CIV 05-6375-TC, 2006 WL 3827457 (D. Or. 2006).

◆   A student enrolled in the University of Michigan's "Inteflex" program – a special six-year course of study leading to both an undergraduate and medical degree. He struggled with the curriculum and failed the NBME Part I, receiving the lowest score in the brief history of the Inteflex program. The university's medical school executive board reviewed the student's academic career and decided to drop him from registration in the program. It denied his request to retake the NBME Part I. The student sued the university in a federal court, claiming due process violations. The evidence showed that the university had a practice of allowing students who had failed the NBME Part I to retake the test up to four times. The student was the only person ever refused permission to retake the test. Nonetheless, the court held that his dismissal did not violate the Due Process Clause. The U.S. Supreme Court agreed. The **Due Process Clause was not offended because "the University's liberal retesting custom gave rise to no state law entitlement to retake NBME Part I."** *Regents of Univ. of Michigan v. Ewing*, 474 U.S. 214, 106 S.Ct. 507, 88 L.Ed.2d 523 (1985).

II. STUDENT SEARCH AND SEIZURE

In New Jersey v. T.L.O., *below, the Supreme Court held the warrant and probable cause requirement of the Fourth Amendment does not apply to school officials who search students suspected of violating a law or school rules. Instead, the legality of a student search depends upon the reasonableness of the search in light of all the circumstances. A search performed by school officials must be "reasonable at its inception" and "not overly intrusive under all the circumstances." A student's age and sex are relevant considerations when evaluating the intrusiveness of a search. The Supreme Court revisited T.L.O. in Safford Unified School Dist. #1 v. Redding, Subsection II.A.3, below. The Court clarified that "justified at its inception" means there are reasonable grounds for suspecting that the search will turn up evidence of a rules violation. Courts in Florida, Washington and Louisiana have held the questioning of a student about contraband may be deemed a Fourth Amendment "search."*

A. Fourth Amendment "Reasonable Suspicion"

1. Searches Based on Individualized Suspicion

◆   A teacher at a New Jersey high school found two girls smoking in a school lavatory in violation of school rules. She brought them to the assistant vice principal's office, where one of the girls admitted to smoking in the lavatory. However, the other girl denied even being a smoker. The assistant vice principal then asked the latter girl to come to his private office, where he opened her purse and found a pack of cigarettes. As he reached for them, he noticed rolling papers and decided to thoroughly search the entire purse. He found marijuana, a pipe, empty plastic bags, a substantial number of one dollar bills and a list of "people who owe me money." The matter was then turned over to the police. A juvenile court hearing was held, and the girl was adjudicated delinquent. She appealed the juvenile court's determination, contending that her constitutional rights had been violated by the search of her purse. She argued that the evidence against her should have been excluded from the juvenile court proceeding.

The U.S. Supreme Court held the search did not violate the Fourth Amendment. It said: "The legality of a search of a student should depend simply on the reasonableness, under all the circumstances, of the search." Two considerations are relevant in determining the reasonableness of a search. First, **the search must be justified initially by reasonable suspicion of a violation.** Second, **the scope and conduct of the search must be reasonably related to the circumstances which gave rise to the search, and school officials must take into account the student's age, sex and the nature of the offense.** The Court upheld the search of the student in this case because the initial search for cigarettes was supported by reasonable suspicion. The discovery of rolling papers then justified the further searching of the purse, since such papers are commonly used to roll marijuana cigarettes. The Court affirmed the delinquency adjudication, ruling the "reasonableness" standard was met by school officials in these circumstances and the evidence was properly obtained. *New Jersey v. T.L.O.*, 469 U.S. 325, 105 S.Ct. 733, 83 L.Ed.2d 720 (1985).

◆ A California student who was searched because he was in a school hallway without a hall pass avoided a juvenile court sentence because the campus aide who detained him could not articulate a reason for performing the search. The Court of Appeal of California held that under ordinary circumstances, a search of a student by a school official must be justified at its inception, reasonably related to the objectives of the search, and not excessively intrusive. In a prior case, *In re Lisa G.*, 125 Cal.App.4th 801 (Cal. Ct. App. 2004), the court of appeal held that disruptive behavior alone did not justify the search of a student. In that case, a teacher failed to articulate a reasonable suspicion of misconduct by a student that was sufficient to justify searching the student's purse. Similarly, in this case, the aide was unable to explain a reasonable suspicion that searching the student would reveal evidence of a crime or violation of a school rule. In the court's view, **"a suspicion that a student was tardy or truant from class, without more, provides no reasonable basis for conducting a search of any kind."** As a result, it found the evidence seized in this case was inadmissible and should have been suppressed. As the lower court had incorrectly declared the student a ward of the court, the judgment was reversed. *In re Diego C.*, No. B232230, 2011 WL 6740151 (Cal. Ct. App. 12/29/11).

◆ A New Hampshire school parking lot monitor observed a student walking away from the school. Three school employees caught up with the student as he crossed a field about 200 yards from the building. He said he did not feel well. The employees persuaded him to return to school, where they searched him under a policy applying to any student who returned to school after leaving an assigned area. An assistant principal asked the student if he "had anything on him that he shouldn't have on school property." The student handed over a small bag of marijuana he had hidden inside a sock. In juvenile proceedings, a New Hampshire family court denied his motion to exclude the marijuana from evidence. On appeal, the Supreme Court of New Hampshire found no distinction between a "search" and the treatment of the student in this case.

According to the court, **courts and schools are to consider a child's age, school record, the extent of the problem to which the search was directed, the exigencies at the time, the probative value and reliability of information justifying the search, and prior experiences with the student**. Consideration of these factors did not support the state's claim that the search was "justified at its inception." There was no record of a drug problem at the school, and no administrator had any prior disciplinary experiences with the student. Since the search was not justified at its inception, it was held unreasonable under the state constitution. *In re Anthony F.*, 163 N.H. 163, 37 A.3d 429 (N.H. 2012).

◆   A California student attended a class, left campus, and then returned to school. An assistant principal learned the student had left and called him to the office. There, the student was asked to empty his pockets based on a school policy subjecting students to searches when they returned to campus after being "out-of-bounds." A plastic bag containing 44 ecstasy pills was found, and a state juvenile court petition was filed against the student for possession of a controlled substance. He sought to suppress the pills from evidence on the theory that the policy of searching all students who leave and return to campus during the day was unlawful. After the court held the school's policy was constitutional, the student admitted possessing a controlled substance and was placed on probation. On appeal, the California Court of Appeal held that Fourth Amendment criminal law principles do not apply to school searches.

Article I, Section 28, of the state constitution recognized rights of students and staff to attend safe, secure and peaceful campuses. **School officials do not investigate violations of criminal law and "must be permitted to exercise their broad supervisory and disciplinary powers, without worrying that every encounter with a student will be converted into an opportunity for constitutional review."** The court held the policy supported the purpose of assuring safe schools. The search was done without touching the student, who was only asked to empty his pockets. As the court found the search consistent with the special need to keep a safe school environment, it found no constitutional violation. *In re Sean A.*, 191 Cal.App.4th 182 (Cal Ct. App. 2010).

◆   Georgia school administrators received a report that an African-American student stole an MP3 player from another student's locker and tried to sell it. A white male stated that he and the African-American student stole the player together after going locker to locker. He accused the African-American student of selling the MP3 player for $40. The assistant principal interviewed the African-American student, who denied the allegations. She then searched his locker and found a dead cell phone that was later determined to be stolen from a middle school in the district. Investigators questioned the African-American student a second time about the stolen MP3 player. He admitted trying to sell it to a friend but claimed he did not steal it and was not aware that it had been stolen. After school officials suspended him for eight days, he sued them.

A federal district court held that the search and seizure claims did not state a Fourth Amendment or due process violation. As for the equal protection claims, they failed because the student did not show that he was "similarly situated" to his white classmate. On appeal, the U.S. Court of Appeals, Eleventh Circuit, affirmed, noting that in cases involving short-term suspensions of 10 days or less, **"once school administrators tell a student what they heard or saw, ask why they heard or saw it, and allow a brief response, a student has received all the process that the Fourteenth Amendment demands."** *Roy v. Fulton County School Dist.*, 288 Fed.Appx. 686 (11th Cir. 2008).

♦   A New York middle school teacher reported that her classroom was being disturbed by a musical noise from a cell phone. The dean of the school arrived to investigate and enforce the school's rule prohibiting cell phone use in class. After a student realized the dean intended to search each student in the room for the source of the noise, he removed a hunting knife with a six-inch blade from his pocket and handed it over to the dean. As he was 15 years old, he was charged in a state family court with the delinquent act of weapons possession. The student moved to suppress evidence of his knife possession, claiming it was unlawfully obtained in violation of the state and federal constitutions. The court denied the motion and adjudicated him delinquent. On appeal, the New York Supreme Court, Appellate Division, held **the dean did not perform a "search" of the student, because he was holding the knife and it was in plain view.**

Even if there was a search, the dean's actions were justified. Asking students to empty their pockets was a non-intrusive, practical means of finding an unauthorized cell phone. The dean had a reasonable basis to believe a student in the class was violating school rules, and that the sound was disruptive. The family court had properly found the dean was trying to restore order, "which is not a law enforcement interest." Accordingly, he required neither probable cause nor reasonable suspicion to justify asking the students to empty their pockets. The appellate court upheld the family court's finding of delinquency. *In re Elvin G.*, 47 A.D.3d 527, 851 N.Y.S.2d 129 (N.Y. App. Div. 2008).

♦   A Florida student felt dizzy at school and lost consciousness in a lavatory. He then told a school monitor he did not feel well. The monitor escorted the student to a school office. The assistant principal later said that the student was quiet, subdued and a little pale. She ordered the student to empty out his pockets and bookbag. After noticing a plastic baggie that appeared to contain marijuana, she called the police. The contents of the bag tested positive for marijuana. The student was arrested and charged with marijuana possession. A Florida court denied his motion to suppress the evidence and adjudicated him delinquent. The student appealed to a Florida District Court of Appeal. The court explained that school officials must have reasonable grounds to suspect that a search will result in evidence that the student has violated the law or school rules. Here, the search was premised upon the student's lavatory incident and his appearance. **The student's pale or quiet appearance alone was "entirely consistent with non-criminal behavior such as illness."** The court reversed the adjudication of delinquency. *C.G. v. State of Florida*, 941 So.2d 503 (Fla. Dist. Ct. App. 2007).

◆ A student informant identified an 18-year-old adult student as one of several students who might be involved in drug dealing at an Ohio high school. The assistant principal summoned the adult student to the office, where he agreed to a pat-down search. Several hundred dollars were found in his wallet, which he claimed was pay from his job. Administrators asked to search his car, and he told them they would only find cigarettes. A search confirmed that the student possessed cigarettes and lighters, and he was suspended for three days.

The school board rejected the student's appeal, and an Ohio common pleas court upheld the suspension. On appeal to the Court of Appeals of Ohio, the student argued the informant's report was an insufficient reason for a search or questioning. Moreover, he admitted having the cigarettes, making a search unnecessary. **The court found a student search is justified at its inception when there are reasonable grounds for suspecting it will turn up evidence of a violation of school rules or a law.** The assistant principal believed the informant was trustworthy, making the search justified at its inception. The search was reasonable in scope because the student admitted contraband would be found in his car. A school policy called for only a warning to adult school district employees who possessed tobacco, while students were subject to suspension. Since students were distinguishable from district employees and could be treated differently, the court found no equal protection violation and upheld the discipline. *Mayeux v. Board of Educ. of Painesville Township School Dist.*, No. 2007-L-099, 2008 WL 754979 (Ohio Ct. App. 3/21/08).

◆ A Pennsylvania student had his cell phone on, in violation of a school policy. When a teacher confiscated the phone, a text message appeared on its screen from another student requesting marijuana. The teacher and an assistant principal then called nine students listed in the cell phone's directory to see if their phones were turned on in violation of school policy. They accessed the student's text messages and voice mail, and used the phone's instant messaging feature. The student stated the district superintendent later told the press that the student was a drug user or peddler, and the family sued the teacher, assistant principal, superintendent and school district in a federal district court. It held the superintendent could not assert absolute immunity for his statements to the press. The teacher and assistant principal also had no immunity for the invasion of privacy claims. **The court agreed with the family that accessing the phone directory, voice mail and text messages, and use of the phone to call persons listed in the directory amounted to a "search or seizure" under the Fourth Amendment.** The court found no basis for the "search," as it was not done to find evidence of wrongdoing by the student, but instead to obtain evidence of possible misconduct by others. The Fourth Amendment claims would proceed. *Klump v. Nazareth Area School Dist.*, 425 F.Supp.2d 622 (E.D. Pa. 2006).

◆ A California school security employee saw three teenagers sitting on the front lawn of a high school during school hours. Because the employee did not recognize any of them, he called a police officer. The officer approached the intruders and asked them for identification. One of them produced identification from another school. The officer decided to escort the three intruders to the office to verify their identities. For his own safety, he decided to pat them down.

The officer discovered a knife with a locking blade on one intruder and confiscated it. The intruder was charged with unlawful possession of the knife on school property. He was charged with a crime, and his case reached the Court of Appeal of California. It held **searches of students are justified if there is reasonable suspicion of a violation of a law, school rule or regulation.** Students may be detained without any particularized suspicion, so long as the detention is not arbitrary, capricious or for the purpose of harassment. Here, the intruder did not attend the school. He had a lesser right of privacy than students who were properly on school grounds. The officer had ample cause to believe the intruder did not belong on campus. The state's interest in preventing violence on a campus outweighed the minimal invasion to the intruder's privacy rights. As the pat-down search was proper, the court affirmed the judgment. *In re Jose Y.*, 141 Cal.App.4th 748, 46 Cal.Rptr.3d 268 (Cal. Ct. App. 2006).

◆ A Massachusetts school administrator saw three students in a parking lot when they should have been in class. A search of one student yielded a small bag of marijuana. A juvenile court denied his motion to suppress the marijuana evidence and found him delinquent. On appeal, the Supreme Judicial Court of Massachusetts explained that **reasonable suspicion is not a hunch or "unparticularized suspicion," but instead requires commonsense conclusions about human behavior.** In this case, the student had recently been truant and failed to bring his mother to a meeting to discuss it. School officials had no evidence he possessed contraband or had violated a law or school rule. The court rejected the argument that the search was appropriate based on the student's truancy. A violation of school rules, standing alone, would not provide reasonable grounds for a search unless the specific facts of the violation created a reasonable suspicion of a violation. As there was no information of an individualized nature that the student might have contraband, any search was unreasonable at its inception and the court vacated the juvenile court order. *Comwlth. of Massachusetts v. Damian D.*, 752 N.E. 2d 679 (Mass. 2001).

2. School Liaison and Resource Officers

In assessing the proper standard for searches conducted by school liaison and resource officers, the courts have focused on what the officer's duties were, who initiated the investigation, who performed the search and the purpose of the search. North Dakota's Supreme Court has held the reasonable suspicion standard applies when a school resource officer acts on his or her own initiative or at the direction of other school officials when there is some educational goal. The probable cause standard applies when municipal officers initiate a search.

◆ A North Dakota school resource officer learned about possible drug use by students a short distance from school, and a security guard was assigned to patrol the area. Two students evaded the guard, who returned to campus and told the resource officer he had "smelled something funny." When the officer followed the students in a patrol car, they walked away. The officer told the principal of their evasive behavior and said he suspected them of drug activity. The principal questioned one of the students in the presence of the officer. The student emptied his pockets, which contained a pipe and synthetic marijuana. He later sought to suppress this evidence in criminal proceedings.

The court applied the "reasonable suspicion" standard for school searches, and the student was convicted of felony charges. On appeal, the Supreme Court of North Dakota held the "reasonable suspicion" standard applies when school officials initiate a search or when police involvement is minimal. **In the court's view, the reasonable suspicion standard applies when a school resource officer acts on his or her own initiative or at the direction of other school officials to further educational goals.** The court found the relevant factors supported applying the reasonable suspicion standard in this case. The resource officer did not initiate the investigation. He notified the principal of his observations and let him decide how to handle the situation. The officer was not involved in the questioning except to instruct the student to put his possessions on the table. As he worked in conjunction with and at the direction of the principal, the court applied the "reasonableness standard." Finding the search was justified at its inception and not excessively intrusive, the court upheld the student's conviction. *State v. Alaniz*, 815 N.W.2d 234 (N.D. 2012).

3. Strip Searches

In Safford Unified School Dist. #1 v. Redding, *below, the Supreme Court discussed the distinction between the "probable cause" standard for police searches and the "reasonable suspicion" standard for school searches. It held "probable cause" requires evidence that raises "a fair probability" or a "substantial chance of discovering evidence of criminal activity." By contrast, the Court held "the standard for school searches could as readily be described as a moderate chance of finding evidence of wrongdoing."*

◆ An Arizona assistant middle school principal questioned a 13-year-old student about knives, lighters and a cigarette found in her planner. When the student denied owning any of the contraband, the assistant principal questioned her about prescription-strength ibuprofen pills and an over-the-counter painkiller. After the student denied knowing about the pills, the assistant principal told her he had received a report from a male student that she was giving pills to others at school. She denied this and allowed the assistant principal to search her belongings. He found no contraband there but told female staff members to further search the student in the nurse's office. An administrative assistant and school nurse asked the student to remove her jacket, socks, shoes, pants and T-shirt. They then instructed her to pull her bra to the side and shake it. Finally, the two staff members told the student to pull out the elastic of her underpants.

No pills were found. The student's mother sued for Fourth Amendment violations. The case reached the U.S. Supreme Court, which held the male student's report created enough suspicion to justify the search of the student's backpack and outer clothing. But asking her to pull away her underwear and expose her breasts and pelvic area made the search **"categorically distinct, requiring distinct elements of justification on the part of school authorities for going beyond a search of outer clothing and belongings."** While the indignity of a search does not necessarily outlaw it, "the suspicion failed to match the degree of intrusion." The assistant principal had no reason to suspect the student was hiding anything in her underwear. The Court stated "the *T.L.O.* concern to limit a school search to reasonable scope requires the support of reasonable suspicion of danger or of resort to underwear for hiding evidence of wrongdoing before a search can reasonably make the quantum leap from outer clothes and backpacks to exposure of intimate parts." Despite the violation, the law of student searches was not so well established as to deprive school officials of qualified immunity. *Safford Unified School Dist. #1 v. Redding*, 557 U.S. 364, 129 S.Ct. 2633, 174 L.Ed.2d 354 (2009).

◆   Two students in an Ohio high school nursing class reported missing cash, a credit card and gift cards. The other 15 or 16 students in the class were taken to the first aid room, where their purses, books, shoes, socks and pockets were searched. After a search of each student's locker, staff members received a report that an unidentified student was hiding the missing items in her bra. The school director then instructed a female instructor to search the students in the lavatory. Eleven students sued the school district, instructors and other school officials in a federal district court for violating their Fourth Amendment rights. The court denied the officials' request for qualified immunity. On appeal, the U.S. Court of Appeals, Sixth Circuit, affirmed the judgment, and the officials appealed to the U.S. Supreme Court. It returned the case to the Sixth Circuit in view of its decision in *Safford Unified School Dist. #1 v. Redding*, above.

The Sixth Circuit held there must be "reasonable grounds for suspecting that the search will turn up evidence that the student has violated or is violating either the law or the rules of the school." **A student handbook policy did not create mutual consent to conduct the strip searches, as the district argued.** There was no waiver of privacy expectations, as some students did not even know about the policy. The court held "students have a significant privacy interest in their unclothed bodies." The severity of the school's need in this case was held "slight." A search for money served a much less important interest than a search for drugs or weapons. The court found the search was unlikely to uncover any evidence and violated the students' rights. As a result, the court again denied the officials' claim to immunity. *Knisley v. Pike County Joint Vocational School Dist.*, 604 F.3d 977 (6th Cir. 2010).

◆   A Georgia high school student violated a ban on electronic communication devices by bringing an iPod and cell phone to class. After confiscating the iPod and putting it in a drawer, the teacher left the room, and a classmate took it from the drawer. When the teacher returned, he found the iPod missing and asked who had taken it. After no student admitted having the iPod, all of them were told to open their book bags, turn out their pockets and untuck their shirts. A classmate later confided the identity of the iPod taker to the assistant principal. He avoided confronting the iPod taker to protect the identity of the informer, and told the school discipline secretary to take each of the girls to a closet where they were to shake out their blouses and roll down their waistbands.

Although the identity of the iPod taker was already known, the secretary told a student to remove her pants and underwear. The student sued the teacher, district and others in a federal district court. It held student searches must be "justified at its inception." **This meant reasonable grounds for suspecting that the search will turn up evidence of a violation of rules must be present.** In *Thomas v. Roberts*, 261 F.3d 1160 (11th Cir. 2001), the Eleventh Circuit considered a strip search of Georgia fifth-graders for $26 in missing cash. *Roberts* put schools on notice that a strip search for non-dangerous contraband violates the Fourth Amendment. Officials lacked individualized suspicion that the student had the iPod, and the assistant principal acknowledged the search was to protect the informant. As the search was not based on individualized suspicion that the student had an iPod, a jury could find a Fourth Amendment violation if she was searched as she claimed. But as the assistant principal was not a "final policymaker" for the district, there could be no district liability on the federal claims. *Foster v. Raspberry*, 652 F.Supp.2d 1342 (M.D. Ga. 2009).

◆   A federal district court held Illinois charter school officials were immune to claims filed by a student who was strip-searched by a security guard and police officer. In *Safford Unified School Dist. v. Redding*, this chapter, the Supreme Court held that a school official searching a student may claim qualified immunity where no clearly established law reveals a constitutional violation. The student could not show the law regarding school strip searches was "clearly established" at the time of the search. *Redding* was not released until after the search in this case. As for the other claims, the court rejected the student's argument that school and municipal officials placed her in a position of danger by allowing the search to go forward. **A single, isolated incident of wrongdoing by a non-policymaker was insufficient to establish municipal liability.** Rejecting other state law claims, the court disposed of many of the student's claims prior to any trial. *S.J. v. Perspectives Charter School*, 685 F.Supp.2d 847 (N.D. Ill. 2010).

◆   A Michigan student told her gym teacher that money had been stolen from her during class. The gym teacher searched backpacks of male students in the class, without success. A male teacher searched the boys in their locker room, instructing them to lower their pants and underwear and remove their shirts. A police officer arrived and told the teacher to continue searching. The principal and a female teacher then searched the girls in their locker room, requiring them to pull up their shirts and pull down their pants. About 25 students were searched, but the stolen money was not discovered. The case reached the U.S. Court of Appeals, Sixth Circuit, which stated that the law regarding strip searches was sufficiently unclear that the teachers and officer were entitled to qualified immunity. After the district court dismissed some of the claims, the students brought a second appeal to the Sixth Circuit. It held that to hold the district liable for not sufficiently training its teachers and maintaining a policy of unconstitutional searches, the students had to show "deliberate indifference." But the teachers had disregarded school policies when performing the search, and **the need for further training was not so obvious that the district could be found "deliberately indifferent" to student constitutional rights**. As a result, the court affirmed the judgment for the school officials. *Beard v. Whitmore Lake School Dist.*, 244 Fed.Appx. 607 (6th Cir. 2007).

◆   An Alabama seventh-grade teacher reported her $450 makeup bag and $12 in cash were missing. The principal, an assistant principal and a counselor told students to empty their book bags and purses and take off their shoes and socks. The principal took some boys into the hallway for questioning. He then found the makeup bag in a trash can. The principal then took the boys to the boys' lavatory, where he told them to drop their pants and raise their shirts. The counselor took the girls to the lavatory and told most of them to do the same. A few girls were told to pull up their bras. Parents of the students sued the school board, principal, assistant principal, and counselor for Fourth Amendment violations. A federal court noted the school handbook warned school officials to avoid group searches where individualized suspicion was lacking. School officials were to call the police and parents if a more intrusive search was required. The policy forbade strip searching. The court found that the officials did not have any individualized suspicion that any student took the makeup bag. The classroom searches, which did not involve the touching of students, were justified, but **a strip search for the possible theft of $12 was unreasonable. The strip searches were intrusive and violated the district's own policy.** As the search was beyond the school officials' authority, they were not entitled to qualified immunity from the Fourth Amendment violation claims. *H.Y. v. Russell County Board of Educ.*, 490 F.Supp.2d 1174 (M.D. Ala. 2007).

◆   Connecticut school officials held a security search prior to the boarding of buses to a senior class picnic. A student was found with a pack of cigarettes, but no action was taken against her. A classmate then reported to a teacher that the student said she planned to hide marijuana in her pants after the security check. The principal instructed the nurse to search the student's underpants. The student's mother arrived and agreed to help with the search after being told the police would be called otherwise. The nurse and mother then performed the search behind a curtain. The student was required to raise her shirt, pull down her bra and skirt, and pull her underpants away from her body. The search revealed no marijuana, and the student was allowed to attend the picnic. She later sued the principal and other officials for constitutional violations. A federal court upheld the search under *New Jersey v. T.L.O.* (this chapter).

The U.S. Court of Appeals, Second Circuit, considered the case and reviewed *Cornfield v. Consolidated High School Dist.*, 991 F.2d 1316 (7th Cir. 1993), an Illinois case that found an intrusive strip search required such a high level of suspicion that it approached probable cause. Here, the factors relied on by the school officials were insufficient to create reasonable suspicion for a strip search. While the teacher may have been entitled to rely on the classmate as a reliable informant, the principal was not. After receiving the tip, the principal did not investigate or try to corroborate the classmate's account. **A history of drug use could be a factor justifying a school search, but the student in this case was not previously disciplined for any drug offense.** While she had cigarettes and a lighter, the court held this had only a tenuous link to a drug possession report. Finding officials lacked reasonable suspicion, the court reversed the judgment. *Phaneuf v. Fraikin*, 448 F.3d 591 (2d Cir. 2006).

4. State Constitutional Cases

In In re P.E.A., *754 P.2d 382 (Col. 1988), the Colorado Supreme Court held the search of a student's car for contraband was justified at its inception. The Supreme Court of New Jersey looked to the Colorado decision in* State v. Best, *below, to support the application of a reasonableness standard to the search of vehicles parked on school property. Officials took action that was reasonably related to the objectives of the search and not excessively intrusive.*

◆ A New Jersey assistant principal (AP) received a report that a high school student was under the influence of drugs. After being taken to the AP's office and interviewed, the student denied any wrongdoing. A search of the student's pockets yielded three white capsules. The AP then searched the student's car and denied his request to call his father. The car search yielded contraband, including a bag containing what appeared to be illegal drugs. A school resource officer arrested the student, who waived his right to remain silent and admitted that the contraband belonged to him. In juvenile proceedings, the student moved to suppress evidence seized from his car as a violation of his right to be free from unreasonable searches and seizures. Based on a finding that the AP's search of the car was reasonably related to a suspicion that the student had drugs and posed a danger to the school, the trial court denied the student's motion.

A state appellate division court affirmed the judgment, and the student appealed to the Supreme Court of New Jersey. On appeal, the court explained that under *New Jersey v. T.L.O.*, this chapter, the school setting required some easing of police search standards in view of the need to maintain school discipline and safety. **The court found no reason to avoid the *T.L.O.* standard in vehicle cases, as "the school setting calls for protections geared toward the safety of students."** The court was not convinced by the student's claim to a greater expectation of privacy in his car than he might have in a locker or purse. A "reasonable grounds" standard applied to the search of a student's car on school property by school authorities. Based on a classmate's statements and his apparent drug use, and the student's statements and possession of pills, it was reasonable for the AP to extend the search to the student's car. The court affirmed the judgment. *State v. Best*, 201 N.J. 100, 987 A.2d 605 (N.J. 2010).

◆ Several people told a Florida middle school principal that a student had been drinking alcohol with a friend at home the day before. Upon interviewing the student, the principal learned that the two girls drank alcohol before school. A sibling of the student had then taken them to school. A child study committee met and found the student was under the influence of alcohol at school. After a hearing, the school board expelled the student for substantially disrupting the orderly conduct of the school and for gross misconduct in violation of a school policy against drinking alcohol. On appeal, a Florida District Court of Appeal found **Section 1006.07 of Florida Statutes and the school's own policy limited the board's power to punish students to conduct occurring on school grounds or during school-provided transportation**. In this case, the consumption of alcohol occurred at the student's residence about 45 minutes before school began. As she argued, the board could not punish her for drinking alcohol at home. There was no evidence that the student was under the influence of alcohol at school or that she behaved in an impaired manner. Since the court found no evidence that the student disrupted the learning environment despite her ingestion of alcohol, she could not be expelled under the school policy. As a result, the court vacated the school board's decision. *A.B.E. v. School Board of Brevard County*, 33 So.3d 795 (Fla. Dist. Ct. App. 2010).

◆ An Oregon student was called to the office and told that an anonymous witness saw him trying to sell drugs. After speaking to his mother, the student agreed to turn his pockets inside out. Marijuana, plastic bags and a pipe were found, and he admitted he had tried to sell marijuana. In juvenile court proceedings, the student claimed any evidence seized by school officials should be excluded from trial because there was no probable cause for a search.

Finding probable cause was unnecessary, the juvenile court held the search was lawful. It also concluded that the student was delinquent. Appeal reached the Supreme Court of Oregon. It discussed Article I, Section 9, of the Oregon Constitution, which prohibits unreasonable searches or seizures. The court held school searches are different from law enforcement searches. **Only searches involving safety concerns justify a departure from the "warrant and probable cause" requirement.** When school officials perceive an immediate threat to safety, they need the ability to take prompt, reasonable steps. School officials have wide latitude to take safety precautions when they have reasonable suspicion based on specific and articulable facts that an individual poses a threat to safety or possesses an item posing such a threat. "Reasonable suspicion" applies to searches for drugs on school property. Since officials reasonably suspected that the student had illegal drugs at the time of the search and that he intended to sell them at school, the judgment was affirmed. *State ex rel. Juvenile Dep't of Clackamas County v. M.A.D.*, 348 Or. 381, 233 P.3d 437 (Or. 2010).

B. Random Search Policies

The U.S. Supreme Court has upheld random testing programs for students seeking to participate in extracurricular activities and use school parking facilities. According to the Court, students participating in extracurricular programs have a reduced expectation of privacy when compared to the general student population, justifying random testing. See Chapter Thirteen for more cases concerning random searches of students in interscholastic athletics.

◆ A New Jersey school district required extracurricular participants and students with school parking privileges to undergo random drug testing. After a student tested positive for drug use, he sought a declaration that the board's policy did not comply with state laws and regulations. An administrative law judge (ALJ) held the policy did not ensure documentation and verification of the random selection procedure and omitted procedures to challenge positive test results. The board was ordered to delete the student's test result. On review, the state education commissioner found that while the policy did not fully comply with state regulations, it did not violate state law. The ALJ's order to delete the test result was reversed, and the board was ordered to correct its policy. Appeal reached the Superior Court of New Jersey, Appellate Division. It found the board's internal grievance procedure complied with state law.

The parents argued that the policy lacked the detailed information required by the law and regulations. While the board policy was flawed to the extent that it did not provide the specificity contemplated by state regulations, the court held there was no violation of the law. It held **the policy still provided a basic outline of procedures and alerted families about how they could obtain more information**. No constitutional concerns were implicated, as the state supreme court had upheld random drug testing in schools in 2003. Since the family was unable to show it was prejudiced by the lack of specificity in the policy, and the policy complied with the law, the court affirmed the commissioner's order. *K.Q. and L.Q. v. Board of Educ. of Gateway Regional High School Dist.*, 2012 WL 1253008 (N.J. Super. Ct. App. Div. 4/16/12).

◆   An Oregon school district responded to increased student drug use by instituting a random drug-testing policy for all students wishing to participate in varsity athletics. A student who wanted to play football refused to sign the drug-testing consent form and was suspended from sports for the season. His parents sued the district in a federal district court. The court upheld the policy, but the Ninth Circuit held it violated the U.S. and Oregon Constitutions. On appeal, the Supreme Court noted students have a lesser expectation of privacy than the general populace, and that student-athletes have an even lower expectation of privacy in the locker room. The Court held the invasion of privacy in this case was no worse than what was typically encountered in public restrooms. Positive test results were disclosed to only a few school employees. **The insignificant invasion of student privacy was outweighed by the district's important interest in addressing drug use by students who risked physical harm while playing sports.** The Court vacated the judgment and remanded the case. *Vernonia School Dist. 47J v. Acton*, 515 U.S. 646 (1995).

◆   An Oklahoma school district adopted a policy requiring all students who sought to participate in extracurricular activities to submit to random drug testing. A student challenged the policy in a federal district court, which awarded summary judgment to the board. On appeal, the Tenth Circuit held student drug use in the Oklahoma district was far from epidemic or an immediate crisis and reversed the judgment. The board appealed to the U.S. Supreme Court, which noted the testing policy was adopted to protect students.

The Court found no reason to limit drug testing to student-athletes, extending *Vernonia* to cover all extracurricular activities participants. Participants in these activities had limited privacy rights, as they voluntarily subjected themselves to certain intrusions on their privacy. They also agreed to abide by extracurricular club rules and requirements that did not apply to the student body at large. The policy's intrusion on student privacy was minimal. Test results could have no impact on student discipline or academics, but could only lead to the limitation of extracurricular activities participation. By contrast, the district and board had an important interest in preventing student drug use. The Court found sufficient evidence of drug use by students to justify the policy. **It deemed the policy a reasonably effective means of addressing legitimate**

concerns in preventing, deterring and detecting student drug use. *Board of Educ. of Independent School Dist. 92, Pottawatomie County v. Earls*, 536 U.S. 822, 122 S.Ct. 2559, 153 L.Ed.2d 735 (2002).

◆ Wyoming's highest court upheld a random drug- and alcohol-testing policy for extracurricular activities participants. It held the privacy rights of the extracurricular participants were more reduced than those of the general population, and **the testing policy was less intrusive than the one upheld by the Supreme Court in** *Vernonia School Dist. 47J v. Acton*, this chapter. *Hageman v. Goshen County School Dist. No. 1*, 256 P.3d 487 (Wyo. 2011).

◆ A federal court held that daily searches of disabled students at segregated facilities operated by a public school special education cooperative violated the Fourth Amendment. **The court found the cooperative's programs were educational and not punitive in nature.** This distinguished the case from *C.N.H. v. Florida*, 927 So.2d 1 (Fla. Dist. Ct. App. 2006), where a court approved of daily pat-down searches at an alternative school where students attended by court order and in lieu of confinement. In this case, the students did not attend school in lieu of detention. **A policy of daily, suspicionless searches was unconstitutional.** A jury would have to decide whether daily searches over a course of years was "highly offensive" under state law principles. *Hough v. Shakopee Public Schools*, 608 F.Supp.2d 1087 (D. Minn. 2009).

◆ An Arkansas district handbook permitted random searches of book bags, backpacks, purses and other containers at all times on school property. A staff member found some marijuana in a student's purse after all the students in her classroom were ordered to wait in the hall during a search. The student sued the district for constitutional rights violations. The case reached the Eighth Circuit, which held students have a legitimate, though limited, privacy expectation in their personal belongings at school. A full-scale search without any suspicion of wrongdoing virtually eliminated their privacy interests. **Searches involving "people rummaging through personal belongings" were much more intrusive than searches involving metal detectors or police dogs.** As the policy was highly intrusive and not justified by any significant school interest, the court held that it violated the Fourth Amendment. *Doe v. Little Rock School Dist.*, 380 F.3d 349 (8th Cir. 2004).

C. Police Involvement

1. *Miranda* Warnings

In Miranda v. Arizona, *384 U.S. 436 (1966), the Supreme Court adopted the criminal rights advisory that has come to be known as the "*Miranda *warning." It is a set of prophylactic measures designed to safeguard the constitutional guarantee against self-incrimination. The advisory includes the right to remain silent, to know that any statement can be used against the person in court, and the right to have assistance of counsel. Failure to issue a* Miranda *warning may result in a juvenile or criminal court order to exclude statements made by a* *detained person as a coercive violation of constitutional rights. If a suspect makes a statement during a custodial interrogation, the government has the burden of showing a voluntary, knowing and intelligent waiver of rights.*

School officials are not agents of the police, as they act to ensure student safety and maintain school order, not combat crime. A duty to issue Miranda warnings arises when a suspect is not free to move and is in "police custody."

◆   A uniformed school resource officer removed a 13-year-old North Carolina seventh-grader from class to question him about break-ins in his neighborhood. A police investigator, an assistant school principal and a school intern were also present for the questioning. Neither the officers nor any school administrators called the student's guardian prior to questioning the student, and nobody told him he was free to leave the room. After the student denied any wrongdoing, an assistant principal urged him to "do the right thing." He also said "the truth always comes out in the end." The resource officer told the student "this thing is going to court," and threatened him with juvenile detention. The student then admitted he had committed the crimes. Only then did the officer inform him he could refuse to answer the questions and that he was free to leave the room.

After offering further details, including the location of the stolen items, the student wrote a statement at the officer's request. After juvenile petitions were filed against the student, his public defender moved to exclude the statements and evidence obtained from the school interview. Finding the student was not "in custody" of the police at the time of the interrogation, the juvenile court denied the motion and found him delinquent. Appeal reached the U.S. Supreme Court, which held that a duty to issue a *Miranda* warning arises if there has been such a restriction on a person's freedom as to render him or her in police "custody." Whether a suspect is in custody depends on the circumstances and on whether a reasonable person would feel at liberty to end the questioning and leave. According to the Supreme Court, **a child's age and the school setting are relevant to the *Miranda* analysis**. If the age of a child suspect is known to the officer at the time of questioning, or would have been objectively apparent to a reasonable officer, consideration of age is consistent with the *Miranda* custody analysis. The Court reversed the judgment and returned the case to a state court to determine if the student was in police custody at the time of the in-school interrogation. *J.D.B. v. North Carolina*, 131 S.Ct. 2394 (U.S. 2011).

◆   An anonymous informant told Wisconsin school officials that a student had drugs at school. He consented to the search of his person, book bag and locker by a school liaison officer and a municipal police officer. When no drugs were found, an assistant principal searched the student's car and found marijuana, a pipe, Oxycontin and cash. She turned over these items to the police, who arrested the student and took him to the police station, where he received his criminal rights warnings, known as "*Miranda* rights." Prior to trial, the student sought to exclude evidence seized from his car and any statements he made during the investigation. He claimed he was "in custody" of the police at the time he was questioned in the parking lot. If this was the case, it was necessary to read him his *Miranda* rights at that time. The court denied the student's motions to suppress his statements and the evidence seized from his car.

On appeal, the Court of Appeals of Wisconsin found *Miranda* **warnings are only required when a person is in police "custody."** Whether a person is in custody depends upon the circumstances. Formal arrest, restraint on freedom of movement, or interrogation that is likely to elicit an incriminating response are examples of "custody" for *Miranda* purposes. Here, while the student was "escorted" to his car by police, an assistant principal was still in control of the investigation, up to and including the search of the car. Finding that a reasonable person would not have considered himself to be in "custody" at the time, the student was not entitled to have his *Miranda* rights read to him in the parking lot. The court also found the search reasonable under the circumstances. *State of Wisconsin v. Schloegel*, 769 N.W.2d 130 (Wis. Ct. App. 2009).

◆   A Tennessee student told a school resource officer that marijuana found in his truck belonged to him. As they returned to the school building, the student also admitted he had left school to smoke marijuana with a friend that morning. The resource officer took the student to juvenile court and charged him. The student later moved to suppress his statements on grounds that she did not inform him of his *Miranda* rights prior to questioning. The juvenile court denied the student's motion, finding the student was not in police custody at the time.

On appeal, the Supreme Court of Tennessee held that **the student was not confined for questioning, and he was not in police "custody."** Thus, his incriminating statements had been properly admitted into evidence. However, since *T.L.O.* was decided, there has been an increased presence of law enforcement officers in public schools. Municipalities have "blended" the traditional duties of school officials and law officers to protect the safety of students and teachers. Based on the resource officer's duties, a new trial would be held to find whether the search required probable cause or reasonable suspicion. *R.D.S. v. State of Tennessee*, 245 S.W.3d 356 (Tenn. 2008).

◆   A Boston middle school student showed a clear plastic bag containing over 50 bullets to other students. The school resource officer confiscated the bullets, and later conducted a pat-down search that yielded no further evidence. The officer then read the student his *Miranda* warnings and asked him to disclose the location of his gun. The student said he did not have a gun. His mother and grandmother arrived at school, and the officer continued questioning the student without informing the adults of the student's *Miranda* rights. After an expulsion hearing the same day, the student led the officer to the gun, which he had hidden in a yard in a residential area. In juvenile delinquency proceedings, the judge found the resource officer had unlawfully failed to provide the student *Miranda* warnings in the presence of an interested adult, as required by state law. The case reached the Supreme Judicial Court of Massachusetts, which noted that the juvenile court judge refused to apply the "limited public safety exception" to *Miranda* established by the U.S. Supreme Court in *New York v. Quarles*, 467 U.S. 649 (1984). Here, the student was only 13 years old.

Juvenile suspects under 14 may not waive their *Miranda* rights in the absence of an interested adult, such as a parent. But this resource officer was faced with an emergency that threatened 890 middle school students and area residents. He reasonably found an immediate need to question the student. The student's possession of 50 bullets was enough to support the inference that a gun was in close proximity. This was valid reason to invoke the public safety exception to *Miranda*. Accordingly, the court reversed the juvenile court order. *Comwlth. v. Dillon D.*, 448 Mass. 793, 863 N.E.2d 1287 (Mass. 2007).

◆   Virginia elementary school students reported to their teacher that a 10-year-old student had brought a gun to school. An assistant principal questioned the student repeatedly in her office and searched her book bag and desk. After no weapon was found, the student was allowed to leave. The next school day, a student witness said the student had thrown a handgun into the woods adjoining the school. School officials called police and resumed the interrogation. Although the student said she felt ill and repeatedly asked for her mother, the officials denied her requests. She claimed they detained her for over one hour and refused to let her go to the lavatory. The officers found no weapon and did not call the student's mother until leaving. The student sued school and police officials in a federal court for due process and Fourth Amendment violations.

Appeal reached the U.S. Court of Appeals, Fourth Circuit. It refused to adopt a general rule requiring school administrators to notify parents during investigations, or to forbid student detentions of a particular length. Virginia law and school board rules required a principal to make reasonable efforts to contact parents or guardians before police interrogations. The Constitution imposed no parental notification duty while a student was detained. When school officials constitutionally seize a student and tell police the basis for their suspicion, the detention is justified at its inception. **When a student detention justifies police involvement, no Fourth Amendment violation occurs.** The officers detained the student only until they determined no guns were on school grounds. The court found no fault with the efforts of the school officials to protect school safety, and it affirmed the judgment. *Wofford v. Evans*, 390 F.3d 318 (4th Cir. 2004).

◆   An Oregon student was suspended from school and subjected to a juvenile court adjudication. A vice principal called the student's mother several weeks later, and told her the student was again in the school office. The mother told the vice principal she was very uncomfortable with him talking to her son without his lawyer present. The next month, school officials questioned the student for two hours after a teacher smelled marijuana smoke coming from a restroom while the student and a classmate were there. The student first denied using marijuana, but later admitted it to the vice principal and other officials. As required by school policy, they reported this admission to municipal police.

After the school board voted for expulsion, the student appealed to an Oregon trial court, claiming he was entitled to *Miranda* warnings when he was questioned by school officials. The court dismissed the case because no police officers were involved and the case was not a criminal prosecution. On appeal, the Court of Appeals of Oregon **found no authority for suppressing evidence in a school disciplinary hearing on grounds of failure to administer** *Miranda* **warnings**. A school expulsion did not resemble the deprivation of liberty present in criminal cases. The differences between a school expulsion and a juvenile proceeding required affirming the judgment. *T.M.M. v. Lake Oswego School Dist.*, 198 Or.App. 572, 108 P.3d 1211 (Or. Ct. App. 2005).

2. Police-Assisted Searches

◆   A Washington school resource officer arrested a student after he observed him with a bag of marijuana. The dean of students "took a passive role" during the arrest. As they waited for a patrol car, the officer noticed the student's backpack was padlocked. When the student refused to give him the key, the officer handcuffed and searched him. He found the key to the padlock, opened the backpack, and found a BB pistol inside. In juvenile court proceedings, the BB gun was used as evidence and the student was convicted of carrying a gun and possessing marijuana at school. In ruling for the state, the juvenile court relied on the "reasonable suspicion" test from *New Jersey v. T.L.O.*, this chapter.

On appeal, the Supreme Court of Washington found educators have a substantial interest in maintaining discipline that often requires swift action. At the time of the backpack search, the officer had already handcuffed the student. Because the student was under his control, there was no need for swift action. There is a fundamental difference between a resource officer and a school administrator, based on the objectives of their searches. **Since the officer's search did not further any educational goals, and he had already arrested and handcuffed the student, the court found no reason to apply the reasonable suspicion standard from *T.L.O.*** Due to overwhelming indicia of police action, the court held the officer needed a warrant to search the backpack. Since there had been no application for a warrant, the court held the search was unlawful and the BB gun could not be used as evidence in the juvenile case. *State v. Meneese*, 174 Wash.2d 937, 282 P.3d 83 (Wash. 2012).

◆   An Idaho student was developmentally disabled and had a form of autism. His school called a police officer to his class twice to observe his aggressive behavior with school staff. During one episode, the student hit the officer while she was trying to calm him. On another day, the student continuously tapped on his desk and was "verbally aggressive" toward teachers. School staff called the officer, who attempted to block the student from exiting, then took him to the floor, handcuffed him and hobbled his legs. The student was sent to a hospital on a "mental hold," while he struggled and remained verbally aggressive. He sued the school district and the police officer, claiming the district was negligent and the officer used excessive force in violation of the Fourth Amendment. A federal district court held that the district and officer were entitled to immunity.

The student appealed to the U.S. Court of Appeals, Ninth Circuit, arguing the district breached a duty to protect him by calling the police officer, creating an unreasonable risk of harm. The court observed that the district did not employ the officer and had no real or apparent authority over her. **The district did not breach an asserted duty to intervene in her handling of the incident.** *Hayenga v. Nampa School Dist. No. 131*, 123 Fed.Appx. 783 (9th Cir. 2005).

◆   A Texas school parking lot attendant told the principal that three students were smoking in a car parked in a school lot. The principal obtained the assistance of a municipal police officer assigned to the high school. The officer patted down the student and found him in possession of marijuana. The state prosecuted the student for possession of marijuana in a drug-free zone. A juvenile court denied the student's pretrial motion to suppress the marijuana. He pleaded no contest to drug possession, was fined and placed under community supervision for one year. The student appealed to the Texas Court of Appeals. On appeal, the court held that **where school officials initiate a search, or police involvement is minimal, the "reasonable suspicion" test applies**, not the more exacting "probable cause" standard applicable to traditional law enforcement searches. Because the student was smoking in the parking lot, wore baggy shorts and refused to empty his pockets, reasonable grounds existed for suspecting a search would turn up evidence of a rules violation. The search was reasonably related to the objectives of the search and not excessively intrusive in view of the student's age and sex. So it did not violate the Fourth Amendment. *Russell v. State of Texas*, 74 S.W.3d 887 (Tex. Ct. App. 2002).

◆   A resource officer was assigned to work at a New Hampshire school by the municipal police department. Administrators agreed to investigate less serious matters, including drug possession, and refer those involving weapons or a threat to school safety to the officer. A teacher observed a student passing tinfoil to a classmate and reported it to the resource officer. The officer referred the student to an assistant principal. The assistant principal and another administrator questioned the student and asked if they could search him. He agreed and they discovered tinfoil that the student admitted "might be LSD." The administrators contacted the resource officer and returned the case to him.

     A state court granted the student's motion to suppress evidence found by the administrators. On appeal, the New Hampshire Supreme Court held **school officials may take on the mantle of criminal investigators if they assume police duties.** That is what occurred in this case, as there was an understanding between the resource officer and school officials on how violations would be investigated. The court cautioned school administrators to "be vigilant not to assume responsibilities beyond the scope of their administrative duties" when establishing working relationships with police. Because an agency relationship existed between the police and school officials, the court affirmed the order for the student. *State of New Hampshire v. Heirtzler*, 789 A.2d 634 (N.H. 2001).

3. Drug-Sniffing Dogs

     In Burbank v. Canton Board of Educ., *a Connecticut court applied a "public smell doctrine" to a search of school lockers and parking lots using police dogs. The court relied on a 1982 Texas case which reasoned that the **use of dogs to sniff for contraband in unattended lockers and cars is not a Fourth Amendment "search" at all**. Odors emanating from a person or property are "considered exposed to the public 'view' and, therefore, unprotected."* Horton v. Goose Creek Independent School Dist., *690 F.2d 470 (5th Cir. 1982).*

◆   At the request of a Missouri school district police director, a sheriff's office sent two deputies with search dogs to a high school. Students from one classroom were instructed to stand at the far end of the hallway during the search. After the classroom was evacuated, a deputy led his dog around the classroom. No drugs were detected, but a student claimed that when he returned to the room, the pockets on his backpack were unzipped. His parents sued school and law enforcement officials in a federal district court, asserting they were deprived of their Fourth Amendment rights. The court held the student was not subjected to a seizure when he was asked to leave the classroom while the dogs sniffed. Officials who were not present at the time faced no liability, as there was no showing that they were directly involved in any violation. It was not shown that there had been improper training or supervision by sheriff's officials, and the court held neither the school district nor the sheriff's department had any policy or custom that caused a constitutional violation. A previous Eighth Circuit case held **there is no municipal liability for unconstitutional custom or usage from a single act**. All the claims against the individual school and sheriff's department officials and both entities lacked merit, and the court found no constitutional violation. *Burlison v. Springfield Public Schools*, No. 10-3395 CV-S-RED, 2012 WL 220205 (W.D. Mo. 1/25/12).

◆ A Connecticut school district policy allowed police to make unannounced searches on school property with drug-sniffing dogs, even without warrants or suspicion of any crime. The policy recited that its inclusion in the student and/or parent handbook was the only notice required to advertise searches. A high school student was arrested as a result of contraband found during a sweep conducted pursuant to the policy. His parents filed a state court lawsuit against the school board. After a hearing, the court found a policy of warrantless and suspicionless drug-dog sweeps on school property without notice to parents did not violate any constitutional rights. It held the use of drug-sniffing dogs was not a "search" under the Fourth Amendment, since "students do not have a reasonable expectation of privacy in the odor or 'aroma' emanating from their unattended lockers" and vehicles. Arguing that the trial court should have reviewed the case under the state constitution, the parents appealed. But when the case reached the Supreme Court of Connecticut, they acknowledged their son had graduated from high school. **Since he was no longer subject to the policy, the case was held moot**, and the appeal was dismissed. *Burbank v. Board of Educ. of Town of Canton*, 299 Conn. 833, 11 A.3d 658 (Conn. 2011).

4. Liability Issues

In Chavez v. Martinez, *538 U.S. 760 (2003), the U.S. Supreme Court held courts cannot award damages against police investigators who wrongly induce suspects to provide incriminating information unless it is actually used in a criminal prosecution. Until compelled statements are used in a criminal case, there is no potential violation of the Fifth Amendment self-incrimination clause.*

◆ The U.S. Supreme Court held that individual immunity from liability is available in a civil rights action under 42 U.S.C. § 1983 not only for permanent, full-time government employees but also for those serving on some other basis, such as under a temporary contract. Applying this rationale, the Court held immunity was available to a private attorney who was hired by a municipality to investigate possible fraud by a firefighter on leave. In the firefighter's civil rights lawsuit, the Ninth Circuit held the attorney could not claim immunity since he was not a city employee. But **the Supreme Court found no reason to create a distinction based on whether a person works for the government full time or on some other basis**. For this reason, the attorney was entitled to claim immunity from liability on Fourth and Fourteenth Amendment violations claims. *Filarsky v. Delia*, 132 S.Ct. 1657 (U.S. 2012).

◆   Four California police officers learned from a high school principal that a student had told a classmate he would "shoot up" the school. He was said to be a victim of bullying and had been absent from school for two days. Concerned that the student was a threat, the police went to his house. When they arrived, they knocked on the door but received no response. Nobody answered the home telephone, and the student's mother hung up her cell phone after a police sergeant identified himself and said he was waiting outside. Soon, the student and his mother came outside and learned that the officers wanted to discuss the threats. The student responded, "I can't believe you're here for that." When the sergeant asked to come inside the house to talk, the mother refused. He asked her if there were any guns in the house, and she went inside. Fearing they were in danger, the officers entered the house. The student's father challenged their authority to be there, and they did not conduct any search. Ultimately, the officers concluded the report about the student was false. Later, the family sued the officers in a federal court for Fourth Amendment violations.

Appeal reached the U.S. Supreme Court, which found none of its prior decisions had "found a Fourth Amendment violation on facts even roughly comparable to those present in this case." It found **a reasonable police officer could read the Court's prior decisions as allowing their entry into a residence if there was a reasonable basis to believe there was an imminent threat of violence**. As a result, the Court found a lower court had correctly held the officers had an objectively reasonable basis for their actions. This included the mother's initial failure to answer the door or the phone, hanging up the cell phone on the sergeant, refusing to answer questions, and running into the house. *Ryburn v. Huff*, 132 S.Ct. 987 (U.S. 2012).

◆   Arkansas teachers grew concerned about a student's behavior and poetry he had written at school. They told the school resource officer, and the student was detained, searched and questioned in the school office. In a federal district court action against the district and school officials, the student asserted "emotional bullying" by unspecified school officials who had detained him.

According to the student, he was emotionally abused and became "totally paranoid" while waiting in the school office. Although the student claimed school officials had a custom of tolerating unconstitutional invasions of student rights, the court disagreed. A false imprisonment claim was no constitutional violation but instead could only be a state tort law claim. And under Arkansas law, this claim would fail because he did not show he was detained without legal authority. In the court's opinion, there was no evidence that he was actually detained. Instead, it appeared that he was not locked in the office as he claimed. **Although an improper seizure was alleged, the court found that teachers had reported the student's conduct out of concern for student safety and**

well-being. When the student met with the resource officer in the morning, he had simply lifted his shirt to show he did not have any weapons. The court found this limited search was reasonable under the circumstances, resulting in dismissal of the Fourth Amendment violation claim. And there was no evidence that the conduct of school officials infringed on the student's speech. In sum, the court found the school had good reason to investigate the student's behavior, and it dismissed the case. *Broussard v. Waldron School Dist.*, No. 2:10-CV-02106, 2012 WL 3815673 (W.D. Ark. 9/4/12).

◆   A Delaware elementary school child was questioned about taking money from an autistic student on their school bus. A vice principal contacted a state trooper and obtained permission from the accused student's parent to discuss the theft. When the interview took place, the student denied taking the money and said another child had taken it. The trooper then interrogated the other child. According to the other child, the trooper told him "11 or 12 times that he had the authority to arrest" him and put him in jail. The trooper also told the child about a place where "bad children were sent." And it was asserted that he threatened to use his handcuffs. The child claimed the interrogation lasted for about an hour, and that it caused him to cry. When the accused child told his mother about the incident, she sued the school board, school district, vice principal, state of Delaware, state agencies and officials. In the court's opinion, the conduct did not support an infliction of emotional distress claim.

As for the false imprisonment and false arrest claims, the court found "the only restraint threatened was arrest, which constitutes a restraint by legal authority." **It also noted the nature of compulsory attendance laws and the need to direct students at school involved some restraint.** In this case, the child admitted that the trooper told him before he entered the room that "he was not in trouble." The court held the child's subjective feelings did not form the basis for finding that he was in the trooper's custody. As the child was not in custody, the court held he was not restrained, defeating the false imprisonment/false arrest claims. As a result, the state entities and trooper prevailed on all the claims. *Hunt v. Cape Henlopen School Dist.*, No. K10-01-049 WLW, 2012 WL 3860808 (Del. Super. Ct. 8/23/12).

◆   An Oregon state child protective services worker and a deputy sheriff interviewed an elementary student at her school. They did so without a warrant or the consent of her parents, based on suspicion that her father had sexually abused her. At some point, the student said she had been abused, and her father was charged criminally. But a jury failed to reach a verdict and the charges were dismissed. Years later, the student's mother sued the social worker and deputy sheriff in a federal court for failing to obtain a warrant in violation of the Fourth Amendment. The court held the officials violated the Constitution, but granted their request for qualified immunity, because Fourth Amendment law on the issue was not clearly established. After the U.S. Court of Appeals, Ninth Circuit, held the officials were entitled to immunity, the officials sought to clarify the Fourth Amendment issue, and they appealed to the Supreme Court.

The Court ruled public officials had a right to appeal decisions that found their conduct violated the Constitution, even though they were

entitled to immunity and would not have to pay monetary damages. An official who was entitled to immunity still had an interest in appealing from an adverse decision in order to "gain clearance to engage in the conduct in the future." So the Court rejected the claim that the employees lacked standing. This action arose under 42 U.S.C. § 1983, a law commonly invoked to obtain damages from public officials for civil rights violations. Fear of Section 1983 liability should not unduly inhibit officials in the discharge of their duties. But the student was nearly 18 years old and had moved to Florida. She would never again be subjected to an in-school interview by Oregon child protection officials. Applying this rationale, the Court held the case was moot. *Camreta v. Greene*, 131 S.Ct. 2020, 179 L.Ed.2d 1118 (U.S. 2011).

◆ A Miami-area high school student was spotted walking away from the campus of a school he did not attend. Police had twice warned him not to enter the school's safety zone, and they arrested him. Prosecutors filed a delinquency petition against the student, and he was charged with trespass in a school safety zone and resisting arrest. He moved to dismiss the petition, arguing that the law unconstitutionally restricted peaceful conduct and communication. The case reached the Florida District Court of Appeal, Third District, which noted that a Florida statute makes it unlawful for any person to enter a "school safety zone" without legitimate business or other authorization at the school from one hour prior to the start of school until one hour after the end of school. The statute allowed those with authorization or legitimate business at a school to remain in a school zone. The student did not show that those seeking to engage in protected speech or assemblies could not receive "authorization." He did not show that persons who had received notices barring them from school safety zones have any First Amendment rights to return to a school safety zone. **The law was clearly intended to protect children, which is a compelling government interest.** The court affirmed the order declaring the student a juvenile delinquent. *J.L.S. v. State*, 947 So.2d 641 (Fla. Dist. Ct. App. 2007).

◆ Parents of an Iowa student who was arrested and detained in a juvenile detention center could not claim any monetary damages in a civil action against her school district. The state court of appeals affirmed a trial court ruling that the district had no duty to notify the parents that their daughter had been arrested. **There was no deprivation of any parental rights, and the parents had no standing to assert a claim based on their child's due process rights.** School officials had made many attempts to contact the parents after the student was detained. *Simmons v. Sioux City Community School Dist.*, 743 N.W.2d 872 (Table) (Iowa Ct. App. 2007).

CHAPTER THREE

Freedom of Speech and Association

I. STUDENTS

Tinker v. Des Moines Independent Community School Dist., *393 U.S. 503 (1969), this chapter, was the first U.S. Supreme Court case to recognize student speech rights in school settings. In it, the Court held that to regulate student speech, school officials must show "the student's activities would materially and substantially disrupt the work and discipline of the school."*

Tinker *remains the starting point in student speech rights cases, and many courts have applied it in analyzing off-campus student speech, including social media sites such as Facebook. In on-campus and curricular settings, the courts have taken a more restrictive view of student speech. The U.S. Court of Appeals, Fifth Circuit, recently noted that "since* Tinker, *every Supreme Court decision looking at speech has expanded the kinds of speech schools can regulate."*

The Supreme Court declined to apply Tinker *in its most recent student speech rights case,* Morse v. Frederick, *551 U.S. 393 (2007), below, noting "the constitutional rights of students in public school are not automatically coextensive with the rights of adults in other settings."*

◆   A New York fifth-grade science teacher asked students to write their wishes on a picture of an astronaut. One student responded: "Blow up the school with the teachers in it." He was suspended for one day in school and five days out of school. In doing so, the principal found the picture had frightened a classmate. The school board upheld the discipline, and the family sued the school district in a federal court for First Amendment violations. After the court dismissed the case, the family appealed to the U.S. Court of Appeals, Second Circuit. It observed that the student had written in crayon and that no prior discipline indicated he was a danger. Additional proceedings were required to determine whether his words presented a foreseeable risk of material and substantial disruption. When the case returned to the district court, it was revealed that the student had previously submitted artwork and stories that included guns and violent themes. In addition, the court heard evidence that the student had been disciplined for pushing and shoving in the hallways. Based on this evidence, the court found the district was entitled to judgment. Again, the parents appealed to the Second Circuit, which assessed the case under *Tinker v. Des Moines Independent Community School Dist.*, this chapter. It held the relevant inquiry was whether facts might reasonably have led school authorities to forecast substantial disruption of (or material interference with) school activities.

The court held *Tinker* **"does not require school administrators to prove that actual disruption occurred or that substantial disruption was inevitable."** It added, "[I]t is not for courts to determine how school officials should respond" to student speech favoring violent conduct. In view of the completed record, the court found school officials could reasonably foresee that the drawing submitted by the student could create substantial school disruption. As for the claim that the punishment was excessive, the court found this was a matter for school officials to determine. Since school officials could reasonably foresee that the drawing submitted by the student could create substantial school disruption, the court affirmed the judgment for the school district. *Cuff v. Valley Cent. School Dist*, 677 F.3d 109 (2d Cir. 2012).

◆   An 18-year-old Alaska high school student observed an Olympic Torch Relay that passed in front of his school. The school principal deemed the relay a school-approved social event or class trip. As torchbearers and camera crews passed, the student and his friends unfurled a 14-foot banner bearing the phrase "Bong Hits 4 Jesus." The principal instructed them to take down the banner, but the student refused to comply. She confiscated the banner and suspended him for 10 days. The district superintendent reduced the suspension to eight days. He found the principal had based the discipline on the banner's advocacy of illegal drug use, and not on any disagreement with the message. The school board also affirmed the suspension, and its decision was upheld by a federal district court.

The U.S. Supreme Court held the case involved "school speech." The relay was held during school hours and was sanctioned by the principal as "an approved social event or class trip." The board's rules were universally applied to school social events and class trips. The banner was directed to the school and was plainly visible to most students. **The principal reasonably determined that the banner would be interpreted by viewers as promoting illegal drug use.** While the message might be regarded as cryptic, offensive, amusing or nonsense, it might advocate the use of illegal drugs. Supreme Court decisions on drug testing of student extracurricular programs have recognized that deterring drug use is an important and perhaps compelling interest. School officials in this case were dealing with a "far more serious and palpable" danger than that faced in *Tinker v. Des Moines Independent Community School Dist.*, below. The Court held that to allow the banner would have sent a powerful message to students that the school was not serious about its anti-drug message and the dangers of illegal drug use. *Morse v. Frederick*, 551 U.S. 393, 127 S.Ct. 2618, 168 L.Ed.2d 290 (2007).

◆ In 1965, a group of Iowa adults and high school students publicized their objections to the hostilities in Vietnam by wearing black armbands during the holiday season. Three students and their parents had previously engaged in similar activities, and they decided to participate in this program. The principals of Des Moines schools became aware of the plan and adopted a policy that **any student wearing an armband to school would be asked to remove it or face suspension.** The three students wore their armbands and were all suspended until they agreed to come back without the armbands. The students did not return to their school until the planned protest period had ended.

The students sued the school district for First Amendment violations under 42 U.S.C. § 1983, seeking to prevent school officials from disciplining them, plus their nominal damages. A federal district court dismissed the complaint and the Eighth Circuit summarily affirmed the decision. On appeal, the Supreme Court stated neither students nor teachers shed their constitutional rights to freedom of speech or expression at the schoolhouse gate. **In order for school officials to justify prohibition of a particular expression of opinion, they must show something more than a mere desire to avoid the discomfort and unpleasantness associated with unpopular viewpoints.** Where there was no evidence that student expression would materially interfere with the requirements of appropriate discipline in the operation of the school, or collide with the rights of others, the prohibition was improper. The expressive act of wearing black armbands did not interrupt school activities or intrude in school affairs. The Court reversed the lower court decisions. *Tinker v. Des Moines Independent Community School Dist.*, 393 U.S. 503, 89 S.Ct. 733, 21 L.Ed.2d 733 (1969).

◆ A Washington high school student gave a speech nominating a classmate for a student election before an assembly of over 600 peers. All students were required to attend the assembly as part of the school's self-government program. **In his nominating speech, the student referred to his candidate in terms of**

an elaborate, explicit sexual metaphor, despite having been warned in advance by teachers not to do so. Student reactions to the speech included laughter, graphic sexual gestures, hooting, bewilderment and embarrassment. When the student admitted he had deliberately used sexual innuendo in his speech, he was informed that he would be suspended for three days and that his name would be removed from the list of candidates for student speaker at graduation. The student sued the school district in a federal district court, claiming his First Amendment right to freedom of speech had been violated.

The court agreed and awarded him damages and attorneys' fees. It also ordered the school district to allow the student to speak at graduation. The decision was affirmed by the Ninth Circuit, under the authority of *Tinker*. On appeal, the Supreme Court reversed the decision, holding that **while public school students have the right to advocate unpopular and controversial views in school, that right must be balanced against the school interest in teaching socially appropriate behavior.** The Constitution does not protect obscene language, and a public school, as an instrument of the state, may legitimately establish standards of civil and mature conduct. *Bethel School Dist. No. 403 v. Fraser*, 478 U.S. 675, 106 S.Ct. 3159, 92 L.Ed.2d 549 (1986).

A. Protected Speech

1. Disciplinary Cases

◆ A Mississippi student asked school administrators if she could attend her high school prom in a tuxedo with her same-sex partner. She was told that only boys were allowed to wear tuxedos to the prom and that girls would be required to wear dresses and could not slow dance together. After the student contacted the ACLU and threatened a lawsuit, the school board met and decided not to host a prom. In a federal district court action, the court found the board had effectively cancelled the prom. It found support for a First Amendment claim based on identity and affiliation with a unique social group. In *Fricke v. Lynch*, 491 F.Supp. 381 (D.R.I. 1980), the court held a male student's desire to take a same-sex date to his prom "had significant expressive content which brought it within the ambit of the First Amendment." Additional support for the student's position came from a state court in Alabama which held in 2008 that a school board could not cancel a prom to prevent a same-sex couple from attending.

Based on clearly established case law, the court found the board violated the student's rights by denying her request to bring her girlfriend as her date to the prom. Since she had been openly gay since eighth grade, the court held her wish to wear a tuxedo and attend the prom with a girl represented an intent to communicate a message that was protected by the First Amendment. While the student established a substantial likelihood of success on the merits of her First Amendment claim, she did not convince the court that the order she was requesting would be in the public interest. A parent-sponsored prom had been offered, and school officials represented that she would be welcome there. Relief was denied as against the public interest. *McMillen v. Itawamba County School Dist.*, 702 F.Supp.2d 699 (N.D. Miss. 2010).

◆   A California student and three others walked out of their middle school with the intent of participating in protests against pending immigration reform measures. The middle school vice principal allegedly threatened them harshly with discipline upon their return, calling them "dumb, dumb and dumber" and warning them of the possible legal consequences of their truancy. He also allegedly threatened them with a $250 fine and juvenile sentencing, but this did not occur. After returning home on the day of the discipline, the student committed suicide, leaving a note that stated "I killed myself because I have too many problems. ... Tell my teachers they're the best and tell [the vice principal] he is a mother f#@(-)ker." The student's estate sued the school district, vice principal and others for constitutional and state law violations. The case reached the U.S. Court of Appeals, Ninth Circuit, which found that **no First Amendment retaliation claim could be based on threats of discipline if it was based on a lawful consequence that was never administered**.

The policy of disciplining truancy violated no First Amendment rights, even if the students sought to leave for expressive purposes. Further, the vice principal's words were not a form of corporal punishment, and nothing indicated that he had a retaliatory or discriminatory motive. Finally, since the suicide was not foreseeable, the estate failed to show negligence. The court affirmed the judgment. *Corales v. Bennett*, 567 F.3d 554 (9th Cir. 2009).

◆   Tennessee students claimed that their varsity football coach humiliated and degraded players, used inappropriate language and required them to participate in a year-round conditioning program that violated school rules. He also apparently hit a player in the helmet and threw away college recruiting letters sent to "disfavored players." One student typed a petition to remove the coach, which eighteen players signed. When the coach learned of this, he summoned players into his office one by one to interview them. Players who signed the petition were allowed to stay on the team if they apologized and said they wanted to play for him. Four players who did not apologize were taken off the team. These students sued the coach, school board and others for First Amendment violations. The case reached the U.S. Court of Appeals, Sixth Circuit, which noted that the players did not dispute their insubordinate actions during a team meeting. "Student athletes are subject to more restrictions than the student body at large." **The petition was a direct challenge to the coach's authority.** Therefore, it was not protected speech and there was no First Amendment violation. *Lowery v. Euverard*, 497 F.3d 584 (6th Cir. 2007).

◆   About 300 Hispanic students walked out of a Texas school to protest immigration reforms pending in Congress. Many wore T-shirts stating "We Are Not Criminals." The school principal, himself Hispanic, learned that some students planned to walk out of school the next day. Other faculty members believed some Caucasian and African-American students planned to wear T-shirts reading "Border Patrol" to antagonize them. The principal announced that any students who wore unauthorized shirts would be sent to the office, but about 130 students walked out of school. These students were suspended for three days. School administrators called most of their parents, but some students did not learn of the suspensions until they reported to school the next day. Many angry parents came to school, demanding to meet with the principal. After some parents refused to leave the building, school security asked them to leave.

Several families sued the district and superintendent in a federal district court for First Amendment violations. The court held **the principal acted to prevent disruption of the educational process**. Students were warned not to wear unauthorized T-shirts on the second day to prevent a possible race riot. "Where school administrators reasonably believe the students' uncontrolled exercise of expression would materially and substantially interfere with the work of the school or impinge upon the rights of other students, they may forbid such expression." The principal did not violate the First Amendment. *Doe v. Grove Public School Dist.*, 510 F.Supp.2d 425 (S.D. Tex. 2007).

2.   Threats and Bullying

In Boim v. Fulton County School Board, *this chapter, the U.S. Court of Appeals, Eleventh Circuit, compared threatening speech to falsely yelling 'fire' in a crowded theater. The court cited* Schenck v. U.S., *249 U.S. 47 (1919), the Supreme Court decision in which Justice Oliver Wendell Holmes stated the famous "yelling fire in a movie house" rule.*

◆   Death threats and insults based on sexual orientation were posted to the website of a California private school student. After some classmates were implicated in the postings, the student's father called the police. Based on a recommendation by the police, the family moved. The private school newspaper reported the postings and revealed the family's new address. The student filed a state court action against the school for negligence, violation of state hate crime laws and related claims. The case was dismissed and arbitrated under an agreement in the private school contract. An arbitrator held the school was not liable for the student postings, even though some of them were made from school computers. Under the arbitration agreement, the prevailing party was entitled to its costs and legal fees. The state court of appeal reversed an award of fees and costs of more than $521,000 which the arbitrator had made to the school. The student filed a separate action in a California court, asserting violation of hate crimes laws, defamation and infliction of emotional distress.

The classmate asserted his comments were of public interest and protected by the First Amendment. He also said he intended the message as "jocular humor." The court denied the classmate's motion to strike the claims under a state strategic lawsuit against public participation (anti-SLAPP) statute. The classmate appealed to the Court of Appeal of California, which held he did not show the student's complaint was subject to the anti-SLAPP statute. **The classmate did not show the message was protected speech.** Even if the message was a teenage joke, the court found it did not concern a public issue. *D.C. v. R.R.*, 182 Cal.App.4th 1190, 106 Cal.Rptr.3d 399 (Cal. Ct. App. 2010).

◆   A New York student was accused of making an insulting remark after a Hispanic student died in a motorcycle accident. Hispanic students confronted him at school, and he was escorted from school for his own protection. In the next few days, the principal denied requests by the student and his mother to read a letter declaring his innocence or to distribute copies of it. Meanwhile, the threats against him continued, and police officers were assigned to protect his house. At a hearing, the superintendent found the student should be expelled for the final weeks of the school year. But the state commissioner of education found insufficient evidence that the student had made an offensive remark.

A federal district court suit was filed against the school district, board members and administrators for constitutional rights violations. After the court held for the district and officials, appeal reached the U.S. Court of Appeals, Second Circuit. It held the officials had qualified immunity from any liability. Even if the student had a right to return to school to address his classmates, the court found it was reasonable for the officials to believe they were acting within constitutional and statutory bounds. There was no question to the court that the student's "mere presence in the school, with or without his speech, would likely result in violence or the threat of violence." **The question was not whether there had been actual disruption, but whether it could be forecast.** It was reasonable for officials to forecast disruption if they readmitted the student. Since their conduct was objectively reasonable, the lower court correctly awarded them qualified immunity. The court affirmed the judgment. *DeFabio v. East Hampton Union Free School Dist.*, 623 F.3d 71 (2d Cir. 2010).

◆ A Minnesota student wrote an essay "detailing a fantasy murder-suicide inspired by the school shooting that took place at Columbine High School." He placed the essay in his folder, and his teacher read it a few weeks later. After the teacher reported the disturbing and graphic content of the essay, a child protection worker obtained an order to place the student in protective custody. The student was taken to a youth mental health facility, where he underwent a psychiatric evaluation. He was found not a threat to himself or others, and he was released after a total of 72 hours in custody. The family sued the school district, teacher, principal, and county law enforcement and child protection officials in a federal court for constitutional rights violations. Claims against the school district, teacher and principal were dismissed, but the family proceeded with speech and Fourth Amendment claims against law enforcement and child protection officials. The case reached the U.S. Court of Appeals, Eighth Circuit, which held **the student's essay was unprotected by the First Amendment, which does not protect a "true threat."** The essay was a serious threat, describing the student's "obsession with weapons and gore, a hatred for his English teacher," an attack at a high school, details of his teacher's murder and the narrator's suicide. *Riehm v. Engelking*, 538 F.3d 952 (8th Cir. 2008).

◆ A Texas student's notebook described a pseudo-Nazi group and a plan to commit a Columbine-style school shooting or a "coordinated shooting" at all schools in the district. The entries were reported to an assistant principal, who issued a three-day suspension for making terroristic threats. The student was then assigned to an alternative school. His parents sued the school district for First Amendment violations. The case reached the U.S. Court of Appeals, Fifth Circuit, which noted that the school environment made it possible for a single armed student to cause massive harm with little forewarning. Recent history demonstrated that threats against schools and students must be taken seriously. **Since school**

administrators could prohibit student speech that advocated illegal drug use, the same rule should apply to speech that threatens violence and massive death to a school population. As student threats against a student body were not protected, the court found no constitutional violation. *Ponce v. Socorro Independent School Dist.*, 508 F.3d 765 (5th Cir. 2007).

◆ A Georgia high school student wrote a passage in her notebook labeled "Dream." It described, in first person, an account of a student's feelings while taking a gun to school, shooting her math teacher and being chased by the police. The student showed the notebook to a classmate. Her art teacher obtained the notebook and read the passage, then spoke with the school liaison officer and principal about it. The officer believed it was "planning in disguise as a dream," and the student was removed from class the next day.

At a meeting of school officials, the student and her parent, the student dismissed the narrative as creative fiction. The principal suspended the student for 10 days and recommended expelling her for threats of bodily harm, disregard of school rules and disrespectful conduct. The school board voted not to expel her, but it affirmed the suspension and retained a record of it. The student sued the school board for violation of her First Amendment rights. A federal district court held for the school board, and the student appealed to the U.S. Court of Appeals, Eleventh Circuit. It held that writing the narrative and showing it to a classmate was reasonably likely to cause material and substantial disruption. In the climate of increasing school violence and government oversight, **the school had a compelling interest in acting quickly to prevent violence on school property**. The court found no First Amendment violation. *Boim v. Fulton County School Dist.*, 494 F.3d 978 (11th Cir. 2007).

◆ A South Carolina teacher claimed a student disrupted her classroom for over two hours and took a swing at her. Officials filed a juvenile delinquency petition against him for violating a state statute "by willingly, unlawfully, and unnecessarily interfering with and disturbing the students and teachers." The student argued the law was unconstitutionally vague and overbroad in violation of the First Amendment. A state court upheld the statute and committed the student to the juvenile justice department. The student appealed to the state supreme court, arguing the law was overly broad because it punished protected speech and was so vague that persons of common intelligence would have to guess at its meaning. The court held **the statute did not prohibit any speech that was protected by the First Amendment**. By its terms, it criminalized "conduct that 'disturbs' or 'interferes' with schools, or is 'obnoxious.'" The statute was not a substantial threat to free speech, and dealt with school disturbances, not public forums. The state had a legitimate interest in preserving discipline and could prohibit conduct interfering with the state's legitimate objectives. *In re Amir X.S.*, 371 S.C. 380, 639 S.E.2d 144 (S.C. 2006).

◆ The U.S. Court of Appeals, Third Circuit, held **"a school's authority to control student speech in an elementary school is undoubtedly greater than in a high school setting."** Accordingly, a New Jersey elementary student who was suspended for saying "I'm going to shoot you" during recess did not show any speech rights violation. Her principal was entitled to discretion in finding threats of violence and simulated firearms use unacceptable. Officials need not provide students the same latitude afforded to adults and need not tolerate speech that is inconsistent with a school's basic educational mission. *S.G., as Guardian of A.G. v. Sayreville Board of Educ.*, 333 F.3d 417 (3d Cir. 2003).

3. Internet Cases

A federal district court in Minnesota offered educators some guidance on out-of-school student speech in an order denying immunity to school officials who disciplined a student for her off-campus Facebook activity. It wrote "Such [off-campus] statements are protected under the First Amendment and are not punishable by school authorities unless they are true threats or are reasonably calculated to reach the school environment and are so egregious as to pose a serious safety risk or other substantial disruption in that environment."

◆   Missouri twin high school students created a website with racist, bullying speech. School administrators linked the twins to the site and suspended them for 10 days. After two hearings, the district suspended the twins for 180 days, allowing them to enroll in a public academy. The twins sued the school district in a federal court and sought a preliminary order to lift the suspensions. At a hearing, they said the postings were satirical, not serious, and they denied being racists. School witnesses claimed the website caused substantial disruption at the school. Numerous attempts were made at school to access the site and teachers said that their students were distracted or upset. Media representatives had come to the school, and two teachers stated that the incident ranked among the most disruptive events of their careers. Although the court issued the order sought by the twins, it found the website had caused considerable disturbance and disruption. In addition, the court found the site was "targeted at" the school. Appeal went before the U.S. Court of Appeals, Eighth Circuit. It held that in prior federal court decisions, it had been found that **Tinker applies to off-campus student speech when it was reasonably foreseeable that the speech would reach the school community and cause a substantial disruption**. In fact, the court held "the location from which the Wilsons spoke may be less important than the district court's finding that the posts were directed at Lee's Summit North." As the postings had caused substantial school disruption, the court vacated and reversed the lower court's contrary order for the students. *S.J.W. v. Lee's Summit R-7 School Dist.*, 696 F.3d 771 (8th Cir. 2012).

◆   A Minnesota sixth-grader said on her Facebook wall that she hated an adult school hall monitor who "was mean to me." While the post was made on a home computer during non-school hours, the principal ordered her to apologize to the hall monitor and assigned her to detention. Later, the student was suspended for one day and prohibited from attending a class ski trip for a Facebook post stating "I want to know who the f%$# told on me." School officials called her to the school office again, and she admitted having an online conversation about sex. After repeated questioning, she revealed some private passwords. Officials then viewed her Facebook wall and private messages. A federal court noted the

Facebook website was inaccessible from school computers. It held a reasonable school official should have known of Supreme Court rulings which hold that student expression may not be suppressed unless it will materially and substantially disrupt school work and discipline. **While the Internet posed new challenges, the court held it did not change the clearly established general rules that have governed student speech rights for decades.** As a result, the officials had no immunity against the student's First Amendment claims. **A Facebook message resembles email and is entitled to an expectation of privacy.** In refusing to dismiss the student's state law privacy and Fourth Amendment claims, the court held there appeared to be no legitimate school interest in searching the student's online conversations. The activity had taken place off campus. As the student had already admitted to a sex-related discussion, the court found no legitimate reason for the search. And as the law in the area was clearly established, officials were not entitled to qualified immunity on the search claim. *R.S. v. Minnewaska Area School Dist. No. 2149,* 894 F.Supp.2d 1128 (D. Minn. 2012).

◆ A Pennsylvania middle school student used a home computer to make a fake profile of her school principal on MySpace.com. The profile stated that the principal was a "married, bisexual man whose interests include 'fucking in his office' and 'hitting on' students and their parents." After investigating, the principal suspended the student for 10 days. She sued the school district for speech rights violations. Appeal reached the U.S. Court of Appeals, Third Circuit. A three-judge panel of the court held that **school authorities need not wait until a substantial disruption occurs in order to curb the offending speech**. Off-campus speech that caused (or reasonably threatened) substantial disruption of, or material interference with a school did not have to satisfy any "geographical technicality." The principal's concern was found valid. Insinuations about him on the profile struck at the heart of his fitness to serve in his position. As the profile was available to 22 middle school students with "friend" status on MySpace.com, the court found it was directly targeted at the school. *J.S. v. Blue Mountain School Dist.,* 593 F.3d 286 (3d Cir. 2010).

Later, the Third Circuit reheard the case and issued a new opinion reversing the judgment. It found that to impose student discipline under *Tinker v. Des Moines Independent Community School Dist.,* this chapter, officials must have "a specific and significant fear of disruption, not just some remote apprehension of disturbance." *Morse v. Frederick,* this chapter, did not endorse the view that school officials may censor any student speech that interferes with a school's educational mission. **The court held the web page did not cause substantial disruption at school.** It held instead that the student created the profile as a joke and took steps to make it private. In fact, the court found the principal's "response to the profile exacerbated rather than contained the disruption in the school." So it held the district violated the First Amendment by suspending the student. While the judgment on the First Amendment claim was reversed, the court held the district did not interfere with parental rights. As district policies were not unconstitutionally vague or overbroad, the court rejected a challenge to them. *J.S. v. Blue Mountain School Dist.,* 650 F.3d 915 (3d Cir. 2011).

◆ A Pennsylvania high school student made a MySpace.com parody of his principal at his grandmother's house, using her computer during non-school hours. He used a photo of the principal from the school website and created bogus answers to survey questions on the site which indicated that the principal was a drug user whose "interests" were "transgender, appreciators of alcoholic beverages." After the principal identified the student as the parody's creator, he suspended him for 10 days, placed him in an alternative program, banned him from extracurricular programs and denied his participation in graduation ceremonies. A three-judge panel of the U.S. Court of Appeals, Third Circuit, held the **school officials did not establish a sufficient nexus between the web page and school disruption**. It found the relationship between the student's conduct and the school was "attenuated," and the judgment was affirmed. *Layshock v. Hermitage School Dist.*, 593 F.3d 249 (3d Cir. 2010).

After a three-judge panel of the Third Circuit decided *J.S. v. Blue Mountain School Dist.*, above, all the judges of the court voted to reconsider the case. On review, the court rejected the district's argument that the student had "entered" school property and "taken" the principal's picture from its website. Noting the student made the profile at his grandmother's house, the court found "it would be an unseemly and dangerous precedent to allow the state, in the guise of school authorities, to reach into a child's home and control his/her actions there to the same extent that it can control that child when he/she participates in school sponsored activities." As the district court found, **the student's speech could not be treated as if it had occurred on campus by virtue of being aimed at the school community**. School officials conceded that the profile did not disrupt the school. It was not foreseeable that the profile would come to the attention of the district and principal, and as no "sufficient nexus" existed between the profile and any school disruption, the court held the discipline was inappropriate. *Layshock v. Hermitage School Dist.*, 650 F.3d 205 (3d Cir. 2011).

◆ A California student made a video off campus that showed some of her friends "ranting" about a classmate. The video was then posted on YouTube. An assistant principal viewed the video and told the student to take it off YouTube. Administrators suspended the student for two days, and she filed a federal district court action against the school district. After issuing two preliminary orders, the court found no Supreme Court case involving school regulation of off-campus student speech, making the state of this legal area unclear. **Most courts have held *Tinker v. Des Moines Independent Community School Dist.*, this chapter, applies to off-campus speech.** It was reasonably foreseeable that the video would make its way to campus, as the student posted it on YouTube and made it readily accessible to the public. The court found existing case law did not provide clear guidance. The mere fact that students were discussing the video was insufficient to meet the *Tinker* disruption standard. Complaints by a student and some parents, and the brief discipline of five students, did not forecast substantial disruption. Despite the absence of actual disruption or a reasonable forecast of disruption on campus, the court held school officials were entitled to immunity because of the unclear state of the law in this area. *J.C. v. Beverly Hills Unified School Dist.*, 711 F.Supp.2d 1094 (C.D. Cal. 2010).

◆   A West Virginia high school student created a MySpace.com web page that ridiculed a classmate. She opened the page to about 100 MySpace "friends," and other students added vulgar criticisms of the classmate. The classmate filed a harassment complaint with the school, which suspended the student for five days and excluded her from social activities for 90 days for violating a school policy against harassment, bullying and intimidation. In a federal district court, the student sued the school district for speech rights and due process violations.

The U.S. Court of Appeals, Fourth Circuit, held schools have some latitude in regulating speech to further educational objectives. In upholding the discipline, the court found that bullying is a major concern in schools. **"Schools have a duty to protect their students from harassment and bullying in the school environment,"** in the court's view. **It was foreseeable that the student's conduct would reach the school via computers, phones or other devices.** The nexus between the speech and school pedagogical interests justified discipline. The court found the speech was materially and substantially disruptive, and it held that speech originating outside of school "but directed at persons in school and received by and acted on by them was in fact in-school speech." *Kowalski v. Berkeley County Schools*, 652 F.3d 565 (4th Cir. 2011).

◆   A Missouri high school student sent instant messages to another student, saying he was depressed and wanted to take guns to school, kill other students, then kill himself. The school principal learned of the electronic conversation and called police. Juvenile proceedings were brought against the student, and he was excluded from school for the rest of the school year. He later sued the school district in a federal court, seeking to clear the discipline from his school record. The court found that the case required a trial. The record did not show that the student substantially disrupted the school. But as he had received a hearing and opportunity to be heard, his due process rights were satisfied. All claims against the superintendent were dismissed. *Mardis v. Hannibal Public School Dist. #60*, No. 2:08CV63 JCH, 2009 WL 1140037 (E.D. Mo. 4/28/09).

The court later found that **the student's instant messages were "true threats" that were not due First Amendment protection**. He should have reasonably known his messages would reach other students. The student's state of mind and access to weapons made his threats believable. He expressed the wish to kill at least five classmates, and told a confidante that he had a .357 magnum pistol. Since a reasonable person would take these messages as "true threats," officials "acted entirely within their permissible authority in imposing sanctions." Contrary to the student's argument, complaints by parents who were scared to send their children to school indicated "substantial disruption." *Mardis v. Hannibal Public School Dist. #60*, 684 F.Supp.2d 1114 (E.D. Mo. 2010).

◆   Connecticut student council members complained about the postponement of a battle-of-the-bands event called "Jamfest." They sent a mass email from a school computer urging recipients to contact the superintendent. A student officer posted an Internet blog stating "jamfest is cancelled due to douchebags in central office." She wrote that the email had "pissed off" the superintendent and caused her to cancel the event, and suggested others "write something or call her to piss her off more." Several students added blog comments, including one that referred to the superintendent as "a dirty whore." The superintendent and principal continued to receive calls and emails about Jamfest. The principal barred the student from class office and from giving a campaign speech.

The student's mother sued the school district for speech rights violations. Appeal reached the U.S. Court of Appeals, Second Circuit. It held that **off-campus conduct could create a foreseeable risk of substantial school disruption. The off-campus character of the speech did not insulate the student from discipline.** The posting was designed to reach the school, and it "foreseeably created a risk of substantial disruption within the school environment." As the student threatened to disrupt efforts to resolve the Jamfest dispute, and she frustrated student government operations, the court affirmed the judgment. *Doninger v. Niehoff*, 527 F.3d 41 (2d Cir. 2008).

After the student graduated, the district court considered her monetary damage claim. It held administrators could bar her from office based on vulgar, offensive off-campus speech that was likely to be heard at school. But the officials were not entitled to immunity for prohibiting students from wearing t-shirts to support her. *Doninger v. Niehoff*, 594 F.Supp.2d 211 (D. Conn. 2009).

4. Confederate Flags

Recent federal appellate court decisions regarding Confederate flag displays at school have interpreted Tinker v. Des Moines Independent Community School Dist. *as not requiring disruption to have **actually occurred** for officials to regulate student speech. Officials may bar Confederate flag displays based on a **forecast** of substantial disruption or material interference.*

◆   A Tennessee school district policy banned Confederate flag items, based on a history of racial conflicts in district schools, some of them involving Confederate flags. A student wore a shirt and belt buckle to school with Confederate flag images and refused to comply with the dress code after several warnings, resulting in a suspension. He sued the school district, its board and school officials in a federal court. The court held for school officials, and appeal reached the Sixth Circuit. Quoting its decision in *Barr v. LaFon*, 538 F.3d 554 (6th Cir. 2008), the court held "*Tinker* does not require disruption to have actually occurred." Courts are to evaluate the circumstances "to determine whether the school's forecast of substantial disruption was reasonable."

As explained in *Barr*, **school officials need not tolerate student speech that is inconsistent with their educational mission.** In view of the record of problems at district high schools which involved Confederate flags, the court held officials reasonably forecast that flag displays would be disruptive. Unlike the display of an anti-war armband in *Tinker*, these **flag displays communicated "a message of hatred toward members of the student body" and thus presented a situation involving "substantial disorder or invasion of the rights of others."** It was reasonable to conclude that future flag displays would likely lead to unrest. Since school officials could reasonably forecast substantial disruption if they allowed Confederate flag items, the court affirmed the judgment. *Defoe v. Spiva*, 625 F.3d 324 (6th Cir. 2010).

◆   A South Carolina student claimed a right to wear Confederate flag clothing that was banned by the school's dress code. She also claimed a right to wear clothing to protest the dress code. She sued school officials in a federal district court, which held for the district on her Confederate flag claim. The parties agreed that she could wear "protest clothing" pending resolution of the case. An appeal was made to the U.S. Court of Appeals, Fourth Circuit, but it found no final order to review. As a result, **the case was returned to the lower court for further proceedings on the question of the protest clothing.** *C.H. v. Heyward*, 404 Fed.Appx. 765 (4th Cir. 2010).

◆   A Texas high school responded to race-related problems by prohibiting Confederate flag displays on school grounds. The number of reported race incidents decreased over the next three years, but racial graffiti remained common in a boys' lavatory. A home-made Confederate flag was raised on the school flagpole on Martin Luther King, Jr. day in 2006. When two students carried purses to school bearing large images of a Confederate flag, they were sent to the office. They were allowed to either go home or have a parent retrieve the purses. They chose to go home, and later sued the principal and school board for violating their constitutional rights. Before the U.S. Court of Appeals, Fifth Circuit, the students argued they did not cause disruption, and that the flag symbolized their ancestry and Christian faith. The court held that **school officials reasonably banned displays of the Confederate flag at school to prevent substantial and material disruption**. The decision was based on the history of racial hostility at the school, some of which involved Confederate flag displays. School officials reasonably anticipated that the flag would cause substantial disruption or material interference, based on evidence of racial hostility and tension. For this reason, the lower court had properly held for the school officials. *A.M. v. Cash*, 585 F.3d 214 (5th Cir. 2009).

◆   A Missouri high school community endured racially charged incidents and violence, leading to the withdrawal of three of the high school's 15-20 African-American students from school. A fight occurred at a high school basketball game after white players used racial slurs during the game. A Confederate flag was displayed near the locker rooms during the game. As a result of these and other incidents, the district superintendent banned students from displaying the Confederate flag on their clothing. Students who wore Confederate items to school were told to change their clothes. They later sued the school district, asserting First Amendment violations. A federal court found no constitutional violation, as there was sufficient evidence of school disruption if the flag was allowed. The students appealed. The U.S. Court of Appeals, Eighth Circuit, held that the numerous racial events at the school made the school's actions constitutionally permissible. The court held *Tinker* **and cases interpreting it "allow a school to 'forecast' a disruption and take necessary precautions before racial tensions escalate out of hand."** As a result of the race-related incidents both in and out of school, the administration had reasonably banned in-school Confederate flag displays. The court affirmed the judgment for school officials. *B.W.A. v. Farmington R-7 School Dist.*, 554 F.3d 734 (8th Cir. 2009).

B. Student Publications

Courts reviewing school speech rights cases typically apply a "forum analysis" to determine the speaker's First Amendment rights. In R.O. v. Ithaca City School Dist., the U.S. Court of Appeals, Second Circuit, found a school newspaper was a "limited public forum" that was subject to reasonable editorial control by the school. Because student publications are not "public forums," school administrators may exercise editorial control over them if a reasonable basis exists for the belief that a publication would materially disrupt class work, involve substantial disorder or violate the rights of others.

◆   Washington students produced a newspaper as part of a journalism course. A "Freedom of Expression" policy permitted opinions that did not substantially disrupt the educational process or interfere with the rights of others. Student editors decided to focus an issue of the newspaper on oral sex. They interviewed students and obtained permission for quotes. Prior to publication, the editors removed quotes from some students who sought anonymity. When the issue was released, at least four students were quoted in an article accompanied by "provocative" photos. Some students were quoted in the article and described their sexual experiences. The principal reprimanded an editor, and the district then revised its policy to require the principal's prior approval of all articles.

A group of parents sued the school district in a state court for negligence and invasion of privacy. A jury found for the district, and the families appealed to the state court of appeals. There, they argued the lower court committed error by deeming the newspaper a "limited public forum." The court held a ruling on the forum was irrelevant, as the case involved tort claims. Nor was it an error for the trial court to admit open forum or First Amendment evidence. **The jury instructions were correct, as they permitted the parents to advance their claim that the district negligently failed to exercise control over the school newspaper.** The court found it was unclear from the pleadings whether each family was seeking between $2 million and $4 million, or if this was a collective sum. Ultimately, the parents sought a collective award of $6.8 million. The court held school district attorneys did not commit misconduct by suggesting these damages were excessive. Rejecting the families' other arguments, the court affirmed the judgment. *M.R.B. v. Puyallup School Dist.*, 169 Wash.App. 837, 282 P.3d 1124 (Wash. Ct. App. 2012).

◆   An Iowa journalism teacher was reprimanded for letting students publish inappropriate material in issues of the high school newspaper. More than a year after the teacher's reprimand, he again allowed students to publish articles the administration found objectionable. An issue depicted a photoshopped picture of a baby smoking a cigarette with the caption "Students Chew, Use Tobacco." A student was depicted in clothes prohibited by the school dress code, and another was quoted as saying he wanted to be like "Jay Z because he is a gangster." The reprimand stated that the issue generated complaints, caused a significant and material disruption to school operations, and encouraged illegal activity. Although the teacher's two-day suspension was withdrawn, he sued the principal and school district in the state court system. In his petition, the teacher asked the court to find that the issues did not violate Section 280.22 of the Iowa code. After the court held for the principal and district, the teacher appealed.

The Court of Appeals of Iowa noted Section 280.22 had been enacted in response to *Hazelwood School Dist. v. Kuhlmeier*. Section 280.22 prohibited students from publishing materials that were obscene, libelous or slanderous. Section 280.22 was intended to increase student speech rights, in the court's opinion. **To permit censorship of student publications, there must be some encouragement of specific unlawful acts or rules violations.** The materials in this case did not encourage such activity. Student quotes were for the most part found humorous, and the court rejected findings that the publications encouraged student lawlessness. The court found no duty to "sanitize student expression when it did nothing more than quote a classmate who questioned a school policy." There was no standard by which the court could assess a claim that the publication did not comply with "professional standards of English and Journalism." As none of the district's arguments had merit, the court reversed the judgment. *Lange v. Diercks*, 808 N.W.2d 754 (Table) (Iowa Ct. App. 2011).

◆ A New York high school newspaper faculty advisor refused to let student editors publish a sexually oriented cartoon and article in the school newspaper. District officials then created publication guidelines for the newspaper. Student editors sought to print the same cartoon in the next issue of the newspaper. Again, the faculty advisor rejected the cartoon. The editors created independent publications without the cartoon and received permission to distribute them.

In a federal court action, the students asserted constitutional violations. Appeal reached the U.S. Court of Appeals, Second Circuit, which stated that the student newspaper was a limited public forum that could be restricted to certain kinds of speakers or subjects. A faculty advisor had always provided guidance to student editors, and the school administration exercised substantial control. **The district's actions were a lawful means of avoiding publication of lewd material that conflicted with legitimate school pedagogical concerns.** The court found the cartoon was lewd and subject to censorship under *Hazelwood School Dist. v. Kuhlmeier* and *Bethel School Dist. No. 403 v. Fraser*. Although the students claimed a right to distribute the independent newspaper on campus, the court held school authorities acted reasonably in barring it. As the authorities acted lawfully under the applicable standards, the court held for the school district. *R.O. v. Ithaca City School Dist.*, 645 F.3d 533 (2d Cir. 2011).

◆ A California high school student editor wrote an editorial for the school paper called "Immigration." He suggested all non-English speakers were illegal aliens. Latino parents complained about the editorial, and the superintendent instructed the principal to retract remaining copies of the paper. Administrators wrote to parents of their regret over the decision to allow the publication. The student then wrote a provocative editorial about race relations titled "Reverse Racism." The principal approved it for publication, but delayed publication until a counter-viewpoint editorial could be presented in the same issue.

The student's action for speech rights violations reached the state court of appeal. It held Education Code Section 48907 protected student expression in school publications. But the section prohibited "material which so incites students as to create a clear and present danger of the commission of unlawful acts on school premises or the violation of lawful school regulations." "Immigration" would not incite students to commit unlawful acts on school grounds, violate school rules, or pose a risk of substantially disrupting school operations. **Schools may only prohibit speech that incites disruption by specifically calling for a disturbance** or because the manner of expression "is so inflammatory that the speech itself provokes the disturbance." While the student was not disciplined, his rights were violated by the principal's statement that "Immigration" had been improperly published. *Smith v. Novato Unified School Dist.*, 150 Cal.App.4th 1439, 59 Cal.Rptr.3d 508 (Cal. Ct. App. 2007).

◆ New Hampshire school yearbook editors considered publishing a picture of a student holding a shotgun and dressed in trap-shooting attire. The yearbook faculty advisor and the school principal encouraged the editors to make their own decision. The staff voted 8-2 not to publish the student's photograph in the senior portrait section of the yearbook. After the student's parents complained, the staff offered to publish the picture in the community sports section of the yearbook. The school board adopted a new publications policy banning the use of "props" in senior portraits. The student sued the board in a federal court, which observed that the editors were not coerced by school officials to reject the picture. The editors believed the display of a firearm would be inappropriate in a school publication, given school policies and recent tragedies such as Columbine. **The editorial judgment exercised by students was sufficiently independent from the school administration to avoid attribution to the school.** Thus, the student could not establish "state action." And while the revised board policy was state action, it was content neutral and viewpoint neutral. *Douglas v. Londonderry School Board*, 413 F.Supp.2d 1 (D.N.H. 2005).

◆ A Missouri high school principal objected to two articles prepared for publication in the school newspaper. Because the principal believed there was no time to edit the articles before the publication deadline, he deleted the two pages on which the articles appeared. Former students who were members of the newspaper staff sued, alleging that their First Amendment rights were violated when the pages were removed from the newspaper before publication.

A federal district court ruled in favor of the school district. The Eighth Circuit reversed, holding that the newspaper was a public forum "intended to be and operated as a conduit for student viewpoint." The U.S. Supreme Court agreed to hear the case and noted that school facilities, including school-sponsored newspapers, become public forums only if school authorities have intentionally opened those facilities for indiscriminate use by either the general public "or by some segment of the public, such as student organizations." The Court determined that since the district allowed a large amount of control by the journalism teacher and the principal, it had not intentionally opened the newspaper as a public forum for indiscriminate student speech. **School officials can exercise "editorial control over the style and content of student speech in school-sponsored expressive activities so long as their actions are reasonably related to legitimate pedagogical concerns."** Because the decision to delete the two pages from the newspaper was reasonable, the Court found no violation of the First Amendment. *Hazelwood School Dist. v. Kuhlmeier*, 484 U.S. 260, 108 S.Ct. 562, 98 L.Ed.2d 592 (1988).

C. Non-School Publications

◆   A Michigan eighth-grader came to school with red tape over his mouth and wrists, a sweatshirt reading "Pray to End Abortion" and leaflets containing abortion statistics. After a teacher sent him to the office for causing a disruption, a guidance counselor told him to remove the tape and change his shirt or hide the message. The student returned to class but attempted to put his sweatshirt back on. The principal then repeated the directive not to wear it. As the student did not have approval to distribute the leaflets, the principal stated he could not hand them out. The principal had to pick up leaflets found in hallways. Although no discipline was imposed on the student, his parents sued the principal, school district and school officials in a federal district court. The parties agreed that the student could not come to school with tape on his mouth or wrists, but could wear the sweatshirt saying "Pray to End Abortion."

The case reached the U.S. Court of Appeals, Sixth Circuit. It held school hallways are "nonpublic forums" that do not possess the attributes of streets, parks and other places that are considered public forums. School facilities may be deemed "public forums" only if authorities open them for indiscriminate use. The school had let the student post leaflets on bulletin boards or hand them out in the cafeteria. The court held the regulation of his speech had been "eminently reasonable." There was no indication of a desire to suppress his anti-abortion viewpoint. **It was reasonable for the school to require prior approval before permitting students to distribute literature at school.** The court held the school policy on distribution of literature was not unconstitutional. *M.A.L. v. Kinsland*, 543 F.3d 841(6th Cir. 2008).

◆   Texas students and parents claimed an elementary school prevented speech about Christian religious beliefs and disallowed distributing religious items or literature at school. They filed a federal district court action against the school district, asserting First Amendment claims. The court held the "disruption" standard from *Tinker v. Des Moines Independent Community School Dist.*, this chapter, did not apply because the provisions being analyzed were content- and viewpoint-neutral. **The policy was not targeted at nonschool materials based on their content or viewpoint.** The power of the principal to review materials was limited in time and scope and there was provision for an appeal. The policy's numerical limit of 10 copies was not arbitrary, as the families urged. Instead, the court found a limit appropriately balanced the school's need to conserve resources with the interest in normal student interactions. The school district had a substantial interest in limiting time, place and manner restrictions to distributions of over 10 copies of an item. A provision delegating power to school principals to determine time, place and manner of distributions of over 10 documents had clear guidelines for principals and did not offer them excessive discretion. The court awarded pretrial judgment to the school district. *Pounds v. Katy Independent School Dist.*, 517 F.Supp.2d 901 (S.D. Tex. 2007).

D. Personal Appearance and Dress Codes

1. Dress Codes

Clothing with expressive content may be protected "speech" under the First Amendment and is subject to the substantial disruption test from Tinker v. Des Moines Independent Community School Dist. *(this chapter). But some courts have rejected claims that items such as T-shirts, jeans and body piercings are expressive at all. Officials may bar messages that materially disrupt school, involve substantial disorder or violate the rights of others. Dress codes implicate the Due Process Clause and must be specific enough to notify students of what speech is unacceptable, while not so broad as to prohibit protected expression.*

In K.J. v. Sauk Prairie School Dist., below, a federal court in Wisconsin upheld a middle school ban on bracelets declaring "I [Heart] Boobies! (Keep A Breast)." In doing so, it disagreed with a Pennsylvania federal court ruling that found the phrase had no inherent sexual connotations. But in the Wisconsin case, the court found "I [Heart] Boobies!" used vulgarity and sexuality to attract attention and provoke conversation. It found the phrase "a ploy that is effective for its target audience of immature middle school students."

◆ A Wisconsin seventh-grader wore a "I [Heart] Boobies! (Keep a Breast)" bracelet at school for most of a semester without disruption. But the principal later said students could no longer wear the bracelets at school and would be disciplined if they did. The school began selling its own bracelets that said "Sauk Prairie Eagles support breast cancer awareness." In a federal court action, the student's mother claimed First Amendment violations. In considering a request for an order to require the school district to allow the bracelets to be worn at school, the court noted the principal's view that the slogan was sexual innuendo that violated the school dress code. He also believed the slogan sexualized the cause of breast cancer awareness. In addition to declaring the bracelets a distraction and inappropriate slang, the principal said that some people, including some teachers, were offended by the slogan. Parents and teachers had told him the slogan was inappropriate and trivialized cancer.

In finding school officials may decide what speech is vulgar, offensive or inappropriate, the court stated **"the Supreme Court has taken the position that courts should show deference to judgments by school administrators about the propriety of putatively lewd or vulgar speech" by students**. Seventh Circuit precedents held that schools must have discretion to decide what messages are appropriate in school, so long as they act reasonably. The court found the bracelet slogan was "sexual innuendo that is vulgar, at least in the context of a middle school." While the phrase promoted a worthy cause, the court held this did not make the phrase "innocuous." Schools have the duty to demonstrate appropriate forms of civil discourse and impart essential lessons of civil, mature conduct. In denying the request for an order to allow students to wear the bracelets, the court held it was reasonable for the school to find the phrase was vulgar and inconsistent with respectful student discourse. *K.J. v. Sauk Prairie School Dist.*, No. 3:11-cv-622-bbc (W.D. Wis. 2/6/12).

◆ Two Illinois students opposed a "Day of Silence" that was meant to bring attention to the harassment of homosexuals. They staged a "Day of Truth" and wore shirts to school saying "My Day of Silence, Straight Alliance" on the front and "Be Happy, Not Gay" on the back. A school official crossed out "Not Gay" based on a school rule forbidding derogatory comments about personal characteristics, including sexual orientation. The students sued school officials in a federal court, asserting First Amendment violations. The court denied their request for a preliminary order allowing them to wear the T-shirts, and they appealed. The U.S. Court of Appeals, Seventh Circuit, found the school sought to prohibit derogatory comments about personal characteristics, not to ban discussion of public issues. While the students were not entitled to a preliminary order suspending school rules, the court found the slogan was "only tepidly negative" and held the students could wear the shirts on a preliminary basis. *Nuxoll v. Indian Prairie School Dist. #204*, 523 F.3d 668 (7th Cir. 2008).

The case returned to the district court, which issued orders in the students' favor and awarded them $25 each for infringement of their constitutional rights. The case then returned to the Seventh Circuit, which found "a handful of incidents years before the T-shirt was first worn" insufficient evidence of school disruption to justify banning the slogan. Evidence of disruption was limited to a single statement by a school official. **Speech cannot be stifled just because it offends others.** To justify prohibiting expression, school officials would have to present facts which might reasonably lead them to forecast substantial disruption. As the damage award was justified, the court held for the students. *Zamecnik v. Indian Prairie School Dist. #204*, 636 F.3d 874 (7th Cir. 2011).

◆ Seven students attending Florida public schools were from families who were members of a group that had gained notoriety by posting a billboard stating "Islam is of the Devil" and announcing a Koran burning day. Although the event was cancelled, the center made T-shirts repeating the "Islam is of the Devil" statement and related messages. When the students wore the anti-Islam shirts to school and a football game, the school district enforced its dress code policy against them. The policy required students to dress in a way that did not disrupt or distract from the educational process and was not offensive to others or inappropriate at school or at school events. The students and parents sued the school board in a federal court. In ruling for the board, the court held school officials did not violate student rights by prohibiting the controversial anti-religious message. The message was not conducive to civil discourse on religious issues and was not appropriate for school. **A school mission was to teach civility to students of different races, creeds and colors.** Moreover, a school is not a public forum, and officials do not have to tolerate student speech that is inconsistent with its basic educational mission. There was evidence that the shirts disrupted the school, causing confrontations and the need for extra security. *Sapp v. School Board of Alachua County, Florida*, No. 1:09cv242-SPM/GRL, 2011 WL 5084647 (N.D. Fla. 9/30/11).

◆ A female Mississippi student wore men's clothing for her senior picture instead of the "drape" required by school policy. After the school district excluded her portrait from the senior portraits section of the yearbook, she sued for sex discrimination under Title IX of the Education Amendments of 1972 and the Equal Protection Clause of the Fourteenth Amendment. **The court held that there was no fundamental right to appear in a yearbook.** While the district claimed the policy was neutral, as both sexes were required to wear specific clothing, the student said the policy amounted to sexual stereotyping. The court found some appeal to both arguments and held that the decision should be made on a more complete record. In addition to the lack of a record, the district had yet to explain its justifications for the policy. Since the court expressed the need to hear the district's rationale for the policy, it denied the motion to dismiss the action. It ordered the parties to attend a mandatory mediation session within 30 days. If mediation failed, the case would proceed. *Sturgis v. Copiah County School Dist.*, Civil Action No. 3:10-CV-455-DPJ-FKB, 2011 WL 4351355 (S.D. Miss. 9/15/11).

◆ A Pennsylvania school district instituted a dress code requiring khaki or navy slacks, golf shirts and certain types of shoes. When students complained about the dress code, they were given a partial waiver based on their religion. Officials allowed logos protesting the dress code, so long as the code was otherwise complied with. Some students wore logos that the district did not view as protesting the dress code, such as Disney or Pokemon characters and the Nike swoosh. After being suspended in-school many times for wearing logos that were not considered as protesting the dress code, a student was expelled from school. His sister was suspended and later withdrew from school.

In a federal case against the school district, the students argued that their clothing had to be considered speech in protest of the dress code. The court awarded qualified immunity to school officials. A trial was held, and the jury found the students were not disciplined for wearing clothing with logos or for "liturgical colors." The court explained that they did not show retaliation for wearing nonconforming clothing. There was a legally sufficient factual basis for the jury to find the students were disciplined only for wearing nonconforming clothing. In the court's view, their conduct was not protected. It held that **for the First Amendment to apply, there must be some intent to convey a message**. No such intent was identified here. As nonconformity with a dress code is not "expressive conduct" that deserves First Amendment protection, the court rejected the students' arguments. *Scicchitano v. Mt. Carmel Area School Dist.*, No. 4:09cv638, 2011 WL 4498842 (M.D. Pa. 9/27/11).

◆ A Texas student wore a shirt to his school with "San Diego" printed on it. After an assistant principal told him this was a dress code violation, his parents brought him a "John Edwards for President '08" T-shirt to wear instead. But as the second shirt had a printed message, it also violated the dress code. Months later, the student sued the school district. By the time a hearing was held, a new dress code was in place. The court dismissed the case but asked to review the new dress code, which extended the ban on messages to polo shirts, and shirts with pro and university team logos or messages. The court later denied a request for an order to prevent enforcement of the dress code, and the case reached the U.S. Court of Appeals, Fifth Circuit. The court held the district did not suppress unpopular viewpoints. Instead, it provided students with more clothing options.

As the dress code was content-neutral, it could be justified if it furthered an important government interest that was unrelated to expression. Among the reasons for adopting the dress code were improving student performance and attendance, instilling self-confidence, decreasing disciplinary referrals and lowering the drop-out rate. All these reasons furthered important government interests. Another valid goal was to promote professional and responsible dress for students preparing for the workforce. **"Federal courts should defer to school boards to decide what constitutes appropriate behavior and dress in public school."** The judgment was affirmed. *Palmer v. Waxahachie Independent School Dist.*, 579 F.3d 502 (5th Cir. 2009).

◆ A California school with a history of conflict over sexual orientation let a Gay-Straight Alliance group hold a "Day of Silence" to "teach tolerance." The 2003 event was accompanied by student fights. A group of students held an informal "Straight-Pride Day" and wore T-shirts with anti-gay slogans. Some students were asked to remove these shirts. Others were suspended for fighting. When the school allowed another "Day of Silence" in 2004, one student wore a T-shirt to school stating "I will not accept what God has condemned." The reverse of the shirt stated "homosexuality is shameful 'Romans 1:27.'" The student was detained in a school conference room for refusing to remove the shirt. Although he was not further disciplined, and no record of the incident was placed in his file, he sued the district and school officials for violating his speech and religious free exercise rights. The case reached the Ninth Circuit.

The court noted that *Tinker v. Des Moines Independent Community School Dist.* (this chapter) allows schools to **"prohibit speech that intrudes upon the rights of other students,"** or collides with the rights of others to be secure **and to be let alone**. The T-shirt collided with other students' rights in the most fundamental way. Speech attacking minority students injured and intimidated them, damaged their sense of security and harmed their learning opportunities. Schools had a right to teach civic responsibility and tolerance, and did not have to permit hateful and injurious speech that ran counter to that message. *Harper v. Poway Unified School Dist.*, 445 F.3d 1166 (9th Cir. 2006).

After graduating, the students tried to pursue their claim for monetary damages. The case returned to the Ninth Circuit which held that the case was moot and that school officials had immunity from any damage claims. *Harper v. Poway Unified School Dist.*, 318 Fed.Appx. 540 (9th Cir. 2009).

◆ A Florida student had piercings and wore jewelry on her body, tongue, nasal septum, lip, navel and chest. She claimed her piercings were a way to express her "non-conformity and wild side" and expressed her individuality. An administrator told the student that her body jewelry violated the school dress code. The student refused to remove the jewelry and was assigned to lunch detention for four days for violating the dress code. She sued. A court ruled against her, and she appealed. The U.S. Court of Appeals, Eleventh Circuit, held that students have speech rights at school, "but those constitutional rights are circumscribed by the special characteristics of the school environment." While the First Amendment protects "symbolic speech," **the Supreme Court has held that it does not apply unless "an intent to convey a particularized message was present."** The student did not show that the First Amendment protected her right to express individuality at school by wearing body-piercing jewelry. Her conduct had insufficient communication to earn such protection, and the board had enforced the dress code in a viewpoint-neutral manner. *Bar-Navon v. Brevard County School Board*, 290 Fed.Appx. 273 (11th Cir. 2008).

◆   A New Jersey school board adopted a uniform policy with significant input from the school community. Students could opt out of the policy for religious and medical reasons. A student tried to opt-out based on "Constitutional Rights, Fundamental Freedom, Individual personal choice and Philosophical Beliefs." Upon being denied this request, he refused to comply, and was suspended. His family sued the board in a state court. Appeal reached a New Jersey Appellate Division Court, which held parents do not have a fundamental right generally to direct how a public school teaches their children. **Dressing as one chose was not expressive conduct that was due constitutional protection.** Here, the student "simply did not want to be told what to wear." The court rejected the parents' claim based upon an asserted right to direct and control every aspect of their child's education. *Dempsey v. Alston*, 405 N.J. Super. 499, 966 A.2d 1 (N.J. Super. Ct. App. Div. 2009).

◆   A Kentucky middle school adopted a policy generally requiring students to wear solid-colored clothing and restricting tight, baggy, revealing, form-fitting or "distressed" clothing. A parent sued the school district, stating his daughter wanted to "be able to wear clothes that look nice on her, that she feels good in and that express her individuality." The U.S. Court of Appeals, Sixth Circuit, held the school could enforce a dress code where the student did not seek to convey any particular message through her clothing. The First Amendment does not apply unless there is a "particularized message." The student here had no message, wanting only to "wear clothes she feels good in." Her First Amendment claim failed. **As for the parent's claim, the court held parents lack a fundamental right generally to direct how public schools teach their children**. *Blau v. Fort Thomas Public School Dist.*, 401 F.3d 381 (6th Cir. 2005).

◆   Arkansas students wore black armbands to protest a mandatory uniform policy for grades seven through 12. After a few students wore armbands over their uniforms, the school disciplined them. One student handed out a flyer criticizing the uniform policy without first obtaining the principal's approval. This violated a district "literature review policy" requiring advance approval by the principal. The students sued the school district and school officials for constitutional violations. A court upheld the uniform policy, and held the school board members were entitled to qualified immunity. On the other hand, the district superintendent and a junior high school principal were denied immunity in their individual capacities for imposing discipline to suppress a particular viewpoint. After a jury awarded nominal damages, the district appealed. The U.S. Court of Appeals, Eighth Circuit, found *Tinker* **was so similar in all relevant aspects that it required a judgment for the students**. *Lowry v. Watson Chapel School Dist.*, 540 F.3d 752 (8th Cir. 2008).

2. Hair Length and Appearance

In Karr v. Schmidt, *460 F.2d 609 (5th Cir. 1972), the Fifth Circuit held that "there is no constitutional right to wear one's hair in a public high school in the length and style that suits the wearer." Karr created a* per se *rule that hair and grooming regulations are constitutional, so long as they are not arbitrary.*

◆ An African-American male student was told to remove braids from his hair, even though no policy prohibited them. The school board revised its dress code to require all students to "wear their hair in a standard, acceptable style." All students were required to wear uniforms. Any hairstyle detrimental to student performance or school activities was prohibited. Male students could not wear their hair in braids, spiked, or in a style distracting to other students. However, females could wear braids. The student claimed that the policy had a disparate impact on African-American males and violated his equal protection, free exercise and speech rights. A federal district court rejected his First Amendment and equal protection claims. A school committee had revised the dress code in conjunction with a school safety policy. **According to the court, the board's policy advanced legitimate concerns for discipline, avoiding disruption and fostering respect for authority.** *Fenceroy v. Morehouse Parish School Board,* No. Civ.A. 05-0480, 2006 WL 39255 (W.D. La. 2006).

◆ A Texas school board adopted a student grooming policy prohibiting boys from wearing their hair below the shirt collar. An elementary school principal observed a third-grade boy with a ponytail and advised him and his mother that he was in violation of the grooming policy. The school board suspended the student for three days for refusing to comply, and it placed him on in-school suspension. The student's mother removed him from school and sued the board for violating the Texas Constitution and state law. A state court permanently enjoined the board from enforcing the policy. But the Supreme Court of Texas held **the grooming policy did not deprive males of equal educational opportunities or impose other improper barriers**. The regulation of hair length and other grooming or dress requirements was not discriminatory on the basis of sex, and the court reversed the judgment. *Board of Trustees of Bastrop Independent School Dist. v. Toungate,* 958 S.W.2d 365 (Tex. 1997).

◆ A fourth-grade Indiana boy wore an earring to school, even after the school board revised its handbook to bar the wearing of jewelry by male students. After a five-day suspension, a hearing examiner recommended transferring the student to another school that did not have similar policies. The board adopted the recommendations, but the student refused to transfer. The family sued the school district in the state court system for a declaration and order prohibiting enforcement of the policy. The Court of Appeals of Indiana rejected an argument that the policy violated equal protection of the law because girls were permitted to wear earrings. Enforcement of a strict dress code was a factor in improving student attitudes. **The policy served the valid educational purpose of instilling discipline and creating a positive educational environment.** *Hines v. Caston School Corp.,* 651 N.E.2d 330 (Ind. Ct. App. 1995).

3. Gang Affiliation

A federal district court held in Brown v. Cabell County Board of Educ., *below, that schools may ban gang-related clothing if there is evidence of a potentially disruptive gang presence at school and gang-related disturbances. Borrowing language from recent Confederate flag cases that apply* Tinker v. Des Moines Independent Community School Dist. *(this chapter), the court held the "test is not whether a student's statement has led to a disturbance or disruption, but whether it could reasonably be expected to lead to one."*

◆   Gang activities at a West Virginia high school escalated when a gang leader was arrested for shooting a police officer. The principal advised staff members that the slogan "Free A-Train" was banned. A student wrote "Free A-Train" on his hands several times and was suspended for 10 days. He sued the school board in a federal court for speech rights violations. The court held schools may ban gang-related clothing if evidence indicates a potentially disruptive gang presence and gang-related disturbances. **Recent federal cases suggest schools may regulate expression if they can reasonably forecast material and substantial disruption at school.** This defeated the student's claim that speech must lead to an actual disruption before school administrators may suppress it. As students and parents expressed fear over the use of the slogan, administrators could reasonably forecast that allowing the student to keep displaying it may have exacerbated the tensions and increased these fears. The court held the "distraction from classes or intimidation from passive displays of support may serve as the basis of a disruption," and found no speech rights violation. *Brown v. Cabell County Board of Educ.*, 714 F.Supp.2d 587 (S.D. W.Va. 2010).

◆   An Illinois school disciplinary code defined "gang activity" as "prohibited student conduct." Gang activity included any act in furtherance of a gang, and use or possession of gang symbols, such as drawings, hand signs and attire. The code stated that gangs and their activities substantially disrupted school by their very nature. A student was suspended three times for drawing gang-related symbols, including an inverted pitchfork and crowns with five points. Each time, the student was informed about the code prohibition on gang symbols and warned of its disciplinary implications. After the third incident, the superintendent notified the student's mother of a proposed expulsion, the date of a hearing and the right of the student to counsel. A school resource officer testified at the hearing that the pitchfork and crowns were gang-related signs.

The school board voted to expel the student for the second half of the school year, and his mother sued. **A federal court held that the student code sufficiently defined the term "gang symbol," using specific examples of prohibited conduct.** The court rejected all of the student's First Amendment arguments. Both he and his mother had been warned that his conduct was a violation before he was expelled. The decision to expel the student after documented violations of the student code was not contrary to the evidence or in conflict with board policy. *Kelly v. Board of Educ. of McHenry Community High School Dist. 156*, No. 06 C 1512, 2007 WL 114300 (N.D. Ill. 1/10/07).

◆   A Kentucky board of education devised a student dress code based on the need to address a school gang problem, promote safety, prevent violence and disputes over clothing, and identify non-students and intruders on campus. The dress code limited the clothing available to students as well as the way it could be worn. Some students who were disciplined for dress code violations sued the school board, and the case reached the U.S. Court of Appeals, Sixth Circuit. It held that **school officials had an important and substantial interest in creating an appropriate learning environment by preventing the gang presence and limiting fights**. The regulation of student expression furthered an important government interest without suppressing free speech. The board believed the dress code would help reduce gang activity, ease tension among students who fought over attire and enhance student safety. The dress code addressed those issues in a manner that was unrelated to the expressive nature of student dress. School officials may control student speech or expression that is inconsistent with a school's educational mission. *Long v. Board of Educ. of Jefferson County, Kentucky*, 21 Fed.Appx. 252 (6th Cir. 2001).

II. EMPLOYEES

A. Protected Speech

In Garcetti v. Ceballos, *547 U.S. 410 (2006) the Supreme Court held its public employee speech cases reflected "the common sense realization that government offices could not function if every employment decision became a constitutional matter."* **A public employee's speech pursuant to official duties is not protected by the First Amendment.** *Under* Garcetti, *courts must first determine if an employee's speech was made pursuant to official duties. If the speech was not made pursuant to official duties, the test from* Pickering v. Board of Educ., *391 U.S. 563 (1968), and* Connick v. Myers, *461 U.S. 138 (1983), applies. Under* Pickering *and* Connick, *employees have First Amendment protection (1) if they speak on matters of public concern and (2) their interest in public comment outweighs the government interest in efficient public service.*

◆   *Garcetti* involved a deputy district attorney in California who examined a search warrant affidavit presented by a defense attorney. He determined that it contained misrepresentations and recommended dismissal. After a heated discussion, the DA's office decided to proceed with the prosecution. Later, the deputy district attorney was transferred and denied a promotion. He sued county officials under 42 U.S.C. § 1983, claiming First Amendment violations. **The U.S. Supreme Court held that "when public employees make statements pursuant to their official duties, the employees are not speaking as citizens for First Amendment purposes."** It was part of the deputy district attorney's job to advise his supervisors about the affidavit, and if his supervisors thought his speech was inflammatory or misguided, they could take corrective action. *Garcetti v. Ceballos*, 547 U.S. 410, 126 S.Ct. 1951, 164 L.Ed.2d 689 (2006).

◆   An Illinois teacher had a confrontation with the parent of a student who recited violent rap lyrics in his class. The teacher said he wanted to report the student to the police for threatening him, but the principal and assistant principal feared the parent would file a lawsuit and did not support him. When the teacher signed a criminal complaint, the student was charged with disorderly conduct. The teacher was soon assigned an unsatisfactory evaluation based on poor interpersonal skills. All the teacher's previous evaluations had been satisfactory. He learned his contract would not be renewed if he did not resign, and he sued the school district, principal and assistant principal in a federal district court for First Amendment violations. In holding for the district and officials, the court held the teacher's conduct did not involve a public concern.

On appeal, the U.S. Court of Appeals, Seventh Circuit, found "a jury could easily find that the real reason" for the teacher's poor evaluation "was the threat of litigation by the student's belligerent father." It noted his complaint was intended at least in part to ensure school safety and to "bring to the public light the fact that such an incident had occurred." **Illinois law required the immediate reporting to law enforcement authorities of a battery or intimidation in school.** The court held the lower court should not have awarded school officials judgment on the ground that the criminal complaint was a purely private matter. When the case returned to the lower court, the school officials could not claim qualified immunity. While school districts are generally not liable for the constitutional violations of school administrators, the court found evidence of a district policy to condone unconstitutional employment terminations. *Gschwind v. Heiden*, 692 F.3d 844 (7th Cir. 2012).

◆   A California high school calculus teacher who lost his claim that he should be allowed to adorn his classroom with religious and patriotic banners was denied review of his case by the U.S. Supreme Court. The case involved complaints about a large banner that read, "IN GOD WE TRUST," "ONE NATION UNDER GOD," "GOD BLESS AMERICA," AND "GOD SHED HIS GRACE ON THEE." Another banner in the teacher's classroom read "All men are created equal, they are endowed by their CREATOR." When the case reached the U.S. Court of Appeals, Ninth Circuit, it held the banners conveyed a religious message. **Since the district acted within constitutional limits when it ordered the teacher to take down the banners, it was entitled to judgment.** *Johnson v. Poway Unified School Dist.*, 132 S.Ct. 1807 (U.S. 2012). A full summary of the case appears in Chapter 4, Section III of this volume.

◆   A New York school district payroll clerk often reported improprieties to her district superintendent. She said a co-worker forged his supervisor's signature to obtain additional pay and that numerous payments were authorized without the required school board approval. The clerk questioned the superintendent's purchase of $500 in district funds to buy chocolates for a gift. Near this time, a consultant hired by the district to help resolve interpersonal problems among staff recognized the clerk as a former employee of another school district.

The consultant informed the superintendent that the clerk's employment had been terminated by three other school districts. But the clerk did not inform her current employer of this history at the time of her job application. When the school board discharged the clerk, she filed a federal court action against school officials. The court denied the district superintendent's motion for immunity, and he appealed. The U.S. Court of Appeals, Second Circuit, held that qualified immunity protects government officials from paying civil damages if their conduct did not violate clearly established statutory of rights of which a reasonable person would have known. **While public employee speech may be protected, the employee must be speaking about a matter of public concern.** In this case, the court found the clerk's speech was made pursuant to her duties and was not protected. Taking a complaint up the chain of command did not transform public employee speech into protected speech made by a private citizen. Since the court found the speech that prompted the clerk's retaliation claim owed its existence to her job duties and was made in pursuit of those duties, it was unprotected. As a result, the superintendent was entitled to qualified immunity. *Ross v. Breslin*, 693 F.3d 300 (2d Cir. 2012).

◆   A New York teacher filed a grievance after school administrators failed to discipline a student who threw books at him. He said the assault of a teacher by a student violated a citywide policy. After the teacher told other teachers of his grievance, he claimed administrators retaliated against him by issuing bad performance reviews and a false report of sexually abusing a student. The board discharged the teacher, and he filed a federal district court case for speech rights violations. Applying *Garcetti v. Ceballos*, above, the court held the grievance was an aspect of the teacher's core duties of maintaining class discipline. It held conversations with other teachers were not within the scope of his employment.

The teacher appealed to the U.S. Court of Appeals, Second Circuit. It found that in addition to finding officials need wide latitude in managing government offices, *Garcetti* held that the First Amendment does not "constitutionalize the employee grievance." Statements made pursuant to official duties are not protected speech. According to the court, when the teacher filed a grievance to complain about his supervisor's failure to issue discipline to a student, he was "speaking pursuant to his official duties and thus not as a citizen." For this reason, the filing of the grievance was unprotected. The court agreed with other federal circuits which have held that, **under *Garcetti*, official duties need not be required by (or included in) an employee's job description**. As a grievance over the decision not to discipline the student was a means to fulfill a primary employment duty, the court held for the board. *Weintraub v. Board of Educ. of City School Dist. of City of New York*, 593 F.3d 196 (2d Cir. 2010).

◆   A probationary California first-grade teacher complained about a student in her class who had severe behavior issues, and she told her principal she felt he should be evaluated for emotional disturbance. She had a poor relationship with the district's special education director, who eventually refused to speak to her without a witness. One of their encounters involved placement of the teacher's own disabled child. Other teachers complained that the teacher used her cell phone during classes and arrived late every day. Just prior to her discharge, the teacher left campus during lunch without permission. After the school board voted not to renew the teacher's contract, she sued the school district and several administrators in a state court under Section 44113 of the state Education Code.

The case reached the Court of Appeal of California, which explained that Section 44113 makes government employees liable for using official authority to interfere with a teacher's right to disclose improper governmental activities. The special education director and other non-supervisors of the teacher were exempt from Section 44113 liability. And the district was exempt from Section 44113 liability, since it was not an employee. But the principal, superintendent and a supervisory assistant superintendent were not exempt under the provision, as they had acted as "supervisory employees." Despite this finding, the court affirmed the decision for the school administrators, because the matters the teacher sought to disclose were not "improper governmental activities." **Her activities on behalf of special needs children were not considered a "protected disclosure" under Section 44113.** The teacher's complaints about unruly students and a failure to perform a timely special education assessment of her own child were unprotected, because they were made in a context of internal personnel or administrative matters. *Conn v. Western Placer Unified School Dist.*, 186 Cal.App.4th 1163, 113 Cal.Rptr.3d 116 (Cal. Ct. App. 2010).

◆ A Washington school employee made comments about her co-workers on an Internet blog. She was then transferred from a curriculum specialist position to a classroom teaching job. She claimed this was retaliation for her posting of blogs on the Internet that included "several highly personal and vituperative comments about her employers, union representatives and fellow teachers." In a federal district court action against the school district's human resources specialist, the employee claimed First Amendment protection for her postings.

The court held for the human resources specialist, and the employee appealed to the Ninth Circuit. The court found the employee's former position required her to enter into trusting mentor relationships with less experienced teachers, to whom she was to give honest, critical and private feedback. Her public blog resulted in complaints from co-workers, and one of them had refused to work with her, even though she had been assigned as her instructional coach. The transfer followed because **the blog fatally undermined her ability to enter into trusting relationships as an instructional coach**. The court found the blog had a harmful effect on the employee's working relationships, and common sense indicated that few teachers would expect to enter into a confidential and trusting relationship with her after reading her blog. Since the lower court properly found the employee's interest in speech did not outweigh the school district's interest in fulfilling its responsibilities, the court affirmed the judgment. *Richerson v. Beckon*, 337 Fed.Appx. 637 (9th Cir. 2009).

◆ A Nebraska school technical support coordinator claimed he was fired for telling staff members about pay irregularities, invalid contracts and funding discrepancies. He filed a federal district court action against the school district for speech rights violations. The case reached the U.S. Court of Appeals, Eighth Circuit, which found the coordinator admitted each instance of speech involved his job duties. **Since speech relating to a public employee's job duties is unprotected by the First Amendment, there was no constitutional violation.** *Anderson v. Douglas County School Dist.*, 342 Fed.Appx. 223 (8th Cir. 2009).

◆   An Idaho security employee advised a high school principal of student drug and weapons violations. He also expressed concern over school safety and emergency policies, which he felt were inadequate. Near this time, the principal took away some of the employee's job duties. The employee wrote a letter to administrators complaining about the principal's unresponsiveness to safety, poor staff training, concealment of safety violations, ineffective enforcement of truancy and sexual harassment policies, and inadequate fire safety planning. At the end of the school year, his responsibilities were combined with those of three other positions in a new position. Another applicant was hired for this job and the employee sued the school district for retaliation in violation of state law and the First Amendment. Appeal reached the Ninth Circuit, which explained that *Garcetti v. Ceballos*, this chapter, required it to determine whether the employee was speaking as a public employee or as a private citizen. But the precise nature of his duties was unclear. There was room for debate regarding whether he wrote the letter as part of his official duties. According to the Ninth Circuit, **the *Garcetti* inquiry was not a purely legal question over which a federal court could award pretrial judgment**. Speech rights present a mixed question of law and fact. There remained questions regarding the nature of the employee's duties, so the court returned the case to the lower court. *Posey v. Lake Pend Oreille School Dist. No. 84*, 546 F.3d 1121 (9th Cir. 2008).

◆   A probationary Indiana teacher told her students that she had honked her car horn to show support for a "Honk for Peace" sign denouncing military involvement in Iraq. Parents complained to the principal, who told all teachers not to take sides in any political controversy. The teacher was not rehired, which she believed was based on her answer in the current events class. She sued the school system in a federal court for violating the First Amendment. The court held for the school system, and the teacher appealed to the Seventh Circuit.

Although the teacher admitted she made the comment while performing her official duties, she claimed academic freedom. The court held public school teachers "must hew to the approach prescribed by principals" and other school administrators. It stated that "the school system does not 'regulate' teachers' speech as much as it hires that speech." **Teachers have to "stick to the prescribed curriculum" and have no constitutional right to interject their own views on curricular subject matter.** They could not use their classes as platforms for their own perspectives. Public school students are a captive audience and they "ought not be subject to teachers' idiosyncratic perspectives." The teacher had been allowed to teach the controversy about Iraq, so long as she kept her opinions to herself. As she could not advocate viewpoints that departed from the curriculum, the court held for the school system. *Mayer v. Monroe County Community School Corp.*, 474 F.3d 477 (7th Cir. 2007).

◆   A Texas high school athletic director and head football coach repeatedly asked for information about athletic activity funds. He wrote memorandums to a school office manager and the principal, seeking immediate funding for a tournament entry fee for a school team, and was soon stripped of his athletic director duties. The district then voted against renewing his coaching contract. The coach sued the district and school officials in a federal district court, asserting that he was retaliated against for engaging in protected speech. Appeal reached the U.S. Court of Appeals, Fifth Circuit, which held **public employee speech cases use a "balancing test" between the speaker's expression and the employer's interests**. However, *Garcetti* "added a threshold layer" to rules set by cases like *Pickering v. Board of Educ.* "Even if the speech is of great social importance, it is not protected by the First Amendment so long as it was made pursuant to the worker's official duties." The coach claimed he wrote his memos as a taxpayer and a father, but the court held the memos focused on daily operations. The coach admitted he needed the information so he could operate the athletic department. As his speech was made in the course of performing his job, it was unprotected by the First Amendment. *Williams v. Dallas Independent School Dist.*, No. 05-11486, 2007 WL 504992 (5th Cir. 2/13/07).

◆ Colorado charter school teachers were hired by a K-8 charter school under contracts indicating that the school board welcomed "constructive criticism" to enhance the school's program. Each teacher received satisfactory evaluations, and their contracts were renewed. The next year, the teachers and a paraprofessional grew concerned about the school's operations, management and mission. They held off-campus meetings to discuss school matters. Parents and others also attended. The teachers expressed their concerns to the board, which invited grievances "without fear of retaliation." However, the teachers contended that their grievances were ignored, and that the principal gave them less favorable job evaluations. Each teacher submitted a resignation letter effective well before the end of the school year. The board discussed the letters during a meeting at which the principal also submitted her resignation. After the principal resigned, the teachers unsuccessfully tried to rescind their own resignations.

The teachers claimed that the board then "blacklisted them from future employment," and they sued. On appeal, the U.S. Court of Appeals, Tenth Circuit, held that **the vast majority of the speech at issue involved personal job duties, and not the public concern**. However, the statements regarding official impropriety, as well as political speech, were matters of public concern. And the teachers' comments about their freedom of speech and expression related to the public concern, so they were constitutionally protected. Their discussions about the future of the school and upcoming elections were also protected. The case was returned to the lower court for it to determine if the discussions outweighed the school interest in avoiding disruption. *Brammer-Holter v. Twin Peaks Charter Academy*, 492 F.3d 1192 (10th Cir. 2007).

B. Personal Appearance and Dress Codes

School officials have considerable authority to regulate employee speech that could be perceived by the public as representing an official school view.

◆ New York City Board of Education (BOE) regulations required school employees to maintain neutrality regarding political candidates while on duty or with students and precluded the distribution, posting or display of materials supporting any political candidate or organizations in BOE buildings or staff mailboxes. BOE teachers claimed that the regulations violated employee speech rights. They sought a federal court order to prohibit enforcement of them. The court held school officials may impose reasonable restrictions on the speech of teachers, unless an open forum has been intentionally opened for indiscriminate use by the public. **Schools have more authority to regulate teacher speech when there is a risk that the public would view it as bearing the school's imprimatur than when regulating personal expression.** As the regulation was neutral and left teachers ample alternatives for expression, the court upheld a ban on political button-wearing by teachers at school. There was no risk of attribution of political views to the BOE when materials were posted in areas not accessible to students, so the BOE was ordered to allow posting of political items on bulletin boards and teacher mailboxes. *Weingarten v. Board of Educ. of City School Dist. of City of New York*, 591 F.Supp.2d 511 (S.D.N.Y. 2008).

Months later, the court considered permanent relief. Only the issue of political buttons remained in dispute. The court noted the Supreme Court has allowed schools to regulate teacher speech in classrooms for legitimate pedagogical reasons. So long as the school acted in good faith and banned buttons for legitimate pedagogical concerns, the regulation was constitutional. Students were a captive audience in their classrooms, and the board found teacher displays of political partisanship were inconsistent with the school's mission. As the board exercised its judgment in good faith, the court accorded it deference and upheld its regulations. *Weingarten v. Board of Educ. of City School Dist. of City of New York*, 680 F.Supp.2d 595 (S.D.N.Y. 2010).

◆ A California school district and the association representing its teachers could not reach a new agreement as their contract neared expiration. The association called for teachers to wear buttons supporting its bargaining position. Most of the teachers taught in self-contained classrooms in which only teachers and students were present. The district superintendent advised teachers of a district policy preventing them from engaging in any political activity during work time. Teachers complied with the directive, but the association filed an unfair practice charge against the district. The state Public Employee Relations Board (PERB) found that the wearing of buttons was not political activity and held that the district had interfered with the teachers' rights. The district appealed to the state court of appeal, which held that **button-wearing was "political activity" that could be barred under the state Education Code**. It was reasonable to prohibit public school teachers from political advocacy during instructional activities. The wearing of union buttons during instructional time was "inherently political." The court held that keeping the labor relations dispute from spilling into the classroom was a proper restriction of political activity and reversed the PERB's decision. *Turlock Joint Elementary School Dist. v. PERB*, 5 Cal.Rptr.3d 308 (Cal. Ct. App. 2003).

◆ *Turlock Joint Elementary School Dist. v. PERB*, above, is limited to instructional time. **A ban on political advocacy could not be enforced in noninstructional settings.** Another California district prohibited employees from distributing partisan election materials on school grounds and from campaigning during work hours. The teachers association objected to the policy and demanded its rescission so that teachers could wear buttons expressing their opposition to a state education finance voter initiative. A state superior court held the policy violated the First Amendment speech rights of teachers.

The Court of Appeal of California held state law allows schools to restrict the political speech of teachers during work hours. Because public school teachers have considerable power and influence in classroom situations and their speech may be reasonably interpreted as reflecting the official view of their school districts, it was reasonable to prohibit them from wearing political buttons in classrooms. This restriction did not violate the First Amendment or the state constitution, as school authorities must have the power to disassociate themselves from political controversy and the appearance of approval of political messages. **But it was unreasonable for the school district to restrict political speech by teachers outside their classrooms.** The court modified the decision so that teachers were prohibited from wearing political buttons only in the classroom. *California Teachers Ass'n v. Governing Board of San Diego Unified School Dist.*, 53 Cal.Rptr.2d 474 (Cal. Ct. App. 1996).

C. Association Rights

The following cases involve claims by or on behalf of individual rights to free association. For additional associational rights cases involving employee associations, collective bargaining, agency fees (fair sharing) and payroll deductions, please see Chapter Eleven, Section I of this volume.

◆ A Kentucky teacher sent many inappropriate letters to a colleague. One threatened her with "increasing danger." The colleague reported this, and the principal investigated. He later reprimanded the teacher and authorized his transfer to another school. The teacher signed a memorandum (MOU) requiring him to stop communicating with the colleague. Three years later, he emailed the colleague about a meeting of a professional organization called the Louisville Area Chemistry Alliance (LACA). The principal reprimanded him for violating the MOU, advised him to stop contacting the colleague and permanently barred him from LACA meetings. In a federal court, the teacher sued the school board. The court held for the board and officials, but the U.S. Court of Appeals, Sixth Circuit, reversed the ban on attending LACA meetings. It affirmed the rest of the judgment for the school board and officials.

In later proceedings, the lower court entered an order preventing the board from barring the teacher from LACA meetings. But it dismissed the claims against the school officials. The teacher appealed again to the Sixth Circuit, which held his association with the LACA was protected by the First Amendment, and that the district's ban was overly broad. As the board had "no tenable explanation for such a sweeping and everlasting prohibition," the board had been properly denied judgment. In developing a reprimand, the principal and a district human resources director did not follow any simple procedure or standard policy. **Since they had used their discretion, the court held qualified immunity applied.** The principal and director were not final policymakers and so could not create liability for the school board. *Baar v. Jefferson County Board of Educ.*, 476 Fed.Appx. 621 (6th Cir. 2012).

◆   A New Jersey teacher was unable to bring a second lawsuit to challenge his school board's policy governing the use of teacher mailboxes. In the first case, a federal district court held **the mailbox policy was a content-neutral limitation on teacher speech**. It also held the challenge was moot. In an effort to revive the case, the teacher deliberately violated the policy and filed a second federal court action. Again, the court upheld the policy, and the U.S. Court of Appeals, Third Circuit, affirmed the judgment. The U.S. Supreme Court later denied the teacher's request to further review the case. *Policastro v. Tenafly Board of Educ.*, 132 S.Ct. 1546 (U.S. 2012).

◆   A Nevada administrative assistant worked for a school district for six years under the supervision of the district's general counsel. After the general counsel said the district superintendent had misused district funds, he was suspended pending dismissal proceedings. Soon, the administrative assistant learned she would be transferred to a temporary position. When the school board held a public meeting to consider whether it would retain the general counsel, the administrative assistant sat next to him. The human resources head told the administrative assistant she had placed her loyalties in question by sitting next to her former supervisor. Later, the administrative assistant was offered a job in the human resources department with a salary freeze. She chose early retirement instead, and she sued the human resources head and the school district in a federal court for retaliation. The case reached the U.S. Court of Appeals, Ninth Circuit, which held a public employer has to reasonably predict the speech would cause disruption to prevail under *Pickering v. Board of Educ.*

There was no evidence that the administrative assistant's association with the general counsel actually disrupted workplace operations. Nor did the district show her relationship with the general counsel might cause future disruption. The school district had punished her for simply showing up at a public meeting and sitting next to her longtime supervisor. The court held the district "cannot pile on other reasons after the fact under the guise of disruption," and it reversed the judgment. A rehearing before all the judges of the Ninth Circuit was denied, but a superceding opinion was issued, again ruling for the administrative assistant. The court held **"an employer may not interfere with an employee's First Amendment rights unless there is evidence that the employee's actions have actually disrupted the workplace or are reasonably likely to do so in the future."** *Nichols v. Dancer,* 657 F.3d 929 (9th Cir. 2011).

◆   A Mississippi school administrator was notified that her contract would not be renewed because she failed to properly investigate and document a sexual misconduct report. In addition to charges that she compromised the investigation, the school district said she made unauthorized calls to the parents of a student who made a similar report. It was claimed that the administrator offered to alter or destroy a memo she wrote as part of the investigation while a lawsuit was pending and committed other misconduct during the investigation. A hearing officer upheld the nonrenewal after she did not appear at her hearing.

In a federal court action, the administrator asserted race discrimination, retaliation, speech rights and Equal Pay Act violations. The superintendent was granted qualified immunity, and the court held for the school district. On appeal, the U.S. Court of Appeals, Fifth Circuit, found the lower court had correctly held for the superintendent. There was no explanation by the administrator of her failure to follow district hearing procedures. **Her speech was unprotected because she admitted her investigation into the second sexual harassment claim was done pursuant to her official duties.** Her race discrimination claim failed because she did not show she was treated less favorably than similarly situated employees. *Alexander v. Brookhaven School Dist.*, 428 Fed.Appx. 303 (5th Cir. 2011).

◆   A California teachers' association placed political endorsements for two school board candidates in school employee mailboxes. While the association was authorized to communicate with its members though their mailboxes, an administrator advised the association that state Education Code Section 7054 prohibited the use of school mail facilities to distribute materials containing political endorsements. The association filed an unfair practice charge with the state Public Employee Relations Board (PERB). The action was dismissed, but appeal later reached the Supreme Court of California. The court found Section 7054 prohibited school districts and community colleges from using funds, services, supplies or equipment to urge support for (or the defeat of) any ballot measure or candidate, including board candidates. **California law stated that "the government may not 'take sides' in election contests or bestow an unfair advantage on one of several competing factions."** The court found Section 7054 was "designed to avoid the use of public resources to perpetuate an incumbent candidate or his or her chosen successor, or to promote self-serving ballot initiatives" that would compromise the integrity of elections.

As "equipment" was intended to include mailboxes such as those used by the district, Section 7054 applied. Permitting the district to restrict political speech did not run afoul of Government Code Section 3543.1, which permits employee organizations to use school bulletin boards, mailboxes and other means "subject to reasonable regulation." Under established First Amendment law, school mailboxes were considered nonpublic forums. The ban on political endorsements was upheld as reasonable. *San Leandro Teachers Ass'n v. San Leandro Unified School Dist.*, 209 P.3d 73, 95 Cal.Rptr.3d 164 (Cal. 2009).

◆   The Colorado Education Association (CEA) and an affiliate recruited members for walks to support a state senate candidate. Two individuals claimed this violated the Colorado Constitution, and challenged the union activity with the Colorado Secretary of State, seeking to impose a $170,000 civil penalty. An administrative law judge (ALJ) rejected the claim and found the unions did not communicate beyond their own membership. The case reached the Supreme Court of Colorado, which held that **unions were expressly permitted to establish political committees and engage in other campaign activities among their members. The court found that campaign spending is a form of speech.** The First Amendment protects political association, and any limitations on political expenditures place a substantial restraint on speech and association. The state constitution's broad membership communication exception protects employee free speech and association rights. There was no evidence that the unions made unlawful expenditures or campaign contributions. The union communicated with members, not voters or the general public. Any indirect benefit to the candidate was permitted by the state constitution, and the court upheld the judgment. *Colorado Educ. Ass'n v. Rutt*, 184 P.3d 65 (Colo. 2008).

III. ACADEMIC FREEDOM

Schools have broad discretion in curricular matters and courts do not closely scrutinize reasonable school board decisions in this area. But once a decision has been made to place a particular book in a school library, the same level of discretion does not apply. In ACLU of Florida v. Miami-Dade County School Board, *below, a federal appeals court held a Florida school board had the authority to determine what books were to appear on school library shelves.*

A. Library Materials

◆ A Miami parent was outraged to find a copy of "Vamos a Cuba" on the shelves of his daughter's public school library. As a former political prisoner from Cuba, he claimed the book was untruthful. After the book was removed from library shelves, the school board chairman said that the book offended the Cuban community. Another board member noted that the board was rejecting its school staff's recommendation due to political pressure. Still another board member suggested that if the board did not vote to remove the book from school libraries, they might find bombs under their cars. A different parent and two organizations sued the board for First Amendment and Due Process violations.

Appeal reached the U.S. Court of Appeals, Eleventh Circuit, which noted the board had found the book was not accurate. The board voted to replace the series with updated books, and the court held it could do so. "Whatever else it prohibits, the First Amendment does not forbid a school board from removing a book because it contains factual inaccuracies, whether they be of commission or omission. **There is no constitutional right to have books containing misstatements of objective facts shelved in a school library.**" Rather than banning the book, the school board was "removing" it from its library shelves. As the board had the sole authority to determine what books were to appear on school library shelves, the court held in its favor. *ACLU of Florida v. Miami-Dade County School Board*, 557 F.3d 1177 (11th Cir. 2009).

In Board of Educ. v. Pico, *below, the Supreme Court held the removal of books from a school library would be unconstitutional if it was motivated by an intent to deny students access to ideas with which school officials disagreed.*

◆ The U.S. Supreme Court held that the right to receive information and ideas is "an inherent corollary of the rights of free speech and press" embodied in the First Amendment. The case arose when a New York school board rejected the recommendations of a committee of parents and school staff it had appointed and ordered that certain books be removed from school libraries. The board characterized the books as "anti-American, anti-Christian, anti-Semitic, and just plain filthy." Students sued the board and its individual members, alleging the board's actions violated their rights under the First Amendment. The Supreme Court noted that while school boards have broad discretion in the management of curriculum, they do not have absolute discretion to censor libraries and are required to comply with the First Amendment. **A decision to remove books from a school library is unconstitutional if it is motivated by an intent to deny students access to ideas with which school officials disagree.** *Board of Educ. v. Pico*, 457 U.S. 853, 102 S.Ct. 2799, 73 L.Ed.2d 435 (1982).

◆ The Children's Internet Protection Act (CIPA) requires public schools and libraries receiving federal assistance to install filtering systems on computers used by children 17 or younger. Two complaints filed in federal courts sought to bar the Federal Communications Commission from implementing the law. A three-judge federal panel found the law unconstitutional. On appeal, the U.S. Supreme Court held Internet access in public libraries is not a public forum. **Libraries have discretion to choose what parts of the Internet they will offer patrons, in the same way they choose which books to put on the shelves**. "A public library does not acquire Internet terminals in order to create a public forum for Web publishers to express themselves, any more than it collects books in order to provide a public forum for the authors of books to speak." CIPA provisions allowed librarians to disable filters when asked by adult patrons. The Court rejected a claim that those seeking sensitive material would be reluctant to ask for unblocking. It held "the Constitution does not guarantee the right to acquire information at a public library without any risk of embarrassment." *U.S. v. American Library Ass'n Inc.*, 539 U.S. 194 (2003).

B. Textbook Selection

◆ A Texas student and the author of an environmental textbook had no constitutional right to compel the state board of education to select a particular textbook, according to the U.S. Court of Appeals, Fifth Circuit. Government can, without violating the constitution, selectively fund programs to encourage activities it believes are in the public interest, and may discriminate on the basis of viewpoint by choosing to fund one activity over another. Schools can thus promote policies and values of their own choosing, free from the forum analysis and the viewpoint-neutrality requirement. Devising the curriculum and selecting textbooks were core functions of the board, which needed to keep editorial judgment over the content of instructional materials for public school classrooms. The court agreed with the board that its selection of curricular materials was government speech. **Students have no constitutional right to compel the selection of classroom materials of their choosing.** *Chiras v. Miller*, 432 F.3d 606 (5th Cir. 2005).

◆ A group of parents whose children attended grade school in an Illinois school district sued for an order to prevent use of the Impressions Reading Series as the main supplemental reading program for grades kindergarten through five. The parents alleged that the series "foster[ed] a religious belief in the existence of superior beings exercising power over human beings" and focused on "supernatural beings" including "wizards, sorcerers, giants and unspecified creatures with supernatural powers." The case reached the Seventh Circuit, which found the parents' argument (that use of the textbook series established a religion) speculative. Although the series contained some stories involving fantasy and make-believe, their presence in the series did not establish a coherent religion. The intent of the series was to stimulate imagination and improve reading skills by using the works of C.S. Lewis, A.A. Milne, Dr. Suess and other fiction writers. **The primary effect of the series was not to endorse any religion; rather the primary effect was to improve reading skills.** Use of the series did not impermissibly endorse religion under the Establishment Clause or the Free Exercise Clause. The court ruled for the school. *Fleischfresser v. Directors of School Dist. 200*, 15 F.3d 680 (7th Cir. 1994).

◆ A teacher in a Michigan public school taught a life science course using a textbook approved by the district's school board. He showed films to his class regarding human reproduction (*From Boy to Man* and *From Girl to Woman*) after obtaining approval from his principal. The films were shown to his seventh-grade classes with girls and boys in separate rooms, and only students with parental permission slips were allowed to attend. Both films had traditionally been shown to seventh-grade students in the school.

But after a board meeting where community residents demanded that the teacher be tarred and feathered for showing the films, the superintendent suspended the teacher with pay pending "administrative evaluation." The board approved this action. The teacher then sued the district for violating his First Amendment and other civil rights. A jury awarded the teacher $321,000 in compensatory and punitive damages. The U.S. Supreme Court reversed the decision and remanded the case. According to the Supreme Court, **an award of money damages may be made only to compensate a person for actual injuries caused by deprivation of a constitutional right.** Awards for abstract violations of the U.S. Constitution were not allowed. *Memphis Community School Dist. v. Stachura*, 477 U.S. 299, 106 S.Ct. 2537, 91 L.Ed.2d 249 (1986).

C. School Productions

◆ A Nevada high school student selected a W.H. Auden poem containing the words "hell" and "damn" for recital at a statewide poetry reading competition. He practiced the poem twice a day for over two months. When the student recited the poem at a competition in the school, the dean of students emailed the English chair that it was objectionable due to inappropriate language. The student recited the poem again at a districtwide competition held off campus.

An administrator reprimanded English department members for allowing the recitation. The student learned he would have to choose a new poem, as the Auden poem had profanity. A federal district court found the recitation of the Auden poem could not be considered vulgar, lewd, obscene or offensive. **Off-campus poetry recitation at a state competition sponsored by national organizations was not school-sponsored speech and was not a part of the curriculum or any regular classroom activity.** Where there was no showing that speech would materially and substantially interfere with appropriate discipline, the court could not uphold restraint by school officials. A poem by a recognized poet, recited at an off-campus student competition authorized by the school, did not present even a remote risk of disruption. *Behymer-Smith v. Coral Academy of Science*, 427 F.Supp.2d 969 (D. Nev. 2006).

In Boring v. Buncombe County Board of Educ., *below, a federal appeals court held the selection of a school play was part of the curriculum, not a matter of public concern for which a teacher could claim constitutional protection.*

◆   A North Carolina high school English and drama instructor won numerous awards for directing and producing student plays. She selected a play for a state competition that depicted a divorced mother with a lesbian daughter and a daughter who was pregnant with an illegitimate child. Her advanced acting class won 17 of 21 possible awards at a regional competition for performing the play. But a parent objected to a scene from the play and the principal forbade students from performing it at the state finals. He later allowed the performance with the deletion of certain scenes. The school board approved a transfer of the teacher to a middle school for violating the district's controversial materials policy. She sued the board and school officials for retaliatory discharge. A three-judge panel of the U.S. Court of Appeals, Fourth Circuit, rejected the board's argument that the First Amendment protects only original expression and not the selection of a play. The panel held that due to the important role that teachers play in society, the First Amendment extended to the selection of plays for high school drama classes. The full court reheard the case and vacated the panel decision, upholding the transfer. **The selection of a school play was part of a public school curriculum, and did not constitute a matter of public concern for which a teacher could claim constitutional protection.** *Boring v. Buncombe County Board of Educ.*, 136 F.3d 364 (4th Cir. 1998).

IV. PARENTAL SPEECH AND ASSOCIATION RIGHTS

The Supreme Court has recognized a fundamental right of parents to direct and control the upbringing of their children. This does not include a parental right to direct and control public school curriculums or enter school campuses without restriction. Courts have approved state actions that intrude on parental liberty, such as sex and health education programs, community service and attendance requirements, uniform policies, and condom distribution programs.

A. Access to School Campuses

◆   The U.S. Court of Appeals, Fourth Circuit, rejected speech and due process violations claims by the parent of a disabled child against a North Carolina school district. According to the parent, school officials released his son from school early without his knowledge, forcing the child to wait for an hour at a neighbor's house. Later, the school banned him from campus, declaring his conduct to be disruptive. The parent was also prohibited from speaking to school staff. A federal court found his claims lacked merit. It held **parents have a limited right to direct their children's education that "does not include**

the unfettered right to access school premises." On appeal, the Fourth Circuit refused to hear the case because the lower court had not entered a final order. *Justice v. Farley*, 470 Fed.App. 136 (4th Cir. 2012).

◆   A non-custodial Iowa parent claimed school officials prevented her from visiting her children at their schools on several occasions. She obtained a state court order allowing "social visitation" with her children for three or four hours on three consecutive days. After she visited one child on the first day, police officers refused to let her approach her ex-husband's house. In a federal district court action against school and police officials, the parent claimed she was treated differently from married parents, in violation of her due process and equal protection rights. After the court held for school and police officials, the parent appealed to the U.S. Court of Appeals, Eighth Circuit. It held her equal protection claims failed because she was not similarly situated to married parents. The terms of her divorce decree made such a comparison improper.

While parents have a right to the care, custody and management of their children, **a one-time, temporary interruption in her visitation rights did not deprive her of a protected interest**. The officers may have misinterpreted their obligations, but they did not violate the Constitution. There was also no error in the dismissal of the due process claim against school officials. Due to relevant portions of the divorce decree, the parent had no fundamental liberty interest in seeing her children at school. School officials reasonably interpreted the court orders to prohibit her from interrupting the school day. As the lower court had correctly found no constitutional violations, the judgment was affirmed. *Schmidt v. Des Moines Public Schools,* 655 F.3d 811 (8th Cir. 2011).

◆   A New Jersey student said her varsity basketball coach routinely criticized her, singled her out due to her weight and went on "profanity-laced tirades" about her and some teammates. Her parent complained to school administrators and appeared at board meetings at least four times to urge action against the coach and to discuss the need to address civility in coaching. At one of the meetings, he spoke against reappointing the coach. Five others spoke in favor of the coaching staff, and the coach was reappointed. Months later, the parent was cut off about 30 seconds into an address to the board at a meeting to consider a policy against behavior diminishing individual dignity and safety. Other speakers were allowed to exceed a five-minute limit on remarks.

The parent filed a state court action against the school board for retaliation and other claims. A jury found the board and school officials liable for negligent supervision, but the court dismissed the daughter's claims. The court refused to reverse a $100,000 verdict for the parent for emotional distress. Appeal reached the Supreme Court of New Jersey, which held there was enough evidence for a jury to find the board president had silenced the parent for his viewpoints. The public comment period of a school board meeting is a public forum that can be limited only if justified without reference to the content of speech. **Once the board opened the floor for discussion, it could not deny the forum to those wishing to express less-favored or controversial views.** The court held the jury was free to find the president's warning revealed antagonism toward a view he did not want to hear. Since the president's motive was not content neutral, the court held the parent established a First Amendment violation. But the evidence of emotional distress was limited to transient embarrassment and humiliation. The case was returned to the trial court to reduce the damage award or to hold a new trial on damages. *Besler v. Board of Educ. of West Windsor-Plainsboro Regional School Dist.*, 201 N.J. 544, 993 A.2d 805 (N.J. 2010).

◆   Four Tennessee high school football players were dismissed from the team after signing a petition stating they hated their head coach and did not want to play for him. They filed an unsuccessful lawsuit against the school board in a federal court (see *Lowery v. Euverard*, this chapter). Parents of the same students filed a new federal court action on their own behalf against the school board and two school officials. A jury held for the board and school officials, and the court ordered the parents to pay the board attorneys' fees and costs of over $87,000 as a sanction for bringing claims that were frivolous and intended to harass school officials. On appeal, the U.S. Court of Appeals, Sixth Circuit, found **a school board meeting was a "designated and limited public forum."**

The forum in this case was "limited," because people did not have to be allowed to engage in every type of speech there. **In a designated public forum, the government may regulate the time, place and manner of speech in a content-neutral fashion.** In this case, the board's content-neutral justifications for the policy had nothing to do with an individual's proposed speech. The policy served a significant government interest in avoiding unstructured, chaotic board meetings. The court rejected claims that the policy was unconstitutionally vague and that the trial court had given the jury improper instructions. As the policy amounted to a content-neutral time, place and manner regulation, the court affirmed the judgment. But since the parents' claims were not frivolous, the court reversed the award of attorneys' fees for the board and school officials. *Lowery v. Jefferson County Board of Educ.*, 586 F.3d 427 (6th Cir. 2009).

◆   An Oklahoma parent agreed to check on another parent's daughter while volunteering at school. After obtaining approval to enter the classroom, the parent checked on the child, then spoke to a paraprofessional and other children for a few minutes. She then went to perform her volunteer duties and was again approached by the other parent to check on her daughter. The parent again looked in on the classroom. A school official sent her a letter banning her from school for five weeks for violating an Oklahoma law regarding "Interfering with Peaceful Conduct of Activities." After a hearing, the school reduced the time the parent was excluded from school, but she sued the district in federal district court for constitutional violations, including an interest in the care, custody and control of her children. The court held school officials were well within their bounds in limiting access, as "parents simply do not have a constitutional right to control each and every aspect of their children's education and oust the state's authority over that subject." **Public education is committed to the control of school authorities.** Federal courts in Kansas, Virginia, New Jersey, Texas and Michigan have held parents have no constitutional right to be on school grounds. *Mayberry v. Independent School Dist No. 1 of Tulsa County, Oklahoma*, No. 08-CV-416-GKF-PJC, 2008 WL 5070703 (N.D. Okla. 11/21/08).

◆   South Carolina legislators considered a bill to offer parents tax credits for private and homeschool expenses. A local school board believed the bill would undermine public school education, and it resolved to express opposition to the bill. The board instructed its director of community relations to communicate its position, and she did so on the district's website. The site was linked to other websites operated by bill opponents. The director emailed school employees and circulated fact sheets and opinions expressing the district's position. A parent sought to use the same channels to voice his support for the bill. The superintendent denied the request, and the parent sued the school district in a federal district court. The case reached the U.S. Court of Appeals, Fourth Circuit. It held government speech is exempt from First Amendment scrutiny.

The Supreme Court has stated that "the government may advocate in support of its policies with speech that is not supported by all." Generally, the government may support valid programs and policies and advocate particular positions. The district had approved a message of opposition to the bill and could deny access to its channels of communications. The district did not create a limited public forum, and the parent's speech rights were not implicated. *Page v. Lexington County School Dist. One*, 531 F.3d 275 (4th Cir. 2008).

B. Curriculum

Courts have repeatedly rejected parental attempts to direct school curriculums through lawsuits. School boards have broad powers to direct and control curriculums. Parental rights to direct and control the education of children do not extend to the selection of the curriculum.

◆   A 16-year-old Oregon student ran away from home and began to live with her grandmother. She was not legally emancipated, and her grandmother lacked legal authority to make her decisions. Over the next year, disputes arose between the school district and parents based on the district's consent to allow the child to attend off-campus school activities without notice or parental permission. According to the parents, school officials and staff violated their rights by failing to follow district policies regarding parental consent and notification, and by actively encouraging her to seek emancipation. They claimed the district undermined their authority, intruded into family matters and permanently harmed family relationships. While the court acknowledged that parents have a due process interest in the care, custody and control of their children, "mere negligence on the part of government officials is not enough" to create a due process violation. As the Ninth Circuit stated in *Fields v. Palmdale School Dist.*, 427 F.3d 1197 (9th Cir. 2005), the right of parents to control their children does not extend beyond the threshold of the school door.

Once parents chose to send their child to public school, their rights to control the child's education were substantially diminished. Issues of public education are generally committed to the control of school officials. In the court's opinion, this defeated the parents' theory that if the district had followed its own policies, their child would have been forced to communicate with them and move back home. Suggestions by a counselor that the student explore emancipating herself and an attempted mediation session did not violate family due process rights. The court dismissed the case, finding no constitutional violations. *Benitez v. Gresham-Barlow School Dist.*, No. 3:12-CV-1003-ST, 2012 WL 3878419 (D. Or. 2012).

◆   A Massachusetts draft guide to selecting and using curricular materials on genocide and human rights referred to "the Armenian genocide." It declared the "Muslim Turkish Ottoman Empire destroyed large portions of its Christian Armenian minority population in the late nineteenth and early twentieth centuries." A Turkish cultural group asked state officials for a "contra-genocide perspective" on Ottoman Armenians. Changes were made to the guide, and Armenian representatives asked the governor "to remove references to pro-Turkish sources." A revised version of the guide had no references to pro-Turkish websites except that of the Turkish Embassy. Turkish-American groups sued the state education commissioner in a federal district court, asserting the revisions were made improperly in response to political pressure. The court held that even if the case had been timely filed, **the guide was a form of government speech that was exempt from First Amendment scrutiny**.

On appeal, the U.S. Court of Appeals, First Circuit, also held the action was untimely and lacked merit. It found the guide was a "virtual school library" for students and teachers that was curricular in nature. The court declined "to hold that any compliant response to an expression of political opinion critical of a school library's selection of books would violate a First Amendment right to free enquiry on the part of library patrons." Schools must prepare students for their role as citizens, and state officials had considerable discretion in public school operations. Federal cases recognize the **government has authority "to choose viewpoints when the government itself is speaking."** The court found it should not interfere with school library selection matters. It held the guide did not implicate the First Amendment, and it rejected the complaining parties' additional arguments. *Griswold v. Driscoll*, 616 F.3d 53 (1st Cir. 2010).

◆   A New Jersey school district did not violate a parent's speech rights by requiring his consent to a policy banning his daughter from underage drinking and drugs as a condition for extracurricular participation. According to the court, **requiring an unconditional consent to the student participation form did not violate the parent's rights**. There was no First Amendment right for a parent to refrain from signing a school permission form "under duress" while dictating that the school allow a student to participate in extracurriculars. (A fuller summary of this case appears in Chapter Thirteen, Section 1). *Doe v. Banos*, 416 Fed.Appx. 185 (3d Cir. 2010).

◆   A New Hampshire taxpayer organization accused a school board of using public resources to engage in one-sided advocacy regarding election matters. The organization sued the board and town in state court, seeking an order to halt the board from sending any mailings on election issues. The court denied relief, finding "the government may use public funds to endorse its own measures." A final judgment for the board and town was affirmed by the state supreme court. The organization and its chairman then filed an action against the town and board in a federal district court, adding new claims and new taxpayers as parties. One claim alleged the town did not permit the organization to link its website to the town website while others were allowed to do so.

The court noted that most of the claims had (or could have) been raised in the state court case. It applied doctrines of *res judicata* and collateral estoppel, which bar claims between the same parties that have already been considered. On appeal, the U.S. Court of Appeals, First Circuit, held the addition of three new taxpayers did not change the outcome. Federal courts must give state court judgments the same effect they have under state law. **The court held the government may "speak for itself" and may use other parties to say its message.** For that reason, the town's decision to disallow the taxpayers from linking to their website was permissible. No similar group was allowed to link to the website. The town did not turn its website into a designated public forum by linking to a community event site. As the lower court had correctly held the remaining claims were barred, the judgment was affirmed. *Sutliffe v. Epping School Dist.*, 584 F.3d 314 (1st Cir. 2009).

◆   A Pennsylvania parent selected 10 Bible verses for her kindergartner to share with his class, including Psalms 118, Verse 14 which states "The Lord is my strength and my song, and is become my salvation." However, the principal informed the parent that reading the Bible to the class would be "against the law of separation of church and state." The parent sued for speech rights violations under the state and federal constitutions. A court held for the district, and the U.S. Court of Appeals, Third Circuit, affirmed. **A kindergarten class is a "unique forum" that is not a place for debate about issues of public importance.** Age and context are relevant, as "the age of the students bears an important inverse relationship to the degree and kind of control a school may exercise." The younger the student, the more control over speech a school could exercise. *Busch v. Marple Newton School Dist.*, 567 F.3d 89 (3d Cir. 2008).

V. USE OF SCHOOL FACILITIES

Schools may establish reasonable rules governing the time, place and manner of speech on school property, as discussed in Chapter Four, Section II. As in religious speech cases, the reasonableness of these rules depends upon the type of forum established by the school. A "limited public forum" exists on property that is generally open for use by the public. Time, manner and place regulations regarding a limited public forum must be content-neutral and narrowly tailored to serve a significant governmental interest. They must also provide for ample alternative channels of communication.

A. Student Organizations and Demonstrations

Student First Amendment rights are not coextensive with those of adults. School demonstrations may be enjoined if they are materially disruptive or invade the rights of others. Many student group access cases interpret the federal Equal Access Act (EAA), 20 U.S.C. §§ 4071-4074, which is more fully discussed in Chapter Four, Section II.C. In the next case, the U.S. Supreme

Court relied on K-12 school law precedents in holding that a state-affiliated California law college could deny official recognition to a Christian student organization because the group violated its school anti-discrimination policy.

◆ Hastings College of Law allowed officially recognized Registered Student Organizations (RSOs) to use college communications channels, office space and email accounts. RSO events were subsidized by student fees. To gain RSO status, groups had to comply with a school nondiscrimination policy. The Christian Legal Society (CLS) did not accept students whose religious convictions differed from its Statement of Faith. The CLS sought an exemption from the nondiscrimination policy, but Hastings denied the request due to noncompliance with the nondiscrimination policy. In a federal district court action, the CLS asserted speech, religious free exercise and due process violations. The court upheld Hastings' policy, and the case eventually reached the U.S. Supreme Court. The Court held regulations on speech are allowed if they serve a compelling state interest. According to the Court, the CLS faced only indirect pressure to modify its policies. The group could still exclude any person for any reason if it decided to forego the benefits of RSO recognition.

Hastings' policy applied to "all comers," which ensured a student was not forced to fund any group that might exclude her. An all-comers requirement helped Hastings "police" its policy without inquiring into the reasons for restricting RSO membership. Social networking sites reduced the importance of RSO channels. As for the CLS's argument that Hastings had no legitimate interest in regulating its membership, the Court held Hastings could "reasonably draw a line in the sand permitting all organizations to express what they wish but no group to discriminate in membership." The policy did not distinguish among groups based on viewpoint; it was "textbook viewpoint neutral." *Christian Legal Society Chapter of the Univ. of California, Hastings College of Law v. Martinez*, 130 S.Ct. 2971, 177 L.Ed.2d 838 (U.S. 2010).

◆ A group of Florida students sought official recognition of a gay-straight alliance club. They claimed their purpose was to promote tolerance and equality among students, regardless of sexual orientation or gender identity. They sought to create a safe, respectful learning environment for all students and to work with the school administration and other clubs to end prejudice and harassment. The principal denied approval of official recognition as a school club with access to school facilities on the same basis as other student clubs.

The club sued the school board in a federal district court, asserting that the school board had violated the EAA. A court explained that the EAA prohibits schools from denying equal access and fair opportunities on the basis of religious, political, philosophical or other content of speech that may be expected at meetings of student groups in limited open forums. The school board claimed the club was "sex-based" and that its speech presented a threat to school order. The court held that **the board did not offer any evidence to refute the club's assertion that it did not discuss sex,** let alone promote sexual activity. The court also rejected the board's claim that the club would interfere with its abstinence-based sex education curriculum. The court ordered the board to recognize the club and grant the privileges given to other student clubs. *Gay-Straight Alliance of Okeechobee High School v. School Board of Okeechobee County*, 483 F.Supp.2d 1224 (S.D. Fla. 2007).

In later activity, the court held the club had a tolerance-based message that did not materially or substantially interfere with discipline in school operations. To justify its refusal to recognize the club as a school organization, the school board had to show more than mere discomfort and unpleasantness associated with an unpopular viewpoint. Despite prevailing, the club did not demonstrate compensable injury, and it was awarded only $1 in nominal damages. *Gonzalez v. School Board of Okeechobee County*, 571 F.Supp.2d 1257 (S.D. Fla. 2008).

◆ An 18-year-old Virginia student distributed anti-abortion flyers at school in his sophomore and junior years as part of a "Pro-Life Day of Silent Solidarity." No disruption was reported. As a high school senior, the student again handed out anti-abortion literature in school hallways and the cafeteria during non-instructional times. The principal called the student to his office to tell him he could only distribute the flyers before or after school. The student contacted a lawyer, and within a month, the district devised a rule for students who were not associated with approved student groups or curricular programs. It gave them no option for distributing non-school materials during the school day. The student sued the district for an order to prohibit the enforcement of the ban on distribution of his materials. A federal court found that the rule virtually banned the circulation of all written materials during the school day. **There was no evidence that the student's anti-abortion literature would cause disruption in the school.** The district had acted with a remote apprehension of disturbance rather than a specific and significant fear of disruption. The student had distributed similar literature the two previous school years without disruption. The rule was unreasonable. The court granted the student's request for a preliminary order preventing the board from enforcing the rule. *Raker v. Frederick County Public Schools*, 470 F.Supp.2d 634 (W.D. Va. 2007).

◆ A Kentucky high school's site-based decision-making council approved a proposal for a gay straight alliance (GSA) club. Students who opposed the GSA club protested, and many parents threatened to remove their children from the school system. The school board then voted to ban all non-curricular clubs. The principal let the GSA club use school facilities as an outside organization, but did not allow the club to meet in homerooms or before school in a classroom. Four other non-curriculum-related student organizations retained access to school facilities during this time. The GSA club and its members sued for an order requiring the board to afford it the same opportunity to use school facilities as other student clubs enjoyed. A federal district court rejected the board's argument that the other organizations were "curriculum related."

A school opens up a "limited open forum" if it allows even one non-curriculum-related student group to use its facilities. A club cannot be denied permission to meet at school during noninstructional time if others may do so. When a limited open forum has been created, a school may prohibit only meetings that materially and substantially interfere with school activities. Here, the school's treatment of the GSA club was a content-based restriction that was forbidden by the EAA. The board could not deny access to its facilities based on the uproar caused by recognition of the GSA club. *Boyd County High School Gay Straight Alliance v. Board of Educ. of Boyd County*, 258 F.Supp.2d 667 (E.D. Ky. 2003).

B. Non-Student Groups

◆ Over time, Utah municipal officials accepted at least 11 monuments for display from private groups or individuals, including a wishing well, fire station, a September 11 monument, and a Ten Commandments monument. A Gnostic Christian organization called "Summum" sought to build a monument on public grounds containing its "Seven Aphorisms," or principles of creation. The organization stated that the Aphorisms had been handed down from God to Moses with the Ten Commandments, but withheld because the people were not ready to receive them. When the city declined Summum's request, the group sought a federal court order directing the city to permit its project.

The court denied the request, but the U.S. Court of Appeals, Tenth Circuit, held that the city had to allow the monument, as parks are traditionally considered public forums for speech. Appeal reached the U.S. Supreme Court, which held that **the First Amendment restricts government regulation of private speech, but does not regulate government speech**. The Court declared that government entities may "speak for themselves." Government entities may exercise the freedom to express their own views when receiving assistance from private sources when they deliver a "government-controlled message." Government speech must comply with constitutional provisions, such as the Establishment Clause, and the government was accountable to the electorate and the political process for its advocacy. When private speech was allowed in a public forum, the government could not place content-based restrictions upon private speech. In this case, the permanent monuments on display were "government speech" that the city could control. A "forum analysis" did not apply to the installation of permanent monuments on public property. The Court reversed the judgment. *Pleasant Grove City, Utah v. Summum*, 555 U.S. 460, 129 S.Ct. 1125, 172 L.Ed.2d 853 (2009).

◆ Anti-abortion activists drove a truck around a California middle school, displaying enlarged, graphic images of early-term aborted fetuses. An assistant principal observed that some students became upset and felt that the pictures on the truck created a traffic hazard, so he contacted the sheriff's department. Two deputies arrived, detained the activists for about 75 minutes and searched their vehicles. Deputies talked with their supervisors about the legality of stopping the display. The assistant principal and a deputy instructed the activists to leave, after reading California Penal Code Section 626.8 to them. Section 626.8 prohibited a person from coming into school buildings or grounds where the person's "presence or acts interfere with the peaceful conduct of the activities of the school or disrupt the school or its pupils or school activities." The activists sued the deputies, the sheriff's department and assistant principal for violating their speech rights and for an unreasonable search and seizure.

A federal district court dismissed the case, and the activists appealed to the U.S. Court of Appeals, Ninth Circuit. The court agreed with the activists that the deputies and assistant principal applied section 626.8 unconstitutionally. **Peaceful public expressions of ideas cannot be prohibited because they may be offensive to others, or simply because bystanders may object.** Any disruption caused by the graphic display was a result of student reaction and discussion. Section 626.8 applied only to interference or disruption caused by the manner of a person's expressive conduct. The law could not be used to infringe upon the lawful exercise of protected speech. Thus, the judgment on the speech rights claim was reversed. While the deputies and assistant principal had violated the activists' speech rights, they were entitled to qualified immunity, since they made a reasonable mistake in believing that Section 626.8 applied. However, the deputies were denied immunity for the long detention of the activists. The investigation should not have taken more than the few minutes needed to check for outstanding warrants. *Center for Bio-Ethical Reform v. Los Angeles County Sheriff Dep't*, 533 F.3d 780 (9th Cir. 2008).

◆   A Montana speaker received $1,000 from a ministerial association to serve as the master of ceremonies at a religious rally held the evening after a school assembly. He claimed that the board reversed a decision to allow him to speak at the assembly in violation of the First Amendment. The U.S. Court of Appeals, Ninth Circuit, held that **the speaker had no protected interest in addressing a public school assembly**. He was not being paid by the board and was thus not deprived of any valuable government benefit. The speaker later gave his speech off school grounds and was paid by the ministerial association. No other federal circuit court had found that permission to speak at a school assembly was a valuable government benefit. *Carpenter v. Dillon Elementary School Dist. 10*, 149 Fed.Appx. 645 (9th Cir. 2005).

◆   The No Child Left Behind Act requires each local educational agency that receives assistance under the Act to provide military recruiters access to secondary student names, addresses and telephone numbers. The section, 20 U.S.C. § 7908, has a parental notice requirement. The Solomon Amendment, applicable to higher education institutions, has no such provision. In 2006, the Supreme Court held that law schools had to provide the military the same access granted to all other employment recruiters under the Solomon Act. It held that the broad and sweeping power of Congress to provide for defense included the authority to require campus access for military recruiters. **Congress was free to attach reasonable conditions to federal funding, and the Solomon Amendment regulated conduct, not speech.** *Rumsfeld v. Forum for Academic and Institutional Rights*, 547 U.S. 47, 126 S.Ct. 1297, 164 L.Ed.2d 156 (2006).

CHAPTER FOUR

Religion and the Public Schools

I. RELIGIOUS ESTABLISHMENT

The Establishment Clause of the First Amendment to the U.S. Constitution prohibits Congress from making any law respecting the establishment of a religion. Because public schools and administrators are subject to this mandate by operation of the Fourteenth Amendment, the courts have struck down practices that improperly entangle public schools with religion.

*The U.S. Supreme Court has set forth various tests in Establishment Clause cases, but has declared **"the touchstone for our Establishment Clause analysis is the principle that the First Amendment mandates government neutrality between religion and religion, and between religion and non-religion."***

In C.F. v. Capistrano Unified School Dist., this chapter, the U.S. Court of Appeals, Ninth Circuit, explained the general rule that government officials are generally shielded by immunity from liability for damages in a civil action, if their conduct does not violate clearly established statutory or constitutional rights of which a reasonable person would know.

A. Prayer and Religious Activity

◆   A Rhode Island high school class presented the school a mural with the text of a "school prayer" in 1963. Years later, an atheist student reported feeling excluded and ostracized because of the prayer mural. She dedicated a Facebook page to discussion of the prayer mural, and this gained attention from the local and national media. By the time the school committee met to consider its legal options, strong community opposition had galvanized against efforts to remove the prayer mural. A federal court characterized the meeting as having the tone of a religious revival, with "a rowdy and belligerent atmosphere." Speakers were openly hostile to the student, and one told her she could "go to hell."

Following the meeting, the student reported bullying and threats at school, on the way home, and online. At a later school committee meeting, members resolved to keep the mural. In response, the student sued the committee in a federal district court for constitutional violations. The court stated that **while Establishment Clause jurisprudence is complex and contentious, neutrality is the guiding principle in Supreme Court cases**. This refers to neutrality with respect to religion and non-religion, as well as to different religions. In the court's view, the committee's purposes for voting to keep the mural were not secular. Maintaining the mural at the school had an effect of advancing religion, and the contentious committee meeting indicated excessive government entanglement with religion. An objective observer, aware of the background and circumstances of the case, would find the mural was an endorsement of religion by the school committee. As the school committee had committed a constitutional infraction, the court ordered the immediate removal of the mural. *Ahlquist v. City of Cranston*, 840 F.Supp.2d 507 (D.R.I. 2012).

◆   The U.S. Supreme Court denied an appeal from a successful challenge to the constitutionality of a Delaware school board's policy of opening its public meetings with a prayer. The U.S. Court of Appeals, Third Circuit, held the policy violated the Establishment Clause. It found Supreme Court school prayer cases reveal a need to protect students from government-endorsed or sponsored religion. **The First Amendment prohibits government religious coercion, and the risk of coercion is heightened in the public school context.** This required the Third Circuit to uphold the challenge. *Indian River School Dist. v. Doe*, No. 11-569, 132 S.Ct. 1097 (cert. denied 1/17/12).

◆   A New York parent claimed a charter school principal forced her child to eat during a fast. She sued the school and its principal in a federal district court for religious discrimination. The complaint claimed the principal defied the parent's instructions, isolated the child in the cafeteria and presented her with food. But the court found the complaint legally deficient. There was no direct claim that the school or the principal were "acting under color of state law," which was necessary to advance a case under 42 U.S.C. § 1983. It was unclear whether charter schools were "state actors" for Section 1983 liability purposes.

While the Free Exercise Clause is "an unflinching pledge to allow our citizenry to explore religious beliefs in accordance with the dictates of their conscience," the court held "not every belief put forward as 'religious' is elevated to constitutional status." **To survive dismissal, the court found there had to be a reasonable possibility that the parent had sincerely held convictions with theological, rather than secular grounds.** She stated no facts concerning her religious beliefs or their importance. Even if the parent's view was believed, the court found a general reference to "familial religious practice" without explanation of the importance of fasting, was insufficient to allege a sincerely held religious belief. As a result, the religious free exercise challenge failed. Regarding the Equal Protection and Establishment Clause claims, the court held the parent did not show intentional discrimination based on a religious belief. While the complaint was deficient, the court held the parent could file a new one alleging facts that supported these claims. *Meadows v. Lesh*, No. 10-CV-00223(M), 2010 WL 3730105 (W.D.N.Y. 9/17/10).

◆ Illinois' "Silent Reflection and Student Prayer Act" allowed a voluntary moment of silence in public school classrooms. In 2007, an amendment to the act provided that "the teacher in charge **shall** observe a brief period of silence" at the start of every school day, "with the participation of all the pupils" in the classroom. It further provided the period "shall not be conducted as a religious exercise but shall be an opportunity for silent prayer or for silent reflection on the anticipated activities of the day." A public high school student sued her school district and state officials in a federal court, which held the act invalid. On appeal, the U.S. Court of Appeals, Seventh Circuit, found the act served the secular purpose of helping calm students and prepare them for their school day. No evidence indicated this was a sham, as the student claimed. Review of the Illinois legislative debate confirmed a secular purpose and an intent to create uniformity across the state. **Nothing indicated the act was motivated by a religious purpose.** Federal courts had upheld similar moment of silence laws in Georgia, Virginia and Texas. Student-led prayer is permissible, and the court upheld the act. *Sherman v. Koch*, 623 F.3d 501 (7th Cir. 2010).

◆ A New Jersey head football coach led his teams in pregame prayers for many years. In 2005, parents began to complain, and administrators told him he could not lead, encourage or participate in student prayers. District guidelines emphasized student rights to pray on school property or at school events, so long as it did not interfere with school operations. However, the guidelines barred school representatives from participating in student-initiated prayers.

After temporarily resigning, the coach agreed to abide by the district's policy. He then sued the district and its superintendent. He emailed team co-captains and asked them if they would like to resume pre-game and pre-meal team prayers. After players voted to continue team prayers, the coach stood with them and bowed his head during pre-meal and pregame team prayers. A federal court found "nothing wrong with remaining silent and bowing one's head and taking a knee as a sign of respect for his players' actions and traditions." The district appealed to the U.S. Court of Appeals, Third Circuit, which noted that the coach's silent expression of support for the team was "not a matter of public concern." His conduct violated the Establishment Clause. In *Board of Educ. of Westside Community Schools v. Mergens*, this chapter, the Supreme Court held that faculty involvement in student religious groups was limited to a "nonparticipatory capacity." **The relevant question is whether a school official has improperly endorsed religion based on what a reasonable observer, familiar with the context and history of the display, would believe.** Since the coach's conduct over 23 years signaled endorsement of religion to any reasonable observer, the judgment was reversed. *Borden v. School Dist. of Township of East Brunswick*, 523 F.3d 153 (3d Cir. 2008).

◆   A New York school district with a Mohawk Indian majority permitted the saying of "Ohen: Ton Karihwatehkwen," also referred to as "the Thanksgiving Address," over a school public address (PA) system. The address acknowledged people, Mother Earth, plants, fruits, grasses, water, fish, medicine, animals, trees, birds, Grandfather Thunders, Four Winds, Elder Brother Sun, Grandmother Moon, stars, Four Beings and a concept sometimes interpreted as "Creator." A parent who was not Mohawk complained that "the address could be a prayer." A district lawyer agreed, but stated that the school could allow student-initiated recitation of the address at a location chosen by students.

The superintendent then let students go to a school auditorium for recitation of the address instead of having it said over the PA system. The saying of the address was discontinued at pep rallies and at school lacrosse games. Mohawk students sued the district and school officials in a federal district court. The court rejected their claim that they were treated differently than students who recited the Pledge of Allegiance. Thanksgiving is not a religious holiday and is unrelated to a specific group or culture. The district did not broadcast Christmas carols or hymns over the PA system or at pep rallies or games. **Here, the district had attempted to promote diversity, pluralism and tolerance for culture, including Mohawk tradition.** The district continued to celebrate Mohawk culture in many ways. Students could still say the address in the auditorium, and their flag and traditional forms of dress were displayed on some occasions. As the district acted reasonably by ending the recitation of the address at rallies, lacrosse games and over the PA system, the court ruled in its favor. On appeal, the U.S. Court of Appeals, Second Circuit, affirmed the judgment. *Jock v. Ransom*, No. 07-3162, 2009 WL 742193 (2d Cir. 3/20/09).

◆   A New York school board directed a principal to have a prayer read aloud by each class in the presence of a teacher at the beginning of the school day. The procedure was adopted on the recommendation of the state board of regents. State officials had composed the prayer and published it as part of their "Statement on Moral and Spiritual Training in the Schools." The parents of 10 students sued the board, insisting that use of an official prayer in public schools violated the Establishment Clause of the First Amendment. The New York Court of Appeals upheld the practice as long as schools did not compel pupils to join in the prayer over the parents' objections. On appeal, the U.S. Supreme Court held that the practice was wholly inconsistent with the Establishment Clause. **There could be no doubt that the classroom invocation was a religious activity.** Neither the fact that the prayer was denominationally neutral nor that its observance was voluntary served to free it from the Establishment Clause. *Engel v. Vitale*, 370 U.S. 421, 82 S.Ct. 1261, 8 L.Ed.2d 601 (1962).

◆ Pennsylvania law required that "[a]t least ten verses from the Holy Bible shall be read, without comment, at the opening of each public school on each school day. Any child shall be excused from such Bible reading, or attending such Bible reading, upon written request of his parents or guardian." A family sued school officials to enjoin enforcement of the laws as violative of the First Amendment. The school commissioner of Baltimore had also adopted a rule that mandated the reading of a chapter of the Bible or the Lord's Prayer at the start of each school day without comment. That rule was also challenged. The U.S. Supreme Court consolidated the cases and held that both rules violated the Establishment Clause. The Court reiterated the premise of *Engel v. Vitale*, above, that **neither the state nor the federal government can constitutionally force a person to profess a belief or disbelief in any religion**. Nor can it pass laws that aid all religions as against nonbelievers. The primary purpose of the statutes and rule was religious. The compulsory nature of the ceremonies was not mitigated by the fact that students could excuse themselves. *Abington School Dist. v. Schempp*, 374 U.S. 203, 83 S.Ct. 1560, 10 L.Ed.2d 844 (1963).

◆ **The U.S. Supreme Court invalidated an Alabama statute allowing meditation or voluntary prayer in public school classrooms.** The case was initiated in 1982 by the father of three elementary students who challenged the validity of two Alabama statutes: a 1981 statute that allowed a period of silence for "meditation or voluntary prayer," and a 1982 statute authorizing teachers to lead "willing students" in a nonsectarian prayer composed by the state legislature. After a lower court found both statutes unconstitutional, the U.S. Supreme Court agreed to review only the portion of the lower court decision invalidating the 1981 statute that allowed "meditation or voluntary prayer." The Court concluded that the intent of the Alabama legislature was to affirmatively reestablish prayer in the public schools. Inclusion of the words "or voluntary prayer" in the statute indicated that it had been enacted to convey state approval of a religious activity and violated the First Amendment's Establishment Clause. *Wallace v. Jaffree*, 472 U.S. 38 (1985).

◆ Two Texas students challenged a number of their school district's practices, including one allowing overtly Christian prayers at graduation ceremonies and football games. The district permitted nondenominational prayers at graduation ceremonies, read by students selected by vote of the graduating class. In response to the complaint, the district revised its policies for prayer at school functions by requiring them to be nonsectarian and non-proselytizing. Shortly thereafter, the district enacted new policies deleting the nonsectarian, non-proselytizing requirements for pre-game invocations and graduation prayers. A federal district court ordered the school district to enact a more restrictive policy, allowing only nonsectarian and non-proselytizing prayers.

The case reached the U.S. Supreme Court, which ruled that student-led, pre-game prayers violated the Establishment Clause. Although the district asserted that students determined the content of the pre-game message without review by school officials and with approval by the student body, school officials regulated the forum. **The majoritarian process for selecting speakers guaranteed that minority candidates would never prevail and that their**

views would be effectively silenced. The degree of school involvement in the pre-game prayers created the perception and actual endorsement of religion by school officials. *Santa Fe Independent School Dist. v. Doe*, 530 U.S. 290, 120 S.Ct. 2266, 147 L.Ed.2d 295 (2000).

B. Instruction of Students

1. Curriculum

◆   A student charged a longtime California history teacher with disparaging Christianity. The student dropped the class and sued the teacher and school district for Establishment Clause violations. The court heard evidence that the teacher had opposed a creationist teacher, who some 20 years earlier had been directed not to teach creationism in science classes. The teacher had accused him of propagandizing students with "religious, superstitious nonsense." Teachers' associations joined the case and asserted qualified immunity on his behalf. The court held for the student regarding the statement about the creationist teacher. But the teacher was granted qualified immunity. On appeal, the U.S. Court of Appeals, Ninth Circuit, held the lower court did not abuse its discretion by granting the teacher qualified immunity, as the law in this area was not "clearly established" at the relevant time. It vacated the ruling on the statement about the creationist teacher. As the court found no case holding a teacher violated the Establishment Clause by appearing critical of religion during a class, the teacher had no fair warning that it was unlawful. **Supreme Court cases recognized the importance of protecting the robust exchange of ideas. The court held "teachers and the schools must try to maintain an atmosphere of free inquiry."** Teachers were entitled to challenge students to foster critical thinking skills and develop their analytical abilities. *C.F. v. Capistrano Unified School Dist.*, 654 F.3d 975 (9th Cir. 2011).

◆   A Delaware Muslim family said a fourth-grade teacher isolated their child by reading Christmas books and telling a candy cane story that was supposed to symbolize Christian beliefs. Classroom discussions deviated from a textbook and framed the events of 9/11 "as a war of Christians versus Muslims." When the student finally complained, her mother asked school officials for an apology and a statement to the class that the child had done nothing wrong. After the ACLU became involved, the teacher agreed to let the student make a class presentation. A transfer of the student followed, but classmates shunned and taunted her. In a federal district court action, the student filed claims under the state and federal constitutions. **The court held the government cannot promote or affiliate itself with any religious doctrine or organization, nor is it permitted to discriminate on grounds of religious belief or practice.**

Pretrial judgment was denied by the court regarding Christian readings and the candy cane story. A reasonable jury might find phrases from the story, such as "Jesus is the pure Lamb of God," and "Jesus is the Christ," lacked any secular purpose and endorsed Christianity. A claim alleging retaliation also required further consideration. But the court found the 9/11 textbook portrayed historic events evenhandedly and served a secular educational purpose that neither enhanced nor inhibited religion. A reasonable jury might find that a transfer to another classroom was an adverse action. An equal protection claim required further consideration, as the court found the teacher read Christmas books to the class every day for a month but did not recognize other religious holidays. *Doe v. Cape Henlopen School Dist.*, 795 F.Supp.2d 522 (D. Del. 2011).

◆ An organization called Islamic Relief sponsored a Minnesota charter academy serving mostly Somali Muslims. The ACLU claimed the academy held prayer sessions in which parents, volunteers and teachers participated. The academy was accused of endorsing Islamic dress codes and dietary practices, and providing buses only at the end of an after-school religious program. The ACLU sued academy officials, Islamic Relief and the state education department in a federal court, asserting that the academy preferred "Muslim" religious practices. The court found Islamic Relief had potential liability under the Establishment Clause due to its role in the traditionally exclusive function of public education. Charter schools were a part of the public school system under Minnesota law, and the state Charter School Law required each sponsor to assure compliance with nonsectarian requirements. The court rejected arguments for pretrial dismissal because the issues raised were factual in nature.

For example, **religious entanglement created by the academy's dress code and the busing schedule required a factual inquiry**. The role played by Islamic Relief in the academy's operations also required further scrutiny. As a result, the case required a trial. After two more years of pretrial activity, the academy was faced with serious financial trouble, and it agreed to dismiss the case. The court approved of a settlement agreement by which the school would be liable for a $267,500 payment to the ACLU. This was to be paid by Islamic Relief. *American Civil Liberties Union of Minnesota v. Tarek Ibn Ziyad Academy*, Civil No. 09-138 (DWF/JJG), 2011 WL 4537962 (D. Minn. 9/29/11).

◆ A New York kindergartner made a poster for a class assignment with his mother's help. She wrote statements on the poster such as "prayer changes things" and "Jesus loves children." The student's teacher did not hang the poster, and the school principal later told her to have the student make a new one. After the mother helped her son make a new poster that also had religious themes, the teacher and principal folded it to obscure the religious content. The mother sued the school district and officials for speech and religious rights violations in a federal court. The court held for the district, and appeal reached the U.S. Court of Appeals, Second Circuit. It found the poster was assigned under specific parameters that the school could regulate in a reasonable manner. **Schools may reasonably regulate speech and activities that are part of the school curriculum.** The Establishment Clause claim was properly dismissed. *Peck v. Baldwinsville Cent. School Dist.*, 426 F.3d 617 (2d Cir. 2005).

The case was returned to the district court, which entered a judgment for the school district and officials. In 2009, the Second Circuit noted the case had been filed 10 years earlier. It held the student now lacked standing to pursue the case because he was seeking an injunction relying on a past, not a future injury. *Peck v. Baldwinsville Cent. School Dist.*, 351 Fed.Appx. 477 (2d Cir. 2009).

◆   A Michigan elementary school held a simulated marketplace event where fifth-graders made products for sale at booths in the school gymnasium. Other students at the school visited the booths and purchased goods with faux school currency. A student accepted his mother's suggestion to sell Christmas candy cane-shaped tree ornaments made of pipe cleaners and beads. His father offered to make cards to attach to the canes, which bore a religious message. The student did not attach a sample card when he submitted his required prototype ornament, and he never told the school he intended to attach the cards.

On the day of the event, the student's teacher learned about the card for the first time. She halted sales of the card, and the principal told the family that the student could not sell ornaments with the card since the event was considered instructional time. However, the student was permitted to sell cards in a school parking lot, but he sold the ornaments without the cards instead. The parents sued the district and principal for speech rights violations. A federal court held for the district, and the U.S. Court of Appeals, Sixth Circuit, affirmed the judgment. The marketplace event was part of the curriculum. **Educators do not offend the First Amendment by exercising editorial control over student speech in school-sponsored events.** The court held the school's desire to avoid a curricular event that might offend parents and other children qualified as a valid educational purpose, and it found the principal's decision to stop the sales of the religious card was based on her reasonable evaluation of legitimate pedagogical concerns. *Curry v. Hensiner*, 513 F.3d 570 (6th Cir. 2008).

◆   A Virginia high school Spanish teacher posted religious content on his bulletin board. A visitor complained, and the principal took down items such as a "National Day of Prayer" poster depicting George Washington kneeling in prayer, and four newspaper clippings discussing the Bible and religion. The school board had no written policy on teacher use of classroom bulletin boards and it relied on principals to decide what could be posted. The principal's primary criterion for assessing postings was relevancy to the curriculum being taught by the particular teacher. The teacher sued the board in a federal court, which held the items were "curricular" in nature and that his speech was unprotected. On appeal, the U.S. Court of Appeals, Fourth Circuit, rejected his assertion that he could post any materials he wished in the classroom. His material was curricular in nature, and not a matter of public concern. **School boards have the right to regulate speech within a compulsory classroom setting.** The school had an interest in preventing in-class teacher speech that interfered with day-to-day operations. Since the materials were likely to be attributed to the school, and the court held the principal could remove them. *Lee v. York County School Division*, 484 F.3d 687 (4th Cir. 2007).

◆   Dover (Pennsylvania) area residents elected two Fundamentalist Christians to their school board. One became the board's president. He sought to include creationism and prayer in the district curriculum and recommended purchasing a textbook advocating "intelligent design." The board accepted 60 copies and forced teachers to use it as a reference text. The board then voted to change the district's ninth-grade biology curriculum so that "students will be made aware of gaps/problems in Darwin's theory and of other theories of evolution, including but not limited to intelligent design." Resident parents sued the board in a federal district court, asserting Establishment Clause violations.

The court held that **the intelligent design policy conveyed a message of religious endorsement**. None of the experts who testified at trial could explain how intelligent design "could be anything other than an inherently religious proposition." The disclaimer singled out evolution from everything else being taught in the district, suggesting evolution was a "highly questionable opinion or hunch." While evolution was "overwhelmingly accepted" by the scientific community, intelligent design had been refuted by peer-reviewed research. The board members conveyed a strong message of religious endorsement. The court entered an order preventing the district from maintaining the intelligent design policy and from requiring teachers to disparage evolutionary theory. *Kitzmiller v. Dover Area School Dist.*, 400 F.Supp.2d 707 (M.D. Pa. 2005).

◆ In 1981, Louisiana legislators enacted "Balanced Treatment for Creation Science and Evolution Science in Public School Instruction," an act providing that any school offering instruction in evolution must include equal time for instruction in "creation science." The act required that curriculum guides be developed and research services supplied for creation science but not for evolution. The stated purpose of the act was to protect academic freedom. A group of parents, teachers, and religious leaders challenged the law. A federal court and the Fifth Circuit both held that the act was an unconstitutional establishment of religion, and Louisiana state officials appealed to the U.S. Supreme Court. The Court addressed the issue of whether the Creationism Act was enacted for a clear secular purpose. It noted that **because the act provided for sanctions against teachers who chose not to teach creation science, it did not promote its avowed purpose of furthering academic freedom**. The Court ruled that "[b]ecause the primary purpose of the Creationism Act is to advance a particular religious belief, the Act endorses religion in violation of the First Amendment." The Creationism Act was therefore declared unconstitutional. *Edwards v. Aguillard*, 482 U.S. 578, 107 S.Ct. 2573, 96 L.Ed.2d 510 (1987).

2. Textbooks

◆ Massachusetts parents objected to their school district's presentation of books portraying diverse families to their children. This included depictions of families in which both parents were of the same gender. Massachusetts law required notification to parents and an opportunity to exempt their children from curriculums that primarily involved human sexuality. State law also mandated that academic standards include respect for cultural, ethnic and racial diversity, but did not mention or provide for notice to parents when a school curriculum included any discussion of homosexuality. Two families sued the school district, claiming that the exposure of their children to books describing diverse families violated a core belief of their religion that homosexual behavior and gay marriage are immoral and violate God's law. They claimed that two books were part of an effort by the public schools to systematically indoctrinate young children into the belief that homosexuality and homosexual marriage are moral and acceptable conduct. The court dismissed the case.

The U.S. Court of Appeals, First Circuit, found "Given that Massachusetts has recognized gay marriage under its state constitution, it is entirely rational for its schools to educate their students regarding that recognition." **Exposure to the books would not prevent the parents from raising their children in their religious beliefs.** Parental rights in the public school context are not absolute, and parents lack constitutional rights to control each and every aspect of their children's education. No federal case had recognized a due process right to allow parents an exemption from exposure to particular books used in the public schools. Requiring a student to read a particular book is not coercive, and public schools are not obligated to shield students from ideas that are potentially offensive. *Parker v. Hurley*, 514 F.3d 87 (1st Cir. 2008).

◆   Georgia school board members were concerned that constituents wanted texts with "alternate theories of the origin of life." The board allowed stickers to be placed on science textbooks reading: "This textbook contains material on evolution. Evolution is a theory, not a fact, regarding the origin of living things. This material should be approached with an open mind, studied carefully, and critically considered." Parents who believed the stickers endorsed religion sued the board in a federal court. It held **an informed, reasonable observer would believe the stickers sent a message of approval to creationists**. As the board impermissibly entangled itself with religion, the court ordered removal of the stickers. On appeal, the Eleventh Circuit found the lower court had improperly relied on a letter from a parent who objected to teaching evolution and a petition submitted to the board prior to its vote to place the stickers on new textbooks. As the record did not show the letter and petition were submitted to the board before the vote, the lower court was advised to issue new findings and conclusions of law and determine if any petition was submitted before the board vote. *Selman v. Cobb County School Dist.*, 449 F.3d 1320 (11th Cir. 2006).

In late 2006, the board agreed to refrain from placing any stickers or labels disclaiming evolutionary theory in textbooks.

3. School Music Performances

In Nurre v. Whitehead, *below, a school district's tradition of letting seniors pick music for their graduation ceremonies was held to be a "limited public forum." But in* Stratechuk v. Board of Educ., South Orange-Maplewood School Dist., *below, a New Jersey holiday concert was not deemed a public forum. Schools are not public forums unless they are intentionally designated as such.*

◆   A Washington school district received complaints about religious music selections at a 2005 high school graduation ceremony. As the 2006 graduation approached, administrators rejected the school wind ensemble's selection of "Ave Maria," believing it created a risk of new complaints. They asked the ensemble to make another selection. A student member of the wind ensemble sued the school district and superintendent for constitutional violations. A federal district court held the district did not violate the student's rights. On appeal, the U.S. Court of Appeals, Ninth Circuit, held that **instrumental music was "speech" for First Amendment analysis**. Schools are not considered public forums for speech unless they are opened up by officials for indiscriminate use. A limited public forum for expression had been opened in this case because of the district's tradition of letting seniors select the music for their graduation ceremonies. In a limited public forum, restrictions can be based on subject matter, so long as any distinctions are reasonable in light of the purpose of the forum. Here, the school district acted reasonably to avoid repeating the prior year's controversy. The court affirmed the judgment for the district. *Nurre v. Whitehead*, 580 F.3d 1087 (9th Cir. 2009).

◆ A New Jersey school holiday activity policy stated that "special effort must be made to ensure the activity is not devotional and that pupils of all faiths and beliefs can join without feeling they are betraying their own faiths." After receiving complaints about religious music at a school concert, the policy was reexamined. A school arts director clarified that music selections representing religious holidays would be avoided. A parent complained this conveyed a message that Christianity was disfavored, and sued. A federal court held for the school district, and appeal went to the U.S. Court of Appeals, Third Circuit.

Applying *Lemon v. Kurtzman*, 403 U.S. 602 (1971), the court found no Establishment Clause violation. As the lower court held, the district's intent was to avoid government endorsement of religious holidays and potential Establishment Clause violations. Although the parent maintained this was a "sham" purpose, the court held **the Constitution did not require schools to promote religion to the maximum extent allowed**. Failure to do so did not make the district "anti-religious," as he claimed. The policy did not preclude religious songs from classrooms or concerts, unless they were specific to a holiday. **School concerts are not public forums**, and as the lower court had correctly found the policy was reasonably related to legitimate pedagogical concerns, the judgment for the school district was affirmed. *Stratechuk v. Board of Educ., South Orange-Maplewood School Dist.*, 587 F.3d 597 (3d Cir. 2009).

C. Commencement Ceremonies

Commencement ceremonies may present complicated questions regarding possible government religious coercion and the private speech rights of student speakers. The leading case in this area is Lee v. Weisman, 505 U.S. 577 (1992). In it, the Supreme Court reaffirmed the principle that the government may not coerce anyone to support or participate in religion, or otherwise act in any way that establishes a state religion or religious faith, or tends to do so.

◆ A Wisconsin school district rented a church sanctuary to hold its graduation ceremonies for over 10 years. It did so because of complaints that its own facilities were too small, uncomfortable and not air-conditioned. A group of students and parents sued the district in a federal court for Establishment Clause violations. After the court denied the families preliminary relief, it held the district did not engage in religious coercion or endorsement and dismissed the case. A three-judge panel of the Seventh Circuit then agreed with the objecting families that the church atmosphere was strongly Christian. But the panel rejected the claim that there had been religious coercion and held any "encounter with religion here is purely passive and incidental to attendance at an entirely secular ceremony." It said there was no unconstitutional church-state entanglement. Months later, a majority of the active judges of the Seventh Circuit voted to review the panel decision. Before explaining its decision, the full court stated that it was not deciding whether any religious institution or church could ever host a graduation ceremony. In the court's view, the involvement of minors, the significance of graduation ceremonies, and religious proselytizing proved too much to withstand an Establishment Clause challenge.

There was evangelical literature in the church lobby, and the walls were decorated with religious banners, symbols and posters. Church literature and decorations were aimed at children and teens, and members staffed information booths during some graduation ceremonies. In reviewing Supreme Court cases, the court found **the key to Establishment Clause review is "the principle that the First Amendment mandates government neutrality between religion and religion, and between religion and nonreligion."** It held the ceremonies violated the Establishment Clause because they caused actual religious coercion and a risk of religious endorsement. As a result, the court reversed the judgment and returned the case to the district court. Beginning in 2010, the school district held high school graduation ceremonies in its newly constructed field house. *John Doe 3 v. Elmbrook School Dist.*, 687 F.3d 840 (7th Cir. 2012).

◆   A Montana school district had no guidelines for valedictory speeches, but a policy declared that administrators would not censor presentations or require particular content. A graduation policy required the district to provide the public with a disclaimer stating that graduation presentations were considered "private expression" and did not reflect an official position. When the superintendent of schools learned a student intended to include some references to her beliefs, he told her not to mention God or Christ. Days before the ceremony, the student and her father met with the superintendent, who had prepared a revised text for her. But the student said she would not change her speech, and she was not allowed to speak. Her state court action reached the Supreme Court of Montana, which found it was the district's unwritten practice to prohibit religious references in student speeches. This was contrary to the district's written policy against censorship in graduation ceremonies. In prior cases, the court had found it "axiomatic" that the government may not regulate speech based on content.

Applying U.S. Supreme Court precedents, **the court found it would be unreasonable to find that the brief mention of personal religious views would materially and substantially disrupt a graduation ceremony**. It was not permissible for school officials to censor the student's intended graduation speech. There was no religious coercion present in remarks about what she had learned in high school. Each of the student's references to God or Christ was prefaced by "I learned," or "my faith," and was "directed to her personal life and beliefs." The court held no objectively reasonable observer of a graduation ceremony would perceive that the student's brief religious references bore the imprimatur of the school district. By ignoring its own policy, the district violated the student's speech rights, and she was entitled to nominal damages. *Griffith v. Butte School Dist. No. 1*, 358 Mont. 193, 244 P.3d 321 (Mont. 2010).

◆ A Connecticut school district held its high school graduation ceremonies at a cathedral. Before the 2010 ceremony, the school board voted to hold the event on school grounds due to a threatened lawsuit. But the board rescinded its vote after lobbying by a religious group that promised free legal representation if the board agreed to hold the ceremonies at the cathedral. Alternative sites were rejected, including a symphony hall that would cost a total of $5,000 less than the cathedral. A federal case was filed to obtain an order prohibiting the board from holding 2010 graduation ceremonies at the cathedral. Among the court's findings was that many large crosses, banners and other religious items would be in view at the cathedral. The court held **a reasonable observer would find selection of the cathedral for graduation ceremonies conveyed a message that the board embraced one religious view**. Observers would see religious objects, symbols and messages in the cathedral. Even with modifications, the cathedral remained a religious environment. By selecting the cathedral, the board sent a message that it was closely linked with a religious mission, and that it favored "the religious over the irreligious, and that it prefers Christians" over others. Any consideration of alternate sites did not appear to be open-minded.

No precise criteria were stated, and the board rejected a cheaper site. And "the uneasy process of attempting to 'secularize' First Cathedral by covering some of its religious imagery" created excessive government entanglement with religion. Government coercion was found, since graduating seniors had no real choice to skip graduation. As the board failed the relevant Establishment Clause tests, the court issued a preliminary order for the students and parents. *Does 1, 2, 3, 4 and 5 v. Enfield Public Schools*, 716 F.Supp.2d 172 (D. Conn. 2010).

◆ A Colorado high school valedictorian submitted a speech for review by her school principal that did not mention religion. But at the ceremony, she encouraged attendees to learn about Jesus Christ and "the opportunity to live in eternity with Him." After the ceremony, the valedictorian learned she would not receive her diploma unless she publicly apologized. Instead of apologizing, she prepared a statement explaining that her speech reflected her beliefs and that it was made without the principal's prior approval. Although the valedictorian submitted the statement and received a diploma, she sued the school district in a federal district court. After the court held for the school district, she appealed to the U.S. Court of Appeals, Tenth Circuit. It applied *Hazelwood School Dist. v. Kuhlmeier*, 484 U.S. 260 (1988), which held **educators do not offend the First Amendment by exercising editorial control over student speech in school-sponsored expressive activities**, "so long as their actions are reasonably related to legitimate pedagogical concerns." Greater control over student speech was appropriate in school-sponsored events because the school community might reasonably perceive them to bear the school's approval. The valedictory speeches were supervised by faculty and were clearly school sponsored.

An order to apologize was reasonably related to learning, and did not violate the valedictorian's rights. There was no substantial burden on the valedictorian's free exercise or equal protection rights, as she was held to the same religion-neutral policies as others. The judgment was affirmed. *Corder v. Lewis Palmer School Dist. No. 38*, 566 F.3d 1219 (10th Cir. 2009).

◆   A Rhode Island student and her father sued their school district in a federal district court to prevent an annual graduation prayer performed by clergy members of various faiths. The court held the clergy-led prayers violated the Establishment Clause of the First Amendment. The defendants appealed to the U.S. Court of Appeals, First Circuit, which agreed with the student that the prayers violated the Establishment Clause and affirmed the judgment.

On appeal, the U.S. Supreme Court held the district violated the Establishment Clause by selecting clergy members to say prayers as part of an official public school graduation ceremony. **The government may not coerce anyone to support or participate in religion, or otherwise act in any way that establishes a state religion or religious faith, or tends to do so.** In this case, state officials directed the performance of a formal religious exercise. The principal decided that a prayer should be given, selected the clergy participant, and directed and controlled the prayer's content. The district's supervision and control of the graduation ceremony placed subtle and indirect public and peer pressure on attending students to stand as a group or maintain respectful silence during the invocation and benediction. The state may not force a student dissenter to participate or protest. The Court rejected the argument that the ceremony was voluntary, and it affirmed the judgment for the student and her parent. *Lee v. Weisman*, 505 U.S. 577, 112 S.Ct. 2649, 120 L.Ed.2d 467 (1992).

D. School Policies

1. The Pledge of Allegiance

Nearly 70 years ago, the U.S. Supreme Court held the states cannot compel citizens to recite the Pledge of Allegiance in West Virginia State Board of Educ. v. Barnette, *319 U.S. 624 (1943). The Court held the First Amendment protects both the right to speak freely and the right to refrain from speaking at all.*

◆   New Hampshire's School Patriot Act required public schools to authorize voluntary student participation in Pledge of Allegiance recitations. Parents claimed routine Pledge recitations in classrooms violated state and U.S. laws and constitutional provisions. A lawsuit was filed against two school districts, as well as state and federal officials, seeking to declare the School Patriot Act unlawful. The court dismissed the federal government from the case and held for the districts and officials. Appeal went before the U.S. Court of Appeals, First Circuit, which found New Hampshire enacted the School Patriot Act shortly after the September 11, 2001 tragedy as "a continuation of the policy of teaching our country's history" to students. The act made student participation in Pledge recitations voluntary. While the parents claimed the Pledge was a "religious exercise," the court disagreed. Supreme Court cases have established that "the Constitution does not require complete separation of church and state." **Neither the Pledge nor the phrase "Under God" was a prayer or a religious reading. Recitation of the Pledge could be distinguished from overt religious activities.** The Patriot Act had a secular purpose of promoting patriotism. Pledge recitation affirmed a belief in a description of the nation, not in a religion. There was no merit to the parents' claim that Pledge recitations made their children outsiders. The court found the act made student participation voluntary. A student could refuse to recite the Pledge for any reason, including a simple desire to be different. No religious endorsement was created by inclusion of the phrase "under God" in Pledge recitations. Silence by students was not an expression of participation, and the court rejected the claim that public schools are obligated to shield individual students from potentially offensive ideas. No equal protection or due process violation was present, as the parents had no right to control public education to the degree sought in this case. Since none of the claims had merit, the court affirmed the judgment. *Freedom From Religion Foundation v. Hanover School Dist.*, 626 F.3d 1 (1st Cir. 2010).

◆ In 2007, Texas legislators added "under God" to the state pledge, which now declares "Honor the Texas flag, I pledge allegiance to thee, Texas, one state under God, one and indivisible." A group of parents sued the governor to challenge inclusion of the phrase "under God" in the pledge. A federal district court upheld the pledge. On appeal, the Fifth Circuit reviewed the legislative history of the bill and found it was intended to mirror the national pledge. The Supreme Court has never ruled on the constitutionality of the national pledge, but the Fifth Circuit has previously found it is a "patriotic exercise designed to foster national unity and pride" and is not a religious exercise. Under tests applied by federal courts, the court found no Establishment Clause violation.

In the court's view, the amendment had a secular purpose. Legislators believed that conformity with the U.S. Pledge was the "safest and smoothest means" to acknowledge "our religious heritage." The court held the bill had secular purposes and was not enacted as a sham to advance Christianity. **The court found no reasonable observer would understand the purpose of the pledge to be religious endorsement.** The words "under God" acknowledged, but did not endorse religion. Applying *Lee v. Weisman*, the court held the pledge did not coerce students to engage in a religious exercise and was not "prototypical religious activity." The court held for the governor, finding even with the addition of "under God," the pledge remained a patriotic exercise with a minimal religious component. *Croft v. Perry*, 624 F.3d 157 (5th Cir. 2010).

◆ California teachers led willing students in daily recitations of the Pledge of Allegiance, as permitted by California Education Code Section 52720. A parent claimed the phrase "under God" in the Pledge offended her disbelief in God, interfered with her parental rights and indoctrinated her child. She filed a federal case against her child's school district. The court held for the parent, and the district appealed to the U.S. Court of Appeals, Ninth Circuit. On appeal, she pursued only claims based on state law and the district's policy. The court held not every mention of God or religion by the state is a constitutional violation. **Complete separation of church and state was not required.** Instead, the court found **the Constitution "affirmatively mandates accommodation, not merely tolerance, of all religions, and forbids hostility towards any."** The child had never recited the Pledge but was seeking to prohibit others from doing so. As the Supreme Court found in *Elk Grove Unified School Dist. v. Newdow*, this chapter, "the Pledge is a patriotic exercise designed to foster national unity and pride." Finding that Congress had an "ostensible and predominant purpose" to inspire patriotism, the court held the Pledge was predominantly a patriotic exercise. For this reason, the phrase "one Nation under God" did not convert the Pledge from a patriotic exercise into a religious one. While California Education Code Section 52720 permitted teachers to lead Pledge recitations, the court noted objectors could sit or stand quietly. Under each of the tests used by the Supreme Court in Establishment Clause cases, the court found no violation. "One nation under God" described the Republic, and it was not an expression of the speaker's particular theological beliefs. The court held neither the state law nor the district policy violated the Establishment Clause. *Newdow v. Rio Linda Union School Dist*, 597 F.3d 1007 (9th Cir. 2010).

◆   Florida's Pledge Statute requires Pledge recitation at all public schools and requires that "civilians must show full respect to the flag by standing at attention." The law exempts students from Pledge recitation upon presenting a signed, written statement from a parent. An eleventh-grade student challenged the law in a federal court, asserting speech rights violations. The court agreed with the student. State education officials appealed. The U.S. Court of Appeals, Eleventh Circuit, held the "standing at attention" provision of the law could not be enforced. **There is a well-established constitutional right to remain seated and silent during Pledge recitations.** But the rest of the statute did not violate the First Amendment. Parents had a fundamental right to control their children's upbringing. They could excuse their children from reciting the Pledge, and school officials had to honor this, even if the students wished to recite the Pledge. Parents could refuse to excuse their children, and those rights would also be honored. According to the court, parental rights to interfere with the wishes of their children trumped school officials' rights to interfere on behalf of the school's interest. *Frazier v. Winn*, 535 F.3d 1279 (11th Cir. 2008).

◆   Virginia law provides for the daily, voluntary recitation of the Pledge and placement of the U.S. flag in each public school classroom. Loudoun County Public Schools implemented the provision through a policy allowing students to remain seated quietly during Pledge recitation if their parents objected. An Anabaptist Mennonite parent asserted that the Pledge indoctrinated his children with a "'God and Country' religious worldview" and violated the Mennonite Confession of Faith. He sued the school system, asserting that the inclusion of the words "under God" in the Pledge made it a religious exercise. A federal district court dismissed the case, finding recitation of the Pledge was a secular activity that neither advanced nor inhibited religion. On appeal, the U.S. Court of Appeals, Fourth Circuit, stated **the Establishment Clause does not require separation of church and state "in every and all aspects."** It rejected the assertion that Pledge recitation was like a prayer. "Fleeting references to God" in a classroom were not unconstitutional. The Establishment Clause did not make unconstitutional the daily recitation of the Pledge in a public school. *Myers v. Loudoun County Public Schools*, 418 F.3d 395 (4th Cir. 2005).

◆   The non-custodial father of a California student sued state, local and federal officials in a federal court, claiming that a 1954 Act of Congress adding the words "under God" to the Pledge violated the Establishment Clause. He also claimed a state law requiring elementary schools to open the day with patriotic exercises and the school district's use of daily Pledge recitations violated the Constitution. The court dismissed the case, but the U.S. Court of Appeals, Ninth Circuit, held the 1954 Act and district policy violated the Establishment Clause.

The court denied a motion by the child's mother to intervene in the case, even though a state family court order granted her the child's exclusive legal custody. She alleged that her daughter was a Christian who did not object to recitation of the Pledge. The case reached the U.S. Supreme Court, which rejected the father's claim to unrestricted rights to inculcate his daughter in his atheistic beliefs. His rights could not be viewed in isolation from the mother's parental rights. Nothing done by the mother or the school board impaired his right to instruct the child in his religious views. **State law did not authorize the father to dictate what others could say or not say to his daughter about religion.** The Court reversed the judgment. *Elk Grove Unified School Dist. v. Newdow*, 542 U.S. 1, 124 S.Ct. 2301, 159 L.Ed.2d 98 (2004).

◆ An Alabama student raised his fist and remained silent while the rest of his class recited the Pledge. The principal told him he could not receive a diploma unless he served three days of detention and apologized to the class. The student sued the teacher, principal and school board in a federal court for First Amendment violations. The case reached the U.S. Court of Appeals, Eleventh Circuit, which noted that *West Virginia State Board of Educ. v. Barnette*, 319 U.S. 624 (1943), established a clear right for students to refuse to say the Pledge. Any reasonable person would have known that disciplining the student for refusing to recite the Pledge violated his First Amendment rights. **Officials may only regulate student expression that materially and substantially interferes with school activities or discipline.** Here, the student was being punished for his unpatriotic views, not for being disruptive. *Holloman v. Harland*, 370 F.3d 1252 (11th Cir. 2004).

2. Other Policies

In 2012, the Fourth Circuit Court of Appeals court upheld a South Carolina school district policy that permitted students to earn two credits for off-campus religious instruction received during time they were released from school. Other courts, including the Supreme Court have upheld released-time programs.

◆ South Carolina's Released Time Credit Act allowed public high school students to earn up to two academic credits for religious classes taken during released time. Credits were to be evaluated using similar criteria to those used for evaluating credits of students who transferred from private to public schools. An unaccredited religious organization approached a school district and offered released-time religious courses for academic credit to high school students. The organization made an arrangement by which it would submit the grades of participating students to a Christian school. The school agreed to review and monitor the organization's curriculum, award student course grades and then transfer the grades to the school district. Over the next three years, about 20 of 1,500 students in the school district participated in the program. Parents of two children objected to the program, and they sued the district in a federal court. The court found the program passed Establishment Clause scrutiny. On appeal, the U.S. Court of Appeals, Fourth Circuit, noted the Supreme Court upheld a released-time program in *Zorach v. Clauson*, see Chapter 15, Section IV.F.

The court held the policy had a secular purpose that did not have a primary effect of advancing or inhibiting religion and did not entangle the state with religion. The court found no requirement for the total separation of church and state. In fact, the Supreme Court has long accepted a "policy of benevolent neutrality" that recognizes a range of state religious accommodations. *Zorach* remained good law. The court held the released-time program did not violate the Establishment Clause, because it did nothing more than accommodate student schedules for their outside religious learning. **Public schools have broad but not unlimited discretion to release students to accommodate their wishes to engage in religious instruction.** Failure to accommodate their religious desires could result in an unconstitutional, religiously hostile environment. *Moss v. Spartanburg County School Dist. Seven*, 683 F.3d 599 (4th Cir. 2012).

◆   A Missouri school allowed the Gideons to distribute Bibles to fifth-grade classrooms during the school day in the presence of a teacher or administrator. Objecting parents sued the school district. The school board then passed a new policy on the distribution of literature at school. The case reached the U.S. Court of Appeals, Eighth Circuit, which noted that the amended policy required organizations to obtain approval from the superintendent prior to distributing literature. If material was approved by the superintendent, it could be distributed in front of school offices or at a table in the cafeteria during non-class times. If a request was denied, the policy specified that the organization could appeal to the school board. **The amended policy was reasonable and did not prohibit the district from neutrally facilitating private Bible distributions.** *Roark v. South Iron R-1 School Dist.*, 573 F.3d 556 (8th Cir. 2009).

◆   A Louisiana elementary school principal informed fifth-grade teachers at his school that the Gideon society would distribute Bibles to the fifth-grade class outside his office. He said that while students did not have to take a Bible, he was acting on instructions from the school board. A student accepted a Bible but claimed she felt pressured to do so because of potential name-calling and teasing from peers if she refused. Her parent sued the school board. A court ruled that **the Bible distribution violated the Establishment Clause.** The student feared peers would say she did not believe in God and call her a "devil worshipper" or "Goth" if she refused a Bible. Concern for religious coercion in elementary grades is strong, based on the impressionability of young students. Elementary school students may not fully appreciate the difference between official and private speech, and a school board policy might be misperceived as endorsement. Allowing the Gideons to have access to an elementary school during a school day to hand out Bibles was "unquestionably religious." The board had no secular purpose for the practice, and it created an impression of religious preference that violated the Establishment Clause. *Roe v. Tangipahoa Parish School Board*, Civ. No. 07-2908, 2008 WL 1820420 (E.D. La. 4/22/08).

◆ A New York school district released Catholic and Protestant students to nearby programs at designated times during the school day. Others remained in classrooms with nothing to do until the released students returned. A family claimed the program led to "abusive religious invective directed against those who did not participate and that the district did not adequately train teachers and principals to protect non-participants from the taunts of program participants."

The family sued the district, asserting the "released time" program violated the Establishment Clause by promoting Christianity over other religions and non-religion. The case reached the Second Circuit, which noted the program authorized by New York Education Law permitted districts to release students, with parental permission, for one hour per week for religious instruction. The U.S. Supreme Court had upheld this law in *Zorach v. Clauson*, 343 U.S. 306 (1952). The program used no public funds and involved no on-site religious instruction. Schools simply adjusted their schedules to accommodate student religious needs. **The court rejected the argument that the school's imprimatur was placed on a program of religious instruction and that churches used the schools in support of their religious missions.** Nothing here suggested that the released-time program was administered in a coercive manner. *Pierce v. Sullivan West Cent. School Dist.*, 379 F.3d 56 (2d Cir. 2004).

3. Immunization

School districts and state educational agencies have a compelling state interest in requiring the immunization of all students in an effort to prevent and control communicable diseases.

◆ A West Virginia law required vaccination for diphtheria, polio, rubeola, rubella, tetanus and whooping cough prior to public school admission. An exception was available for those who presented a certificate from a "reputable physician" showing immunization was impossible or improper. A parent obtained a certificate from a child psychiatrist, and her child began to attend a public preschool. The school nurse challenged the certificate, and the parent sued state and county education and health and human services entities and officials.

Finding the board of education and state department of health and human services were entitled to immunity, the court held in their favor. On appeal, the U.S. Court of Appeals, Fourth Circuit, found it was unnecessary to determine the sincerity of the parent's beliefs. As for her federal claims, the Supreme Court had rejected similar arguments in *Jacobson v. Massachusetts*, 197 U.S. 11 (1905) and *Prince v. Massachusetts*, 321 U.S. 158 (1944). In *Prince*, the Court rejected a religious-based claim to be free from compulsory vaccination. According to the court, **the state's wish to prevent the spread of communicable diseases was a compelling interest**. The state law did not unconstitutionally infringe on the parent's religious free exercise rights. Recent cases indicated that religious freedom must yield to the compelling societal interest in controlling contagion through mandatory inoculation. The court held students can be required to undergo immunization before attending school. *Workman v. Mingo County Board of Educ.*, 419 Fed.Appx. 348 (4th Cir. 2011).

◆   A New York high school denied a student's request for a waiver allowing him to attend school without undergoing immunization pursuant to New York Public Health Law Section 2164(9). The section exempts students from state immunization requirements if their parents hold "genuine and sincere religious beliefs" which are contrary to immunization. The student appealed the district's decision to forbid him from competing or practicing with the lacrosse team, which he had done in years past without obtaining an immunization. While the appeal was pending before the state commissioner of education, he sued the district for violating his religious free exercise rights. He claimed that the district's policy had a discriminatory impact on students whose religious convictions prohibited immunization. The court disagreed, finding that **the district's responsibility for ensuring student safety was rationally based**. It was "firmly established that there is no constitutional right to participate in extracurricular sporting activities." The district did not violate the student's equal protection or religious free exercise rights. *Hadley v. Rush Henrietta Cent. School Dist.*, No. 05-CV-6331T, 2007 WL 1231753 (W.D.N.Y. 4/25/07).

◆   New York parents refused immunizations based on their religious beliefs, asserting that their genuine and sincere beliefs fulfilled the legal requirements for a state law religious exemption. School officials met with the family to discuss their position. The parents stated that use of aborted fetal tissue made immunization unholy and violated God's supreme authority. However, they cited no biblical authority for this claim. The school district denied the request.

A federal court noted the parents did not know the basis for their religious objection. The district sought pretrial judgment on that ground. The court found the Second Circuit has emphasized the limited function of the judiciary in determining whether beliefs are to be accorded First Amendment protection. To assess a person's religious sincerity, the Second Circuit used a subjective test under which the person's claim must be given great weight. **So long as the person conceived of his or her beliefs as religious in nature, the subjective test was met.** It was not appropriate to award pretrial judgment when a person's subjective state of mind was at issue. Since the family had presented evidence of a sincerely held religious belief against immunization, the court denied pretrial judgment. *Moses v. Bayport Bluepoint Union Free School Dist.*, No. 05 CV 3808 (DRH) (ARL), 2007 WL 526610 (E.D.N.Y. 2/13/07).

II. USE OF SCHOOL FACILITIES

Courts use a "forum analysis" when considering the use of school facilities by students, clubs and non-students. A "limited public forum" exists whenever a government agency voluntarily opens up its facilities or programs for public use. The "forum" may be a bulletin board, public address system, or the use of classrooms for meetings during noninstructional time. Once a district makes the decision to open a limited public forum, any restriction it places on speech must be reasonable, and there can be no viewpoint discrimination. The nature of the forum determines the limits that may be placed on speech by intended users. For cases on the forum analysis and secular speech, see Chapter Three, Section V.

The No Child Left Behind (NCLB) Act requires school districts to certify to their state educational agencies "that no policy of the local educational agency prevents, or otherwise denies participation in, constitutionally protected prayer in public elementary schools and secondary schools." The requirement is a condition of receiving federal funds and is codified at 20 U.S.C. § 7904.

♦ A Tennessee fourth-grader met with classmates during school recess time to read and discuss the Bible. A parent called to complain about the meetings, and a teacher told students not to meet that day. Later, the school principal told the teacher there was to be no "organized Bible study" during recess, and the fourth-grader got the impression that students could not have any Bible study meetings during recess. Meanwhile, the school board met and issued a policy allowing students and school employees to express religious views "within the parameters of current law." But no parents tried to meet with school officials.

After a media blitz, a district press release acknowledged the principal's belief that students should not have structured activities during recess, as this would defeat the purposes of having a break from the school day. The family sued the superintendent, principal and board in a federal court for constitutional rights violations. After a trial, a jury reached a verdict for the board. When the case reached the U.S. Court of Appeals, Sixth Circuit, it noted **the parents admitted they had filed their lawsuit without any personal knowledge that the principal interrupted the Bible study group**. They based their complaint on the statements of their son and a fourth-grade classmate. Although the court found the lower court had made some errors, it found no reason to disturb the jury verdict or the lower court's post-trial rulings. Ample evidence showed that students still read and discussed the Bible during recess. As this likely led to the verdict for the board of education, the court found no reason for a new trial. *Whitson v. Knox County Board of Educ.*, 468 Fed.Appx. 532 (6th Cir. 2012).

A. Assemblies and School-Sponsored Events

♦ Ohio high school students had a band that performed mostly Christian songs. The father of one student was a school board member and the band's manager. He sought approval for a band performance at a school-wide assembly during school hours. The district superintendent first approved the performance but cancelled it after a school attorney warned her of Establishment Clause problems. The board member appeared in a television interview. He said "together we can bring religion back into the schools." The board then asked another band that performed secular music to perform at the assembly. Band members sued the school district in a federal court, asserting their appearance was cancelled because of disapproval of their Christian message.

The court rejected the band members' claim that the assembly was a public forum in which the district had to maintain viewpoint neutrality. The assembly was not a "forum" of any kind, and for that reason, the district was not subject to any neutrality requirement. The school district "was entitled to exercise editorial control" over it. When the school itself was the speaker, educators were entitled to exercise greater control to assure the views of speakers were not erroneously attributed to the school. **The school district could discriminate**

against the band members because of their Christian religious identity. The court awarded pretrial judgment to the school district. *Golden v. Rossford Exempted Village School Dist.*, 445 F.Supp.2d 820 (N.D. Ohio 2006).

◆   A New Jersey school district hosted after-school talent shows called "Frenchtown Idol." The shows were held at 7:00 p.m. in the school auditorium and were entirely voluntary. Students were invited to develop their own performances at home and received no school credit for participating. Three teachers reviewed all song lyrics, skits, and acts. A student submitted "Awesome God" as her talent show selection. The district superintendent found this inappropriate for the show because of its "overtly religious message and proselytizing nature." She found the song was "the musical equivalent of a spoken prayer." The music teacher informed the student that she could not sing "Awesome God" at the show and offered her two songbooks to select a replacement song, even if it was a religious one. The student sued the board in a federal district court for constitutional rights violations. The court found the talent show was not a "school-sponsored production." **Speech taking place in the show "was the private speech of a student and not a message conveyed by the school itself."** The board could not engage in viewpoint discrimination.

Any restrictions on speech had to be viewpoint neutral and reasonable in view of the purposes served by the forum. Here, the exclusion of speech simply because it was controversial or divisive was "viewpoint discrimination." The court rejected the school board's argument that it had to exclude the song to avoid an Establishment Clause violation. It was unlikely an audience would perceive the student's song to be the expression of anyone's view but her own. The court awarded pretrial judgment to the student. *Turton v. Frenchtown Elementary School Dist. Board of Educ.*, 465 F.Supp.2d 369 (D.N.J. 2006).

B. Student Groups

In Child Evangelism Fellowship of Minnesota v. Minneapolis Special School Dist. No. 1, *below, a federal court held a school's interest in avoiding Establishment Clause violations was no reason to treat private after-school student religious speech differently from other student speech. In* Good News Club v. Milford Cent. School, *533 U.S. 98 (2001), and* Lamb's Chapel v. Center Moriches Union Free School Dist., *508 U.S. 384 (1993) the Supreme Court rejected similar efforts by schools as "viewpoint discrimination."*

◆   A Minnesota school district provided after-school access to transportation and food services to a Child Evangelism Fellowship (CEF) group for eight years. During this time, the CEF held after-school meetings at an elementary school and used district facilities to distribute its advertising. The group was a community partner under a state law on after-school enrichment programs. A school site coordinator became concerned about prayer and proselytizing at CEF meetings, and the group was removed from the after-school program. Attendance for CEF meetings declined from 47 students to five after the action. Meanwhile, other community partners, such as scouting groups and boys/girls clubs, were allowed to remain in the after-school program. The CEF sought a federal court order to set aside the district's action as impermissible viewpoint discrimination. Appeal reached the U.S. Court of Appeals, Eighth Circuit.

A decline in attendance at CEF meetings from 47 to five students in two years convinced the court that the group would suffer irreparable harm in the absence of a court order. **The government may not regulate speech when it is based on the speaker's ideology or opinion.** The CEF had been removed from the after-school program because of its religious viewpoint, while similar groups with a secular message, like the scouting groups, were allowed to remain. This was impermissible viewpoint discrimination, and the court held that excluding the group on this basis was unconstitutional. Speech by CEP members was private, and the Constitution did not prohibit private religious conduct during non-school hours. As it appeared the CEF had a valid First Amendment claim, the court held the group was entitled to preliminary relief. *Child Evangelism Fellowship of Minnesota v. Minneapolis Special School Dist. No. 1*, 690 F.3d 996 (8th Cir. 2012).

◆ A New York City Department of Education (DOE) policy allowed outside groups to use school premises for purposes described by state law, but forbade use of school property for religious services or religious instruction. In 1994, the school board denied an application by a church to use a middle school for Sunday services. A federal district court dismissed an action by the church asserting the denial of its application was discriminatory, and in 1997, the U.S. Court of Appeals, Second Circuit, affirmed the judgment for the board. In 2001, the U.S. Supreme Court held a different New York school district violated the Constitution by excluding a Christian children's organization from its facilities for after-school meetings. See *Good News Club v. Milford Cent. School*, below. After the release of *Good News Club*, the church which had lost the 1994 lawsuit filed a new federal court action against the New York City DOE.

While the church's action was pending, the city board adopted a new rule that "prohibited use of school property for religious worship services, or otherwise using a school as a house of worship." Applying *Good News Club*, the court held for the church. After more district court activity, the case returned to the Second Circuit. It held **the school was a limited public forum from which expression could be excluded only on the basis of reasonable, viewpoint-neutral rules.** The board's new rule prohibited using school facilities for religious worship services and using a school as a house of worship. But the church's application declared that it intended such a use. According to the court, the conduct of religious worship services was "quite different from free expression of a religious point of view, which the Board does not prohibit." Worship services had "the effect of placing centrally, and perhaps even of establishing, the religion in the school." As the exclusion applied to the conduct of worship services and not to the free expression of religious views associated with it, the court found no viewpoint discrimination. The church was not open to the general public and excluded people who were not baptized, excommunicated or who advocated Islam. Rejecting a claim that the rule was hostile to religion, the court upheld the policy. *Bronx Household of Faith v. Board of Educ. of City of New York*, 650 F.3d 30 (2d Cir. 2011).

◆   A New York student submitted a request to use school facilities for private religious club meetings after school hours. The superintendent denied the request, stating that this use of facilities amounted to school support of religious worship. The club sued the school in a federal district court, which issued an order preventing the school from prohibiting the club's use of school facilities. The U.S. Court of Appeals, Second Circuit, later held that the school's denial of access was permissible because it was based on content rather than viewpoint.

The club appealed to the U.S. Supreme Court, which observed that **the nature of the forum determines the limits that a school may place on speech taking place in the forum**. The school had established a limited public forum in which it could reasonably seek to avoid identification with a particular religion. While the school was not required to allow all speech, limits on speech could not be based upon viewpoint and had to be reasonable in light of the purpose of the forum. The school's policy broadly permitted speech about the moral and character development of children. The school had excluded the club from its facilities solely because of its religious viewpoint. This resulted in unconstitutional viewpoint discrimination. "Speech discussing otherwise permissible subjects cannot be excluded from a limited public forum on the ground that the subject is discussed from a religious viewpoint." Club meetings took place after school hours and were not school sponsored. No risk of coercion was present, because students had to obtain permission from their parents to attend meetings. The school failed to show any risk of school endorsement of religion. The Court reversed the judgment. *Good News Club v. Milford Cent. School*, 533 U.S. 98, 121 S.Ct. 2093, 150 L.Ed.2d 151 (2001).

◆   A South Carolina school district charged the Child Evangelism Fellowship of South Carolina fees to use its facilities for Good News Club meetings after school. Many other users had free access to school facilities, including parent-teacher and district organizations, booster clubs, political parties, the SADD, 4-H, FFA and FHA. After paying the district over $1,500 during a two-year period, the Good News Club sought a waiver from the fee. The district denied the request, and the club sued it in a federal district court. The board eliminated a "best interest of the district" waiver provision from the policy. A new provision waived fees for organizations that had used its facilities for at least 20 years. Only scouting groups met this requirement. The case reached the Fourth Circuit, which held the provision unconstitutional. The government may not regulate speech based on its content or the message it conveys. **Once government facilities are opened for private speech, an agency may not discriminate based upon the viewpoint of the speaker.** The "best interest of the district" provision was subjective and "a virtual prescription for unconstitutional decision making." And the revised provision incorporated the viewpoint discrimination built into the earlier "best interest" provision, under which the scouting groups initially got access. *Child Evangelism Fellowship of South Carolina v. Anderson School Dist. Five*, 470 F.3d 1062 (4th Cir. 2006).

◆   An Oregon school district let Boy Scout representatives make presentations during school lunch periods when students were required to be present. School employees helped the Scouts by quieting children, directing attention to the

Scout representative and helping fasten hospital-style bracelets on students with information on Scout meetings. Staff also distributed Scout flyers in classes and put Scout information in school newsletters. An atheist parent objected to these practices and filed a discrimination complaint against the district under an Oregon statute. The state superintendent of public instruction investigated the complaint, but found no substantial evidence of discrimination. The case reached Supreme Court of Oregon, which noted that the case did not involve the Constitution. It instead concerned a state law prohibiting discrimination based on religion (or other protected grounds) in public school programs, services or activities. Class time and lunch periods were "school activities." However, handing out Boy Scout flyers and making presentations did not amount to discrimination against the student, because it did not treat him differently than others because of religion. **The flyers and other information were distributed to all students, with no mention of a religious affiliation.** The lunchroom presentations were neutral, making no mention of religion. The court reversed the judgment. *Powell v. Bunn*, 341 Or. 306, 142 P.3d 1054 (Or. 2006).

C. The Equal Access Act

The federal Equal Access Act (EAA), 20 U.S.C. §§ 4071-4074, governs student use of secondary school facilities during noninstructional time. It makes it unlawful for a public secondary school to deny equal access to facilities, if the school maintains a "limited open forum." A limited open forum exists where student groups have been accorded the right to meet in noncurricular groups on school grounds during noninstructional time.

◆ New York religious club members claimed school officials rejected their application to form a Bible club for budgetary reasons and because the school was "a secular school." After eight months, the club found a volunteer advisor and began to meet on school grounds every two weeks. A school district policy required student groups to be supervised during meetings. While a paid advisor normally served this function, the district determined it could not pay the club's advisor without violating federal law. More than two years after it began meeting at school, the club and its members sued school administrators and accused them of violating the club's right to organize and meet at the school.

The court found **nothing in the EAA is to be construed to authorize the expenditure of public funds beyond the "incidental cost of providing space for student-initiated meetings."** The school district had altered its policy by requiring an unpaid volunteer, but nothing in the EAA required "incidental costs" to be uniform. Since the change in policy meant an advisor's stipend was "not a necessary, subordinate cost of meeting," the court found the claim for a paid advisor would require expending public funds beyond what was "incidental." As a result, the district prevailed on the EAA claim. Additional challenges by the students under the Free Exercise and Free Speech clauses also failed. The court asked the parties to submit evidence to help it to resolve the remaining Equal Protection Clause claim. *Youth Alive v. Hauppauge School Dist.*, No. 08-CV-1068 (NGG)(ALC), 2011 WL 4628751 (E.D.N.Y. 9/30/11).

◆   A Nebraska high school student wanted permission to begin a Christian Club. The school permitted its students to join, on a voluntary basis, a number of groups and clubs that met after school. Each of these clubs had faculty sponsors. However, the student who wished to start the Christian Club did not have a faculty sponsor. School administrators denied her request because she did not have a sponsor and because they believed a religious club at the school would violate the Establishment Clause. The student sued the school board and administrators in a federal district court. She alleged a violation of the EAA.

The court held for the school, holding the other clubs related to the school's curriculum and thus, the school did not have a "limited open forum" as defined by the EAA. Appeal reached the U.S. Supreme Court, which stated the other clubs did not relate to the school's curriculum. **The school had to provide a limited open forum to all students wishing to participate in groups.** The EAA provided that schools could limit activities that substantially interfered with their orderly conduct. The Court also stated **the EAA did not violate the Establishment Clause because it had a secular purpose and limited the role of teachers who work with religious clubs**. The Court held the school had violated the EAA. *Board of Educ. of Westside Community School v. Mergens*, 496 U.S. 226, 110 S.Ct. 2356, 110 L.Ed.2d 191 (1990).

◆   A Minnesota gay tolerance organization claimed a school district violated the EAA by denying it access to school facilities enjoyed by other noncurricular groups like cheerleading and a synchronized swimming club. A federal court granted the organization's request for preliminary relief, finding cheerleading and synchronized swimming, like the tolerance group, were "noncurricular."

On appeal, the U.S. Court of Appeals, Eighth Circuit, found a limited open forum exists under the EAA when at least one noncurriculum-related group is allowed to meet on school grounds during non-instructional time. It agreed with the gay tolerance group that cheerleading and the synchronized swimming club were not curriculum related. The school offered no courses for these activities, and they were not required for any course. Accordingly, the gay tolerance group could use the same facilities. A school district could categorize cheerleading and synchronized swimming classes as "curriculum related" by awarding P.E. credits. A more drastic option would be to "wipe out all of its noncurriculum related student groups and totally close its forum." *Straights and Gays for Equality v. Osseo Area Schools-Dist. No. 279*, 471 F.3d 908 (8th Cir. 2006).

The case returned to the lower court, which issued a permanent order for the gay tolerance club to have the same access to meetings, communications and other school facilities as recognized curricular groups. The district appealed again to the Eighth Circuit, which affirmed the judgment for the organization. **Placement of favored student groups as student government subgroups did not automatically make them "curriculum related."** This would make it far too easy for a school to circumvent the EAA. *Straights and Gays for Equality v. Osseo Area Schools-Dist. No. 279*, 540 F.3d 911 (8th Cir. 2008).

◆   A Washington school district required student clubs to submit their proposals for official recognition to the Associated Student Body (ASB) council for approval. Students attempted to form a Bible club for several years and submitted three different applications. The ASB denied the application based on the club's proposal to make announcements over the public address system and decorate the school in a biblical theme. The ASB later rejected applications by the club based on its name – "Truth," and its restriction of voting membership to those who professed belief in the Bible and Jesus Christ. After the ASB voted down a second application, the club sued the school district and school officials. A federal court awarded pretrial judgment to the district, finding club membership restrictions were a legitimate reason to deny recognition.

The club appealed to the Ninth Circuit, which ordered the district court to reconsider several claims. It noted that many of the 30 ASB-recognized student clubs had selective membership criteria, including the Earth Club, Gay-Straight Alliance and National Honor Society. Significantly, two honor clubs at the school had gender-exclusive memberships. **The Bible club's membership restrictions inherently excluded non-Christians in violation of the district's non-discrimination policies, making denial of recognition consistent with the EAA.** The club did not show the district's non-discrimination policy restricted ASB status on the basis of religion or the content of speech. To the extent that the district allowed waivers to other groups, there remained an issue of fact to consider. The court reversed and remanded the case for further review. *Truth v. Kent School Dist.*, 542 F.3d 634 (9th Cir. 2008).

D. Non-Student Use

◆   The Good News Club (GNC) held after-school evangelical programs for elementary school students in public schools. Students could only participate if they had prior written parental permission. Meetings were free and students did not raise funds for the GNC. A Virginia school board adopted a new facilities use policy in response to legislation allowing the Boy Scouts to use school facilities. The policy gave the superintendent discretion to waive facilities use fees, and the board waived fees for city or county agencies and groups affiliated with those agencies. All school groups and school-sponsored activities were granted a waiver, as were Boy and Girl Scouts and other patriotic organizations. Local charitable organizations and partners were also exempted from the fee. By contrast, the GNC paid $12.50 per hour to use school facilities. After paying to use school facilities for about six months, the GNC sued.

A federal court noted that the **government does not have to allow all speech on all its property at all times, but once it has opened up facilities to private speech, there can be no discrimination based on the viewpoint of a speaker**. Here, the policy gave the superintendent "complete unfettered discretion in deciding who benefits from the fee-waiver." This improperly allowed the superintendent to decide which organizations could have a fee waiver. As a result, the GNC was entitled to a preliminary order waiving the fees. *Child Evangelism Fellowship of Virginia v. Williamsburg-James City County School Board*, Civ. No. 4:08cv4, 2008 WL 3348227 (E.D. Va. 8/08/08).

◆   A Maryland school district allowed many nonprofit groups to distribute flyers to teachers, who then placed them in student cubbies. The district did not let the Child Evangelism Fellowship distribute flyers for student meetings of the

Good News Club through this forum. The club sued. A federal district court granted the club's request for preliminary relief concerning bulletin boards, open houses and other events, but denied its request to distribute flyers based on the risk of an Establishment Clause violation. On appeal, the U.S. Court of Appeals, Fourth Circuit, reviewed evidence that the district had allowed over 225 groups to distribute flyers in 18 months. Other religious groups, such as the Salvation Army, Jewish Community Center and YMCA were allowed to circulate flyers. **Here, the role of teachers in placing the materials in student cubbies during school hours did not create an Establishment Clause risk.** The risk of religious endorsement was no greater than the risk of a perception of hostility toward religion if the group was not allowed to distribute its flyers. The court reversed the lower court order. *Child Evangelism Fellowship of Maryland v. Montgomery County Schools*, 373 F.3d 589 (4th Cir. 2004).

The board then revised its take-home mail policy. Under the revised policy, materials and announcements of five organizations could be approved for display or direct distribution to students. The case returned to the Fourth Circuit, which found that the new policy gave too much discretion to the school district to control the take-home flyer forum. As the new policy did not require viewpoint neutrality, the court again reversed the judgment. The district could restrict the number or content of messages in the forum in a viewpoint-neutral or reasonable manner. It could also eliminate the flyer forum by reserving it solely for government messages. *Child Evangelism Fellowship of Maryland v. Montgomery County Public Schools*, 457 F.3d 376 (4th Cir. 2006).

◆   A New York school district issued regulations allowing social, civic, or recreational uses of its property as well as limited use by political organizations, but provided that the school not be used for religious purposes. An evangelical church sought permission to use school facilities to show a film series on traditional Christian family values. The district denied permission to use its facilities because the film was religious. The church filed a lawsuit in a federal court alleging the district violated the First Amendment. The court found the district's action "viewpoint neutral," and the U.S. Court of Appeals, Second Circuit, agreed. The church appealed to the U.S. Supreme Court, which **held the exclusion of subject matter based on its religious content would impermissibly favor some viewpoints or ideas at the expense of others. Therefore, the regulation discriminated on the basis of viewpoint.**

The exclusion of the church from using school property was not viewpoint neutral. Next, the Court determined that since the film series was not to be shown during school hours and was to be open to those outside the church, the public would not perceive the district to be endorsing religion. Since use of school facilities by the church did not violate the test from *Lemon v. Kurtzman*, permission by the district would not violate the Establishment Clause. The film had a secular purpose, its primary effect did not advance religion, and the showing of the film would not "foster excessive state entanglement with religion." Thus, speech about "family and child related issues" from a religious perspective could be aired on public school grounds. The Court reversed the lower court decisions. *Lamb's Chapel v. Center Moriches Union Free School Dist.*, 508 U.S. 384, 113 S.Ct. 2141, 124 L.Ed.2d 352 (1993).

E. Religious Literature and Symbols

In McCreary County v. American Civil Liberties Union of Kentucky, *545 U.S. 844 (2005), the U.S. Supreme Court struck down the display of the Ten Commandments at county courthouses in Kentucky. In* McCreary County, *the Court held it would look to the events leading up to a Ten Commandments display to assess its constitutionality. It found substantially religious objectives by the Kentucky counties. In another 2005 case,* Van Orden v. Perry, *545 S.Ct. 677 (2005), the Supreme Court allowed a display of the Ten Commandments on a monument at the Texas Capitol. The Court explained the display was "a far more passable use of those texts than was the case in* Stone [v. Graham], *below, where the text confronted elementary school students every day."*

◆   Texas parents claimed two elementary principals violated the constitutional rights of their children. Two incidents involved students trying to distribute pens and pencils with religious messages at school. One child's family claimed her principal told her three times to stop handing out religious materials. The parents sued the principals in a federal court for constitutional violations. The court denied the principals' request for qualified immunity. While the case was pending, the district adopted a new policy allowing students to distribute materials. The families sought pretrial judgment, and the court upheld the new policy. On appeal, the Fifth Circuit upheld the new policy as content-neutral and supported by legitimate school interests. Claims involving the new policy were returned to the lower court. A three-judge Fifth Circuit panel held the principals should be denied qualified immunity. But the opinion was later withdrawn and a majority of the court's judges voted to rehear the case. A new decision was issued stating that "qualified immunity protects government officials from civil damages when their actions could reasonably have been believed to be legal."

For officials to lose their immunity, there must be a violation of a "clearly established" constitutional right. Courts were to ask whether the law clearly put reasonable officials on notice of what conduct was prohibited. To attain "clearly established" status, existing legal authority must "define the contours of the right in question with a high degree of particularity." In this case, **the principals were entitled to qualified immunity as "clearly established law did not put the constitutionality of their actions beyond debate."** *Morgan v. Swanson*, 659 F.3d 359 (5th Cir. 2011).

◆   A suburban Kansas City school district routinely granted requests by non-profits to send informational flyers home with elementary students. When the volume of requests became burdensome, the district published a new procedure that limited "backpack distributions" to nonprofit groups and approved events sponsored by civic groups that directly benefitted the district. Community organizations could take advantage of a one-time opportunity to distribute flyers on two distribution dates near the beginning of the school year. Despite knowing of the one-time distribution rule, a religious group did not timely ask to distribute flyers promoting its summer soccer camp. Although the district permitted the group to post its flyer on the district's website, the group sued the district in a federal district court for constitutional violations. Finding the school district did not have a policy or practice of letting the general public distribute flyers at schools, the court dismissed the group's claims. The group appealed to the U.S. Court of Appeals, Eighth Circuit, which held the group had no constitutional right to free distribution of flyers to public school students.

Contrary to the group's arguments, distribution of flyers was a "limited forum," not a "public forum." As the lower court had correctly observed, **a public entity may impose reasonable, viewpoint-neutral restrictions on speech in a limited public forum**. After requests to distribute flyers were turned down as untimely, the group was allowed to use the district website. Nothing indicated the district's response was based upon or influenced by religion. Since the district adopted reasonable restrictions on the distribution of flyers, the court found no First Amendment violation, and the judgment for the district was affirmed. *Victory Through Jesus Sports Ministry Foundation v. Lee's Summit R-7 School Dist.*, 640 F.3d 329 (8th Cir. 2011).

◆ Las Cruces Public Schools employed an insignia incorporating three crosses that was used on official vehicles and other school district property. A taxpayer challenged the use of the crosses in a federal court, which noted that "Las Cruces" is Spanish for "the crosses." The city had long used crosses in its official insignia, as did non-religious and private entities. The crosses were in a part of the insignia that was less than two inches wide. And the school district did not use the symbol to proselytize. The insignia was locally recognized as having a secular purpose, and it did not advance religion or entangle the government with religion. The taxpayer appealed to the Tenth Circuit, which noted that the insignia was also used by the area chamber of commerce and many private businesses. **The "Establishment Clause enshrines the principle that government may not act in ways that aid one religion, aid all religions or prefer one religion over another."** Of primary importance was whether the government intended to endorse religion or had the effect of endorsing religion. An objective observer would not conclude that the city adopted the logo with the purpose of endorsing Christianity. Compelling evidence established that the symbol was not religious. The policy ensured compliance with Establishment Clause principles, and the court affirmed the lower court judgments. *Weinbaum v. City of Las Cruces, New Mexico*, 541 F.3d 1017 (10th Cir. 2008).

◆ New York City's holiday display policy did not permit creches (nativity scenes). The policy allowed the display of secular holiday symbols, including "Christmas trees, Menorahs, and the Star and Crescent." Displays could not "appear to promote or celebrate any single religion or holiday." The Catholic League for Religious and Civil Rights protested the absence of creches from holiday displays in city schools. After the city refused to change the policy, a Catholic parent of two elementary students sued. She claimed that the policy promoted Judaism and Islam and disapproved of Christianity. After a federal court upheld the policy, the U.S. Court of Appeals, Second Circuit, held the decision to represent Christmas with secular symbols, rather than creches, did not show hostility to Christianity. **The menorah and the star and crescent were religious symbols, but they did not depict a deity while a nativity scene did.** The policy had a secular purpose "to teach the lesson of pluralism."

Promoting tolerance and respect for diverse customs did not violate the Religion Clauses of the First Amendment. The policy avoided a religious message by requiring any symbol or decoration to be displayed simultaneously with others reflecting different beliefs or customs. Objective observers would perceive the promotion of pluralism, not religion. The court affirmed the judgment for the city. *Skoros v. City of New York*, 437 F.3d 1 (2d Cir. 2006).

◆ A Kentucky statute required the posting of the Ten Commandments on the wall of each public school classroom in the state. A group of citizens sought an injunction against the statute's enforcement, claiming it violated the First Amendment's Establishment and Free Exercise Clauses. The Kentucky state courts upheld the statute, finding it was secular and did not advance or inhibit any religion and did not entangle the state with religion. Utilizing the test from *Lemon v. Kurtzman*, **the U.S. Supreme Court struck down the statute. The Court held the posting of the Ten Commandments had no secular purpose.**

Kentucky state education officials insisted the statute served the secular purpose of teaching students the foundation of western civilization and the common law. The Court stated, however, the pre-eminent purpose was plainly religious in nature. **The Ten Commandments undeniably came from a religious text**, despite the legislative recitation of a secular purpose. The Court noted the text of the Commandments was not integrated into a course or study of history, civilization, ethics, or comparative religion, but simply posted to induce children to read, meditate upon, and perhaps, to venerate and obey them. The Court held it made no difference that the cost of posting the commandments was paid for through private funds and that they were not read aloud. *Stone v. Graham*, 449 U.S. 39, 101 S.Ct. 192, 66 L.Ed.2d 199 (1981).

III. LIMITATIONS ON EMPLOYEE RELIGIOUS ACTIVITY

The Free Exercise Clause of the First Amendment provides that Congress shall make no law prohibiting the free exercise of religion. Courts examining the rights of school employees to engage in religious speech follow the First Amendment analysis from Garcetti v. Ceballos *and* Pickering v. Board of Educ., *discussed in Chapter Three, Section II, with the additional consideration of the employee's right to freely exercise religion. For cases involving religious discrimination against employees, see Chapter Eight, Section V.*

◆ A veteran California high school calculus teacher put large banners in his classroom with religious and patriotic slogans. A colleague complained to the school principal, who met with the teacher twice and warned him that expressing a religious viewpoint might make his students feel uncomfortable. Eventually, the school board approved an order directing the teacher to remove the banners and to review district procedures and the state education code. He sued the school district and several officials in a federal district court for state and federal constitutional violations. Agreeing with the teacher, the court held the school district had a limited public forum for teacher speech in their classrooms and had impermissibly limited his speech based on viewpoint.

Appeal reached the U.S. Court of Appeals, Ninth Circuit. It held the lower court had erroneously applied a "pure forum-based analysis." It should have applied public employee speech rights cases such as *Pickering v. Board of Educ.*, 391 U.S. 563 (1968) and *Garcetti v. Ceballos*, 547 U.S. 410 (2006), among others. Applying the *Pickering* line of cases, the court found no basis for ruling for the teacher. The banners plainly conveyed a religious message. The court held **the teacher took advantage of his position to press his views upon "the impressionable and captive minds before him."** He could not promote a religious viewpoint when speaking as a public employee. Since the district acted within constitutional limits when ordering the teacher to take down the banners, it was entitled to judgment. The court returned the case to the district court with instructions to enter judgment for the district and officials. *Johnson v. Poway Unified School Dist.*, 658 F.3d 954 (9th Cir. 2011).

◆   Employees of the Texas Education Agency (TEA) provided support to the state board of education. The board set curricular and graduation requirements for state public schools and determined which textbooks to purchase. TEA staff members were told "not to advocate a particular position on curriculum issues" and to refrain from participating in matters under deliberation. A TEA Director of Science for the Curriculum Division directed the state K-12 science program. Her supervisor instructed her not to communicate with people outside the TEA regarding the state education board's science curriculum deliberations. But she disobeyed the order when she forwarded an email to 36 teachers and teacher organizations concerning a presentation critical of teaching creationism in public schools. Finding the director had violated TEA's neutrality policy, the supervisor recommended employment termination, and she resigned.

The director sued the TEA and state education commissioner in a federal district court, which held for the TEA and the commissioner. On appeal, the U.S. Court of Appeals, Fifth Circuit, held the First Amendment mandates government neutrality among various religions and non-religion. The director claimed the TEA neutrality policy established religion by deeming creationism to be a subject matter for the board to consider in setting the state science curriculum. But the court found no evidence of religious advancement. **A TEA policy against employee speech about possible subjects to be included in the curriculum did not primarily advance religion.** The court held the policy preserved the role of TEA staff to support the board. As the court found no circumstances under which a TEA director's inability to speak about potential subjects for the state curriculum could be perceived as state endorsement of religion, it affirmed the judgment. *Comer v. Scott*, 610 F.3d 929 (5th Cir. 2010).

◆   A Wisconsin guidance counselor prayed with students, destroyed school literature about condoms, and ordered literature advocating abstinence without her supervisor's permission. The school superintendent later informed her that her contract would not be renewed. The counselor sued, asserting that her non-renewal was based on hostility to her religious beliefs. Her case reached the U.S. Court of Appeals, Seventh Circuit, which held she was let go because of her conduct, not her religious beliefs. In the court's view, it was easy to understand the imprudence of retaining a guidance counselor who threw out school materials and substituted her own without asking permission. U.S. Department of Education guidelines prohibit teachers, administrators and other school employees from "encouraging or discouraging prayer, and from actively participating in such activity with students." Finding that **"teachers and other public school employees have no right to make the promotion of religion a part of their job description,"** the court held that the Constitution is not a license for uncontrolled teacher expression. *Grossman v. South Shore Public School Dist.*, 507 F.3d 1097 (7th Cir. 2007).

◆   A South Dakota school district let the Good News Club hold meetings on school grounds under its community use policy. A teacher attended the club's first meeting at her school. The principal told her she could not attend future meetings, warning that her participation might be perceived as an establishment of religion. She sued. A court held that the district had engaged in viewpoint discrimination by excluding her from meetings. While the district could bar the teacher from club meetings at her own school, no Establishment Clause concerns applied to meetings at other schools. The court issued a permanent order allowing the teacher to attend meetings at schools other than her own. The U.S. Court of Appeals, Eighth Circuit, held that **the teacher's participation in after-school club meetings was private speech that did not put the district at risk of violating the Establishment Clause**. Nonparticipants left the building by the time meetings were held, and student participants had parental permission. No reasonable observer would perceive the teacher's presence at club meetings in her own school or any other school to be a state endorsement of religion. The court reversed the decision in part and affirmed it in part, holding for the teacher on all issues appealed. *Wigg v. Sioux Falls School Dist. 49-5*, 382 F.3d 807 (8th Cir. 2004).

◆   A Pennsylvania instructional assistant often wore a small crucifix to work over a six-year period without disruption or controversy. Her supervisor did not notice the crucifix until "someone in the teachers union" reported it. The district suspended the assistant for violating its policy and a state law prohibiting public school teachers from wearing religious items while performing their duties. She sued for reinstatement and a declaration that the policy was unconstitutional.

A federal court noted that district policy forbade employees from wearing religious symbols, but allowed nonreligious jewelry. The district's policy was overtly averse to religion, as it punished religious items while "permitting its employees to wear jewelry containing secular messages or no messages at all." **The policy constituted impermissible viewpoint discrimination because it was directed only at religious speech.** It had a discriminatory purpose and effect that was not justified by any government interest. The court rejected the district's arguments based on potential criminal liability and threatened violations of the Establishment Clause. The section did not apply to the instructional assistant, since she was not a certificated teacher. No reasonable observer would view the district as endorsing religion if it allowed employees to wear unobtrusive crucifixes or similar jewelry. The assistant was entitled to reinstatement and an order preventing the district from enforcing its policy. *Nichol v. ARIN Intermediate Unit 28*, 268 F.Supp.2d 536 (W.D. Pa. 2003).

IV. FINANCIAL ASSISTANCE AND VOUCHER PROGRAMS

The U.S. Supreme Court upheld an Ohio law authorizing public funding of a private school voucher program in Zelman v. Simmons-Harris. *The case may be contrasted to cases like* Committee for Public Educ. and Religious Liberty v. Nyquist, *413 U.S. 756 (1973), where the Court held direct aid from states to sectarian schools "in whatever form is invalid."*

While Zelman *found no Establishment Clause violation in the Ohio program, the case did not resolve the constitutionality of voucher programs under state constitutional provisions, which is for state courts to decide.*

◆ A Tennessee education board voted to eliminate an alternative school and the jobs of three teachers – one of whom also served as the principal. Two weeks later, it voted to contract with a religious school for public alternative school services. The teachers sued the board and its members for constitutional rights violations. A federal court held the teachers had no standing to challenge the contract. On appeal, the U.S. Court of Appeals, Sixth Circuit, explained that a party seeking to file a federal action must show "an injury in fact" that is "concrete and particularized," "actual or imminent" and "fairly traceable" to the actions of the party being sued. It must further be shown that a court order can remedy the injury being alleged. A party must present claims that are more than simply generalized grievances. While the teachers asserted the injury of losing their jobs, they did not identify an injury. They had a close relationship with their students, but could not pursue claims on behalf of them. Unlike the district court, the Sixth Circuit held **two of the teachers, as resident taxpayers, had municipal taxpayer standing and could pursue an Establishment Clause claim**. In reversing the standing decision as to the two teachers who were resident taxpayers, the court found the board "should not be able to evade suit simply because it was cheaper to violate the Constitution." *Smith v. Jefferson County Board of School Commissioners*, 641 F.3d 197 (6th Cir. 2011).

◆ The Ohio General Assembly adopted the Ohio Pilot Scholarship Program in 1995 in response to a federal court order to remedy problems in the Cleveland School District. The program made vouchers of up to $2,500 available for Cleveland students to attend public or private schools, including schools with religious affiliations. The state supreme court struck down the program on state constitutional grounds in 1999. Legislators cured these deficiencies and reauthorized the program for 1999-2000. A new lawsuit was filed in a federal court, which permanently enjoined the state from administering the program.

The Sixth Circuit affirmed the judgment, and state officials appealed. The U.S. Supreme Court held the program allowed government aid to reach religious institutions only because of the deliberate choices of the individual recipients. Any incidental advancement of religion, or perceived endorsement of a religious message, was attributable to the individual recipients, not to the government. The New York program struck down in *Committee for Public Educ. and Religious Liberty v. Nyquist*, 413 U.S. 756 (1973), gave benefits exclusively to private schools and the parents of private school enrollees. Ohio's program offered aid directly to a broad class of individual recipients defined without regard to religion. **Where government aid is religiously neutral and provides direct assistance to a broad class of citizens that in turn directs funds to religious schools through genuine and independent private choices, the program is not readily subject to an Establishment Clause challenge.** *Zelman v. Simmons-Harris,* 536 U.S. 639, 122 S.Ct. 2460, 153 L.Ed.2d 604 (2002).

◆   Arizona's Scholarships for Pupils with Disabilities allowed students with disabilities to attend a private school or a school outside their residence school district. Legislators also enacted a Displaced Pupils Choice Grant Program, which permitted children in foster care to attend a private school of their choice. Under the Disabilities Program, parents of a disabled student could apply for scholarships if they were not satisfied with their child's progress in a public school the prior year. After the parents selected a school, they received checks from the state that were restrictively endorsed to their school of choice. The program allowed both sectarian and nonsectarian schools to participate, and schools were "not required to alter their creed, practices or curriculum" to do so. Objectors to the programs sued the state superintendent of public instruction for violating two provisions of the state constitution.

On review, the Supreme Court of Arizona explained that Arizona Constitution Article 9, Section 10, the "Aid Clause," has no equivalent under the U.S. Constitution. The Aid Clause was "aimed at placing restrictions on the disbursement of public funds to specified institutions, both religious and secular." The court distinguished the voucher programs from a state tax credit program for contributions to school tuition organizations. The Aid Clause was primarily designed to protect the public fisc and public schools, and **the scholarship programs provided aid to private schools in violation of the Aid Clause.** *Cain v. Horne,* 220 Ariz. 77, 202 P.3d 1178 (Ariz. 2009).

◆   Opponents of Florida's Opportunity Scholarship Program (OSP) sued state officials in a Florida court for violating three state constitutional provisions. The Supreme Court of Florida held that the OSP was unconstitutional under the "no aid" provision, Article I, Section Three of the Florida Constitution. The OSP violated the state constitution's uniformity requirement by diverting public funds into "separate private systems parallel to and in competition with the free public schools that are the sole means set out in the Constitution for the state to provide for the education of Florida's children." Paying tuition for students to attend private schools was a substantially different manner than the one prescribed in the state constitution. OSP funding was taken directly from each school district's appropriated funds, reducing the funds available to the district. No OSP provision ensured private schools were "uniform." While public schools were held accountable for teaching certain state standards and to teach all basic subjects, private schools were not required to do so and could even hire teachers who did not possess bachelor's degrees. **"Because voucher payments reduce funding for the public education system, the OSP by its very nature undermines the system of 'high quality' free public schools."** The court struck down the OSP program. *Bush v. Holmes,* 919 So.2d 392 (Fla. 2006).

◆ Swan's Island, Maine, had no high school of its own and did not contract with another district to educate resident secondary students as permitted by state law. Two Swan's Island students went to a private religious school at their parents' expense. Swan's Island then adopted a policy for a monthly tuition subsidy for year-round residents with children enrolled in private high schools. The parents received subsidies for a full school year, until the Maine Attorney General's Office found the policy violated state law. The town suspended the program, and the parents sued Maine officials in the state court system. A trial court held for the state. On appeal, **the Maine Supreme Judicial Court held state law barred the payment of any public funds, whether state or municipal, from reaching sectarian schools**. The legislature had considered and rejected a bill that would have repealed the law. This reaffirmed the state's public policy against the public funding of sectarian schools. The court affirmed the judgment. *Joyce v. State of Maine*, 951 A.2d 69 (Me. 2008).

◆ In 1980, Maine restricted public funding to nonsectarian schools for school districts that contract with private schools to educate their high school students. The state's highest court upheld the provision against a challenge by parents who sought public funding for their children to attend religious schools. *Bagley v. Raymond School Dep't*, 782 A.2d 172 (Me. 1999). After the Supreme Court issued *Zelman v. Simmons-Harris*, this chapter, another group of parents sought court approval of public funding for their children to attend religious schools. The U.S. Court of Appeals, First Circuit, held that even after *Zelman*, **the Constitution did not require Maine to fund tuition at sectarian schools**. *Eulitt v. State of Maine*, 386 F.3d 344 (1st Cir. 2004).

   Another group of parents filed a challenge to the provision in a state court. The case reached the Supreme Court of Maine, which found the state law was not motivated by religious discrimination, and held the provision did not burden or inhibit the free exercise of religion in any constitutionally significant way. *Anderson v. Town of Durham*, 895 A.2d 944 (Me. 2006).

◆ The Colorado Opportunity Contract Pilot Program was enacted to meet the educational needs of low-achieving students in the state's highest poverty areas. Participation was mandatory for any district that had at least eight schools with poor academic ratings. Voucher opponents sued the state in a case that reached the Supreme Court of Colorado. It found local boards retained no authority under the pilot program to determine which students were eligible to participate or how much funding to devote to it. In fact, the program deprived school districts of all local control over instruction. And it violated the local control provision of the state constitution by requiring districts to pay funds, including some locally raised tax revenues, to parents who paid them to nonpublic schools in the form of vouchers. The program violated the state constitution, as **"local control" required school districts to maintain discretion over any instruction paid for with locally raised funds**. *Owens v. Colorado Congress of Parents, Teachers and Students*, 92 P.3d 933 (Colo. 2004).

CHAPTER FIVE

Academic Practices

I. CURRICULUM AND GRADING

Educators have considerable discretion in academic, curricular and grading matters. Courts do not subject official decisions in these areas to close judicial scrutiny. For religious challenges to curriculums, please see Chapter Four, Section I.B.1. Constitutional challenges on secular grounds appear in Chapter Three, Section IV.B. Testing is considered in Section IV of this chapter. For cases involving students with disabilities see Chapter Six.

A. Curriculum

◆ A West Virginia school board offered single-sex education in middle schools for reading, math, social studies and science. As the board sought to expand the program, the parent of three sixth-grade girls asked a federal court to halt its implementation for 2012-13. In her view, the single-sex program violated the Equal Protection Clause and Title IX of the 1972 Education Amendments. The court noted 2006 federal regulations interpreted Title IX as allowing single-sex programs that are "completely voluntary." Schools offering

175

such programs must offer "a substantially equal coeducational class or extracurricular activity in the same subject." Classes or extracurricular activities must be "substantially equal" and schools are subject to periodic evaluations to assure that single-sex classes or activities are based on genuine justifications.

While the regulations did not define "completely voluntary," the court held parents had to affirmatively assent before a child could be placed in single-sex classrooms. **The district's opt-out opportunity was held insufficient to meet the requirement that single-sex classes be "completely voluntary."** Also, the district did not offer the opt-out until just before the school year began. This suggested to the court that any choice was not voluntary. In the court's view, the parent was likely to succeed on the legal merits of her case, and her children would suffer irreparable harm if no order was issued. By contrast, the district would suffer little harm by reinstating the coeducational programs it had operated for years prior to 2010. Since the order sought by the parents would prevent a continuing violation of Title IX, the court held in her favor. *Doe v. Wood County Board of Educ.*, 888 F.Supp.2d 771 (S.D. W.Va. 2012).

◆ After review by a school committee, the Seattle School Board selected the "Discovering" math textbook series. Before voting, the board considered emails from teachers and community members who stated various opinions. Some objected due to "an experimental, inquiry-based method of teaching math" that allegedly did not help all students. Although the Washington Superintendent of Public Instruction had approved the Discovering series earlier in the year, a curriculum study by the state board of education found the series was "mathematically unsound" and overemphasized calculator use. After hearing public testimony at three meetings, the board approved the series by a 4-3 vote.

Three taxpayers filed a state superior court action against the board. The court upheld the challenge, and the board appealed. The state court of appeals first noted that the challengers carried "a heavy burden," because the decision was based on complex and technical facts at the heart of the board's expertise. The board was aware of the criticism of the series but also knew that some mathematicians viewed the series favorably. The adoption committee, which included many experienced district teachers, had recommended the series. The court said its role was not to weigh their credibility. **As there was no showing that the board failed to give due and honest regard to the recommendation to approve the text series, the court reversed the judgment.** *Porter v. Seattle School Dist. No. 1*, 248 P.3d 1111 (Wash. Ct. App. 2011).

◆ A Louisiana school board approved a middle school principal's request to try single-sex classes for a term as "an experiment for his doctoral dissertation." He collected data indicating significant academic improvement and a decline in behavioral problems in the single-sex classes. Impressed with the numbers and unaware of inaccurate data reporting, the board approved single-sex education at all district middle schools. A parent who objected to single-sex classes for his children sued the board for violating regulations implementing Title IX of the Education Amendments of 1972, and the Equal Protection Clause. A federal court held the principal "fudged a bunch of the numbers" to conclude that single-sex education improved student academic performance. While the U.S.

Department of Education (DOE) authorized single-sex education options in 2006 guidance, a condition for this was that instruction be fully voluntary.

There was evidence that after voluntary single-sex classes were offered, the principal called parents who had selected coed classes and convinced many of them to return their children to single-sex classrooms. The parent claimed that the coed classes were "disproportionately filled with students with special needs and Individual Education Plans (IEPs)." Others said the school "threatened to abandon their child's IEP if they elected the single-sex class." Although the court found many problems with the program and "an extreme lack of oversight," it found no intentional discrimination, and denied injunctive relief. But the board was ordered to follow a 10-step plan to implement single-sex education. This required better notice to parents about single-sex education, more coed classes, and better gender distribution of students and IEP services. **Objecting parents were allowed to move their children to coeducational public schools.** The Fifth Circuit held that as the school year was almost over, the injunctive order was moot. But the claims for monetary damages were not moot, and the case was returned to the district court to review claims under the DOE regulations as well as the remaining constitutional and statutory claims. *Doe v. Vermilion Parish School Board*, 421 Fed.Appx. 366 (5th Cir. 2011).

◆ Section 51210 of the California Education Code requires not less than 200 minutes of physical education (PE) in elementary schools every 10 school days. A parent claimed his child's school district refused to comply with this requirement, and he said the state department of education (CDE) permitted the district to avoid its duty. He sued the district and CDE in the state court system. But a state superior court held Education Code Section 51210 did not create a mandatory duty. Appeal reached the Court of Appeal of California, which held the repeated use of the word "shall" in Section 51210 indicated its mandatory nature. Having decided there was a mandatory duty for the district to provide 200 minutes of PE each 10 school days, the court held the student and his father had shown they had special interests sufficient to confer standing on them.

Section 51210 was enacted to protect student health and welfare and to establish a common curriculum to encourage districts to develop programs incorporating education guidelines and standards. Among the legislative findings was that "most children lead inactive lives." Moreover, the percentage of overweight children had more than doubled in recent years. Based on these findings, the court found the student and parent had sufficient interests to pursue the case. A final claim by the CDE was that the family had to exhaust available administrative remedies before a court could compel agency action through a writ of mandate. But the CDE did not specify any grievance procedure that was available to them. The case was returned to the superior court so the family could make a more complete request for relief. *Doe v. Albany Unified School Dist.*, 190 Cal.App.4th 668, 118 Cal.Rptr.3d 507 (Cal. Ct. App. 2010).

◆ A Washington fourth-grade student was part of his school district's highly capable program. At his parents' request, he was allowed to skip to grade six the next school year. In the next three years, the student completed grades six, seven and eight. His father then objected to a proposal to promote him to grade nine and suggested that he enroll in one eighth-grade class. He asked the school district to designate his son a ninth-grader for academic purposes, and an eighth-grader for athletic and estimated graduation date purposes. After the school district denied the father's request, he sued the district in a state court. The court held for the district, and appeal reached the Court of Appeals of Washington.

On appeal, the father stated the athletic issue had been resolved. His only concern was his son's academics and his wish for a 2013 graduation date. The court found the question was not "ripe" and thus inappropriate for a court order. Under the state constitution, the student had a right to be "amply provided with an education" through a general and uniform system of public schools. While state public schools were open to qualified individuals ages 5-21, the court found this did not translate into a constitutional right to remain in public school until age 18 via grade retention. Graduation depended upon completion of required credits, and many events could affect a district's decision to graduate a student. **School boards were vested with the final responsibility for providing student opportunities and creating policies to ensure the quality of education programs.** Promoting the student to grade nine and assigning him an estimated graduation date of 2012 did not violate any constitutional rights. *McColl v. Sequim School Dist.*, 152 Wash.App. 1066 (Wash. Ct. App. 2009).

B. Bilingual Education

In Lau v. Nichols, 414 U.S. 563 (1974), the U.S. Supreme Court held non-English-speaking students in San Francisco schools could claim protection under Title VI of the Civil Rights Act of 1964. Non-English speakers cannot be denied meaningful opportunities to participate in educational programs.

◆   As a result of claims by African-American students against nine Texas school districts in 1971, broad aspects of the Texas educational system were placed under federal court supervision. Mexican-American students intervened in the case in 1972, and the nine districts were required to provide them equal educational opportunities. The Texas Education Agency was ordered to study the needs of all minority students in the state. In 1981, the court ordered state officials to offer bilingual instruction to limited-English proficient students, based on "*de jure* discrimination" and violation of the Equal Educational Opportunities Act (EEOA). The U.S. Court of Appeals, Fifth Circuit, reversed the judgment in 1982, expressing concern that no school districts were parties.

In 2006, the Mexican-American intervenors reopened the case, and the court found violations of both the 1971 order and the EEOA. It ordered the state to create a new monitoring system and language programming to fulfill EEOA requirements. State officials appealed to the Fifth Circuit, which found a new monitoring system and secondary LEP language program for all the districts would require an extraordinary effort in a very short time. To prove a violation of the 1971 order, the intervenors would have to show the action flowed from a *de jure* segregated system. This was not shown, as **Texas at no time separated Anglo and Mexican-Americans by law.** Because *de jure* segregation of Mexican-American students was not shown, the 1971 order could not be enforced by the intervenors. As for an EEOA violation, the lower court had failed to address the instructions issued in 1982. At that time, the Fifth Circuit found little reason to resolve the case on a statewide basis. **Problems varied by district and would by necessity present local questions for each individual district.** Since the issues raised by the intervenors could not have been properly addressed in the absence of the individual school districts, the court returned the case to the district court. *U.S. v. State of Texas*, 601 F.3d 354 (5th Cir. 2010).

◆ Nine California school districts challenged a state board policy requiring English language testing of limited English proficient (LEP) students on state tests. According to the districts, English language testing of LEP students was not "valid and reliable" as required by the No Child Left Behind (NCLB) Act, and they faced sanctions for failing to meet adequate yearly progress. The Court of Appeal of California noted that **the NCLB Act did not require native language testing of LEP students.** Students had to be provided reasonable accommodations on assessments. To the extent practicable, assessments were to be "in the language and form most likely to yield accurate data on what such students know and can do in academic concern areas, until such students have achieved English language proficiency." In 1998, California voters had enacted Proposition 227 to require English instruction of public school students with very limited exceptions to promote the rapid development of English for LEP students. The NCLB Act "invites each state to make its own judgment call in fashioning a testing program for its LEP students" consistent with NCLB Act requirements. State board decisions were entitled to deference, and the board had engaged in a deliberative policymaking process to determine how LEP students would be tested. *Coachella Valley Unified School Dist. v. State of California*, 176 Cal.App.4th 93, 98 Cal.Rptr.3d 9 (Cal. Ct. App. 2009).

◆ After California enacted Proposition 227, LEP students brought a federal court action against state officials, asserting Proposition 227 violated the Equal Protection Clause. The court found no constitutional violation. On appeal, **the Ninth Circuit found nothing in the record indicating that Proposition 227 was race-motivated.** The state's bilingual education system did not operate to remedy identified patterns of racial discrimination but was instead intended to improve the educational system. The reallocation of political authority represented by Proposition 227 addressed educational, not racial issues, and the fact that most of California's LEP student population was Latino did not create a viable equal protection claim. The court affirmed the judgment. *Valeria v. Davis*, 307 F.3d 1036 (9th Cir. 2002).

◆ New Mexico enacted the Bilingual Multicultural Education Act (BMEA) to ensure equal educational opportunities for students by making local school districts eligible for bilingual instruction. To qualify for the program, districts had to provide for the educational needs of linguistically and culturally different students, including Native American students. The Albuquerque Public School District operated the Alternative Language Services (ALS) program pursuant to the BMEA, providing bilingual education for limited English proficient students. The U.S. Department of Education's Office for Civil Rights, which oversees Title VI compliance, reviewed the ALS program and entered into an agreement for corrective action with the district. The agreement established new procedures for identifying and serving limited English proficient students.

A group of Albuquerque students in the ALS program sued the district in a federal court, asserting the BMEA and ALS program were discriminatory, since they classified and placed students on the basis of race or national origin. The case reached the U.S. Court of Appeals, Tenth Circuit. It held **the BMEA did not violate the Equal Protection Clause or Title VI.** There was no evidence that the district violated the agreement with the Office for Civil Rights by forcing students to participate in the ALS program without notice or consent. The ALS program and the BMEA did not violate the federal Equal Education Opportunity Act's mandate to take appropriate action to overcome language barriers that impede equal participation by its students. *Carbajal v. Albuquerque Public School Dist.*, 43 Fed.Appx. 306 (10th Cir. 2002).

C. Grading

In Regents of Univ. of Michigan v. Ewing, *474 U.S. 214 (1985), the Supreme Court held courts may not override academic decisions unless there is "such a substantial departure from accepted academic norms as to demonstrate that the person or committee responsible did not actually exercise professional judgment." An Ohio court held a school district did not have to change grades even though the teachers who assigned them had deviated from school policy.*

◆   A Texas student-athlete enrolled in an engineering graphics class but rarely attended. Based on discussions with the family and an expectation that the student would improve his performance, the teacher issued him a passing grade for the first marking period. A few days later, the student dropped the class, and the teacher changed the grade to fail. By that time, report cards had already been issued showing the student had passed. After the student's parents complained, the teacher was told to reinstate the passing grade. He refused and later claimed an assistant principal forced him to illegally change the grade to keep the student eligible for sports. The teacher said he reported the grade change and illegal attendance records to a board member, the area superintendent and the school district's office of professional responsibility. He stated that as a result of his reporting, he was unjustly reprimanded, given a negative performance evaluation and forced to obtain a lower-paying position in another district.

The teacher sued the district in a state court under the Texas Whistleblower Protection Act (WPA). Appeal reached the state court of appeals, where he claimed he had reported a violation of the state's "no pass, no play" rule. But the court agreed with the district that the teacher never made such a report. He did not assert that the student had participated in any games or events when he should have been suspended. The teacher also claimed the district violated a state penal code section prohibiting tampering with a governmental record. The court held this claim failed because **student report cards are required by the education code and are not deemed "government records" under the penal code.** As a result, the court affirmed the judgment for the district. *Wilson v. Dallas Independent School Dist.*, 376 S.W.3d 319 (Tex. Ct. App. 2012).

◆   A New Jersey student failed her freshman English class. She also claimed her English teacher made an inappropriate remark to her in the presence of other students and a teacher's aide. An informal meeting was held, at which the student and her family were informed that the failing grade would stand and she would have to go to summer school to obtain a passing grade. She went to summer school, earned a passing grade, and was promoted to the next grade. Instead of filing an appeal with the state commissioner of education to contest the failure, the student's attorney engaged in negotiations with school officials to review the matter. When a petition was filed near the end of the next school year, it was dismissed as untimely. **A state appellate court refused to interfere with the decision, noting that local educators had informed the student of the correct appeal procedure.** *H.H. v. Board of Educ. of Township of Wall,* 2011 WL 499859 (N.J. Super. Ct. App. Div. 2/15/11).

◆   An Ohio student just missed A grades in two advanced placement classes. She said her calculus teacher improperly averaged grades and claimed her writing teacher incorrectly weighted grades. This violated a general school board policy requiring that full-year grades be weighted and semester grades be averaged. After the teachers declined to change the grades, the student and her father met with the principal and later with the school superintendent, school board and counsel. The board heard the teachers' explanations for assigning the grades and then approved the grades. The state education department denied the student relief, and she filed a state court complaint. Before the court, the calculus teacher said he had used his grading method for years and had told the principal when he began to use it. The writing teacher also stated that she had obtained approval for her grading policy and had been using it for about 10 years. A judgment was issued for the school district, and the student appealed.

The Court of Appeals of Ohio held that to obtain relief, the student had to establish a "clear legal right." But she only cited state laws and rules requiring schools to keep records and issue diplomas. Under either version of the grading guidelines, **the court found teachers had discretion to create alternative grading systems and report them to the principal**. The board had followed its policies by discussing the matter with the family, and the principal and superintendent reviewed the case. Both teachers used the same grading method for all their students and did not treat the student differently from others. As she did not show her grades were unfair or arbitrary, her request for a court order had been properly dismissed. *Hingel v. Board of Educ. of Austintown Local School Dist.,* No. 08 MA 258, 2009 WL 4547721 (Ohio Ct. App. 11/23/09).

◆   An Arkansas middle school student participated in his school's accelerated reader program, in which students could win prizes or awards by reading books and taking tests based on them. He stated that he read four of five books in the *Harry Potter* series because of the high points assigned to the books. After the student scored 100% on each of the tests, his reading teacher accused him of cheating, stating it was impossible to read the books in one week. The student's classroom teacher agreed and confronted him about cheating. The student's mother sought reinstatement of the scores. The school principal permitted only one score to be reinstated, finding no obligation to reinstate the others under program incentive rules. The student sought a court order requiring the principal and teachers to reinstate the cancelled scores, apologize publicly and by letter, and prevent them from "further humiliating and using coercive tactics."

The court dismissed the case and awarded the school district $1,500 in attorneys' fees. The student appealed to the state supreme court, which held that **no law compelled school officials to reinstate scores in voluntary reading programs**. The court found "a general policy against intervention by the courts in matters best left to school authorities." Reinstatement of test scores was left to the discretion of school officials. As the student had no legal remedy available, the court affirmed the judgment, including the award of attorneys' fees. *T.J. v. Hargrove*, 362 Ark. 649, 210 S.W.3d 79 (Ark. 2005).

◆   A Michigan student ranked first in his class at the end of his junior year. He maintained dual enrollment in his high school during his senior year but took no classes there. The student worked as a paralegal in his mother's law office for an employer-based course taken through a county intermediate district. Although an "A" was the highest possible grade under the intermediate district policy, the student's high school district allowed A+ grades. The student's mother awarded him an A+ for the employer-based course, but his report card indicated an A. The high school district refused the mother's request to change the grade, and the student sued for due process violations. A state court held for the district. Before the state court of appeals, the student argued that a high school district policy allowing grades to be weighted or adjusted did not apply to intermediate district courses. The court stated that **a district's board of education had authority to implement a grading system under Michigan law**. The paralegal training course was administered by the intermediate school district, not the high school, so the highest possible grade was an A. The high school district's policy prevented weighting or adjustment of the grade. Since the student had no vested property interest in an A+ and no legal right to a particular grade, the court affirmed the judgment. *Delekta v. Memphis Community Schools*, No. 249325, 2004 WL 2290462 (Mich. Ct. App. 2004).

◆   **An Ohio school district did not violate a student's rights by suspending her for excessive tardiness** under an attendance policy that assigned students failing grades for poor attendance. An Ohio appeals court upheld the policy as a constitutional means of promoting good attendance. According to the appeals court, under state law, school policies are generally left to the discretion of the school board. The board policy in this case promoted attendance for academic performance and provided sanctions for excessive unexcused absences. It distinguished between excused and unexcused absences and was neither unreasonable nor unconstitutional. *Smith v. Revere Local School Dist. Board of Educ.*, No. 20275, 2001 WL 489980 (Ohio Ct. App. 2001).

◆   A California middle school music teacher assigned three students conduct grades of "needs improvement" or "unsatisfactory." Parents complained about the poor conduct grades, which made the students ineligible for honor society and field trips. The principal then changed the grades to "satisfactory" without consulting the teacher. The teacher filed a grievance that was denied at all three levels, culminating with the school board. The teacher and his collective bargaining association sued the district and principal in the state court system. The California Court of Appeal noted that the state Education Code provides that **a grade assigned by a classroom teacher is final and can be changed only in limited circumstances such as clerical or mechanical mistake**, or where the assignment is characterized by bad faith or incompetency. The court rejected the district's argument that the code section did not apply to citizenship grades. Even if citizenship marks were not considered grades, the district had exceeded its authority in changing them. *Las Virgenes Educators Ass'n v. Las Virgenes Unified School Dist.*, 102 Cal.Rptr.2d 901 (Cal. Ct. App. 2000).

II. STUDENT RECORDS

Under the Family Educational Rights and Privacy Act of 1974 (FERPA), 20 U.S.C. § 1232g, parents and eligible students have rights to access their education records and protect the records from access by unauthorized persons.

FERPA applies only to "education records," which are records "directly related to a student" that are "maintained by an educational agency or institution or by a party acting for the agency or institution."

On December 2, 2011, the U.S. Department of Education revised FERPA regulations to permit a limited directory information policy in which schools specify the parties or purposes for which information is disclosed. The amended regulations include student email addresses in the term "directory information" and create new sanctions for the improper redisclosure of protected data.

FERPA regulations state when personally identifiable information may be disclosed without consent by a parent or eligible student. "Personal identifiers" may indirectly identify students without stating names. This includes a student's date and place of birth, mother's maiden name, or "information that, alone or in combination," may allow identification by a person in the community.

Records that originate from a school, or are created by nonschool entities, may become education records if they are "maintained" by a school. Notes used only as a personal memory aid and kept in the sole possession of the maker are outside FERPA's coverage. As amended in 2011, FERPA regulations declare that as states develop and refine their information management systems, it is critical to take steps to protect personally identifiable information on students.

A FERPA regulation at 34 C.F.R. Part 99.31(a)(1) requires educational institutions to "use reasonable methods to ensure that school officials obtain access to only those education records in which they have legitimate educational interests." This regulation permits educational agencies to disclose education records to another institution without consent, even after a student has enrolled or transferred, for reasons related to enrollment or transfer.

FERPA allows educational agencies to enter into agreements with organizations that conduct studies and redisclose personally identifiable information from education records. Provisions of the 2011 regulations restrict the redisclosure of personally identifiable information by requiring agreements to include provisions for destroying all personally identifiable information by contractors or other third parties when the information is no longer needed for the purposes for which the study was done. Further disclosures must be in accordance with agreements to other parties and for specified purposes.

To assure that information that is "redisclosed" by an educational agency or institution remains protected by FERPA, the amended regulations declare an intent to enforce the act not only against the educational agency, but against a third party recipient of the information. A FERPA enforcement tool is the Secretary of Education's declared ability to issue a cease and desist order, and to terminate federal funding eligibility "under any applicable program."

If the Secretary finds that a third party outside an educational agency or institution has violated FERPA regulations, the offending educational agency or institution may not allow the third party violator access to personally identifiable information from education records for at least five years.

Under 34 C.F.R. Part 99.36, personally identifiable information from an education record may be disclosed to parents and other appropriate parties in connection with "health and safety emergencies." A student's social security number or student identification number is personally identifiable information that may not be disclosed as directory information under 34 C.F.R. Part 99.3.

In Gonzaga Univ. v. Doe, 536 U.S. 273 (2002), this chapter, the U.S. Supreme Court held FERPA does not authorize private lawsuits. Analogous state laws protect student records and may create greater student rights.

The Health Insurance Portability and Accountability Act (HIPAA) was enacted to ensure continued health insurance for persons changing jobs, and to address the problem of health information confidentiality. Under federal regulations, records covered by FERPA are exempt from HIPAA. However, since schools typically provide services deemed to be within HIPAA definitions, schools may be considered "covered entities" under HIPAA in some situations. Several federal court decisions have held HIPAA does not create a private right of action for individuals to bring lawsuits. These include Dominic J. v. Wyoming Valley West High School, 362 F.Supp.2d 560 (M.D. Pa. 2005), Runkle v. Gonzales, 391 F.Supp.2d 210 (D.D.C. 2005), and Swift v. Lake Park High School Dist. 108, No. 03 C 5003, 2003 WL 22388878 (N.D. Ill. 2003).

A. Student and Parental Rights

◆ A 16-year-old Texas student said some of her coaches interrogated her about her relationship with an 18-year-old woman. One coach accused her of spreading a rumor that the 18-year-old was the coach's ex-girlfriend. She said the coaches yelled at her, called her a liar and threatened to sue her. Eventually, the student admitted dating the 18-year-old. She said the coaches threatened to tell her mother she was gay and had a relationship with the 18-year-old. The student's mother reported the coaches to the school athletic director, principal and district superintendent, but she said they did not investigate. The student then sued the district and coaches in a federal court for privacy rights violations.

Under the district's version of the facts, the student was openly gay and did not try to keep this a secret. It was asserted that the student broke a team rule by riding to practice with the 18-year-old. She also disregarded other rules. Significantly, the coaches said the relationship between the student and an 18-year-old was a potential crime which they had to report. In reviewing the case, the court found the parties had strikingly different accounts of the incident and the coaches' reasons for disclosing information to the student's parent. Because of this factual dispute, the court denied the coaches qualified immunity. Prior **decisions by the Fifth Circuit Court of Appeals and the Supreme Court indicate a person has a reasonable expectation in the privacy of her sexual orientation.** A factual dispute about the coaches' motivation prevented any finding at this point regarding a legitimate interest in disclosure. In future proceedings, the court would obtain more facts and try to determine whether the coaches acted reasonably, and whether the district was liable for constitutional violations and failure to train its employees. *Wyatt v. Kilgore Independent School Dist.*, No. 6:10-cv-00674-JDL, 2011 WL 6016467 (E.D. Tex. 11/30/11).

◆ An African-American student petitioned the New Jersey Department of Education to reverse a 10-day suspension for possessing a knife at school. He claimed white students at the school were only suspended three to five days for similar conduct. After the suspension was upheld, the student's father filed a state court action against the school district for civil rights violations. He also filed a series of requests for public records and court actions seeking statistics about violent incidents in the district to support his discrimination claim. These requests were made under the state Open Public Records Act (OPRA). When the district provided copies of disciplinary records, the father made an OPRA request for additional records that he believed were in the district's possession. When this request did not yield the records sought, he filed another state court action. This time, he demanded the names of police departments and officers who responded to 47 weapons-related incidents in district schools from 2001 to 2007. The school district disputed that there were 47 weapons incidents and provided records for a lower number. A state trial court eventually resolved the three OPRA actions in favor of the district. It found 249 incident reports sought by the father did not exist. In the civil rights case, the court held for the district.

Appeal went before a New Jersey appellate court, which consolidated the OPRA cases with the civil rights action. It held there was no denial of access to records. The court found the father had received all the records he was due. The OPRA and common law claims for access to documents "kept the parties in a continuous, multi-faceted battle" and complicated the litigation. As for the civil rights claim, **the court found the student did not show any discrimination in his discipline or the report to the police. A 10-day suspension was not significantly different from the suspensions imposed on white students,** and the court affirmed the judgment. *O.R. v. Kniewel*, Nos. L-2293, L-2380-07, L-2686-06, L-2316-06, 2010 WL 1191088 (N.J. Super. Ct. App. Div. 3/17/10).

◆ A New Jersey high school teacher wanted to use a student psychiatric evaluation "as a tool" to teach his class about "The Catcher in The Rye." He obtained a student's psychological evaluation from the school social worker and distributed copies of it to the class as a template for their projects. A friend of the student recognized the evaluation and told the student's family about it. The school administration collected and destroyed the evaluation copies, but the student's parents said he was shocked and embarrassed and became asocial. Due to diabetes, anxiety and depression, the student had already been homeschooled for a significant time. In a federal court action against the board of education, school staff members and school administrators, the parents asserted constitutional claims, violations of student privacy rights laws, and negligence.

In pretrial activity, **the court held there is a right to privacy under the Due Process Clause** of the Fourteenth Amendment. **The evidence of privacy rights violations by the teacher and social worker supported claims under the state and federal constitutions.** The court held no reasonable juror could find disclosure of a student's psychiatric evaluation was merely negligent. Federal privacy laws did not create a private right of action. The First and Fourth Amendment claims were dismissed, as disclosing student data did not implicate either amendment. And the failure-to-train claims arising under the state and federal constitutions failed as there was no evidence that supervisors knew of the disclosure. But due to the evidence of privacy rights violations by the teacher and social worker, the state law claims against them could proceed. *L.S. and R.S. v. Mount Olive Board of Educ.*, 765 F.Supp.2d 648 (D.N.J. 2011).

◆   A group of students accused of underage alcohol consumption at a house party could not pursue claims against law enforcement officers for violating the Family Educational Rights and Privacy Act (FERPA). According to the students, the sharing of information about their criminal activity between sheriffs' officials and their school district violated their privacy rights. But a federal district court explained **that there is no private right of action to enforce FERPA in a court**. The U.S. Supreme Court foreclosed any such action in *Gonzaga Univ. v. Doe*, this chapter. *Green v. Arpaio*, No. CV-10-1481-PHX-GMS, 2010 WL 5279911 (D. Ariz. 12/17/10).

◆   A Washington private school student intended to teach in the state's public school system after his graduation. At the time, the state required new teachers to obtain an affidavit of good moral character from the dean of their college or university. When the university's teacher certification specialist overheard a conversation implicating the student in sexual misconduct with a classmate, she commenced an investigation of the student and reported the allegations against him to the state teacher certification agency. She later informed the student that the university would not provide him with the affidavit of good moral character he needed for certification as a Washington teacher.

The student sued the university and the specialist under state law and 42 U.S.C. § 1983 for violating FERPA. A jury awarded him over $1 million in damages. The case reached the U.S. Supreme Court, which held that **FERPA creates no personal rights that can be enforced in a court under Section 1983**. Congress enacted FERPA to force schools to respect students' privacy with respect to education records. It did not confer enforceable rights upon students. The Court reversed and remanded the case to a state court for further proceedings. *Gonzaga Univ. v. Doe*, 536 U.S. 273 (2002).

◆   An Oklahoma parent learned that teachers asked students to grade each other's assignments and then call out the results in class. She asserted that the policy was embarrassing to her children and sued the school district and school administrators for violations of FERPA and the Due Process Clause. A federal district court held the policy did not violate any constitutional privacy rights and that the practice of calling out grades did not involve "education records" within the meaning of FERPA. A federal appeals court reversed the judgment.

The U.S. Supreme Court accepted the district's petition to review the case. It observed that an "education record" under FERPA is one that is "maintained by an educational agency or institution or by a person acting for such agency or institution." According to the court, student papers are not "maintained" within the meaning of FERPA when students correct them or call out grades. **The word "maintain" suggested that FERPA records were kept in files or cabinets in a "records room at the school or on a permanent secure database."** The momentary handling of assignments by students did not conform to this definition. The appeals court committed error by deciding that a student acted for an educational institution under FERPA when assisting with grading. Because Congress did not intend to intervene in drastic fashion with traditional state functions by exercising minute control over teaching methods, the Court reversed and remanded the case. *Owasso Independent School Dist. No. I-011 v. Falvo*, 534 U.S. 426 (2002).

◆ A 21-year-old Iowa teaching assistant and coach exchanged text messages with a ninth-grader. The two had sexual contact, and the student told a friend. When her mother learned about the relationship, she met with the district superintendent. During their meeting, he took a full page of notes, which were later shown to a school attorney. The coach was placed on administrative leave and reported to the police, and a criminal investigation was begun. The mother claimed the superintendent identified the student in discussions with the school board, administrators and staff and that a board member spoke publicly about the incident. A lawsuit was filed against the school district for privacy rights violations. A state court held the superintendent's notes were not a "confidential public record" under Iowa Code Section 22.7. Appeal reached the Court of Appeals of Iowa, which explained that Iowa Code Chapter 22 establishes a right of access to governmental records and requires that certain categories of government records be kept confidential. Since the superintendent's notes were made as part of his official duties, they were school records. But the court noted he relied on his memory when speaking with the board and staff, not his notes. **Section 22.7 "is not a general privacy law that prohibits public officials from discussing information that is neither a record itself nor derived from a record."** Section 22.7(18) of the state code did not give the mother a cause of action. Her verbal report was not filed with a designated investigator. There was no merit to the claim that a state administrative provision governing child abuse reports by school employees was violated. As a result, the court affirmed the judgment for the school district. *V.H. v. Hampton-Dumont Community School Dist.*, No. 09-0364, 2009 WL 5126111 (Iowa Ct. App. 12/30/09).

◆ A divorced New Hampshire mother did not have physical custody of her child. In addition to claiming lack of appropriate notice when her son missed school, she claimed an individualized education program (IEP) team member violated her rights by exchanging confidential medical information with her son's physician against her wishes. In a federal district court action, the mother asserted due process violations. The court reviewed evidence that the child's father had primary residential responsibility for the child. A family court order directed the school to call both parents in an emergency. The mother had refused to sign a release for her son's medical records and told IEP team members not to contact medical providers. But the father had signed a release that would allow a physician to exchange medical records with the school.

The father had residential responsibility for the child through a proceeding that provided full due process to the mother. **There was no constitutional right to notification from the school whenever the child was released to his father.** The mother did not claim interference with her custody rights or a transfer of custody sufficient to trigger constitutional concerns. Even if such rights existed, the court held school officials would have immunity. There was no merit to a claim against the father. The court dismissed the case. *Vendouri v. Gaylord*, Civil No. 10-cv-277-SM, 2010 WL 4236856 (D.N.H. 10/26/10).

◆   An Illinois student's parent requested all test questions from honors biology exams. He was offered an opportunity to examine test booklets at school or at home and to hand-copy test questions, so long as they were returned the next day and no photo-copies were made. The parent sued the school district in the state court system, seeking a declaration that the booklet was a "student record" under the state School Records Act. A trial court held that the booklets did not come under the Act, as they were devoid of any student marks or other identifying information. The Appellate Court of Illinois affirmed the decision.

While the case was pending, the parent requested copies of his daughter's algebra exams. The district provided him the parts of exam booklets with the student's answers and calculations, but it blocked the test questions. The parent filed a new action. This time, the appellate court noted the student had written her name, and wrote answers and calculations on the test booklets. **As they contained student markings and other identifying information, the booklets were "student records."** The marked-on algebra test booklets were covered by the Act, so the parent had a right to inspect and copy them. Unlike federal law, the state act allowed parents to "copy" student records, not just "inspect and review" them. *Garlick v. Oak Park and River Forest High School Dist. #200*, 389 Ill.App.3d 306, 905 N.E.2d 930 (Ill. App. Ct. 2009).

◆   A New York school district superintendent told staff members they had a duty to inform parents about student pregnancies. He said a student's disclosure of pregnancy to staff members was unprotected by any privilege and might trigger legal reporting obligations. Staff members who learned of a student's pregnancy "should immediately" report it to a school social worker, who should then "encourage" the student to disclose a pregnancy to her parents. If a student would not inform her parents, the memorandum stated that a social worker "should offer to meet with the parents and the student to help the student inform her parents" and/or offer to inform the student's parents in the student's absence. If a student continued refusing these prompts, the social worker "should inform the student that she/he will inform the parents." The district teachers' association sued the school board and superintendent on behalf of students. A federal court held the association lacked standing to file the action.

On appeal, the U.S. Court of Appeals, Second Circuit, held **the association did not establish any risk of civil liability or professional discipline**. The superintendent stated that he would not discipline staff members for their actions with respect to parental pregnancy notification. The memorandum was non-mandatory, and the court affirmed the judgment for the school board. *Port Washington Teachers' Ass'n v. Board of Educ. of Port Washington Union Free School Dist.*, 478 F.3d 494 (2d Cir. 2007).

B. Media Requests

FERPA's general definition of "education records" is: "those records, files, documents and other materials which – (i) contain information directly related to a student; and (ii) are maintained by an educational agency or institution or by a person acting for such agency or institution." This includes personally identifiable information that may reveal a student's identity. **Courts have held that records pertaining to a single student meet these criteria, but statistical compilations do not.** *Thus, compiled student disciplinary hearing information could be released to the media under FERPA and the state Open Records Act in* Hardin County Schools v. Foster, *40 S.W.3d 865 (Ky. 2001).*

◆ A Washington student with a severe peanut allergy died on a school field trip after he ate a school lunch with peanut products. The district superintendent revealed that the district had provided the peanut products despite knowing of his severe allergy. The district and family entered into mediation, and the family accepted $960,000 in return for a release of all claims. The parties made a joint press release and agreed that the district and staff would decline to comment to the press about the case. The district denied a newspaper publisher's request for 75 documents, including its investigation report, the settlement agreement and investigation notes by the investigator and school attorneys. The school district, family and student's estate sought a state court order exempting the records from public disclosure. The case reached the Supreme Court of Washington, which held **the Washington Public Records Act requires agencies to make public records available for public inspection and copying, unless an exemption applies**. The documents sought were classified as "work product," prepared in anticipation of the lawsuit and were exempt from disclosure. Teachers and a volunteer nurse chaperone were "clients whose communications with the attorneys were privileged." Even if the documents were not protected from disclosure as "work product," they were protected by the attorney-client privilege. *Soter v. Cowles Publishing Co.*, 174 P.3d 69 (Wash. 2007).

◆ Montana students were disciplined for shooting others on school property with plastic BBs. The school board held a closed hearing to consider their discipline. The board opened the session after deciding on the discipline, then returned to closed session to take the action it discussed. A newspaper publisher noted that the board's previous practice had been to publicly reveal the nature of the student discipline while referencing students with an anonymous number. After the district superintendent refused a further request for information about the discipline, the publisher sued the school district in the state court system.

Appeal reached the Supreme Court of Montana, which found "student records" included student names and addresses, birth days, achievement levels and immunization records. Each school board must maintain a record of any discipline that is educationally related. **Courts in Ohio, Missouri and Georgia have held that disciplinary records are not "education records" as defined by FERPA.** Courts in Indiana and Wisconsin have held that once the names of students are blocked out, they are no longer "education records." The court decided that FERPA did not prevent the public release of student disciplinary records after student names were blocked. As there was no basis for refusing the publisher's request for information under FERPA or state law, the lower court decision was reversed. *Board of Trustees, Cut Bank Public Schools v. Cut Bank Pioneer Press*, 337 Mont. 229, 160 P.3d 482 (Mont. 2007).

◆ A *Chicago Tribune* reporter requested over a million records on current and former Chicago public school students. The request included personal data such as school, medical or special education status, attendance, race, transportation status, free or reduced-cost lunch status, class rank, grade average, bilingual education status, date of birth, and standardized test scores. The board of education denied the request as burdensome and as a high risk of disclosing personal information in violation of federal and state laws including the Freedom of Information Act (FOIA) and Student Records Act. The *Tribune* sued the board, and the case reached the Appellate Court of Illinois. It noted the FOIA required public bodies to comply with record requests unless an exemption applied. **FOIA's student records exemption was a *per se* rule that did not require a case-by-case balancing of the competing interests in public information and individual privacy.** The clear language of the FOIA created an exemption from disclosure for student files. Most of the data requested by the *Tribune* was considered private and confidential. Because the request was entitled to the *per se* exemption, the board had properly denied it. *Chicago Tribune Co. v. Board of Educ. of City of Chicago*, 332 Ill.App.3d 60, 773 N.E.2d 674 (Ill. App. Ct. 2002).

C. Electronic and Video Records

In S.A. v. Tulare County Office of Educ., a California school district did not violate state and federal education record requirements by refusing to provide parents all emails that personally identified their son in an electronic format. A federal court held emails had a "fleeting nature" and were not "education records" unless they were placed in a student's permanent file.

◆ A Pennsylvania student discovered webcam photos and screenshots of himself on a school laptop. The school district agreed to disable the security tracking software on the laptop, but the student and others pursued a federal district court case. The court prohibited the district and its agents from remotely activating webcams on laptop computers issued to students. Under the court order, the school district could not remotely capture screenshots of laptops, except for maintenance, repairs or trouble-shooting. **The district could use an alternate means to track lost, stolen or missing laptops.** A global positioning system or other anti-theft device that did not permit the activation of webcams or capture screenshots was permitted. The order prevented the district from accessing any student-created files on laptops, such as emails, instant messages, internet use logs and web-browsing histories. Under the court order, the district was required to adopt official policies governing the use, distribution and maintenance of student laptops. It was further required to issue regulations for student privacy on laptops and to train staff on the oversight and enforcement of the policies. Under the order, the school district would have to provide students and their parents an opportunity to view images already taken from webcams. Such images were to be destroyed when the process was completed. *Robbins v. Lower Merion School Dist.*, No. 10-665, 2010 WL 1976869 (E.D. Pa. 5/14/10).

◆ Parents of students attending the Whitney E. Houston Academy (a New Jersey performing arts school) signed a form consenting to the videotaping, photographing or sound recording of their children "in classroom, playground, auditorium activities or productions." Consent was given with knowledge that recordings might appear in the media or be used for school exhibits and public relations. The academy PTA presented a play and videotaped it. Copies of the videotape were later made available for sale through the PTA. A student who had a non-speaking role tripped during the show. Her parent sued the PTA for invasion of her daughter's privacy rights. A state court found no evidence that the PTA had received a commercial benefit and that it had acted with a charitable purpose. On appeal, a state appellate court noted that since the PTA was a charitable organization, the parent would have had to show her child's likeness was used for financial or commercial benefit. **An invasion of privacy claim requires proof that a party has used the likeness of another person without consent for commercial benefit, and proof of damages.** It was not sufficient for the parent to simply claim that the recording of her daughter, by itself, established a claim for appropriation of her likeness. The lower court had correctly held for the PTA. *Jeffries v. Whitney E. Houston Academy P.T.A.*, No. L-1389-07, 2009 WL 2136174 (N.J. Super. Ct. App. Div. 7/20/09).

◆ A California child with autism received special education from a county special education agency. His parents asked for copies of "any and all electronic mail sent or received" by the agency concerning or personally identifying their child. They then clarified that they sought emails in their electronic format. The county sent the parents hard copies of emails that had been printed and placed in their child's permanent file, but it refused to provide electronically formatted emails. The parents complained to the state department of education (DOE) and later filed a federal district court case for state and federal records violations.

The court found the Individuals with Disabilities Education Act (IDEA) required the county to provide parents a child's "education records." It held **only those emails that personally identified the child and were "maintained" by an educational agency were "education records" under the IDEA and FERPA.** DOE had correctly found the county produced the child's education records by providing hard copies of all the emails that personally identified him and were maintained in his permanent file. Only those emails that were both maintained by the county and which personally identified the student were considered to be "education records." The court held that emails in electronic format were not "maintained" by the county. **Emails had a "fleeting nature" and were not "education records" unless they were placed in a student's permanent file.** The county did not "unlawfully purge" emails without notice to the parents. *S.A. v. Tulare County Office of Educ.*, No. CV F 08-1215 LJO GSA, 2009 WL 3126322 (E.D. Cal. 9/24/09).

◆ A Tennessee school board approved of the installation of video surveillance cameras throughout a middle school building. An assistant principal discovered that cameras had been placed to record areas of locker rooms where students dressed for sports activities. Four months later, a visiting girls' basketball coach complained to the school principal after her team members noticed a camera. The principal incorrectly assured the coach that the camera was not activated. The camera was on, and it recorded images of students changing their clothes.

Some of the students and their parents sued the school board, the director of schools, the principal and the assistant principal. The case reached the U.S. Court of Appeals, Sixth Circuit, which held there is a Fourth Amendment "right to shield one's naked body from view by members of the opposite sex." **Even in locker rooms, the students retained a significant privacy interest in their unclothed bodies.** Students using locker rooms had a reasonable expectation that no one would videotape them without their knowledge. Video surveillance is inherently intrusive. A reasonable school administrator would know that students had a privacy right against being surreptitiously videotaped while changing clothes. For this reason, the court held the principal and assistant principal were not entitled to qualified immunity from liability. *Brannum v. Overton County School Board*, 516 F.3d 489 (6th Cir. 2008).

◆ A surveillance video camera on a school bus videotaped a fight by two Washington elementary students. The school district denied a request by the parents of a student for a copy of the tape. It claimed the videotape was exempt from public disclosure under the state's Public Disclosure Act (PDA). A state court agreed with the district's decision not to disclose the tape. The videotape contained information that would allow a viewer to identify a student, and the tape was "maintained" by the district for potential discipline. Appeal reached the Supreme Court of Washington, which found the videotape was a "public record." Since the district was an "agency" under the PDA, it had to disclose the tape unless an exemption applied. A PDA exemption applied to materials in a student's permanent file, such as "grades, standardized test results, assessments, psychological or physical evaluations, class schedule, address, telephone number, social security number, and other similar records." In this case, the court found the videotape differed significantly from records "maintained "in student personal files. Because **the videotape could not be legally withheld as a student file document**, the court reversed the judgment. *Lindeman v. Kelso School Dist. No. 458*, 162 Wash.2d 196, 172 P.3d 329 (Wash. 2007).

◆ A New York court held **a videotape of a student fighting with a teacher during school was not an education record under FERPA**. The school district had voluntarily disclosed it to the police. Under FERPA, education records are "records, files, documents and other material which contain information directly related to a student." FERPA is intended to protect records relating to a student's performance and does not apply to a videotape recorded to maintain the school's security and safety. The student's rights to appeal his suspension outweighed the district's interest in protecting the confidentiality of school records. The court granted the student's request to release the videotape. *Rome City School Dist. Disciplinary Hearing v. Grifasi*, 10 Misc.3d 1034, 806 N.Y.S.2d 381 (N.Y. Sup. Ct. 2005).

◆ A Florida court held that **videotapes of students on school buses were "records and reports" under the school code**. In previous cases, the court had used FERPA's definition of "personally identifiable information." But FERPA calls for the denial of eligibility for federal funds only if an educational agency violates federal privacy requirements. The Florida Code went beyond FERPA by protecting students against the release of any personal information contained in records or reports permitting the personal identification of a student. The state code protected as confidential even those records or reports that were redacted of any personally identifying information. *WFTV, Inc. v. School Board of Seminole*, 874 So.2d 48 (Fla. Dist. Ct. App. 2004).

III. REFORM LEGISLATION

A. The No Child Left Behind Act of 2001

The No Child Left Behind (NCLB) Act of 2001 reauthorized the Elementary and Secondary Education Act (ESEA) of 1965. It requires the states to use academic assessments to annually review school progress and determine if "adequate yearly progress" (AYP) has been made under state standards. The AYP requirement is a condition for the receipt of Title I funds under the ESEA.

Schools that fail to achieve AYP for two consecutive years are designated for "school improvement." If a school does not make AYP after two years of improvement status, it is subject to "corrective action." This may entail replacing teachers or an entirely new curriculum. A school failing to make AYP after a year of corrective action must be "restructured." This involves replacing staff, converting to charter school status or surrendering direct control to state officials. NCLB Act notice and transfer provisions are triggered when schools are identified for improvement, corrective action or restructuring.

A federal regulation defining "highly qualified teacher" under the No Child Left Behind (NCLB) Act was declared in violation of Congressional intent because it permitted some California teachers to become highly qualified without obtaining full state certification.

◆ Under the NCLB Act, alternative-route teachers meet the "highly qualified teacher" designation only by obtaining "full state certification." But a federal regulation, 34 C.F.R. Part 200.56(a)(1)(i), permitted an alternative-route teacher to gain "highly qualified" status without first obtaining "full state certification." Students, parents and two nonprofit organizations claimed the regulation and a parallel California state education regulation allowed a disproportionate number of intern teachers to teach in minority and low-income California schools. The challengers said California intern teachers lacked "full state certification," which is part of the definition of a highly qualified teacher under the NCLB Act.

A federal district court heard evidence that the state's intern teachers were concentrated in schools that served low-income and minority students. But the court upheld the regulation. On appeal, the U.S. Court of Appeals, Ninth Circuit, held the federal regulation impermissibly expanded the highly qualified teacher definition of 20 U.S.C. § 7801(23) to include alternative-route teachers in the process of obtaining full certification. Since 34 C.F.R. Part 200.56(a)(2)(ii) was inconsistent with congressional intent, the court invalidated it. The state and federal regulations permitted California and its school districts to ignore the disproportionate number of interns teaching in schools in minority and low-income areas, and the court held the challengers could pursue the case. *Renee v. Duncan*, 623 F.3d 787 (9th Cir. 2010).

Congress later expanded the definition of "highly qualified teacher" to include an alternative-route teacher who demonstrated satisfactory progress toward full certification. The case then returned to the Ninth Circuit. It held that as long as the congressional act was in effect, the challenged regulation would be consistent with the NCLB Act. In addition, the challengers were not entitled to judicial enforcement of a particular NCLB Act reporting requirement, and could not claim their attorneys' fees for prevailing during the 2010 court activity. *Renee v. Duncan*, 686 F.3d 1002 (9th Cir. 2012).

◆ A federal appeals court refused to review Connecticut's challenge to federal interpretations of the No Child Left Behind Act. According to Connecticut officials, the NCLB Act's "unfunded mandates provision" required the state to be fully funded for any costs of complying with the NCLB Act. It stated it was currently spending $41.6 million of its own funds to comply with the act. The court ruled against the state, which appealed. The U.S. Court of Appeals, Second Circuit, held arguments regarding the unfunded mandates provision were not ready for judicial review. This claim could be decided once there was an administrative record. The district court was entitled to find the disposition of the proposed plan amendments and request for waivers was not arbitrary or capricious. An NCLB Act provision stated that approval of a state plan should not be declined before a hearing. **But the pending legal issue was the meaning of the unfunded mandates provision, which was not yet ripe for review.** Since the court held that claim was not ready for review, it found no reason to order a hearing on the plan amendments before arguments about the unfunded mandates provision were heard. *Connecticut v. Duncan*, 612 F.3d 107 (2d Cir. 2010).

◆ The number of Newark, New Jersey schools "in need of improvement" under the NCLB Act increased from 37 in 2003-04 to 51 in 2006-07. An audit revealed that Newark Public Schools did not meet its NCLB Act obligation to notify parents of their rights to obtain transfers and supplemental educational services (SES) for their children. A group of Newark parents filed a class action suit against the school system, asserting NCLB Act violations. A federal court held that the Act did not create individually-enforceable rights and dismissed the complaint. On appeal, the U.S. Court of Appeals, Third Circuit, explained that the NCLB Act was enacted by Congress under its Spending Clause powers. As with other Spending Clause legislation, the NCLB Act offered federal money to the states in return for an agreement by the states to perform specific actions. **Unlike federal civil rights legislation, the NCLB Act's "penalties" section did not offer any remedy in the event of noncompliance.** Instead, states that failed to meet the Act's requirements were subject to withholding of funds by the Secretary of the U.S. Department of Education. Thus, the parents lacked a private right of action to enforce the Act's provisions. *Newark Parents Ass'n v. Newark Public Schools,* 547 F.3d 199 (3d Cir. 2008).

◆ The NCLB Act's "Unfunded Mandates Provision" prevents the Act from being construed to authorize an officer or employee of the federal government to mandate that a state or state subdivision spend funds or incur costs not paid for under the Act. School districts from Michigan, Texas and Vermont joined the National Education Association (NEA) and NEA affiliates in a federal action against the Secretary of the U.S. Department of Education, seeking a federal court declaration that she was misinterpreting the Unfunded Mandates Provision. They argued that states need not comply with NCLB Act requirements where federal funding did not cover the increased costs of NCLB Act compliance. A federal court refused to interpret the NCLB Act to excuse states from complying with requirements of the Act that imposed additional costs on states. **The states had to comply with the NCLB Act regardless of any federal funding shortfall.** On appeal, the U.S. Court of Appeals, Sixth Circuit, reached a tie vote, meaning that the lower court's decision stood. As a result, the judgment for the Secretary was affirmed. *School Dist. of City of Pontiac v. Secretary of U.S. Dep't of Educ.,* 584 F.3d 253 (6th Cir. 2009).

◆ Illinois school districts and parents sued the U.S. Department of Education in a federal court, arguing that certain NCLB Act requirements were in conflict with those of the Individuals with Disabilities Education Act (IDEA). The court held the districts and parents lacked standing to bring the case. It held the IDEA and NCLB Act established voluntary programs and that school districts could solve any problem created by the laws by turning down federal funds. Appeal reached the U.S. Court of Appeals, Seventh Circuit. It held the districts and parents had standing to proceed with the case because they had no option but to follow the state's lead. Both federal laws required states to opt in or opt out for a year or more at a time. Once a district accepted a grant it had to comply with all program requirements. This was sufficient to establish standing. But the claim of the districts and parents was too weak to pursue any further. **The IDEA had to give way to the NCLB Act if there was truly any conflict between the laws.** The 2004 IDEA amendments were designed in part to conform the IDEA to the NCLB Act, not to displace it. If there was any conflict between the 2001 NCLB Act and IDEA enactments from between 1970 and 1990, the NCLB Act would prevail. The court dismissed the case. *Board of Educ. of Ottawa Township High School Dist. 140 v. Spellings,* 517 F.3d 922 (7th Cir. 2008).

◆   Pennsylvania's education secretary identified 13 schools in the Reading School District as failing to achieve AYP. The NCLB Act requires districts to report the test scores of four subgroups when the number of students in the subgroup exceeds a state-designated number. The secretary had established this "N" number at 40, based on several computer studies. The district claimed that the secretary arbitrarily set the N number and did not provide adequate assistance. The Commonwealth Court of Pennsylvania found no evidence to contradict the secretary's selection of the number 40 as appropriate. Plus the secretary provided the district with adequate technical assistance. **The state was not required to provide all the assistance specified in the NCLB Act at the moment a school was identified for improvement.** *Reading School Dist. v. Dep't of Educ.*, 855 A.2d 166 (Pa. Commw. Ct. 2004).

The school district then sent the department its plans to bring six schools into compliance. It submitted a cost estimate for the plan in excess of $26 million for 2003-2004. The district estimated it would receive about $8 million in federal funding, and it asked the state education department for the shortfall. The department did not respond to the request for funds, but found six schools and the district as a whole failed to achieve AYP for 2003-2004 and would be placed on level-one or level-two sanctions for 2004-2005. The district appealed, asserting that the department did not provide federal funds to implement the act, mandatory technical assistance to sanctioned schools, or Spanish language testing on a required statewide assessment. Appeal reached the commonwealth court again, which held that the department violated the district's due process rights by limiting the grounds for appeal in its policy. *Reading School Dist. v. Dep't of Educ.*, 875 A.2d 1218 (Pa. Commw. Ct. 2005).

B. State Reform Acts

Alabama's Students First Act (SFA) replaced the state's Fair Dismissal Act in 2012. Former law provided employees with a hearing to review school board termination or transfer actions. And hearing officers were allowed to determine whether such actions were "arbitrarily unjust." Under the SFA, employees still receive a hearing to appeal a school board's decision, but hearing officers are now required to defer to the employment decisions of education boards.

◆   In 2010, the Chicago Board of Education responded to significant budget deficits by laying off 1,289 teachers. Federal funding was later increased, and 715 teachers were rehired. Some teachers who were not rehired complained that many positions were being filled by new hires rather than by laid-off tenured teachers. The Chicago Teachers Union (CTU) filed a federal court action against the board for due process violations. After the court held for the CTU, the U.S. Court of Appeals, Seventh Circuit, affirmed. The Seventh Circuit later reheard the case and certified certain questions of state law to the Supreme Court of Illinois. It noted Illinois School Code Section 34-18(31) empowered the Chicago Board of Education to make rules for layoffs and recalls. But as a district human resource director admitted, no such rules were ever formulated.

Section 34-84 of the School Code authorized merit-based appointments and promotions of teachers in Chicago, and it described the process for removing tenured teachers for cause. In contrast to the CTU's argument, **Section 34-84 created no rights for laid-off teachers to continue in employment in preference to equally- or less-qualified teachers**. In the court's view, there was no preferential right of laid-off Chicago teachers to a vacant position over less-qualified, inexperienced teachers. Section 34-18 only authorized the board to create recall procedures and did not create any substantive rehire rights. Finally, the court rejected the CTU's arguments that the board was required to publish regulations governing layoff procedures. As the laws did not give laid-off tenured teachers the rights they claimed, the court held for the board. *Chicago Teachers Union v. Board of Educ. of the City of Chicago*, 963 N.E.2d 918 (Ill. 2012).

◆   An Alabama special education coordinator found a small bag in her car that later proved to be marijuana. Her daughter had a history of drug use and had recently borrowed the car. After parking on a campus lot, the employee brought the bag into the office and asked a co-worker if she thought it was marijuana. That morning, the employee left the substance in her desk drawer when she went to a doctor's appointment. The co-worker then told another employee about the substance, and they informed an administrator. Police were called, and a field test determined the substance was marijuana. The next day, the employee admitted bringing the substance into school. Although she was not charged with a crime, the board suspended her without pay for 90 days. A hearing officer later found she did not intend to have an illegal substance on board property. He found the suspension had been "manifestly unjust." Appeal then reached the Court of Civil Appeals of Alabama. It found the hearing officer had applied an "arbitrary and capricious" standard of review. But **the state's Students First Act required the hearing officer to give deference to the board's decision**, which was based on a zero-tolerance policy against drug possession on campus. As the board argued, the hearing officer did not give appropriate deference to the board, and the court reversed the judgment. *Chilton County Board of Educ. v. Cahalane*, No. 2110532, 2012 WL 3631143 (Ala. Ct. Civ. App. 8/24/12).

◆   Due to a history of low test scores, the Duquesne City School District was placed on Pennsylvania's education empowerment list in 2000. It was declared a financially distressed school district, and its management and operations were placed under a special board of control. In 2007, the special board of control eliminated the district's only high school. After the state department of education approved the action, the board laid off 18 district employees. No agreements to enroll high school students were made with neighboring school districts. Six weeks after the school closure, the General Assembly enacted Act 45 of 2007, which gave the state education secretary authority to designate two or more districts to accept high school students from a distressed district.

Act 45 required that employees who were furloughed by the closure of a high school be hired on a preferential basis by a district within three miles of the distressed district. Employees of districts located within three miles of Duquesne City School District noted only Duquesne met all of Act 45's requirements. They claimed Act 45 was a "special law" that violated the state constitution. Appeal reached the Supreme Court of Pennsylvania. **It held**

Article III, Section 32 of the state constitution prohibits local or special laws regulating school districts. Duquesne was the only member of the initial class of districts described by Act 45, and no other district could meet Act 45's criteria unless "a highly improbable convergence of events" transpired. The court held the class of districts created by Act 45 was substantially closed to new members. The practical effect of the law was to assure that affected Duquesne staff members would be given preferential hiring treatment. Parts of Act 45 were "special legislation" that were prohibited by the state constitution. *West Mifflin Area School Dist. v. Zahorchak*, 4 A.3d 1042 (Pa. 2010).

◆   In 1998, the Missouri legislature passed SB 781 as part of a settlement in a long-running federal lawsuit to desegregate St. Louis public schools. SB 781 created the Transitional School District (TSD) to handle the transition from federal court supervision to local control. SB 781 further provided that if the St. Louis school district lost its accreditation after the restoration of control to the city board, the general authority over the school district transferred back to the TSD. This provision was carried forward into law as Section 162.1100 of the Revised Statutes of Missouri. The St. Louis school district's performance was at or below minimally acceptable levels after 1994, and in 2006, the state board reestablished the TSD. When the district lost its accreditation, it sued the state board. Meanwhile, a special administrative board took control of St. Louis public schools. After a trial, the state board prevailed. The district appealed to the Supreme Court of Missouri, arguing that Section 162.110 was special legislation that violated the state constitution. The court disagreed. While Section 162.1100 created a classification that was characteristic of special legislation, the state constitution was not violated. *Board of Educ. of City of St. Louis v. Missouri State Board of Educ.*, 271 S.W.3d 1 (Mo. 2008).

◆   The Kentucky Education Reform Act (KERA) created site-based councils to provide greater accountability and decentralize school management. A KERA provision, KRS § 160.345(2)(h), required site-based councils to select principals from applicants recommended by the district superintendent. A superintendent fired a high school principal for poor performance. He received nine applications for the resulting vacancy, including one from the former principal. The superintendent forwarded only three applications to the site-based council. The council asked for the others, but the superintendent refused and appointed one of his three candidates as interim principal. A state court ordered the superintendent to forward all nine applications, and the council then recommended rehiring the former principal. The state supreme court consolidated the case with that of an assistant principal who claimed she was passed over for a vacancy due to gender. It held neither superintendent had the authority to limit the pool of "qualified applicants" under Section 160.345(2)(h). **Site-based councils were created in direct response to widespread mismanagement caused by an overly centralized system of school governance.** Superintendents had to send site-based councils the applications of all applicants who met state law requirements, including the assistant principal and the fired principal. *Young v. Hammond*, 139 S.W.3d 895 (Ky. 2004).

◆   In 1993, Maryland's state education board adopted school performance standards that mandated reporting requirements and improvement plans for each public school. Schools that did not meet the standards were placed under the direct control of the local school board. If they failed to improve under local reconstitution, they were designated for "state reconstitution." By 2000, the state board had placed 97 Maryland schools under local reconstitution, 83 of which were in Baltimore. The state board reconstituted three low-performing Baltimore schools, but their performance remained stagnant after three years.

The state board hired a private company to provide the school's curriculum, instructional services, support personnel, teaching tools, special education and other services. The company hired and managed the professional staff for the three schools. The collective bargaining agent (CBA) for school employees sued the state education board in a state court, arguing the board could not adopt regulations creating student performance standards and reconstitution. The court held the board was statutorily authorized to contract with the company. On appeal, the Court of Appeals of Maryland rejected the CBA's claim that state law did not authorize the state reconstitution regulations. State laws enacted in 1997, 1999 and 2000 recognized that **under state reconstitution, public school teachers might be employed by private entities**. The court affirmed the judgment. *Baltimore Teachers Union v. Maryland State Board of Educ.*, 379 Md. 192, 840 A.2d 728 (Md. 2004).

C. Charter Schools

1. Legislation

Charter school laws were among the first of the educational reforms of the 1990s to be tested in the courts. They have survived numerous legal challenges asserting violations of state and federal constitutional provisions. But the Supreme Court of Georgia held the state Charter Schools Commission Act was not a constitutional exercise of legislative power, as it permitted legislators to create general K-12 schools that would duplicate efforts by locally controlled schools and compete for the same students.

◆   Georgia's Charter Schools Commission Act deemed a "commission charter school" to be a public school within the state system of K-12 education. Charter school opponents filed a state court suit against state officials, arguing that the commission charter schools violated local education control provisions of the state constitution. The case reached the Supreme Court of Georgia, which considered a claim that the act was unconstitutional because it authorized schools that were not "special" under Georgia Constitution Article VIII, Section V, Paragraph VII(a). The opponents claimed the act permitted charter schools to compete with the state's regular public K-12 education system by serving the same types of students and not offering any education that was "special."

According to the court, local education boards had exclusive control over the establishment and maintenance of the general K-12 public education system. Examples of "special schools" authorized in a 1966 state law included vocational trade schools, schools for exceptional children, and schools for adult education. "Special school" was a constitutional phrase, not a statutory phrase that the legislature could define. "Special school" language did not permit the General Assembly to create general K-12 schools that would duplicate efforts by locally controlled schools or compete for the same students. **Since charter schools offered a K-12 public education to any student in the state, they did not qualify as "special schools."** Accordingly, the court held Article VIII, Section V, Paragraph VII(a) could not be interpreted as relinquishing the historical exclusivity of local control over general K-12 public education. As all the state's arguments failed, the court held for the challengers. *Gwinnett County School Dist. v. Cox*, 289 Ga. 265, 710 S.E.2d 773 (Ga. 2011).

◆   A Texas open-enrollment charter school employee claimed he was fired as the result of his refusal to perform an illegal act. He sued the school under the Texas Whistleblower Protection Act (WPA). After a state court dismissed the case, the employee appealed to the Court of Appeals of Texas. He argued the school was subject to the WPA, which prohibits local governmental entities from taking adverse personnel action against employees. Public school districts and state political subdivisions were "local governmental entities" under the WPA. While the court found the WPA was a "broad remedial measure intended to encourage disclosure of governmental malfeasance and corruption," it held **the WPA was inapplicable to open-enrollment charter schools**. State law defined "charter schools" as "public schools," not "public school districts." While open-enrollment charter schools were subject to laws governing public schools, the court held this did not subject them to laws applying to "public school districts." A charter school had no jurisdiction outside its own campus. Since an open enrollment charter school was neither a school district nor a state political subdivision, the court held the case was properly dismissed. *Ohnesorge v. Winfree Academy Charter School*, 328 S.W.3d 654 (Tex. Ct. App. 2010).

◆   In 2006, Florida Statutes Section 1002.335 established the state Schools of Excellence Commission as an independent state entity with power to authorize charter schools throughout the state. Local boards thus lost their former power to authorize charter schools. At least 31 local school boards filed resolutions with the state board, seeking to retain their former authority to authorize charter schools. The state board permitted only three local boards to retain this authority. Several boards then appealed. According to a state district court of appeal, article IX section 4 of the Florida Constitution requires school boards to operate, control and supervise all free public schools within their districts. The court held **Section 1002.335 "permits and encourages the creation of a parallel system of free public education escaping the operation and control of local elected school boards."** It vested a commission of state board appointees with the powers of operation, control and supervision that were reserved to local boards. Rejecting the state board's arguments that the new law furthered the goals of systemic uniformity and efficiency, the court found Section 1002.335 in "total and fatal conflict" with article IX, section 4 of the Florida Constitution, and held the act unconstitutional. *Duval County School Board v. State Board of Educ.*, 998 So.2d 641 (Fla. Dist. Ct. App. 2008).

◆ A South Carolina academy applied to a school district to open as a charter school for the 2004-05 school year. The district's board gave the academy conditional approval, contingent upon finding a site in the district prior to August 2003. The academy notified the board that it had located a site in the district, and the board paid it over $87,000. But the academy obtained another site, and the state education department approved it. The academy was not ready to open when public schools opened for the 2004-05 school year. It tried to open in a temporary location, but when the school district reported this to the education department, the department directed the academy's closure. The academy obtained a conditional certificate to hold classes in an alternate facility. The school board held a hearing and ruled that the academy had not met four conditions for approval and that it had no contract with the district.

Although the academy did not meet the conditions, it appealed to the state board of education, which affirmed the local board's decision. On appeal, the Supreme Court of South Carolina reviewed the state Charter School Act and held that **a conditional charter did not confer due process rights on a charter applicant**. Even if there was a lack of due process, the local board had remedied this by holding a hearing. The academy was required to meet the terms of its application. *James Academy of Excellence v. Dorchester County School Dist. Two*, 376 S.C. 293, 657 S.E.2d 469 (S.C. 2008).

◆ A Pennsylvania resident requested an auditor's report and financial statements from a charter school. He also sought information about the written arrangement between the school and a private management entity. The school claimed it was not an agency of the commonwealth and that the state Right-to-Know Act did not apply to it. The management entity denied the resident's request for records on grounds that it was a private company. The resident sued the school for disclosure. A state common pleas court held for the resident and ordered the school to provide copies of the requested records.

On appeal, the Supreme Court of Pennsylvania held that the Right-to-Know Act required "agencies" to make public records accessible for inspection and duplication. Among the agencies required to disclose records were the offices, departments, boards or commissions of the executive branch. **School districts were similar to the entities explicitly listed in the Right-to-Know Act and they qualified as "agencies."** Charter schools were independent public schools created for the essential governmental service of education. As organizations performing essential governmental functions, charter schools were "agencies" covered by the Right-to-Know Act. The court affirmed the judgment. *Zager v. Chester Community Charter School*, 594 Pa. 166, 934 A.2d 1227 (Pa. 2007).

◆ A Wisconsin "virtual academy" was established as a charter school to provide curriculum by Internet and mail to students statewide. The academy's administrative offices were within the district that established it. The Wisconsin Education Association Council sued the establishing school district, state superintendent of instruction and others, claiming that the school violated state charter school, open enrollment and teacher certification statutes. A court held for the district and state superintendent. On appeal, the state court of appeals found academy students studied and completed assignments under the direction of their parents, who were not licensed. This violated the law. Academy teachers worked from their homes across the state, not just in the district. This also violated the law because **the charter school law prohibited a school board from establishing a charter school located outside the district**. While the academy's offices remained in the district, the statutory term "school" could not be construed to exclude the teachers and students making up the academy. The court also reversed the trial court's decision on the open enrollment issue. As operation of the academy violated three Wisconsin laws, the court reversed the judgment. *Johnson v. Burmaster*, 307 Wis.2d 213, 744 N.W.2d 900 (Wis. Ct. App. 2007), review denied, 749 N.W.2d 662 (Wis. 2008).

◆ Massachusetts law authorized "Commonwealth" and "Horace Mann" charter schools. Horace Mann charter schools were subject to approval by local school committees, but Commonwealth schools were independent of a school committee. The law charged the board of education with the final determination on granting charters and allowed the board to revoke charters. A school committee that served four towns approved an application for a Commonwealth charter school focusing on advanced learning in math and science. The school committees of three towns sued the board, and the case reached the Supreme Judicial Court of Massachusetts. It held the board had the final decision to grant a charter. **No state law or regulation permitted appeals from a board decision.** Public hearings are legislative, not adversary in nature. The legislature did not intend school committees to obtain judicial review in Commonwealth charter school cases. Local school committees could make the process unworkable and unwieldy and played a limited role in the application process. *School Committee of Hudson v. Board of Educ.*, 448 Mass. 565, 863 N.E.2d 22 (Mass. 2007).

◆ The Ohio Federation of Teachers, Ohio Congress of Parents and Teachers, and the Ohio School Boards Association sought a state court ruling that community schools violated the Ohio Constitution. The case reached the Supreme Court of Ohio, which rejected the claim that community schools diverted funding from public schools. The General Assembly had authority to spend tax revenues to further a statewide system of schools. There was no violation of state constitutional provisions for local control of city school boards and local revenue. **The General Assembly did not intrude upon local powers by creating community schools.** *Ohio Congress of Parents and Teachers v. State Board of Educ.*, 111 Ohio St.3d 568, 857 N.E.2d 1148 (Ohio 2006).

2. Applications

The Louisiana state Board of Elementary and Secondary Education was allowed to immediately terminate a charter school's contract after an investigation indicated the school had jeopardized student health and welfare.

◆ Louisiana's Board of Elementary and Secondary Education (BESE) voted to terminate and revoke a charter, following an investigation of a school for lack of supervision, failure to investigate sexual behavior and failure to report child abuse. Also documented was the school's failure to evaluate two students for disability and failures to document – and follow up on – incidents involving the safety, health and welfare of students at the school. Later, the BESE petitioned a state court, asserting the BESE violated provisions of the charter contract and the state Charter School Law and Open Meetings Law. Appeal reached the Court of Appeal of Louisiana, which noted the charter contract permitted termination of the charter based on the BESE's determination that the operator had failed to comply with specified obligations. Nothing required the procedure in the charter contract to comply with state charter-school provisions. The BESE could use separate procedures to revoke the charter since the health, safety and/or welfare of students was at issue. **The BESE could immediately revoke the charter once it determined that the health, safety or welfare of students was threatened.** There was no violation of the state Open Meetings Law, as it was not shown that the BESE took action at a meeting that was not open to the public. As a result, the judgment for the BESE was affirmed. *Pelican Educ. Foundation v. Louisiana State Board of Elementary and Secondary Educ.*, 97 So.3d 440 (La. Ct. App. 2012).

◆ After New Jersey's commissioner of education denied a charter application, a member of the group that proposed the school appealed to a state court. When the case reached a state appellate court, it was noted that the group had submitted several previous charter school applications that were denied as deficient. The district superintendent estimated that $2 million would be diverted from district schools if the charter school opened. The application had conflicting information regarding course requirements, did not fully address state high school graduation requirements and failed to specify a process for curriculum development in the nine areas of the New Jersey state core curriculum content standards. The commissioner was concerned that a charter school could undermine school district integration efforts. **Included in the commissioner's findings was that the goals and objectives of the charter school plan were weak.** A distance learning component did not identify a specific model or explain how it would be implemented. It was not error for the commissioner to credit the district superintendent's concerns. There was no merit to the applicant's argument that the No Child Left Behind Act required the granting of the application because the district's high school was identified as a school in need of improvement. In the court's view, the application was correctly denied. *In re Proposed Quest Academy Charter School of Montclair Founders Group*, 2012 WL 1836117 (N.J. Super. Ct. App. Div. 5/22/12).

◆ An Ohio church sought to sponsor community schools (known elsewhere as charter schools). But the state education department found it ineligible, since neither the church nor its parent, Presbyterian Church USA, was an "education-oriented" entity as required by Section 3314.02(C) of the revised state code. The case reached the Supreme Court of Ohio. It noted Section 3314.015(B) of the state code made "final" a department determination regarding an entity's status as "education-oriented." Section 3314.015(B)(3) made a department determination regarding "education-oriented" status appealable. Community school provisions did not say department decisions were "not appealable." They only stated that they were "final." **A key to review by appellate courts is that there is a "final" order from which a party may appeal.** "Final" meant the opposite of "not appealable." Since the community school provisions did not prohibit an appeal by the church, the court reversed the judgment and returned the case to the lower courts for further activity. *Brookwood Presbyterian Church v. Ohio Dep't of Educ.*, 127 Ohio St.3d 469, 940 N.E.2d 1256 (Ohio 2010).

◆ A Maryland school board charter review committee rejected a charter application as incomplete. In a 10-page letter, the committee described the deficiencies and sought clarification from the applicant in 50 areas. After the application was resubmitted, the committee found only eight of its concerns had been satisfied. Charter school representatives met with the committee to discuss the school application. Using a county public school "analytical scoring rubric," the board assigned the application only 189 of 530 possible points. After the board voted down the application, it sent the applicants a breakdown of its evaluation criteria, the scoring rubric and the score. Charter school applicants appealed to the Maryland State Board of Education (MSBE), which held the process had been fair. Appeal reached the Court of Special Appeals of Maryland.

The court found **the Maryland Public Charter School Program vested county education boards with primary chartering authority and that the MSBE had broad authority over the administration of public schools.** Prior MSBE rulings permitted local boards to withhold charter application scoring rubrics, so long as the process was otherwise explained. As the MSBE found, the committee explained the deficiencies in a 10-page letter and held four meetings to discuss its action. The court found the MSBE's review of the local decision was consistent with its prior cases. An argument that the local board was "generally opposed to granting a charter" did not show local bias made the board unable to make a fair and impartial decision. As the court found nothing illegal, arbitrary or capricious about the denial of the application, it held for the board. *Board of Educ. of Somerset County v. Somerset Advocates for Educ.*, 189 Md.App. 385, 984 A.2d 405 (Md. Ct. Spec. App. 2009).

◆ A Florida charter school application stated that students who scored at or above the 25th percentile in norm-referenced tests would be considered as having demonstrated acceptable student performance standards. The local board denied the application, finding that this measure would render the school unaccountable and that the 25th percentile was lower than its own standards. Moreover, the academy did not make reasonable enrollment projections and had overestimated its capital budget by $1 million. The academy appealed to the state Charter School Appeals Commission, where it asserted the 25th percentile had been a typographical error and should have been the 51st percentile.

The commission found no requirement that a school grade be a part of a charter application, and no substantial evidence of a deficiency. The state board then granted the application. On appeal, the District Court of Appeal of Florida found the application was not deficient. **There was no state law requirement for a school "A" goal.** The academy offered to correct its typographical error, and the application was sufficient with respect to student assessment and accountability. The academy overcame any reason for denying the application regarding budget and class size. **The state charter school law did not permit the state board to open charter schools.** Once a charter application was granted, the school board had control over the process. The board had authority to revoke a charter, and it still operated, controlled and supervised schools in the district. The court affirmed the state board's decision. *School Board of Volusia County v. Academies of Excellence*, 974 So.2d 1186 (Fla. Dist. Ct. App. 2008).

◆   South Carolina applicants submitted a charter school application and met with a state Charter School Advisory Committee to review compliance with the state Charter Schools Act. The committee voted to certify the application, but the board for the school district in which the charter school was to be located voted to deny it at a public hearing. The board found the application deficient in at least seven areas; thus, it would adversely affect other students in the district. The case reached the Supreme Court of South Carolina. The court explained that the Charter School Act permitted the denial of applications that did not meet the specific requirements of S.C. Code Sections 59-40-50 or 59-40-60, failed to meet the spirit or intent of the act, or that adversely affected the other students in the district. Instead of providing a written explanation of the reasons for denial of the application, and citing specific standards, the local board had only spoken in generalized terms. **The local board had clearly failed to meet the act's requirements.** The judgment for the applicants was affirmed. *Lee County School Dist. Board of Trustees v. MLD Charter School Academy Planning Committee*, 371 S.C. 561, 641 S.E.2d 24 (S.C. 2007).

◆   A Florida charter school concentrated on serving poor children, many of whom had failed at other schools. Its operator applied for two new charters. The board denied the application under a policy that required applicants already having charters from the board to demonstrate a record of success in operating an exemplary charter school for the past two fiscal years. "An exemplary charter school" was one with at least a "B" grade or significant annual learning gains. The school board found the existing charter school to be non-exemplary based on its financial and academic performance. The school received a "D" grade for 2003-04 and was projected for a D or F in 2004-05. A state district court of appeal upheld the denial of the application. The Charter School Law required applicants to demonstrate how their schools would use "guiding principles" and meet a state-defined purpose. Among other things, charter applicants had to provide a detailed curriculum plan showing how students would be provided with services to meet state standards. The local board's policy of requiring "exemplary performance" was a practical and reasonable approach to testing an applicant's academic and financial abilities. **Competent, substantial evidence indicated that the application was fiscally and academically non-compliant**, and there was good cause to deny it. *Imhotep-Nguzo Saba Charter School v. Dep't of Educ.*, 947 So.2d 1279 (Fla. Dist. Ct. App. 2007).

◆   Illinois charter school applicants submitted a proposal for a school that would offer unemployed high school drop-outs opportunities to earn a diploma while acquiring vocational skills. Participants would divide time between school and work at low-income housing sites. The state board noted that the district had a $32.65 million deficit and faced additional budget cuts if it lost a pending voter referendum. It found the proposal not economically sound. A state court affirmed this decision, and appeal reached the Supreme Court of Illinois. The court **found that the terms of a proposed charter, including funding issues, must permit both the school and the district to be financially secure.** It agreed with the state board's interpretation of the law as requiring proposals to meet all 15 statutory requirements. As the proposal was not in the best interests of students in the district, the court affirmed the board's decision. *Comprehensive Community Solutions v. Rockford School Dist. No. 205*, 216 Ill.2d 455, 297 Ill.Dec. 221, 837 N.E.2d 1 (Ill. 2005).

3. Operations and Finance

California's highest court held an arbitrator had no authority to deny or revoke a school charter. And it held collective bargaining provisions could not be construed to allow an arbitrator to make an award in conflict with state law.

◆   A collective bargaining agreement (CBA) between the Los Angeles Unified School District (LAUSD) and the United Teachers of Los Angeles (UTLA) contained procedures intended to minimize disruptions to employees working at schools that were being converted to charter schools. Among the provisions was a section requiring LAUSD to disclose the operator of a charter school to employees of the proposed school. Other CBA provisions provided employees and the community a chance to review plans for charter school conversions, and a full disclosure of charter school employment conditions. After LAUSD approved the conversion of a high school into a charter school, the UTLA filed grievances on behalf of teachers, claiming LAUSD did not abide by the CBA.

A state superior court denied the UTLA's petition to compel arbitration. Appeal reached the Supreme Court of California, which noted that Section 47611.5 of the state Education Code declares **"the approval of a charter school petition shall not be controlled by a collective bargaining agreement."** And the state Educational Employment Relations Act prohibits negotiations when education code sections would be replaced, set aside or annulled. A CBA proposal that altered the state statutory scheme would be non-negotiable if it replaced or set aside an education code provision. **An arbitrator had no authority to deny or revoke a school charter in the state.** According to the court, the UTLA had failed to identify which CBA provisions had been violated. Although no arbitrator could award relief that controlled, delayed or obstructed the approval or denial of a charter petition, the court held some of the grievances were potentially subject to arbitration. It returned the case to the superior court so the UTLA could clarify the CBA provisions at issue and decide whether enforcing them would conflict with the education code. *United Teachers of Los Angeles v. Los Angeles Unified School Dist.*, 54 Cal.4th 504, 278 P.3d 1204, 142 Cal.Rptr.3d 850 (Cal. 2012).

◆   The Cincinnati City School District auctioned nine vacant school buildings with deed restrictions preventing use of the property for a school purpose. The purchasers of one building obtained a conditional-use approval to reopen the school as a charter school. In a state court, the board of education sought an order declaring the deed restriction valid and enforceable. By the time it did so, the purchasers had invested more than $100,000 in preparing to open a charter school. Appeal reached the Supreme Court of Ohio. It held state law required a local board to offer charter schools the opportunity to purchase unused school buildings "suitable for use as classroom space" before they were offered for sale to other parties. Another provision required school boards to offer real property to start-up community schools in their territories if the property had not been in use for one full school year. These laws indicated that **the general assembly had a preference for giving charter schools the opportunity to operate out of unused public school buildings**. The deed restriction frustrated the state's intention to make classroom space available to community schools. In view of the strong public interest in community schools, the court held the deed restriction unenforceable as against public policy. *Cincinnati City School Dist. Board of Educ. v. Conners*, 132 Ohio St.3d 468, 974 N.E.2d 78 (Ohio 2012).

◆ An Indiana teacher applied to work at a charter school in Oklahoma. He interviewed twice in Oklahoma and sent his professional references and other materials. The teacher said the school then advised him it had registered him for a national teacher's conference, and it issued him a cell phone. He said the school sent him a letter of intent, which he signed and returned. According to the teacher, the letter of intent conveyed a term of employment, communicated an intent that he would be discharged only for good cause, and stated a salary offer. But the charter school principal rescinded the job offer, and the teacher suspected this was because of his sexual orientation. In a state court action for breach of contract, the teacher claimed he reasonably relied on the school's promise of employment by making preparations to move to Oklahoma.

Finding no employment contract was made, the court dismissed the case. On appeal, the Court of Appeals of Oklahoma found the teacher had stated the elements of an implied contract. It was relevant that the school issued him a cell phone and enrolled him in a national teachers' convention, then sent him a letter of intent. **The teacher's signing of the letter and taking steps toward moving to Oklahoma were evidence of acceptance of an employment offer.** There had been specifics such as a stated minimum salary and a limitation on employment termination to just cause in accordance with specified procedures. As the teacher had asserted a sufficient claim for breach of an implied contract, and relied in good faith on that contract, the court reversed the judgment. *Sexton v. Kipp Reach Academy Charter School*, 260 P.3d 435 (Okla Ct. App. 2011).

◆ Pennsylvania's Charter School Law requires school districts to pay a charter school an amount for each resident student who attends the charter school. Charter schools also have the ability to set the grades or age levels to be served. A school district contested a deduction by the state for refusing to pay a cyber charter school on behalf of a four-year-old who had enrolled in the school as a kindergartner. The district noted its kindergarten program had an age threshold of five, and that the cyber student did not meet this requirement.

After a state administrative appeal, the secretary of the state department of education held for the charter school. The case eventually reached the state supreme court. It noted the state code gave school districts the discretion to maintain kindergarten programs for children between the ages of 4 and 6. If a school board decided to maintain a kindergarten program, the board had a state-law right to decide the age of eligibility. Under the state code, a child was entitled to enroll in a public school district of residence only if the district's minimum entrance requirements were met. As a four-year-old, the student was not allowed to attend the district's schools. Children were not statutorily entitled to attend kindergarten and could enroll only if a district had decided to provide it. The court held that **when faced with a conflict in enrollment policies, the cyber charter school was bound by the policy of a district of residence**. For this reason, the district did not have to pay for the child's admission to the cyber charter school. *Slippery Rock Area School Dist. v. Pennsylvania Cyber Charter School*, 31 A.2d 657 (Pa. 2011).

◆   In 2000, the New York Department of Labor decided that charter schools were generally not considered to be public entities. Thus, a state prevailing wage law for those working on public projects did not apply. But in 2007, the department issued an opinion letter declaring the prevailing wage law should apply to charter school projects. Soon, the state commissioner of labor notified the Charter Schools Institute and state education department that the prevailing wage laws would be enforced for new charter school projects after a specified date. Charter schools and supporting organizations filed a state court action for a declaration that the commissioner's new position exceeded her authority and an order declaring the prevailing wage laws inapplicable to charter schools.

A state trial court held a charter agreement was a public contract and that charter school construction and renovation projects were public works. An appellate division court reversed the judgment, and appeal reached the state's highest court. The New York Court of Appeals found the prevailing wage laws applied to public agency contracts for the employment of laborers, workmen or mechanics on "public works projects." According to the court, a charter agreement was not a contract for public work. **A charter was an authorizing agreement by which an agency determined a charter applicant was competent for state licensure.** While the court held New York charter schools bore some similarities to public entities, the prevailing wage law identified only four covered public entities. None were educational entities such as charter schools. Finding the prevailing wage law did not apply to charter schools, the court affirmed the appellate division's judgment. *New York Charter School Ass'n v. Smith*, 15 N.Y.3d 403, 940 N.E.2d 522, 914 N.Y.S.2d 696 (N.Y. 2010).

◆   A Cincinnati community school sponsor placed a school on probation, then suspended it from operating. The sponsor gave the school a statutory written notice of its right to request an informal hearing within 14 days, but the school sought a direct appeal to the state education department. Asserting the school waived its appeal rights, the sponsor advised the department that the contract was terminated. Unable to continue operating, the school appealed to the state supreme court, which found that the state code permitted a sponsor to terminate a community school contract upon 90 days' written notice. Notice must include reasons for the action and a statement that the school may request an informal hearing within 14 days. A school may appeal from an adverse decision to the state education board. **A community school contract was terminated upon the passage of 90 days after the date of a sponsor's notice.** As the sponsor complied with statutory requirements, the court held that the school was not entitled to relief. *State ex rel. Nation Building Technical Academy v. Ohio Dep't of Educ.*, 123 Ohio St.3d 35, 913 N.E.2d 977 (Ohio 2009).

◆   A Florida school board voted to terminate two charter schools with long histories of financial mismanagement. The board indicated the action was for "good cause" under Florida law, based on the severity of recent audit findings. A charter provision permitted termination upon 24 hours' notice, but the school operators claimed the procedural protections of the state Administrative Procedure Act (APA). Appeal reached the Supreme Court of Florida, which noted that **the law permits the immediate termination of charters for "good cause" shown,** or when the health, safety or welfare of the students is threatened. School boards did not have to follow the APA when facing circumstances involving the health, safety or welfare of students, or where other good cause necessitated immediate action. *School Board of Palm Beach County, Florida v. Survivors Charter Schools*, 3 So.3d 1220 (Fla. 2009).

◆   A 2005 New York Charter School Law amendment directed the state comptroller to audit all school districts and charter schools in the state. Several New York City charter schools filed a state court challenge to the comptroller's authority to do the audits. The case reached the Court of Appeals of New York, which found the legislature designated the state board of regents and chartering entities as the public agents authorized to supervise and oversee charter schools. **Charter school audits could not be construed as "incidental to the audits of school districts."** The state comptroller could not claim the power to conduct the audits on the basis of the receipt of state funds and the performance of a governmental function. Once paid to a charter school, public funds were no longer under state control. As a check on their accountability, charters had to be renewed each five years and could be lost if educational standards were not met. The court ruled for the charter schools. *In re New York Charter Schools Ass'n v. DiNapoli*, 13 N.Y.2d 120, 914 N.E.2d 991 (N.Y. 2009).

◆   A Texas private school converted to an open-enrollment charter school. The charter school board hired the subsidiary of a management company to run the school under a five-year contract. The parent management company's president signed the contract, which assigned claims to the management company to collect fees owed to the subsidiary. Relations strained between the school operators, the management company and the subsidiary, and the contract was ended after only one year. The company sued for breach of contract, and a state court awarded it a directed verdict of $250,899 and attorneys' fees. On appeal, the Court of Appeals of Texas affirmed the damage award for management fees owed to the subsidiary. It then considered a claim regarding unlawful "advances" by the parent company. **State law prohibited the governing body of an open-enrollment charter school from accepting a loan from a management company under contract to manage a charter school.** By law, the "advances" were prohibited loans, voiding the contract. Even if that contract was valid, the parent could not show a contract existed without proving its own illegal conduct. For this reason, the lower court should have granted the school operators a directed verdict on that claim. *Academy of Skills & Knowledge v. Charter Schools, USA*, 260 S.W.3d 529 (Tex. Ct. App. 2008).

◆ Baltimore's school board rejected applications for funding by three different charter schools. Appeals came before the state board of education (SBE), and then the Maryland Court of Appeals. The court found the SBE's calculation of an "average cost" included students who would receive Title I or special education funds or services. This would in turn require the charter schools to adjust their budgets. The SBE acted within its discretion by deciding the cases. Allowing local boards to decide "what funding is commensurate with the amounts disbursed to the other public schools" risked disparate local methods of implementing a uniform law and undercut the SBE's authority to interpret the education law. The legislature must have envisioned that the SBE would have primary authority to interpret the law. **The law's "commensurate funding" language necessarily had a per-student basis, and there was no error in the SBE's use of an average per-student approach.** As a result, the SBE decisions were upheld. *Baltimore City Board of School Commissioners v. City Neighbors Charter School*, 400 Md. 324, 929 A.2d 113 (Md. 2007).

◆ A Texas corporation operated three "distance learning" charter schools in California. Families of students enrolled in the schools claimed the schools did not provide computers, instruction, assessment, review, curriculum, equipment, supplies or services, but collected over $20 million in state funding. The families asserted that the corporation aggressively recruited poor rural districts to approve charter schools. The districts then intentionally failed to perform their oversight duties. The families sued the corporation and chartering districts for breach of contract, misrepresentation, constitutional violations and misuse of taxpayer funds. They added a claim under the California False Claims Act (CFCA) for submission of fraudulent claims and an Unfair Competition Law (UCL) claim for unfair and deceptive business practices. The case reached the Supreme Court of California, which held **charter school operators were "persons" who could be held liable under the CFCA.** And UCL purposes were served by subjecting the charter school operators to deceptive business practices claims. *Wells v. One2One Learning Foundation*, 39 Cal.4th 1164, 48 Cal.Rptr.3d 108, 141 P.2d 225 (Cal. 2006).

◆ The Individuals with Disabilities Education Act (IDEA) and the Elementary and Secondary Education Act (ESEA) authorize state recipients of federal funds to distribute grant money to local educational agencies (LEAs). Public charter schools are within the definition of an LEA under both laws. A U.S. Department of Education audit of the Arizona Department of Education (ADE) concluded the ADE had improperly awarded ESEA and IDEA funds to for-profit entities that operated charter schools in the state. The Arizona State Board for Charter Schools and several for-profit charter school operators petitioned for review. A federal district court held that the statutes expressed a congressional mandate that in order to receive federal funds, charter schools must be nonprofit. The state board and the schools appealed. The Ninth Circuit affirmed. **Only nonprofit institutional day or residential schools are eligible for federal funding under the ESEA and IDEA.** Congress clearly intended to "prohibit the funding of for-profit schools, charter or otherwise." *Arizona State Board for Charter Schools v. U.S. Dep't of Educ.*, 464 F.3d 1003 (9th Cir. 2006).

IV. TESTING

A Texas school district employee who was found to have falsified student dropout reports for reporting to the state was unable to show that other school officials violated his constitutional rights by putting him up to the misconduct.

◆   A Texas school district network specialist had the ability to upload student dropout data to a program used to report to the Texas Education Agency. He claimed an assistant principal and the school principal put him up to deleting student names from the school's dropout list. A report reflected 30 dropout records were changed on a day when only the network specialist had logged on to the computer system. A local news station reported the record falsification, and the school district investigated. A report concluded that the specialist knowingly changed student dropout data without authorization. He was later reassigned twice and then indicted by a grand jury for altering a government record. Officials arrested the specialist, but a second grand jury indictment was dismissed. He sued the administrators in a federal district court.

After the case was dismissed, the specialist appealed to the U.S. Court of Appeals, Fifth Circuit. It considered a Fourth Amendment claim based on the initiation of criminal charges without probable cause. But the specialist did not assert he was either seized or arrested and did not show he was subjected to an "unreasonable seizure." There was evidence that he admitted changing dropout data on a specific date, which established probable cause for his indictments. Even though the specialist claimed the prosecutor learned of a document he called "the smoking gun," the court found this did not show the administrators knowingly withheld evidence. **While the specialist claimed a due process violation, the court found no right to be free from criminal prosecution that is unsupported by probable cause.** The judgment was affirmed. *Cuadra v. Houston Independent School Dist.*, 626 F.3d 808 (5th Cir. 2010).

◆   Cincinnati Public Schools (CPS) spent $809,000 to hire a testing agency to develop exams for students in grades 9 - 11. CPS kept the exams in a secure area at a central location prior to administration. Students and staff members were forbidden from copying exams, and exams were collected immediately after being administered. A CPS teacher grew concerned over the design, implementation and scoring of the exams. About 60 other CPS teachers signed a petition seeking copies of the ninth grade exam. CPS denied the request, arguing that the exams had secure and copyrighted material. After mediation failed, the teacher sought a special order, called a "writ of mandamus," from the

Supreme Court of Ohio. The court held that this remedy is available to compel compliance with the Ohio Public Records Act. Since the semester exams were created to fulfill CPS policy decisions, the Public Records Act applied. CPS had spent a great amount of money in developing the exams, and CPS had taken steps to maintain their secrecy. **As the exams were trade secrets, CPS did not have to disclose them to the teacher.** *State ex rel. Perrea v. Cincinnati Public Schools*, 123 Ohio St.3d 410, 916 N.E.2d 1049 (Ohio 2009).

◆   Arizona's Proposition 203 required all children in state public schools to be instructed in English. It specified a standardized, nationally normed written test of academic subject matter, administered in English. State officials claimed the U.S. Department of Education (DOE) agreed to permit appeals of adequate yearly progress (AYP) calculations on grounds that student test scores could not be a valid, reliable indicator of academic proficiency due to language deficiencies. A DOE monitoring team found that Arizona improperly used the NCLB Act appeals process to remove assessment scores from AYP calculations. The DOE ordered the state to cease this use of appeals and to use practices minimizing language barriers to LEP students. The state education department sued the DOE for breach of an oral agreement to permit appeals for LEP students. The court agreed with the DOE's argument that **a breach of contract claim could not be based on a claim that the DOE promised to interpret the NCLB Act a certain way.** However, the state could amend its complaint to add an Administrative Procedures Act claim regarding its state plan amendment under the NCLB Act. *Horne v. U.S. Dep't of Educ.*, No. CV-08-1141-PHX-MHM, 2009 WL 775432 (D. Ariz. 3/23/09).

◆   In 2003, the California state board of education announced that all public school students graduating in spring 2006 would have to pass both the language arts and mathematics parts of the California High School Exit Exam to receive a diploma. Districts had to offer supplemental instruction to all students who did not demonstrate sufficient progress toward passing. The legislature appropriated $20 million in supplemental funding for districts with the highest percentage of students who had not yet passed the exam. The state superintendent of public instruction distributed supplemental funding only to districts in which 28% or more of the class of 2006 had yet to pass the exam.

A state court lawsuit was filed on behalf of 47,000 students who had yet to pass at least one part of the exam but had satisfied other diploma requirements for spring 2006. The state court of appeal held that **the state superintendent of public instruction had authority to give priority to the schools with the highest numbers of students who failed both parts of the exam.** The court found nothing arbitrary in the allocation of a limited sum of money to benefit school districts that appeared to have the greatest need. *O'Connell v. Superior Court of Alameda County,* 47 Cal.Rptr.3d 147 (Cal. Ct. App. 2006).

◆   A Maryland principal intern was accused of misconduct when taking a Praxis Series School Leaders Licensure Assessment Test. When she took the test, a site administrator submitted irregularity reports based on her failure to stop writing in her test booklet when time was called. The Educational Testing

Service (ETS) then cancelled her scores and returned her fee. The intern sued the ETS and the site administrator for breach of contract and other claims. The judge awarded pretrial judgment to the ETS on the breach of contract claim and dismissed all of the intern's remaining claims. The intern appealed to the state court of special appeals, which noted that **the ETS reserved the right to cancel a test score for misconduct**. However, the court agreed with the intern that a jury should be allowed to determine if her test scores had been cancelled in bad faith. The court reversed the judgment and remanded the case to the trial court. The intern would have to "surmount a gigantic hurdle" unless she could show that the administrator had some motive to lie. *Hildebrant v. Educational Testing Service*, 171 Md.App. 23, 908 A.2d 657 (Md. Ct. Spec. App. 2006).

◆   A Florida district court of appeal upheld an administrative ruling **rejecting charges that a teacher provided inappropriate assistance to her students during the Florida Comprehensive Assessment Test**. The state education practices commission filed a complaint against the teacher for providing answers and other help to her students on the test. However, after a hearing, an administrative law judge found all of the commission's student witnesses not credible. The judge accepted the testimony of the lone student who testified for the teacher. The commission held another hearing and issued a final order suspending the teacher's certification. The court of appeal held that the commission had improperly modified the judge's findings. As substantial evidence supported the judge's decision, the complaint was dismissed. *Stinson v. Winn*, 938 So.2d 554 (Fla. Dist. Ct. App. 2006).

◆   The Massachusetts Education Reform Act specified a comprehensive diagnostic assessment of students in the fourth, eighth and tenth grades, with satisfaction of the tenth-grade examination a high school graduation requirement. Although student failure rates were as high as 53% in some core areas on the first MCAS administration in 1998, the board made the English, math, science and social studies parts of the exam a graduation requirement for students in the class of 2003. The board planned to phase other subjects into the graduation requirement and to raise the threshold scaled score over time. A group of students from the class of 2003 sued, challenging the regulation requiring them to pass the MCAS exam as a graduation prerequisite.

The court denied a request for an order prohibiting the state education board from enforcing the regulation. The students appealed to the Supreme Judicial Court, which held that **the board had the authority to gradually incorporate core areas in the MCAS examination, and to test students in English and math before doing so in other areas**. The regulation largely accomplished the Reform Act goal of holding educators accountable through required academic standards, curriculum frameworks and competency determinations. The legislature twice ratified the MCAS exam appropriating substantial funds for remediation programs. This indicated acceptance of the board's phase-in approach. The court affirmed the lower court decision. *Student No. 9 v. Board of Educ.*, 440 Mass. 752, 802 N.E.2d 105 (Mass. 2004).

V. EDUCATIONAL MALPRACTICE

Claims of educational malpractice have, for the most part, failed. Courts have been reluctant to interfere with a school's internal operations.

◆   A Florida family claimed that Osceola County School Board employees told them Celebration School provided "a quality education based upon a time-tested and successful curriculum known as 'best practices.'" After moving to the Town of Celebration and enrolling their children in Celebration School, the parents became disenchanted with the school and placed their children in private schools. They sued the school board for misrepresentation. The case reached a Florida district court of appeal, which found the claims for fraudulent inducement and negligent misrepresentation were not "educational malpractice claims." The trial court should have allowed the parents to amend their complaint to allege sufficient facts and attempt to prove each element of these claims. However, **the trial court had properly dismissed the family's claim under the Florida Constitution, which guarantees a high quality free public education**. There was no benchmark for determining how to define a "high quality education." This determination was for the legislature to make. *Simon v. Celebration Co.*, 883 So.2d 826 (Fla. Dist. Ct. App. 2004).

◆   A group of parents sued the Denver Public Schools and its superintendent for failing to provide students with a quality education. The complaint asserted that the school system failed to provide course books, failed to impose adequate discipline on students, improperly used credit waivers to inflate graduation rates, maintained a pattern of poorly performing schools, and used "dumbed-down" standards for measuring school performance. It also alleged damages for intellectual and emotional harm, diminution of educational and career opportunities, discrimination, and asserted that parents were forced to send their children to private or alternative schools. A court dismissed the case on grounds that the constitutional and statutory claims were not justiciable. The state court of appeals agreed to review the contract claim and distinguished it from contract claims against private schools. Contract claims attacking the general quality of public education have been rejected because they are not truly based in contract but instead seek damages for educational malpractice.

Public school students have not individually contracted with their school systems for specific educational services and cannot assert breach of contract claims. There was no enforceable promise to provide a curriculum, books or other educational services in this case. The court held the matter was political in nature and not within the power of the courts to decide. No court in the nation has recognized a breach of contract claim rooted in legislative policy. The court affirmed the judgment for the board and superintendent. *Denver Parents Ass'n v. Denver Board of Educ.*, 10 P.3d 662 (Colo. Ct. App. 2000).

CHAPTER SIX

Students with Disabilities

I. THE IDEA

The Individuals with Disabilities Education Act (IDEA) imposes obligations on the states and requires compliance with IDEA procedures as a condition of receiving federal funds. To receive IDEA funds, states must maintain a policy assuring that all children with disabilities have access to a free appropriate public education (FAPE). "FAPE" refers to special education and related services provided at public expense that meet state educational agency standards in conformity with an individualized education program (IEP).

Local educational agencies (LEAs) receiving IDEA funds must make satisfactory assurances that they are identifying and providing special education services to resident students with disabilities.

In Board of Educ. v. Rowley, *this chapter, the U.S. Supreme Court held the IDEA establishes only a basic floor of opportunity for students with disabilities, and imposes no requirement on school districts to maximize student potential.*

Rowley *limits a court's inquiry to two things – whether the district has complied with IDEA procedural protections, and whether the IEP was reasonably calculated to enable the student to receive educational benefits. If a school district satisfies this two-part inquiry, the court's analysis is at an end.*

A. IDEA Substantive Requirements

◆ A Texas student had a 142 IQ and above-average math and social studies abilities, but he had poor writing, handwriting and spelling skills. As a tenth-grader, he had above-average grades and passed all parts of a state-mandated exam. But the next year, he stopped relying on a district-provided spell-checker in his regular classes. The student continued earning above-average grades, but he failed the written composition part of the state exit-level English test. In his senior year, he attended general education classes with 30 minutes of special education monitoring per semester. During the school year, the student's parents became convinced that he was incapable of performing college-level work. To delay his graduation and preserve his eligibility for school, the student dropped an economics class that was required for graduation. His parents had him reevaluated, and they began looking into a Massachusetts private school.

Although the district urged the student to graduate and obtain a waiver of the exit exam if necessary, the student enrolled in the Massachusetts school, where he remained for the summer and another school year. A hearing officer held the IEPs had insufficient transitional planning for entry into college and did not address the student's learning disability. A federal court agreed, and the case reached the U.S. Court of Appeals, Fifth Circuit. **It held a student's "whole educational experience, and its adaptation to confer 'benefits' on the child, is the ultimate statutory goal" under the IDEA.** Using this "holistic perspective," the court held the school district had customized the student's IEP on the basis of his assessments and his performance. Applying *Board of Educ. v. Rowley*, 458 U.S. 176 (1982), the court held the student's IEPs were reasonably calculated to enable him to earn passing marks and advance in grade. *Klein Independent School Dist. v. Hovem*, 690 F.3d 390 (5th Cir. 2012).

◆   A California student's parents claimed their child had a greater capacity for progress than what was reflected by her school district's proposed IEPs. After two due process hearings, the case went before the U.S. Court of Appeals, Ninth Circuit. It held the IDEA does not require any particular educational approach. Further, the district was not required to offer the Applied Behavioral Analysis program urged by the parents. Instead, **the eclectic educational approach of the district met the IDEA's substantive requirements**. As the IEPs were tailored to the student's needs, based on accepted autism education principles and consistent with IDEA objectives, the court held for the school district. *K.S. v. Fremont Unified School Dist.*, 426 Fed.Appx. 536 (9th Cir. 2011).

◆   A New York student with hearing impairments sought the provision of a sign-language interpreter from her school district. She had residual hearing and was an excellent lipreader, which allowed her to attain above-average grades and to advance through school easily. A federal court held that the disparity between the student's achievement and her potential to perform as she would if not for her disability deprived her of a free appropriate public education. This decision was affirmed by the U.S. Court of Appeals, Second Circuit, and the U.S. Supreme Court agreed to review the case. The Court found no requirement in the IDEA that public schools maximize the potential of each student with a disability. The opportunities provided to each student by their school varied from student to student. The IDEA was primarily designed to guarantee access to students with disabilities to allow them to meaningfully benefit from public education. The IDEA protected the right to access education by means of its procedural protections, including the annual IEP meeting and review process. In IDEA cases, courts were to limit their inquiry to **whether the district had complied with IDEA procedural protections and whether the IEP was reasonably calculated to enable the student to receive educational benefits**. If the district satisfied this two-part inquiry, the court's analysis was at an end and the district was entitled to judgment. *Board of Educ. v. Rowley*, 458 U.S. 176 (1982).

◆   The parents of a Minnesota child sought to have accommodations provided for extracurricular activities in which she might wish to engage. However, they did not identify any specific activity at that time. The student later identified volleyball and after-school clubs as activities she was interested in. Her parents also sought accommodations so she could attend an off-campus fifth-grade graduation party. The district refused to provide accommodations relating to the party since it was a private event sponsored by the parent-teacher organization. A lawsuit filed by the parents reached the Minnesota Supreme Court, which held that **the student did not have to prove that she would receive educational benefits from extracurricular and nonacademic activities in order to qualify for supplemental aides and services**. In the court's view, the

IEP team would have to consider whether the extracurricular and nonacademic activities were appropriate for her. *Independent School Dist. No. 12, Centennial v. Minnesota Dep't of Educ.*, 788 N.W.2d 907 (Minn. 2010).

◆   A New Jersey high school student designated as "other health impaired" received special education and did well in his classes but tested poorly in standardized tests. His parents became concerned with his education and requested a due process hearing, where they noted that his reading skills were at a third-grade level. His teachers and other school employees testified that standardized test scores were unreliable and that academic progress was a better indicator of success, but an administrative law judge disagreed and ruled for the parents. A federal court reversed that decision, but **the Third Circuit held the student's good grades did not indicate that he was making educational progress**. In this case, the school district failed to incorporate necessary recommendations made by the parents' experts and by the student's teachers and evaluators. *D.S. v. Bayonne Board of Educ.*, 602 F.3d 553 (3d Cir. 2010).

◆   A Washington student with learning disabilities attended regular classes and progressed from grade to grade. Her parents became dissatisfied with her education and found an independent evaluator who suggested that no public school in the state could provide her an adequate education. The parents enrolled their daughter in a Massachusetts private school and sought tuition reimbursement from their school district. A federal court held an administrative law judge improperly relied on *Board of Educ. v. Rowley*. According to the court, *Rowley* was superseded by post-1982 IDEA amendments. **The case reached the Ninth Circuit, which held the *Rowley* standard is still appropriate for determining whether a child has received an appropriate education.** Congress never disapproved of *Rowley* in any of the amendments to the IDEA. *J.L. v. Mercer Island School Dist.*, 575 F.3d 1025 (9th Cir. 2009).

◆   A Tennessee school board violated the rights of a student with autism by failing to consider Lovaas programming and improperly staffing his IEP team meetings. The Sixth Circuit held **"meaningful educational benefit" had to be gauged in relation to the student's potential**. The IDEA's legislative history supported exceeding the "meaningful educational benefits" standard where there was a "difference between self-sufficiency and a life of dependence" for a child. *Hamilton County Dep't of Educ. v. Deal*, 392 F.3d 840 (6th Cir. 2004).
    The case returned to a lower court, which held district IEP proposals were appropriate for the student. The parents appealed an award of half their request for Lovaas service reimbursement. The Sixth Circuit affirmed the decision. As the district's IEPs were reasonably calculated to offer the student a meaningful educational benefit, the reduction in reimbursement was reasonable. *Deal v. Hamilton County Dep't of Educ.*, 258 Fed.Appx. 863 (6th Cir. 2008).

◆   Colorado parents claimed their school district did not address their autistic son's inability to generalize skills he learned at school. Despite his apparent progress toward IEP goals and objectives, his home behavior was "unevenly tempered," and they placed him in a residential school. The case reached the

U.S. Court of Appeals, Tenth Circuit, which held the substantive IDEA standard for a free appropriate public education is not onerous. **Congress did not impose any greater substantive educational standard than would be necessary to make access to education "meaningful."** *Rowley* rejected "self-sufficiency" as a substantive IDEA standard. The IDEA was not designed to remedy a poor home setting or to make up for some other deficit not covered by the act. Generalization across settings was not required to show educational benefit. The school district did not have to do more than provide an IEP that enabled the child to make measurable and adequate gains in the classroom. *Thompson R2-J School Dist. v. Luke P.*, 540 F.3d 1143 (10th Cir. 2008).

B. Procedural Protections

1. IEPs and Team Meetings

The individualized education program (IEP) is the IDEA's most important procedural protection. The IDEA requires adequate notice to parents and opportunities for parental participation in the development of a student's IEP. A school district "must include the parents of a child with a disability in an IEP meeting unless they affirmatively refuse to attend."

In A.G. v. Placentia-Yorba Linda Unified School Dist., *320 Fed.Appx. 519 (9th Cir. 2009), the Ninth Circuit held the IDEA does not require a child's most current teacher to attend an IEP meeting. Rather, it requires a special education teacher or provider who has actually taught the child to attend the meeting. The court rejected a claim by parents that there was an IDEA violation and held not all of their child's special education teachers needed to attend IEP meetings.*

◆   In a case consolidating actions by two New York students with autism, the Second Circuit Court of Appeals held that **an IDEA provision requiring that IEPs be updated annually did not mean that an IEP was inappropriate simply because it did not change significantly on an annual basis**. Although the photocopying of one student's goals was found "disturbing," the school's witnesses had explained that the goals remained appropriate. The parents participated in IEP meetings and provided the school with private evaluations, which were appropriately reviewed. An argument by the parents that the school department had predetermined a placement was not supported by the evidence. In fact, some witnesses had testified that the student would thrive in the program that was being proposed. As a result, the court held for the school department. *M.H. v. New York City Dep't of Educ.*, 685 F.3d 217 (2d Cir. 2012).

◆   A New Jersey student split time between regular education classes and special education programs during his first two years of elementary school. When his school district sought to place him in a full-time autism program, his parents rejected the proposal and requested an IDEA due process hearing. After an administrative law judge (ALJ) held for the school district, a federal court held the school district did not meaningfully include the parents in the IEP process. As a result, the court found the IEPs violated the IDEA because they were predetermined. On appeal to the U.S. Court of Appeals, Third Circuit, the court found clear evidence of predetermination. **Since the IEPs were created without parental participation or input, an IDEA procedural violation was present.** For this reason, the judgment for the parents was affirmed. *D.B. and L.B. v. Gloucester Township School Dist.*, 489 Fed.Appx. 564 (3d Cir. 2012).

◆   California parents claimed their son's school district violated the IDEA by staffing IEP meetings with his teacher from three years earlier. The dispute reached the U.S. Court of Appeals, Ninth Circuit, which held the IDEA required that an IEP team include "not less than 1 special education teacher, or where appropriate, not less than 1 special education provider of such child." The IDEA did not require the participation of a child's current special education provider in IEP team meetings. Instead, **an IEP meeting was procedurally valid as long as it included not less than one special education teacher or provider who had actually taught the student.** Next, the court found no merit to the parents' claim that the district violated the IDEA by not notifying them who would attend IEP meetings. It rejected their argument that failure to invite them to informal meetings and supply them a draft of IEP goals and objectives was an IDEA violation. This did not hamper their ability to contribute to the discussion of goals and objectives at IEP meetings. As any IDEA violations that may have occurred were harmless, the court held for the school district. *Mahone v. Carlsbad Unified School Dist.*, 430 Fed.Appx. 562 (9th Cir. 2011).

◆   **The U.S. Court of Appeals, Third Circuit, found no requirement in 20 U.S.C. Section 1414(d)(1)(B) for inclusion on an IEP team of an expert in a child's specific disability.** Although a New Jersey parent claimed his child's IEPs had no objectively measurable goals, the court found any such error did not warrant compensatory education. There was no error in the district court's finding that any flaws in the IEPs did not affect the rights of either the student or parent. As the student was not deprived of any educational opportunity, a lower court judgment for the board was affirmed. *Rodrigues v. Fort Lee Board of Educ.*, 458 Fed.Appx. 124 (3d Cir. 2011).

◆   The parents of a Vermont student with a disability asserted that their school district violated the IDEA because the student's applied media instructor, a regular education teacher, missed some IEP meetings. They claimed that his increased presence might have led to a different placement. After they began due process proceedings, the case reached the Second Circuit, which ruled against them. **The court held the absence of a regular educator at any given IEP meeting is not necessarily a procedural violation of the IDEA.** In this case, the applied media instructor's participation was held appropriate under the circumstances. He attended some meetings, and the parents decided to enroll their child in a particular applied media course without regard to his opinion. Thus, they suffered no harm. *K.L.A. v. Windham Southeast Supervisory Union*, 371 Fed.Appx. 151 (2d Cir. 2010).

◆   The parents of a New York student who had problems in large groups attended committee on special education (CSE) meetings at which the student's IEP was changed from a classroom of 24 students to a 12:1:1 setting. The parents rejected the proposed IEP, placed the student in a private school and then sought tuition reimbursement. A federal court found the IEP procedurally deficient because the student's special education teacher did not attend the CSE meetings. But the Second Circuit found **the IEP coordinator at the student's school had attended the CSE meetings along with the student's general education teacher** and that the IEP was reasonably calculated to provide educational benefits. No tuition reimbursement was awarded to the parents. *A.H. v. Dep't of Educ. of City of New York*, 394 Fed.Appx. 718 (2d Cir. 2010).

◆ Parents of an autistic preschool child were denied a ruling that school officials "predetermined" a placement and failed to provide him intensive one-on-one therapy. The U.S. Court of Appeals, Fourth Circuit, affirmed a lower court order finding the school considered information from the parents at IEP meetings. A hearing officer found the parents "derailed the IEP process" by preventing thorough discussions, and many of their own suggestions were adopted in the IEP. **Use of a draft IEP did not show predetermination.** The court affirmed a judgment for school officials under several disability laws. *J.D. v. Kanawha County Board of Educ.*, 357 Fed.Appx. 515 (4th Cir. 2009).

◆ A California school district scheduled an IEP meeting without first checking the parents' availability. The parents had a history of not attending meetings, and they did not return a signed copy of the IEP meeting notice. The mother asked the district to reschedule the meeting, but the district met in her absence. The parents filed an administrative action against the district for IDEA procedural violations. When the case reached the Ninth Circuit, it held that regardless of the parents' history and the reason for their unavailability on the date in question, the district had an affirmative duty to comply with the IDEA. It held **a school district "must include the parents of a child with a disability in an IEP meeting unless they affirmatively refuse to attend."** By proceeding with the IEP meeting in the parents' absence, the district violated the IDEA. *Drobnicki v. Poway Unified School Dist.*, 358 Fed.Appx. 788 (9th Cir. 2009).

◆ The parents of an autistic student in California claimed that their district violated the IDEA because no teacher from the student's private school attended IEP team meetings. The case reached the Ninth Circuit, which held the district provided a valid IEP. **The exclusion of a private school teacher from IEP team meetings did not result in lost educational opportunities for the student.** The stay-put provision of the IDEA required the district to maintain the student's current placement during the appeals process. *Joshua A. v. Rocklin Unified School Dist.*, 319 Fed.Appx. 692, 559 F.3d 1036 (9th Cir. 2009).

◆ A Connecticut student with serious emotional disturbance had increasing behavioral problems as he entered middle school. He was transferred to a state-approved special education day school, where he achieved good grades. His parents sought a private school placement, fearing he was not being sufficiently challenged. After an evaluation, the school board adopted several of the parents' suggested changes to the IEP, and offered a placement in a regional school for students with emotional and behavioral difficulties. The parents rejected the IEP, and the case reached the Second Circuit. It held schools comply with the IDEA when parents have adequate opportunities to participate in IEP development. **Nothing in the IDEA requires that parents consent to an IEP.** Because the initial and revised IEPs were sufficient, the board had offered an appropriate IEP. *A.E. v. Westport Board of Educ.*, 251 Fed.Appx. 685 (2d Cir. 2007).

◆   Ohio parents disagreed with the IEP prepared for their autistic son and placed him in a private school. They filed a due process hearing request but lost at two administrative levels. Without an attorney, they appealed. A federal court held for the school district, and the Sixth Circuit later held they could not pursue the case without hiring an attorney. **The U.S. Supreme Court heard the parents' appeal, and held the IDEA accorded them independently enforceable rights.** As it would be inconsistent with the statutory scheme to bar them from asserting enforceable rights in federal court, the Court reversed the judgment. *Winkelman v. Parma City School Dist.*, 550 U.S. 516 (2007).

2. Notice and Hearing Requirements

A federal regulation at 34 CFR Part 300.504 requires schools to provide a copy of IDEA procedural safeguards to parents once per school year, and upon initial referral or evaluation for special education, the filing of a due process complaint, or other parental request. Schools and school districts may place procedural safeguard notices on their websites. There is a two-year limitation period on the filing of IDEA complaints. A party appealing from an adverse due process hearing decision must appeal within 90 days from the date of the hearing officer's decision, unless the state has its own limitation period.

◆   While incarcerated, the father of a child with a disability attempted to challenge a decision that the student did not need additional special instruction. A federal district court held that **non-custodial status did not automatically divest the father of all parental rights**. On appeal, the Second Circuit ruled that the lower court would have to decide whether the mother should be joined as a necessary party by examining state law and the divorce decree. *Fuentes v. Board of Educ. of City of New York*, 136 Fed.Appx. 448 (2d Cir. 2005).

The case returned to the district court, which held the father lacked legal standing. He filed another appeal. The Second Circuit rejected the father's claim that the IDEA created a presumption that biological parents have a right to sue under the IDEA, so long as a custody decree did not restrict those rights. The court certified a state law question to the state's highest court regarding the extent of the parent's right to participate in education decisions. *Fuentes v. Board of Educ. of City of New York*, 540 F.d 145 (2d Cir. 2008).

The New York Court of Appeals held that **while a non-custodial parent has the right to participate in a child's education, that parent does not have the right to "control educational decisions"** absent an express provision in the custody agreement. The father could thus not pursue a challenge to the provision of services to his child. *Fuentes v. Board of Educ. of City of New York*, 12 N.Y.3d 309, 907 N.E.2d 696 (N.Y. 2009).

◆ A Maryland student with learning disabilities and a speech impairment attended private schools for years. His parents then sought to place him through the Montgomery County Public Schools. The district evaluated him and drafted an IEP that would have placed him in one of two district middle schools. The parents rejected the offer and requested a hearing. An administrative law judge (ALJ) held the parents had the burden of persuasion in the case. As a result, the district won. The case reached the U.S. Supreme Court, which explained that the party filing the lawsuit, who seeks to change the state of affairs, should be expected to bear the burden of proof. **The Court held parents who challenge their children's IEPs in special education due process hearings have the burden of proving the IEPs are inappropriate.** The Court affirmed the judgment, holding the burden of proof in an administrative hearing to challenge an IEP is on the party seeking relief. *Schaffer v. Weast*, 546 U.S. 49 (2005).

When the case returned to a federal district court, the parents challenged the student's eighth-grade IEP with evidence of changes made to his grade ten IEP. The school district countered with evidence that the student had graduated with a 3.4 grade point average. The court ruled for the district, and the Fourth Circuit affirmed the judgment. Using the tenth-grade IEP to challenge the eighth-grade IEP would promote a hindsight-based review that conflicted with the IDEA's structure and purpose. *Schaffer v. Weast*, 554 F.3d 470 (4th Cir. 2009).

C. Implementation of IEPs

*In a Texas case, the U.S. Court of Appeals, Fifth Circuit, described a test for assessing whether a school district has adequately implemented an IEP. The court assessed whether education was being provided in a coordinated and collaborative manner by key stakeholders and whether the student was receiving positive academic and nonacademic benefits. A **student challenging the adequacy of an IEP must demonstrate that school authorities failed to implement substantial or significant IEP provisions.** Houston Independent School Dist. v. Bobby R., 200 F.3d 341 (5th Cir. 2000).*

◆ The U.S. Court of Appeals, Second Circuit, held **the New York City Department of Education could not use employee testimony regarding the services described in student IEPs to alter the terms of a deficient IEP.** The case involved three students with autism who were initially offered public school placements in classrooms with a 6:1:1 student/teacher/paraprofessional ratio. In each case, the parents sought 1:1 services. All the families prevailed after hearings before impartial hearing officers, but each decision was later reversed by a state review officer. In each case, the review officer relied on testimony by school department staff about the services that would have been provided if the student attended the public school placement described in the department's IEP. When the cases reached the Second Circuit, it held testimony may not be used support modifications that materially differ from a written IEP.

School officials could not rehabilitate or amend a deficient IEP with "after the fact testimony regarding services that do not appear in the IEP." In each case, the department failed to complete an adequate functional behavioral assessment (FBA) and behavior intervention plan for the student and excluded parent counseling from the IEP. A practice of routinely omitting FBAs would violate state law. Since even minor violations could cumulatively result in the denial of FAPE, the court held **"school districts are well-advised to ensure the IEP complies with the checklist of requirements specified by state regulations."** In conclusion, the court held the adequacy of an IEP is to be considered prospectively as of the time of the placement decision and not in hindsight. *R.E. v. New York City Dep't of Educ.*, 694 F.3d 167 (2d Cir. 2012).

◆   The U.S. Court of Appeals, Ninth Circuit, rejected claims by a student whose parents accused their school district of allowing a pair of students who harassed their son transfer with him to a different school. They also said his program was improperly changed and that aversive interventions were used in violation of the IEP and state law. In affirming the decision for school officials, the Ninth Circuit held **the officials did not deny the student a FAPE and were entitled to select the method for implementing his IEP**. *B.D. v. Puyallup School Dist.*, 456 Fed.Appx. 644 (9th Cir. 2011).

◆   Due to a learning disability, an Illinois student had an IEP from grade five forward. His parent said a special education teacher was not always present in his general education classes as specified in his IEP, and that not all of his IEP accommodations were consistently provided. A general education teacher refused to accept an assignment he had completed with a teacher's help. The student's mother filed a due process request and convinced a hearing officer that the student had been denied all the support to which he was entitled for significant time periods. **But a federal court found no evidence of intentional discrimination and no evidence that the district had refused to offer him an IEP to accommodate his disability.** It held the Americans with Disabilities Act addresses disability discrimination, not special education services. *Brown v. Dist. 299-Chicago Public Schools*, 762 F.Supp.2d 1076 (N.D. Ill. 2010).

II. DISCIPLINE OF STUDENTS WITH DISABILITIES

A. Discipline as a Change in Placement

The IDEA, at 20 U.S.C. § 1415(k)(G), states that disciplinary removals of over 10 school days, or a pattern of removals that exceeds 10 days in a school year, may constitute a "change in placement." Students who violate a student code of conduct may be placed in appropriate interim alternative settings. And 20 U.S.C. § 1415(k) allows schools to consider any unique circumstances on a case-by-case basis when determining whether to order a change in placement for a student with disabilities who violates a student code of conduct.
There are "special circumstances" in which schools may remove a student to an interim alternative educational setting for up to 45 days, regardless of whether the behavior leading to discipline is a manifestation of a disability. The "special circumstances" are: weapons possession, the sale, use or possession of drugs; or infliction of serious bodily injury while at school, on school grounds, or at a school event. A hearing officer reviewing a disciplinary

removal may return the child to his or her placement, or order a change in placement to an appropriate interim alternative setting for not more than 45 school days. To do so, the hearing officer must find maintaining the current placement is "substantially likely to result in injury."

In Honig v. Doe, *below, the U.S. Supreme Court held that while a school district cannot unilaterally change the placement of a disabled student it feels is dangerous,* **the district can use "its normal procedures for dealing with children who are endangering themselves or others," such as "time-outs, detention, the restriction of privileges," or suspension.**

◆ Two emotionally disturbed California students were suspended for five days for misbehavior including destruction of school property, assault and making sexual comments to classmates. Pursuant to state law, the suspensions were continued indefinitely pending expulsion proceedings. The students sued the school district in U.S. district court, claiming the suspensions violated the "stay-put" provision of the IDEA, which provides that a student must be kept in his or her "then-current" educational placement during the pendency of an IDEA proceeding. The court issued an injunction preventing the expulsion, and the school district appealed. The U.S. Court of Appeals, Ninth Circuit, held the indefinite suspensions constituted a prohibited "change in placement" without notice under the IDEA. On appeal, the U.S. Supreme Court held the purpose of the "stay-put" provision was to prevent schools from changing a child's placement over parental objections until all IDEA proceedings were completed.

While the IDEA provided for interim placements, there was no emergency exception for dangerous students. **Where a disabled student poses an immediate safety threat, school officials may temporarily suspend him or her for up to 10 school days.** Indefinite suspensions violated the "stay-put" provision. The Supreme Court modified the decision, holding that suspensions of up to 10 school days do not constitute a change in placement. And it held **a school district can use "its normal procedures for dealing with children who are endangering themselves or others," such as "time-outs, detention, the restriction of privileges," or suspension.** The Court also held that states could be required to provide services directly to disabled students where a local school district fails to do so. *Honig v. Doe*, 484 U.S. 305 (1988).

B. Manifestation Determinations

A manifestation determination review is required when disciplinary action would result in a disabled child's removal from school for over 10 days in a school year. **The student's IEP team must perform the review.** *Parents and school IEP team members are to determine "if the conduct in question was caused by, or had a direct and substantial relationship, to the child's disability." If so, the team must determine if the conduct was a direct result of a failure to implement the IEP.* **If the team finds the child's behavior is not a manifestation of a disability, the disciplinary procedures applied to non-disabled children may be applied to the child.**

A student whose misconduct is not a manifestation of a disability is still entitled to regular disciplinary procedures. If the team finds the misconduct is related to the child's disability, it may still seek the parents' agreement to change the placement. A local education agency (LEA) that disciplines a student with disabilities must continue to provide the student with a free appropriate public education if a placement is changed. This is irrespective of whether the child's behavior is found to manifest a disability.

◆   A Missouri student who had "violent rages" at school was suspended from school twice. His mother voluntarily educated him at home for two months. After he returned to school, the IEP team met and decided he should only attend school for half days. He was suspended again for violent behavior, and his mother withdrew her consent for special education. While the student was attending a regular classroom, he assaulted a student and was suspended for five days. When the student returned to school, he was notified of his reassignment to an alternative program. In a due process proceeding, a hearing officer found there was no change in placement, and no manifestation hearing was required.

On appeal, a federal court held a "change in placement" "will only occur when a fundamental change in the educational program occurs." A disciplinary removal for more than 10 consecutive days, or a "pattern" of removals of more than 10 days in a school year, is a change in placement requiring a manifestation determination. But **a manifestation determination is needed only if the change in placement is disciplinary in nature**. In this case, the mother voluntarily requested homeschooling, so none of the time out of school during those two months counted toward the 10-day removal threshold. The shortened school days did not count as days of suspension, as the action was not taken for disciplinary reasons. The alternative school placement was simply a transfer from one school to another. Five days of suspension had occurred after the mother withdrew her consent for special education and the student was in a regular education program. The long time gap between suspensions led the court to find there was no "pattern of suspensions." Rejecting the parents' other arguments, the court held for the school district. *M.N. v. Rolla Public School Dist. 31*, No. 2:11-cv-04173-NKL, 2012 WL 2049818 (W.D. Mo. 6/6/12).

◆   A Michigan student assaulted another student. An investigation determined his actions were intentional and not a manifestation of his disability, and he was suspended for 180 days. After the school board upheld the discipline, the case reached the Court of Appeals of Michigan. The court described the assault as an "extreme bullying incident." It explained that **school officials have wide discretion to create rules to maintain order and discipline**. Michigan law specified that if a student in grade six or above commits an assault against another student, the school board "shall suspend or expel the pupil from the school district for up to 180 school days." In conformity with state law, the school board had a policy to enforce this provision. Adequate notice of a 180-day suspension was provided based on the state law and school board policies. Moreover, the handbook allowed adjustment of the term of suspension based on the circumstances. Since there was no arbitrary or capricious conduct by the board, the court affirmed the discipline. *Stansky v. Gwinn Area Community Schools*, No. 305287, 2012 WL 5290301 (Mich. Ct. App. 10/25/12).

◆   Two Florida students with disabilities who were removed from their school for misconduct unrelated to their disabling conditions were unable to obtain federal court relief. The U.S. Court of Appeals, Eleventh Circuit, upheld a lower court decision for their school board. **It held the board did not violate the IDEA by refusing to pay for a private school placement after the students were removed from their placements.** In addition to finding no IDEA violation, the court found the board did not discriminate against the students under Section 504 of the Rehabilitation Act. *Lewellyn v. Sarasota County School Board*, 442 Fed.Appx. 446 (11th Cir. 2011).

◆   A South Dakota student fought with another student and brought a knife to school. An IEP team found his misconduct was not a manifestation of his learning disability. After missing four days of school, he was placed in an alternative educational setting. His grandmother asked for a board hearing but was told that was not possible because the student was no longer suspended. In his alternative placement, he received two hours of instruction four days a week instead of his usual 30 hours per week. An IDEA action was filed, which reached the U.S. Court of Appeals, Eighth Circuit. It explained that the change of a student's placement "is primarily an educational, not a disciplinary, decision." In the court's view, the student had been suspended for four days.

The assistant principal had explained the charges and given the student an opportunity to respond. As suspensions of 10 days or less trigger only minimal due process protection, due process had been satisfied. The IEP team could have placed the student in an interim alternative educational setting if it had chosen. The team could also place him in an alternative educational setting with parental consent. This is what had actually occurred, as the grandmother agreed to the change. **Federal law states that IEP teams must determine any interim alternative educational placement.** Once the IEP team changed the student's placement with the grandmother's consent, the team, and not the school board, "became the decision-maker authorized to change his placement" under 34 C.F.R. Part 300.530(d)(5). By agreeing to the change in placement, the grandparent "gave the IEP team, rather than the District's school board, control of the situation." As the district did not violate the student's rights, the judgment was reversed. *Doe v. Todd County School Dist.*, 625 F.3d 459 (8th Cir. 2010).

◆   A District of Columbia student who was eligible for special education taunted a substitute teacher and refused to follow instructions. Because he had two prior infractions in the same school year, he was suspended for 54 days and placed in an alternative educational setting. A manifestation determination review found his behavior was not a manifestation of his disability. After a hearing officer reduced the suspension to 10 days, an assistant district superintendent increased it to 45 days. Another hearing officer found that the alternative placement was not appropriate under the IDEA and reduced the suspension to 11 days. **When the district challenged that decision, the D.C. Circuit upheld it because the alternative placement denied the student a FAPE.** The hearing officer did not exceed his authority in modifying the suspension. *District of Columbia v. Doe*, 611 F.3d 888 (D.C. Cir. 2010).

◆ Along with several friends, an emotionally disabled Virginia student vandalized his school by shooting the building and some school buses with paintball guns. The principal recommended that he be expelled, which triggered an IDEA manifestation determination review. The review committee found his behavior was not a manifestation of his disability. A hearing officer recommended suspending the student for the rest of the year. His parents objected and sought due process. The hearing officer found no IDEA violation, and a federal court agreed. **There was no IDEA requirement that the review committee members know the student personally.** And the student was not drawn into the vandalism by his friends. Rather, he had been an instigator. *Fitzgerald v. Fairfax County School Board*, 556 F.Supp.2d 543 (E.D. Va. 2008).

◆ A Pennsylvania student who was eligible for a Section 504 plan but not an IEP under the IDEA caused a bomb scare at his school. The school district denied his parents' request for a manifestation determination hearing and expelled the student. The parents sued the school district in a federal court, which held **a manifestation determination is required for discipline under the IDEA, but not Section 504**. While a manifestation determination is one way to comply with Section 504 requirements, the law does not mandate this. As a result, the student had not been denied due process by the failure to conduct a manifestation determination. *Centennial School Dist. v. Phil L.*, 559 F.Supp.2d 634 (E.D. Pa. 2008).

C. Delinquency and Juvenile Justice

A federal regulation at 34 C.F.R. Part 300.535(a) explains that special education protections do not shield students who commit crimes or juvenile offenses from law enforcement efforts. The regulation states "[n]othing in this part prohibits an agency from reporting a crime committed by a child with a disability to appropriate authorities or prevents [s]tate law enforcement and judicial authorities from exercising their responsibilities with regard to the application of Federal and State law to crimes committed by a child with a disability." In the following case, the Court of Appeals of Michigan rejected a student's claim that this regulation violated his due process rights.

◆ A Michigan student with Tourette's Disorder was suspended several times. School officials petitioned a county court to declare him guilty of school incorrigibility. After the court found him guilty, he appealed. The state court of appeals found the student engaged in repeated and escalating misconduct that disturbed others. Moreover, the educational agency did not have to provide his special education and disciplinary records prior to filing a juvenile petition. In a separate proceeding, an administrative law judge had held the juvenile petition was not a "change in placement." Since the student did not appeal from that finding, he could not attack it now. In any event, he was not removed from school for more than 10 consecutive school days or a series of removals totaling more than 10 school days in one school year. So the court found a manifestation determination hearing was unnecessary. Section 712A.2 of the state code did not require evidence of willful violations and did not exempt violations based on a juvenile's disability. **The IDEA does not prevent schools from reporting crimes by disabled students to appropriate officials.** As sufficient evidence supported an adjudication of guilt, the judgment was affirmed. *In re Nicholas Papadelis*, No. 291536, 2010 WL 3447892 (Mich. Ct. App. 9/2/10).

◆   A Georgia school district assigned a one-on-one assistant to an aggressive autistic student for an after-school daycare program and also devised a behavior intervention plan for him. A custodian with a special needs son received training and served as the assistant, but often had to be away to attend to his own child. On a day when the custodian was absent, the student became agitated and left the building. Eventually, several staff members placed him in his time-out room, where he hit the window and kicked the walls. A police officer handcuffed him until his father could come and pick him up. The father later sued for disability discrimination under Section 504 and the ADA, but **a federal court found no evidence of intentional discrimination against the student**. At most, staff members acted negligently. *J.D.P. v. Cherokee County, Georgia School Dist.*, 735 F.Supp.2d 1348 (N.D. Ga. 2010).

◆   A New Mexico student with a learning disability skipped class 136 times in a semester, used drugs and alcohol, was arrested for attacking family members and sent to a juvenile detention center. An evaluation recommended "placement in reg-ed with support." The student's school district deemed this an "interim IEP" for her ninth-grade year. But the district did not revise the "interim IEP" prior to the school year and did not update her last functioning IEP. The student had serious disciplinary problems and 65 unexcused absences in her first term. She was suspended for fighting and failed all her classes. In a special education proceeding, a hearing officer found the district did not deny the student a FAPE. She enrolled in ninth grade at a different high school where she consistently attended school and earned a 4.0 grade point average. But the student resumed skipping classes, used drugs and alcohol and stopped attending school when her mother kicked her out of the house. Her special education case reached a federal court. It held **any loss of educational opportunity was the result of her own behavior, not school errors**. On appeal, the U.S. Court of Appeals, Tenth Circuit, held any IDEA violation was immaterial because of her truancy and misconduct. The student had largely rejected the services offered to her, and the district had to provide her a FAPE if she returned to school. *Garcia v. Board of Educ. of Albuquerque Public Schools*, 520 F.3d 1116 (10th Cir. 2008).

◆   An Illinois student who received special education and related services was charged with lighting fireworks and throwing them at others. A juvenile court adjudicated him delinquent and placed him on probation. When he violated probation, his probation officer recommended a residential placement. His mother moved to a new school district, which was notified that it should appear in juvenile court regarding its potential liability for funding the student's placement. The juvenile court agreed with the probation officer that the student should be residentially placed, and ordered the district to fund the placement. The district challenged the decision in a state court and won. The Illinois Supreme Court held that **the student's placement was not made under the**

School Code, but under the Juvenile Court Act. It was made to remedy a probation violation, not the student's educational needs. Also, the district was not given the opportunity to show that it could educate the student. The state had to fund the placement. *In re D.D.*, 819 N.E.2d 300 (Ill. 2004).

◆ A New York principal initiated a family court proceeding to determine if a student was in need of supervision based on 16 unexcused absences from school during a two-month period. The court ordered a school committee on special education to conduct an evaluation. It found that the student was emotionally disturbed and had a disability. After the court placed him on probation for a year, he appealed. The New York Supreme Court, Appellate Division, held the **adjudication of the student as a child in need of supervision was not a change in placement** under the IDEA. His placement was not changed, and he was simply ordered to attend school and participate in his IEP. *Erich D. v. New Milford Board of Educ.*, 767 N.Y.S.2d 488 (N.Y. App. Div. 2003).

III. PLACEMENT OF STUDENTS WITH DISABILITIES

A. Identification and Evaluation

The IDEA requires each local education agency to identify and evaluate students with disabilities in its jurisdiction. After a district identifies a student as disabled, it must develop and implement an individualized education program (IEP). The IEP must be reasonably calculated to provide educational benefits and where possible, to include the student with nondisabled students.

Parents may request the initial evaluation of a child for special education and related services, as may the state or the local educational agency (LEA).

An evaluation is to take place within 60 days of receiving parental consent, or within the relevant state time frame. LEAs are exempt from the 60-day requirement in transfer cases or if a parent "repeatedly fails or refuses to produce the child for the evaluation." Parents who do not allow an evaluation of their children, or who refuse special education and related services, will be barred from later asserting IDEA procedural protections in disciplinary cases.

A special education evaluation must use a variety of assessment tools and strategies to gather relevant functional, development and academic information. The IDEA Amendments of 2004 prohibited exclusive reliance on the "severe discrepancy" model when assessing a student's eligibility for special education based on a specific learning disability.

Lack of appropriate instruction in reading or math may not be used to make an IDEA eligibility determination. And a lack of English proficiency is specifically excluded from entering into eligibility determinations.

◆ A Pennsylvania student struggled with reading and misbehaved regularly in his half-day kindergarten classroom. He repeated kindergarten but made little progress in an intensive full-day program. In first grade, the student's behavior problems continued. His teacher believed it was too soon to discuss special education testing. A school evaluator found the student had attention deficit hyperactivity disorder

(ADHD) but did not need special education because of it. His grades improved in grade two, but he fought with others at school and on his bus.

A private neurological evaluation diagnosed the student with ADHD, and the district found him eligible for special education. His parents requested a due process hearing. After due process proceedings, the case reached the U.S. Court of Appeals, Third Circuit. It held the IDEA requires an initial evaluation when a disability is suspected. In this case, the court found no unwarranted delay or deficiency in the initial evaluation. It held the school "was not required to jump to the conclusion" that the student's misconduct indicated a disability. School staff offered extra help and worked closely with the parents. Evidence showed the student was progressing. He received substantial accommodations and one-on-one tutoring as recommended by his neurologist. Since "**schools need not rush to judgment or immediately evaluate every student exhibiting below-average capabilities**," the court found no IDEA child-find violation and held for the district. *D.K. v. Abington School Dist.*, 696 F.3d 233 (3d Cir. 2012).

◆   The Ninth Circuit held a California school district could best decide how to assess a bilingual student for IDEA eligibility. His parents said he had a learning disability, but the district only designated him "at risk for retention." In the court's view, the IDEA requires safeguards to ensure testing procedures are not racially or culturally discriminatory. But a blanket rule barring a district from considering other factors in determining whether a child has a specific learning disability would "upset the balance IDEA attempts to achieve." For that reason, the court held **schools had to review the relevant materials available on a child, then make a reasonable choice between valid but conflicting test results in determining if a severe discrepancy existed**. A post-hearing evaluation obtained by parents was "additional evidence concerning relevant events" after the hearing. The case was returned to a lower court, which was to consider whether the report was relevant to whether the district violated the IDEA. *E.M. v. Pajaro Valley Unified School Dist.*, 652 F.3d 999 (9th Cir. 2011).

◆   A Hawaii student struggled with reading in grades 2-4. After obtaining private tutoring at her own expense, her mother requested a response to intervention (RTI) model to determine if the child had a learning disability. Although the Hawaii Department of Education (DOE) agreed to an in-depth achievement evaluation, it declined to use the RTI model. A DOE evaluation team found the student ineligible for special education because her assessment reports indicated no "severe discrepancy" between her IQ and achievement on standardized tests. Following administrative proceedings, the case reached the U.S. Court of Appeals, Ninth Circuit. The court noted that scientific research has criticized the severe discrepancy model. Congress did away with exclusive reliance on the severe discrepancy model in the 2004 IDEA reauthorization.

Although the reauthorized IDEA did not require an alternative model to determine if a student had a specific learning disability, the IDEA expressly authorized the RTI model. **IDEA regulations issued in 2006 prohibited states from requiring school districts to use a severe discrepancy model and compelled them to use the RTI model.** Federal regulations prohibited Hawaii from requiring exclusive reliance on the severe discrepancy model. Use of this model was a procedural violation of the IDEA. Hawaii had since issued new special education regulations permitting the RTI model. A lower court would have to determine whether the student was eligible for special education. *Michael P. v. Dep't of Educ., State of Hawaii*, 656 F.3d 1057 (9th Cir. 2011).

◆   The U.S. Court of Appeals, Eighth Circuit, reviewed 34 C.F.R. Part 300.8(c)(4)(i), a federal regulation defining "emotional disturbance" under the IDEA. **A student seeking special education eligibility for "emotional disturbance" must exhibit one of five listed characteristics "over a long period of time and to a marked degree that adversely affects a child's educational performance."** The court held a student was qualified for special education under the IDEA because his bipolar disorder caused an "inability to build or maintain satisfactory interpersonal relationships with peers and teachers," one of the five characteristics which may adversely affect educational performance under the regulation. He had behavior disorders and a history of threats and suicidal comments from the time he entered district schools in fifth grade. *Hansen v. Republic R-III School Dist.*, 632 F.3d 1024 (8th Cir. 2011).

◆   After an evaluation, a Pennsylvania second-grader was thought to have ADHD. But there was no discrepancy between his ability and his achievement, so he was not placed in special education. By the seventh grade, the student's performance declined and at the end of the eighth grade, he was evaluated again and found to have ADHD. His performance continued to decline over the next two years, and he dropped out of school. The student's parents filed an IDEA action against the school district for failing to timely identify him as disabled. A federal court, and later the Third Circuit ruled against the parents, finding that **the school district did not rely solely on an ability/achievement analysis in determining that the student did not need special education at an earlier age**. The district did not violate its child-find duty under the IDEA. *Richard S. v. Wissahickon School Dist.*, 334 Fed.Appx. 508 (3d Cir. 2009).

◆   A New York student with ADHD was sexually abused by a cousin and was later suspended for fighting and drug possession. His grades dropped out of the honor roll range, but he continued to pass his classes. His parents placed him in a boarding school for troubled students. The committee on special education met and determined the student did not meet the IDEA criteria for severe emotional disturbance. His parents appealed, and the case reached the Second Circuit. The court held for the school district, ruling that **even if the student exhibited some of the symptomology for an emotional disturbance, his symptoms did not affect his academic performance**. Instead, drug use appeared to be at the root of his school problems. *Mr. and Mrs. N.C. v. Bedford Cent. School Dist.*, 300 Fed.Appx. 11 (2d Cir. 2008).

◆   A Pennsylvania student with autism spectrum disorder had a behavioral crisis while in a private school funded by the district. **A reevaluation led to an evaluation report that used boilerplate language, listing generic goals and principles that might work for any child rather than specifying the student's needs and issues.** The IEP also contained much of that boilerplate language. When the parents sought due process, a hearing officer determined that both the IEP and the private school placement were inappropriate. The case reached a federal court, which agreed that the IEP and the private school were inappropriate. A new IEP would have to be developed. *A.Y. and D.Y. v. Cumberland Valley School Dist.*, 569 F.Supp.2d 496 (M.D. Pa. 2008).

◆ A Texas student with ADHD received special education services until the fourth grade, after which he no longer needed them. He performed well in school but had behavioral problems through the seventh and eighth grades. He nevertheless passed all his classes and met the statewide standards required by the Texas Assessment of Knowledge and Skills. After he robbed a school concession stand he was placed in an alternative setting. His mother requested a due process hearing, alleging that the district failed to identify him as a student with a disability. The case reached the Fifth Circuit Court of Appeals, which held that even though the student had a qualifying disability (his ADHD), he did not need special education services as a result. **His behavioral problems resulted from non-ADHD occurrences, such as family problems.** *Alvin Independent School Dist. v. Patricia F.*, 503 F.3d 378 (5th Cir. 2007).

◆ A Maine student excelled academically but began having problems with peers and depression. In sixth grade, she skipped school, inflicted wounds on herself and had peer problems. After attempting suicide, she was hospitalized and later diagnosed with Asperger's Syndrome. A school pupil evaluation team identified her as a qualified individual with a disability under Section 504, but found her ineligible for special education under the IDEA. Her parents enrolled her in a private school. In the lawsuit that arose over her education, **the First Circuit held that even though the child did not have academic needs, she could still be eligible for special education under the IDEA**. Her condition adversely affected her educational performance in nonacademic areas, and she was entitled to compensatory education for the period during which she was deemed ineligible. But she was not entitled to tuition for the private placement. *Mr. I. v. Maine School Administrative Dist. No. 55*, 480 F.3d 1 (1st Cir. 2007).

◆ The foster parents of an HIV-positive Maryland student told her about her condition for the first time just before her fifth-grade year. Over the next two years, she cut herself, heard voices telling her to stab herself, was hospitalized at five institutions and finally diagnosed with a psychotic condition. She missed a lot of school, and her academic performance declined during sixth grade. Her mother requested an IEP meeting to determine her eligibility under the IDEA. The IEP team found that while the student engaged in inappropriate behavior or had inappropriate feelings, she did not qualify for special education because her condition caused no adverse educational impact. Eventually the dispute reached the Fourth Circuit, which held the student was eligible for special education. **Her emotional disturbance affected her educational performance**, despite contrary testimony from school district experts. *Board of Educ. of Montgomery County, Maryland v. S.G.*, 230 Fed.Appx. 330 (4th Cir. 2007).

B. Child Find Obligation

The IDEA's "child find" obligation requires the states, through their local educational agencies (LEAs), to "identify, locate, and evaluate all children with disabilities residing within their boundaries." The child find obligation is triggered as an individualized duty to a child when an educational agency "has knowledge" that the child has a disability. Under the pre-2004 IDEA, students who were not declared eligible for IDEA services often made successful claims for IDEA procedural protections when their schools sought to discipline them.

Under current 20 U.S.C. § 1415(k)(5)(b), a school may be deemed to have knowledge that a child is disabled only if: (i) before the behavior leading to discipline, the child's parent "has expressed concern in writing" to a teacher or to supervisory or administrative personnel that the child is in need of special education or related services; (ii) the child's parent has requested an individual initial evaluation to determine if the child has a disability; or (iii) the child's teacher, or other school personnel, "has expressed specific concerns about a pattern of behavior demonstrated by the child, directly to the director of special education of such agency or to other supervisory personnel of the agency."

The "child find" duty of each state applies to children with disabilities who are homeless or wards of a state. LEAs must "conduct a thorough and complete child find process" to determine the number of parentally placed students with disabilities attending private schools in the LEA. Child find efforts must be designed to ensure the equitable participation of parentally placed private school children. LEAs must "undertake activities" for parentally placed private school students similar to activities for public school students. Services to parentally placed students may be provided at private schools, including religious schools, "to the extent consistent with law." LEAs and private schools must have "timely and meaningful consultation" for that purpose.

◆   A California student had poor grades and scored below the first percentile on standardized tests. She failed all her tenth-grade academic classes. Teachers said she was "like a stick of furniture" and that her work was "gibberish and incomprehensible." They reported she played with dolls, colored with crayons and sometimes urinated on herself in class. Due to her parent's reluctance, the school district "decided not to push" a special education evaluation. A third-party counselor recommended that the district test the student for learning disabilities, but she was instead promoted to grade eleven. Early in the school year, the mother requested an assessment and an IEP meeting. Later, the district found the student IDEA-eligible. The parent sought a due process hearing, resulting in a decision in her favor. After a federal court upheld the decision, the case reached the U.S. Court of Appeals, Ninth Circuit. There, the district asserted there was no parental right to file a claim unless an IDEA notice provision specifically applied. The court reviewed 20 U.S.C. § 1415(b)(6)(A) and held **a party may present a complaint to a court or hearing officer with respect to any matter relating to the identification, evaluation or placement of a child**. As a result, the court held the child find claim advanced by the parent was recognizable. *Compton Unified School Dist. v. Addison,* 598 F.3d 1181 (9th Cir. 2010).

◆   The parents of a Connecticut student with a nonverbal learning disability believed their school district should have diagnosed their son as IDEA-eligible for the fourth grade. However, the district did not find him eligible until it created an IEP for his sixth-grade year. The parents placed their son in a private school and eventually sued for tuition reimbursement. A federal district court held they failed to prove that district officials "overlooked clear signs of disability and were negligent in failing to order testing." **The IDEA child find provision does not impose liability for every failure to identify a child with a disability, and nonverbal learning disabilities are difficult to identify.** On appeal, the Second Circuit found the student's Connecticut Mastery Test scores indicated he was performing at goal in math and reading and was "proficient" in writing. And his lowest grade before being removed for a private school placement was a C+. The judgment for the school board was affirmed. *A.P. v. Woodstock Board of Educ.*, 370 Fed.Appx. 202 (2d Cir. 2010).

◆   A Delaware student had a Section 504 plan, but failed third-grade math. Upon learning their child would be retained in grade three, her parents sought a full range of assessments. One indicated she had a severe discrepancy in reading comprehension. They placed the child in a Christian school and requested a due process hearing, seeking reimbursement for their costs. The case reached the U.S. Court of Appeals, Third Circuit. It found the evidence at the time the parents sought an evaluation did not show their child's Section 504 plan was failing. Her grades were improving in all subjects. School officials could not have known that the student would later fail to advance in grade and fail a state test. While some of her programs were available to others, it appeared to the court that her curriculum was tailored to her needs. Her teacher "provided extra support at every turn." Although the parents argued that the IEP put into place by the district was deficient, the court held **a lower court had properly found the student had no other IDEA-qualifying disabilities in math and writing**. Finding the IEP was adequate, the court denied tuition reimbursement. *Anello v. Indian River School Dist.*, 355 Fed.Appx. 594 (3d Cir. 2009).

◆   An Ohio student was diagnosed with ADD, ADHD, oppositional defiant disorder and absence seizures. He was finally diagnosed with Asperger's syndrome in eighth grade. A dispute arose over the student's IEP, and his parents filed an IDEA action, asserting that the district's failure to diagnose Asperger's syndrome amounted to a violation of the act. **A federal court held that the district's failure to correctly label the student's disabilities did not violate the IDEA.** The student received special education from his second-grade year to the present. **The IDEA does not require schools to place students in specific categories. It only requires that they be given an appropriate education**, which the student received. *Pohorecki v. Anthony Wayne Local School Dist.*, 637 F.Supp.2d 547 (N.D. Ohio 2009).

◆   The mother of Nevada preschool twins with speech and other developmental difficulties took them to a free screening session at a private learning center, which referred them to their school district. The district referred the mother to a "Child Find Day" about six weeks later and did not give her a copy of her IDEA procedural safeguards. The children were not responsive at the Child Find Day, and assessments were scheduled for two months later. Meanwhile, the private center determined that the children had autism. The district eventually agreed with that diagnosis. A hearing officer determined that the district had failed to timely evaluate the children, but on appeal, the Ninth Circuit held that **the delay between when the twins were evaluated and began receiving services was reasonable**. As a result, the mother was entitled to be reimbursed only for the $1,670 she spent on private evaluations. *JG v. Douglas County School Dist.*, 552 F.3d 786 (9th Cir. 2009).

C. Least Restrictive Environment

The IDEA requires placing students with disabilities with non-disabled peers to the extent possible. This is known as the least restrictive environment (LRE) requirement. Each IEP must explain the extent to which a child will not participate in regular education classes. In analyzing the LRE requirement, many courts rely on Oberti v. Board of Educ. of Borough of Clementon School Dist., *995 F.2d 1204 (3d Cir. 1993).* Oberti *evaluated whether the district made reasonable efforts to accommodate a student in regular classes, whether appropriate supplemental aids and services were made available, and the possible negative effects for other students if the student remained in regular education classes. While the IDEA has a strong preference for placements in the LRE, the U.S. Court of Appeals, Seventh Circuit, held in* Beth B. v. Van Clay, *282 F.3d 493 (7th Cir. 2002), that the Act does not require a regular classroom placement that would provide an unsatisfactory education.*

In McLaughlin v. Holt Public Schools Board of Educ., *320 F.3d 663 (6th Cir. 2003), the Sixth Circuit found an IDEA regulation requiring placement "as close as possible to the child's home" did not apply if a necessary program was unavailable at a neighborhood school.*

◆ A severely disabled 14-year-old Texas student was placed in the general education science and social studies classes his parents requested. Even though he had aides and modified assignments, he grew overwhelmed in these classes, and team members kept recommending special education for these subjects. When independent experts evaluated the student and recommended special education science and social studies for him, the parents became enraged. The student was removed from the general education classes over their objection, and they filed a due process hearing request. A hearing officer found the special education placements appropriate. Later, a federal court found the student did not benefit academically from mainstream social studies and science classes.

On appeal, the U.S. Court of Appeals, Second Circuit, held that a primary IDEA goal is to place disabled students in the least restrictive environment. In this case, **the student was interfering with other students in his general education classes**. Evidence indicated he did not benefit from the setting, was becoming increasingly frustrated and overwhelmed, and was unable to pay attention. As the student's classes became more difficult, his problem behaviors increased. He refused to work on assignments, needed constant help and prompting, and eventually "shut down and refused to work at all." In affirming the judgment, the court noted the student would remain in the general education classes in which he was having success and would be with non-disabled peers for activities, lunch and special assemblies. *J.H. v. Fort Bend Independent School Dist.*, 482 Fed.Appx. 915 (5th Cir. 2012).

◆   An 18-year-old Pennsylvania student with multiple disabilities was non-verbal and not toilet trained. Her district proposed placing her in a full-time life skills class and in mainstream school assemblies, lunch, homeroom and recess. Her parents requested a due process hearing, asserting the placement was too restrictive. A hearing officer agreed with them and ordered compensatory education, but an appeals panel held that the student required a regular education setting only for lunch, recess, physical education, homeroom, music, art and a single academic class. The award of compensatory education was reversed. A federal district court and later the Third Circuit upheld that decision, noting that **the student was making progress in her life skills class and her frequent loud vocalizations had a negative effect on other students**. *A.G. v. Wissahickon School Dist.*, 374 Fed.Appx. 330 (3d Cir. 2010).

◆   A New Hampshire student with mental retardation, orthopedic impairment and other disabilities attended a rehabilitation day center for four years under an IEP. When she was 19, the IEP team recommended a continued placement there. But her parents refused to consent to the IEP and withdrew her from school. They sought a home- and community-based program to help her with basic life skills and community interaction. The case reached the First Circuit, which ruled for the school district. It found **the student's behavior appeared to be improving and the day center was a less restrictive placement than the home service setting the parents wanted**. Further, the IEP called for a significant increase in services in the area of pre-vocational skills. *Lessard v. Lyndeborough Cooperative School Dist.*, 592 F.3d 267 (1st Cir. 2010).

◆   A 14-year-old Arizona student suffered a traumatic brain injury that confined him to a wheelchair and made him dependent on caregivers for daily activities. His IEP team determined that he had a better chance of achieving his IEP goals if he were placed at a particular private day school 35 miles away. His parents objected, seeking instead to keep him in his neighborhood school with his non-disabled peers. A special education hearing officer found that the student failed to respond despite the district's best efforts and that the private day placement was best for him. The Arizona Court of Appeals agreed. **The student's severe disability made continued mainstreaming inappropriate.** *Stallings v. Gilbert Unified School Dist. No. 41*, No. 1 CA-CV 08-0625, 2009 WL 3165452 (Ariz. Ct. App. 10/1/09).

◆   A Connecticut school district behavioral consultant notified the parents of a student with Down syndrome that his behavior problems were making it more difficult to keep the student in a regular classroom. A performance and planning team drafted an IEP that called for only 60% regular classroom placement instead of the 80% urged by the parents. The district hired a consultant who recommended gradually increasing the student's time in regular classrooms to

80%, and the district agreed to increase the time to 74%. However, the parents were determined to achieve 80% time in regular classrooms. A federal district court and the Second Circuit eventually upheld the IEP, noting that while mainstreaming is an important objective, it has to be weighed against the need for an appropriate education. **Mandating a percentage of time in regular classes would be inconsistent with the individualized approach of the IDEA.** *P. v. Newington Board of Educ.*, 546 F.3d 111 (2d Cir. 2008).

◆ The mother of a Kansas student with Down syndrome challenged the IEP proposed for his entry into high school, as it would require a long bus ride to a high school in another town. She sought to place him in the high school in their town. An educational cooperative serving eight school districts ran a "level program" or "cluster system" using a functional educational approach. A hearing officer and a federal court found that the Level IV program at the distant high school was the least restrictive placement and that the neighborhood school had no teachers qualified to teach the student. The student's inability to focus in regular classrooms was documented, and the Level IV program provided a continuum of placements and support services. **Although neighborhood placements are preferred under the IDEA and implicate the least restrictive environment, they are not an enforceable right.** *M.M. v. Unified School Dist. No. 368*, No. 07-2291-JTM, 2008 WL 4950987 (D. Kan. 11/18/08).

D. Change in Placement and the 'Stay-Put' Provision

The IDEA "stay-put" provision requires school districts to provide parents prior written notice of any proposed change in a disabled student's placement. If the parents wish to contest the change, a hearing must be granted. During a challenge to a change in placement, the child is to remain in the "then-current" educational placement pending the outcome of the proceeding.

In Hale v. Poplar Bluff R-I School Dist., *280 F.3d 831 (8th Cir. 2002), the Eighth Circuit* **held the transfer of a Missouri student to a different school building for fiscal reasons did not constitute a change of placement that violated the stay-put provision.**

◆ A Pennsylvania student had a specific learning disability. His parents and the school district disagreed on a placement after his third-grade year. Over the next two years, his third-grade IEP became his stay-put placement under the IDEA. The district proposed providing the student with itinerant learning support primarily in a regular classroom instead of the daily hour of resource room support specified in the third-grade IEP. The parents rejected that proposal, arguing that it amounted to a change in placement. After a due process proceeding, the case reached the U.S. Court of Appeals, Third Circuit. It held that the school district had provided the same services to the student in the inclusive setting, on a daily basis and with the same special education teacher. Thus, **providing the student with itinerant learning support was not a change in placement that violated the IDEA's stay-put provision.** *In re Educ. Assignment of Joseph R.*, 318 Fed.Appx. 113 (3d Cir. 2009).

◆   The parents of a Texas student with disabilities disagreed with the district's proposed IEP for grade two and placed her in a private school. They sought due process and obtained a ruling from the hearing officer that the district did not make an appropriate placement. Thus, the parents were entitled to tuition reimbursement. **By the time the administrative ruling was issued, the school year was nearly over.** When the district appealed to a federal court, the parents did not ask for tuition reimbursement for another school year. As a result, when the court ruled on the case over a year later, it held that they were not entitled to tuition reimbursement. However, the Fifth Circuit reversed, finding that **another year of tuition was due under the stay-put provision.** *Houston Independent School Dist. v. V.P.*, 582 F.3d 576 (5th Cir. 2009).

◆   Florida triplets with autism received IDEA Part C services from the state's early intervention program until they turned three. When they "aged out" of Part C eligibility and the responsibility for their special education needs passed to IDEA Part B, their school district became obligated to provide them with IEPs. Because their school district did not have their IEPs in place, their parents sought to use the IDEA's stay-put provision to continue their individual family service plans (IFSPs). A federal court held **a student's Part C placement is not his or her current educational placement for stay-put purposes.** The Eleventh Circuit later affirmed the judgment, ruling the IDEA did not provide for the continued provision of services to the triplets pursuant to their IFSPs. *D.P. v. School Board of Broward County,* 483 F.3d 725 (11th Cir. 2007).

◆   An Ohio school district made addendums to a student's IEP in three consecutive months during his sixth-grade year. The third addendum sought to phase out a point reward system used to reinforce his behavior. The addendum also stated if the target behavior was not maintained, the original IEP would be reinstated. The parents did not learn that the addendum was being implemented until the district sent them a certified letter several days after the IEP meeting.

A due process hearing officer found that the student's sixth-grade IEP included the third addendum, rendering it the student's "stay-put" placement pending the outcome of the due process hearing. The case twice reached the state appeals court. In its second opinion, the court held the addendum was neither a fundamental change in nor an elimination of a basic element of the IEP. It held for the school district, holding that **not every change to an IEP constitutes a change in placement.** *Stancourt v. Worthington City School Dist.,* Nos. 07AP-835, 07AP-836, 2008 WL 4151623 (Ohio Ct. App. 9/9/08).

◆   A Virginia special education student with an emotional disability attended a gifted and talented program in an elementary school. He persuaded a classmate to place a threatening note in another student's computer file stating "death awaits you." The district assembled a manifestation determination review committee, which found no relationship between the student's disabilities and the threatening note. It recommended expelling the student, but the district instead transferred him to a gifted and talented program at a nearby school for the remainder of the year. His parents objected to the transfer decision and requested a due process hearing. The hearing officer ruled against the parents, and the Fourth Circuit affirmed, noting that **the student's transfer to a nearly identical program at a nearby school did not implicate the IDEA's stay-put provision**. The court also held his IEP was appropriate. *A.W. v. Fairfax County School Board*, 372 F.3d 674 (4th Cir. 2004).

The student later used his cell phone to take pictures up a classmate's skirt without her knowledge. The school suspended the student for 10 days and recommended expelling him. The IEP team determined his misconduct was not a manifestation of his disability. A hearing officer then ruled he should be suspended for 18 days and reassigned to another school. The school board agreed and offered interim services, but the parents appealed to a federal court, seeking money damages. The court dismissed their lawsuit, noting that they failed to exhaust their administrative remedies. *A.W. v. Fairfax County School Board*, 548 F.Supp.2d 219 (E.D. Va. 2008).

E. Other Placement Issues

1. Behavior Problems

◆ A Texas student with autism and other disorders regressed significantly in the summer before her ninth-grade year. Her IEP was revised, but her behavior and academic problems increased. She ran away from school and had sexual contact with other students in a lavatory. Her parents sought to place her at a residential school, and a hearing officer agreed with their decision. A federal district court also affirmed the residential placement, awarding over $110,000 in tuition plus $36,000 in attorneys' fees to the parents. But the Fifth Circuit found **the parents had not yet shown that the residential placement was necessary for educational (rather than medical or behavioral) reasons**. The court returned the case to the lower court for further proceedings. *Richardson Independent School Dist. v. Michael Z.*, 580 F.3d 286 (5th Cir. 2009).

◆ A New York school district offered an autistic student support from a special education teacher for part of the day and a program assistant for the rest of the day. However, he had behavioral and lack-of-focus problems and his parents placed him in a private school. They sued for tuition reimbursement, alleging that the district violated the IDEA because it failed to offer a functional behavioral assessment (FBA). A hearing officer found that the district should have offered an FBA, but a state review officer reversed. The case reached the U.S. Court of Appeals, Second Circuit, which observed that three key district officials had testified that an FBA was not necessary. **The IEP adequately addressed the student's behavior, and the parents were not entitled to tuition reimbursement.** *A.C. and M.C. v. Board of Educ. of Chappaqua Cent. School Dist.*, 553 F.3d 165 (2d Cir. 2009).

◆ A Pennsylvania student with worsening psychological problems attended private schools at the district's expense. After she was kicked out of a residential school in New Mexico, her parents placed her in a psychiatric residential treatment center that provided no educational services. Her parents sought reimbursement for the costs. The case reached the Third Circuit, which held that the district did not have to pay for the treatment center placement because her admission there was necessitated by her acute medical condition. And her medical and educational needs could be separated. Further, once the student's condition stabilized, the district began providing services again. *Mary v. School Dist. of Philadelphia*, 575 F.3d 235 (3d Cir. 2009).

◆ The mother of a New York student with Asperger's disorder signed him up for a private school before the school district prepared an IEP for the upcoming year. The IEP, when completed, maintained his "other health impaired" classification, but placed him in a more restrictive special education class. The mother sought tuition reimbursement and a hearing officer found that the district's failure to obtain a functional behavior analysis (FBA) entitled the mother to tuition reimbursement. A review officer reversed, and a federal court agreed that the lack of an FBA was not fatal to the IEP. **School districts must consider using positive behavioral interventions and supports as well as other strategies to address behavior, so the mere failure to conduct an FBA did not violate the IDEA.** *Connor v. New York City Dep't of Educ.*, No. 08 Civ. 7710 (LBS), 2009 WL 3335760 (S.D.N.Y. 10/13/09).

◆ A Minnesota student with emotional and behavioral disabilities was suspended several times for fighting with other girls. Her suspensions added up to more than 10 days out of class. The district offered homeschooling services, but the student's mother rejected the offer. After conducting a functional behavioral assessment, the district offered to place the student in an emotional behavioral disability setting that included boys. The mother rejected this placement as well, preferring an all-girl setting. An administrative law judge held the district denied the student an appropriate education because of the suspensions and the district's failure to modify her IEP. But the Eighth Circuit found **the mixed-gender setting was appropriate given that all the student's serious behavior problems involved altercations with girls.** *M.M. v. Special School Dist. No. 1*, 512 F.3d 455 (8th Cir. 2008).

2. Extended School Year Services

◆ A dispute arose between a New Jersey school district and the parents of a student over extended school year services (ESY) and transportation. A federal court ruled for the district on the ESY and transportation claims, but it awarded 17 days of compensatory education due to the district's failure to serve the student for the same number of days at the start of his fifth-grade year. The family then sought costs and attorneys' fees of $118,787. The court modified the award but still granted them all their costs and $71,850 in attorneys' fees. Even though they were successful on only one claim, their claims were all related. *L.T. v. Mansfield Township School Dist.*, No. 04-1381 (NLH), 2009 WL 1971329 (D.N.J. 7/1/09).

◆ A Pennsylvania school district offered an incoming kindergartner with autism an IEP that included applied behavioral analysis (ABA) therapy and verbal behavior (VB) services in an autistic support class. But the IEP reduced the student's ABA therapy from his early intervention IEP and also reduced his occupational therapy. His parents challenged the IEP and reached a settlement in which the student was to receive two hours of ABA and VB therapy a day. The district then provided three hours of therapy a day, exceeding interim IEP requirements. Later, the district proposed reducing the ABA/VB therapy for the rest of the school year and a summer extended school year program. A federal court held the district could provide less than three hours of ABA therapy a day and did not have to provide over 1.5 hours a day in the summer. **It had already provided more ABA therapy than the interim IEP required.** *Travis G. v. New Hope-Solebury School Dist.*, 544 F.Supp.2d 435 (E.D. Pa. 2008).

◆   A multiply disabled 11-year-old Massachusetts student had attended a seven-week summer program called "Active Healing" at district expense since her kindergarten year. But the program was not approved by the state. After a seizure caused the student to regress, her mother sought a 12-week extended evaluation at Active Healing. The district refused to pay for the evaluation because the program was unapproved, and the mother sought administrative review. A hearing officer ruled that the district had to pay for the evaluation, but a federal court disagreed. **Despite the past history of the district funding the summer program, it could not be ordered to pay for the extended evaluation at an unapproved program.** *Manchester-Essex Regional School Dist. v. Bureau of Special Educ. Appeals*, 490 F.Supp.2d 49 (D. Mass. 2007).

◆   The IEPs for a Kentucky student with cerebral palsy and delayed cognitive development addressed his ongoing behavior issues. His parents believed he was regressing and sought direct occupational therapy for him as well as a summer placement. Ultimately, the district rejected extended school year (ESY) programming for the student's next school year. The parents unilaterally placed the student in a residential facility that offered summer programs and requested a due process hearing. A hearing officer ruled for the district, but an appeals board and a federal district court reversed his decision. On further appeal, **the Sixth Circuit reversed the lower court decision, holding ESY programming was the exception, not the rule.** The parents would have to show that ESY was necessary to avoid something more than "adequately recoupable regression." *Kenton County School Dist. v. Hunt*, 384 F.3d 269 (6th Cir. 2004).

◆   A Virginia student with autism received ESY services prior to entering kindergarten. In kindergarten, he progressed in all but two of the 27 goals stated in his IEP. His parents sought to continue the one-on-one services he received during the summer, but were unable to agree with their school district on an IEP. A hearing officer and a federal court both ruled that the purpose of ESY services was to make reasonable progress on unmet goals. The court found that the district's IEP was adequate. The Fourth Circuit Court of Appeals held that **ESY services are necessary only when the regular school year benefits to a student will be significantly jeopardized in the absence of summer programming.** The court remanded the case to the hearing officer for a redetermination of the appropriateness of ESY services using the correct standard. *J.H. v. Henrico County School Board*, 326 F.3d 560 (4th Cir. 2003).

3. Transfer Students

The IDEA allows schools to conduct an evaluation of any student who transfers from a school outside the state before becoming obligated to develop a new IEP. When parents repeatedly refuse a school's efforts to conduct an individual evaluation of a child, the school is relieved of the obligation to convene an IEP meeting and is not considered in violation of the IDEA.

In Johnson v. Special Educ. Hearing Office, *287 F.3d 1176 (9th Cir. 2002), the Ninth Circuit held that when a disabled student transfers from one public agency to another, the receiving agency must provide a program that conforms with the last agreed-upon placement, but does not have to replicate it.*

◆   A New Jersey couple moved to Montana after a doctor found their child's performance had an autistic component. In New Jersey, an IEP had been crafted to provide the child with speech/language therapy. The IEP team at his Montana school refused to consider a New Jersey doctor's evaluation and reduced the student's speech/language therapy. After two months, the IEP team referred the student to a child development center for free autism testing. Five months later, a report came back confirming that his behavior was consistent with autism spectrum disorder. At this point, the school year was almost over. The IEP team met to develop an IEP for the next year and determined that the student did not need extended school year services. The parents brought an IDEA challenge that reached the Ninth Circuit. The court of appeals held that the **referral of the student to the child development center did not comply with the IDEA. The school district had failed to meet its obligation to evaluate the student.** *N.B. and C.B. v. Hellgate Elementary School Dist.,* 541 F.3d 1202 (9th Cir. 2008).

◆   A California student with a cochlear implant received one-on-one deaf and hard of hearing services in his family's home. When his family moved to Nevada, the school district there offered the services in his neighborhood school under an interim IEP. His parents objected, asserting the location violated the California IEP. They hired a private service provider and sought reimbursement from the Nevada school district. A hearing officer and then a federal district court held that the school district had offered comparable services to the transfer student. **The IDEA did not require the Nevada district to adopt the California IEP in its exact form.** *Sterling A. v. Washoe County School Dist.,* No. 3:07-CV-002450LRH-RJJ, 2008 WL 4865570 (D. Nev. 11/10/08).

◆   A Louisiana school district transferred a student with deafness from his neighborhood school to a cluster school located about four miles further from home. His parents claimed the transfer was a "change in placement" that required prior written notice. When the case reached the Fifth Circuit, it held **a change in a school site at which an IEP is implemented is not a "change in placement" under the IDEA.** The few changes resulting from the transfer, such as riding a special bus and sharing a transliterator with another student instead of having his own, were not fundamental changes to the IEP. *Veazey v. Ascension Parish School Board,* 121 Fed.Appx. 552 (5th Cir. 2005).

◆   When a student with autism moved to Rhode Island, his new school district assembled an IEP team and proposed an interim IEP within two weeks of the parents' first contact. The district wanted to place the student in a self-contained classroom that used a modified TEACCH method. The parents rejected the IEP and notified the district that they would be placing their son in a private school. A due process hearing officer ruled for the parents, but the First Circuit Court of Appeals ruled for the district, noting that **the IDEA did not require the best possible education for students with disabilities**. Here, the IEP was reasonably calculated to provide an appropriate education. The classroom was half the size of the student's previous placement, and the teachers had extensive experience and training with autistic children. *L.T. on Behalf of N.B. v. Warwick School Committee*, 361 F.3d 80 (1st Cir. 2004).

◆   A Seattle first-grade student with mild mental retardation and Down syndrome was assigned to a unique classroom combining special education and general education students. Her mother moved and sought a regular education placement for her. The new district offered a temporary placement in a self-contained special education class until it could perform an evaluation. Two months into the school year, the student had yet to attend class. In a due process challenge, the hearing officer upheld the district's temporary placement as the closest approximation to the student's last IEP. Later, the Ninth Circuit held the district's placement was appropriate. **The temporary placement was not a "take it or leave it" proposition, but was rather designed to get as close to the student's previous unique placement as possible pending an evaluation.** The temporary IEP conferred educational benefits on the student. *Ms. S. and her Daughter G. v. Vashon Island School Dist.*, 337 F.3d 1115 (9th Cir. 2003).

F. Residency Issues

The IDEA mandate to provide a free appropriate public education extends to all children with a disability residing in the area served by a local educational agency. Disputes among school districts and other agencies are generally resolved through interagency agreements. Occasionally, parents fail to establish a clear domicile, raising residency issues.

◆   A Kansas school district provided two children special education for some time. It determined they were not district residents because they did not sleep at their mother's rental unit. As a result, the district demanded the immediate withdrawal of the children from school. The parent requested an IDEA hearing and submitted an affidavit of residency. When it was learned that the children again stopped sleeping within district boundaries, the district filed a state court action for fraud. The mother sued the district and its special education services director in a federal court, which held for the district and found the special education director was entitled to qualified immunity. After a trial, the court dismissed the IDEA claim. On appeal, the U.S. Court of Appeals, Tenth Circuit, affirmed the judgment on the IDEA claim but vacated the judgment on all the others. The lower court again held for the district and director, and a second appeal went to the Tenth Circuit. It found the parent had abandoned the IDEA claims. The lower court had correctly held she lacked standing to challenge the nonresident admissions policy, since **she never actually sought admission for the children as nonresidents**. Even if she had standing, there was evidence that her children were absent from school due to illness and not the district's conduct. *D.L. v. Unified School Dist. No. 497*, 596 F.3d 768 (10th Cir. 2010).

◆   The mother of a Michigan special education student sought to enroll him in a neighboring school district, which had accepted 67 applications from nonresidents under the state's school choice law. However, because the process was less streamlined for special education students due to the higher costs, the two districts were unable to reach an agreement and the neighboring district rejected the student's application. His mother sued for discrimination and the case reached the Sixth Circuit. The court of appeals held that the school choice law did not violate equal protection. **There was a rational reason for the stricter transfer requirements for special education students.** *Clark v. Banks*, 193 Fed.Appx. 510 (6th Cir. 2006).

IV. RELATED SERVICES

Related services include the provision of sign-language interpreters, transportation, speech pathology, psychological and counseling services, and physical and occupational therapy. The IDEA requires school districts to provide services that are necessary for students with disabilities to receive educational benefits, but excludes medical services from coverage except where required for evaluation or diagnostic purposes. See 20 U.S.C. § 1402 (26).

A. Generally

◆   An Iowa student suffered a spinal cord injury that left him quadriplegic and ventilator dependent. For several years, his family provided personal attendant services at school. A family member or nurse performed catheterization, tracheostomy suctioning, repositioning and respiratory observation during the school day. When the student entered the fifth grade, his mother requested that the district provide him with continuous, one-on-one nursing services during the school day. The district refused, and the family filed a request for due process. An administrative law judge held the school district was obligated to reimburse the family for nursing costs incurred during the current school year and to provide the disputed services in the future. The case reached the U.S. Supreme Court, which held that the requested services were related services, not medical services. The court based its decision in the IDEA definition of related services, its holding in *Irving Independent School Dist. v. Tatro*, this chapter, and the IDEA purpose of making special education available to all disabled students. The Court held that **since the disputed services could be performed by someone other than a physician, the district was obligated to provide them**. *Cedar Rapids Community School Dist. v. Garret F. by Charlene F.*, 526 U.S. 66, 119 S.Ct. 992, 143 L.Ed.2d 154 (1999).

◆ A West Virginia student with medical problems suffered abuse and neglect at the hands of his parents. He was placed in foster care. A state court conducted a review of his pending abuse and neglect petition, and ordered his school board to provide and pay for a full-time nurse even though the board received no notice or opportunity to appear at the review hearing. The state's highest court held the board should have been given notice and an opportunity to help shed light on the best interests of the student. **School records showed that the student had not suffered a seizure in two years and that he had not had a full-time nurse assigned to him for four of his 11 years in the school system.** *State of West Virginia v. Beane,* 680 S.E.2d 46 (W. Va. 2009).

◆ **The U.S. Supreme Court ruled that clean intermittent catheterization (CIC) is a related service not subject to the "medical service" exclusion of the IDEA.** The parents of an eight-year-old girl born with spina bifida sued their local Texas school district after it refused to provide CIC for the child at school. The parents tried to force the district to train staff to perform the procedure. After a U.S. district court held against the parents, they appealed to the U.S. Court of Appeals, Fifth Circuit, which reversed the district court ruling. The district then appealed. The Supreme Court affirmed the court of appeals' ruling that CIC is a supportive related service, not an excluded medical service. *Irving Independent School Dist. v. Tatro,* 468 U.S. 883 (1984).

◆ A Tennessee student with profound bilateral hearing loss received a cochlear implant at the age of 14 months. Her school district later developed an IEP for her, offering to place her in a new collaborative program that was being developed with Head Start. The school district also proposed to discontinue the mapping service (optimization of the implant) it had been providing for the student. The parents objected and requested a hearing. A hearing officer held that the district's placement met IDEA requirements, but ruled that it had to continue the mapping services. **A federal court held that the 2004 IDEA Amendments excluded the mapping of a cochlear implant as a related service under the IDEA.** The regulations clarified that position in October 2006, so the district had to pay for mapping the implant until that time. *A.U. v. Roane County Board of Educ.,* 501 F.Supp.2d 1134 (E.D. Tenn. 2007).

B. Level or Location of Services

◆ A Pennsylvania student with learning disabilities received special education in reading, math and writing. In the sixth grade, his parents placed him in a private school and sought tuition reimbursement as well as compensatory education for the prior two years. After a federal court upheld the student's sixth-grade IEP, the U.S. Court of Appeals, Third Circuit, agreed that it addressed his deficiencies. **A lack of occupational therapy in the student's seventh-grade IEP was attributable to the delay by the parents in providing an occupational therapy evaluation.** Once they did so, a revised IEP provided for reevaluation of his potential needs within 30 days of his return to a district school. *Souderton Area School Dist. v. J.H.,* 351 Fed.Appx. 755 (3d Cir. 2009).

◆ A California student with multiple disabilities could not swallow food, instead receiving nutrition through a surgical opening in his stomach called a gastrostomy tube or "G-tube." His mother claimed he developed a severe reflux disorder from liquids, necessitating that he be fed only pureed foods. She used a syringe plunger even though standard medical practice called for using a gravity methodology. A dispute arose over the method of feeding her son. She kept him at home for a while, then sought compensatory education. A federal district court ultimately ruled that the mother could not dictate the method to be used to feed her son. **No doctor prescribed the plunge method, and the mother never provided evidence that the gravity method would not work.** No compensatory education was due. *C.N. v. Los Angeles Unified School Dist.*, No. CV 07-03642 MMM (SSx), 2008 WL 4552951 (C.D. Cal. 10/9/08).

◆ A Maryland student with disabilities received two types of medication from the school nurse under an agreement signed by her treating/prescribing psychiatrist. When teachers and other staff members observed that the student was lethargic and drowsy, the psychiatrist prescribed another medication. However, the student's fatigue continued. The nurse sought clarification from the doctor on giving the student medication when symptoms contraindicated further drug administration. The parents told the doctor not to provide further information to the nurse or other district employees regarding the student's medical condition and treatment. The district then refused to continue medicating the student. When the parents challenged that decision, they lost. The Court of Appeals of Maryland held that the dispute was about medical treatment and not special education. **The nurse could not be forced to medicate the student without free communication with the doctor.** *John A. v. Board of Educ. for Howard County*, 400 Md. 363, 929 A.2d 136 (Md. 2007).

◆ A Georgia student with a disability complained that words became fuzzy or three dimensional when he tried to read. A behavioral optometrist diagnosed accommodative and convergence disorder, and recommended visual therapy to reduce vision loss. The district refused to pay for such therapy on the grounds that the student was receiving a free appropriate public education. The parents paid for the therapy, then sought due process. An administrative hearing officer and a federal court found that the parents were entitled to reimbursement for the therapy as a related service. The Eleventh Circuit agreed. **Although the student's condition had not yet caused poor academic performance, it did prevent him from receiving a free appropriate public education.** *DeKalb County School Dist. v. M.T.V.*, 164 Fed.Appx. 900 (11th Cir. 2006).

◆ A hearing-impaired Louisiana student attended a public school with the assistance of a cued speech transliterator to supplement spoken information in his classes. Although other hearing-impaired students in the district who used American Sign Language attended their neighborhood schools, the cued speech transliterator served at a centralized location. The student achieved substantial academic benefit there, but his parents wanted him to attend his neighborhood school for social reasons. The school district denied a transfer request, but a federal district court held the student was entitled to attend his neighborhood school with the transliterator. The Fifth Circuit held the student's IEP satisfied the IDEA, and his parents were seeking the neighborhood placement for primarily social reasons. **They did not have veto power over the district's decision to provide the transliterator only at the central location.** *White v. Ascension Parish School Board,* 343 F.3d 373 (5th Cir. 2003).

◆   A South Dakota student who suffered epileptic seizures was provided transportation to and from school by her district as a related service under the IDEA. She was accompanied by a nurse during the ride. Although parents could designate different pick-up and drop-off sites within a specific school area, students were not transported outside the boundary unless it was necessary to obtain an educational benefit under an IEP. The district denied a request by the student's mother to drop her off at a day care center outside the boundary. The state Office of Special Education ordered the district to pay for transportation to the day care center, but a hearing examiner ruled it was not necessary. Later, the Eighth Circuit affirmed the decision that **the district did not have to provide transportation to the day care center.** The request was for the mother's convenience and was not necessary to provide the student educational benefit. *Fick v. Sioux Falls School Dist. 49-5,* 337 F.3d 968 (8th Cir. 2003).

C. Provision of Related Services at Private Schools

◆   An Arizona student attended a school for the deaf from grades one through five and a public school from grades six through eight. During his public school attendance, a sign-language interpreter was provided by the school district. The student's parents enrolled him in a parochial high school for ninth grade and asked the school district to continue providing a sign-language interpreter. The school district refused, and the student's parents filed an IDEA action.

The U.S. Supreme Court held the Establishment Clause did not exclude religious institutions from publicly sponsored benefits. If this were the case, religious groups would not enjoy police and fire protection, or have use of public roads and sidewalks. Government programs that neutrally provide benefits to broad classes of citizens are not subject to Establishment Clause prohibition simply because some religiously affiliated institutions receive an attenuated financial benefit. **Providing a sign-language interpreter under the IDEA was part of a general program for distribution of benefits in a neutral manner to qualified students.** A sign-language interpreter, unlike an instructor or counselor, was ethically bound to transmit everything said in the way it was intended. The Court reversed the decision. *Zobrest v. Catalina Foothills School Dist.,* 509 U.S. 1, 113 S.Ct. 2462, 125 L.Ed.2d 1 (1993).

◆   A New York first-grader with ADHD sought a 1:1 aide at his private school, and administrative rulings agreed that the aide would be sent to the private school. The district then sought a court ruling that the aide should be provided only at the public school. The Supreme Court, Appellate Division, held state law permitted a school district to provide services at a private school. It ruled that the decision must be made on a case-by-case basis, with the student's needs in the least restrictive environment serving as a guide. The New York Court of

Appeals affirmed the judgment, finding **the state's dual enrollment statute was intended to offer private school students with disabilities "equal access to the full array of specialized public school programs."** *Board of Educ. of Bay Shore Union Free School Dist. v. Thomas K.*, 14 N.Y.3d 289 (N.Y. 2010).

◆   The parents of a student at the Delaware School for the Deaf requested a general education placement with a full-time American Sign Language interpreter and a private school placement with a small class size when their child's performance declined. Their district responded that a sign-language interpreter would be provided only if the student attended district schools. After the parents placed their son in a private school, a hearing officer held that the district should have provided a sign-language interpreter. A federal court held that **nothing in the IDEA or its regulations conferred upon parentally placed private school students an individual right to receive special education and related services that they would receive in public schools.** The IDEA only required school districts to allocate a proportional share of IDEA funds to private schools, which the district had done here. *Board of Educ. of Appoquinimink School Dist. v. Johnson*, 543 F.Supp.2d 351 (D. Del. 2008).

V. TUITION REIMBURSEMENT

If a school district is unable to provide special education services to a student with a disability in its own facilities, it must locate an appropriate program in another district, hospital or institution. When a private placement is required, the district may become responsible for tuition and other costs.

A. Private School Tuition Claims

◆   Despite an expert's contrary recommendations, a California school district prepared an IEP for a student with autism that placed her in a large general education classroom for half of her school day. The parents objected to the IEP and placed her in a private setting where she would attend a class with between six and eight students. After administrative proceedings, a federal court held the district denied the student a free appropriate public education. It also approved of the private school located by her parents. Later, the U.S. Court of Appeals, Ninth Circuit, noted **the district's IEP proposal would have placed the student with 24 peers.** As the court found the IEP inappropriate, it held for the parents. *Solana Beach School Dist. v. Ka. D.*, 475 Fed.Appx. 658 (9th Cir. 2012).

◆   A student attended Oregon public schools through grade eleven. He had problems paying attention and finishing work, but he was able to pass his classes with help at home from family members. The school district evaluated him but found him ineligible for special education and related services. After he experienced multiple behavioral problems, a psychologist determined that he had ADHD, depression and other issues. His parents enrolled him in a three-week wilderness program and then a private residential school. They then requested a due process hearing. A hearing officer found the student was eligible for special education under the IDEA but held the school district only had to pay for the residential placement, not the wilderness program or the evaluation.

On appeal, the Ninth Circuit Court of Appeals held the student was not categorically barred from seeking tuition reimbursement. The U.S. Supreme Court agreed to review the case and found the district's failure to provide an IEP of any kind was at least as serious a violation of its IDEA responsibilities as a failure to provide an adequate IEP. **The Court rejected the school district's argument that the student had to receive special education and related services from the district before advancing any claim for tuition reimbursement.** *Forest Grove School Dist. v. T.A.*, 557 U.S. 230 (2009).

The case was returned to a federal district court, which held the school district did not have to pay the student's tuition. It reasoned that the parents had failed to notify the district of their private school selection until well after making it. Moreover, the district had found that the student did not need special education or even a Section 504 plan. And the parents seemingly chose the private school because of the student's drug use and behavioral problems. *Forest Grove School Dist. v. T.A.*, 675 F.Supp.2d 1063 (D. Or. 2009).

A second appeal was made to the Ninth Circuit, which agreed with the lower court that the placement was made to address the student's drug abuse, opposition and misconduct – and not his education. The U.S. Supreme Court then denied review on their claim to private school tuition reimbursement. *T.A. v. Forest Grove School Dist.*, No. 11-630, 132 U.S. 1145 (cert. denied 1/23/12).

◆   An adopted student in Maryland with learning disabilities and emotional disturbance exhibited suicidal tendencies and clinical depression. Her IEP team placed her in a private special education day school. She later self-mutilated and attempted suicide. Her parents placed her in a residential school, even though a school psychologist found that she should be placed in a therapeutic school for students with serious emotional issues. The parents sought reimbursement, but a federal court and later the Fourth Circuit ruled against them. **The placement was based on the parents' desire to ensure the student did not harm herself. It was not made for educational reasons and was not the least restrictive environment** because she made progress in the day school when her mental health issues stabilized. *Shaw v. Weast*, 364 Fed.Appx. 47 (4th Cir. 2010).

◆   A Virginia student with autism and a significant communication disorder made little progress in public schools, mastering only one IEP objective in six years. His parents requested a due process hearing, suggesting a one-on-one Lindamood-Bell Center placement. After a hearing, the school board acknowledged the student should be classified as having multiple disabilities but refused to provide one-on-one instruction. The parents placed him in the Lindamood-Bell program for four years and then sought tuition reimbursement. A hearing officer found three of the IEPs were invalid but also found the center to be an inappropriate placement. **A federal court agreed, but the Fourth Circuit vacated and remanded the case for a year-by-year IEP analysis.** If the center was appropriate, tuition reimbursement might be awarded. *M.S. v. Fairfax County School Board*, 553 F.3d 315 (4th Cir. 2009).

◆   An Oregon student with ADHD and depression made progress in school but engaged in defiant and risky behavior at home. Her parents sought a more restrictive placement for her, but the school district ruled it out because she was earning good grades when she did her work. Her parents unilaterally placed her in a residential facility, but she was expelled for having sex with another student. Her parents then placed her in an out-of-state facility and sought tuition reimbursement, which the Ninth Circuit denied. It held **the student did not require residential placement for any educational reason. She was not disruptive in class and was well regarded by teachers.** *Ashland School Dist. v. Parents of Student R.J.*, 588 F.3d 1004 (9th Cir. 2009).

◆   The parents of a Colorado three-year-old with autism rejected the draft IEP offered by their school, which would have placed their son in an integrated setting, and kept their son at home with the one-on-one therapy program he had been receiving. The district failed to finalize the IEP for that year. The next year, the parents again rejected the district's IEP calling for an integrated placement with five hours of discrete trial training a week. The school district finalized that IEP, but the parents selected a private school, then sought tuition reimbursement. A hearing officer held for the school district, but a federal court found the parents entitled to tuition for the first year because the district failed to finalize the IEP. The Tenth Circuit reversed the judgment, noting that IDEA procedural violations were not sufficient for the parents to prevail in this case. **A procedural violation must result in lost educational opportunities to justify an award of tuition.** The court remanded the case (returned it to the district court) for further consideration of that issue. *Sytsema v. Academy School Dist. No. 20*, 538 F.3d 1306 (10th Cir. 2008).

When the case returned to the district court, it held that the unfinished IEP failed to offer the student needed one-on-one services. As a result, the parents were entitled to an award of their tuition costs. *Sytsema v. Academy School Dist. No. 20*, No. 03-cv-2582-RPM, 2009 WL 3682221 (D. Colo. 10/30/09).

◆   A South Carolina ninth-grader with a learning disability attended special education classes. Her parents disagreed with the IEP devised by their school district. The IEP called for mainstreaming in regular education classes for most subjects. The parents requested a due process hearing and unilaterally placed the student in a private school. A hearing officer held that the IEP was adequate. After the student raised her reading comprehension three full grades in one year at the private school, the parents sued the district for tuition reimbursement. A U.S. district court held the educational program and achievement goals of the proposed IEP were "wholly inadequate" under the IDEA. Even though the private school was not approved by the state education department, it provided the student with an excellent education that complied with IDEA substantive requirements. The parents were entitled to tuition reimbursement.

The U.S. Supreme Court held that the failure of the school district to provide an appropriate placement entitled the parents to tuition reimbursement, even though the private school was not on any state list of approved schools. This was because the district denied the student FAPE and the private education provided to her was found appropriate by the district court. South

Carolina did not release a list of approved schools to the public. Under the IDEA, parents unilaterally place children in private schools at their own risk. To recover tuition costs, parents must show the placement proposed by the school district violates the IDEA and that the private school placement is appropriate. The Court upheld lower court decisions for the parents. *Florence County School Dist. Four v. Carter*, 510 U.S. 7, 114 S.Ct. 361, 126 L.Ed.2d 284 (1993).

◆   The parents of a child with a disability did not waive their claim for reimbursement of the expenses involved in unilaterally placing their child in a private school during the pendency of proceedings to review the child's IEP. The case involved a learning disabled child who was placed in a public school special education program against the wishes of his parents. The parents requested a due process hearing and, prior to the resolution of their complaint, placed their child in a private residential school. The parents then sought reimbursement for their expenses. A federal appeals court found the IDEA stay-put provision did not bar claims for reimbursement. The U.S. Supreme Court held that barring reimbursement claims in cases of unilateral parent placement would be contrary to the IDEA, which favors proper interim placements. However, **parents who unilaterally change a child's placement during the pendency of proceedings do so at their own financial risk**. If the courts ultimately determine a child's IEP is appropriate, the parents are barred from obtaining reimbursement for any interim period in which the placement violated the IDEA. The Court affirmed the appellate court ruling. *Burlington School Committee v. Dep't of Educ.*, 471 U.S. 359, 105 S.Ct. 1996, 85 L.Ed.2d 385 (1985).

B. Parental Conduct

The IDEA discourages unilateral conduct by school districts and parents alike. The IDEA allows for the reduction or denial of reimbursement to parentally placed private school students, if the parents fail to give at least 10 days notice of the intended placement, do not make the child available to designated school employees for an assessment and evaluation before the child's removal from public school, or if a judge so rules.

In M.C. ex rel. Mrs. C. v. Voluntown Board of Educ., *226 F.3d 60, 68 (2d Cir. 2000), the U.S. Court of Appeals, Second Circuit, found that "courts have held uniformly that reimbursement is barred where parents unilaterally arrange for private educational services without ever notifying the school board of their dissatisfaction with their child's IEP." And in* Frank G. v. Board of Educ. of Hyde Park, *459 F.3d 356 (2d Cir. 2006), the court held it is inequitable to permit reimbursement when parents have not timely requested it.*

◆   Alaska parents of a child with autism were vigorous advocates of his rights. As the student neared grade three, the parties were unable to develop an IEP for him, and the parents filed a due process hearing request. Although they were invited to an IEP meeting, they did not attend. Instead, the parents offered their written comments and suggestions for the IEP. A hearing officer ordered the school district to keep the student in the writing instruction placement sought by the parents. When they tried to include writing instruction in a draft IEP, the school district postponed further efforts to update an IEP until a final decision by the hearing officer. Due to the impasse, the district relied on the second-grade IEP, with third-grade lessons and materials. After a hearing, the hearing officer found the student had regressed in several areas. She held the district denied the student a FAPE. She awarded the parents their math and reading tutoring costs.

When the case reached the U.S. Court of Appeals, Ninth Circuit, it held the district had a duty to review and revise the student's IEP at least annually. Nothing in the IDEA made this duty contingent on parental cooperation. The IDEA, its regulations, and case precedents emphasized parental involvement and advocacy, even when this did not align with a school's recommendations. **Although the parents had been zealous advocates for their child, the court found it would be antithetical to IDEA purposes to penalize them for exercising their rights under the act.** It held the district could have continued working with the parents on an IEP or revised the IEP and filed its own due process request to seek approval of its proposal. As the district could not "ignore its affirmative duty under the IDEA by postponing its obligation to revise the outdated IEP," the court held the district had violated the IDEA with a "take it or leave it" approach. As a result, it reversed the decision regarding denial of FAPE and held the parents were entitled to reimbursement for their tutoring costs. *Anchorage School Dist. v. M.P.*, 689 F.3d 1047 (9th Cir. 2012).

◆ The mother of a Delaware student with disabilities placed him in a private school after a dispute about his IEP. The district agreed to fund the placement for one year and began the formal IEP process for the next year. However, the mother failed to return a form requesting permission to evaluate her son until midway through the summer. She also claimed she could not attend an IEP meeting because of scheduling conflicts. She then returned her son to the private school and refused to further participate in the IEP process, asserting that a free appropriate public education (FAPE) was denied because the IEP was not in place at the start of the school year. A federal district court ultimately ruled against her when she sued for tuition reimbursement, noting that **the delays were at least partly her fault and did not deny her son FAPE.** On appeal, the Third Circuit affirmed, noting that not all procedural violations of the IDEA result in a denial of FAPE. Here, the parents' non-cooperation caused the delay. *C.H. v. Cape Henlopen School Dist.*, 606 F.3d 59 (3d Cir. 2010).

◆ A New York school department's committee on special education developed an IEP for a student with autism. The IEP stated that the student would attend school in District 75 (a group of schools for students with disabilities) but did not specify which school he would attend. Instead, a citywide placement officer would make that determination. The student's parents objected to the school that was eventually proposed, but instead of visiting a second school they enrolled their son in a private school. When they sought tuition reimbursement, a federal court and later the Second Circuit ruled against them. Under the circumstances, **the IDEA did not require the school district to name the particular location for receiving special education services.** *T.Y. v. New York City Dep't of Educ.*, 584 F.3d 412 (2d Cir. 2009).

◆   A New Hampshire student had a learning disability in math. Her IEP team suggested a private school placement, and her parents agreed. The next year, they requested due process, claiming the district had denied her a FAPE for the prior five years. They withdrew the student from school and began homeschooling her. The district threatened to file truancy charges against them unless they registered her as a homeschooled student. When the case finally reached a federal district court, **the court held that the parents acted unreasonably during the IEP process; thus, any delay in developing an IEP did not violate the IDEA.** Also, the truancy threat did not amount to a denial of FAPE. *Kasenia R. v. Brookline School Dist.*, 588 F.Supp.2d 175 (D.N.H. 2008).

◆   The parents of a Maine student placed her in a private residential facility before the district could evaluate her. They then demanded a due process hearing and met with the district to consider her eligibility for IDEA services. The hearing was delayed while an independent evaluation was conducted. At an IEP meeting, the parents insisted on a therapeutic residential placement while the district asserted that a nonresidential public school setting would be appropriate. The parents challenged the district's placement, claiming it failed to offer the student a finalized IEP. A federal district court and the First Circuit ruled for the district, noting that the IEP was never finalized because the parents disrupted the IEP process. **Their fixation on a residential placement at district expense caused the breakdown of the IEP process.** *C.G. and B.S. v. Five Town Community School Dist.*, 513 F.3d 279 (1st Cir. 2008).

VI. TRANSITION AND GRADUATION

Transition services describe "a results-oriented process, that is focused on improving the academic and functional achievement of the child with a disability ..." The IDEA requires a statement of a student's transition service needs for the IEP of each student with a disability no later than the age of 14, or earlier if appropriate. See 34 C.F.R. Part 222.50. The 2004 IDEA Amendments urged increasing emphasis on the provision of effective transition services for disabled students, in view of their increasing graduation rates.

A. Transition Plans

◆   A New York preschooler received 30-35 hours per week of home-based Applied Behavioral Analysis (ABA) therapy from his school district, with speech and occupational therapy. The committee on special education (CSE) recommended a special education placement but without the ABA sessions. His parents rejected the IEP and sought due process. A hearing officer ruled for the school district, and the Second Circuit held the district did not have to provide home-based ABA therapy. **Appropriate supports and services were included in the IEP to ease the student's transition to school.** And the parents failed to show that the CSE had predetermined a kindergarten placement. *T.S. and S.P. v. Mamaroneck Union Free School Dist.*, 554 F.3d 247 (2d Cir. 2009).

◆ A New Hampshire school district prepared an IEP for an 18-year-old student that was nearly 60 pages long and contained nine pages of transition services. The parents rejected the IEP but refused to make any modifications to the plan or even to specify which parts of it were objectionable other than to say they disagreed with the behavior aspects of the IEP. The district unsuccessfully tried to put the rest of the IEP into effect and then filed an administrative due process request. A hearing officer ruled for the school district, and a federal district court affirmed the judgment, ruling **the district did not have to comply with the parents' unspecified vision of a perfect IEP.**

The district had offered the student a detailed and comprehensive IEP that more than adequately addressed his needs. The mother appealed to the U.S. Court of Appeals, First Circuit. The court agreed with school officials that the student's IEP should be put into effect. **The IDEA does not require transition plans to be articulated as a separate component of an IEP. Nor were behavior plans necessary unless certain disciplinary actions had been taken.** Thus, the first proposed IEP, which discussed a behavior plan, did not violate the IDEA. *Lessard v. Wilton Lyndeborough Coop. School Dist.*, 518 F.3d 18 (1st Cir. 2008).

◆ After a Pennsylvania student with disabilities turned 16, his new IEP left sections of his mandatory transition plan largely blank, instead noting that he would meet with a school counselor to discuss his prerequisites for college and other issues. At the next IEP team meeting, the district offered the student an alternative special education day placement at an in-state private school. His parents instead opted for a residential school in New York. When they sought tuition reimbursement, the district failed to submit the due process request for more than three months. However, a hearing officer still ruled in favor of the district, finding the proposed placement appropriate. A federal court and the Third Circuit affirmed the judgment. **The dispute over the transition plan and the delay in submitting the due process request did not add up to an IDEA violation where the proposed IEP was appropriate.** *Sinan v. School Dist. of Philadelphia*, 293 Fed.Appx. 912 (3d Cir. 2008).

◆ An Illinois student with Rett Syndrome engaged in self-injurious behavior and sometimes struck others. In her first year of high school, she head-butted two staff members, breaking their noses. The district sought a special education setting, but the parents objected, instead settling for keeping the student at home. Eventually she was returned to her neighborhood school, where she made limited academic progress. When the district again tried to place the student in a special education setting, the parents requested a hearing, asserting that the IEP meeting was a sham to mask a "predetermined placement." A hearing officer, a federal court and the Seventh Circuit all ruled for the district. The parents received a meaningful opportunity to participate in the development and review of their daughter's IEP. **While the district did not include a transition plan in the IEP, the student was unable to benefit from one at the time**, so the lack of a transition plan did not violate the IDEA. *Board of Educ. of Township High School Dist. No. 211 v. Ross*, 486 F.3d 267 (7th Cir. 2007).

B. Graduation

The 2004 IDEA amendments relieved schools of a duty to seek an evaluation before terminating the eligibility of a student who has graduated with a regular diploma or become too old to be eligible for a free appropriate public education (FAPE). When an eligible child graduates or "ages out" of school, the school district must give the child a summary of his or her academic achievement and functional performance, with recommendations for assistance in meeting the child's postsecondary goals.

◆   An Indiana school district offered special education to a learning disabled student until his parents decided to homeschool him. They sought to reintegrate him into public schools and obtained private evaluations showing that he had autism. But the school district did not identify an autism spectrum disorder until the student was 17 and awarded him a diploma at age 19. His parents challenged the graduation, asserting he should continue to receive special education. A federal court, using the stay-put provisions of the IDEA, ordered the district to continue educating the student in a college preparatory program. **The parents' challenge to the validity and good faith of the decision to graduate their son warranted a stay-put placement.** *Tindell v. Evansville-Vanderburgh School Corp.*, No. 309-cv-00159-SEB-WGH, 2010 WL 557058 (S.D. Ind. 2/10/10).

◆   An Illinois sophomore with Type 1 diabetes and a social anxiety disorder began missing school and took classes at a community college. She sought reimbursement for her tuition there, but a federal court and the Seventh Circuit ruled against her. The student had a Section 504 plan in place for her diabetes but was not IDEA eligible. **There was no medical evidence that she stopped attending high school because her anxiety had worsened, and she was unable to establish a medical basis for her better attendance and performance at the community college.** As a result, the parents' request for community college tuition reimbursement was properly denied. *Loch v. Edwardsville School Dist. No. 7*, 327 Fed.Appx. 647 (7th Cir. 2009).

◆   The parents of a California student waited until after he graduated to file a Section 504 claim against the school district. Appeal reached the Ninth Circuit. It held that despite differences between Section 504 and the IDEA, **a party seeking relief that is also available under the IDEA must exhaust administrative remedies to the same extent as for IDEA claims.** *Fraser v. Tamalpais Union High School Dist.*, 281 Fed.Appx. 746 (9th Cir. 2008).

◆   An Oregon student with a Section 504 plan had ADHD but did not qualify for an IEP. He was suspended for accessing a school database to change his grades. A hearing was conducted to consider expulsion, but his father claimed he received improper notice and thought the meeting was just for fact-finding. The school district agreed to further investigate, and the family filed a Section 504 complaint, challenging the suspension and seeking restoration of class credit. A hearing officer ordered the district to give the student the opportunity to recover lost credits. The student graduated with a regular diploma but sued the district under Section 504 and the IDEA, seeking to modify his final grades and requesting money damages. A federal court dismissed the case, holding that **even though he had graduated, he should still have pursued administrative remedies** before suing. *Ruecker v. Sommer*, 567 F.Supp.2d 1276 (D. Or. 2008).

◆ A 19-year-old Florida student had Asperger's syndrome and was non-verbal. His senior-year IEP identified writing as a priority need. At an IEP meeting held three months before the end of the year, the district proposed eliminating goals requiring him to complete written work. It also advised the parents their son would graduate at the end of the year, if he received all of his academic credits. The parents rejected the proposal to graduate their son and to eliminate his written work. They requested a new IEP meeting or mediation and new evaluations. Days before graduation, the board advised the parents it would hold an IEP meeting to discuss a diploma and review the IEP. It then informed them the graduation ceremony was the day before the IEP meeting.

An administrative law judge rejected the parents' request for stay-put relief, but a federal district court held their due process request before graduation triggered the stay-put provision. The board appealed to the Eleventh Circuit. It rejected the district court's finding that the board had misled the parents by scheduling an IEP meeting the day after their son's graduation. There was no evidence that the board did not intend to hold the meeting if the student failed to graduate. **The district court should not have back-dated a stay-put injunction.** The court vacated the decision and instructed the district court to decide if a preliminary order should be issued. *Sammons v. Polk County School Board*, 165 Fed.Appx. 750 (11th Cir. 2006).

The case returned to the district court, which held that the student, now 22, was not entitled to stay-put protection or compensatory education. *Sammons v. Polk County School Board*, No. 8:04-cv-2657-T-24-EAJ, 2007 WL 4358266 (M.D. Fla. 12/10/07).

◆ A Washington student became pregnant as a high school senior. She failed a quiz near the end of the year and was barred from the graduation ceremony. The district superintendent later met with the family and suggested a Section 504 plan to increase the student's point total for the failed course. A resulting increase in points for the class allowed her to graduate. She and her family sued the district and school officials, alleging discrimination and due process violations. A jury found that the district violated the student's due process rights and awarded her $5,000, with over $31,000 in attorneys' fees and costs. However, the jury found no discrimination. On appeal, the Court of Appeals of Washington found that **no state or federal law created an entitlement for students to attend graduation ceremonies.** The student received an opportunity to meet with the principal to resolve her grievance prior to the ceremony. She was not deprived of any interest protected by the Constitution. *Nieshe v. Concrete School Dist.*, 128 Wash.App. 1029 (Wash. Ct. App. 2005).

◆ The parents of a Pennsylvania student with dyslexia, memory disorder and ADHD agreed with their school district on a twelfth-grade IEP that called for transition services in a college preparatory program in Maryland. The district did not provide the transition services, but it recommended that the student be graduated. The parents objected, and the IEP team met without them to finalize an IEP with no transition services. The Commonwealth Court of Pennsylvania held **the district failed to provide agreed-upon transition services, then scheduled the student's graduation.** It ordered the district to provide him a year of compensatory education in the college prep program. *Susquehanna Township School Dist. v. Frances J.*, 823 A.2d 249 (Pa. Commw. Ct. 2003).

◆ An Illinois school district improperly decided to graduate a high school student with multiple disabilities on the basis of his accumulation of required credits instead of his progress toward his individualized goals. As the district committed several violations of the IDEA with respect to the student's educational program and IEPs, it was required to reimburse him for private school costs and provide compensatory education at a private school until he reached age 22. The violations included designing IEPs with vague and immeasurable goals, not changing IEP goals from year to year despite regression, and failure to develop a timely transition plan. **To be eligible for graduation, the student had to meet general graduation requirements and make progress on his IEP goals and objectives.** *Kevin T. v. Elmhurst Community School Dist. No. 205*, No. 01 C 0005, 2002 WL 433061 (N.D. Ill. 3/20/02).

VII. SCHOOL LIABILITY

A. IDEA Claims

1. Compensatory Education

Compensatory education is the belated provision of necessary educational or related services to a student to which the student was entitled, but which the education agency failed to provide. Compensatory education may be awarded to students who are over the statutory age of entitlement (usually 21) to prohibit education agencies from indefinitely delaying the provision of necessary services until the student is beyond school age.

◆ The parents of an 11-year-old Pennsylvania student who had never attended public schools requested an evaluation for special education after obtaining a private evaluation. They did not sign the consent forms for a public evaluation, instead enrolling the student in a private school recommended by their evaluator. Eventually the district was able to conduct an evaluation and prepare an IEP, which the parents rejected. They sought compensatory education for the delay, claiming that they had asked for an evaluation during the student's kindergarten year. The case reached the Third Circuit, which ruled against the parents. It noted that **they were not entitled to compensatory education because they had no intention of placing their son in public school. There was no evidence they had asked for an evaluation during kindergarten.** *P.P. v. West Chester Area School Dist.*, 585 F.3d 727 (3d Cir. 2009).

◆   A Texas student with multiple disabilities had an IEP that included a goal to initiate communications about his need to go to the bathroom. The district used a voice-output device for him to communicate this need and gave a device to the parents for home use, explaining its proper use to his mother. The student regressed in his ability to use the device at home and in his extended school year program, and he wet the bed every morning. His parents challenged the IEP's schedule of in-home and parent training. A federal court held **the student's regression in toilet training was not a failure to implement a significant portion of the IEP**, and thus no compensatory training was due. *Clear Creek Independent School Dist. v. J.K.*, 400 F.Supp.2d 991 (S.D. Tex. 2005).

◆   A District of Columbia student with multiple disabilities who was making progress required new evaluations. However, they were not performed. After six months, the student's mother requested a due process hearing. A hearing officer determined that the district had failed to provide the student with a FAPE, but limited compensatory education to the two-month period prior to the hearing request. The mother appealed. A federal court noted that **the school district had failed to show it was providing the services required by the IEP and did not conduct a reevaluation required by the IDEA**. Accordingly, the court held the student was entitled to compensatory education for the entire three-year period at issue. *Argueta v. Government of District of Columbia*, 355 F.Supp.2d 408 (D.D.C. 2005).

◆   A 19-year-old Tennessee student with no hands, one foot and cerebral palsy was dropped while school district attendants were attempting to move him from his wheelchair. His parents received his complete academic record for the first time and filed a due process complaint. A federal district court held the system violated the IDEA by not relaying information from the student's assessments. After he received a special education diploma, the Sixth Circuit ordered the district court to decide whether the case was moot. The district court held **the compensatory education claim was based on an assertion that the school system had denied a FAPE at a time when the student remained eligible for services**. Though he was now 24 and had a special education diploma, his compensatory education request involved past violations and the case was not moot. On appeal, the Sixth Circuit agreed, and found an IDEA procedural violation. *Barnett v. Memphis City Schools*, 113 Fed.Appx. 124 (6th Cir. 2004).

2. Monetary Damages, Costs and Fees

In Ortega v. Bibb County School Dist., *397 F.3d 1321 (11th Cir. 2005), the U.S. Court of Appeals, Eleventh Circuit, restated a longstanding rule that tort-type personal injury claims for damages are unavailable under the IDEA. But many attorneys representing students and their parents often add claims alleging disability discrimination and tort damages to IDEA actions.*

Claims involving any matter relating to the identification, evaluation or placement of a child, or the provision of a free appropriate public education, are subject to the IDEA's administrative exhaustion requirement.

◆   Maryland parents sued their school board in a federal court, claiming their autistic child was attacked by a male peer and suffered black eyes and a swollen lip. They claimed the same student had previously attacked their child and that they communicated their child's fears to school officials and his teacher, but the perpetrating student was allowed to sit near him. The court explained that the parents' failure to request a due process hearing was fatal to their IDEA and Section 504 claims. Claims for damages did not excuse an administrative hearing. **Tort-like damages are inconsistent with the IDEA's statutory scheme, which exists to assure the provision of a free appropriate public education.** A Section 504 claim for disability discrimination was also subject to the exhaustion requirement, since it was linked to an IDEA claim. In addition, the parents did not assert any disability discrimination by the board. While they asserted constitutional rights violations, the court found this claim only amounted to a restatement of the IDEA claim. *Wright v. Carroll County Board of Educ.*, Civ. No. 11-cv-3103, 2012 WL 1901380 (D. Md. 5/24/12).

◆   A Pennsylvania student had academic difficulty during her school career. By the fifth grade, she was receiving 45 minutes of daily learning support. In the second half of the year, the district reevaluated her and found her ineligible for special education. A due process hearing officer ruled that the district violated the IDEA and ordered compensatory education as well as reimbursement for an independent education evaluation. A review panel largely affirmed the decision. When the district appealed to a federal district court, the parents sought money damages. **The court ruled that the IDEA does not permit compensatory damages but ruled they might be available under Section 504.** The case would move forward. *Breanne C. v. Southern York County School Dist.*, 665 F.Supp.2d 504 (M.D. Pa. 2009).

◆   Parents of a New York student with disabilities sought tuition reimbursement. After winning at administrative and federal court levels, they sued to recover $29,350 in fees for assistance provided by an educational consultant. A federal court awarded $8,650 in fees, allowing only those charges accumulated between the hearing request and the administrative ruling. **The U.S. Supreme Court found that nothing in the IDEA made clear to the states that accepting federal funds would make them responsible for reimbursing parents for expert witness fees.** The fees were not reimbursable costs. *Arlington Cent. School Dist. Board of Educ. v. Murphy*, 548 U.S. 291, 126 S.Ct. 2455, 165 L.Ed.2d 526 (2006).

◆   The mother of a Nevada student with autism took her son to a childhood autism program ordered by a hearing officer as compensatory education. The district was required to pay "all out-of-pocket expenses" – nearly $65,000. When the mother sought an additional $26,515 to fully compensate her for wages and benefits she lost while transporting her son to the program, the Supreme Court of Nevada held that she was not entitled to them. **Out-of-pocket expenses did not include lost income.** *Gumm v. Nevada Dep't of Educ.*, 113 P.3d 853 (Nev. 2005).

B. Discrimination Claims

The Americans with Disabilities Act (ADA), 42 U.S.C. § 12101, et seq., and Section 504 of the Rehabilitation Act of 1973, 29 U.S.C. § 794, are federal statutes prohibiting discrimination against persons with disabilities. Both acts require schools and their employees to make "reasonable accommodations" for qualified individuals with disabilities, but no institution is required to lower its academic standards in order to do so. As the Eighth Circuit Court of Appeals held in Sonkowsky v. Board of Educ. for Independent School Dist. No. 721, *327 F.3d 675 (8th Cir. 2003),* **to create liability under Section 504 or the ADA, there must be evidence of bad faith or gross misjudgment by school officials.**

◆   A Pennsylvania student with bipolar disorder reported frequent peer harassment at her school. She reported one girl called her "psychotic" and a "slut." One of the harassers was suspended and stopped going to school. Eventually, the student left school and received homebound instruction. She then graduated and later attended college. The student sued her former district and school officials in a federal court, asserting violations of the ADA and Section 504 of the Rehabilitation Act. The court dismissed the case, and appeal reached the U.S. Court of Appeals, Third Circuit. It agreed with the lower court that the student did not qualify for federal disability law protection, because she did not show she had a substantially limiting impairment. While the student's bipolar disorder was a mental or physical impairment, the court agreed with the lower court that **she did not demonstrate that her limitations substantially limited her ability to interact with others, care for herself, concentrate on school work or sleep.** Since the court did not find she was significantly restricted in a major life activity, it affirmed the judgment for the school district. *Weidow v. Scranton School Dist.,* 460 Fed.Appx. 181 (3d Cir. 2012).

◆   An Indiana student began having allergic reactions to perfume. Some of his reactions involved rashes and swelling, while others required hospitalization. When the student reported his reactions to the school, he could not give details such as who sprayed perfume or what fragrances triggered his reactions. The principal instructed staff to advise students not to spray perfumes in classrooms or hallways. Periodic school announcements were made that spraying should be confined to the lavatories. A school newspaper article alerted the community to the situation and discouraged excessive use of perfume and hallway spraying.

But the principal refused to issue a written policy against spraying perfume in school. In his senior year, the student was hospitalized due to significant allergic reactions at school. He remained at home for his education to avoid further such reactions. In a federal court action for disability discrimination, the court found no intentional discrimination. Instead, the school was working to control the problem. Suggestions by the school included separate parking and school entry for the student, permission for him to leave classes early to avoid others, changing his schedule and allowing different arrival times. Since he had graduated (with high honors) by the time the case reached court, his claim for an injunction was moot. **As the school did nothing to cause the reactions and did not intentionally discriminate against him, the court found for the**

school system. It held the school's refusal to enact a "written no spray policy" was reasonable. *Zandi v. Fort Wayne Community Schools*, No. 1:10-CV-395-JVB, 2012 WL 4472006 (N.D. Ind. 9/13/12).

◆   Hawaii sisters were diagnosed as autistic when they were pre-schoolers. According to their parent, the Hawaii Department of Education (DOE) found the girls eligible for special education but did not implement or design IEPs for them. He alleged the school system "warehoused" them in their first years of school. A federal district court dismissed the family's discrimination case. On appeal, the U.S. Court of Appeals, Ninth Circuit, noted a distinction between a free appropriate public education under the IDEA and Section 504. **To establish Section 504 liability, the family had to show the DOE intentionally discriminated against the students or was deliberately indifferent to their rights.** Evidence supported the claim that the girls could not access the benefits of a public education without autism-specific services. There was evidence that the DOE was on notice that they required services but failed to provide them. Failure to act despite knowledge of the likelihood of harm was evidence of deliberate indifference. Rejecting the DOE's arguments regarding claims under Section 504 and regulations published under Section 504, the court returned the case to the district court. *Mark H. v. Hamamoto*, 620 F.3d 1090 (9th Cir. 2010).

◆   A Kentucky student with diabetes attended her neighborhood school, which did not have a nurse working there. Because the student required insulin shots, her mother arranged to have someone give them to her. However, the mother then sought to have the school district hire a nurse for the neighborhood school. The district instead offered to transfer the student to a nearby school where a nurse worked. The mother rejected this option because of the extra transportation time it would involve. She later sued the district in a federal district court for Rehabilitation Act and ADA violations. The court ruled against her, noting that **the school district had offered a reasonable accommodation, which the mother had refused.** *B.M. v. Board of Educ. of Scott County, Kentucky*, Civ. No. 5:07-153-JHM, 2008 WL 4073855 (E.D. Ky. 8/29/08).

◆   A Pennsylvania student began having behavioral problems in elementary school and was diagnosed with ADHD and oppositional defiant disorder. He took medication that helped him in class, and he performed at grade level in reading, writing, math, science and social studies. In grade seven, the district found him eligible for a Section 504 accommodation plan. The student's behavior deteriorated; he threatened to shoot a teacher and burn down the school, and he was suspended. His parents asserted that the district had failed him under both the IDEA and Section 504. After a hearing officer found the school district had adequately addressed the student's attention and organization problems, the parents sued. **A federal court held that the student did not have a serious emotional disturbance so as to be entitled to IDEA disciplinary protections like a manifestation determination.** He understood the consequences of his behavior, and the school district accommodated his needs. *Brendan K. v. Easton Area School Dist.*, No. 05-4179, 2007 WL 1160377 (E.D. Pa. 4/16/07).

◆   A Wyoming student with cerebral palsy attended school in a district that initially did not have accessible buildings. The district hired a full-time aide to assist her during the school day. During her entire school career, the student continued to have accessibility issues. The district did not make accessible seating in the school gym available, and locked her out of a school building because an accessible door was not working. Also, during her senior year, her aide frequently missed school due to a personal situation. When the student sued the district under Section 504 and the ADA, the district sought to have the case dismissed. The court refused to do so, noting that **the mere hiring of the full-time aide did not mean that the district had not intentionally discriminated against the student**. A trial would have to be held. *Swenson v. Lincoln County School Dist.*, 260 F.Supp.2d 1136 (D. Wyo. 2003).

C. Negligence and Civil Rights Claims

In order to hold school districts liable for negligence, there must be some act or omission that creates a foreseeable risk of harm. Civil rights actions require an injured party to show violation of a clearly established right, and often, "conscience-shocking" conduct. Many of these cases are decided on the basis of immunity, a concept more fully discussed in Chapter Twelve.

◆   A Colorado student with Down syndrome was placed in a class for students with severe disabilities, where students sat in "wrap-around desks" with bars to prevent them from pushing their chairs out. Staff members said they used the desks for a few minutes at a time for discipline and to ensure students remained on task and were not disruptive. The student's mother said she observed her child in a desk for an hour with the bar in place. Concerned over the child's lack of progress, she revoked her consent for the desk. But school staff continued using the desk, and the student was sent home with a broken arm. The parent removed her child from school and filed an administrative claim against the district. A hearing officer found the student was denied a free appropriate public education and held the use of the desk was prohibited by state law. The case reached the U.S. Court of Appeals, Tenth Circuit. It found the wrap-around desk did not bind students in a way that implicated the Fourth Amendment.

In the court's view, **the desk did not involve a restriction on movement that was distinguishable from typical school custodial settings**. There was no due process violation, as the student's liberty interest in freedom from bodily restraint was not implicated. Her disabilities presented unique challenges, and it was conceivable that use of the special desk was a rational response to them. According to the court, due process rights are not "triggered by every time-out and after-school detention." Nothing indicated any intent to harm the student, and the court found the absence of a deliberate intent by school staff was decisive. *Ebonie S. v. Pueblo School Dist. 60*, 690 F.3d 1051 (10th Cir. 2012).

◆   A New York student with a history of behavior problems that included aggression at home, setting fires, stealing and threatening others attended school under an IEP. He made better social progress after being placed in a community residence and displayed no aggressive behaviors for two years. When he was 11 years old, he called a kindergartner his girlfriend while on a school bus. Her mother asked that they be separated. Later, he exposed himself to the kindergartner and forced her to touch him. Her mother sued the district for negligence. The Court of Appeals of New York ruled that she could not recover for her daughter's injuries because **the molestation by the 11-year-old was not foreseeable**. His past conduct did not indicate any sexually aggressive behavior. *Brandy B. v. Eden Cent. School Dist.*, 934 N.E.2d 304 (N.Y. 2010).

◆   A New York City special education teacher initiated a Type Three referral to remove an aggressive student from her class, and she contemplated quitting because of his behavior. Her supervisors told her to "hang in there" because referral could take up to 60 days. Forty-one days after initiating the referral, the student attacked another child and the teacher intervened, sustaining injuries. She sued the city for negligence, alleging that a "special relationship" supported her claim. A jury awarded her over $512,000, and appeal reached the state's highest court. **According to the New York Court of Appeals, no special relationship existed between the teacher and the board that would create a cause of action for negligence.** *DiNardo v. City of New York*, 13 N.Y.3d 872, 921 N.E.2d 585, 893 N.Y.S.2d 818 (N.Y. 2009).

◆   A disabled California student had an IEP that called for full-time adult supervision. She had held hands with a male student on more than one occasion and went with him unsupervised to a greenhouse on campus, where he made sexual advances toward her. Her family sued the district for negligence and lost. The California Court of Appeal held that **the student's IEP did not require the district to supervise her every minute she was on campus**. Further, the hand-holding did not make it foreseeable that the male student would make sexual advances toward her during one brief, unsupervised period. *M.P. v. Chico Unified School Dist.*, No. 138462, 2009 WL 226005 (Cal. Ct. App. 2/2/09).

◆   An assistant principal in North Carolina called a disabled student's mother to report some sexual experimentation between the student and another boy. The mother believed the contact was not consensual and she sued the school board for negligence, also asserting state constitutional claims. The school board sought immunity, but the North Carolina Supreme Court held the lawsuit could proceed. **Sovereign immunity was created by the courts, but constitutional rights trumped them.** And granting immunity to the board would leave the student and his mother without an adequate state remedy. *Craig v. New Hanover County Board of Educ.*, 678 S.E.2d 351 (N.C. 2009).

◆   A disabled female student in Ohio rode the bus home every afternoon with three disabled male students. No bus aide accompanied them because none was required by any of the students' IEPs. The student was abused by a male student during the rides home. A bus aide present on the morning drive eventually discovered the abuse, and the parents ultimately sued the district for her injuries. They claimed that a state law "motor vehicle exception" to immunity allowed them to sue, while the district asserted that the exception applied only to the action of driving the bus. On appeal, the Ohio Supreme Court held **immunity** protected the school district. The motor vehicle exception applied only to the driving of the bus and not the supervision of students by the driver. *Doe v. Marlington Local School Dist. Board of Educ.*, 907 N.E.2d 706 (Ohio 2009).

◆ The mother of a Virginia child with cerebral palsy and a seizure disorder became concerned that the student's teacher was improperly confining her to a wheelchair for most of the day. She hid recording equipment in the child's wheelchair, got information that corroborated her concerns and then sued the teacher, the school board and the superintendent for violating her child's right to bodily integrity under the Due Process Clause. The defendants sought immunity, but the Fourth Circuit held that they were not entitled to it. **The student had a clearly established right to be free from bodily restraint, and the mother alleged that the confinement was intentional and excessive.** If staff members indeed restrained the child for hours at a time as alleged, they would have violated clearly established law. The court remanded the case for further proceedings. *H.H. v. Moffett*, 335 Fed.Appx. 306 (4th Cir. 2009).

◆ A Minnesota student with an emotional-behavioral disorder and a history of sexually inappropriate behavior was supposed to sit alone behind the bus driver, and his transportation form included that directive. However, the form did not detail his past history. He was allowed to move back in the bus at some point, and he sexually assaulted another student. When the other student sued the district, the Minnesota Court of Appeals held that **the district had immunity with respect to its decision to withhold the student's prior history of sexual misbehavior.** But as for the failure to follow directions and keep the student in the seat behind the driver, the bus service had no immunity. *J.W. v. 287 Intermediate Dist.*, 761 N.W.2d 896 (Minn. Ct. App. 2009).

◆ A 15-year-old Tennessee student with depression, ADHD, bipolar disorder and schizophrenia jumped off a moving school bus after the driver refused to allow him to get off at a location that was not designated as a bus stop. The student died from the fall. His mother sued school officials, claiming disability discrimination and civil rights violations. A federal district court and the U.S. Court of Appeals, Sixth Circuit, ruled against her. The Sixth Circuit held **the school board had no policy or custom of deliberate indifference to student rights, and its conduct was not the moving force or cause of the death.** *Hill v. Bradley County Board of Educ.*, 295 Fed.Appx. 740 (6th Cir. 2008).

◆ A learning-disabled Colorado high school student told her mother she did not want to attend school anymore because boys teased her. The mother told the principal that certain boys were "bothering" her daughter. Later, the student told a school counselor that one boy had repeatedly called her to ask for oral sex and that two boys had coerced her into sexual conduct. The school resource officer then investigated, but the mother refused to cooperate on "advice of counsel." The district attorney then declined to prosecute the case. The student had a psychotic episode that required hospitalization. The family sued the school district under Title IX. **The Tenth Circuit held for the district, finding it did not have actual knowledge of the sexual harassment until the student told** the counselor about it. Nor did the district have a policy of allowing peer sexual harassment. And the district was not required to discipline the boys for sexual harassment. *Rost v. Steamboat Springs RE-2 School Dist.*, 511 F.3d 1114 (10th Cir. 2008).

◆   An Ohio school aide supervised an autistic student who had previously injured fellow students on the bus. The aide rode with the student on the bus, and was hit and bitten by the student on one occasion. Later, the aide accompanied the student on a field trip to a bowling alley, where the aide intervened to protect another student from the autistic student's attack. The aide was injured. She sued the school board for negligence and civil rights violations, asserting a "state created danger" theory. A federal court and the Sixth Circuit ruled in favor of the school board, noting that **the school district did not create the danger or increase the risk to the aide**. The board was simply attempting to discharge its duties under the IDEA. *Hunt v. Sycamore Community School Dist. Board of Educ.*, 542 F.3d 529 (6th Cir. 2008).

◆   A Michigan student with multiple disabilities, including a seizure disorder, had to be harnessed into seats when traveling in a vehicle or a wheelchair. During a field trip, the student suffered a seizure and became unresponsive on a school bus. Later, he suffered another seizure on the bus, and neither the attendant nor the driver could perform CPR. Emergency responders arrived 10 minutes later and took the student to a hospital, where he died the next day. Litigation in the state court system reached the Michigan Court of Appeals. It found **the board was entitled to immunity because school officials did not act with "gross negligence," which is defined as conduct so reckless as to amount to a disregard for safety**. *Lofton v. Detroit Board of Educ.*, No. 276449, 2008 WL 4414255 (Mich. Ct. App. 9/30/08).

◆   A Nevada student had tuberous sclerosis and autism and was non-verbal. An IDEA lawsuit was brought on his behalf against his school district and teacher. In it, he alleged that his teacher slapped him repeatedly and body-slammed him into a chair. The student also claimed that school officials knew about his teacher's violent conduct but did nothing to prevent it. The teacher and the school district asked for qualified immunity, but a federal court and the Ninth Circuit refused to grant it. **The court held that no reasonable special education teacher would believe it was lawful to seriously beat a disabled four-year-old.** The case was allowed to proceed. *Preschooler II v. Clark County School Board of Trustees*, 479 F.3d 1175 (9th Cir. 2007).

D. Abuse and Neglect

◆   A Nevada teacher of autistic students was charged with abusing children. Classroom aides and parents who reported incidents to school officials said the school district failed to act and the teacher was allowed to stay in the classroom for more than a year while continuing to abuse students. In a federal court, the families charged the district with civil rights violations and negligence. Finding no "deliberate indifference" by school officials, the court held for the district.

But three months later, it issued a new order for the families. It held that if a jury found the parents' claims were true, **there would be evidence of "deliberate indifference" to the students' civil rights that would create liability under the Constitution and federal disability protection laws.** If true, the charges would also support a negligent supervision claim. As a result, the court denied the district's request for judgment. *Ferguson v. Clark County School Dist.*, No. 2:08-CV-31 JCM (GWF), 2012 WL 2000688 (D. Nev. 6/5/12).

◆ California parents complained to school officials that a teacher's aide had assaulted their disabled child and bruised his ribs. School staff members largely dismissed their complaints. When the parents reported that the aide was stepping on the student's toes, a school nurse found only that he had a fungus on his toes and said the likely cause was wearing shoes that were too small. After the student complained that the aide sexually assaulted him, the parents sued the school district in the state court system. When the case reached the California District Court of Appeal, it noted the family's claim that a special education teacher and a vice principal witnessed some misconduct by the aide.

The student had shown bruises to staff members, but they claimed the mother caused them. **All district employees are mandated reporters of suspected child abuse or neglect who must make reports to the appropriate agency if they know or suspect a child has been the victim of abuse or neglect.** While the district had minimized the parents' repeated complaints, the court found it knew about many of them. The court reversed the judgment, holding the district had "purportedly conducted its own investigation and dismissed these complaints out of hand, instead of following the procedure mandated under the Penal Code." *Ali A. v. Los Angeles Unified School Dist.*, Civil Action No. B221099, 2011 WL 72957 (Cal. Ct. App. 1/11/11).

◆ A Minnesota special education teacher took a student to her resource room as a result of a behavior incident, as specified in her IEP. On the way, she denied the student lavatory use, and the student had an accident. An investigation found that the incident was a lapse in judgment, so the teacher was not disciplined. The student's mother sued the school district for child abuse and neglect. A federal court and the Eighth Circuit ruled against her, noting she failed to allege anything done by the teacher that was "shocking to the contemporary conscience." There was no due process or Fourth Amendment violation. **The student's IEP, which included a behavior intervention plan, stated she was to be taken to her resource room if she had a behavior incident.** The teacher was complying with this instruction at the time of the accident. *C.N. v. Willmar Public Schools, ISD No. 347*, 591 F.3d 624 (8th Cir. 2010).

◆ A Florida student with autism sued his former teacher and school board based on five incidents of corporal punishment. He claimed that she violated his due process rights and the Rehabilitation Act by abusing him in class, and he pointed to her suspension and later conviction on one count of child abuse. But the court found four of the incidents were related to the student's refusal to go to a "cool-down room" or his calling the teacher names or threatening her. The fifth incident involved her tripping him, which was not corporal punishment. In each case of corporal punishment, **the teacher used restraint on the student only until he calmed down or agreed to comply with her instructions.** *T.W. v. School Board of Seminole County, Florida*, 610 F.3d 588 (11th Cir. 2010).

◆ A Georgia student with emotional and behavioral issues and ADHD made suicidal comments to staff members but told a school psychologist he was just kidding. He was hospitalized for two weeks and released. The school placed him in its time-out room for most of two days due to disruptive behavior. He made suicidal threats again. After picking a fight with another student, the student was sent to the time-out room again, and he hanged himself. His parents sued the school system and state department of education, but the Georgia Court of Appeals found **no official disregarded his rights in a manner that could be deemed deliberately indifferent.** *King v. Pioneer Regional Educ. Service Agency*, 688 S.E.2d 7 (Ga. Ct. App. 2009).

◆ A Minnesota student's IEP team determined she was ineligible for extended school year services, but it provided curb-to-curb transportation and an aide for one summer. The next summer, it required the student to use general education transportation without an aide. A driver sexually abused her, and the parents sued the school district for violating Section 504. A federal district court and the Eighth Circuit held for the district, as **discontinuation of the aide and abuse by the driver did not amount to discrimination. The district did not act with bad faith or gross misjudgment.** School officials had followed the IEP, which stated that the student was ineligible for ESY and related services. *M.Y. v. Special School Dist. No. 1*, 544 F.3d 885 (8th Cir. 2008).

E. Service Animals

◆ An Illinois autistic student had daily tantrums, an eating disorder and episodes of running on impulse. A doctor prescribed a service dog, which was obtained two years later. This calmed the student greatly. However, at a preschool IEP meeting, district officials told his mother the service dog could not accompany him to school because even though the dog was hypoallergenic, another student was highly allergic to dogs. The family sought a preliminary injunction to temporarily allow the student to bring the dog to school. **The Appellate Court of Illinois agreed with the family that the student would suffer irreparable harm if he could not have the service dog in class, and it issued an order in his favor based on state law.** *Kalbfleisch v. Columbia Community Unit School Dist., Unit No. 4*, 920 N.E.2d 651 (Ill. App. Ct. 2009).

Later, the family sought an order that would allow the dog to accompany the student to school. The Appellate Court of Illinois held **the dog met the state's definition of a "service animal" even though the commands to assist the student came from staff members and not the student himself.** The student could bring the dog to school. *K.D. v. Villa Grove Community Unit School Dist. No. 302*, 936 N.E.2d 690 (Ill. App. Ct. 2010).

CHAPTER SEVEN

Employment Practices

I. EMPLOYEE PRIVACY

A. Technology and Surveillance

Courts reviewing public employee privacy cases balance legitimate employee privacy expectations against the government interest in supervision, control and workplace efficiency. While Fourth Amendment principles apply to searches and seizures by government employers, the courts have held that a public employee's expectation of privacy in the workplace may be reduced by actual office practices, work procedures or rules. Acceptable use policies are an example of such office practices. In O'Connor v. Ortega, 480 U.S. 709 (1987), the U.S. Supreme Court held public employees have a reasonable expectation of privacy in their workspaces, desks and file cabinets. The O'Connor Court announced a case-by-case standard for evaluating employee privacy cases.

In City of Ontario, California v. Quon, *below, the Supreme Court held a California police department did not violate an officer's privacy rights by reviewing text messages on his department-owned pager. In so ruling, the Court held* **cases applying to government searches of employee offices, including** O'Connor v. Ortega, **applied to electronic communications.**

◆ A California police department informed employees that they had "no expectation of privacy or confidentiality when using" department-owned pagers capable of sending and receiving text messages. An officer's monthly pager usage exceeded his allotment. A supervisor found many messages on the officer's pager were not work-related and some were sexually explicit. The officer sued the department for Fourth Amendment violations. The U.S. Supreme Court agreed to review the case and noted that a public employer's search is reasonable if justified at its inception and not excessively intrusive.

The search in this case was justified at its inception, as there were reasonable grounds for investigating pager use. The supervisor ordered the search to see if the character limit on pagers was sufficient for department needs. As this was a legitimate, work-related reason, the Court found no Fourth Amendment violation. Review of the text messages was not excessively intrusive. Supervisors took care to investigate only pager usage that took place during work hours. The officer and others had received no assurances of privacy and had limited privacy expectations. **The text-message search did not violate the officer's rights or the rights of those with whom he communicated.** The Court noted "the judiciary risks error by elaborating too fully on the Fourth Amendment implications of emerging technology before its role in society has become clear." *City of Ontario, California v. Quon*, 130 S.Ct. 2619, 177 L.Ed.2d 216 (U.S. 2010).

◆ An Ohio teacher was found to have engaged in conduct unbecoming to the teaching profession. She signed a "last chance agreement" acknowledging her improper use of school computers for excessive emailing during instructional time and inappropriate emails. Among other sanctions, the superintendent of schools notified the Ohio Department of Education that the teacher would be suspended without pay for 45 days. A citizen made a public records request to see emails and documentation supporting the discipline. But the superintendent refused to provide copies of emails, claiming they were not "public records." The citizen filed a state court action seeking an order requiring the district to produce the emails. A state court held the teacher's use of a public email system for private purposes did not render her emails "public records" under state law. On appeal, the Court of Appeals of Ohio held a "public record" is a document, device or item created or received by a state agency (or coming under agency jurisdiction) that serves to "document the organization, functions, policies, decisions, procedures, operations or other activities of the office." Emails discovered during an investigation were "public records" under state law. **Since the emails were used to support disciplining the teacher, they were "public records," regardless of their private content.** *State of Ohio v. Jackson City School Dist.*, No. 10CA3, 2011 WL 1770890 (Ohio Ct. App. 5/5/11).

◆   Parents of severely disabled Illinois students claimed a special education teacher and classroom aide verbally and physically abused their children. They claimed their children were screamed at, degraded, force-fed, pushed, slapped and abandoned in a time-out room or a lavatory. An investigation forced the resignation of the teacher and aide, but the parents raised new concerns. To help prevent future abuse incidents, the school board proposed installing security cameras with both audio and video in classrooms. A group of special education teachers sued the board under the Illinois Eavesdropping Act and the Fourth Amendment. A federal district court held a "search" occurs under the Fourth Amendment when an expectation of privacy that society would consider reasonable is infringed upon. Teachers had no reasonable expectation of privacy in a classroom, and the court found nothing private about the communications taking place there. It held instead that **a "classroom in a public school is not the private property of any teacher,"** and held for the board. *Plock v. Board of Educ. of Freeport School Dist. No. 145*, 545 F.Supp.2d 755 (N.D. Ill. 2007).

After the federal case was dismissed, a state court held the audio-taping of classrooms violated the Illinois Eavesdropping Act. On appeal, the Appellate Court of Illinois held "eavesdropping" occurred when a person knowingly and intentionally used a device to hear or record a conversation, or when a conversation was intercepted, retained or transcribed without the consent of all parties. A "conversation" was defined as "any oral communication between two or more persons." This definition applied regardless of whether one or more of the parties intended a communication to be "private under circumstances justifying that expectation." The court found this broad language defeated the board's claim that teaching did not constitute a "conversation" as defined in the Act. **As the Act defined "conversation" to include any oral communication, the trial court had ruled correctly for the teachers.** *Plock v. Board of Educ. of Freeport School Dist. No. 145*, 920 N.E.2d 1087 (Ill. App. Ct. 2009).

◆   A New Mexico assistant principal's wife installed a recording device on her home phone. She recorded a graphic, sexual conversation between her husband and his secretary. The school district obtained the tape, then non-renewed the assistant principal's contract, offering him a teaching job instead. He accepted an administrative job in another New Mexico school district, then sued his former school district's board, superintendent and other officials for defamation and violations of federal law. A court held for the board and officials, and the assistant principal appealed to the U.S. Court of Appeals, Tenth Circuit. He asserted a liberty interest that was violated by use of an illegally obtained recording of his phone conversation. However, the assistant principal's employment was not terminated. **His one-year contract was fulfilled, and he found a better paying job in another school district. This defeated a claim that his opportunities were foreclosed.** The court affirmed the judgment. *Castillo v. Hobbs Municipal School Board*, 315 Fed.Appx. 693 (10th Cir. 2009).

◆   A Connecticut principal had a history of conflict with her superintendent. When she returned from a medical leave, she learned that he had used her computer, accessed her email and sent a copy of a letter from her attorney to his own email inbox. The principal sued the superintendent for speech and privacy rights violations. In pre-trial activity, the court noted that while email carried risks of unauthorized disclosure, **confidential information may generally be communicated through un-encrypted email with a reasonable expectation of confidentiality and privacy**. The school district's acceptable use policy (AUP) notified system users of a "limited privacy expectation in the contents of their personal files on the district system."

AUP language prohibited users from unauthorized access to the system, including logging onto another person's account or using an open account to access another person's files. This prompted the court to find that the principal had a reasonable expectation of privacy in her work emails. The superintendent's use of the principal's email did not appear to be the type of "routine monitoring" permitted by the AUP. Since the court found his conduct was not objectively reasonable, he would not enjoy immunity in further proceedings. *Brown-Criscuolo v. Wolfe*, 601 F.Supp.2d 441 (D. Conn. 2009).

◆ A California teacher submitted a workers' compensation claim for a back injury. She underwent disc replacement surgery and got married while still on disability leave. The School Insurance Program for Employees (SIPE) and the teacher's school district hired an investigator to surreptitiously attend her wedding and obtain videotape of her. The investigator went to the wedding and represented himself as a guest. He videotaped the ceremony and the reception. The day after the wedding, the investigator videotaped the teacher and her husband while they sunbathed on the balcony of a rented room. The teacher sued the school district, SIPE and others for invasion of privacy and negligence.

The court dismissed the case, and the teacher appealed. The Court of Appeal of California rejected the teacher's claim that SIPE and her district "intended to harass her," not to conduct an investigation or disciplinary action. The investigation was part of a judicial or administrative proceeding that was "cloaked in immunity" because it was an essential step to an administrative proceeding. For this reason, **the district and SIPE were entitled to immunity** and there was no liability for either agency under the Government Code. The court also ruled against the teacher on her claims for invasion of privacy. The conduct of the district and SIPE was within the scope of Government Code immunity. *Richardson-Tunnell v. School Insurance Program for Employees (SIPE)*, 157 Cal.App.4th 1065, 69 Cal.Rptr.3d 176 (Cal. Ct. App. 2007).

◆ A 2006 Michigan law required the state education department to use all available technology to compare registered educational personnel with conviction records maintained by the state police department. The education department attempted a database comparison before the law went into effect. A state official sent a letter to local school officials identifying teachers with criminal convictions. The letter said that teachers having a "listed offense" must be dismissed. The state official later stated that it was expected that the comparison would result in some "false hits" because some data fields, such as Social Security numbers, might match. The Michigan Education Association (MEA) claimed the department was releasing inaccurate criminal history records, and it sued state officials to prohibit the release of information. The court issued an order for the MEA that would prevent the department from releasing the comparison data to local school officials. Despite the order, the state distributed lists of convicted teachers to local officials. A teacher who was an MEA member sued, asserting a host of negligence claims on behalf of all certified teachers with criminal convictions. The case reached the Michigan Court of Appeals, which held the state governmental tort liability act conferred immunity on state officials acting within the scope of their authority. **The officials were attempting to comply with school safety legislation.** *Frohriep v. Flanagan*, 275 Mich.App. 456, 739 N.W.2d 645 (Mich. Ct. App. 2007).

On review, the Supreme Court of Michigan held a chief academic officer and supervisor of client services did not qualify for immunity, reversing part of the appellate decision. *Frohriep v. Flanagan*, 480 Mich. 962 (Mich. 2007).

B. Employee Search and Seizure

Searches and seizures conducted by school authorities implicate the Fourth Amendment. Because these searches are not carried out to enforce criminal laws, the courts consider them "administrative searches," which may be justified by the need to protect student safety and ensure order in schools.

1. Drug Testing

◆   Mississippi first-grade students reported that their teacher was lying on her classroom floor with her eyes closed. An assistant superintendent instructed her to undergo a drug test pursuant to district policy. After initially refusing a test, she agreed to take one, and it indicated she had used opiates. She also admitted taking Xanax and Ambien, resulting in notice that she would be dismissed for refusing to take the drug test and for neglect of duty and insubordination. At a hearing, the school board voted for employment termination, based on the teacher's own testimony of a positive drug test and statements by other teachers.

A state chancery court held the board action was arbitrary and capricious, and appeal reached the Supreme Court of Mississippi. A district policy defined "reasonable suspicion" as a belief that an employee was using or had used drugs or alcohol. Reasonable suspicion was based on "abnormal conduct or erratic behavior while at work, absenteeism, tardiness or deterioration in work performance." **The court held state law committed the entire matter to the discretion of the school board. Under this standard, the decision was not arbitrary and capricious.** District policy stated the consequences for those who refused to take a drug test upon request. The board had relied on the policy's clear language when it discharged the employee, and the court found its decision was well-reasoned. There was ample evidence that the teacher had refused to take the drug test. Since the board had the prerogative to select the appropriate punishment, including employment termination, the court upheld the decision. *Smith County School Dist. v. Barnes*, 90 So.3d 63 (Miss. 2012).

◆   A Texas teacher claimed her principal took her to a drug-testing facility because he believed she was under the influence of an illegal substance. Testing reflected no substance use, and she filed an incident report with the local police concerning the principal. When the district superintendent notified the teacher that her contract would not be renewed, she filed a grievance against the district. She later filed a lawsuit against the district, principal and other officials. A federal district court held the school officials were entitled to immunity for the teacher's state law false imprisonment claim. This was because she was also asserting the claim against the school district itself. Immunity applied to claims against the school district for punitive or exemplary damages. **A school district could only be liable for civil rights violations based on actions for which it was actually responsible.** The teacher claimed that an official district policy or custom was the moving force in the violation of her federally protected rights. If her claims were true, the teacher raised a valid question of her right to relief. As a result, the court denied the district's motion to dismiss the federal claims. *Catlett v. Duncanville Independent School Dist.*, No. 3:09-CV1245-K, 2010 WL 2217889 (N.D. Tex. 5/27/10).

◆   A West Virginia school board implemented a random, suspicionless drug-testing policy on employees in 47 "safety-sensitive positions," including teachers, coaches, cabinetmakers, handymen, plumbers and the district superintendent. Teachers and their employees' association sought to prevent implementation of the policy. A 19-year veteran teacher testified that he never witnessed a school employee coming to work in an impaired state. And the district superintendent admitted there had been no instances of any student injuries due to a drug- or alcohol-impaired teacher. A federal court found drug testing is a "seizure" under the Fourth Amendment. When a state agency conducts a search, there must ordinarily be individualized suspicion of wrongdoing. The U.S. Supreme Court has found that special safety needs outweigh employee privacy interests where there are major safety concerns such as a risk of great harm to people and property. But **the teachers and other school employees in this case did not have a reduced privacy interest by virtue of their public employment**. They were not in "safety-sensitive" positions. The risk of harm stated by the board was speculative, and it did not outweigh the employees' privacy interests. The court issued a preliminary order preventing implementation of the policy. *American Federation of Teachers - West Virginia, AFL-CIO v. Kanawha County Board of Educ.*, 592 F.Supp.2d 883 (S.D. W.Va. 2009).

2.   Individualized Searches

The special need of public employers to protect the public safety allows them to avoid the Fourth Amendment warrant and probable cause requirement. In O'Connor v. Ortega, *480 U.S. 709 (1987), the Supreme Court held the search of a public employee's office was reasonable when the measures adopted were reasonably related to the objectives of the search and not excessively intrusive.*

◆   A Massachusetts high school electronics shop teacher admitted to police investigators that he let students leave pornographic materials in a drop folder on his computer. He also admitted storing copyrighted movies and computer viruses on his computer, along with a collection of porn. A detective executed a search warrant and found files on the teacher's computer with pirated movies, hacking tools and child pornography. The teacher appealed a conviction for possessing child pornography to the Supreme Judicial Court of Massachusetts. It noted that computer files can easily be destroyed and a school search was less intrusive than searching the teacher's home. He had no reasonable expectation of privacy in the computer's open share files, which were accessible to all network users. **There was no probable cause to search private computer files** based on items found on an unauthorized computer that a student had connected to the school computer network. The fact that pirated movies had been passed from the student's computer to his did not suggest the teacher's private files had child pornography. The court reversed the conviction. *Comwlth. v. Kaupp*, 453 Mass. 102, 899 N.E.2d 809 (Mass. 2009).

◆   Maryland law officers charged a 26-year-old teacher with sex crimes after a 17-year-old student at his high school reported their sexually oriented text, telephone and instant message communications. The teacher had emailed the student sexually explicit pictures of himself. She came to his classroom, where he exposed his penis to her. A few weeks later, the student reported the teacher's conduct, and police persuaded her to place a one-party consent call to him. In the course of the call, the teacher admitted exposing himself. Police then obtained a search warrant for his residence, vehicle, cell phone and computers. A state court denied his motion to suppress evidence found through the warrant. A jury found him guilty of sexual abuse of a minor, indecent exposure and telephone misuse. The teacher appealed to the Court of Special Appeals of Maryland, which held that **the search warrant application identified reasonable grounds to believe that evidence of a crime could be found in his house**. Enough evidence was present to reasonably infer that the teacher used home computers to communicate with students and that this evidence remained in the house. As a result, the court affirmed the judgment. *Ellis v. State of Maryland*, 185 Md.App. 522, 971 A.2d 379 (Md. Ct. Spec. App. 2009).

◆   A longtime New York teacher was found guilty of having an inappropriate relationship with a female student in 1990. In 1998, he was accused of sexually harassing a student, and was later arrested for stalking the student from the 1990 incident. The district suspended the teacher without pay and reassigned him to an administrative job. He was instructed to remove his personal belongings from his classroom so it could be used by another teacher. Administrators and custodians cleaned out the classroom. When the teacher came to retrieve his property, he claimed some items were missing, including tests, quizzes and other teaching materials. He sued the district for constitutional rights violations. The case reached the Second Circuit, which ruled for the district. Many persons had access to the classroom, and the teacher acknowledged that his property was commingled with school materials. **His suspension greatly reduced, if not eliminated, any reasonable expectation of workplace privacy he might have had**, and the district's demand that he remove personal items put him on notice that he had no remaining expectation of privacy in the classroom. Further, tests, quizzes and homework problems stored in the classroom and file cabinet were the district's property. *Shaul v. Cherry Valley Springfield Cent. School Dist.*, 363 F.3d 177 (2d Cir. 2004).

3. Employee Examinations

◆ Students, parents and colleagues complained that a Connecticut teacher used foul language, made sexual remarks to students, yelled and "breached school security." The district placed him on paid administrative leave, pending an investigation. The board later found that the teacher violated its standards of conduct, but could return to work under a remediation plan that included an independent psychiatric evaluation and the release of unrestricted medical records from 13 years earlier. Instead, the teacher obtained three medical and psychiatric opinions stating he was able to return to work. He sued the board for a court order allowing his return. A federal court held for the school board. After the teacher agreed to an examination by a board psychiatrist and released his medical records to the psychiatrist, but not to the board, he returned to his job. He nevertheless appealed, and the Second Circuit held that **a person's psychiatric health data and substance abuse history is intimate information protected by a right of confidentiality**. The teacher had a protected privacy right in his medical records and did not have to disclose them without sufficient justification. The board's demand for medical records was arbitrary. The court remanded the case for a determination of whether his substantive due process rights were violated. *O'Connor v. Pierson*, 426 F.3d 197 (2d Cir. 2005).

◆ A Florida assistant middle school principal became involved in a loud and angry dispute with a uniformed school resource officer in front of students. He was suspended and later discharged after protesting a reprimand by the school board. The board required him to undergo a psychological examination. The assistant principal claimed race and disability discrimination, speech rights violations and retaliation by his school board. He commenced a federal discrimination lawsuit. **A federal district court found the examination was job-related and necessary and was not a violation of federal disability law.** Moreover, the assistant principal did not establish a claim because he did not suffer an "injury-in fact," which is required to recover monetary damages in any lawsuit. The Eleventh Circuit affirmed the judgment for the school board. *Mickens v. Polk County School Board*, 195 Fed.Appx. 928 (11th Cir. 2006).

C. Personnel Records

State data privacy acts are intended to protect the confidentiality of public employee personnel files. In Laramie County School Dist. No. One v. Cheyenne Newspapers, Inc., *below, the Wyoming Supreme Court held that while state freedom of information acts vary, most courts have held that documents including the names, positions and salaries of individual employees are available for public review. By contrast, personal information such as address, age, date of birth or Social Security number are private.*

Courts in states including Washington, New Hampshire and Iowa have held that the public is entitled to inspect documents with individual public employee names, positions and salaries. For additional cases involving open meeting laws, see Chapter Fourteen, Section IV.C. of this volume.

1. Media Access

◆   A newspaper publisher made a request under the Wyoming Public Records Act (PRA) for school district employment records that would reveal employee names and salaries. A district assistant superintendent denied the request, asserting the state education code required him to publish only the salaries of employees by category and made it unlawful to disclose individual employee names and salaries. A state court held for the publisher on the question of the PRA disclosure. On appeal, the Supreme Court of Wyoming explained that the PRA generally mandates disclosure – not secrecy – for public records. The act is based on a legislative policy of making agency records available to the public. A PRA provision states that **employment contracts describing the terms and conditions of employment of public officials and employees "are not considered part of a personnel file and shall be available for public inspection."** It seemed obvious to the court that an employee salary is a "term of any employment contract," requiring the disclosure of employee salaries. It held the publisher was entitled to the names and salaries of district employees. *Laramie County School Dist. No. One v. Cheyenne Newspapers, Inc.*, 250 P.3d 522 (Wyo. 2011).

◆   An Illinois resident asked for a copy of a school district superintendent's employment contract under the state Freedom of Information Act (FOIA). A school district record-keeper denied the request on the grounds that the contract was part of the superintendent's personnel file. The resident sued in an Illinois circuit court, which held that employment contracts found in personnel files were *per se* exempt from disclosure under the FOIA. On appeal, the Supreme Court of Illinois explained that the FOIA intends to open governmental records to public scrutiny. A superintendent's contract was a "public record" under the FOIA. An exemption protected "information, that if disclosed, would constitute a clearly unwarranted invasion of personal privacy." The court found that the district was incorrect in asserting that the superintendent's contract was *per se* exempt from disclosure. Since any employment contract contained terms and conditions of employment, "by its very nature, **the superintendent's employment contract, as a whole, constitutes 'information that bears on his public duties.'"** Placing the contract within a personnel file did not insulate it from public disclosure, so the resident prevailed. *Stern v. Wheaton-Warrenville Community Unit School Dist. 200*, 233 Ill.2d 396, 910 N.E.2d 85 (Ill. 2009).

◆   A Wisconsin school board held a public hearing to consider discharging a teacher for viewing adult website images on his work computer. After the board voted for discharge, a newspaper requested access to exhibits presented at the hearing. The teacher's union filed a grievance to challenge the discharge action. In preparation for the grievance, the district assembled the images viewed on his work computer and put them on a CD. The newspaper filed an Open Records Request for the CD. The teacher sought a court order prohibiting release of the requested information. He argued that the materials sought by the newspaper were off limits as part of a current investigation and because they had copyrighted images. The court found the Open Records Law has a presumption of complete public access that is overcome only in exceptional cases. An exception exists for "materials to which access is limited by copyright." The newspaper claimed that the teacher could not raise the copyright objection, since he did not own the copyrights. The Supreme Court of Wisconsin held that the teacher could assert the copyright exception. But the board's release of the memorandum and CD was a "fair use" of the copyrighted materials, and the records could be disclosed. **The state's "presumption of complete public access" to records outweighed the teacher's privacy and reputation interests.** *Cedarburg Educ. Ass'n v. Cedarburg School Dist.*, 300 Wis.2d 290, 731 N.W.2d 240 (Wis. 2007).

◆   A Pennsylvania court granted a preliminary order prohibiting the public release of school employee home addresses. While the state Open Records Law did not specifically exempt employee home addresses from public release, the court relied on a state constitutional right of privacy. Independent constitutional rights of privacy protected individuals from the disclosure of personal matters in which there was a "legitimate privacy expectation." Legitimate privacy expectations are those that society recognizes as reasonable. The court found **it is generally accepted that persons have privacy interests in their home addresses**. It added that "disclosure of personal information, such as home addresses, reveals little, if anything about the workings of government." *Pennsylvania State Educ. Ass'n v. Wilson*, 981 A.2d 383 (Pa. Commw. Ct. 2009).

◆   An Alabama teacher could not appeal an adverse Open Records Act ruling after a state circuit court held that **her school board had to disclose disciplinary information in her personnel file to a newspaper**. Her position that the Alabama Open Records Act did not require disclosure to the newspaper was not being contested by her school board. On appeal, the Supreme Court of Alabama found no live controversy between the teacher and board. Unless parties have conflicting interests, the case is likely to yield an advisory opinion and the controversy is academic. As there was no controversy between the teacher and board, the court vacated the judgment and dismissed the appeal. *Fenn v. Ozark City Schools Board of Educ.*, 9 So.3d 484 (Ala. 2008).

◆   A newspaper asked three Washington school districts for copies of records relating to teacher sexual misconduct in the prior 10 years. The districts notified 55 current and former teachers that their records had been gathered. Thirty-seven of the teachers asserted that the disclosure of records identifying them as subjects of sexual misconduct violated their privacy rights. A state court ordered the districts to disclose the identities of all the teachers whose misconduct was substantiated, or had resulted in some discipline, and where a district's investigation was inadequate. The court held that 15 teachers could claim exemption from disclosure of their names, but the 22 others could not. "Letters of direction" to the teachers did not have to be disclosed.

   On appeal, the Supreme Court of Washington explained that allegations of sexual misconduct by a teacher were "personal information" under the state's Public Records Act (PRA). **Disclosing a public school teacher's identity for an unsubstantiated sexual misconduct allegation was a violation of privacy rights under the PRA.** On the other hand, no privacy rights were violated when complaints about specific misconduct were substantiated after an investigation. Letters of direction had criticisms and observations of teachers and thus constituted personal information. They could not be released to the public if they simply guided future conduct and did not identify incidents of substantiated misconduct. The court ruled that a teacher's identity should be released only when an allegation of sexual misconduct was substantiated or when the misconduct resulted in discipline. *Bellevue John Does 1-11 v. Bellevue School Dist. #405*, 189 P.3d 139 (Wash. 2008).

◆ The Supreme Court of South Carolina held that a school board violated the Freedom of Information Act (FOIA) by refusing to provide information sought by a publisher during the selection process for a superintendent. The publisher sought all materials gathered by the district "relating to not fewer than the final three applicants under consideration," as permitted by the FOIA. But the board released information on only two finalists, citing privacy concerns. The court rejected the claim that state law mandated the disclosure of material only for "final applicants," even if this was less than three persons. **FOIA language was not subject to limitation by a district seeking to avoid disclosure** by naming less than three "finalists." *New York Times Co. v. Spartanburg County School Dist. No. 7*, 374 S.C. 307, 649 S.E.2d 28 (S.C. 2007).

◆ A Montana newspaper sought documents relating to employee disciplinary actions under the "right to know" provisions of the Montana Constitution and state law. A state court held that the employees had no reasonable expectation of privacy in their conduct as public employees and that any interest was exceeded by the interest in disclosure. The employees appealed, and the Supreme Court of Montana dismissed the appeal as premature. The trial court then dissolved the stay and ordered the district to release designated documents to the newspaper. The district released the documents, and the teachers appealed to the supreme court a second time. They did not request a stay and the documents were released to the newspaper, which published them. **The supreme court refused to consider the teachers' claim that they had reasonable expectations of privacy in the documents. The issue was moot in view of the publication of the documents by the newspaper.** *In re Petition of Billings High School Dist. No. 2*, 335 Mont. 94, 149 P.3d 565 (Mont. 2006).

2. Disclosure to Third Parties

Most state freedom of information laws include privacy exemptions that closely track the federal Freedom of Information Act (FOIA). In American Civil Liberties Union Foundation of Iowa v. Records Custodian, Atlantic Community School Dist., below, the court held school employee disciplinary records are exempt from disclosure under state law. It noted courts in Illinois, Massachusetts, Oregon, New Hampshire and New York have found that school employee disciplinary records are a part of an employee's personnel file. In the following case, the Supreme Court of Kentucky held a school board could not call an executive session to consider an "exit strategy" and consulting contract for a departing superintendent.

◆ Because of a change in board membership, a Kentucky superintendent decided to resign before his contract expired. He sought to resign under favorable terms and do consulting work as an independent contractor. At a board meeting held before the new board members took their posts, a closed session was held to draft a consulting contract for the departing superintendent. An open session was then held where the board voted to accept his resignation and authorized a one-year consulting contract paying over $40,000 more than his previous salary.

A trial court held the closed session to draft the consulting contract violated the Kentucky Open Meetings Act (OMA), and it enjoined further payments on the contract. But it held the OMA permitted closed-session discussions of the superintendent's resignation. On appeal, the Supreme Court of Kentucky held **the board violated the OMA when it discussed the consulting contract in a closed session. The lower court had erred in holding the board could discuss the resignation of the superintendent in a closed session.** According to the court, the OMA did not permit the secret discussion of general personnel matters. Resignation was not among the OMA's listed personnel exceptions. On the other hand, the lower court had correctly held the personnel exception did not allow secret negotiation of a consulting contract. Independent contractors were not "employees," so the matter had to be discussed in an open session. The later vote in open session did not cure the defect. As it was appropriate for the lower court to void the contract and stop the payments, that part of the judgment was affirmed. *Carter v. Smith*, 366 S.W.3d 414 (Ky. 2012).

◆ Two Iowa school employees strip-searched female students in an attempt to find $100 in cash that a classmate reported as missing. The state American Civil Liberties Union (ACLU) Foundation made a formal request to identify the employees and find out more about the incident. The school district provided only the employee names. The ACLU Foundation petitioned a state court for an order requiring the district to comply with its records request. The court held the employee discipline reports were exempt from disclosure under the state Open Records Act and dismissed the case. On appeal, the state supreme court stated the act created a right to examine public records. But **the act exempted over 60 categories of records from disclosure – including "personal information in confidential personnel records" of public bodies** such as school districts. Unlike the federal Freedom of Information Act, the Iowa Open Records Act had no qualifying language requiring courts to determine whether the disclosure of a document would constitute a clearly unwarranted invasion of privacy. In prior cases, the court had found **employee performance evaluations in confidential personnel files were exempt from disclosure under the act**. The discipline records in this case were like performance evaluations and were exempt from disclosure. *American Civil Liberties Union Foundation of Iowa v. Records Custodian, Atlantic Community School Dist.*, 818 N.W.2d 231 (Iowa 2012).

◆ A California high school math teacher was investigated and reprimanded for sexually harassing a student. He was placed on administrative leave for a month pending the result of a school investigation. An attorney investigated, but the student's parents did not allow her to be interviewed. Among the findings of the investigation was that the teacher had violated a board policy prohibiting sexual harassment of students. He was prohibited from interacting with the student who had accused him of harassment. The incident was reported to a law enforcement agency, as required by a school district policy. But no criminal charges were filed against the teacher, and he was allowed to return to his job.

Two years after the investigation, a parent of two children who resided in the district requested the investigation report, a copy of the letter of reprimand and any other public records regarding complaints about improper behavior by the teacher toward students. The teacher petitioned a state superior court to prevent the disclosure. It granted a temporary restraining order but later denied his request for a preliminary order. It held the documents were subject to disclosure under the California Public Records Act (CPRA). On appeal, the state court of appeal observed that the state constitution guarantees individual privacy rights but assures a public right of access to information held by public agencies. In general, the CPRA specified access rights to any public record. But personnel records were among 29 categories of exempt documents. The court held **the CPRA required the release of the investigation report and disciplinary record, as the public interest in disclosing them outweighed the teacher's privacy interest**. *Marken v. Santa Monica-Malibu Unified School Dist.*, 202 Cal.App.4th 1250, 136 Cal.Rptr. 3d 395 (Cal. Ct. App. 2012).

◆   A New York teachers union asked six charter schools for full names, titles, salaries and home addresses of their teachers, instructors and faculty members. The schools denied the request in part, stating full compliance would constitute an invasion of personal privacy rights under state Freedom of Information Law (FOIL) provisions. After exhausting administrative appeals, the union sued the charter schools under the FOIL. A state court ordered the charter schools to disclose the names, and appeal reached the New York Court of Appeals. It held charter schools were subject to the FOIL and were thus required to maintain records containing employee names, public office addresses, titles and salaries.

State law generally permitted public inspection of documents, but access could be denied to records that "if disclosed would constitute an unwarranted invasion of personal privacy." This included the "sale or release of lists of names and addresses if such lists would be used for commercial or fund-raising purposes." **While the union had the right to solicit members, the court held it could not rely on the FOIL to do so.** It was clear that the union's "intent in requesting the teacher names is to expand its membership and, by extension, obtain membership dues." Ordering disclosure of the teacher names "would do nothing to further the policies of FOIL." The fact that a record had to be "maintained" did not mean it had to be disclosed. The request for teacher names was denied. *In re New York State United Teachers v. Brighter Choice Charter School*, 15 N.Y.3d 560, 940 N.E.2d 899 (N.Y. 2010).

◆   A Vermont school superintendent recommended discharging a principal during his contract term based on performance issues. After a public hearing, the school board decided to retain the principal but also voted to investigate his job performance. Several months later, the superintendent assigned the principal a poor performance evaluation and again recommended discharge. This time, the board met in executive session with the principal and superintendent. After the principal refused to resign, the board placed him on paid administrative leave. Instead of revealing the reasons for the decision, board members explained the decision was based on performance and a prior investigation. After a hearing, the board voted against renewing the principal's contract. He sued the board for due process and contract violations, race discrimination and defamation. The court held for the board, and the principal appealed. The Supreme Court of Vermont affirmed. **A decision not to rehire a non-tenured employee does not implicate a protected interest.** Evidence supported the trial court's findings that the principal was not stigmatized by the board action. *Herrera v. Union No. 39 School Dist.*, 975 A.2d 619 (Vt. 2009).

◆   A Texas school district received a request for all records on a teacher. It provided some documents but withheld others, including one memorializing a meeting with the principal. The district sought a ruling from the state attorney general, who found the memorandum was not a "document evaluating the performance of a teacher" and thus not "confidential" under the state Public Information Act. The district then asked for the opinion of a state court, which found the memorandum was confidential and exempt from disclosure. The case reached the Court of Appeals of Texas. It held that to withhold information under the Public Information Act, the government must show the requested information is either not subject to the Act or is exempt under one of the Act's exceptions. **Teacher evaluations are exempt from public disclosure under Section 21.355 of the act.** The memorandum touched on performance issues discussed at the meeting. It gave the teacher corrective direction and referred her to school policies. The court held the memorandum "evaluated" the teacher because it reflected the principal's judgment, gave her correction and provided for further review. The judgment for the school district was affirmed. *Abbott v. North East Independent School Dist.*, 212 S.W.3d 364 (Tex. Ct. App. 2006).

3.   Electronic Communications

Courts in Wisconsin, Florida, Michigan and Arizona have held that emails do not become public records just because they were sent or received using a school email address or because they are retained on a school computer. The Arizona Supreme Court has held "only those documents having a substantial nexus with a government agency's activities qualify as public records."

Courts in Arizona, Arkansas, Colorado, Florida, Idaho, Ohio, Tennessee, Washington and Michigan have found the contents of public employees' personal emails are not public records. A Florida court held that, although digital in nature, "there was little to distinguish a personal email from personal letters delivered to public employees through a government post office box and stored in a government-owned desk." Times Publishing Co. v. City of Clearwater, 830 So.2d 844 (Fla. Dist. Ct. App. 2002). And in Howell Educ. Ass'n MEA/NEA v. Howell Board of Educ., 287 Mich. App. 228 (Mich. Ct. App. 2010), the Court of Appeals of Michigan stated a general rule that a public school's possession and retention of electronic data in its email system does not "convert" teacher emails into public records that are subject to disclosure.

◆   A news reporter requested copies of all emails sent in a 30-month period to and from the email addresses of nine Pennsylvania school board members, the district superintendent, and a general school district address. In response, the district stated the request was not sufficiently specific. It stated that some of the emails were protected from disclosure by state or federal law and that others were exempt as they involved "internal pre-decisional deliberations." Following administrative proceedings, the case reached the Commonwealth Court of Pennsylvania. It held the emails were district "property" under its acceptable use policy. Not all emails on a district server automatically became "public records." **Only emails that documented district transactions were "public records."** But the court agreed with the reporter that the request in this case was appropriately limited with respect to the type of record requested and the time frame and scope of emails sought. The request was specific enough because the district had already identified potential records stated in the request. In ruling for the reporter, the court directed the school district to provide him all emails from the specified accounts that "document a transaction or activity of an agency and that were created, received or retained pursuant to law or in connection with a transaction, business or activity of the agency for the period specified." No record involving private activities was subject to disclosure. *Easton Area School Dist. v. Baxter*, 35 A.3d 1259 (Pa. Commw. Ct. 2012).

◆   A Wisconsin taxpayer sought the contents of all emails sent by teachers on school computers over 13 months. After the district advised teachers it intended to disclose their emails to the requester – without regard to content – they filed a state court action to block the disclosure. A state circuit court held the personal emails sent on the school system were "records" under the Wisconsin Public Records Law. Appeal reached the state supreme court, which noted the district's Internet use policy permitted employees to make occasional personal use of their school email accounts. **The court found no other state court has held that personal emails should be released to members of the public.** To be a "record" under the Public Records Law that was available for public inspection, the court held the content of the document must have a connection to a government function. The court found the personal emails in this case had no such connection and were not "records" under the Public Records Law. Personal emails were not "records" simply by virtue of being sent or received on government email and computer systems. Flexible workplace policies allowing occasional personal email use were "in line with the mainstream of professional practice." Agreeing with the teachers, the court held the disclosure of their personal email was neither a proper nor intended effect of the law. *Schill v. Wisconsin Rapids School Dist.*, 786 N.W.2d 177 (Wis. 2010).

◆   During heated collective bargaining negotiations reported by the media, a Michigan individual sought all emails sent to and from three teachers who also served as officers for the local education association. The teachers and their unions sued to block the district from complying with the request for emails. A state court held emails generated through the school's email system and retained or stored by the district were public records under the state Freedom of Information Act (FOIA). The Court of Appeals of Michigan held that under the

FOIA, a "public record" is a "writing prepared, owned, used, in the possession of, or retained by a public body in the performance of an official function."

But the court explained that "mere possession of a record by a public body does not render the record a public document." Emails have to be stored or retained by the school in performance of an official function to come within the FOIA's definition of "public record." The personal emails in this case had nothing to do with school operations. Retention of emails by the school system was a "blanket saving of all information" that did not distinguish among personal and official purposes. The email system backup was not an "official function" which made all emails public records. As union communications by the teachers did not concern their official capacities as public employees, the court held **the union-related emails were not "public records" under the FOIA**. *Howell Educ. Ass'n MEA/NEA v. Howell Board of Educ.*, 287 Mich.App. 228 (Mich. Ct. App. 2010).

◆ A Florida high school teacher was suspended for exchanging emails and instant messages with students that were sexually explicit and made derogatory comments about staff members and school operations. An administrative law judge allowed a board expert to inspect the hard drives of the teacher's home computers to discover if they had relevant data for use in a formal termination hearing. The teacher appealed, arguing that production of the home computer records would violate his Fifth Amendment right against self-incrimination and his privacy rights. The court agreed with the teacher that the request for wholesale access to his personal computers would expose confidential communications and extraneous personal information such as banking records. There might also be privileged communications with his wife and his attorney.

An earlier Florida decision held that **a request to examine a computer hard drive was permitted "in only limited or strictly controlled circumstances," such as where a party was suspected of trying to purge data**. Other courts had permitted access to a computer when there was evidence of intentional deletion of data. There was no evidence that the teacher was attempting to thwart the production of evidence in this case. The broad discovery request violated the teacher's Fifth Amendment rights and his personal privacy, as well as the privacy of his family. The court reversed the order allowing unlimited access to the teacher's home computers. *Menke v. Broward County School Board*, 916 So.2d 8 (Fla. Dist. Ct. App. 2005).

◆ A Tennessee citizen sought to view and inspect a county education board's digital records of Internet activity, including emails sent and received, websites visited, and the identity of Internet service providers conducted during school hours or stored on school-owned computers. A judge reviewed the requested records privately, and found they were not accessible under the state Public Records Act (PRA). The citizen appealed to the Court of Appeals of Tennessee, asserting that the digital records or documents were open to public inspection because they had been made during business hours or were stored on the school's computers. The court found the PRA favored disclosing public records, including documents, papers, electronic data processing files and other material "made or received pursuant to law or ordinance or in connection with the transaction of official business by any governmental agency." **The PRA did not limit access to records based on the time a record was created or the place the record was produced or stored.** The citizen's argument that the material he sought was produced during business hours and on school-owned computers was not relevant. The trial judge properly inspected documents in private to decide if they were "made or received pursuant to law or ordinance or in connection with the transaction of official business." Placement of a document in a public employee's file did not make it a "public record." The judgment was affirmed. *Brennan v. Giles County Board of Educ.*, No. M2004-00998-COA-R3-CV, 2005 WL 1996625 (Tenn. Ct. App. 2005).

II. EMPLOYEE QUALIFICATIONS

A. Certification and Licensure

In Morrison v. State Board of Educ., *1 Cal.3d 214, 82 Cal.Rptr. 175, 461 P.2d 375 (1969), the California Supreme Court found "before any act could be deemed a ground for discharge, it must bear directly on the teacher's fitness to teach and must cause a clearly discernible detriment to the school and to its students." Michigan and California courts relied on* Morrison *in recent cases involving teacher misconduct off school grounds. Arizona and Pennsylvania courts have upheld decisions to revoke professional licenses based on misconduct that relates to a teacher's fitness to teach, even for misconduct that did not result in a conviction or that occurred off campus.*

In Board of Educ. of City of Chicago v. Cady, *307 Ill.Dec. 872, 860 N.E.2d 526 (Ill. App. Ct. 2006), the court held that an Illinois teacher's certificate must contain an endorsement for the particular subject the teacher intends to teach.*

◆   A college dropout used false documents to convince an Ohio school district that he had graduated with honors from a state university and held a valid state teaching license. He was hired for a substitute teaching job, and he ignored the district's requests for proof of his degree and state teaching license. After three years of substitute teaching, the district hired him for a full-time job. When it was learned that the dropout had never graduated from college and had falsified his professional qualifications, he was charged with six felony counts of forgery and tampering with records. He pled guilty to two counts, was sentenced to four years of community control and ordered to pay restitution of $21,837. A hearing officer later recommended denying the dropout's application for a provisional teaching license and declaring him permanently ineligible to apply for a permit or licensure in the state of Ohio. The case reached the state court of appeals, which held **state law granted the board the authority to refuse to license an applicant, limit a license, or suspend/revoke a teaching license**. It held the board had discretion to permanently bar an applicant from licensure or from any position requiring licensure. *Haynam v. Ohio State Board of Educ.*, No. L-11-1100, 2011 WL 6365144 (Ohio Ct. App. 12/16/11).

◆   After 30 years of law practice, a Kansas lawyer was convicted of stealing money and lying to an investigator during his disbarment procedure. His prison sentence was later erased from state criminal records, but his disbarment was not subject to erasure. After being released from prison, the lawyer took classes and tried to obtain state teaching licensure. But his application was denied by a state professional practices commission, which found his felony convictions and disbarment violated the public trust and confidence. The state board of education upheld the decision, as did a state trial court. On appeal, the Court of Appeals of Kansas cited the board's findings that the lawyer had engaged in repeated acts of dishonesty over an extended time period while in a position of public trust. His felonious conduct and resulting disbarment were still relevant. **It was within the board's discretion to rule on an applicant's efforts at rehabilitation as well as fitness to be a member of the teaching profession.** Five years of rehabilitation did not mean the applicant was fit to teach. Substantial evidence supported the board's findings, and the court affirmed the denial of his application for a state teaching license. *Wright v. Kansas State Board of Educ.*, 46 Kan.App.2d 1046, 268 P.3d 1231 (Kan. Ct. App. 2012).

◆   An Arizona court upheld a decision by the state Professional Practices Advisory Committee refusing to approve an applicant for certification to teach in the state. At a hearing of the committee, it was revealed that he was convicted of driving under the influence of alcohol three times in the 1970s and 1980s. In addition, **the applicant was convicted of disorderly conduct, unlawful possession of a firearm and phone harassment**. Although the committee noted the applicant's candor and sincerity in addressing his alcohol abuse, he raised concerns about his professional state of mind by making stereotyped statements about racial groups. A state court dismissed the applicant's appeal and refused to grant him additional time after granting him several extensions. On appeal, the state court of appeals agreed with the lower court that he did not comply with court rules and orders to file papers. *Houston v. State Board of Educ.*, No. 1 CA-CV 10-0634, 2011 WL 5926675 (Ariz. Ct. App. 11/22/11).

◆   In 2006, his fourth year as an elementary educator, a Florida teacher pushed a third-grader out of his classroom. In a criminal misdemeanor proceeding, the teacher pled guilty to battery of a minor. The school board voted to suspend him, but an administrative law judge found the conduct of pushing a child by the fingertips was not shown to be intentional or reasonably expected to cause harm. After the hearing, the commission adopted the ruling, finding the teacher did not violate the state code of ethics or principles of professional conduct.

After the commission issued its decision, the school board reinstated the teacher. In 2008, the Florida legislature amended Section 1012.795 of the state code by requiring the commission to revoke the educator certificate of any teacher convicted of misdemeanor battery on a minor. The commission filed a new proceeding to permanently revoke the teacher's educator certificate based on the prior incident. A second hearing was held, and the commission ordered the permanent revocation of the teacher's educator certificate. On appeal, the Florida District Court of Appeal found no legislative intent to apply Section 1012.795 retroactively. When the teacher pled guilty to battery, the law had yet to be amended. **The court found he had a vested property interest in his educator certification.** Since retroactive application of the law would impair the teacher's vested rights, the court reversed the commission's order. *Presmy v. Smith*, 69 So.3d 383 (Fla. Dist. Ct. App. 2011).

◆ A nonprofit center that contracted with the New York City Department of Education (DOE) hired an employee who admitted she had been convicted of first-degree robbery at age 17. After her parole, she earned a college degree, did volunteer work, and started a family. The DOE conducted a security clearance and allowed only five minutes for the employee to submit documentation and a statement explaining the events and circumstances of her conviction. After the DOE denied her application for continuing employment at the nonprofit center, she filed a lawsuit against the DOE which reached the New York Court of Appeals. It held state law generally makes it unlawful for employers to deny a license or employment application based on a criminal offense. An exception allows an employer to reject applicants where the licensure or the employment of a former offender would "involve an unreasonable risk to property or to the safety or welfare of specific individuals or the general public." **Employers are required to consider eight factors regarding the "unreasonable risk" exception.** State law required the DOE to consider any information she produced in determining whether to apply the "unreasonable risk" exception. As the DOE did not consider all of the employee's information, the court held in her favor. *Acosta v. New York City Dep't of Educ.*, 16 N.Y.3d 309 (N.Y. 2011).

◆ A California teacher was subject to suspension of her teaching credential after her third DUI conviction. While the third incident resulted in a 30-day jail sentence, the court allowed her to fulfill the time at home and at work in the classroom by wearing an ankle bracelet. She was placed on probation and ordered to participate in an alcohol education program. Two years later, the California Commission on Teacher Credentialing found cause to suspend the teacher's credential for 60 days. An administrative law judge (ALJ) held the commission did not prove unprofessional conduct and recommended dismissal of the charge. In doing so, the ALJ relied on a test for the discipline of teachers created by the state supreme court in *Morrison v. State Board of Educ.*

But the commission rejected the ALJ's decision, as did a state trial court. The Court of Appeal of California held it was appropriate to consider six of the seven *Morrison* factors, including the "adverse effect upon students and teachers" of the misconduct. **The court held any conduct used as a ground for the suspension of a professional license must demonstrate unfitness to practice that profession.** Statutory terms such as "immoral or unprofessional conduct" and "moral turpitude" are almost unlimited in scope. The court found the legislature did not grant the commission power to let employers dismiss employees on the basis of personal, private conduct that might be deemed objectionable. Students might observe the teacher's ankle bracelet, so it was likely her conviction had an adverse affect on them. As the lower court order was correct, it was affirmed. *Broney v. California Comm'n on Teacher Credentialing*, 184 Cal.App.4th 462, 108 Cal.Rptr.3d 832 (Cal. Ct. App. 2010).

◆   A Kentucky teacher injured her head in a bicycling accident and had post-concussive syndrome, memory and attention problems, sleep loss, depression, anxiety, irritability and outbursts of anger. She later confronted students playing basketball outside her school, and a parent filed a complaint against her, stating she had threatened to kill them. After an investigation, her contract was terminated for conduct unbecoming a teacher. A teacher tribunal affirmed the termination action, as did the state court system. The Kentucky Education Professional Standards Board (KEPSB) then revoked the teacher's teaching certificate for 10 years. Based on the basketball incident, the teacher was also convicted of terroristic threatening. A state court fined the teacher $4,500 and ordered her to refrain from abusive conduct with the victims. She appealed the decision to revoke her teaching license to a state court, which held terroristic threats were reason enough for revocation. On appeal, the state court of appeals affirmed the judgment. **State law permitted the revocation, suspension or refusal to renew or issue a teaching certificate for reasons including physical or mental incapacity** preventing a teacher from performing duties with "reasonable skill, competence or safety." The KEPSB and circuit court had found the teacher lacked the capacity to safely carry out her duties. *Macy v. Kentucky Educ. Professional Standards Board*, Nos. 2008-CA-002234-MR, 2008-CA-002293-MR, 2010 WL 743668 (Ky. Ct. App. 3/5/10).

◆   An Arkansas teacher pleaded no contest to a charge of misappropriation of about $36,000 from a county conservation district. She was ordered to repay the money and serve a 60-month probationary term. The Arkansas State Board of Education then denied the teacher's request to obtain licensure. Two years after the conviction, the court expunged (erased) the offense from her record. The teacher again sought certification, and the board again denied her request for a waiver that would allow her to obtain it. She petitioned a state court for review, but the court affirmed the decision. The state court of appeals found that under Section 6-17-410 of the Arkansas Code, an "individual's underlying conduct shall be deemed as a matter of law never to have occurred" when an offense is expunged. An individual may also state that no such conduct ever occurred.

   While the teacher claimed the statute prevented the board from considering the offense, the court disagreed. **A state licensure and renewal law prohibited licensure of a person who has a report in the Child Maltreatment Central Registry or has pled guilty (or no contest) to, or has been found guilty of offenses including felony theft.** It appeared to the court that the state General Assembly intended to make ineligible for licensure those whose records were expunged. There was no abuse in the board's decision to deny the teacher licensure or to deny a request for a waiver. *Landers v. Arkansas Dep't of Educ.*, 2010 Ark.App. 312 (Ark. Ct. App. 2010).

◆   A Florida teacher attempted suicide at her school. The state commissioner of education brought a complaint against her, and she asked for a hearing after sanctions were sought against her teacher's certificate. An administrative law judge (ALJ) found insufficient evidence to show others were present at the time of the suicide attempt. Although the school superintendent asked that the ALJ order the teacher to participate in a recovery network program for counseling, the request was rejected. Instead, the ALJ found the teacher guilty of misconduct and recommended a reprimand and two years of probation. A final order required her to enter counseling. A Florida district court of appeal agreed with the teacher that the reasons for modifying the ALJ's order were not stated. It returned the case to the education practices commission for review and to complete the record by stating the particular reasons for the modification and decide if the penalty was warranted. **Failure by the commission to state its reasons for modifying the ALJ order was a fundamental error and a due process violation.** *Withers v. Blomberg*, 41 So.3d 398 (Fla. Dist. Ct. App. 2010).

◆   A Texas teaching intern had a one-year probationary contract as part of a program that required a favorable principal evaluation and a continued offer of employment in order for her to obtain alternative certification. But the principal recommended that she repeat her internship and be assigned to another school district. It was recommended that certification be denied and that the intern repeat her internship. After filing unsuccessful grievances, she appealed to the state commissioner of education. The commissioner ruled that he lacked the authority to review the grievances, and the intern appealed. On appeal, the state court of appeals noted state law limited the commissioner's authority to review school board decisions to actions that violated the school laws of the state or contractual provisions. The court rejected the claim that the principal's failure to recommend certification violated the school rules of Texas. It held the law did not impose a duty on the school board, principal or course provider. Nor did it confer any rights or privileges on the intern. There was no merit to the intern's breach of contract claim. **Her employment was conditioned on satisfactory participation in the certification program.** The court held the commissioner had properly dismissed the case. *McCandless v. Pasadena Independent School Dist.*, No. 03-09-00249-CV, 2010 WL 1253581 (Tex. Ct. App. 4/2/10).

◆   A California school board classified teachers and counselors holding less than a regular teaching credential as "temporary employees." It voted to lay off 225 employees classified as probationary or temporary for budget reasons, and most of them pursued their hearing rights. An administrative law judge upheld the layoffs, and the teachers association sued the district. Appeal reached the state court of appeal, which held **employees who were qualified to teach were not "temporary employees" simply because they were not yet fully accredited**. It rejected the district's claim to discretion to classify employees as "temporary," based on their certification status. The district had to classify as "probationary employees" any teachers who were employed in positions requiring certification qualifications, unless they were classified as permanent employees or substitutes. **Teachers holding emergency permits and satisfying other conditions of state law could be classified as probationary employees.** Probationary employees with emergency or specialist permits accrued no credit toward permanent status, and state law required interns who were reemployed in a succeeding school year to be classified as "permanent." *Bakersfield Elementary Teachers Ass'n v. Bakersfield City School Dist.*, 145 Cal.App.4th 1260, 52 Cal.Rptr.3d 486 (Cal. Ct. App. 2006).

◆   The Court of Appeal of California held **state law deems a probationary teacher reelected for the next school year, if she is employed for two consecutive years** in a position requiring certification qualifications and is not given a contrary notice by March 15. It held a teacher could not be denied probationary employee status by virtue of internship work, as this required certification. The court rejected a school district's assertion that work under a university intern credential did not count toward the two-year tenure requirement. It held a district had to reinstate a teacher who had worked under an internship credential. She had finished her second complete consecutive school year of employment in a position requiring certification qualifications at the time she received a late notice of non-reelection. *Peoples v. San Diego Unified School Dist.*, 41 Cal.Rptr.3d 383 (Cal. Ct. App. 2006).

◆   A Delaware school district employed a media specialist who had originally worked as a librarian. Over time, her duties came to include teaching reading and language skills to students. Eight evaluations of the specialist's classroom performance found her instructional planning and strategies unsatisfactory. District officials held post-evaluation conferences but notified her she would be discharged for incompetence and neglect of duty. After a hearing, the board discharged the specialist. She appealed to a state superior court, which found it was proper to evaluate her using a Lesson Analysis Form based on the Delaware Performance Appraisal Standards for teachers. The evaluations were properly conducted during appraisal periods. She declined opportunities to change her improvement plan and remained uncooperative while superficially complying with her plan. On appeal, the Supreme Court of Delaware affirmed the decision. It found **library functions had changed from an emphasis on cataloging to providing complementary teaching of reading and language skills**. The district required its librarians to teach, and it was reasonable to evaluate the specialist in instructional situations. *Squire v. Board of Educ. of Red Clay Consolidated School Dist.*, 911 A.2d 804 (Table) (Del. 2006).

◆   The Iowa Board of Educational Examiners held a hearing to consider charges that a teacher told her daughter to blow into an interlock ignition device so she could drive her car while intoxicated. She admitted asking the girl to blow into the device. She admitted using marijuana, but not in her daughter's presence. The board suspended her certification for not less than three years, and a state court affirmed the judgment. On appeal, the Court of Appeals of Iowa held **the board only needed proof of a founded child abuse report to suspend or revoke a teaching certificate**. The board did not have to determine if a teacher actually committed the acts substantiating a founded report. The court rejected her assertion that the abuse complaint was unrelated to her fitness to teach because it only involved her own child. The report against the teacher involved illegal activities that threatened the health and safety of a child and set an extremely poor example. As any founded child abuse report against a teacher had some relevance to licensure, the court affirmed the judgment. *Halter v. Iowa Board of Educ. Examiners*, 698 N.W.2d 337 (Table) (Iowa Ct. App. 2005).

◆ **The non-renewal of a tenured Oklahoma teacher's contract because of her failure to earn certain continuing education credits was not a deprivation of her due process and equal protection rights.** The teacher persistently refused to comply with her district's continuing education requirements. After several years, the Oklahoma Legislature mandated certain salary increases for teachers regardless of compliance with the requirements. The district then threatened the teacher with dismissal unless she fulfilled them. The teacher failed to do so, and the district fired her. The Supreme Court held for the school board, noting it made every effort to give the teacher a chance to meet the requirements. There was no deprivation of equal protection since all teachers were obligated to obtain the credits, and the sanction of contract non-renewal was rationally related to the district's objective of enforcing the continuing education obligation of its teachers. *Harrah Independent School Dist. v. Martin*, 440 U.S. 194, 99 S.Ct. 1062, 59 L.Ed.2d 248 (1979).

B. Testing and Reform Legislation

The No Child Left Behind Act required all teachers of "core academic subjects" to be "highly qualified" by the end of the 2005-2006 school year. A "highly qualified" teacher holds a bachelor's degree, is fully licensed by the state, and demonstrates knowledge in the subject area taught. The "full state certification" requirement does not include emergency, temporary or provisional licenses. The states are responsible for devising rigorous tests for current teachers in their academic subject areas, and subject knowledge and teaching skills for basic curriculum areas for new elementary teachers.

A No Child Left Behind (NCLB) Act provision formerly permitted alternative-route teachers to meet the "highly qualified teacher" designation only through "full state certification." Congress later expanded the definition of "highly qualified teacher" to include alternative-route teachers who demonstrated satisfactory progress toward full state certification. A federal regulation, 34 C.F.R. Part 200.56(a)(1)(i), encompasses this interpretation and was upheld in Renee v. Duncan, *623 F.3d 787 (9th Cir. 2010). A summary of the case appears in Chapter Five, Section III.A.*

◆ Two Washington special education teachers refused to give mandated tests to severely disabled students. One skipped a training session for the Washington Alternative Assessment of Student (WAAS) portfolio. The other teacher wrote to a state agency, stating that the test was "inauthentic" and a "ridiculous" requirement for her students. In a meeting with the teachers prior to the WAAS testing, the principal directed them to either attend the WAAS training or face insubordination charges. Despite this warning, the teachers missed a key WAAS deadline. Later, both were suspended without pay for 10 days. No parent objected to the WAAS before the testing. After a hearing, a hearing officer found sufficient cause to suspend the teachers. A state superior court affirmed the decision, and the teachers appealed to the Court of Appeals of Washington. It found that during the relevant time frame, the teachers had only justified their action by criticizing the WAAS regime. They did not assert they were motived by parental objections until they were faced with the possibility of discipline.

The teachers were told several times to administer the WAAS and were informed that failure to do so would be considered insubordination. State case law held that **"a teacher is insubordinate if she willfully refuses to obey a reasonable regulation governing her conduct."** Since the teachers had refused to give the test after being directed to do so, the court found sufficient cause for the unpaid 10-day suspensions, and it affirmed the judgment. *Griffith v. Seattle School Dist. No. 1*, 266 P.3d 932 (Wash. Ct. App. 2011).

◆   An Ohio teacher gave her students a worksheet with problems similar or identical to those on a current Ohio Achievement Test (OAT). She reviewed the math portion of the OAT while students worked on the reading portion, changed the directions on a practice worksheet and distributed copies to other teachers. When doing so, the teacher said "don't let the students take this home," and "destroy this when you are done." Similarities in the worksheet and the actual test problems were then noticed. The Ohio State Board of Education notified the teacher of its intent to suspend her teaching certificates for violating a state statute and regulations regarding test security. A hearing officer recommended suspending her teaching certificates for one year. The case reached the Court of Appeals of Ohio, which noted that **state law forbade revealing to any student specific questions known to be part of a statutory student achievement test**.

The statute prohibited persons from helping a student to cheat in "any way." According to the teacher, sixth-grade math concepts could only be tested in a limited number of ways. Materials created by teachers to teach standardized concepts were necessarily similar to the standardized test. The teacher also said the practice worksheet questions were not taken verbatim from the OAT. The court rejected her argument that the statute only prohibited verbatim disclosure of OAT questions and affirmed the decision to suspend her teaching certification for a year. *Luscre-Miles v. Dep't of Educ.*, No. 2008P-0048, 2008 WL 5330522 (Ohio Ct. App. 12/19/08).

◆   The Educational Testing Service (ETS) administers the Praxis Series School Leaders Licensure Assessment Test. Test takers acknowledge in writing all ETS testing policies. An ETS bulletin addresses the consequences of violating testing rules and procedures. The document states that ETS "reserves the right to cancel any test score when, in ETS's judgment, a testing irregularity occurs." Scores could be invalidated for misconduct, which included working on a test after time had been called. A principal intern paid ETS $465 to take the test, and she agreed to the testing conditions. When she took the test, a proctor noted that she twice failed to stop writing when the allotted time had passed and she was told to stop writing. The proctor submitted an "irregularity report" to ETS, which cancelled the intern's Praxis scores. She sued ETS for "malicious defamation" and breach of contract. The court held for ETS, finding the contract reserved to ETS the right to make judgment calls. There was no evidence of defamation or negligence. On further appeal, the Court of Appeals of Maryland agreed that **under the terms of the contract, ETS had the right to rely on the proctor's report and to cancel test scores**. *Educ. Testing Service v. Hildebrant*, 399 Md. 128, 923 A.2d 34 (Md. 2007).

◆ **A Florida district court of appeal upheld an administrative ruling rejecting charges that a teacher provided inappropriate assistance to her students during the Florida Comprehensive Assessment Test.** The state education practice commission filed a complaint against the teacher for providing answers and other help to her students on the test. But after a hearing, an administrative law judge found all of the commission's student witnesses not credible. The judge accepted the testimony of the lone student who testified for the teacher. The commission held another hearing and issued a final order suspending the teacher's certification. The state court of appeal then held that the commission had improperly modified the judge's findings, and it dismissed the complaint. *Stinson v. Winn*, 938 So.2d 554 (Fla. Dist. Ct. App. 2006).

C. Residency, Anti-Nepotism and Patronage Policies

In Ambach v. Norwick, *441 U.S. 68, 99 S.Ct. 1589, 60 L.Ed.2d 49 (1979), the U.S. Supreme Court held teaching in the public schools is a state function so bound up with the operation of the state as a governmental entity as to permit exclusion from that function of those who have not become part of the process of self-government.*

The Ambach *case involved a Connecticut law that required public school teachers in the state to be U.S. citizens. Two teachers challenged the law in the federal court system. The Court found the Constitution required only that the citizenship requirement bear a rational relationship to a legitimate state interest. In the Court's view, a rational relationship existed between the educational goals of the state and its desire that citizenship be a qualification to teach in the state.*

◆ A certified Massachusetts school business administrator claimed he was passed over for several jobs in favor of applicants who lacked certification. He claimed the commissioner of the department of education granted hardship waivers to numerous uncertified applicants without scrutinizing them. According to his state court complaint, hardship waivers were automatically granted electronically. A trial court found the commonwealth and department of education had immunity, and the claims were barred under the Massachusetts Tort Claims Act. On appeal, the state court of appeals found the Education Reform Act of 1993 allowed a school district to hire only certified school business administrators. Waivers of certification were permitted if a district established that compliance would be a great hardship.

The court held the practice was not an exercise of discretion, because the commissioner divested himself of discretion and "no discretion was involved." According to the complaint, the waiver practice was automatic and violated the act. Discretion for granting waivers should entail "weighing alternatives and making choices with respect to public policy." The administrator claimed due process and equal protection violations, noting that in some cases, friends of appointing authorities were rewarded. The trial court did not rule on the constitutional claims but if true, such actions would be an abuse. The court returned the case to the trial court for further activity. *Nordberg v. Massachusetts Dep't of Educ.*, 76 Mass.App.Ct. 216 (Mass. App. Ct. 2010).

◆   An investigation of a Kentucky school superintendent revealed he resided in Ohio in violation of KRS Section 160.350(2). The school board, district and superintendent sued commonwealth officials for a declaration that the law violated equal protection principles and restricted a fundamental right to travel. After a Kentucky circuit court ruled for the commonwealth, the case came before the state court of appeals. It held that KRS Section 160.350(2) **imposed a permissible residency requirement**. There was no requirement that superintendents reside in Kentucky for a certain number of years. Kentucky residence became a condition of employment that could occur even after hiring, undercutting the claim that the law improperly restrained rights to travel. There was a rational basis for requiring superintendents to live in the commonwealth, and no equal protection violation. *Newport Independent School Dist./Newport Board of Educ. v. Comwlth. of Kentucky*, 300 S.W.2d 216 (Ky. Ct. App. 2009).

◆   A Texas teacher claimed she was denied a promotion because her children attended private schools. The district superintendent stated that the school district required the children of all school administrators to attend public schools. In the teacher's federal action, a court awarded qualified immunity to the superintendent, but the Fifth Circuit reversed. Meanwhile, the teacher was promoted twice and became a high school principal. The case returned to the district court, which found that the delayed promotions deprived her of future salary increases, since she would have earned a higher salary in future years had her administrative career begun earlier. Here, the superintendent had enforced an illegal patronage policy. However, the teacher failed to prove her claims against the district. The case returned to the Fifth Circuit, which held that **school districts have no vicarious liability for federal civil rights violations under 42 U.S.C. § 1983. They are liable only for unconstitutional conduct by policymakers,** and the superintendent was not a policymaker. *Barrow v. Greenville Independent School Dist.*, 480 F.3d 377 (5th Cir. 2007).

    The court then awarded the teacher over $654,000 in attorneys' fees and costs. The superintendent appealed to the Fifth Circuit for the third time. The court rejected his claim that the lower court had applied an improper standard in analyzing his actions. Public school employees have a protected right to place their children in private schools. The court refused to reduce the damage award and upheld the award of attorneys' fees. *Barrow v. Greenville Independent School Dist.*, No. 06-10123, 2007 WL 3085028 (5th Cir. 10/23/07).

◆   A New Jersey school board's anti-nepotism policy applied to the immediate families of school board members, school administrators and board employees. However, the policy stated that it "shall have no effect on tenured employees." The board notified an untenured teacher that her one-year teaching contract would not be renewed after she married a tenured teacher in the district. Both teachers sued the board under the state Law Against Discrimination (LAD). They added federal due process and equal protection claims. The board presented evidence that the policy had the legitimate purpose of eliminating conflicts of interest that could arise when employees were married to each other. A state court agreed with the board, and the teachers appealed. A New Jersey appellate court held **the untenured teacher's contract was not**

renewed because of her relationship to a tenured teacher, not on the basis of her marital status. The LAD was not designed to prohibit bias based on specific family relationships, even though the relationship itself existed by reason of a marriage. The teacher's due process claim failed. She was not tenured and had no right to continued employment beyond her current contract. There was a rational basis for the policy, and it was reasonably related to avoiding conflicts of interest, discord and favoritism. *Wowkun v. Closter Board of Educ.*, No. C-103-05, 2006 WL 1933475 (N.J. Super. Ct. App. Div. 2006).

III. VOLUNTARY EMPLOYEE LEAVE

A. Family and Maternity Leave

The Family and Medical Leave Act (FMLA), 29 U.S.C. §§ 2601–2654, grants eligible employees 12 weeks of leave in a one-year period for specific disabling health problems of employees and their families, including a family member's serious illness or a childbirth. A primary FMLA protection requires employers to restore employees who return from FMLA leave to the same job, or a comparable one with equivalent pay, benefits and working conditions, unless they are unable to perform an essential function of the position. The FMLA authorizes monetary damage awards against violating employers.

Employees must provide employers with enough information to place them on notice that FMLA-qualifying leave is needed. In Curcio v. Collingswood Board of Educ., *No. Civ.A. 04-5100 (JBS), 2006 WL 1806455 (D.N.J. 2006), the court held federal regulations create a lenient standard for what constitutes FMLA notice. Employees do not have to mention the FMLA to have protection.*

Employers must issue employees (1) a generalized notice of their FMLA rights posted in the employer's premises; and (2) a customized notice of FMLA rights and procedures for employees who indicate a need to take FMLA leave.

In Hunter v. Valley View Local Schools, *the U.S. Court of Appeals, Sixth Circuit, examined an FMLA regulation at 29 C.F.R. Part 825.220 which forbids employers from using the taking of FMLA leave as a negative factor in actions like hiring, promotion or discipline.* **FMLA leave cannot be counted under "no fault" attendance policies. Federal regulations note "the common understanding" that teachers often work outside their classes or at home.**

In Donnelly v. Greenburgh Cent. School Dist. No. 7, *below, the U.S. Court of Appeals, Second Circuit, held that federal law places the burden on employers to maintain accurate records of hours worked by their employees.*

◆ A New York teacher became ill and underwent gallbladder surgery, and he missed 17 school days in a year. After he returned from leave, his principal assigned him a "needs improvement" rating for professional responsibility, in part due to excessive absences. Based on the principal's recommendation, the district denied the teacher tenure, and he resigned. The applicable collective bargaining agreement (CBA) stated that the regular working day for all district teachers was not to exceed 7.25 hours. As calculated under the CBA, the most the teacher could have worked in the school year before tenure was denied was

1,247 hours. Since an employee must work at least 1,250 hours during the prior 12-month period to be FMLA-eligible, the teacher was three hours short of qualifying for coverage, if the calculation was based solely on the CBA.

Relying exclusively on the CBA, a federal court found the teacher ineligible for FMLA leave. On appeal, the U.S. Court of Appeals, Second Circuit, held that **employers who do not maintain accurate records of the hours worked by their employees have the burden of showing an employee has not worked the hours needed for FMLA coverage**. It was improper for the lower court to restrict the computation of hours for FMLA eligibility solely by reference to the CBA. A jury was entitled to decide whether the teacher had worked at least three hours beyond the CBA maximum. In assessing FMLA eligibility, a court should count hours devoted to activity that was "an integral and indispensable part" of the job's principal activity. This includes preparing lessons, helping students, and grading work. The court held the proximity in time between the teacher's poor job performance evaluations and his medical leave raised an inference of retaliation. A jury could consider whether he had been denied tenure in retaliation for his FMLA-protected activity. *Donnelly v. Greenburgh Cent. School Dist. No. 7*, 691 F.3d 134 (2d Cir. 2012).

◆   A Pennsylvania teacher began maternity leave in October of a school year. Her school district placed her on sick leave that was also designated as unpaid child-rearing leave. When the teacher returned to work the next fall, the district denied her a salary-step increase, asserting that as she was not present in her classroom, she was not "in service for at least one marking period" under the collective bargaining agreement. An arbitrator held the agreement incorporated FMLA terms and required employees to take FMLA leave for child bearing. In ruling for the teacher, the arbitrator held the last five days of the first marking period, during which she used her accrued paid sick leave, were "in service." This leave could be concurrent with sick leave. On appeal, the Commonwealth Court of Pennsylvania held that employees who received paid sick leave were engaged in the performance of their duty for a period of 10 days under state law. The court rejected the school district's assertion that the teacher could not concurrently be on FMLA leave and sick leave. It held **the FMLA protected jobs and assured equality to employees on equivalent leave status**. Nothing in the FMLA authorizes an employer to consider an employee on FMLA leave to be in a "no pay status" when paid sick leave is being used. As the arbitrator had correctly found the teacher was on paid sick leave during the last five days of the first marking period, the court upheld the award. *Tredyffrin/Easttown School Dist. v. Tredyffrin/Easttown Educ.*, 56 A.3d 17 (Pa. Commw. Ct. 2012).

◆   An Ohio custodian missed significant time from work after an auto injury in 2003. Over the next three years, she took intermittent periods of FMLA leave and underwent three rounds of surgery. When the custodian returned to work, her doctor imposed permanent work restrictions on her. The school district placed her on involuntary unpaid medical leave. The district superintendent stated the leave was based on the doctor's restrictions and "excessive absenteeism." The custodian sued. Following another period of involuntary leave, she returned to work. The court held for the district, finding that regardless of any FMLA violation, the custodian would have been placed on involuntary leave due to her work restrictions. On appeal, the U.S. Court of Appeals, Sixth Circuit, noted that **employers cannot discriminate or retaliate against an employee for taking FMLA leave**. The court found that the school district had used the custodian's leave as a negative factor in its decision. This violated the FMLA. Testimony by the superintendent admitting that involuntary leave had been imposed due to her excessive absenteeism was direct evidence of a retaliatory motive. The court remanded the case for a determination of whether the district would have inevitably laid off the custodian. *Hunter v. Valley View Local Schools*, 579 F.3d 688 (6th Cir. 2009).

◆ A part-time Massachusetts school employee worked as a school monitor for several years. Her husband became ill, and she requested FMLA leave to help him. According to the employee, the deputy superintendent said she did not have to "worry about rushing to return." But soon after the death of her husband, her job was terminated, for the stated reason that monitors were no longer needed. Although the employee had not worked enough hours in the prior 12 months to be covered under the FMLA, she sued, asserting that she could pursue FMLA claims based on the deputy superintendent's assurances. A federal district court held for the school district, and the employee appealed.

On appeal, the First Circuit explained that **to be eligible under the FMLA, an employee must have worked at least 1,250 hours in a 12-month period before taking leave**. The employee here had worked only 554 hours in the previous 12 months. While she claimed she received assurances by the deputy superintendent that she could take leave, she never sought written confirmation. Even if the employee was unaware that she was ineligible for FMLA leave, she "let matters lie," without insisting on written confirmation. The court noted that as of January 16, 2009, employers must provide employees with written rulings on their FMLA requests. See 29 C.F.R. Part 825.300(d). But the amended FMLA regulation did not apply to this case, since the events occurred in 2004-05. *Nagle v. Acton-Boxborough Regional School Dist.*, 576 F.3d 1 (1st Cir. 2009).

◆ An Arkansas employer exceeded FMLA minimum requirements by allowing employees to take 30 weeks of unpaid leave. It denied an employee's request for additional time off for treatment of Hodgkin's disease. The employer never notified the employee that 12 of her 30 weeks of leave were considered "FMLA leave." The employer discharged her when she did not return to work after she exhausted 30 weeks of leave. The employee sued, alleging violations of a U.S. Department of Labor regulation that does not count leave taken against an employee's FMLA entitlement if the employer does not designate it as "FMLA leave." Appeal reached the U.S. Supreme Court, which held that the regulation imposed a penalty on employers that was contrary to the law's remedial design, without regard to harm the employee might suffer from lack of notice. **A "categorical penalty" was incompatible with the FMLA and invalid because it fundamentally altered the law.** The court struck down the regulation and affirmed a judgment for the employer. *Ragsdale v. Wolverine World Wide Inc.*, 535 U.S. 81, 122 S.Ct. 1155, 152 L.Ed.2d 167 (2002).

The Pregnancy Discrimination Act, 42 U.S.C. § 2000e(k), prohibits employers from discriminating against employees on the basis of pregnancy and requires them to treat pregnancy the same as any other disabling illness for all employment-related purposes, including health benefits.

◆ A Pennsylvania teacher asked her school district for an 11-month maternity leave. Six months after delivering her child, she asked to return to work early due to financial obligations. The district denied the request, stating it had hired a long-term substitute. The teacher filed a grievance. In deciding it, the district applied a child-rearing leave provision of the parties' collective bargaining agreement (CBA), rather than a childbearing provision. Under the childbearing provision, a return to work was permitted in emergencies. There was no similar language in the childrearing provision. An arbitrator found leave was taken under the CBA childbearing provision and that there was a financial emergency. He held the district should have allowed the teacher to return to work early. Appeal reached the Commonwealth Court of Pennsylvania, which rejected a district claim that the CBA's separate sections were discriminatory. The district had negotiated the terms of the CBA and could not argue the arbitration award violated a public policy against sex discrimination. The childbearing leave provision had been in all the CBAs of the parties since 1977. **Male teachers could take child-rearing leave under the CBA.** "Emergency" included a financial emergency, and the court held for the teacher. *West Allegheny School Dist. v. West Allegheny Educ. Ass'n*, 997 A.2d 411 (Pa. Commw. Ct. 2010).

◆ The U.S. Supreme Court held **a school board rule requiring maternity leaves at mandatory and fixed time periods violated the Due Process Clause**. Two cases were involved in this appeal to the Supreme Court. In both cases school district rules required mandatory leaves at a fixed time early in pregnancy. The Court said that the rules were unconstitutional. The test in this case and other similar cases is that the maternity policy, in order to be valid, must bear a rational relationship to legitimate school interests. If there is a relationship, the rules pass constitutional examination; if not, they are unconstitutional and cannot be enforced. *Cleveland Board of Educ. v. LaFleur,* 414 U.S. 632, 94 S.Ct. 791, 39 L.Ed.2d 52 (1974).

B. Compensatory, Vacation and Sick Leave

◆ New Jersey legislators passed a series of reform laws to reduce property taxes and address excessive benefits for high-level school administrators. State regulations were issued to implement the laws, including a regulation limiting payments for accumulated unused sick leave to $15,000. The state association of school administrators filed a challenge to the new regime. The case appeared before a state administrative tribunal, and appeal reached the Supreme Court of New Jersey. It noted the regulations applied only to new contracts and did not affect existing agreements or alter the terms of employment retroactively.

Contrary to the administrators' argument, the law did not deprive any official of property, and the prospective sick leave cap was a valid exercise of legislative authority. The court rejected a challenge to another provision of the sick leave regulation barring the payment of unused sick leave to an estate or beneficiary if an employee died before retirement. **Such a restriction was not arbitrary or capricious and was intended to bring supplemental compensation for school administrators in line with that of other state employees and current law.** A law governing supplemental compensation did not supersede or repeal an existing cap on sick leave payments, and a challenge based on an alleged violation of state tenure statutes also failed. As the new regime represented a legislative policy judgment, and the new regulations tracked the statutes faithfully, the court upheld them. *New Jersey Ass'n of School Administrators v. Schundler*, 221 N.J. 535, 49 A.3d 860 (N.J. 2012).

◆ A Maine principal worked for a district for 17 years. His final employment contract stated that upon retirement from the school system, he would be paid for up to 30 days of accumulated vacation time. At the end of the school year, the principal retired, and the district paid him for 30 days of unused vacation time. He filed a state court action against the school department, asserting he had "accumulated" 178 days of vacation time and claiming 148 more days of unused vacation time under 26 M.R.S. Section 626. A state court held for the school department, and the principal appealed. The Supreme Court of Maine held that while Section 626 created a statutory right for former employees to claim unpaid wages, the "entitlement to payment is governed solely by the terms of the employment agreement." Section 626 did not modify or supercede the terms of an employment agreement. The principal claimed his contract allowed him to accrue unlimited amounts of vacation time because of the use of the word "accumulated" in the relevant provision. Under that theory, he was entitled to be paid for all 178 days of vacation he had accumulated. Instead, the court found **the plain language of the contract limited the principal to 30 days of vacation pay upon retirement**. Since the lower court did not commit error in finding he was not entitled to further payments, the court affirmed the judgment. *Richardson v. Winthrop School Dep't*, 983 A.2d 400 (Me. 2009).

◆ A Louisiana teacher was unintentionally hit and knocked unconscious by students who rushed out of a class to fight each other in a hallway. After being on paid leave for a year, the teacher sued the board for refusing to pay him sick leave benefits for longer than one year under the "assault" provision of La. R.S. Section 17:1201(C), which would entitle him to leave without a reduction in pay for the duration of his disability. The case reached the Court of Appeal of Louisiana. It noted the "assault pay" provision of Section 17:1201(C) permits a teacher to remain on sick leave without a pay reduction and with no reduction in sick leave days while disabled by an assault or battery. **The section has a "physical contact" provision that permits teachers to receive unreduced sick leave for up to one calendar year, if they are injured while helping to prevent a student injury.** The court held the "assault pay" provision applied whenever a teacher was the victim of a battery by a student. The provision was not limited to situations when a teacher was the intended victim of an assault. The board had to pay for his leave during the duration of his disability. *Stoshak v. East Baton Rouge School Board*, 959 So.2d 996 (La. Ct. App. 2007).

◆   A Washington education employees' union required field representatives to use sick leave and vacation time in partial-day increments. After the union deducted leave from one representative's employee leave bank 79 times, he sued it under the state Minimum Wage Act (MWA) and the FLSA for failure to pay him overtime. A federal court held the representative was exempt from the MWA and FLSA as an administrative employee. He appealed to the Ninth Circuit, which affirmed the decision concerning the FLSA claim but asked the Washington Supreme Court to answer certain state law questions. The state court held the MWA exempted executive, administrative and professional employees from its overtime pay requirements by allowing the payment of fixed salaries. To qualify as an exempt employee, an employee must meet both a "duties test" and a "salary basis test." Employees must show their pay is "subject to improper deductions" to prove they are not paid on a salary basis. An employer's single improper salary deduction did not prevent a finding that an employee was paid on a salary basis. **The partial-day deductions from accrued leave banks did not create an automatic violation of the MWA**, but could be considered by a lower court in determining whether the representative was exempt from its requirements as an administrative employee. *Webster v. Public School Employees of Washington Inc.*, 60 P.3d 1183 (Wash. 2003).

◆   Texas county deputy sheriffs agreed individually to accept compensatory time off in lieu of cash compensation for overtime. The county implemented a budgetary protection policy under which supervisors set a maximum number of hours that could be accumulated. Employees were advised of the maximum and asked to take voluntary steps to reduce compensatory time accumulations. Supervisors could require employees to take their compensatory time at scheduled times. The deputies sued, alleging that the compelled use of compensatory time violated the Fair Labor Standards Act (FLSA). The U.S. Supreme Court noted that the FLSA guaranteed that an employee could make some use of compensatory time upon request. However, **the FLSA did not expressly or impliedly limit a public employer from scheduling employees to take time off work with full pay**. As the FLSA was silent on employer-compelled compensatory time use, the Court held for the county. *Christensen v. Harris County*, 529 U.S. 576, 120 S.Ct. 1655, 146 L.Ed.2d 621 (2000).

IV. REASSIGNMENTS, TRANSFERS AND SUSPENSIONS

Subject to state laws and the terms of any applicable collective bargaining agreement, courts have evaluated reassignment, transfer and suspension cases on the basis of whether the action violates the law or contract, or is arbitrary and capricious or an abuse of discretion.

◆   An Arizona school board temporarily suspended a teacher without pay for an unspecified matter, and he sued in a state court to contest the discipline. The court affirmed the discipline, and appeal went before the Court of Appeals of Arizona. On appeal, the court declared that in civil cases such as this one, the right to appeal is not absolute but exists only by statute. According to the teacher, Section 12-2101(A)(1) of Arizona Statutes gave him a right to appeal. But a review of the statute led the court to rule that Section 12-2101(A)(1) did not apply to the appeal of a decision by a school district governing board. It did not matter to the court that the school district and prior decisions by state courts had assumed that Section 12-2101 created appellate jurisdiction. **Although teachers had a right to seek review of a district governing board's disciplinary decision to a superior court, the law did not provide for further appeal.** The court found the modern statute restored the law to a mid-20th-century version of the law, under which no appeal rights were expressly available. Since the law did not confer jurisdiction on the appeals court to review the decision, the court affirmed the judgment. *Anderson v. Valley Union High School Dist. #22*, 229 Ariz. 52, 270 P.3d 879 (Ariz. Ct. App. 2012).

◆   A Tennessee teacher was head coach of a high school girls' basketball team for 17 years. Parents and players complained about his use of profanity, sexually suggestive remarks and racial slurs. The school principal and director of schools removed the teacher from his coaching duties, but he retained tenure as a teacher. The teacher's union filed a grievance on his behalf. An arbitrator found that the coaching assignment had to comply with the applicable collective bargaining agreement, as the position was a "professional advantage." Thus, the arbitrator held the teacher had to be paid for his coaching supplement for the 2001-02 school year. Rather than pursuing another grievance, the teacher sued the board of education in the state court system.

The case reached the Supreme Court of Tennessee, which noted the state's Educational Improvement Act (EIA) implemented a corporate model under which school directors had authority to assign, suspend, dismiss or transfer teachers. **Directors retained the power to transfer a teacher's coaching responsibilities without regard to collective bargaining agreements.** The term "teacher" did not extend to contracts for coaching duties, as there was no state certification of coaches. State law protections covered a person's status as a "professional employee," but not non-licensed positions. As a result, the teacher's coaching position was unprotected by the collective bargaining agreement, and the school board prevailed on that question. *Lawrence County Educ. Ass'n v. Lawrence County Board of Educ.*, 244 S.W.3d 302 (Tenn. 2007).

◆   A Pennsylvania school administrative assistant complained to the school board president of a pattern of inappropriate sexual behavior by the district superintendent. The superintendent was suspended with pay, and an attorney was hired to investigate the complaint. The attorney interviewed witnesses and then held an informal hearing. Based on his recommendation, the board suspended the superintendent without pay or benefits. He sued the district for reinstatement. His case reached the state supreme court, which held that **the Pennsylvania School Code's removal provision did not divest school boards of their implied authority to suspend superintendents accused of serious misconduct**. Action could be taken against superintendents without pay and benefits, within the constraints of procedural due process. *Burger v. Board of School Directors of McGuffey School Dist.*, 839 A.2d 1055 (Pa. 2003).

◆   A Rhode Island teacher was placed on paid administrative leave near the end of a school year, pending an investigation into a sexual harassment charge. Over three months later, the district superintendent issued him a reprimand letter stating the language he used had been unprofessional and in violation of the department's harassment policy. The teacher was allowed to resume his teaching duties upon completing a course. His union requested a grievance to have the reprimand letter removed from district records. Because of various delays, the teacher then petitioned a state court, asserting that he should have received a pre-suspension hearing prior to being placed on paid administrative leave. The case reached the Rhode Island Supreme Court, which held that **the teacher was not entitled to a hearing as a "suspended" employee because he continued to be paid while on administrative leave and thus was never suspended.** *Martone v. Johnston School Committee*, 824 A.2d 426 (R.I. 2003).

V.   REPORTING ABUSE AND NEGLECT

*State child protection laws require teachers and other mandatory reporters to report suspected child abuse or neglect, and afford immunity for good-faith reports. New York recently amended its child abuse reporting law to clarify that mandated reporters who work for a school must report suspected child abuse or maltreatment **themselves**. Schools are not to designate an agent to make reports on behalf of a mandated reporter and are prohibited from putting any conditions upon child abuse or maltreatment reports by mandated reporters. New York's highest court has suggested that teachers and other state-mandated reporters of child abuse and neglect "ought to err on the side of caution and make a report" if they reasonably suspect child abuse or neglect.*

◆   A California school security guard said she saw a student and teacher leave campus together in his truck. She also observed the teacher running his fingers through the student's hair. Although three staff members said they had reported concerns about the two to the school principal, she denied receiving the reports. None of the school witnesses stated that they reported their suspicions to the police or child protective services. In a state court, the student sued the school district and several employees, including the teacher. After a trial, a jury found the district had reasonable suspicion of child abuse but failed to report it. As a result, the court awarded the student damages of $650,000.

On appeal, the Court of Appeal of California explained that the mandatory reporting requirements of state Penal Code Section 11166 required teachers, school administrators, security staff and others to report their knowledge or observations of suspected child abuse or neglect to authorities. **Failure by a mandated reporter to comply with Section 11166 was a misdemeanor, and no supervisor could impede or inhibit reporting.** The court held the jury was properly instructed that the district was liable for harm caused by the wrongful conduct of employees who were acting within the scope of their employment. In addition, the district could be held liable for employee misconduct under the doctrine of *respondeat superior*. **All mandated reporters were required to make a report of reasonably suspected child abuse or neglect based on an**

objective standard. If the standard was met, a mandated reporter was required to report reasonably suspected child abuse or neglect to the police or to child protective services authorities. *Wieder v. San Diego Unified School Dist.*, No. D056376, 2011 WL 6372878 (Cal. Ct. App. 12/20/11).

◆ A California teacher formed close relationships with four third-graders and developed a "husband-wife" relationship with the grandmother of one of them. He cultivated relationships with other third-graders and their single mothers. The teacher molested the boys until one of them finally told a neighbor. After the teacher's arrest, he pled guilty to criminal sexual abuse. In a state court case, the families asserted negligence by the district and failure to comply with mandatory reporting duties. After a trial, jurors voted against the families.

On appeal, the Court of Appeal of California found that the principal did not investigate possible abuse because the grandmother had consented to the teacher's relationship with the boys. The families claimed a teacher who was not named in the complaint knew of extensive off-campus contact between the teacher and his victims. But the court found it was speculative that investigation of this information would have led to an earlier discovery of the abuse. As a result, it upheld the rejection of a proposed instruction to consider the conduct of employees not named in the complaint. **The court found no merit to the families' claim that district training of staff on pedophile behavior would have led staff to promptly recognize the teacher's "grooming" behavior** prior to his abuse. As a result, the judgment for the school district was affirmed. *A.J. v. Victor Elementary School Dist.*, No. E049404, 2011 WL 1005009 (Cal. Ct. App. 3/22/11).

◆ A New York student's misbehavior included class interruptions, fighting, bringing contraband to school and throwing objects at classmates. He signed a behavior contract that placed him on probation. But he continued to fight with others, vandalize school property, and talk about blowing up things. After the student brought a makeshift metal weapon to school, administrators requested that he undergo a psychiatric evaluation. In response to an English assignment to write an essay, the student wrote about getting drunk, smoking, doing drugs and breaking the law. He also wrote about shooting himself.

After the principal reported his concerns to the state Child and Family Services (CFS) department, a CFS worker insisted that the parents take their son to a hospital for a psychiatric evaluation. A CFS investigation found the principal's report to be unfounded. The parents homeschooled their son for the rest of the year and sued the principal and school district. A federal court rejected claims that the principal violated the student's speech rights by disciplining him for the essay and found no violation of the parents' rights. On appeal, the U.S. Court of Appeals, Second Circuit, held **the state interest in encouraging teachers to protect students was so powerful that immunity from civil and criminal liability was required whenever they reported suspected abuse in good faith**. State law exposed teachers to criminal and civil liability when they willfully failed to make a child abuse report. By its nature, an abuse/neglect report was protective, not disciplinary. If a report to the CFS could result in constitutional liability, administrators would be exposed to civil liability no matter what they did. Since the principal had a legal obligation to report suspected child abuse and neglect, the judgment was affirmed. *Cox v. Warwick Valley Cent. School Dist.*, 654 F.3d 267 (2d Cir. 2011).

◆   A Texas court acquitted a teacher of charges of indecency with a child. He then sought expunction (erasure) of records relating to the charges. Some of the records were in the possession of the Texas Education Agency (TEA). A court ordered the TEA to return all files and records pertaining to the teacher "arising out of the transaction of indecency with a child" and his subsequent arrest. The Court of Appeals of Texas noted that an agency may possess and retain documents related to an acquitted defendant that are not subject to expunction. Child abuse reports and internal investigations were subject to expunction if they referenced police records and files relating to the arrest. **The TEA could have files pertaining to the teacher that were separate from those relating to his criminal investigation, arrest and prosecution.** State law did not intend to erase all evidence of underlying misconduct. While evidence of a criminal investigation, arrest and prosecution was to be expunged, TEA documents from its internal investigation were not. *Texas Educ. Agency v. T.G.F.*, 295 S.W.2d 398 (Tex. Ct. App. 2009).

◆   California first-graders claimed a substitute molested them at a Central School District (CSD) school. The students sued CSD and three other school districts that formerly employed the substitute, claiming each failed its mandatory duty to report suspected child abuse. One of those districts argued that it had no duty to protect students not in its district from potential abuse in the future. The district argued the Supreme Court of California refused to find such a broad duty under the state Reporting Act in *Randi W. v. Muroc Joint Unified School Dist.*, 14 Cal.4th 1066, 60 Cal.Rptr. 263 (1997). After considering 2000 amendments to the Reporting Act, the court held that the legislature did not intend to overcome the *Randi W.* rule that **"future victims were not within the class of persons intended to be protected by the statute."**
On appeal, the Court of Appeal of California noted that the first-graders did not attend the former district at the time of the misconduct. Nor was the substitute under the former district's supervision at that time. The Reporting Act protected children in the custodial care of the person charged with abuse, not all those who might be abused by the same offender in the future. According to the court, *Randi W.* was not intended to extend liability to all children who might conceivably be harmed, even years later, for a reporter's failure to report suspected injury to a child. *P.S. v. San Bernardino City Unified School Dist.*, 94 Cal.Rptr. 788 (Cal. Ct. App. 2009).

◆   A Kentucky kindergartner reported to her mother that another girl in her class had "put her finger up my butt" while they were at school. The mother called the teacher, who assured her the girls would be separated. But the kindergartner later reported that the other girl had been "up my butt" during a classroom reading group. The teacher immediately questioned the other girl, who admitted touching the kindergartner. The teacher was unable to find an administrator for advice at this time, so she carried on with her instructional duties. That evening, the kindergartner told her aunt that the girl had fingered her genitals. The kindergartner's mother reported the improper touching to the school principal the next day. After a conference, the other girl admitted she had "accidentally touched" the kindergartner between the legs.

The principal deemed the incidents to be accidents and did not report them to child protection authorities. The kindergartner reported more conduct by the other girl of a sexual nature. A physical examination of the kindergartner found she had some irritation of the vagina. Medical personnel then reported their observations to the police. The mother sued the school district, teacher and district's insurer for negligently failing to report and investigate. A state court found the teacher's supervision of the children was in good faith and was a discretionary function. The board and teacher were entitled to state law immunity. On appeal, the Court of Appeals of Kentucky held that **it is well-established state law that public school teachers may be held liable for negligent supervision of students**. As the lower court had given no analysis of the discretionary acts issue, the court vacated the judgment and returned the case to the trial court. *Nelson v. Turner*, 256 S.W.3d 37 (Ky. Ct. App. 2008).

◆   An Ohio teacher was investigated for inappropriately touching and making sexual remarks to a ninth-grader. The principal determined the student was lying and took no action. The allegation was not reported to the police or a child services agency. Three years later, the teacher sexually assaulted another ninth-grader in a school athletic equipment room. The student and her parents sued the school board, alleging that its failure to report the first incident violated mandatory state abuse and neglect reporting requirements. A court held that the board was entitled to sovereign immunity. The Court of Appeals of Ohio affirmed the sovereign immunity ruling and determined that state law created a duty only to a specific child. Failure to report the 1996-97 incident could result in liability to that child, but not a different one. The Supreme Court of Ohio found that **teachers and school officials have a special responsibility to protect students committed to their care and control**. They should appreciate that all students are in danger when an abuse report is received about a teacher. A school board could be held liable for failing to report sexual abuse of a minor student by a teacher, when the failure caused the abuse of another minor student by the same teacher. *Yates v. Mansfield Board of Educ.*, 102 Ohio St.3d 205, 808 N.E.2d 861 (Ohio 2004).

◆   A New Jersey principal covered his school office windows in violation of a state law and always kept the door locked. The district superintendent did not monitor this and other violations, and the school board took no action to ensure he complied with the law. A school secretary frequently heard the principal taking pictures of students in his office but failed to report it because he was her "superior." Other staff observed many questionable incidents involving the principal and male students, but no one reported him. Law enforcement investigators arrested the principal for suspected child abuse and found 176 photographs in his office of male students with their legs spread in a chair. The parents of two student victims sued him, and a jury returned a verdict of $275,000 for each student, adding over $100,000 for their parents.

The court entered a judgment of over $775,000 against the board, and the case reached the Supreme Court of New Jersey, which upheld the trial court's liability finding against the board. Here, the **board did not fulfill its most basic obligation of protecting students and did not implement even rudimentary reporting procedures**. The board "grossly disregarded critical information" requiring scrutiny of the principal's activities. School nurses and others breached their independent state law obligation to report child abuse to the appropriate state agency. *Frugis v. Bracigliano*, 827 A.2d 1040 (N.J. 2003).

◆ A South Dakota elementary school counselor met several times with a third-grader, who said that her father had asked her to touch his penis. The counselor discussed the student's statements with a high school guidance counselor and decided the third-grader's reports were probably untrue, based on the student's tendency to fabricate or exaggerate. District policy forbade employees from speaking with parents about abuse allegations, but the counselor discussed the child's statements with the parents. Over a year later, the father pled guilty to sexually assaulting a neighbor child.

The sheriff's office questioned the counselor, who admitted contacting the parents. The state then brought criminal charges against the counselor for failing to report child abuse. The charges were eventually dismissed, but the district notified the counselor of its intent to fire her. The Supreme Court of South Dakota found no evidence to support the district's conclusion that the failure to report child abuse was a breach of the counselor's contract. When the board voted to discharge the counselor, it failed to make the required findings of fact in support of its decision. **In the absence of a finding in the record that the counselor suspected child abuse, the court held the board action was arbitrary, capricious and an abuse of discretion.** *Hughes v. Stanley County School Dist.*, 638 N.W.2d 50 (S.D. 2001).

CHAPTER EIGHT

Employment Discrimination

I. EQUAL PROTECTION

The Equal Protection Clause of the Fourteenth Amendment to the U.S. Constitution commands that no state shall "deny to any person within its jurisdiction the equal protection of the laws." Courts have held an equal protection claim may proceed based on intentional government conduct that improperly treats a person differently than other "similarly situated" persons.

The Supreme Court has construed the Equal Protection Clause as prohibiting only intentional discrimination by government entities and their agents. An intent requirement was imposed by the Court in Washington v. Davis, *426 U.S. 229 (1976), a case which involved a verbal skills test by a police department that resulted in the rejection of a disproportionately high percentage of African-American applicants. Due to the history of official segregation before* Brown v. Board of Educ., *347 U.S. 483 (1954), all government classifications based on race are subject to strict judicial scrutiny.*

◆   A North Dakota school district granted a teacher's request for time off so she could take a vacation to Greece. Her request included four unpaid days. When the time arrived for the teacher's vacation, the district scheduled a school day to make up for a storm cancellation. The teacher did not work on that day. The next week, the district cancelled school in response to imminent flooding. Since school was considered open, the teacher had to use personal leave time for her vacation. But the district paid teachers who did not request leave for this period, treating them as if school had been in session. The teacher challenged the district's decision, stating that she should have been paid like all other teachers in the district who did not teach during the flood period.

The case reached the Supreme Court of North Dakota. It noted the relevant collective bargaining agreement did not explain the rights and duties of the parties if unpaid leave was granted and a scheduled school day was later cancelled. The court held the contractual relationship of the parties was altered when the district granted the teacher unpaid leave. She was released from the obligation to completely fulfill her teaching requirements, and the district was relieved of its duty to pay her salary during her absence. Both parties received a benefit and there was no breach of contract. **There was no equal protection violation, since the teacher was treated the same as other teachers who requested leave and were absent during the flood cancellation week.** *Godon v. Kindred Public School Dist.*, 798 N.W.2d 664 (N.D. 2011).

◆   A Michigan school district retained a married male and laid off an unmarried female when budget problems required combining their duties into a single position. The female worked as a district director of transportation, while the male was the building and grounds supervisor. The district deemed the male better qualified to hold the consolidated position. It noted that the building and grounds job required considerable training, while the director of transportation job did not. The female sued the district in a state court for discrimination under the state civil rights act. The court held for the district, and she appealed to the state court of appeals. It found statements by administrators that the married employee was a "head of household" with "a family to support" did not amount to age, sex or marital status discrimination. Many heads of household are unmarried, and they may also be female. And the building and grounds position required specialized knowledge and training that the unmarried employee could not quickly obtain. **Concerns for the budget and the belief that the married employee was better qualified for the job were found to be legitimate, nondiscriminatory reasons for hiring him.** As a result, the judgment for the district was affirmed. *Swartz v. Berrien Springs Public School Dist.*, No. 286285, 2009 WL 4163539 (Mich. Ct. App. 11/24/09).

◆   An Ohio educational service center (ESC) employee said she was injured in an on-the-job traffic injury. The Ohio Industrial Commission decision found no fraud in her workers' compensation claim. The ESC did not appeal to the court system. Instead, it asked the state industrial commission to find fraud and terminate the employee's participation in the compensation fund. Two hearing officers found no evidence of fraud and the commission denied further appeal. The ESC appealed to a state trial court, which dismissed the case. The case then came before the Supreme Court of Ohio, which noted that the commission had found no evidence of employee fraud. The ESC argued that employers did not receive equal protection under the law because only a claimant whose right to participate in the fund had been terminated could appeal an administrative decision to the court system. The court held that when an employee's right to participate in the fund was granted, an employer had a right to appeal, and when the right was terminated, an employee had a right to appeal. **There was no equal protection violation, because both employers and employees had appeal rights from an adverse commission ruling.** *Benton v. Hamilton Educ. Service Center*, 123 Ohio St.3d 347, 916 N.E.2d 778 (Ohio 2009).

◆   An Oregon state employee complained that a co-worker subjected her to repeated problems. A supervisor directed the co-worker into diversity and anger management training, but he was eventually promoted into a job the employee also wanted. After the employee's position was eliminated, she sued the state agency, co-worker and a supervisor. The court allowed a jury to hear her equal protection claim based on a "class of one" if she could prove she was irrationally singled out due to animosity by the co-worker and supervisor, and treated differently than others who were similarly situated to her. A jury found the co-worker and supervisor intentionally treated her differently than similarly situated employees for improper reasons and awarded her $425,000 in damages. The U.S. Supreme Court held that people may advance equal protection claims based on a "class of one" if there is intentional government conduct that treats a person differently than other similarly situated persons without any rational basis. But that kind of protection did not apply in public employment cases. **The "class of one" theory was simply a poor fit in the public employment context.** The theory was contrary to the presumption of at-will employment and would "constitutionalize the employee grievance." *Engquist v. Oregon Dep't of Agriculture*, 553 U.S. 591, 128 S.Ct. 2146, 170 L.Ed.2d 975 (2008).

◆   A part-time Colorado drama teacher was hired for a one-year employment term at a higher pay grade than her qualifications required. After being rehired for a second year, she declared herself a school board candidate. According to the teacher, the superintendent combed through her personnel file, then initiated a review of her salary and qualifications. After the board voted to reduce the teacher's salary to the level her experience and education supported, it complied with a media request for her personnel files under the state Open Records Act.

Voters elected another candidate for the board, and at the end of the year, the teacher's part-time position was changed to a full-time language arts, speech and drama position. She was not qualified for the job and was not rehired when her contract expired. A federal court awarded pretrial judgment to the district. On appeal, the Tenth Circuit considered the teacher's equal protection claim in view of *Engquist v. Oregon Dep't of Agriculture*, above. **Her equal protection argument failed under *Engquist*. "Government offices could not function if**

every employment decision became a constitutional matter." There was no merit to the teacher's claim that she was not rehired based on an improper motive. Evidence indicated she was unqualified for the new position. All the information furnished to the media had to be disclosed under Colorado law. *Pignanelli v. Pueblo School Dist. No. 60*, 540 F.3d 1213 (10th Cir. 2008).

II. RETALIATION

Title VII and other laws protecting employees from workplace discrimination have anti-retaliation provisions that attempt to prevent employer interference with employee efforts to "secure or advance enforcement of the Act's basic guarantees," including freedom from discrimination. Burlington Northern & Santa Fe Railway Co. v. White, *548 U.S. 53 (2006). Disability retaliation claims filed under the Americans with Disabilities Act (ADA) and Section 504 of the Rehabilitation Act use the analytical framework that is used in Title VII cases.*

The U.S. Supreme Court has given a broad interpretation to the anti-retaliation provision of Title VII of the Civil Rights Act of 1964. Retaliation claims are not limited to employment-related activity or to discrimination claims that the employee has initiated. Retaliation is a separate offense from discrimination, and an employee "need not prove the underlying claim of discrimination for the retaliation claim to succeed." Sullivan v. Nat'l R.R. Passenger Corp., *170 F.3d 1056, 1059 (11th Cir. 1999).*

◆ An African-American teacher taught physical education and coached basketball in a Kansas school district for over 15 years. He lost his job as the girls' coach based on a report of inappropriate conduct. He then lost his job as the boys' coach due to poor performance. He continued teaching for the district. In 1991, the teacher filed an unsuccessful discrimination and retaliation suit against the district. In 1996, he moved to Texas, but he returned to Kansas in 2000 and sought reemployment in the district. After learning that he would not be rehired, the teacher filed another lawsuit against the district, which was dismissed as untimely. Undeterred, the teacher applied for three more jobs in the district in 2009. He claimed two school board members made unfavorable comments about him, both of which referenced his past lawsuits against the district. In a third lawsuit, the teacher claimed the district's decision not to rehire him in 2009 was based on race discrimination and retaliation. A federal district court dismissed the case. Appeal reached the U.S. Court of Appeals, Tenth Circuit, which held that **the retaliation claim was highly speculative and largely based on the inadmissible comments attributed to board members regarding his litigiousness**. As the lower court had correctly held for the school district, the court affirmed the judgment. *Brown v. Unified School Dist. No. 501*, 459 Fed.Appx. 705 (10th Cir. 2012).

◆ An African-American Virginia library supervisor who claimed she was demoted in retaliation for a complaint to the school board about the district superintendent lost a discrimination and retaliation case against her school board. She had complained to the board that the superintendent made racial comments about her "good hair" and complexion. Near this time, her position was eliminated and she was demoted to a teaching job. A federal court dismissed the supervisor's Title VII case, and the U.S. Court of Appeals, Fourth Circuit, upheld the decision. It held Title VII forbids only objectively offensive behavior that is sufficient to alter the conditions of employment. **Teasing and offhand remarks are insufficient to meet Title VII liability standards.** While the supervisor was offended by the comments, the court found the first was innocuous and was not an insult. The second was mainly a reference to the superintendent's dark complexion, not the supervisor's lighter tone. *Session v. Montgomery County School Board*, 462 Fed.Appx. 323 (4th Cir. 2012).

◆   An applicant who sought to work as a Dallas school district police officer did not show the district declined to hire him because he had filed civil rights complaints against previous employers. Affirming a lower court judgment for the district, the U.S. Court of Appeals, Fifth Circuit, found no support for his retaliation theory. Instead, there was evidence that **the applicant was not hired because another police department had fired him after an internal affairs investigation revealed misconduct.** Since he was listed as a "no rehire," the court found he was automatically disqualified from employment by the district. *Cornish v. Dallas Independent School Dist.*, 412 Fed.Appx. 732 (5th Cir. 2011).

◆   A Florida teacher filed a Title VII discrimination lawsuit against her school board. She later resigned, but continued participating in a volunteer mentoring program in county schools for six months. At that time, the board prohibited the teacher from volunteer work. She alleged violations of Title VII. After a trial court held for the board, the District Court of Appeal of Florida held the lower court correctly found volunteers are not protected by Title VII, which applies to employment relationships. But **Title VII applied in this case because of the prior relationship of the parties.** Under *Robinson v. Shell Oil Co.*, 519 U.S. 337 (1997), former employees enjoy Title VII protection when they can establish the elements of a Title VII claim. The lower court committed error in dismissing the claim, as the teacher's status as a former employee qualified her for coverage. The case was returned to the lower court for further proceedings. *Gates v. Gadsen County School Board*, 45 So.3d 39 (Fla. Dist. Ct. App. 2010).

◆   A veteran Tennessee school HR officer was asked if she had witnessed any inappropriate behavior by the district's employee relations director. She described several instances of his sexually harassing behavior. Two other employees reported that the director sexually harassed them. While the school agency took no action against the employee relations director, it fired the HR officer and the two other employees. The HR officer sued the agency for violating Title VII. Her case reached the U.S. Supreme Court, which stated that Title VII makes it unlawful for an employer to discriminate against any employee who has opposed any practice made unlawful by Title VII. Another provision made it unlawful for an employer to retaliate against an employee who participated in a Title VII investigation. A person could "oppose" conduct by responding to someone else's questions. A contrary rule would undermine protection from workplace discrimination. The Court held for the HR officer, finding **the anti-retaliation provisions of Title VII extended to employees who answered questions during an internal investigation.** *Crawford v. Metropolitan Government of Nashville and Davidson County, Tennessee*, 555 U.S. 271, 129 S.Ct. 846, 172 L.Ed.2d 650 (2009).

◆ A Tennessee railway employee complained about her supervisor's sexually harassing comments. The company disciplined the supervisor but also transferred the employee to a less desirable position. A superior said her reassignment reflected complaints by co-workers that a "more senior man" should have the "less arduous and cleaner job of forklift operator." The employee filed a Title VII complaint, and the company suspended her without pay for insubordination. The Supreme Court held that Title VII's anti-retaliation provision bans a wide variety of employer conduct intended to restrain employees in the exercise of protected activities. **Although Title VII does not create a general civility code for the workplace, the jury properly found that the reassignment and suspension amounted to retaliation.** The reassignment was "materially adverse" to the employee, who went unpaid for 37 days during which she was uncertain of her employment status. *Burlington Northern & Santa Fe Railway Co. v. White*, 548 U.S. 53, 126 S.Ct. 2405, 165 L.Ed.2d 345 (2006).

◆ The U.S. Court of Appeals, Ninth Circuit, rejected an Arizona teacher's retaliation claims based on her advocacy for Native American students at her school. The court noted that **the school board had offered her a new contract immediately after her criticisms were published** by the local news media. This precluded an inference of retaliation. School administrators correctly argued that the teacher's conduct was insubordinate. This included taking a day off without permission and referring supervisors to her lawyer in response to their lawful directions. The teacher also threatened to call the police if her immediate supervisor spoke to her. The court found no retaliatory motive. *Avent v. Tempe Union High School Dist. No. 213*, 359 Fed.Appx. 744 (9th Cir. 2009).

III. SEX DISCRIMINATION

A. Title VII of the Civil Rights Act

Title VII prohibits employment discrimination based on race, color, sex, religion or national origin. To show discrimination in a Title VII case, an employee must show some "adverse employment action." This occurs if there is "a materially adverse change in the terms of employment." The Supreme Court held an adverse impact or effect is not sufficient to show a violation of the Equal Protection Clause. Proof of intent to discriminate is required. Since it is difficult to prove intentional discrimination, civil rights statutes such as Title VII are a more common basis for employment discrimination claims.

◆ A Texas school district fired a teacher based on charges that she had sexual contact with male students. Criminal charges against her ended in a mistrial. The State Board of Educator Certification investigated the case and sought to revoke the teacher's certification. After a hearing, an administrative law judge found her testimony was credible while that of her accusers was not. As a result, the state board allowed her to keep her certification. In a separate lawsuit against the school district, the teacher claimed discrimination in favor of males.

Near this time, the district denied the teacher's applications for French and English teaching jobs. Her requests to volunteer at her daughter's school were also denied. The teacher sued the school district in a federal court, claiming she was not rehired or allowed to volunteer due to her gender and because she had filed the sex discrimination lawsuit. Appeal reached the U.S. Court of Appeals, Fifth Circuit. It found the district had legitimate, non-retaliatory reasons for the decision not to rehire the teacher. The district had decided to offer online French instruction, eliminating the need to hire a French teacher. And **the teacher would not have been rehired for an English teaching position regardless of her lawsuit, based on the charges of sexual conduct with students**. As the court found the teacher did not show she was not rehired for arbitrary, retaliatory or discriminatory reasons, it held for the school district. *Ogletree v. Glen Rose Independent School Dist.*, 443 Fed.Appx. 913 (5th Cir. 2011).

◆   A Texas school district outsourced the management of its custodial services department, resulting in the loss of five field supervisor positions. A private service that contracted to run the department eliminated the field supervisor position and replaced it with an area custodial supervisor (ACS) position. A female administrator with 20 years of experience in the district obtained an interview, but claimed she was told that only men would be hired for the job.

All eight ACS positions went to male applicants. The administrator was the only former field supervisor not selected. She was reassigned to a facility supervisor position, and she filed a discrimination charge against the school district with the EEOC. She then received her first negative performance review. When her discrimination and retaliation case reached the U.S. Court of Appeals, Fifth Circuit, it found no direct evidence of discrimination. But it held that the administrator raised an inference of discrimination regarding the first ACS offering based on a former supervisor's statements. The court noted evidence that she had received satisfactory or better ratings on all her performance reviews and was a field supervisor for three years in a position nearly identical to the ACS jobs. Three of the men hired for ACS jobs lacked the district's minimum education and experience requirements. **As the administrator raised sufficient doubt about the district's stated reasons for not hiring her, the judgment was reversed and the case was returned to the district court.** *Gillaspy v. Dallas Independent School Dist.*, 278 Fed.Appx. 307 (5th Cir. 2008).

◆   An African-American employee served as a secretary to several Mississippi school superintendents over a 10-year period. After a superintendent resigned, no immediate replacement was hired. The employee claimed she assumed many of the superintendent's duties for the next two years, when a white male became a "central office administrative coordinator." She said the coordinator performed substantially the same job she did, but for a higher salary. She quit and sued the school system for race and gender discrimination under Title VII, and the Equal Pay Act (EPA). A jury returned a verdict for the school district, and the court found the case baseless and frivolous. It ordered the employee to pay the school district's fees and costs, which exceeded $154,000. On appeal, the U.S. Court of Appeals, Fifth Circuit, found nothing to indicate the employee's working conditions were so intolerable that she was forced to quit. Instead, she was disgruntled that a white, high-level administrator received greater benefits than she did. **The coordinator had greater responsibilities than the employee, such as supervising several departments and managing grants.** The lower court did not abuse its discretion by ruling for the district. But as the case was not frivolous, the award of attorneys' fees and costs was reversed. *Stover v. Hattiesburg Public School Dist.*, 549 F.3 985 (5th Cir. 2008).

◆ After teaching high school Spanish for three years, a Tennessee teacher expected to gain tenure. She claimed her principal sexually harassed her, and filed a complaint against him with the EEOC. Soon, the district notified her of her employment termination. With the help of her union, the teacher appealed to a school administrator. The administrator found the election to non-renew the teacher's contract would stand, but said she would be rehired and gain tenure if she met evaluation requirements. After teaching another year, she received tenure. The teacher sued the school district for sex discrimination under Title VII. A jury found the delay in granting tenure was not an "adverse employment action." The teacher appealed to the Sixth Circuit, which found **the teacher did not lose any tangible benefits or income as a result of the initial denial of tenure.** While she was initially denied tenure, she had another chance to prove herself. She was no worse off with respect to seniority, income or benefits despite being granted tenure after her fourth year, rather than her third. As the teacher lost no income or benefits and did not claim her job had been materially changed, the judgment was affirmed. *Shohadaee v. Metropolitan Government of Nashville and Davidson County*, 150 Fed.Appx. 402 (6th Cir. 2005).

B. Pregnancy Discrimination

The Pregnancy Discrimination Act, 42 U.S.C. § 2000e(k), is an amendment to Title VII prohibiting employment discrimination on the basis of pregnancy. The act requires employers to treat pregnancy the same as disabling illnesses for purposes of health benefits programs and all other employment-related purposes. For more cases involving health-related leaves of absence, please see Chapter Seven, Section III.

◆ A Chicago teacher was a probationary assigned teacher (PAT) at a high school. Due to budgetary reasons, the school lost 1.2 special education positions during the teacher's second year. The principal identified the teacher as "the least effective special education PAT" at the school and recommended contract non-renewal. The teacher claimed she had already told the principal of her pregnancy by this time. Later in the month, the recommendation was approved by the school board. The teacher filed a federal agency discrimination charge against the board and principal. The teacher was rehired following her pregnancy, but she was again found deficient in her methods of instruction and classroom management. The principal recommended that she not be rehired, and she filed another agency complaint against the board and principal. She then filed a federal district court action, asserting pregnancy discrimination and violations of the Family and Medical Leave Act (FMLA), among other claims.

The court explained that claims filed under Title VII of the Civil Rights Act of 1964 may be based on indirect evidence. Although the teacher challenged the principal's reasons for finding her "the least effective PAT," the court rejected this claim. As the Seventh Circuit has held, **the fact that an employer was mistaken or based its decision on bad policy is irrelevant to whether the stated reason for an action is a pretext**. Since courts do not sit in review of an employer's appraisal of an employee's qualifications, the teacher was unable to show pregnancy discrimination. Her FMLA claim failed because the board rehired her after she took her pregnancy leave. As none of the teacher's claims had merit, the court held for the board and principal. *Silverman v. Board of Educ. of City of Chicago*, No. 08 C 2220, 2010 WL 3000187 (N.D. Ill. 7/26/10).

◆ A private corporation based pension calculations on a seniority system that relied on years of service, less uncredited leave. Employees who took pregnancy leave earned less retirement credit than was available for other kinds of medical leave. A group of California employees sued the corporation, and the case reached the Supreme Court. It observed that the Pregnancy Discrimination Act (PDA) (added to Title VII in 1978) made "clear that **it is discriminatory to treat pregnancy-related conditions less favorably than other medical conditions.**" On the effective date of the PDA, the corporation replaced its old plan with a new one providing the same credit for pregnancy leave as for others in the future. But the plan did not retroactively adjust pre-PDA credits. Each of the employees thus received less service credit for a pre-PDA pregnancy leave than she would have for general disability leave, as well as a lower pension benefit. The Court held that the employer did not violate the PDA by paying disparate benefits calculated in part under an accrual rule that applied only to pre-PDA leave. The corporation's pension payments were in accord with a *bona fide* seniority system. *AT & T Corp. v. Hulteen*, 556 U.S. 701 (2009).

◆ A Washington custodian took maternity leave in 1998. The district's family leave policy stated employees need not be reinstated to a specific job if the job was eliminated due to restructuring or a reduction in force. The custodian took maternity leave again in 1999, and experienced complications with twins. The district allowed her to structure a leave of over nine months by using sick days, family leave, holidays and unpaid leave. The district demolished buildings and built new ones during the custodian's second leave. It reduced daily custodial hours from 13 to nine district-wide and reallocated this time between two part-time custodians. The district then hired a full-time custodial employee from another school system. The custodian sued the district for gender, pregnancy and family status discrimination. A state court held **the district did not need to reinstate an employee whose job was eliminated by a restructuring or reduction in force caused by a lack of funding or work**. The district showed the action was based on construction projects, not discrimination. *Ackerman v. Quilcene School Dist. No. 48*, 117 Wash.App.1087 (Wash. Ct. App. 2003).

◆ A Maine school district hired a teacher on a probationary basis after she served as a long-term substitute for most of one school year. Although she experienced classroom management issues, her performance improved during the year and she received a second probationary contract. At the time the teacher received the second contract, she was pregnant. She missed the first weeks of her second probationary year due to her pregnancy. Upon resuming her duties, she received a poor evaluation due to her messy and disorganized classroom. The teacher showed improvement during the year, and she eventually received recommendations for a continuing contract. She became pregnant again during her second probationary year and, without explanation, the board replaced her with a teacher who was not pregnant.

The teacher sued the board in a federal district court. The court refused to dismiss the case, noting **Title VII prevents an employer from discharging an employee on the "categorical fact of her pregnancy," or in retaliation for taking an authorized maternity leave**. Here, the board asserted that the teacher was not good enough to deserve tenure. But the principal and superintendent had given her good evaluations when her case came up for review. And a board member who was alleged to be unaware of the teacher's pregnancy saw her frequently when the signs of her advancing pregnancy were unmistakable. The teacher pointed out inconsistencies and weaknesses in the statements of four board members, and she showed a financial motive for her termination. The court held she produced sufficient evidence to make a trial necessary. *Johnson v. School Union No. 107*, 295 F.Supp.2d 106 (D. Me. 2003).

C. Equal Pay and Gender

The Equal Pay Act requires employers to pay males and females the same wages for jobs involving "equal skill, effort, and responsibility, and which are performed under similar working conditions, except where such payment is made pursuant to (i) a seniority system; (ii) a merit system; (iii) a system which measures earnings by quantity or quality of production; or (iv) a differential based on any other factor other than sex." The act has been interpreted to require only that the jobs under comparison be "substantially" equal. Strict equality of the jobs under comparison is not required. Claimants may also bring sex-based wage claims under the Equal Protection Clause.

Title VII states that it is not an unlawful employment practice for an employer to apply "different standards of compensation ... pursuant to a bona fide seniority ... system ... provided that such differences are not the result of an intention to discriminate because of ... sex."

◆ A Georgia school board began to receive complaints about a varsity softball coach. Administrators notified her in writing of the need to improve her performance and advised her of specific behavior to avoid, such as making disparaging remarks about team members. When complaints continued, the school board fired the coach. She sued, asserting she was fired in violation of Title VII. She also asserted a violation of the Equal Pay Act (EPA). The court ruled for the school system, and the coach appealed. The U.S. Court of Appeals, Eleventh Circuit, explained that an EPA claimant must show that the employer paid persons of different genders different wages for equal work in jobs requiring similar skill, effort and responsibility and under similar conditions. The lower court had agreed with the school system that the softball coach could not compare her job with that of the varsity boys' baseball coach, as his team played 13 more games and had five to 10 more players than the softball team. The court of appeals held **reasonable minds could differ as to whether the coaching jobs were substantially similar**. So the district court had incorrectly dismissed that part of the case. But since the coach did not present any evidence that she was fired because of her gender, her Title VII claim failed. *Hankinson v. Thomas County School System*, 257 Fed.Appx. 199 (11th Cir. 2007).

♦ Two female Pennsylvania school employees claimed they were paid less than male teachers with less seniority. Both males received full credit for their past employment history, and one had insisted on a certain starting wage. Although a female teacher had 13 years of experience at the time she was hired, and a female librarian had 12, they did not receive full credit for this time, based on lapses in their employment history. The females sued the school district for violating the Equal Pay Act. A jury unanimously held for the district, and the employees appealed. The U.S. Court of Appeals, Third Circuit, affirmed. Here, the district introduced sufficient evidence that **the disparity in pay was not caused by gender, but by the particular certification possessed by one male teacher, his salary demand, and the collective bargaining agreement**. *Henderson v. Chartiers Valley School*, 136 Fed.Appx. 456 (3d Cir. 2005).

♦ A Massachusetts school district hired a female teacher in its technical division in 1993. She began at a salary level for employees with five years of experience, and she had the highest starting salary of any teacher hired by the division up to that time. A male technology teacher with four years of teaching experience and 18 years of contracting experience was then hired at a wage that was the same as that of an employee with seven years of teaching experience.

In a state court action, the court awarded over $60,000 to the employee and over $115,000 to a female colleague. On appeal, **the Supreme Judicial Court of Massachusetts noted that the state equal pay act allowed for variations in rates of pay based on seniority**. In this case, the collective bargaining agreement authorized the superintendent to set the salaries of new teachers. There was evidence that four male technical teachers who were hired before the females all received three years of credit, even though their relevant work experience varied. As the lack of uniformity in starting salaries among the employees did not establish wage discrimination, the court held for the district. *Silvestris v. Tantasqua Regional School Dist.*, 446 Mass. 756 (Mass. 2006).

♦ A female Michigan coach served for 10 years as a girls' varsity basketball coach. She also coached the boys' junior varsity for eight years and was an assistant coach of the boys' varsity team for eight years. The coach applied for the boys' varsity head coaching position when the incumbent retired. The only other applicant was a less experienced male teacher who had coached the boys' freshman team for two years. District hiring committee members expressed concerns about complaints from the community if it hired her for the boys' varsity job. The school board president voiced similar concerns, and the male teacher was hired for the job. The coach sued the school district for sex discrimination under Title VII and the state's Elliott-Larsen Civil Rights Act.

A jury returned a verdict of $455,000 for the coach. The court ordered the district to name her coach of the boys' varsity basketball team, but it reduced the award by $210,000. On appeal, the Sixth Circuit Court of Appeals **rejected the district's assertion that it had legitimate, nondiscriminatory reasons for not hiring the coach**. It found direct evidence that gender was a factor in its decision. The board president and the superintendent made similar comments about hiring a female coach, and the superintendent admitted that board members opposed her application. The court affirmed the judgment. *Fuhr v. School Dist. of City of Hazel Park*, 364 F.3d 753 (6th Cir. 2004).

D. Sexual Harassment

Sexual harassment is a form of sex discrimination that violates Title VII. Harassment creating a hostile work environment entails discriminatory behavior if a reasonable person, as well as the victim, would find it hostile. See Harris v. Forklift Systems, Inc., *510 U.S. 17 (1993).*

The Supreme Court held Title VII is violated if an employee is "exposed to disadvantageous terms or conditions of employment to which members of the other sex are not exposed." In Burlington Industries, Inc. v. Ellerth, *524 U.S. 742 (1998), and* Faragher v. City of Boca Raton, *524 U.S. 775 (1998), **the Court held Title VII creates employer liability for sexual harassment by supervisors**. Where no adverse employment action occurs, the employer may avoid liability by showing it used reasonable care to prevent and promptly correct harassment, and the employee unreasonably failed to use available employer remedies.*

◆   A Minnesota custodian claimed her supervisor said that he did not want women on his crew and made comments like "the only place for women is the kitchen and the bedroom." She said he also separated work areas for men and women and barred women from talking to each other unless they were on break.

A private investigator hired by the school district found complaints by the custodian and others about the supervisor lacked merit, and the custodian filed a state court action for violations of the Minnesota Human Rights Act. After the court dismissed the case, appeal reached the Supreme Court of Minnesota. It held that **since the state statutory definition of "discrimination" specifically included sexual harassment, the act permitted a hostile work environment claim**. While a hostile work environment claim can be made under the state act, the claim was not proven in this case. The custodian did not show harassment affecting a term, condition or privilege of employment so severe or pervasive as to alter her job conditions and create an abusive work environment. While the supervisor's conduct was inappropriate and offensive, it was not hostile or abusive. Male custodians also complained about his behavior, and he did not appear to have unreasonably interfered with the custodian's ability to do her job. A lower court judgment for the district was affirmed. *LaMont v. Independent School Dist. #728*, 814 N.W.2d 14 (Minn. 2012).

◆ A Virginia instructional aide was admonished by school administrators for hugging students, smoking in a parking lot, submitting incorrect timesheets, and leaving a cigarette lighter in a special education resource room. According to the employee, the school had an official "zero-tolerance" hugging policy that was only enforced against males. He claimed to be an undercover FBI agent and said he wished to videotape "little burning children coming out of the school." A school board personnel supervisor met with him and offered to let him resign. When the employee refused, the supervisor fired him for charges including failure to meet expectations, inappropriate conduct with students and inability to comply with an improvement plan. The employee sued the school board in a federal court, asserting it enforced an anti-hugging policy only against males. Apart from the employee's own statements, the court found no evidence of any discriminatory policy. **There was no evidence that he was performing his job duties at a level that met the board's legitimate expectations**, and the court held for the school board. *Schroeder v. Roanoke County School Board*, No. 7:08cv00468, 2008 WL 5043474 (W.D. Va. 11/25/08).

◆ An executive secretary had a long-term sexual relationship with a future Mississippi school superintendent. After his election, the superintendent created a job for her. The secretary claimed the superintendent began to sexually harass her shortly after she began her job. In his second year as superintendent, she claimed he raped her in his office. The incident was reported, as were phone harassment charges, but the case was not prosecuted. The secretary took an extended medical leave and returned to work in an elementary school. She claimed this was in retaliation for reporting the assault and harassment, and she sued the school district and superintendent. A federal court dismissed the Title VII claim against the district, noting the secretary was not an "employee" under Title VII's "personal staff exception." **The Fifth Circuit held the statutory term "employee" excluded a person chosen by an elected official to be on the officer's personal staff.** As the superintendent was an elected official and he had hand-picked the secretary, she did not meet the statutory definition of "employee." The court rejected the secretary's arguments that she was not a part of the superintendent's personal staff. He had created the job for her and did not interview anyone else for it. The secretary was hired outside the normal hiring process, and the Title VII exception applied. The court affirmed the judgment. *Saddler v. Quitman County School Dist.*, 278 Fed.Appx. 412 (5th Cir. 2008).

◆ A South Dakota school employee claimed that a male co-worker made suggestive comments to her and asked her to feel his penis. She did not report the misconduct. After three years, a female co-worker complained about the male to a supervisor. The female employee then made a written complaint of the harassment. After an investigation, the district suspended the male without pay and directed him into counseling, threatening to fire him if he did not stop his harassment. When he continued his harassment, he was suspended again, but with no threat of termination. Again he continued his harassing behavior.

The female employee resigned, and at a farewell party, she told the superintendent that harassment was a factor in her resignation. She later sued the school district for sexual harassment. The case reached the U.S. Court of

Appeals, Eighth Circuit, which explained that **an employer may be liable for sexual harassment under Title VII if it knew or should have known of misconduct, but failed to take proper remedial action**. The court found sufficient evidence that sexual harassment continued after the district took remedial action in this case. And the second remedial action had "backtracked" from the threat to immediately terminate his employment. Thus, the female employee was due further consideration of her claims that decreasing the threat of sanctions was a negligent response that increased the harassment. *Engel v. Rapid City School Dist.*, 506 F.3d 1118 (9th Cir. 2007).

◆ A Nevada employee met with two male supervisors to review psychological evaluation reports from job applicants. She claimed one supervisor read a report that an applicant commented to a co-worker, "I hear making love to you is like making love to the Grand Canyon." The employee claimed one supervisor then said, "I don't know what that means." She said the other supervisor responded, "Well, I'll tell you later," and the two males chuckled. The employee was transferred to another job 20 months later. She sued the school district for sexual harassment. When the case reached the U.S. Supreme Court, it held no reasonable person could have believed the single incident violated Title VII. Sexual harassment is actionable only if it is so severe or pervasive as to alter terms and conditions of the victim's employment and create an abusive working environment. The supervisor's comment and the other male's response amounted to "an isolated incident" that could not be considered serious. There was "no causality at all" between the job transfer and the employee's complaint. **There must be a close proximity in time between an employer's knowledge of an employee's protected conduct and an adverse employment action**, if this is the employee's only evidence of retaliation. *Clark County School Dist. v. Breeden*, 532 U.S. 268, 121 S.Ct. 1508, 149 L.Ed.2d 509 (2001).

E. Sexual Orientation

In Oncale v. Sundowner Offshore Services, *523 U.S. 75 (1998),* **the U.S. Supreme Court held that same-sex harassment is a violation of Title VII.** *Title VII is not a general code of workplace civility, but covers conduct that is severe or pervasive enough to create an objectively hostile or abusive work environment. No language in Title VII bars a sex discrimination claim when the complaining party and alleged perpetrators are of the same sex.*

◆ A New York teacher lived with her male partner for more than 30 years, but they did not marry. Her school board voted to extend dependent healthcare benefits to same-sex domestic partners of employees, and she sought coverage for her partner. The board denied coverage because the policy did not cover opposite-sex partners. The teacher and her partner registered their domestic partnership with Westchester County and filed a complaint with the county human rights commission for unlawful discrimination based on sexual orientation and marital status, in violation of the county Human Rights Law.

After a hearing, the commission ordered the employer to discontinue its policy of covering only same-sex domestic partners. Damages of $24,178 were awarded, and an appeal came before a New York Appellate Division Court. It found **eligibility for the domestic partner healthcare benefits sought did not turn upon marital status**. Recipients of same-sex domestic partner benefits had the same marital status as the teacher and her partner. The court held the extension of benefits to only same-sex domestic partners could be justified. It noted that the reason for offering healthcare benefits to same-sex domestic partners was that they could not obtain benefits from their partners by becoming lawfully married in the state. Unlike same-sex domestic couples, the teacher and her partner could legally marry in New York and obtain the coverage they sought. As a result, the court annulled the commission's decision. *In re Putnam/Northern Westchester BOCES v. Westchester County Human Rights Comm'n*, 81 A.D.3d 733, 917 N.Y.S.2d 635 (N.Y. App. Div. 2011).

◆ Two female Wyoming school administrators lived as a couple and were employed by the same school district as middle school assistant principals. A student claimed she saw them holding hands and walking into a Victoria's Secret store during a school field trip. Both administrators denied the report, but they lost their jobs during a school district reorganization the next school year. They sued the school board and superintendent for employment discrimination based on sexual orientation. A court found the superintendent's actions were unconstitutional, but that the law on sexual orientation discrimination was not clearly established at the time of his conduct. A jury awarded the administrators $160,515, and the court held the district liable for it. The U.S. Court of Appeals, Tenth Circuit, held the superintendent was not the final policy-maker for the district. **Since the law on sexual orientation discrimination was not clearly established at the relevant time, neither he nor the district could be held liable to the administrators.** *Milligan-Hitt v. Board of Trustees of Sheridan County School Dist. No. 2*, 523 F.3d 1219 (10th Cir. 2008).

◆ A Minnesota teacher was placed on administrative leave near the end of his probationary period, then discharged. He sued the school district in a state court, asserting that he had reported many incidents of bad behavior by students during his three years with the district, including taunts that he was homosexual. The teacher claimed a right to be free from any abuse or harassment by students in the school environment under a state statute and the district's own policies.

The case reached the Court of Appeals of Minnesota, which rejected the teacher's argument that the statute created an absolute legal duty for school districts. The section required the commissioner of education to maintain a model policy on discrimination, harassment and violence. **School boards were required to adopt and conspicuously post their policies and verify they conformed to state requirements.** The teacher did not argue that the school district violated a particular part of the statute. Here, the district investigated three incidents of student harassment, two of which involved students who implied he was homosexual. The district disciplined the students and informed the parents. District policymaking and enforcement required discretion. The trial court had properly held that the district was protected by discretionary immunity. The court affirmed the judgment. *Malone v. Special School Dist. No. 1*, No. 2004 CA 00347, 2005 WL 3289468 (Minn. Ct. App. 2005).

IV. RACE AND NATIONAL ORIGIN DISCRIMINATION

A. Race Discrimination

As the Supreme Court noted in St. Mary's Honor Center v. Hicks, *509 U.S. 502 (1993), intentional discrimination can be inferred from a disbelief of the employer's stated reason for adverse employment action. Title VII's bona fide occupational qualification (BFOQ) exception allows employers to use sex, religion or national origin as a hiring criterion if one of those characteristics is a "bona fide occupational qualification necessary to the normal operation of that particular business or enterprise." A BFOQ defense will fail unless the qualification at issue is a matter of "necessity," not merely employer convenience. Successful assertion of a BFOQ defense will result in dismissal of a discrimination claim. Race can never be a BFOQ.*

◆ A Kentucky school principal stated that an African-American teacher grew angry and defensive at a meeting about an incident with a student. After the meeting, the principal issued the teacher a "Form E-2" meeting summary that was not a formal reprimand. The teacher filed a grievance with the board of education and filed charges of race and age discrimination with state and federal agencies. After the dismissal of the agency cases, he sued the board and school officials in a federal court for civil rights violations. Appeal reached the U.S. Court of Appeals, Sixth Circuit. It held that to prevail on a race discrimination claim, it must be shown that there was "a materially adverse change in the terms of one's employment." This means a significant change in employment status. In this case, the teacher admitted he was not fired, demoted, or subjected to a reduction in pay or other benefits. The meeting held to discuss the student's behavior was not an adverse employment action. **Other courts have held that a written reprimand is not a materially adverse employment action unless there is some consequence, such as a demotion or suspension.** The teacher did not show he was issued a Form E-2 for discriminatory purposes or that the form was issued as a pretext for discrimination. As there was no adverse employment action, the court held for the board of education. *Creggett v. Jefferson County Board of Educ.,* 491 Fed.Appx. 561 (6th Cir. 2012).

◆ A longtime Colorado school administrator was the only Hispanic principal in her school district. In nine years of work at a school with over 70% Hispanic students, she earned excellent evaluations. The school district contemplated controversial policy changes, including an English Language Learners (ELL) policy that stressed English immersion. The superintendent met with the principal and questioned her support for the new policy, and sought the name of a person who had emailed erroneous misinformation about it. The principal refused to provide the name, and the superintendent recommended that her employment be terminated. Following a hearing before a panel, a board voted to accept the termination recommendation. In a federal court action against the school district, the principal asserted she was fired because of her Hispanic heritage. The court held her insubordination gave the district a legitimate, nondiscriminatory reason for acting and found no evidence of bias.

On appeal, the Tenth Circuit held the superintendent gave the principal ample notice of what constituted "insubordination." She sent the principal a letter explaining that refusal to provide the requested information and to comply with specific instructions was insubordination. After receiving three chances, the principal did not comply with the superintendent's request. **A court is not to second-guess an employer's honestly held judgment about what information is needed from an employee and the consequences for failing to disclose it.** As a result, the court affirmed the judgment against the principal. *Jaramillo v. Adams County School Dist. 14,* 680 F.3d 1267 (10th Cir. 2012).

◆   A Florida teacher of African-American and Caucasian descent served as a middle school science teacher and coach. He then worked as a high school physical education teacher and basketball coach. At some point, he filed a federal agency charge against his school district for discrimination. After being transferred to a middle school science-teaching position, the teacher sued the district for violation of his First Amendment rights, creation of a hostile environment and race and gender discrimination. A federal court held for the school district, and he appealed to the U.S. Court of Appeals, Eleventh Circuit. According to the teacher, he was reassigned to a middle school based on his race. In the court's view, he did not prove he suffered "adverse employment action." **An adverse employment action involves "a serious and material change in the terms, conditions or privileges of employment."** While a transfer can be an adverse employment action if it involves a reduction in pay, prestige or responsibility, "a temporary change in work assignment that creates no tangible harm and does not alter the employee's permanent job title, is not legally adverse." Since the teacher did not show his transfer resulted in any tangible harm, he failed to make out a federal case for employment discrimination. The court held for the school district. *Nash v. Palm Beach County School Dist.,* 469 Fed.Appx. 712 (11th Cir. 2012).

◆   A Texas substitute teacher/teaching assistant sought to become a fully certified teacher in a school district. But school administrators documented his failure to actively monitor and properly supervise students. Despite instructions to the contrary, the employee remained seated in his classes while he wore sunglasses. After being notified of these shortcomings, he claimed white female teaching assistants were allowed to sit in their classrooms, and that others wore sunglasses in their classes. A complaint emerged that he allowed students to have a "paint fight" in class while he sat idly wearing his sunglasses. School administrators advised the employee to resign or face dismissal. When he learned he would not be offered a position for the next school year, he sued the school district in a federal court. A magistrate judge found scant evidence of discrimination. The employee was not qualified for a permanent teaching job since he lacked proper certification. He also did not show he was paid less than others in his position. Appeal reached the U.S. Court of Appeals, Fifth Circuit.

In the court's opinion, the discipline came in response to the employee's failure to properly supervise a classroom and his habit of sitting and wearing sunglasses while in the classroom. He did not present any evidence to refute this explanation. Moreover, the district showed it had paid the employee according to its pay scale for all teaching assistants and substitutes. And it proved he was not offered a permanent teaching job because he was not qualified for one. **As the employee was not rehired due to his failure to correct his behavior, the court held the case was properly dismissed.** *Hatch v. Del Valle Independent School Dist.*, 496 Fed.Appx. 417 (5th Cir. 2012).

◆ An African-American media specialist claimed a Georgia school district passed her over for a promotion she deserved. She was 64 years old and had worked for the school board for 10 years. A hiring committee included three African-Americans, and three of its five members were at least as old as the specialist. None of the applicants for the position fully satisfied the hiring criteria. A white male who was 20 years younger than the specialist was hired for the job.

In a state court action, the specialist claimed the board discriminated against her on the basis of her age, race and Muslim religion. But the board's director of personnel, herself an African-American woman, testified that the decision was not based on the specialist's age, race or religion. Although the specialist believed she was more qualified than the selected applicant, she admitted that she had no information showing that her age, race, religion or gender impacted the board's decision. After the court held for the board, the specialist appealed to the Court of Appeals of Georgia. It found no evidence of discriminatory intent. **Speculation by the specialist that her qualifications were superior to those of the selected candidate did not support a discrimination lawsuit.** As there was no evidence that race, gender or age bias was the board's true reason for rejecting her, the court held for the board. *Jones v. Valdosta Board of Educ.*, 732 S.E.2d 830 (Ga. Ct. App. 2012).

◆ A federal district court in Kansas refused to overturn the discharge of an African-American school custodian who was the subject of complaints and an investigation for inappropriate involvement with a student, falsifying a report and sexual harassment. **Although the custodian claimed he was unlawfully fired based on his race, the court found the district had nondiscriminatory reasons for acting.** An investigation revealed that female teachers had complained about unwanted physical contact and that one of his interactions with a student led to a sexual abuse charge and the placement of his name on the state's central registry for child abuse and neglect. *Thomas v. Unified School Dist. #501*, No. 11-4040-SAC, 2012 WL 1893502 (D. Kan. 5/23/12).

◆ An African-American employee was unable to convince the U.S. Court of Appeals, Eleventh Circuit, that a Georgia school district unlawfully denied her a promotion, reassigned her to a temporary position and told a prospective employer not to hire her based on her race and sex. As a lower federal court had held, **the employee was not reassigned to a temporary position but was assigned to a job with a voter-approved source of funding.** There was no support for her claim that a prospective employer was told not to hire her because she had filed another lawsuit. *Gibbs-Matthews v. Fulton County School Dist.*, 429 Fed.Appx. 892 (11th Cir. 2011).

◆   An African-American school counselor was unable to convince the U.S. Court of Appeals, Third Circuit, that a Pennsylvania school system discharged him because of racial bias. He was fired after being arrested for possession of marijuana. Asserting that the system treated him differently than white employees, he filed a federal action. A U.S. district court dismissed the action, and the Third Circuit issued a brief opinion affirming the judgment. It found no evidence that similarly situated white employees were treated more favorably. And **the district's zero-tolerance policy regarding staff drug use was a legitimate, nondiscriminatory reason for the discharge**. *Wayne v. Glen Mills Schools*, 442 Fed.Appx. 667 (3d Cir. 2011).

◆   The U.S. Court of Appeals, Fifth Circuit, rejected a Louisiana teacher's claim that he was not rehired because of race or sex discrimination. He was hired to fill a teaching position for a teacher who was on a one-year sabbatical leave. When that teacher returned, the vacancy was eliminated. **As the people who did not rehire the teacher were the same people who hired him in the first place, the court found there was a strong inference that any reasons given by the board were not a pretext** for unlawful discrimination. There was substantial evidence that the teacher could not maintain order and discipline in his classes. *Watkins v. Johnson*, 428 Fed.Appx. 331 (5th Cir. 2011).

◆   An Arkansas school district employee sought a promotion from a lower-level purchasing job to a buyer position. Job requirements included a college degree and five years of public purchasing experience. None of the candidates for the job had a college degree, but all were granted interviews. Before any interviews, the superintendent withdrew the job announcement. A second job announcement was issued that deleted the college degree requirement and changed the title to "buyer/fixed asset administrator." A candidate with 20 years of purchasing experience was selected for the new position. The employee believed she was denied an interview based on race discrimination, and also believed the new title was "phony" and specifically tailored for the selected candidate. She sued the district, and the case reached the U.S. Court of Appeals, Eighth Circuit. It found the selected candidate had many years of relevant experience. **Even if the employee met the minimal job requirements, the district had a legitimate non-discriminatory reason for not hiring her.** *Dixon v. Pulaski County Special School Dist.*, 578 F.3d 862 (8th Cir. 2009).

◆   An African-American teacher was suspended for five days for calling a referee "the n-word" at a Virginia high school basketball game. While the teacher was initially told the referee and the NAACP had filed a complaint against her, she later learned no complaint was actually filed. **She filed a grievance, then a federal district court action against the school district, claiming "use of the 'n-word' between African-Americans is culturally acceptable."** The court rejected her due process and related claims that the NAACP charge had been used to coerce an admission of guilt. In a brief order, the U.S. Court of Appeals, Fourth Circuit, affirmed the judgment. *Parker v. Albemarle County Public Schools*, 332 Fed.Appx. 111 (5th Cir. 2009).

◆   A New Mexico teacher of African-American heritage accused the principal of treating him more harshly than others. The teacher's classroom was observed as out of control and disorganized. The principal placed him on a professional growth plan but the teacher rejected it. He claimed the principal yelled at him and suggested he might be involved in the theft of a laptop. The teacher sued the school district, superintendent and principal in a federal court for race discrimination. On appeal, the U.S. Court of Appeals, Tenth Circuit, held **an "adverse employment action" is one that significantly changes employee status,** such as hiring, firing, failing to promote, reassignment, or a substantial change in benefits. Placement on a growth plan and a reprimand angered and embarrassed the teacher, but did not affect his compensation or employment terms. As he failed to prove his performance was not the genuine reason for the reprimand and growth plan, the court ruled for the school district and officials. *Anderson v. Clovis Municipal Schools*, 265 Fed.Appx. 699 (10th Cir. 2008).

B. National Origin Discrimination

Title VII of the Civil Rights Act of 1964 permits institutional liability based on a supervisor's conduct. To prevail in a Title VII case, there must be evidence of an "abusive working environment" that is sufficiently severe or pervasive to alter the conditions of employment.

◆   Chicago school administrators conducted observations of an Indian-born teacher's classroom and found it was out of control. Students walked around the room, used bad language and lacked direction. Some made noises or yelled. Seats were overturned, and few students were doing any work. Shortly after the observations, the teacher took a sixth-month medical leave. When the board declined to renew the teacher's contract, she filed a federal case against the board and principal. The court rejected each of the claims, and the teacher appealed to the Seventh Circuit. It noted that the principal had also recommended not rehiring four American-born teachers. The court found the teacher did not produce sufficient evidence of discrimination. **The facts showed she was not rehired because she could not control her class.** As the evidence did not support a national origin bias claim, the court held for the board. *Dass v. Chicago Board of Educ.*, 675 F.3d 1060 (7th Cir. 2012).

◆   A teacher from Poland began working in the English as a Second Language (ESL) program of the Chicago Public Schools under a one-year contract. When the teacher complained that Hispanic students at the school were treated better than Polish students, she said the principal made anti-Polish remarks and gave her a notice for insubordination based on her refusal to follow the ESL teaching schedule. After a confrontation with the principal in which she said he called her a "stupid Polack," she complained to administrators. The principal assigned the teacher to a classroom with mostly Spanish-speaking students. At the end of the school year, her contract was not renewed and she sued the school board. The case reached the U.S. Court of Appeals, Seventh Circuit, which found no evidence that the board knew of any retaliatory basis for non-renewal. But the court held the teacher made a sufficient case for national origin discrimination based on anti-Polish comments to avoid pretrial judgment. A jury would have to decide if her account of the principal's derogatory remarks was to be believed. **Unlike constitutional claims, Title VII creates liability based on a supervisor's conduct and does not require action by a final policy-maker.** *Darchak v. City of Chicago Board of Educ.*, 580 F.3d 622 (7th Cir. 2009).

◆ An Iowa Spanish teacher she was not rehired because parents complained that students could not understand her English. She cited emails complaining about her accent and use of Spanish in class. After the principal told her that her contract would not be renewed, she sued the district, arguing that she was forced to resign due to a hostile work environment. A federal court found none of the claims of discriminatory or harassing conduct involved conduct by the district. Instead, parents and students were the perpetrators. **The teacher did not establish a hostile environment or that the district knew of any harassment.** She did not report any harassment based on national origin. As there was substantial evidence that the teacher had classroom management issues, the court held for the school district. *Lizama Lidon v. Anamosa Community School Dist.*, No. C08-45 EJM, 2010 WL 2293387 (N.D. Iowa 6/7/10).

◆ A Pennsylvania college professor, born in Iraq, was a U.S. citizen and a Muslim. He sued his employer under Title VII and 42 U.S.C. § 1981 after being denied tenure. Appeal reached the U.S. Supreme Court. It noted that Section 1981 states: "[a]ll persons ... shall have the same right to make and enforce contracts ... as is enjoyed by white citizens ..." The Court found that under Section 1981, Arabs, Englishmen, Germans and other ethnic groups are not to be considered a single race. Based on the history of Section 1981, it concluded Congress "intended to protect from discrimination identifiable classes of persons who are subjected to intentional discrimination solely because of their ancestry or ethnic characteristics." The Court affirmed the decision. **If the professor could prove he was subjected to intentional discrimination because he was Arab, rather than solely because of his place of origin or religion, he could proceed under Section 1981.** *St. Francis College v. Al-Khazraji*, 481 U.S. 604, 107 S.Ct. 2022, 95 L.Ed.2d 582 (1987).

◆ A Native American teacher claimed her principal told her she was "geographically, racially, culturally, and socially out of place" at their Utah school. He gave her bad evaluations and eventually recommended her contract not be renewed. The teacher claimed the principal made a racially derogatory remark to her on her last day of work, and she sued the district in a federal court. The case reached the U.S. Court of Appeals, Tenth Circuit, which held **a supervisor's statement may show a discriminatory motive in a Title VII case.** Under certain circumstances, the employer may be held liable if a decisionmaker who discharges the employee "merely acted as a rubber stamp, or the 'cat's paw' for a subordinate employee's prejudice," even if the supervisor had no discriminatory motive. The "cat's paw doctrine" did not apply if the decisionmaker made an impartial investigation, as had occurred in this case. *Natay v. Murray School Dist.*, 119 Fed.Appx. 259 (10th Cir. 2005).

C. Affirmative Action

Government entities, including school districts, must comply with the Equal Protection Clause of the Fourteenth Amendment, and with Titles VI and VII when devising affirmative action programs. The U.S. Supreme Court struck down a no-minority-layoff (or "affirmative retention") clause in a Michigan teacher collective bargaining agreement in Wygant v. Jackson Board of Educ.

◆   A Connecticut city used written and oral exams to fill vacancies for lieutenant and captain firefighter jobs. It ranked and promoted applicants by the "rule of three." It also hired a company to design its tests so minority candidates would not be disadvantaged. After a lieutenant exam, all 10 of the top-scoring candidates were white. Also, under the rule of three, seven whites and two Hispanics were eligible for promotion, while none of the black candidates reached that level. The city threw out the test results, and the formerly eligible white firefighters sued for race bias. The case reached the U.S. Supreme Court, which held that **the city could not intentionally discriminate against one group so as to avoid a lawsuit for unintentional bias by another group,** unless it could show that the test was not job-related. It held for the firefighters, reversing two lower court decisions for the city. *Ricci v. DeStefano*, 557 U.S. 557, 129 S.Ct. 2658, 174 L.Ed.2d 490 (2009).

◆   A city board of education's affirmative action plan called for the layoff of non-minority teachers with greater seniority than some minority teachers. A federal court held that the importance of providing minority teachers as "role models" for minority students as a remedy for past "societal discrimination" justified the layoff provision. The U.S. Supreme Court held the non-minority teachers were unfairly discriminated against in violation of the Equal Protection Clause. It rejected the "role model" justification because such a theory would allow racially based layoffs long after they were needed to cure the ills of past bias. Even if the board had sufficient justification for engaging in remedial or "benign" racial bias, laying off white teachers was too drastic and intrusive a remedy. **While hiring goals and promotion policies favorable to minorities are acceptable under the Equal Protection Clause, the actual laying off of a certain race of employees was unconstitutional.** "Denial of future employment is not as intrusive as loss of an existing job." *Wygant v. Jackson Board of Educ.*, 476 U.S. 267, 106 S.Ct. 1842, 90 L.Ed.2d 260 (1986).

◆   A Los Angeles high school teacher sought a transfer to a magnet school on the same campus. According to the teacher, the principal of the high school told him he need not apply for the transfer, because the teacher was of "the wrong ethnic origin." The teacher did not formally apply for the transfer, instead relying on this statement. He sued the principal, school district, school board, district superintendent and union for equal protection violations. A federal district court held the policy did not violate the teacher's equal protection rights, and he appealed. The U.S. Court of Appeals, Ninth Circuit, found it uncertain whether the transfer policy would have even affected the teacher. The principal's statement might be "wholly irrelevant" if he lacked decision-making power. He was the principal of the high school, not the magnet school. **The transfer policy could be modified based on an applicant's qualifications. LAUSD might have accepted the teacher's application based on need, his qualifications, or another reason.** Since there were many unanswered questions about the transfer policy, the case was returned to the district court. *Friery v. Los Angeles Unified School Dist.*, 448 F.3d 1146 (9th Cir. 2006).

V. RELIGIOUS DISCRIMINATION

Title VII prohibits employment discrimination on the basis of religion, but exempts religious employers from coverage. The U.S. Supreme Court has held that an employer discharges its duty under Title VII by making a reasonable accommodation of an employee's religious needs, but no duty to accommodate arises where it would work an undue hardship upon the employer.

◆ A Washington school employee, who was a devout Christian, believed the district superintendent wanted her to lie to an independent contractor who was her immediate supervisor. According to the employee, the superintendent became physically threatening when she objected. She said the superintendent touched her and jabbed her finger at her, yelling and cursing with arms flailing. As the employee believed the superintendent was instructing her to tell lies to the contractor, she refused to comply with the superintendent's instructions.

Later, the employee complained to school board members and told them she could not file a formal complaint because staff members were "beholden" to the superintendent. When the superintendent again told the employee to lie to the contractor, she refused, citing religious requirements. This resulted in further threats and yelling by the superintendent. Following a short personal leave, the employee quit. She sued the school district and superintendent in a state court for religious discrimination. Appeal reached the Court of Appeals of Washington, which noted the employee had filed the action under the state Law Against Discrimination (LAD). **As the LAD did not recognize a religious "failure to accommodate claim," the action had to be dismissed.** The court rejected the employee's invitation to import federal standards from Title VII. Although she claimed retaliation by the superintendent, the court found any such treatment was of short duration and was not "adverse employment action." *Short v. Battle Ground School Dist.*, 279 P.3d 902 (Wash. Ct. App. 2012).

◆ A New York teaching assistant had problems with co-workers, was found unreceptive to supervision and was reassigned twice. A principal denied his request to leave school for prayers, but then allowed him to use personal time. He greeted Muslim students in Arabic with a traditional greeting meaning "peace be upon you." At a parent-teacher conference, the employee greeted a young Muslim child by picking her up, hugging her and kissing her on the forehead. The child's mother believed this was inappropriate, and the principal issued the employee a counseling memorandum advising him not to speak Arabic at school or to bring a Quran into classrooms. A school building committee issued a memorandum to the staff stating that only English should be spoken, as the school was an English-as-a-second-language facility. The employee posted a copy of the memorandum and discussed it in non-school Internet discussion groups. After the employee received a poor evaluation, he was denied tenure.

A federal district court found the posting of the counseling memorandum was not a matter of public concern that was entitled to constitutional protection. Legitimate reasons existed for denying tenure, as conflicts with staff members led to reassignments and the employee was unreceptive to supervision. Posting the memorandum disregarded confidentiality concerns relating to the Muslim child's family. **A Title VII religious discrimination claim failed, as the district offered the employee reasonable accommodations for prayers.** He was allowed to use personal time and lunch breaks to attend Friday prayers. As the district provided nondiscriminatory reasons for denying the employee tenure, the court held in its favor. *Mustafa v. Syracuse City School Dist.*, No. 5:05-CV-813, 2010 WL 4447774 (N.D.N.Y. 11/1/10).

◆ An Indiana elementary school principal argued with a Jewish teacher on her staff and allegedly said "Heil Hitler" with her arm outstretched to several staff members who had raised their hands in a meeting. The principal also did not excuse the teacher from an "All Student Sing-Along" with Christian carols, or the school's first ever "Staff Ham Breakfast." Conflict between the principal and teacher escalated, and the teacher filed a religious harassment complaint against her. A new superintendent notified the principal that her contract would not be renewed. She sued the school system for unlawful termination and religious discrimination. The case reached the U.S. Court of Appeals, Seventh Circuit, which found that **when an employer has a legitimate, nondiscriminatory reason for firing an employee, "it simply doesn't matter" if the employee presents allegations of discrimination.** The school system had a legitimate, nondiscriminatory reason for not rehiring the principal. *Larson v. Portage Township School Corp.*, 293 Fed.Appx. 415 (7th Cir. 2008).

◆ An Arkansas school district required a teacher to attend in-service trainings at a Christian college where an opening prayer was said. He objected to mandatory prayers at teacher training meetings and the display of a Bible and scriptural quotes in the superintendent's office. The superintendent refused to remove the displays. The teacher sued the district, superintendent and other school officials in a federal court, which held that prayers at mandatory faculty meetings and in-service trainings violated the Establishment Clause. However, the Bible and framed scripture displays, as well as religious jewelry and T-shirts worn by students and staff, were protected by the Speech and Free Exercise Clauses. The case reached the Eighth Circuit, which noted that the Constitution forbids the government from conveying a message that it endorses a particular religious position. **The prayers at mandatory meetings and trainings unconstitutionally conveyed religious endorsement.** The court precluded prayers at mandatory meetings, regardless of whether the teacher was present. *Warnock v. Archer*, 380 F.3d 1076 (8th Cir. 2004).

The teacher later attended a baccalaureate ceremony at a district high school that included an invocation and benediction by ministers. The court granted his motion for contempt, finding that school employees had planned and supervised the ceremony where prayers were offered. The school district appealed to the Eighth Circuit, which affirmed the order, based on ample evidence that school employees were involved in almost every aspect of the event. *Warnock v. Archer*, 443 F.3d 954 (8th Cir. 2006).

◆   A Connecticut high school teacher belonged to a church that required members to refrain from secular employment on designated holy days. He missed about six school days each year for religious purposes, but the relevant collective bargaining agreement allowed only three days of paid leave for religious observation. Although the agreement allowed three days paid leave for "necessary personal business," the district said it could not be used for religious purposes. The teacher repeatedly asked for permission to use three days of his "necessary personal business" leave for religious purposes. He offered to pay for a substitute if the school board would pay him for the extra days that he missed. The board rejected this, and the teacher sued the board, alleging the policy on "necessary personal business" leave was religious discrimination.

The U.S. Supreme Court held that the school district did not need to accept the teacher's proposals, even if this would not cause "undue hardship." **The board was only bound to offer a fair and reasonable accommodation of his religious needs.** The collective bargaining agreement policy of allowing three days paid leave for religious purposes, but excluding additional days of "necessary personal business" leave for religious purposes, would not be reasonable, if paid leave was provided "for all purposes *except* religious ones." Because the lower courts had not decided whether the "necessary personal business" leave policy had been administered fairly in the past, the Court remanded the case for resolution of that question. *Ansonia Board of Educ. v. Philbrook*, 479 U.S. 60, 107 S.Ct. 367, 93 L.Ed.2d 305 (1986).

On remand, the Second Circuit held that the accommodation was reasonable. *Philbrook v. Ansonia Board of Educ.*, 925 F.2d 47 (2d Cir. 1991).

VI. AGE DISCRIMINATION

The federal Age Discrimination in Employment Act of 1967 (ADEA), 29 U.S.C. § 621 et seq., is part of the Fair Labor Standards Act. It prohibits the use of age as a criterion for employment with respect to persons age 40 and over, and applies to institutions with 20 or more employees that "affect interstate commerce." The ADEA contains an exception allowing the use of age as an employment criterion "where age is a bona fide occupational qualification reasonably necessary to the normal operation of the particular business."

In Jones v. Oklahoma City Public Schools, *this chapter, the Tenth Circuit held the ADEA, like other federal anti-discrimination laws, has a "causation requirement." While age need not have been the only factor in an employment decision, it must be shown that "age was the factor that made a difference." The Supreme Court held the "ADEA's requirement that an employer take adverse action 'because of' age [means] that age was the 'reason' that the employer decided to act."* Gross v. FBL Financial Services, Inc., *129 S.Ct. 2343 (U.S. 2009).*

A. Employment Decisions

◆   A 42-year-old New York woman sought employment as a school librarian, but the school district hired a 35-year-old man instead. She filed discrimination claims with a federal agency, but she did not pursue a lawsuit. Another librarian position opened up in the district four years later, and the woman applied. This time, a school selection committee chose a 32-year-old female for the job.

The woman filed a second federal agency charge and then sued the district for violating the ADEA. The district superintendent was unable to offer pretrial testimony due to a grave illness, but he made a sworn statement shortly before he died. He explained that the woman was not interviewed due to her history of working short-term jobs. He also said her job skills were inferior to those of the selected candidate. After the court held for the school district, the woman appealed to the Second Circuit. It found testimony by other district witnesses corroborated the superintendent's statement that the woman was not interviewed because of her spotty employment record, not because of her age. Evidence showed the applicant had worked in 12 librarian or education jobs in the 10 years before she applied to the district. By contrast, the candidate who was hired for the second job opening had worked for six years at an elementary school, had a master's degree in library science and had completed a librarian internship. **This evidence led the court to hold that a jury could find the school district did not discriminate against the woman when it selected someone younger for the job.** As a result, the court held for the district. *Bucalo v. Shelter Island Union Free School Dist.*, 691 F.3d 119 (2d Cir. 2012).

◆   After 27 years with a school district, a Texas employee was discharged. She said she was fired in retaliation for engaging in protected activities and that she was discriminated against because of her race, national origin, age and gender. The employee was 48 years old at the time of discharge, and she was replaced by a person who was three years older. A state court held she did not make out a valid preliminary case of age discrimination, but it refused to dismiss the case. When the case reached the Supreme Court of Texas, it explained that the Texas Human Rights Law is essentially identical to federal law. It noted the Eleventh Circuit has held that **an age discrimination lawsuit can succeed where a person was replaced by an older worker, if it can be shown that the replacement was put into the job to avoid an age discrimination lawsuit.**

In *O'Connor v. Consolidated Coin Caterers Corp.*, 517 U.S. 308 (1996), the Supreme Court held an inference of age bias "cannot be drawn from the replacement of one worker with another worker insignificantly younger." While being replaced by an older worker was not fatal to her claim, the employee failed to show she was unlawfully replaced because of her age. A greater inference of bias exists when there is a large discrepancy in the ages of the two employees. In the court's view, an inference of bias cannot be drawn from replacement by an "insignificantly younger" worker. And no such inference can be drawn from replacement by an insignificantly older worker. As a result, the court held that the employee could not make out a valid preliminary case of age bias. *Mission Consolidated Independent School Dist. v. Garcia*, 372 S.W.3d 629 (Tex. 2012).

◆   An Oklahoma school district eliminated a longtime administrator's job and reassigned her to an elementary principal job at a similar pay rate. Her vacation benefits were immediately affected and the next year, her salary went down by about $17,000. A month after the administrator was reassigned, a new position called "executive director of teaching and learning" with job duties similar to the administrator's former job was created. At the time of her reassignment, the administrator was nearly 60 years old. A 47-year-old employee was hired for the newly created job. The administrator sued the school district in a federal district court for violating the ADEA. After the court held for the district, she appealed to the U.S. Court of Appeals, Tenth Circuit. It found the ADEA requires an employee to show that "age was the factor that made a difference" in an "adverse employment action." **The requirement was satisfied in this case because the administrator lost salary and went to a job with a significantly different status and different duties.** If an employee shows a factual dispute regarding the truth of an employer's reason for acting, a jury can infer the employer had a discriminatory reason. According to the Tenth Circuit, the lower court should have allowed the case to go to a jury. Since it did not, the judgment was reversed. *Jones v. Oklahoma City Public Schools*, 617 F.3d 1273 (10th Cir. 2010).

◆   A Maryland teacher with extensive experience teaching English, Spanish, German and French was turned down for a foreign language teaching position. After learning that younger teachers were hired to fill vacancies for which she qualified, she sued the school board for age discrimination. A state court found the teacher's ADEA claim was barred by Eleventh Amendment immunity. On appeal, the state court of special appeals reversed the judgment, finding the board had waived its Eleventh Amendment Immunity. The Court of Appeals of Maryland held a state statute barred county education boards from raising a sovereign immunity defense to any claim of $100,000 or less. **As the state expressly waived its immunity for any and all claims of $100,000 or less, the teacher could pursue claims against the board.** *Board of Educ. of Baltimore County v. Zimmer-Rubert*, 409 Md. 200, 973 A.2d 233 (Md. 2009).

◆   A demoted 63-year-old Louisiana special education director was not forced from her job based on age, race or sex, according to the Fifth Circuit Court of Appeals. Although the director claimed she was replaced by a younger man of a different race, the school board stated that she mishandled the reporting of her school system's special education to state authorities. **Her only evidence of age bias was the superintendent's remark that the board sought to project an image of youth and vitality when recruiting new teachers.** A state law claim was returned to a lower court so it could explain its reason for dismissal. *Crary v. East Baton Rouge Parish School Board*, 340 Fed.Appx. 239 (5th Cir. 2009).

◆   An atomic power laboratory in New York decided to cut 31 jobs. It did so in part by ranking employees on job performance, flexibility and criticality. The flexibility factor assessed whether the employees' skills were transferable. The criticality factor assessed the importance of the employees' skills to the lab. When 30 of the 31 people laid off were age 40 or older, an ADEA lawsuit ensued. A jury ruled that the layoff process had a disparate impact on older employees, but the Second Circuit reversed, finding the employees should have been required to prove that the selection process was unreasonable. The Supreme Court held **the burden should have been on the employer to prove that its layoff process used reasonable factors other than age.** *Meacham v. Knolls Atomic Power Laboratory*, 554 U.S. 84, 128 S.Ct. 2395, 171 L.Ed.2d 283 (2008).

◆   A New York school district defeated an age discrimination case by explaining that **the person selected for a teaching job had a better interview than the complaining party.** The complaining party was rejected for two teaching jobs and claimed this was based on age discrimination. The U.S. Court of Appeals, Second Circuit, affirmed a lower court finding that she did not make out a preliminary showing of age discrimination. The district's non-discriminatory reason was sufficient to avoid further proceedings in the case. *Boyer v. Riverhead Cent. School Dist.*, 343 Fed.Appx. 740 (2d Cir. 2009).

◆   A 60-year-old Nebraska teacher sought a full-time teaching job after her workload was reduced. She applied for four vacancies in the same district. Two of the jobs required special education certification, which she lacked. Another included coaching duties. The district hired younger female candidates. The teacher sued, asserting age bias and First Amendment violations. The case reached the Eighth Circuit Court of Appeals, where the district argued that the people who were hired were all better qualified than the teacher. The court agreed. **No inference of bias arises when younger applicants are more qualified than or similarly qualified to an older candidate.** The teacher's First Amendment claims lacked merit, as she did not raise any issue of public concern. *Wingate v. Gage County School Dist. No. 34*, 528 F.3d 1074 (8th Cir. 2008).

B.   Wages and Benefits

In Gross v. FBL Financial Services, *557 U.S. 167 (2009), the U.S. Supreme Court held* **age discrimination claimants must show age was the sole reason for an employer's adverse action under the Age Discrimination in Employment Act (ADEA).** *Relying in part on* Gross, *the U.S. Court of Appeals, Tenth Circuit, held a 54-year-old Utah teacher did not show she was not rehired solely because of her age in* Reeder v. Wasatch County School Dist., *below.*

◆   A pair of Kansas school custodians claimed their positions were eliminated due to age discrimination and not "serious budgetary problems," as the district claimed. When the case reached the U.S. Court of Appeals, Tenth Circuit, it held the action was untimely. In the court's opinion, the custodians should have sued when they first learned their jobs were being eliminated. At that time, they agreed to transfer to vacant custodial positions at a lower pay grade. In ruling against the custodians, the court focused on the time they had first learned of discriminatory actions, not when they were actually laid off a few years later.

The court examined a recent federal amendment known as the Lilly Ledbetter Fair Pay Act. This law allowed parties to file "discrimination in compensation" claims but did not alter existing law requiring employees to file an action within 300 days of when they first learned of injury. **They cannot wait until years later, when the "consequences of the acts become most painful."** *Almond v. Unified School Dist. #501*, 655 F.3d 1174 (10th Cir. 2011).

◆ A 54-year-old Utah provisional teacher's contract was not renewed. She claimed "student interns who had almost no teaching experience" were being hired as replacements for herself and other teachers over the age of 40. In a federal action, the teacher claimed ADEA violations and conspiracy by the district and its officials. According to the U.S. Court of Appeals, Tenth Circuit, the fact that interns were paid half the salary of a regular teacher did not necessarily relate to age. **The court held "the desire to save money is not a motive prohibited by the ADEA."** Any savings would be "age-neutral." There was no evidence linking the teacher's age with eligibility for retirement or the cost of benefits. As she did not show a correlation between the district's desire to save money and her age, the court affirmed the judgment. *Reeder v. Wasatch County School Dist.*, 359 Fed.Appx. 920 (10th Cir. 2009).

◆ Near the end of his 23-year career, a custodian and building operator at a Kansas school district was diagnosed with a ruptured aneurysm and took three months of Family and Medical Leave Act (FMLA) leave. Two years later, the employee had a heart attack and underwent bypass surgery, which forced him to take 12 weeks of FMLA leave plus three weeks of unpaid leave. Later, he had an abdominal hernia at work and missed additional months of work time. According to the employee, the district's human resources director told him "he was too old" and was "getting on in age." Another administrator discussed health and early retirement options with the employee, and he filed age and disability discrimination charges against the district. The case reached the U.S. Court of Appeals, Tenth Circuit, which noted that **the employee was not discharged or demoted but had retired**. While he could bring a lawsuit based on "constructive discharge," he did not show he was forced into retirement, and only asserted undesirable treatment. There was contrary evidence that administrators made no threats, but only suggested that he retire. *Lara v. Unified School Dist. # 501*, 350 Fed.Appx. 280 (10th Cir. 2009).

◆ An Iowa school district offered an early retirement incentive package to teachers who had worked for 20 years and had reached the age of 55. The plan was announced as a way to show appreciation for services rendered and save the district funds. Among other things, teachers had to be at least age 55 and have 20 years of experience of continuous contract service in the district by the end of the current school year to qualify. A teacher with 30 years of experience in the district would not reach 55 until three months after the end of the school year. The school board found her ineligible for the plan, and she sued for age discrimination in violation of the Iowa Civil Rights Act (ICRA).

The case reached the Supreme Court of Iowa, which noted that state law expressly allowed early retirement plans with minimum age requirements. It held **ICRA provisions relating to age discrimination did not apply to retirement plans or benefit systems unless they were a subterfuge to avoid the ICRA**. There was no evidence of age-related discrimination by the district, as it had a legitimate reason for setting the minimum age for plan participants at 55. The district committed no ICRA violation by expanding the pool of qualified employees when it later lowered the years of service requirement to 15. Iowa law gave school districts discretion to set the age for early retirement benefits and did not require them to offer the same plan each year, or to offer plans at all. As a result, the court held for the district. *Weddum v. Davenport Community School Dist.*, 750 N.W.2d 114 (Iowa 2008).

◆ Veteran Mississippi police officers challenged their city's revised pay policy because it gave proportionately higher raises to officers with fewer than five years of tenure. They claimed the policy had a disparate impact on them. The U.S. Supreme Court held that **the officers could sue for disparate impact bias under the ADEA**. To win, the officers would have to identify a "specific test, requirement, or practice with the pay plan that ha[d] an adverse impact on older workers." The city claimed that the differential was justified by the need to make junior officers' salaries competitive. The Court determined that the policy was based on reasonable factors other than age and thus did not violate the ADEA. *Smith v. City of Jackson*, 544 U.S. 228, 125 S.Ct. 1536, 161 L.Ed.2d 410 (2005).

◆ Kentucky created a disability pension plan that favored county and state "hazardous" workers who took disability retirement before they became eligible for a pension. An employee became eligible for normal or disability retirement at age 55. He worked until he became disabled at age 61, at which point the plan calculated his retirement pay as if he had retired without a disability. He sought the higher benefits available for employees who retired with a disability and sued under the ADEA when he was unsuccessful. The U.S. Supreme Court held that **Kentucky's disability retirement pension plan could favor younger workers because it did not discriminate against employees on the basis of age**. The plan had a clear non-age-related rationale for its disparity – to treat a disabled employee as if he became disabled after, rather than before, he became eligible for normal retirement. Age factored into the calculation only because the normal retirement rules permissibly considered age. *Kentucky Retirement Systems v. EEOC*, 554 U.S. 135, 128 S.Ct. 2361, 171 L.Ed.2d 322 (2008).

VII. DISABILITY DISCRIMINATION

A. Federal Law

Rehabilitation Act Section 504 bars any federal funding recipient from discriminating against an "otherwise qualified individual with a disability." An otherwise qualified individual with a disability can perform the "essential functions" of the job "with reasonable accommodation" of a disability. But employers need not accommodate a disability if it creates an undue hardship.

Congress enacted the Americans with Disabilities Act (ADA) in 1991 to extend disability protection to most public and private employees who worked for employers with at least 15 employees. Congress contemplated that the same legal analysis applied in Section 504 and ADA cases. But Congress found in 2008 that the Supreme Court was interpreting the ADA differently from Section 504, and it acted to broaden certain ADA definitions. The 2008 Amendments defined the term "disability" to mean "a physical or mental impairment that substantially limits one or more major life activities" of an individual.

In 2010, the U.S. Department of Justice amended ADA regulations for public entities. A key provision requires use of design standards consistent with guidelines published by the U.S. Architectural and Transportation Barriers Compliance Board. A new rule defined "service animal" as a dog that has been individually trained to do work or perform tasks for the benefit of an individual with a disability. Apart from a limited exception permitting use of trained miniature horses, only individually trained dogs qualify as "service animals."

In 2011, the U.S. Equal Employment Opportunity Commission (EEOC) issued Regulations and interpretive guidance on the 2008 amendments to the Americans with Disabilities Act (ADA). According to the EEOC guidance, the primary purpose of the 2008 ADA amendments was to make it easier for people with disabilities to obtain ADA protection. The EEOC states the primary issue in ADA cases should be whether an employer is meeting its legal obligations and whether discrimination has occurred, not whether an individual meets a qualifying definition of disability. The guidance offers definitions of physical, mental and psychological impairment that include lists of qualifying impairments. Some of the major life activities are caring for oneself, performing manual tasks, seeing, hearing, sleeping, walking, standing, speaking, breathing, learning, reading, concentrating, thinking, communicating, interacting with others and working. Under the 2011 guidance, it is unlawful for a covered entity to use qualification standards, employment tests or other selection criteria that screen out individuals with disabilities or classes of individuals with disabilities. A defense is offered in the guidance for employers who can show an individual's claimed impairment is both transitory and minor. Federal Register, Vol. 76, No. 58, Page 16978, March 25, 2011. 29 C.F.R. Part 1630.

◆ For about 15 years, a substitute teacher worked for Albuquerque Public Schools (APS). She then began to bring a registered service dog to school with her. When APS learned the teacher was doing so, it ordered her to stop. Later, APS denied the teacher's formal request to bring the service dog to school and suspended her for one week. Although no doctor had ever diagnosed her with severe asthma, she sued APS for violating the state Human Rights Act (HRA) and the ADA. A federal court held for APS, and the teacher appealed.

The U.S. Court of Appeals, Tenth Circuit, noted the attempts to bring the service dog to school had taken place before the January 1, 2009, effective date of the ADA Amendments Act of 2008. The court found the act was intended to remove constraints on the definition of "disability" created by Supreme Court interpretations of the ADA. Since the events in this case took place before the effective date of the 2008 act, pre-2008 standards applied. In any event, the lower court had held the teacher was not "disabled" under federal law. As for the state HRA claim, the lower court had found New Mexico state courts apply the same standards as those used for the ADA. And the teacher presented no medical testimony that she had severe asthma. Instead, she relied on her own assessment. **The court said that even if state law standards applied, the state supreme court probably would not apply the ADA amendments retroactively.** As a result, the court held for the APS. *Latham v. Board of Educ. of Albuquerque Public Schools*, 489 Fed.Appx. 239 (10th Cir. 2012).

◆   An Idaho special education teacher had a history of depression and bipolar disorder. In order to renew her teaching certificate, she had to complete six hours of professional development training over a five-year period, including three hours of college credit. During the summer before her certification was to expire, the teacher experienced major depression that rendered her unable to take the required classes. Her request for provisional authorization was denied by the district superintendent and board of trustees. The district then hired one of two certified special education teachers who were available for work. At a board hearing, the teacher testified at length about her history of mental illness and how her depressive episode prevented her from completing the credits. But the board voted to discharge her because of her lack of action over five years.

In a case that reached the Ninth Circuit Court of Appeals, the teacher asserted the board had a duty to honor her request for provisional certification as a "reasonable accommodation." The court reviewed a federal regulation defining "qualified individual with a disability." Under the regulation, the individual must be able to perform the "essential functions" of a position, with or without reasonable accommodation. **The court found no requirement for an employer to provide any reasonable accommodations to an individual with a disability who could not meet job prerequisites on their own.** Since an individual who could not satisfy job prerequisites could not be considered "qualified" under the ADA, the teacher was not entitled to protection. As a result, the court held for the school board. *Johnson v. Board of Trustees of Boundary County School Dist. No. 101*, 666 F.3d 561 (9th Cir. 2011).

◆   A Connecticut teacher was unable to convince the Second Circuit Court of Appeals that her bad back, fatigue and insomnia rendered her disabled under federal law definitions. **While the teacher claimed her ability to stand or walk was limited, the court found no medical evidence supported her claim.** Without medical evidence, the court held she could not show she had a disability. Moreover, the teacher's school district had a "well-chronicled" reason for dismissing her based on her "chronic tardiness and ineffective teaching." Since the board's stated reasons were not found to be a pretext for discrimination, the district prevailed on the ADA discrimination claim. And because the teacher could not show she had a disability under the ADA, her reasonable accommodation claim failed. As for the accommodations she sought, she did not show 10 extra minutes to report for work would help her. It would be unreasonable to have someone on call when she could not arrive on time. *Farina v. Branford Board of Educ.*, 458 Fed.Appx. 13 (2d Cir. 2011).

◆   A teacher sought accommodations for part of the New York State Teacher Certification Examinations. She sought accommodations for a written assignment known as the LAST, identifying herself as dyslexic and seeking a dictionary, extra time, frequent breaks and an oral examination. The National

Evaluation Systems (NES), which contracted with the state to administer the LAST, rejected the requests. The teacher underwent a full neuropsychological evaluation and made later attempts to gain accommodations from the NES. By the time the NES agreed to provide her accommodations such as a reader, extended time and breaks, and a separate testing room, she had lost her teaching position. A federal court explained that an employer or service need not make an accommodation if doing so would fundamentally alter the nature of the service, program or activity. **If an examinee seeks an accommodation that would preclude accurate evaluation of abilities measured by the test, it is not unlawful to deny the accommodation.** The ability to spell, punctuate, capitalize and write a paragraph was an inherent part of the LAST. As exempting the teacher from the LAST writing, spelling and punctuation requirements would not put her on a level playing field with non-disabled persons, the court held for the department and the NES. *Falchenberg v. New York State Dep't of Educ.*, 567 F.Supp.2d 513 (S.D.N.Y. 2008).

◆ A Kentucky teacher suffered a head injury in a bicycling accident. She suffered various ailments, including outbursts of anger. At one point, she confronted a group of students playing basketball unsupervised outside the school. The students claimed that she threatened to kill them and made inappropriate comments about their families and their sexual activity. After an investigation, the school superintendent notified her that her contract was being terminated for conduct unbecoming a teacher. The state court system upheld the decision, and the state Education Professional Standards Board then revoked her teaching certificate for 10 years. The state convicted the teacher on criminal charges of terroristic threatening as a result of the basketball incident. She sued the school board for civil rights violations. A federal court held for the board, and the teacher appealed to the Sixth Circuit. The court held that **an employer may fire an employee for disqualifying conduct, even if that conduct occurs as a result of a disability.** As the board fired the teacher for threatening the group of boys and making inappropriate remarks, it had a legitimate, nondiscriminatory reason for firing her. So the court affirmed the judgment. *Macy v. Hopkins County School Board of Educ.*, 484 F.3d 357 (6th Cir. 2007).

◆ A Georgia school bus driver who suffered panic attacks was not protected by the Americans with Disabilities Act (ADA). She could be discharged since she could not perform her job without a reasonable accommodation. The driver claimed her school board had to accommodate her disability, but a federal court found that the board did not commit any discrimination against her. The U.S. Court of Appeals, Eleventh Circuit, upheld the ruling, finding that **the driver did not have a disability as defined in the ADA.** *Albright v. Columbia Board of Educ.*, 135 Fed.Appx. 344 (11th Cir. 2005).

◆ A Missouri teacher worked as an exceptional education case manager. This required frequent visits to several schools, extensive walking and stair-climbing and repetitive handwriting. She was injured in a car accident and two slip-and-fall incidents, one of which occurred at a high school. The teacher went on medical leave, returning to her case manager position after four months, but she was unable to perform physical tasks required by the job. Her disability discrimination case reached the Eighth Circuit. It held **temporary impairments with little or no long-term impact are not disabilities under the ADA**. There was no evidence that the teacher had a long-term or permanent disability or could not perform a broad range of jobs in various classes. *Samuels v. Kansas City Missouri School Dist.*, 437 F.3d 797 (8th Cir. 2006).

◆ A Texas teacher was hospitalized for depression in a mental institution during her third year of probationary employment for a school district. She took medical leave for over three months. When the school board voted not to rehire her for the following school year, she asserted ADA violations based on having a record of depression or being regarded by the district as disabled. She sued the district in a federal court, which ruled for the district. On appeal to the U.S. Court of Appeals, Fifth Circuit, she argued that her leave and hospitalization proved a record of disability. The court disagreed. Hospitalization itself does not establish a record of mental disability. A presumption that temporary hospitalization is disabling would be contrary to ADA goals. Here, the teacher's condition did not cause a substantial limitation in a major life activity. She was not disabled within the meaning of the ADA. The evidence showed that **the teacher's depression was treatable with medication and did not prevent her from working**. Her leave and hospitalization did not establish a disability and did not prove that the district regarded her depression as preventing her from performing her job. The court affirmed the judgment. *Winters v. Pasadena Independent School Dist.*, 124 Fed.Appx. 822 (5th Cir. 2005).

◆ Congress exceeded its authority by allowing monetary damage awards against the states in ADA cases, according to a 2001 U.S. Supreme Court decision. The Court held that Congress did not identify a history and pattern of irrational employment discrimination against individuals with disabilities by the states when it enacted the ADA, and therefore, the states were entitled to Eleventh Amendment immunity from such claims. As a result, **two University of Alabama employees were unsuccessful in their attempt to recover money damages under the ADA from their employer** for disability discrimination they claimed to have been subjected to. *Board of Trustees of Univ. of Alabama v. Garrett*, 531 U.S. 356 (2001).

◆ The U.S. Supreme Court held that tuberculosis and other contagious diseases may be considered disabilities under Section 504. The case involved a Florida elementary school teacher who was discharged because of the continued recurrence of tuberculosis. She sued her school board under Section 504 in a U.S. district court. The case reached the U.S. Supreme Court, which held **tuberculosis is a disability under Section 504 because it affects the respiratory system and the ability to work, which is a "major life activity."** The Court reasoned the teacher's contagion and physical impairment resulted from tuberculosis. It would be unfair to allow employers to distinguish between a disease's potential effect on others and its effect on the employee to justify discriminatory treatment. Discrimination based on the contagious effects of a physical impairment would be inconsistent with the purpose of Section 504.

The case was returned to a lower court to determine whether the teacher was otherwise qualified for her job and if the board could reasonably accommodate her. *School Board of Nassau County v. Arline*, 480 U.S. 273 (1987).

The district court then held the teacher was "otherwise qualified," as **she posed no threat of transmitting tuberculosis** to others. The court ordered her reinstatement or $768,724 in wages, representing her earnings until retirement. *Arline v. School Board of Nassau County*, 692 F.Supp. 1286 (M.D. Fla. 1988).

In *Bragdon v. Abbott*, 524 U.S. 624 (1998), the Supreme Court held an individual with HIV was entitled to the protections of the ADA, despite the fact that she was not yet symptomatic.

B. State Statutes

State civil rights laws including the Florida Civil Rights Act and California Fair Employment and Housing Act are construed by courts in a similar manner as the Americans with Disabilities Act and Section 504 of the Rehabilitation Act. They all bar discrimination against individuals based on a disability.

◆ **A Michigan school social worker with fecal incontinence could not convince the Sixth Circuit that her employer violated state and federal laws protecting people with disabilities.** The social worker had exhausted a three-year cap on her leave, and there was evidence that she could not perform her job even with accommodations. It was not error for a lower court to have permitted questioning of the social worker on the potential danger to students of abruptly leaving them alone while she used a lavatory, and the risks that they could come into contact with germs. The court did not give improper jury instructions or commit error by allowing evidence that the social worker had obtained disability benefits. It was also not error to refuse to overturn a jury verdict for the school district. The judgment was affirmed. *Hubbard v. Detroit Public Schools*, 372 Fed.Appx. 631 (6th Cir. 2010).

◆ A Florida school district conducted a criminal background check on a teaching applicant and learned he had misrepresented his record. Without revealing that the applicant was twice convicted of driving under the influence, the district human resources director notified a school principal and vice principal that the application was inaccurate. A school district committee decided the teaching applicant would need to provide proof of treatment to qualify for employment. The job was reposted, and a qualified candidate with many years of teaching experience was soon hired. The day after she was hired, the teaching applicant gave the district his treatment records. The human resources director advised him that he had been requalified as an applicant, but the applicant made an administrative complaint against the district, asserting that he was not hired based on his "perceived disability" of alcoholism.

After an administrative hearing, the case reached a Florida District Court of Appeal. It noted that **to be "perceived" as having a disability, the teacher had to show his perceived disability involved a major life activity that was "substantially limiting."** There was no evidence that the district perceived him as "disabled." Once the applicant provided proof of treatment, he was requalified for job vacancies. The district had a neutral policy and did not discriminate against the applicant based on a perception of disability. *St. Johns County School Dist. v. O'Brien*, 973 So.2d 535 (Fla. Dist. Ct. App. 2007).

◆ A Washington school employee who wore hearing aids was hired as a part-time assistant cook at a high school but soon transferred to a middle school to work more hours. However, she did not get along with her supervisor, and she returned to the high school after only nine days. She filed a complaint with the school district, but it investigated and found no harassment or discrimination. Dissatisfied, the employee sued the school district for violating the Washington Law Against Discrimination. She then transferred to a school where she could work full time. There, the employee disregarded the food services director's instruction to use sick time to have a hearing aid repaired. The director claimed the employee had to leave for safety reasons, and escorted her out of a training session. She quit and added retaliation and constructive discharge claims.

A state court held for the school district, and the employee appealed. The state court of appeals noted that **when using her hearing aids, the employee's impairment did not have a substantially limiting effect on her abilities**. Evidence indicated that her disability was easily accommodated. The brief conflict with the middle school supervisor was investigated immediately and resolved. Each of the employee's transfer requests had been granted. An undesirable work situation alone did not support a claim for constructive discharge. Nothing supported the employee's claim that the safety-based order to repair her hearing aid was a deliberate act that had forced her to quit. *Townsend v. Walla Walla School Dist.*, 196 P.3d 748 (Wash. Ct. App. 2008).

◆ The Sixth Circuit has held that **a disease or condition caused by illegal drug use is not a disability unless the individual has successfully completed a supervised rehabilitation program and no longer uses illegal drugs.** In a case involving an Ohio school bus driver who tested positive for marijuana use after driving disabled children to school, the court found little medical evidence of drug addiction. And she failed to show she had a disability or any indication that the district regarded her as a drug addict. *Rhoads v. Board of Educ. of Mad River Local School Dist.*, 103 Fed.Appx. 888 (6th Cir. 2004).

◆ A California school district offered employee health coverage from several group health maintenance organizations, including PacifiCare. Although the PacifiCare plan specifically excluded in vitro fertilization (IVF) treatment from coverage, it covered many other forms of infertility treatment. A teacher's wife was unable to become pregnant due to polycystic ovarian disease. One of her doctors requested pre-authorization for IVF, despite being aware that it was not covered by the teacher's PacifiCare plan. The teacher and his wife began IVF treatment at their own expense and filed a discrimination charge against the district, alleging a violation of the California Fair Employment and Housing Act (FEHA). A state superior court awarded judgment to the district.

The state court of appeal affirmed. It held that broad distinctions applying to the treatment of dissimilar conditions, and pertaining to individuals with and without disabilities, are not "distinctions based on disability." While the distinctions might have a greater impact on certain individuals, they were not intentional disability discrimination and did not violate the ADA. **The discrimination alleged by the teacher was not genuinely based on fertility, because the plan covered many other forms of infertility treatment.** IVF was an expensive treatment used only when others failed. The court explained that if the FEHA and the similar ADA prohibited treatment-based distinctions, they would mandate comprehensive health coverage for all job-related disabilities. This was not the intent of FEHA. Federal case law interpreting the ADA did not prohibit treatment-based distinctions. *Knight v. Hayward Unified School Dist.*, 132 Cal.App.4th 121, 33 Cal.Rptr.3d 298 (Cal. Ct. App. 2005).

VIII. DISCRIMINATION AGAINST VETERANS

State veterans preference acts prohibit discrimination against veterans, but do not require the hiring of unqualified preference-eligible veterans. The Uniformed Services Employment and Reemployment Rights Act (USERRA) prevents employers from using an applicant's membership in a branch of the uniformed services as a motivating factor in employment decisions.

◆   An Alabama school board did not violate the federal Uniformed Services Employment and Reemployment Rights Act by failing to hire a National Guard member as an administrator. The U.S. Court of Appeals, Eleventh Circuit, held the board hired the most qualified candidate for the job and stated **an employer violates the act if an applicant's membership in a branch of uniformed service is a motivating factor in an employment decision.** In this case, the board had legitimate reasons for not hiring the guardsman. *Gambrill v. Cullman County Board of Educ.*, 395 Fed.Appx. 543 (11th Cir. 2010).

◆   A New York elementary principal who was an Army reservist submitted six requests for brief military service leave in one year. During leaves, she could not perform her duties as principal, and board members and the superintendent expressed displeasure over her absences. The principal refused to comply with a board member's request to place his child in a "looping class" so the child could remain with the same teacher for the next grade. The superintendent then told her to place the child in the looping class. Later, the superintendent notified the principal he would recommend her employment termination to the board for inaccessibility to staff and parents, failure to meet with clerical staff, and failure to timely complete class lists. The board discharged her, and she sued the school district under the Uniformed Services Employment and Reemployment Rights Act (USERRA), the state Military Law, and the First Amendment. A federal court dismissed the claims against the board under USERRA and the New York Military Law. On appeal, the U.S. Court of Appeals, Second Circuit, held that **the principal could not pursue her USERRA action against individual board members under 42 U.S.C. § 1983**. The court dismissed the appeal and remanded the case to the district court for further proceedings. *Morris-Hayes v. Board of Educ. of Chester Union Free School Dist.*, 423 F.3d 153 (2d Cir. 2005).

◆   An untenured Kansas teacher and Vietnam-era veteran worked for a school district for three years. After learning he would not be rehired due to performance deficiencies, he followed the recommendation of his principal to submit a resignation letter in lieu of non-renewal. He then sued the district and superintendent for violating the Kansas Veteran's Preference Act (VPA), his federal due process rights and defamation. The court held for the district on all claims, and the teacher appealed. The Court of Appeals of Kansas stated that the VPA pertained to appointments and reductions in force, not resignations. Resignation could not be considered a reduction in force. The teacher did not show he was equally qualified to any employee retained by the district.

The teacher admitted the principal's recommendation for non-renewal was based on performance deficiencies. **As the VPA provided no relief for untenured school employees who resigned under the threat of non-renewal, the court affirmed the judgment on the VPA claim.** The teacher also failed to prove defamation, as no defamatory information was communicated to a third party. And he could not prove that his contract was not renewed in retaliation for promoting or endorsing his teacher's association, in violation of his First Amendment speech rights. Key district officials were not even aware of his advocacy for the association. The trial court had correctly held for the district and superintendent. *Richardson v. Dietrich*, 105 P.3d 279 (Kan. Ct. App. 2005).

◆   A Pennsylvania school district twice rejected a veteran for employment. The second time, he advanced to the fourth step of the district's five-step hiring process. A letter sent by the district informed the veteran he was not selected, but did not state a reason. He sued the district in a state court, which held that the district was a "local agency" under the Pennsylvania Local Agency Law. The letter informing the veteran of its decision was an "adjudication" by a local agency that had to be appealed within 30 days. Since the veteran did not file suit for 90 days after the date of the letter, the court dismissed the case. The case reached the Supreme Court of Pennsylvania. It found the Veterans' Preference Act created vested rights. But to enjoy a preference, a veteran had to possess the minimum job qualifications. **The act did not require the hiring of unqualified preference-eligible veterans.** As no decision had been made concerning the veteran's qualifications, the court reversed the judgment and returned the case to the trial court to assess whether the district was trying to circumvent the act. *Merrell v. Chartiers Valley School Dist.*, 855 A.2d 713 (Pa. 2004).

CHAPTER NINE

Employment Termination, Resignation and Retirement

I. BUDGET REDUCTIONS AND REDUCTIONS IN FORCE

In recent years, a number of states have enacted legislation to modify or partially displace their traditional experience-based tenure laws. Other states continue to consider legislation that makes performance a consideration in teacher tenure decisions. Alabama's Students First Act (SFA), which replaced the state Fair Dismissal Act, is one example. Prior to July 1, 2011, the Fair Dismissal Act provided tenured employees a hearing to review termination or transfer actions by local education boards. Hearing officers were formerly allowed to determine whether such actions were "arbitrarily unjust." Under the SFA, employees still receive a hearing to appeal local board decisions, but hearing officers are now required to give deference to board decisions.

Courts in Montana and New Mexico permit the retention of junior teachers if retaining more senior teachers would seriously affect educational programs. And the California Education Code permits the retention of junior teachers with "special skills and competence," even if more senior teachers are similarly certified. A 2011 Florida act linked instructional employee retention and compensation with student performance. Under the act, Florida school boards retain employees based on program needs and performance evaluations during reductions in force. Within programs being reduced, employees are released by the order of their evaluations, with the lowest-rated employees going first.

Landmark 2010 Colorado legislation tied tenure decisions to student performance. Provisions of the law phase in through 2013-14 and will make it possible for teachers to lose tenure if they receive consecutive poor evaluations.

◆ An Alabama school district policy granted tenured employees a "one-time recall right to a position for which he or she is certified and legally qualified" in the event of a reduction in force (RIF). An assistant principal (AP) who lost her job due to an RIF accepted a teaching job. Later, she noticed that less-senior employees were being placed into AP positions in the district, and she filed a state court action against the board of education and the district superintendent. Other APs in the district who were laid off joined the action, seeking back wages, benefits, reinstatement, and restoration of their progress toward tenure.

After a hearing, the court held the APs were entitled to back wages and should be offered AP positions as they became available. A later order granted them monetary and equitable relief, including the immediate reinstatement of two individuals to AP positions, with back wages and benefits. On appeal, the Supreme Court of Alabama found the APs lacked tenure as APs but had tenured status as teachers. **They had been notified that the RIF policy would be implemented and that they should look to return to classroom jobs.** Since 1920, state courts have found county boards of education to be local agencies of the state that have absolute immunity under the Alabama Constitution. Since the board was an agency of the state, the trial court judgment was void, and the claims against the superintendent were also barred. *Board of School Commissioners of Mobile County v. Weaver*, 99 So.3d 1210 (Ala. 2012).

◆ A California school district hired a school community liaison employee in 1989. She became a permanent employee after a six-month probationary period. In 2008, the district eliminated its school community liaison positions. The employee was laid off and placed on a 39-month reemployment list. She accepted a lower-paying job as a campus monitor, and she was required to serve another six-month probationary period. Before the employee's probationary period was over, the district released her. In a state court, she claimed she did not lose permanent status when she was laid off as a community liaison.

The case reached the state court of appeal, which found Section 45298 of the state Education Code did not address the permanent status of a laid-off employee who is reemployed in a lower-paying job. Section 45298 addressed reemployment in the 39 months when a laid-off employee must be reemployed in preference to new applicants. The court rejected the employee's theory that a classified employee gains permanent status in a district when a probationary period is completed in any position. It held that **"permanence is attained in classification rather than generally by employment with a school district."** The employee did not have permanent status when she was reemployed. Since she had no right to notice and a hearing before the termination of her employment as a probationary employee in 2008, the court held for the school district. *California School Employees Ass'n v. Governing Board of East Side Union High School Dist.*, 193 Cal.App.4th 540 (Cal. Ct. App. 2011).

◆   Two Delaware school counselors provided classroom guidance lessons on violence and bullying prevention, social skills, self-esteem, test anxiety and other topics. Their school district decreased its level of services and terminated all full-time counselors. At a hearing, a school official stated that vendors under contract would give the district more flexibility to meet student needs and could be used "as needed." The counselors filed a state court challenge that reached the Supreme Court of Delaware. Like the hearing officer, the court found the termination action was based on an increased need for clinical and therapeutic mental health counseling. Despite the counselors' claim that they provided clinical and therapeutic counseling, the court found their primary job was to provide classroom services. There was a reduction in the number of employees as the result of a decrease in services in the district. **The counselors were not qualified to perform the services for which the board planned to contract.** They did not attempt to counter the official's statement that they did not have the credentials and experience to provide mental health and therapeutic counseling services. As a result, the court held for the school district. *Furrow v. Board of Educ. of Christina School Dist.*, 12 A.3d 1154 (Table) (Del. 2011).

◆   Clay County, Nebraska, reduced a veteran art teacher's job to .5 full-time equivalency (FTE) in 1997 due to low student enrollment. She kept her .5 FTE job in Clay County and taught .5 FTE in Aurora Schools. In 2008, an art teacher resigned from Clay Center School District, and that district agreed to share an art position with Clay County. Clay Center advertised the job, but the veteran teacher did not apply for it. A probationary teacher was hired to work .5 FTE for Clay Center and Clay County, and Clay County advised the veteran teacher that her position would be eliminated. It voted to reduce its art program to 0 FTE and to contract with Clay Center for an art teacher. At a hearing, the school board found a reduction in force was necessary due to changed circumstances related only to the teacher, who was unqualified for any other district position.

A Nebraska county court vacated the decision, and appeal reached the Supreme Court of Nebraska. It held a teacher's contract may be terminated only for reasons stated in Nebraska law. **A "reduction in force" had been held to involve contract termination "due to a surplus of staff."** The county court had correctly found no reduction in force due to a surplus in staff. Clay County simply planned to replace the veteran teacher. The district was not reducing its staff based on reduced need. It only changed the method by which it secured the services of a .5 FTE art teacher to save money. This was not by itself a legal basis for terminating a tenured teacher's contract. *Miller v. School Dist. No. 18-0011 of Clay County, Nebraska*, 278 Neb. 1018, 775 N.W.2d 413 (Neb. 2009).

◆ A New Mexico teacher was in her third year of employment with a school district and had a good record. However, the superintendent notified her that he was recommending her discharge under a reduction in force (RIF) because of shortfalls in state funding and the discontinuation of federal grant money. The school board discharged the teacher, and an arbitrator found that the RIF constituted "just cause" under state law. On appeal, the Supreme Court of New Mexico explained that unless there were personal grounds for discharging a teacher, a school board had to affirmatively show that no position was available for which the teacher was qualified to support discharge by RIF. So the board had to affirmatively show that no position was available for the teacher. Nothing indicated the board had considered whether any other positions were available. Discharge, unlike contract non-renewal, resulted in job loss in the middle of a school year. Given this hardship, **a board had to show it could not financially endure the school year to justify a mid-year discharge**. *Aguilera v. Board of Educ. of Hatch Valley Schools*, 139 N.M. 330, 132 P.3d 587 (N.M. 2006).

◆ An Iowa school district terminated the contract of a longtime elementary principal due to declining enrollment, budget problems, a reduction of positions and a realignment of the school organization. The grade 7-12 principal became superintendent and the new superintendent's brother was hired as the grade 7-12 principal. When the ousted principal challenged the realignment, the school board upheld her discharge, and a state court affirmed the decision. On appeal, the Supreme Court of Iowa had to decide if termination was supported by "just cause" for the reasons stated. It held **"just cause" under state law included legitimate reasons relating to personnel and budgetary requirements**. Here, the district showed enrollment had declined over 25 percent since 1999. Projections indicated further reductions, and the district had lost about $1 million in annual revenues. As the evidence substantiated a district strategy to gradually reduce its administrative staff, the judgment was affirmed. *Martinek v. Belmond-Klemme Community School Dist.*, 772 N.W.2d 758 (Iowa 2009).

In a separate case, the state supreme court held neither state law nor the contract allowed termination prior to the end of the contract term. *Martinek v. Belmond-Klemme Community School Dist.*, 760 N.W.2d 454 (Iowa 2009).

◆ A Montana school superintendent recommended budget cuts for the district and devised reduction in force (RIF) criteria that stated a preference for multiple endorsements "due to the versatility of using teachers in more than one area." The school board voted to discharge a teacher who was endorsed to teach only social studies. He sought arbitration, arguing that two less experienced teachers were rehired. The arbitrator held for the board, and the case reached the Supreme Court of Montana. It held **teacher tenure rights must be balanced against a school board's authority to manage the district in a financially responsible manner**. A reduction in revenue was "good cause" for the RIF. The board had considered alternatives and was not required to take actions that negatively affected operations and educational programs to preserve a teacher's bumping rights. The court noted that a teacher with multiple endorsements is especially valuable to a small rural district. The teacher's dismissal was upheld. *Scobey School Dist. v. Radakovich*, 332 Mont. 9, 135 P.3d 778 (Mont. 2006).

II. IMMORALITY AND OTHER MISCONDUCT

In Broney v. California Comm'n on Teacher Credentialing, *108 Cal.Rptr.3d 832 (Cal. Ct. App. 2010), the court held statutory terms such as "immoral or unprofessional conduct" and "moral turpitude" are almost unlimited in scope. To avoid arbitrary results, the court looked to* Morrison v. State Board of Educ., *1 Cal.3d 214 (1969). In* Morrison, *the California Supreme Court found **"before any act could be deemed a ground for discharge, it must bear directly on the teacher's fitness to teach"** and cause a clearly discernible detriment to a school and its students. Michigan and California courts have relied on factors listed in* Morrison *in recent cases involving teacher misconduct off school grounds.*

A. Sexual Misconduct

◆   A Kentucky teacher had worked for 10 years without major disciplinary issues when administrators heard rumors that he engaged a high school senior in sexual relations. Other students confirmed the reported relationship, and the student eventually did so as well. School officials made a report to state law enforcement officers, who investigated further. A former student then came forward with a report that she too had engaged in sex with the teacher while she was attending the high school. District officials suspended the teacher pending a criminal investigation. After a jury acquitted the teacher of criminal charges, he returned to teaching at a different school. Later, the district fired him, and he contested the action before a tribunal. A hearing officer affirmed a finding by the tribunal that the teacher had engaged in inappropriate sexual relations with a student. The teacher's appeal reached the Court of Appeals of Kentucky.

In the court's opinion, many of the teacher's objections had to be dismissed due to vagueness. As for the rest of the appeal, the court found the tribunal's findings deserved deference. **There was enough evidence to support the finding that the teacher had sex with the students.** While he claimed he should have been allowed to present evidence of his criminal acquittal to the tribunal, the court found this had no bearing on the administrative case. As there were no due process violations, the court affirmed the discharge. *Drummond v. Todd County Board of Educ.*, 349 S.W.3d 316 (Ky. Ct. App. 2011).

◆   A West Virginia board of education investigated charges that a school bus driver was having a sexual relationship with a high school student. As a result of the investigation, the driver was fired. He appealed to the state public employees grievance board. Witnesses testified at a hearing, including a parent, a school clerk, the student and the driver. Although the student claimed she had a sexual encounter with the driver, he vehemently denied this. The hearing officer found the student's testimony inconsistent. She could not provide details of a sexual encounter that she claimed had occurred. Since the board had the burden of proving such a relationship, the hearing officer held for the driver. A state circuit court reinstated the discharge action. On appeal, the West Virginia Supreme Court of Appeals noted that a hearing officer's findings had to be upheld if they were supported by substantial evidence. **In disciplinary matters, the employer had the burden of establishing the charges by a preponderance of the**

evidence. As the evidence was equal, the board did not meet its burden of proof, and the court reinstated the hearing officer's decision. *Darby v. Kanawha County Board of Educ.*, 227 W.Va. 525, 711 S.E.2d 595 (W.Va. 2011).

◆   Kentucky employees did not show they were forced to quit when they were suspended and had "sexually charged allegations" raised against them. One was a middle school principal who was reassigned to a teaching position pending the investigation. The other was charged with "moral turpitude" involving students and possibly employees. While the employees claimed the charges were false and designed to humiliate them, the state court of appeals found no objective person would believe they were subjected to intolerable working conditions. Both were advised that they would be reinstated if the investigations did not lead to charges, but both resigned. The employees failed to show they were defamed or subjected to hostile work environments. In fact, **the district superintendent was legally required to report any action against their teaching certificates**. The appeal was dismissed as without merit. *Cvitkovic v. Freeman*, No. 2008-CA-001647, 2010 WL 3292906 (Ky. Ct. App. 8/6/10).

◆   A Delaware art teacher had worked for a school district for eight years when he had sexual relations with a 17-year-old former student who no longer attended district schools. On one occasion, he called in sick and met the student at his home. She later told a friend about the relationship, and her parent reported it to state police. The teacher was charged with fourth degree sexual rape based on the student's age and his position of trust, authority or supervision over her. But the charge was dropped. The board discharged the teacher for immorality, and the case reached the Supreme Court of Delaware. The court found that substantial evidence supported the school board's decision. **There was a nexus between the sexual relationship and the teacher's fitness to teach.** His positive work reviews predated the disclosure of his misconduct and he discounted the sexual nature of the relationship. It made no difference to the court that the student no longer attended school in the district. The teacher had compromised his position of trust and his status as a role model, and the court upheld the teacher's firing for immorality. *Lehto v. Board of Educ. of Caesar Rodney School Dist.*, 962 A.2d 222 (Del. 2008).

B. Misconduct, Immoral Conduct and Moral Turpitude

Misconduct that may lead to employment termination includes immoral or criminal conduct, moral turpitude, and neglect of duty. A Florida court has held moral turpitude requires an "intent to defraud or deceive." In Beebee v. Haslett Public Schools, *239 N.W.2d 724 (1976), Michigan's Supreme Court held that if a teacher's off-campus conduct is at issue, there must be some link between the out-of-school acts and in-school behavior to justify employee discipline.*

◆   An openly gay Washington high school teacher claimed a former student harassed him. After school officials investigated, it was found that both parties had used epithets and sworn at each other. The teacher was issued a letter of probable cause for discharge based on harassment of a former student, retaliation and dishonesty during the investigation. A hearing officer later found the teacher lied but found no cause for discharge, as the conduct cited in the district's termination letter had no adverse impact on the teacher's effectiveness.

A state court denied the school district's appeal and awarded the teacher $38,774 in attorneys' fees. The state court of appeals reversed the decision, and the teacher appealed to the Supreme Court of Washington. It held the district lacked statutory rights to appeal an adverse decision by a hearing officer. Instead, its recourse was a constitutional claim. As a result, the court reversed the appeals court decision and reinstated the award of attorneys' fees for the teacher. In doing so, the court restated its longstanding rule that **"sufficient cause for a teacher's discharge exists as a matter of law where the teacher's deficiency is unremediable and (1) materially and substantially affects the teacher's performance; or (2) lacks any positive educational aspect or legitimate professional purpose."** *Federal Way School Dist. No. 210 v. Vinson*, 172 Wash.2d 756, 261 P.3d 145 (Wash. Ct. App. 2011).

◆ A tenured California teacher who placed a graphic advertisement on Craigslist seeking homosexual relations was unable to overturn his employment termination based on unfitness for service and immoral conduct. Although the state Commission on Professional Competence and a trial court reinstated the teacher, the state court of appeal found evidence of unfitness to serve as a teacher as well as immoral conduct. The teacher did not use school resources to place the advertisement, and he had a good employment record. Still, the conduct was adequate grounds for termination. It held "'evident unfitness for service' connotes a fixed character trait" that presumably cannot be remedied. A parent and an educator had seen the ad, and the school principal stated she had lost confidence in the teacher's ability to serve as a role model. There was evidence that he had previously posted five or six similar Internet ads soliciting sex. *San Diego Unified School Dist. v. Comm'n on Professional Competence*, 194 Cal.App.4th 1454, 124 Cal.Rptr.3d 320 (Cal. Ct. App. 2011).

◆ A Florida court reversed a school board's decision to fire a school nurse who left a seizure-prone, quadriplegic student he had been tube-feeding to assess whether another child was having a seizure. The board sought to fire the nurse for not following safe procedures and failing to provide first aid. An administrative law judge (ALJ) found that a teacher had called the nurse to assess the other child but did not know the nurse was tube-feeding the quadriplegic student. The ALJ recommended a written reprimand, but the board voted for termination. On appeal, a state district court of appeal held the board could not modify the ALJ's findings unless they were not based on competent substantial evidence. As a result, the court reversed the decision. *Resnick v. Flagler County School Board*, 46 So.3d 1110 (Fla. Dist. Ct. App. 2010).

◆ A Michigan teacher was photographed while simulating oral sex with a mannequin at a bachelor/bachelorette party. The pictures were taken without her knowledge and posted on a website. Two years later, students at her school accessed the photos, which were then removed from the website. But the teacher was suspended and then discharged for engaging in lewd behavior contrary to the moral values of her community. The case reached the state court of appeals, which held the discipline of a tenured teacher must be based on reasonable and just cause under state law. **Just cause must be shown by significant evidence proving unfitness to teach,** and the focus of the evidence is the effect of the questioned activity on the teacher's students. Courts in Michigan, California and other states with similar tenure laws have focused on incompetence and inefficiency, as they directly affect students. The court held that where conduct, outside school and not involving students, was the basis for discipline, a serious question existed as to whether a school could impose discipline without showing the conduct had **"an adverse effect upon the educational process."** The photos created gossip, but as testimony showed parents had not lost respect for the teacher, the court held in her favor. *Land v. L'Anse Creuse Public School Board of Educ.*, No. 288612, 2010 WL 2135356 (Mich. Ct. App. 5/27/10).

◆ A Delaware teacher was charged with misconduct and/or immorality, including selling grades to students for cash, sleeping during the day and swearing in front of students at a school football game. The most serious charge was that he asked one of his students for a ride to a dangerous area to purchase drugs. At the time, the teacher' driving privileges were suspended due to a DUI conviction. A hearing officer found his statements "incredible." Grade books supported charges that the teacher had raised the final grades of two students for cash. Appeal reached the Supreme Court of Delaware. **The court found state law permitted the admission of any evidence pertinent to the written reasons for a teacher's dismissal.** As the board could hear all evidence that could conceivably throw light on a controversy, a due process claim failed. All the incidents considered by the hearing officer were related to the grounds provided in the termination notice. State law permitted the board to consider a teacher's performance throughout his employment term. Board procedures satisfied due process, and substantial evidence supported the decision. *Bethel v. Board of Educ. of Capital School Dist.*, 985 A.2d 389 (Table) (Del. 2009).

◆ A California school district began termination proceedings against a high school teacher for inappropriate conduct. One incident involved his decision to remove a high school student from his classroom for wearing a shirt that said "Israeli Police." Officials claimed he made disparaging remarks about Israel, used physical force upon students, made inappropriate sexual comments to females, and used profanity and threats. A district commission on professional competence (CPC) found the teacher engaged in unprofessional conduct, but dismissal was not warranted. The Court of Appeal of California found the teacher incorrectly believed a student's "Israeli Police" shirt violated the school dress code. However, his demands to remove the shirt were rooted in the desire to maintain classroom order. Sexual comments to female students were found by the CPC to be "friendly banter." The teacher's conduct after being transferred did not show such unfitness to teach as to warrant dismissal. **He acknowledged his misconduct, was unlikely to repeat it and was not a danger to students.** *Santa Barbara School Dist. v. Commission on Professional Competence*, No. B199525, 2009 WL 73621 (Cal. Ct. App. 1/13/09).

◆ A Florida school hired a teacher six months after he was involved in an accident in which a seven-year-old child was killed. A highway patrol arrest affidavit stated he was driving recklessly and jockeying for position in traffic at a high speed when he lost control of his van. The teacher pleaded no contest and was found guilty of vehicular homicide. He was placed on probation for five years and assigned 500 hours of community service. For unstated reasons, the teacher's school board waited more than four years to initiate dismissal proceedings for committing a "crime of moral turpitude." The board dismissed the teacher, and the action was upheld by an administrative law judge. On appeal, the District Court of Appeal of Florida noted that while the teacher had operated his vehicle in a reckless manner that was likely to cause death or great bodily harm, his actions were not deemed "moral turpitude." **Moral turpitude had the essential element of intent to defraud or deceive.** Since the school board failed to prove moral turpitude, the court reversed the judgment and reinstated the teacher. *Cisneros v. School Board of Miami-Dade County*, 990 So.2d 1179 (Fla. Dist. Ct. App. 2008).

◆ A Missouri teacher brought her children, ages 2, 10 and 11, to a casino and left them in her car for 45 minutes while she went inside. When she returned, the police had arrived, and she was charged with endangering the welfare of a child. The teacher pleaded guilty and completed a year of probation. The school board rehired her, even after it learned about the incident. The state education department sought to suspend the teacher's teaching certificate, but it offered no further evidence about the incident. The teacher claimed that the weather was mild, and that she went into the casino to contact a friend and did not gamble.

The state education commissioner recommended a 90-day suspension of her teaching certificate. The state board found the discipline was appropriate, based on a guilty plea to a crime involving moral turpitude. Appeal reached the Court of Appeals of Missouri, which explained that the board could discipline the teacher only if her offense involved "moral turpitude." **Moral turpitude has been defined as "an act of baseness, vileness, or depravity in the private and social duties" which a person owes others or society.** As the teacher did not plead guilty to a crime that necessarily involved moral turpitude, and because the education department presented no evidence on the issue, the court held that the board should have dismissed the case. *Brehe v. Missouri Dep't of Elementary and Secondary Educ.*, 213 S.W.3d 720 (Mo. Ct. App. 2007).

◆ An Oregon teacher tried to commit suicide after learning her husband had a girlfriend and wanted a divorce. She rammed her vehicle into her husband's vehicle and damaged the girlfriend's house. She voluntarily committed herself for psychiatric treatment and officials charged her with four crimes, three of which were dropped. The other provided for dismissal if she completed her term of probation. The school board voted to dismiss the teacher, and she appealed to the state Fair Dismissal Appeals Board (FDAB). An FDAB hearing panel heard testimony from a psychologist who said the teacher's conduct was isolated and unlikely to reoccur. The board had let two other teachers return to work after suicide attempts, and another returned after entering into a diversion agreement for domestic violence charges. The FDAB panel found the dismissal had been "unreasonable." **On appeal, the Supreme Court of Oregon stated**

that contract teachers may be dismissed only for immorality or neglect of duty. The FDAB did not determine whether the board had applied an excessive remedy. The court returned the case to the panel for further consideration. *Bergerson v. Salem-Keizer School Dist.*, 341 Or. 401, 144 P.3d 918 (Or. 2006).

◆ An Oklahoma teacher who was threatened with discharge returned to work after he settled his state court lawsuit. When the superintendent stated he would "write him up for not reporting to his assigned area," the teacher said "if you do, I'll beat the shit out of you" in a threatening manner. The superintendent left to obtain a witness, and the teacher again threatened him. The teacher then said he was sick and left school for the day. The school board voted to terminate his contract for moral turpitude, and he sued it in a state court. When the case reached the Oklahoma Supreme Court, it held **"moral turpitude" under state law involved a level of conduct that was more than "mere impropriety."** It was not a catch-all for all offensive, inappropriate or unprofessional conduct. While the teacher's threats were "unprofessional, unwise and unacceptable," there was no moral turpitude. *Ballard v. Independent School Dist. No. 4 of Bryan County, Oklahoma*, 77 P.3d 1084 (Okla. 2003).

C. Criminal Conduct

Utah's highest court upheld the firing of a school maintenance supervisor after a police investigation confirmed he performed contracting work for his private business and used a school district vehicle during work hours. The court found it "disingenuous" for the supervisor to argue that as long as he had his cell phone with him, he was still "working" for the district. Misrepresentations regarding his work hours were held to be sufficient grounds for termination for cause. Oman v. Davis School Dist., 956 F.3d 956 (Utah 2008).

◆ Louisiana law enforcement officers obtained a search warrant and raided an alternative school principal's residence. They found cocaine, marijuana, a gun, counterfeit money and drug paraphernalia. After the raid, the principal was placed on leave and subjected to a drug test. He was charged with attempted perjury and possession of unlawful items. The school board scheduled a tenure hearing. In addition to possession of the unlawful items, the board charged him with trying to obtain perjury from a person, failing to timely submit to drug testing, and engaging in unlawful activities in the presence of a former student.

A hearing was held in the principal's absence, and the board placed him on leave without pay. When the hearing resumed, he sought postponement until the criminal case ended and argued that the district attorney should not be allowed to represent the board. Board members voted to fire the principal and a state court upheld the decision. On appeal, **the Court of Appeal of Louisiana found "absolutely no evidence" of misconduct by the hearing officer**. It was not a "conflict of interest" for the district attorney to represent the board while also prosecuting the criminal charges. There was sufficient evidence to support dismissal and no reason to delay the discharge hearing pending the criminal matter. *Sias v. Iberia Parish School Board*, 74 So.3d 800 (La. Ct. App. 2011).

◆   An Arizona district superintendent who was discharged after being arrested for shoplifting a bottle of wine lost an appeal of his due process case in the U.S. Court of Appeals, Ninth Circuit. The court held there was no violation of the Arizona Open Meetings Law, as the superintendent failed to allege a quorum of board members took legal action outside of a public meeting when it considered the termination of his employment. As for the superintendent's due process claims, the court found they were based on the speculative and unsupported assertion that the board did not adequately disclose evidence and witnesses during the proceedings. **The superintendent had failed to attend his own hearing.** As there was no proof of bias, and he did not show stigmatizing conduct, the judgment for the board was affirmed. *Mohr v. Murphy Elementary School Dist. 21 of Maricopa County*, 449 Fed.Appx. 650 (9th Cir. 2011).

◆   An Oklahoma special education teacher accused a student of typing the word "jackass" on his computer, which the student denied. The student then left the classroom, as he had often done in the past. The teacher went to look for him, fearing the student might leave school grounds. He found the student in the school office and slapped him twice on the face. The teacher stated that he did not intend to harm the student, and he went to the student's home to apologize to the family. The school district discharged the teacher under the state Teacher Due Process Act, asserting physical or mental abuse of a child. A state court held that he did not violate the act and ordered him reinstated. The school district appealed to the Supreme Court of Oklahoma, which noted that the student was often a disciplinary problem at school. He was on medication and had social interaction problems. The teacher had apologized to family members, who said they would be satisfied if he taught the student again. **He had begun counseling, and his counselor testified that the incident was unlikely to ever be repeated.** The court affirmed the judgment for the teacher. *Hagen v. Independent School Dist. No. I-004*, 157 P.3d 738 (Okla. 2007).

◆   A South Carolina teacher was arrested for possessing crack cocaine in 1988, but authorities dismissed his case. In 2000, the teacher was arrested "in his car in a well-known drug area" while his passenger attempted to buy crack. Charges against the teacher were dropped when the passenger pled guilty. After the 2000 incident, the teacher was placed on administrative leave, pending an investigation into the arrest and "similar behavior in the past." The superintendent advised him by letter his contract was being terminated. At the teacher's school board hearing, the superintendent said the termination was based solely on the teacher's unfitness. The board upheld the discharge, and the teacher appealed. A state court held that being arrested but not convicted for two criminal charges was not substantial evidence of unfitness to teach. The case reached the state supreme court, which noted that **two drug arrests, 12 years apart, neither resulting in charges, did not support a finding of unfitness to teach**. This was especially true when the district did not contend the teacher ever used, possessed or sold illegal drugs. He was entitled to reinstatement with back pay and benefits from the date of his suspension. *Shell v. Richland County School Dist. One*, 362 S.C. 408, 608 S.E.2d 428 (S.C. 2005).

D. Neglect of Duty

Court review of tenure proceedings is limited to an inquiry into whether the school board or state agency has complied with statutory requirements and whether the administrative findings are supported by substantial evidence.

◆   A Louisiana teacher served her district for 16 years before being assigned to teach social studies and language arts at a middle school. The principal repeatedly explained that if teachers needed to send students to his office for discipline, they were to call him to have the students escorted to the office. The principal reprimanded the teacher twice during the opening weeks of the school year for sending students unescorted to his office for discipline. The principal sought to discipline the teacher, who refused to sign reprimand forms related to her policy violations. The school board found substantial evidence to support her discharge. A state trial court upheld the board's decision, and the teacher appealed. The case reached the Supreme Court of Louisiana, which noted that state law permitted the removal of a tenured teacher for willful neglect of duty. Here, the principal's warnings to the teacher against sending unescorted students to the office for discipline adequately explained school policy. There was substantial evidence to support the board's decision that her **repeated failure to follow these directions constituted willful neglect of duty**. The court upheld the board's action dismissing the teacher. *Wise v. Bossier Parish School Board,* 851 So.2d 1090 (La. 2003).

◆   A Louisiana teacher was a tenured vocational instructor whose only area of certification was shop mechanics. He was suspended with pay after he reported the theft of a loaded gun from his wife's car – which he had parked outside his classroom. A state trial court affirmed the board's decision to fire the teacher for willful neglect of duty, as did the state court of appeal. The Supreme Court of Louisiana reversed the lower courts, finding **no rational basis to discharge the teacher for neglect of duty simply because of the theft of the loaded gun from his wife's car**. It ordered the board to reinstate him to his former position, with all salary and benefits. Instead of rehiring the teacher, the board notified him it had discontinued shop mechanics from the curriculum. As this was his only area of certification, the board terminated his employment, retroactive to a date four years earlier. The teacher again appealed to the supreme court, which found no evidence that the board had complied with its mandate to reinstate the teacher to his former position with all salary and benefits. The teacher should have been considered reinstated as of the date of his last paycheck until he was formally advised of his employment termination. The court amended the judgment to require the board to pay him for this four-year period, with interest. *Howard v. West Baton Rouge Parish School Board,* 865 So.2d 708 (La. 2004).

◆   A Texas teacher checked out a district vehicle for a soccer clinic. Before he went to the clinic, a witness saw him leaving a store with beer and getting into the vehicle. When the principal confronted him about it, the teacher admitted buying beer while using the vehicle. He submitted his resignation after being formally reprimanded, but later rescinded it. The superintendent recommended not renewing his contract, and the school board voted for non-renewal after a hearing. The state education commissioner held **the teacher was "in the course and scope of his employment while he was in possession of alcohol."** A Texas court affirmed the decision, and the teacher appealed. The state court of appeals held it could not substitute its judgment for the commissioner's and could only review it to determine if it was supported by substantial evidence. The teacher had admitted his error and said he was acting within the scope of his duties to attend the clinic. He agreed it was reasonable to assume he was acting for the school when the school day began. As the commissioner's decision was supported by substantial evidence, the court affirmed it. *Simpson v. Alanis*, No. 08-03-00110-CV, 2004 WL 309297 (Tex. Ct. App. 2004).

E. Misuse of Technology

A Florida case held requests to examine employee computer hard drives were permitted "in only limited or strictly controlled circumstances," such as where a party was suspected of trying to purge data. Menke v. Broward County School Board, 916 So.2d 8 (Fla. Dist. Ct. App. 2005). Other courts have upheld such access only when there was evidence of intentional deletion of data.

◆   A Wisconsin teacher's school district and union had a history of acrimony. During his two years as union president, the teacher facilitated a report that was extremely critical of the superintendent and revealed a "no confidence vote" by teachers. After the teacher experienced computer problems, his computer was reimaged. When reimaging was needed again, the superintendent directed that monitoring software be placed on the computer. Soon, the teacher disabled his safe search filter and typed "blonde" into a search box. The search yielded 20 pornographic images, although none were actually accessed. But the teacher admitted previously viewing pornography on his school computer, and the board met to consider discipline. At his hearing, the teacher read a statement to the board instead of testifying. The board voted to discharge him, but an arbitrator rescinded the action. The case reached the U.S. Court of Appeals, Seventh Circuit, which found the teacher received a hearing and opportunity to clear his name, but decided not to testify. He received all the process he was due. While relations between the district and union were "contentious, combative and miserable," the court held **the district had legitimate, nondiscriminatory reasons for firing the teacher.** By viewing pornography on his school computer, the court found he violated a district policy, and this had nothing to do with his union activity. *Zellner v. Herrick*, 639 F.3d 371 (7th Cir. 2011).

◆   A New Jersey teacher resigned after the end of his one-year contract. Two students who had been in his class told a school guidance counselor the teacher had accessed pornographic websites on his classroom computer. The district superintendent ordered an investigation, and a school technology director found some sites viewed on the teacher's computer that might be pornographic. A detective obtained arrest warrants for the teacher, who admitted viewing adult websites on his school computer. A grand jury indicted the teacher for endangering the welfare of a child and official misconduct. He pleaded guilty to unauthorized computer use. The teacher sued the detective, school board, district superintendent, administrators and families for malicious prosecution and negligence. **A federal court held the teacher did not show school officials played any role in a constitutional violation. Their actions were reasonable in response to the allegations.** *Grendysa v. Evesham Township Board of Educ.*, No. Civ.A. 02-1493 (FLW), 2005 WL 2416983 (D.N.J. 2005).

◆   A Texas teacher found a "Teacher Evaluations" icon on a classroom computer. Students later discovered documents involving employee reprimands on the computer's hard drive. The teacher recognized some of the information as confidential and inappropriate for students, but he read it with them. A student saved the personnel documents on floppy disks, and the teacher gave them to his attorney without telling school administrators. The district discharged the teacher, and the Court of Appeals of Texas upheld the discharge. It noted that the state education commissioner had defined **"good cause" as the failure to perform employment duties that a "person of ordinary prudence would have done under the same or similar circumstances."** The court upheld the commissioner's finding of good cause. The teacher did not dispute that he discovered confidential records and allowed students to review and download them. *Tave v. Alanis*, 109 S.W.3d 890 (Tex. Ct. App. 2003).

III. INCOMPETENCE

A. Teaching Deficiencies

An Ohio court has held that recommendations in teacher evaluations "must be specific enough to alert a reasonable person to the need for change." California law authorizes the midyear dismissal of a teacher only if specific instances of unsatisfactory performance are not timely corrected. And Nevada law requires school administrators to notify employees in writing whenever it is necessary to admonish the employee, along with the reasons. Reasonable efforts to assist the employee must be made to correct the deficiency.

◆   A review of an Arkansas school district by the state education department found a recent graduate did not actually complete his graduation requirements. The district superintendent reprimanded a high school guidance counselor in writing and admonished him to review transcripts and set up a system to avoid such a mistake in the future. A private audit found many current seniors at the school were not on track to graduate because they were not taking a fourth math credit as mandated by new state requirements. A school board hearing was held to consider non-renewing the counselor. He said that he was never told of the new requirement and had relied on the district's most recent policy and a student handbook indicating that graduating seniors needed only three math credits. After the board voted not to renew the counselor's contract, he filed a state Teacher Fair Dismissal Act action. A trial court ruled in his favor.

On appeal, the Court of Appeals of Arkansas held **the state Fair Dismissal Act required "just and reasonable cause" for adverse employment action** or discipline. The act calls for a written evaluation of each teacher annually and an opportunity for remediation. In this case, the court held the counselor fulfilled his job duties and reasonably relied on the current student handbook. Nothing indicated the board gave him assistance to correct the deficiencies noted by the district superintendent. Administrators did not notify the counselor of the new math requirement, and there was only one evaluation in his personnel file despite his 14 years of service. He was entitled to a full year of back wages. *Bismarck School Dist. v. Sims*, 2012 Ark. App. 239 (Ark. Ct. App. 2012).

◆ A California probationary teacher's evaluations indicated her performance could be "refined," but she was not told it was unsatisfactory, or that failure to improve would result in dismissal. After her second evaluation, the principal told her the school board had discussed her discharge. He gave the teacher a report which lauded her for creating a "pleasant feeling tone" in classes, but criticized her for allowing students to spend too much time off task. Eight days after the second observation, the district notified the teacher of her dismissal for unsatisfactory performance. The board finalized the dismissal at a hearing, and the teacher sued. A court held that the district did not comply with the state Education Code and ordered the teacher reinstated with lost wages and benefits. The Court of Appeal of California held the dismissal of probationary employees during a school year for unsatisfactory performance required a written notice to the teacher identifying particular instances of unsatisfactory performance 90 days prior to any notice of dismissal. **Here, the district did not provide the teacher a timely written notice of unsatisfactory performance or an opportunity to correct specified deficiencies.** *Achene v. Pierce Joint Unified School Dist.*, 176 Cal.App.4th 757, 97 Cal.Rptr.3d 899 (Cal. Ct. App. 2009).

◆ An Ohio trial court ordered a school board to rehire a teacher. It held her evaluations did not give her specific recommendations for improvement and the means to obtain assistance. Comments such as "see me before next observation" did not satisfy state law. The principal found that the teacher lost control of one class, and noted many of her students wandered around, slept or otherwise failed to participate in classes. The state court of appeals held that the board had to rehire her. **Recommendations in teacher evaluations "must be specific enough to alert a reasonable person to the need for change."** The state supreme court refused to review the case. *Cox v. Zanesville City School Dist. Board of Educ.*, 105 Ohio St.3d 1466, 824 N.E.2d 93 (Ohio 2005).

◆ A Nevada school district admonished a teacher for failing to follow district procedures for testing English language learners. She was provided training and mentoring, and her caseload was reduced by 50%. After a second admonition, the district provided the teacher one-on-one training and feedback on testing procedures. After a third admonition, the district suspended the teacher and advised her that her contract would not be renewed. She sought arbitration, claiming the district violated state law by dismissing her only eight days after the last admonishment. The arbitrator upheld the non-renewal. On appeal to the Supreme Court of Nevada, the teacher argued that she should have been allowed to improve her job performance after the final admonition. The court held the law required a "reasonable time for improvement, which must not exceed three months for the first admonition." **The teacher was admonished many times for the same unprofessional conduct.** There was no violation of the law since all the admonishments were for the same type of conduct. The district provided the teacher assistance for over a year to correct her deficient performance, including training, mentoring and reduction of her workload. She received a reasonable time to improve her performance, but was unable to do so. *Clark County Educ. Ass'n v. Clark County School Dist.*, 131 P.3d 5 (Nev. 2006).

◆ A Missouri school district fired a resource teacher whose individualized education programs were incomplete. District administrators had worked with her before and after issuing her a notice of deficiencies. The district special education director met with the teacher weekly and made additional efforts to assist her. She received extensions for job target deadlines. In her state court action, the state court of appeals held the district complied with each of the state Tenure Act's requirements. There was no merit to the teacher's claim that her termination was improperly based on "non-teaching, non-substantive processing of burdensome administrative paperwork." **Missouri case law defines "incompetency and inefficiency" as the "inability to perform professional teaching duties in a manner acceptable to the Board."** Timely completion of required paperwork was "inextricable from a special education teacher's professional teaching duties." Failure to comply with paperwork requirements could result in the denial of an appropriate education to a student. *Hellmann v. Union R-XI School Dist.*, 170 S.W.3d 52 (Mo. Ct. App. 2005).

B. Procedural Problems

Even before the sweeping amendments to Florida law in 2011, the state required that assessment procedures for instructional personnel be "primarily based on the performance of students assigned to their classrooms." Assessments had to "primarily use data and indicators of improvement in student performance assessed annually." In Sherrod v. Palm Beach County School Board, *963 So.2d 251 (Fla. Dist. Ct. App. 2006), a school board that did not primarily base its decision on the performance of students in a teacher's classroom was held in violation of state law.*

◆ Ohio elementary school staff members accused their principal of altering student answers on the Ohio Achievement Tests. She denied wrongdoing, but the board placed her on administrative leave pending an investigation. Before her contract term ended, the board voted for non-renewal. It did not notify the principal of a meeting at which it took the action. Nor did it hold an executive session or await the outcome of a state education department investigation.

After the education department exonerated the principal, the board refused to hold a meeting to discuss her contract. She sued the board in a state court, seeking a determination that her request for a meeting was covered by state code Section 3319.02(D). A state trial court held for the board, and its decision was affirmed by the court of appeals. The case then came before the Supreme Court of Ohio. It found Section 3319.02 was a remedial statute that required school boards to notify administrators of the date of contract expiration and the right to request a meeting with the board. There were no temporal restrictions on an administrator's meeting request and no requirement that a request follow a final evaluation. **When an administrator's contract was not renewed, Section 3319.02(D) allowed a request for a board meeting to discuss the reasons for non-renewal before a final evaluation or receipt of a board hearing notice.** The principal had received good evaluations in her first year before being placed on leave. As the board did not satisfy its obligation to hold a meeting to discuss her contract renewal as required by Section 3319.02(D), the court reversed the judgment and returned the case to the trial court. *Carna v. Teays Valley Local School Dist. Board of Educ.*, 131 Ohio St.3d 478, 967 N.E.2d 193 (Ohio 2012).

◆ A Florida school board brought formal discharge proceedings against a career contract teacher with many classroom and communication problems. The teacher was then transferred to a different school. There were new complaints about excessive and inappropriate use of R-rated videos, failure to timely post and enter grades into the system, and failure to provide timely instruction on covered materials. The teacher was charged with failing to properly control students and was put on probation. He was transferred to another school, where he failed to follow lesson plans and had no required text for students. After a formal hearing, the school board fired the teacher. He appealed to the Florida District Court of Appeal, which explained that under state law, the assessment procedure for instructional personnel must be primarily based on the performance of students. **Assessments "must primarily use data and indicators of improvement in student performance assessed annually."** Here, the school board did not primarily base its decision on the performance of students in the teacher's classroom. The court rejected the board's argument that a teacher may be discharged if factors other than student performance are "properly deemed more crucial." The statute required primary reliance on standardized tests and left no discretion for teacher assessment. The court ruled for the teacher. *Sherrod v. Palm Beach County School Board*, 963 So.2d 251 (Fla. Dist. Ct. App. 2006).

◆ A newly tenured Nebraska high school principal claimed he was fired and denied due process because he was not evaluated as frequently as specified by state law. The Nebraska Court of Appeals rejected his argument concerning the number of evaluations he had. The discharge occurred after he acquired tenure, and the district had properly evaluated him during the year. There was evidence that the district had thoroughly evaluated the principal and offered to assist him, but that he did not respond professionally. He was advised of his deficiencies and given an opportunity to correct them. The court reviewed evidence that the principal misled the superintendent about an incident that required police intervention. He was also dishonest to parents, students and police concerning another incident, and he was slow to discipline a teacher for accessing pornographic websites at school. **The court found substantial evidence of incompetence, neglect of duty and performance issues that supported the finding of just cause for termination.** *Montgomery v. Jefferson County School Dist. No. 0008*, No. A-01-1018, 2003 WL 1873713 (Neb. App. 2003).

IV. INSUBORDINATION AND OTHER GOOD CAUSE

A. Insubordination

In Barnes v. Spearfish School Dist. No. 40-2, *this chapter, the Supreme Court of South Dakota defined "insubordination" as "a willful disregard of an employer's instructions" or an "act of disobedience to the proper authority," such as "refusal to obey an order that a superior officer is authorized to give." Similarly, in* Ketchersid v. Rhea County Board of Educ., *174 S.W.2d 163 (Tenn. Ct. App. 2005), the Court of Appeals of Tennessee held "insubordination" included the refusal to carry out specific assignments made by a principal.*

◆ A California teacher was charged with defiance and disrespect toward his principal. An evaluator noted his frustration with students caused him to be unprofessional at times. A student said the teacher had called the principal a "slut" who had "slept her way into the position." In other incidents with students and colleagues, he used profanity. After the teacher fled from his classroom when the principal tried to evaluate him, he was placed on leave and barred from the school. Near this time, the district served him with notice of intent to dismiss him for "evident unfitness for service." But the state Commission on Professional Competence found no cause to dismiss him. Appeal reached the Court of Appeal of California. It reviewed *Morrison v. State Board of Educ.*, 1 Cal.3d 214 (Cal. 1969), in which the state supreme court found seven factors are relevant when applying the "evident unfitness for service" standard. **Among the factors was "the likelihood that the conduct may have adversely affected students or fellow teachers and the degree of such adversity anticipated."**

The evidence indicated that despite the teacher's unprofessionalism, he was not unfit for service. While his conduct hurt his relationship with the principal, the court found this did not make him unfit for service. Unprofessionalism by itself was not "evident unfitness for service." The court held for the teacher. *Sweetwater Union High School Dist. v. Comm'n on Professional Competence*, No. D058832, 2012 WL 687841 (Cal. Ct. App. 3/2/12).

◆ A Massachusetts teacher argued with her principal. She then found a substitute and left the building. She went to a hospital and told a psychiatrist that she had "the urge to kill" the principal. To comply with a state law, the remark was reported to police. When the school learned of this, the teacher was placed on leave. A court order was then obtained to bar her from the school. The school committee discharged the teacher for insubordination, conduct unbecoming a teacher and incapacity. An arbitrator found she had not engaged in conduct warranting termination under state law. A state court affirmed the award, and the case reached the state court of appeals. There, the school committee argued the arbitrator had substituted his judgment for that of the committee and did not consider the best interests of the students. **But the court found that after the argument with the principal, the teacher did not attack or threaten her.** She instead found a substitute and sought treatment. Her statements to the psychiatrist were made in the context of trying to seek treatment. The court held she "plainly intended to threaten no one." As the court found no reason to question the arbitrator's conclusions, it affirmed the award. *School Committee of Boston v. Underwood*, 82 Mass.App.Ct. 1113 (Mass. App. Ct. 2012).

◆ Throughout his long career with an Ohio school district, a teacher earned positive job evaluations. After 20 years of service, he used a "Tesla Coil" to make a mark on a student's arm. The board found the mark resembled a cross and lasted almost two weeks. An investigation of the teacher revealed concerns by administrators about his religious activities. A district administrator said she had received complaints about the teacher for much of her 11 years as a board employee. She noted that for much of this time, he failed to follow the required curriculum. A board resolution stated that the teacher had taught creationism and intelligent design in his science classes. In response, the teacher requested a hearing, contending he was the victim of intentional religious discrimination.

After a 38-day hearing, a referee recommended discharging the teacher. He found the teacher had interjected his religious beliefs into the curriculum and was insubordinate. The board adopted the referee's report and voted for dismissal. Later, the Court of Appeals of Ohio held that **state law permits termination of a tenured teacher's employment for willful and persistent violations of reasonable board regulations** and for other good and just cause. It found the evidence supported the findings and held that "repeated violation of the Constitution of the United States is a 'fairly serious matter' and is therefore, a valid basis for termination" of the teacher's contract. He "repeatedly acted in defiance of direct instructions and orders of the administrators." The court affirmed the board's discharge decision. *Freshwater v. Mount Vernon City School Dist. Board of Educ.*, 2012 -Ohio- 889 (Ohio Ct. App. 3/5/12).

The state supreme court allowed the teacher an opportunity to review the case. *Freshwater v. Mt. Vernon City School Dist. Board of Educ.*, 132 Ohio St.3d 1461, 969 N.E.2d 1230, 2012 -Ohio- 3054 (appeal granted 7/5/12).

◆ A Kentucky teacher was suspended for knocking a banana from a student's hands. A school tribunal found he had violated a written directive instructing him to exhibit professional and appropriate behavior and refrain from touching students. The tribunal found contract termination appropriate, and a Kentucky court upheld the decision. According to the Court of Appeals of Kentucky, the insubordination charge was unsupported by a proper written record. **Section 161.790(1) of the state revised statutes requires supervisors to support charges against a teacher with a written record of performance.** The record "must be specific to the individual teacher and the circumstances leading up to the charge." The court found no evidence that the teacher had touched the student. It found the student took a banana from the teacher, disobeyed his instructions to put it down, and then tried to eat it. The teacher knocked the banana down without touching him. He was not advised of any deficiencies as required by school policy, and he received no directive regarding expected behavior. The judgment was reversed due to lack of notice, the administration's failure to comply with its own procedures and other errors. *Raley v. Ohio County Schools*, No. 2009-CA-001358-MR, 2010 WL 3361125 (Ky. Ct. App. 8/27/10).

◆　A California teacher had a single subject teaching credential in music and was her school's only music teacher. A 2002 state audit found her district out of compliance with state law because some teachers without an English Language Learners (EL) certification were assigned to teach EL students. The district created a plan for all teachers to obtain EL certification. A collective bargaining provision required all certificated staff to obtain EL certification by the end of 2005 or face employment termination. The music teacher repeatedly refused to sign a commitment to receive EL training. After the district fired her, the Court of Appeal of California held her arguments trivialized the dilemma faced by the district, which was subject to penalties if it assigned an EL student to an improperly certified teacher. The Legislature recognized that EL students have the same rights to quality education as all other California students. **The district could discharge the teacher for unprofessional conduct, evident unfitness for service, and persistent refusal to obey reasonable district regulations.** The teacher was not guaranteed employment or tenure. *Governing Board of Ripon Unified School Dist. v. Commission on Professional Conduct,* 177 Cal.App.4th 1379, 99 Cal.Rptr.3d 903 (Cal. Ct. App. 2009).

◆　A South Dakota teacher's first evaluation noted "excellent" performance. But she disagreed with other comments on the evaluation and did not sign it. She submitted a written response challenging each of the principal's comments, except the observation that she was an excellent teacher. During the next three years, she refused to sign evaluations and responded to them in writing. The school board later deemed these responses "confrontational" and "insolent."

The next school year, the principal grew concerned that the teacher was talking about personnel issues with other staff. He informed her this was inappropriate and had to stop. The teacher responded that the principal "undermines his own authority and imposes a low morale on the teachers by his own inappropriate actions." The teacher was reprimanded in writing for performance deficiencies and her intentional and willful failure to heed warnings or to follow performance expectations. After the teacher's fourth year in the district, her contract was not renewed because of her insubordination. The teacher appealed, and the Supreme Court of South Dakota noted that **insubordination is "a willful disregard of an employer's instructions" or an "act of disobedience to the proper authority," such as refusal to obey a superior's order.** The hearing had produced a wealth of testimony and documentation supporting the board's action. The court affirmed the judgment. *Barnes v. Spearfish School Dist. No. 40-2,* 725 N.W.2d 226 (S.D. 2006).

◆　The Supreme Court of North Carolina declined to review lower court decisions that upheld a school board's decision not to rehire a teacher who squirted her principal with a water pistol at a school-sponsored event. The state court of appeals found no evidence that the principal was biased. The action was based on several instances of misconduct and was not arbitrary. **The record indicated that the teacher's contract was not renewed because she was a counterproductive force to faculty morale at her school.** *Davis v. Macon County Board of Educ.,* 360 N.C. 645, 638 S.E.2d 465 (N.C. 2006).

B. Conduct Unbecoming a Teacher

In Board of Educ. of Fayette County v. Hurley-Richards, *below, the Court of Appeals of Kentucky held previous Kentucky cases in which "conduct unbecoming a teacher" was justified always involved some kind of dishonest or corrupt behavior. Examples included a teacher falsifying time records, teachers smoking marijuana off campus with 15-year-old students, a teacher calling in sick to work at another job, a teacher whose behavior led to six violent criminal convictions, and a teacher who photographed a partially nude student.*

◆ A veteran teacher who challenged his dismissal for conduct unbecoming a teacher was denied reinstatement by the Supreme Court of North Dakota. Although he said he was denied a fair hearing, the court found an "independent investigation" by a board member and communications between school board members and the community outside the hearing did not hinder his pursuit of the case. **Prior to the discharge, a school administrator had worked with the teacher for seven years on fostering positive relations with students.** Among the incidents leading to the discharge was an outburst within the earshot of students. He called a student "stupid," told another student she had to lose weight and commented about "skinny Ethiopian women." *Kilber v. Grand Forks Public School Dist.*, 820 N.W.2d 96 (N.D. 2012).

◆ A New Jersey special education teacher had worked in her school district for eight years and had a good record. She said that an eight-year-old student in her class had hit her "many times in the past." On a day when the student was agitated and acting aggressively, the teacher said he slapped her and that she reflexively slapped him across the face with her open hand. The school board suspended her without pay and sought to discharge her for conduct unbecoming a teacher. An administrative law judge (ALJ) held a hearing and accepted her account. While the ALJ found the teacher had engaged in unbecoming conduct, he found a single, isolated incident did not warrant dismissal. Instead, a 120-day unpaid suspension with the loss of salary increments for a full school year was recommended. Later, the state education commissioner increased the penalty by four months. A state appellate division court later found **it was not arbitrary or capricious for the commissioner to find that slapping an eight-year-old special education student across the face was unbecoming conduct**.

The court agreed with the commissioner that the teacher's "intolerable conduct and unprofessional behavior validated the very impulses and violence that the student has difficulty controlling." Since the commissioner intended to deprive the teacher of a year's salary increments as a penalty, the court also agreed with the board's request to delay the sanction until a school year in which pay increases were scheduled. *Matter of Tenure Hearing of Craft*, No. 24-2/11, 2012 WL 2579497 (N.J. Super. Ct. App. Div. 7/5/12).

◆ A Kentucky elementary school teacher reprimanded two sibling children for running in the hallway. One of the students ran down the hallway again and told the teacher she could not tell him what to do. He then began pulling his sibling's hair. The teacher put an arm around the student and directed him to the school office. As she did so, the student complained that she was choking him. Another teacher observed the incident and did not intervene. Later, the school district suspended the teacher, and she was notified of contract termination. An administrative tribunal modified the discipline to suspension through the end of the school year. A Kentucky county court found the tribunal's conclusions were unsupported by the evidence. It held the teacher's actions served to maintain school order. In addition, the teacher believed the student presented a risk to others, and that this was a reasonable reason for physical restraint.

On appeal, the Court of Appeals of Kentucky noted the teacher had been charged with conduct unbecoming a teacher under Section 161.790 of the state revised code. When viewing Section 161.790 as a whole, **"conduct unbecoming a teacher" meant "something more than one incident of physically coercing an unruly child to the office."** Because the law grouped the term with "immoral character," the court held **"conduct unbecoming a teacher" was the type of conduct having the appearance or suggestion of immorality**. Prior disciplinary cases involving a finding of "conduct unbecoming a teacher" had always been based on some dishonest or corrupt behavior. As no facts indicated such conduct in this case, the judgment for the teacher was affirmed. *Board of Educ. of Fayette County v. Hurley-Richards*, No. 2010-CA-000840-MR, 2011 WL 3862217 (Ky. Ct. App. 9/2/11).

◆   Ohio school administrators placed a junior high school teacher on leave of absence after investigating charges that he accessed sexually oriented websites on school computers and viewed them with students. The school board resolved to suspend him without pay or benefits, but agreed to delay his hearing until criminal proceedings were complete. The teacher was convicted of several felonies, fined $5,000 and jailed for nearly a year. When the state education department sought to revoke his teaching certificate, he alleged due process violations. A hearing officer found the teacher had sexually abused students, provided them with alcohol and sexually explicit books and movies, let a student view sexually oriented websites on a school computer and "brutalized" at least two students. This conduct was criminal, immoral and unbecoming to a teacher under state law. The state board revoked the teacher's eight-year teaching certificate, and his permanent certification. On appeal, the Ohio Court of Appeals held **he could not be employed as a teacher because he was convicted of one of the crimes listed as disqualifying under state education law**. After his teaching certificates were revoked, the board could not maintain his contract. *Huntsman v. Perry Local School Dist. Board of Educ.*, No. 2004 CA 00347, 2005 WL 1519344 (Ohio Ct. App. 2005).

◆   A Florida teacher had several incidents involving contact with students and was then directed to report physical confrontations and avoid the appearance of intimidating students. He tried to pass candy out to his students in a class, but they became disruptive and rushed toward him. The teacher refused repeated attempts by one student to take more candy. When the student persisted, the teacher struck or shoved him. An administrative law judge (ALJ) conducted a hearing and found that the teacher's use of force was reasonable and lawful. The board modified the ALJ's findings and rejected a recommendation to reinstate the teacher. He sued for reinstatement. A state district court of appeal observed that a school board may not reject an ALJ's findings unless it finds they were not based on competent, substantial evidence or did not comply with the law. Evidence indicated that students crowded the teacher and that the student persisted in attempting to get more candy after the teacher told him he could have no more. **The teacher did not violate the board's previous directive against touching students in a manner that served no educational purpose.** As his actions were not misconduct, gross insubordination, willful neglect of duty, or conduct unbecoming a teacher, the court reversed the board's decision. *Packer v. Orange County School Board*, 881 So.2d 1204 (Fla. Dist. Ct. App. 2004).

V. RESIGNATION AND RETIREMENT

An employee's resignation ends contractual and tenure rights. It may not be withdrawn if the school board has relied on it and hired a replacement. For example, a Minnesota teacher who resigned after earning continuing-contract (tenured) status in a school district could not regain this status when he resigned, worked elsewhere for a year, and then returned to the district.

A. Resignation

◆   After seven years with a Kansas school district, a teacher agreed to leave during a school year in return for a lump sum and insurance payments for five years. A school attorney drafted a written agreement based on discussions at a board meeting, but modifications to it were made in an email exchange. Later, the teacher changed her mind and sought a statutory due process hearing before the board. She reported for work on the day which was to have been her date of termination under the agreement reached at a prior board meeting. The district did not hire a substitute, and the teacher finished out the school year. The board then voted to non-renew her contract, and the school district petitioned a state court for a declaration that the parties had made an oral contract that barred a statutory due process hearing. Appeal reached the Supreme Court of Kansas.

The court found several factors indicating no contract was formed at the first board meeting. A contract exists if there is an unconditional acceptance of the exact terms of an offer. But the parties had communicated by email that there was no "meeting of the minds." A district policy stated that resignations would be considered if they were in writing. **The board did not accept the teacher's resignation in writing, and the meeting minutes did not document a resignation. The court held the board did not prove a contract existed.** Even if one could be found, it was rescinded, as the teacher showed up for work and completed her assignment for the year. *Unified School Dist. No. 446, Independence, Kansas v. Sandoval*, 295 Kan. 278, 286 P.3d 542 (Kan. 2012).

◆   An Alaska teacher arrived late to school and appeared intoxicated. Her principal sent her to an assessment program for alcohol testing. After her blood alcohol level was found to be 0.155, she was assigned to a treatment program. The teacher violated program rules. She was allowed to sign a "last chance agreement," but she violated it as well. After the treatment program discharged the teacher, the district initiated termination proceedings. Upon the advice of a union representative, she resigned. The teacher secretly recorded a telephone conversation with a district human resources director in which the director said that the teacher would be ineligible for rehiring. But he added "you wouldn't have anything negative on your record if you were to apply somewhere else."

The district later refused to provide the teacher a recommendation she sought for another district. In a state court case against the district, she sued for disability discrimination and breach of contract. A trial court held for the school district, and appeal reached the state supreme court. It found the director's promise in the resignation agreement "covered anything negative." **As the teacher raised the possibility that the comments violated the agreement, the court reinstated the contract claim.** But the court held the district's refusal to provide a recommendation to other school districts did not violate the resignation agreement. The trial court would have to reconsider whether the district had immunity. The director's statements could be an implied waiver of the district's right to disclose information about her. But the teacher could not prevail on her disability discrimination claim. The school district stated a legitimate, nondiscriminatory reason for discharging her. Upon learning that she had alcoholism, the district offered her rehabilitation assistance. She was threatened with firing only after she violated the last chance agreement. *Boyko v. Anchorage School Dist.*, 268 P.3d 1097 (Alaska 2012).

◆ A Minnesota teacher worked for a school district from 2000 to 2007. He earned continuing-contract status under state law when he completed his third consecutive year of teaching in the district. After the teacher worked for another employer in 2007-08, he returned to the district for the 2008-09 school year. His contract did not refer to continuing-contract status, stating that its duration was subject to Section 122A.40 of Minnesota Statutes. In April 2009, the school board non-renewed the teacher's contract, effective at the end of the school year.

The case reached the Court of Appeals of Minnesota, which held that under Section 122A.40, teachers are initially subject to a three-year probationary period. During this period, a school board may renew or non-renew a teacher's contract as it sees fit. After completing a probationary period, a teacher had a "continuing contract" with the district that could be terminated only for cause after a hearing or written resignation. After completing a probationary period in a district, "the probationary period in each district in which the teacher is thereafter employed shall be one year." According to the court, the phrase "each district in which the teacher is thereafter employed" included the district in which a teacher completed a three-year probationary period. **A teacher was subject to an additional one-year probationary period of state law upon resignation** and was subject to a one-year probationary period upon returning to the same district. *Montplaisir v. Independent School Dist. No. 23*, 779 N.W.2d 880 (Minn. Ct. App. 2010).

◆ A Colorado teacher had an annual contract that permitted her school district to recover "all damages provided by law" for job abandonment or breach of contract. The district could withhold up to one-twelfth of her annual salary to pay the cost of finding a replacement if she did not provide notice of resignation

30 days prior to a school year. The teacher learned of a personal conflict and advised the district she could not maintain her assignment. The district withheld the teacher's final paycheck. In a state court action, she asserted the district was limited to recovering its actual costs rather than her full paycheck. The case reached the Colorado Supreme Court, which held **the law intended to reimburse districts for their actual cost outlays, not the cost of salaries they would have had to pay in any event**. The teacher tried to resolve a personal conflict in good faith and had tried to comply with district procedures when she resigned. As a result, the district was entitled only to its actual cash outlay. *Klinger v. Adams County School Dist. No. 50*, 130 P.3d 1027 (Colo. 2006).

◆ Certificated Maryland public school employees generally have to provide written notice of a contract termination by May 1. Two teachers submitted written resignations after this deadline. The school board withheld their last paychecks for violating their contracts and replaced them with substitutes. The superintendent upheld the forfeiture provisions, and the board affirmed her decision. A state board upheld the provision, finding it was designed to further the legitimate public purpose of deterring late resignations that deprived local boards of the time needed to recruit and hire replacements at the last minute. It also defrayed some recruiting and hiring costs and the costs of hiring substitute teachers. Appeal reached the Court of Appeals of Maryland, which noted that **the forfeiture provision in the teaching contracts was a reasonable forecast of just compensation, and was binding and could not be altered to correspond to actual damages**. As no evidence indicated the enforcement of the forfeiture provision was arbitrary, the court affirmed the action. *Board of Educ. of Talbot County v. Heister*, 392 Md. 140, 896 A.2d 342 (Md. 2006).

B. Retirement

As in resignation cases, an employee's notice of retirement is typically binding as it cuts off the employee's contractual rights. A school board may not have to rehire an employee who tries to rescind a valid retirement notice.

◆ A South Dakota teacher had worked for her district for 39 years when she learned her position would be reduced from full time to half time the next school year. She retired at the end of the year, took pay for her unpaid sick leave and began receiving benefits from the state retirement system. She came out of retirement before the start of the next school year and signed a one-year probationary contract for the half-time position she had previously rejected. Near the end of the school year, the board did not renew her contract and did not provide her a hearing. The teacher claimed she had no break in service and thus retained her continuing contract status, entitling her to due process protections. She sued the board, and the Supreme Court of South Dakota held that her arguments overlooked her voluntary retirement and her acceptance of a one-year probationary contract. **Her resignation was "a complete termination of her employment relationship"** with the district and terminated her tenure rights. *Wirt v. Parker School Dist. #60-04*, 689 N.W.2d 901 (S.D. 2004).

◆   The Ohio Supreme Court held that **a retired bus mechanic was entitled to reinstatement after his school board illegally abolished his position**, laid him off and outsourced his duties to a private company. Since the board acted illegally, his retirement was considered involuntary. The mechanic retired because of the board's illegal action to abolish his position and outsource his work to a private company. His conduct in applying for retirement benefits did not indicate an intent to give up his continuing public employment rights, and he reapplied for his position as soon as he became aware of his potential right to reinstatement. The court remanded the case for resolution of the mechanic's claim for back wages and benefits. *State of Ohio, ex rel. Stacy v. Batavia Local School Dist. Board of Educ.*, 779 N.E.2d 216 (Ohio 2002).

◆   After 20 years of service, a Minnesota teacher submitted a notice of his retirement. He soon changed his mind and applied for the vacancy he created. The district superintendent wrote the teacher that he was now a probationary teacher subject to employment termination on the last day of the school year. The letter noted the teacher's seniority date was the first day he resumed teaching, and he signed a document designating him as a long-term substitute. Next, the district approved his employment as a probationary teacher. Near the end of the school year, the school board resolved not to renew his contract. The teacher petitioned the Minnesota Court of Appeals, which rejected his claim to continuing contract status. A substitute teacher cannot attain continuing contract status without first being offered, then accepting, a continuing contract. The teacher signed a document advising him he was a long-term, probationary substitute with no continuing contract rights. He was clearly advised that he could regain continuing contract rights only if he were hired for the following school year. **As the teacher had terminated his own contractual rights by retiring and did not reactivate them by resuming his duties, the court affirmed his employment termination.** *Thomas v. Independent School Dist. No. 2142*, 639 N.W.2d 619 (Minn. Ct. App. 2002).

◆   Three Indiana teachers told their district in 1997 that they would retire the next year and accept early retirement benefits under a 1995-1997 master contract. The board and teachers association negotiated a master contract for 1997-2000 that dramatically reduced early retirement benefits. The retirees sued the association for breach of the duty of fair representation, and the board for breach of contract for failing to pay benefits under the 1995-1997 contract.

The court dismissed the complaint, ruling that it should have been filed with the Indiana Education Employment Relations Board (IEERB). The case reached the state supreme court, which held the retirees had to file their unfair representation claims with the IEERB. The state Certificated Educational Employee Bargaining Act recognized a right of school employees to organize and collectively bargain, creating a method to resolve labor disputes through the IEERB. But this ruling did not mean that the trial court had no jurisdiction over the breach of contract claim. **The IEERB had no power to consider a breach of contract claim concerning the board's liability for early retirement benefits.** By dismissing the breach of contract claim, the trial court had denied the retirees the only forum in which the claim could be heard. The trial court was ordered to retain the breach of contract claim. No action was to be taken until the IEERB decided the unfair representation claim. *Fratus v. Marion Community Schools Board of Trustees*, 749 N.E.2d 40 (Ind. 2001).

C. Retirement Benefits

The 2010 Patient Protection and Affordability Act and the Healthcare and Education Reconciliation Act are expected to have implications on school district compensation policies, retirement plans and collective bargaining agreements. The acts have timelines that will eventually require public school retirement plans to comply with requirements of the Employee Retirement Income Security Act (ERISA). Well-publicized provisions extending insurance coverage of dependents up to age 26, prohibiting insurer exclusions for preexisting health conditions and establishing state health insurance exchanges take full effect in 2014. A Patient Protection and Affordability Act provision applies to group health plans and health insurance coverage in which an individual was enrolled on March 23, 2010, the date of enactment of the act.

◆ A Michigan teacher signed an employment contract with the district in May 1968. He assumed coaching duties in the summer of 1968, before he drew a paycheck from the district. In August 1968, the U.S. army inducted him into service, and he served as a combat medic in Vietnam. In 1970, the teacher was honorably discharged. Upon his return to Michigan, the school district hired him. A formal seniority date of September 3, 1968, was assigned, and he worked for the district until 2008. At that time, the district recognized him for 40 years of service. But the Michigan Public School Employees Retirement System denied his application for intervening active-duty service credit, and it rejected the 1968 hire date. The case reached the Court of Appeals of Michigan, which found the state code made a "member" of the retirement system eligible for up to six years of service credit for time spent in the armed forces toward membership in the state retirement system. **To qualify, an employee had to resume public school employment within 24 months after being discharged or released from active duty.** According to the court, the retirement board did not take into account relevant case law definitions. As the teacher met statutory definitions when he was inducted into the army, he was a "member" of the public school employees retirement system as of 1968, and he was entitled to the intervening military service credit he sought. *McCloughan v. Public School Employees Retirement System*, Docket No. 300750, 2011 WL 6378825 (Mich. Ct. App. 12/20/11).

◆ An Oklahoma school district offered an early retirement plan to encourage highly paid senior employees to retire so they could be replaced by lower-paid employees. Eligible retirees were to receive 10% of their salaries plus healthcare benefits. Plan documents said the plan could end "because of lack of funds," but did not explain what would justify termination. In 2002, the district declared a financial crisis that would likely eliminate plan benefits. The school board then voted to terminate payments to retirees but to continue paying for their health insurance. Seventy-nine retirees sued the school district in the state court system for breach of contract. A jury found the retirees proved the district had sufficient revenues to continue paying them benefits and returned a $1.4 million verdict in their favor. On appeal, the Supreme Court of Oklahoma noted that the state constitution required political subdivisions, such as school districts, to carry all "corporate operations on a pay-as-you-go basis." Indebtedness was prohibited beyond a current year. Under state law, **a party demonstrating municipal liability in a contract action had to prove the municipality's ability to pay the claim so that any judgment did not exceed constitutional debt limits**.

Since the retirees did not submit evidence proving the district's legal indebtedness for the fiscal year in which the judgment was issued, a lower court had correctly found lack of compliance with state law. So the judgment was void. But the verdict was supported by competent evidence. The trial court would have to consider evidence establishing the district's actual indebtedness for the year the judgment was issued. *Ahlschlager v. Lawton School Dist., Independent School Dist. 008 of Comanche County*, 242 P.3d 509 (Okla. 2010).

◆   A Pennsylvania school district employee pension plan based retirement benefits on years of service and the employee's average salary in the final years of employment. The plan was administered by the Public School Employees Retirement System (PSERS). Two district employees were approved for leaves of absence to serve in executive union positions for five years. They received pay that was between 44% and 55% higher than what they would have received in their regular employment. When the employees filed retirement applications, the PSERS calculated retirement benefits based on salary levels corresponding to their school district positions. This sharply reduced the retirement benefits the employees expected. The employees appealed to the public school employees' retirement board, which denied their request to use wages earned as union executives in their retirement calculations. Appeal reached the Supreme Court of Pennsylvania, which held **state law did not suggest union employees should receive greater retirement benefits than others who chose to stay in their school positions**. It appeared that the law intended to equalize the playing field by providing retirement benefits for school employees without regard to union service. The court affirmed the retirement board's decision. *Kirsch v. Public School Employees' Retirement Board*, 985 A.2d 671 (Pa. 2009).

◆   An Ohio school janitor suffered an on-the-job fall from a ladder, resulting in back and nerve injuries. After the janitor's treating physician certified her as unable to perform her job duties for 12 months, the state School Employees Retirement System (SERS) ordered a medical examination. It found that nothing precluded her from continuing her custodial work. A SERS medical advisory committee granted her a personal appearance to present her case, but then found that she was not permanently disabled. It denied her application for disability-retirement benefits. The janitor obtained a second medical opinion stating that she could not return to work. The SERS committee denied the janitor's request for a second personal appearance before it, and determined that **the janitor was able to perform her employment duties and was not incapacitated for a period of at least 12 months**. Some 12 years after the fall, the case reached the Supreme Court of Ohio, which found no denial of due process. Despite being denied a second appearance before the SERS, the janitor was allowed reconsideration. Evidence did not show a disabling condition during the 12 continuous months after his application. *VanCleave v. School Employees Retirement System*, 120 Ohio St.3d 261, 898 N.E.2d 33 (Ohio 2008).

◆ An Ohio teacher worked as a special education teacher for over 18 years. He applied for disability retirement benefits due to an inner eyelid infection that caused a film over his eyes. The medical review board of the state teachers retirement system certified the teacher as having an "ongoing" disability. An ophthalmologist selected by the board later found that he was not capable of resuming regular full-time service, and that his benefits should continue. The board questioned these findings, and he clarified that it was unreasonable to expect the teacher to return to his duties after a 17-year absence. But he did not consider the teacher to be totally and permanently disabled based on his medical examination. The medical review board then terminated the teacher's disability retirement benefits. On appeal, the Supreme Court of Ohio held the retirement board did not abuse its discretion and upheld its decision. State law provided that if the board agreed with an examining physician's report that a recipient was no longer incapable of returning to work, disability benefits should be terminated. **The ophthalmologist's examination revealed no incapacitating medical disability.** His conclusion was not based on medical factors, but on the passage of time since the initial disability determination. *Ackerman v. State Teachers Retirement Board*, 117 Ohio St.3d 268, 883 N.E.2d 445 (Ohio 2008).

◆ A New York school superintendent served a school district for about seven years under employment contracts that provided for lifetime health insurance coverage "upon his retirement from the District." He notified the district of his intent to retire from the district, but took a job as a superintendent of another New York district for a salary increase. The district deemed the separation to be a "resignation," then informed the superintendent that because he had resigned, he was not entitled to lifetime health benefits. The superintendent sued the district in a state court for breach of contract, seeking over $450,000.

The court dismissed the complaint, and the superintendent appealed to the New York Supreme Court, Appellate Division. The court found that the contract permitted termination by either retirement or resignation, making it clear the terms were not synonymous. **While health insurance benefits would be provided in the event of retirement, no reference was made to resignation. The superintendent did not change his status by applying for retirement benefits.** Instead, he took a similar position in a neighboring county. As this action was within the recognized definition of "resignation," the court affirmed the judgment for the school district. *Bauersfeld v. Board of Educ. of Morrisville-Eaton Cent. School Dist.*, 846 N.Y.S.2d 809 (N.Y. App. Div. 2007).

◆ A Montana school superintendent obtained assurances from his school board that he could retire with lifetime health insurance premiums for himself and his wife under a contract addendum. Six years later, a board made up of all new members voted to terminate the superintendent's premium payments. He sued the school district in a federal court, asserting violations of state law and due process. The case reached the U.S. Court of Appeals, Ninth Circuit, which held that **the district's arguments to void the contract failed**. The former superintendent had provided adequate consideration for the contract addendum by continuing to work for the district for six weeks after its execution. *McCracken v. Lockwood School Dist. #26*, 208 Fed.Appx. 513 (9th Cir. 2006).

VI. UNEMPLOYMENT BENEFITS

School employees are not entitled to unemployment benefits between academic years, if there is a reasonable assurance of teaching for the school the next year. An employee must work a minimum amount of time to qualify for benefits, but if the employee has committed misconduct resulting in dismissal or left a job without good cause, benefits will typically be denied.

A. Eligibility Requirements

◆ A substitute teacher who signed a renewal application and substitute teacher agreement with a Florida school district was held ineligible to receive state unemployment compensation benefits between consecutive school years. Affirming an administrative order denying benefits, the state court of appeal held **unemployment benefits are not payable for teaching services at educational institutions for a period between academic years or terms, if the person seeking benefits performed instructional services and had a contract** or reasonable assurance that the person would continue the services in the next year or term. By signing the agreement, the teacher acknowledged a reasonable assurance of being reemployed the next year. *Brown v. Florida Unemployment Appeals Comm'n*, 81 So.3d 646 (Fla. Dist. Ct. App. 2012).

◆ A Pennsylvania teacher earned $126.34 per day with 10 sick days for her work as a long-term substitute for a school district. At the end of the school year, she accepted placement on the day-to-day substitute list and applied for unemployment compensation benefits. The state Unemployment Compensation Board of Review (UCBR) found the teacher had no reasonable assurance of returning to work under the Unemployment Compensation Act. On appeal, the state supreme court stated **a school employee is not entitled to unemployment benefits between academic years, if there is a reasonable assurance of performing services in an instructional, research or administrative capacity for the school in the second year**. In this case, the UCBR had found the teacher did not have reasonable assurance of returning to work for the district. Her employment as a day-to-day substitute teacher was substantially less favorable than those for a long-term substitute. State law was not intended to "eliminate the payment of benefits to school employees during summer months," as the district argued. The decrease in the teacher's income was not caused by the summer vacation, but by the district's decision to offer her a position with fewer wages, hours and benefits. As a result, the court held she was entitled to benefits. *Slippery Rock Area School Dist. v. Unemployment Compensation Board of Review*, 603 Pa. 374, 983 A.2d 1231 (Pa. 2009).

◆   A West Virginia custodian worked for his school district during the summer as a painter for several years. The school board did not offer him employment for the summer one year, and he filed a claim for unemployment compensation benefits. The West Virginia Department of Employment Security declared the employee disqualified from benefits on the basis of the existence of reasonable assurances that he would be working for the school board that fall. The department's board of review reversed this decision, finding that he was entitled to benefits since he had worked for the school district in prior summers and was effectively laid off. The case reached the Supreme Court of Appeals of West Virginia, which held that **service personnel employed by school boards are ineligible for unemployment unless they hold a second, separate contract for the summer months or show the existence of a continuing contractual relationship**. Since the employee failed to show he had a continuing contract for the summer break, he was not entitled to receive benefits. *Raleigh County Board of Educ. v. Gatson*, 468 S.E.2d 923 (W. Va. 1996).

B. Misconduct

While the Supreme Court of Florida has found an employee's absence without authorization is "inherently detrimental to the employer's interests," a Virginia court has held "mere absence without leave is not disqualifying misconduct." In the next case, a North Dakota teacher was unable to collect unemployment benefits after being removed for poor evaluations, complaints by the community, and performance issues such as not following the curriculum.

◆   A newly hired North Dakota teacher reported that two students had been raped. She was assured that the report was unfounded. An evaluation of the teacher noted she required improvement in several areas. Midway through the school year, the district superintendent placed her on administrative leave for continuing to talk about alleged rapes of students at school. She returned to work, but was soon found in violation of directives to refrain from discussing personal matters, teach only the curriculum, follow the chain of command and stop making false accusations about student rapes. The school board voted to remove her prior to the end of her contract. The teacher sought unemployment benefits, which were denied based on her non-renewal for misconduct.

Appeal reached the Supreme Court of North Dakota. The court explained that state law disqualified an employee who was discharged for employment misconduct. **"Misconduct" included the deliberate violation or disregard of standards of behavior which an employer had a right to expect.** Under North Dakota law, non-renewal of a teaching contract ordinarily did not rise to the level of misconduct. But in this case, there was evidence that the teacher was discharged for reporting unsubstantiated conduct, and for repeatedly and deliberately violating directives. She was also the subject of complaints from the community. Her own writings indicated she was insolent and unwilling to yield to reasonable employer directives. As the evidence indicated she deliberately disregarded her employer's interests, the court affirmed the denial of benefits. *Schmidt v. Job Service North Dakota*, 756 N.W.2d 794 (N.D. 2008).

◆   A Nevada school district fired an in-school suspension teacher for being absent without leave eight times in five weeks. She filed an unemployment compensation claim, which was granted. The district challenged the award of benefits, maintaining that it admonished the teacher and that excessive absences amounted to misconduct. The teacher stated that her absences were required to see a doctor and to take care of a sick child, whose illness was the result of a continuing medical condition that the school knew about. A hearing referee found the principal more credible than the teacher and held that the discharge was based on attendance problems and failure to notify the district of her absences, in violation of a district policy. A review board reversed the decision, and appeal reached the Supreme Court of Nevada.

According to the court, an employee's absence will be misconduct in unemployment compensation cases "only if the circumstances indicate that the absence was taken in willful violation or disregard of a reasonable employment policy" or lacked an appropriate notice. The court found that the school district had the burden to show the teacher's conduct disqualified her from benefits. **An absence without leave was not disqualifying misconduct. The district would have to show that the teacher's absences were excessive.** Since the board failed to consider whether the absences were "excessive" and whether the first five absences were justifiable, the case was returned to the board for further activity. *Clark County School Dist. v. Bundley*, 148 P.3d 750 (Nev. 2006).

◆   A discharged teacher received unemployment benefits while appealing her dismissal. The Oregon Fair Dismissal Appeals Board held that the dismissal was unlawful and ordered the school district to reinstate her with back pay. The district asserted a right to set off unemployment benefits received by the teacher against her back pay award. It claimed the quarterly payments it made to the state employment department for the Unemployment Compensation Trust Fund justified the offset. The board agreed with the district, finding the district's contributions to the trust fund made it a reimbursing employer. The case reached the Supreme Court of Oregon, which reviewed ORS § 342.905, the statute under which setoff was approved. The court found the board could reinstate a teacher if the charges were untrue or there were inadequate grounds for dismissal. **While Section 342.905 authorized back pay awards for wrongfully discharged employees, nothing permitted the board to set off unemployment compensation against back pay** with money received under an unrelated benefit program. The district had not itself paid unemployment compensation benefits to the teacher. Any such issue was between the teacher and the employment department. As the district did not pay the compensation benefits it now sought to set off, the judgment was reversed. *Zottola v. Three Rivers School Dist.*, 342 Or. 118, 149 P.3d 1151 (Or. 2006).

◆   A Pennsylvania school district suspended a substitute teacher without pay for violating its policy prohibiting weapons on school property. She submitted a claim for unemployment benefits that was denied by a state unemployment compensation referee, who found no justification for inadvertently bringing guns to school when called to work as a substitute on short notice. The case reached the Supreme Court of Pennsylvania, which explained that **a finding of**

"willful misconduct" was necessary to disqualify unemployment compensation benefits. Section 402(e) of the Unemployment Compensation Law did not define "willful misconduct," but previous state court decisions characterized it as disregard for an employer's interests, deliberate violation of employer rules, or disregard for the employer's standards of behavior. Employee negligence could result in a finding of willful misconduct only when it showed intentional disregard for the employer's interest or an employee's duties or obligations. Since the district could not show the teacher's actions were intentional or deliberate, she was not disqualified from benefits. *Grieb v. Unemployment Compensation Board of Review*, 827 A.2d 422 (Pa. 2003).

◆ The Court of Appeals of Minnesota upheld the **denial of unemployment compensation benefits to a custodian who did not lock the exterior doors to his school several times.** After being suspended with a written warning, he yelled at a supervisor and threatened her when she complained about him. The court of appeals held the custodian was properly denied unemployment benefits. His repeated failure to lock exterior doors and his insubordination was misconduct showing both a substantial lack of concern for his employment and a violation of reasonable standards of behavior. *Ashong v. Independent School Dist. #625*, No. A04-1623, 2005 WL 1432203 (Minn. Ct. App. 2005).

VII. WORKERS' COMPENSATION

Workers' compensation (also known as industrial insurance) is typically the exclusive remedy for an employee injured in the course and scope of employment. A significant part of the litigation in this area focuses on whether an injured employee may assert tort claims for more money than what is available under workers' compensation law by showing intentional conduct or a deliberate or conscious failure to act for the employee's safety.

In Richard v. Washburn Public Schools, *below, the Supreme Court of North Dakota was presented with the question of whether sexual harassment was an "injury" under the state Workforce Safety and Insurance Act. It found courts in other states are divided on whether sexual harassment is an "injury by accident" under their workers' compensation laws. Illinois and South Carolina courts have held it may be, while courts in Arizona, New Mexico, Virginia and Wisconsin have held otherwise.*

◆ A 16-year-old North Dakota student worked as a part-time custodian for her school district. She said her supervisor twice put her in a "chokehold," but she did not tell anyone about either incident. Later, she claimed the supervisor told her to "bend over" as he pushed her by the neck from behind. The student told her mother about the third incident. The mother then reported it to the principal, who took no action, in disregard of policy regarding sexual harassment reports. The student did not make a report to the superintendent, as the principal suggested. She said the supervisor later asked her about kissing her boyfriend, put his hands in her pants and pulled her toward him. This time, the mother reported the incident to the superintendent.

Two years later, the student sued for negligence, assault and battery. Finding the state's two-year statute of limitations barred the assault and battery claims, the court dismissed them. It held the supervisor's conduct was not foreseeable and found the negligent supervision and retention claims were barred by the exclusivity provisions of the state Workforce Safety and Insurance Act. On appeal, the Supreme Court of North Dakota held that there are exceptions to the exclusive remedy provisions of the act. **A workplace injury was compensable only if a physical injury was determined with reasonable medical certainty to be at least 50% of the cause of the condition.** In this case, the student's complaint described inappropriate conduct by the supervisor, including sexual comments and touching. According to the court, the essence of her action was to recover for non-physical injuries. It held **the school district did not show the student suffered injuries that were compensable under the state workers' compensation act.** For that reason, the act's exclusive remedy provisions did not bar the claim. A claim for negligent supervision of an employee arises when an employer fails to exercise ordinary care in supervising the employment relationship to prevent foreseeable misconduct of an employee. The court found sufficient evidence of negligent supervision for the student to proceed with this claim, which was returned to the lower court. *Richard v. Washburn Public Schools*, 809 N.W.2d 288 (N.D. 2011).

◆ A Texas school employee hurt himself on the job and then sought benefits for back and shoulder injuries. While admitting the injury, his employing school district disputed compensation issues. Administrative proceedings led to a decision for the employee. In a state court lawsuit, the district sought review, and the employee counterclaimed for his attorneys' fees under a state law that authorized attorneys' fees for claimants who successfully defended appeals "on an issue in which judicial review is sought" by an insurer. The district, which was self-insuring under the state workers' compensation act, then abandoned its defense of the administrative action, in what is called a "nonsuit." A jury then found the employee should get more than $50,000 for attorneys' fees, most of which were incurred prior to the nonsuit. Appeal reached the state supreme court, which held state law did not allow claims or damage awards against state political subdivisions unless they were specifically authorized by the Tort Claims Act. In a prior case, the court had held that any waiver of governmental immunity must be clear and unambiguous. **Since attorneys' fees were not listed in the law waiving governmental immunity, the court held there had been no waiver of immunity.** For this reason, the claim for fees was barred. *Manbeck v. Austin Independent School Dist.*, 381 S.W.3d 528 (Tex. 2012).

◆ A Florida school policy created a team of specially trained first responders. The policy prohibited teachers who were not members of the team from intervening in fights and other school crises. A fight broke out in a classroom of disabled students. Instead of waiting for team members, the classroom teacher tried to separate the students. She was drawn into the fight and fell on her knee. In a state court lawsuit against the school board, the teacher claimed intentional conduct by the board that qualified for an exception to the exclusivity provision of the state workers' compensation law. She argued that the board's actions were substantially certain to cause her injury. A jury found the intentional tort exception did not apply, and the teacher appealed to the state court of appeal, claiming the school board had covered up dangerous situations in the past. She also said the lower court should have let the jury know about a post-incident miscarriage and should have let jurors know of the shooting death of a teacher at the same school two years earlier. But the court of appeal instead found **the teacher voluntarily inserted herself into the fight in disregard of school policy, despite her knowledge that students with disabilities may act out violently**. As the lower court held, the board was entitled to judgment on the grounds of workers' compensation exclusivity. *Patrick v. Palm Beach County School Board*, 50 So.3d 1161 (Fla. Dist. Ct. App. 2010).

◆   A New Jersey alternative high school counselor helped a security officer try to break up a fight between students. The counselor was pinned against a wall and pushed to the floor for 15 to 20 minutes until police arrived. He claimed the incident upset him so much that he feared returning to school. He applied for disability benefits. While the counselor was pursuing his claim, he worked as an adjunct professor at two county colleges, and occasionally performed as a musician in coffee shops and jazz clubs. Two professionals diagnosed the counselor with post-traumatic stress disorder (PTSD). A psychiatrist appointed by the New Jersey Board of Trustees of the Teachers' Pension and Annuity Fund determined the counselor did not have PTSD. An administrative law judge (ALJ) denied an application for accidental disability benefits. On appeal, a New Jersey appellate court found that **disability did not result from "an experience that was either terrifying or horror inducing, nor did it involve any actual or threatened death or serious injury."** As the counselor was not disabled from teaching or other employment, the court held he could not show he was permanently disabled. The state supreme court has held where no qualifying traumatic event occurred, the potential for accidental disability benefits based on a mental disability was eliminated. As the ALJ had correctly applied the law, the denial of benefits was affirmed. *Janetta v. Teachers' Pension and Annuity Fund*, 2011 WL 3241581 (N.J. Super. Ct. App. Div. 8/1/11).

◆   An Ohio educational service center (ESC) employee was hurt in a work-related auto accident. The Bureau of Workers' Compensation granted her claim to participate in the state workers' compensation fund. The ESC asked the state industrial commission to find fraud and terminate the employee's participation in the fund. Hearing officers found no evidence of fraud, and the commission denied further appeal. The ESC appealed to a state court of common pleas, which dismissed the case. On appeal, the Supreme Court of Ohio held **only commission decisions involving employee participation rights can be appealed to the court system**. In this case, the commission had found no evidence of employee fraud and the employer did not appeal from this finding. As the commission had refused to reconsider the claim, the employee's right to participate in the fund had been conclusively determined. The lower court had correctly dismissed the case. *Benton v. Hamilton Educ. Service Center*, 123 Ohio St.3d 347, 916 N.E.2d 778 (Ohio 2009).

◆   A North Carolina teacher had consistent problems managing her classroom and maintaining order. After negative performance evaluations and failed action plans, the teacher missed a meeting with her principal to address her performance problems. She refused to sign a warning letter, left school, and did not return to work. A psychologist diagnosed her with generalized anxiety disorder (GAD) and medically excluded her from work. The teacher submitted a workers' compensation claim, asserting GAD was an occupational disease caused by her "hostile and abusive" classroom. The state industrial commission found that **the teacher failed to show that her GAD was due to causes and conditions characteristic of her job**. It denied her claim. Appeal reached the Supreme Court of North Carolina, which held that an employee satisfies the workers' compensation statute by showing work exposed the employee to a greater risk of contracting an occupational disease than members of the general public. Here, the commission determined that her psychologist's report was not believable, and she did not bring him to testify on her behalf. Without his testimony, the teacher had no expert medical evidence to support her claim. *Hassell v. Onslow County Board of Educ.*, 661 S.E.2d 709 (N.C. 2008).

◆   A California student established a pattern of pushing others and making sexual innuendos to girls. His parents repeatedly rejected any special placement as they did not want their son "labeled." The student later told classmates he wanted to "put a bullet in the head" of his teacher, the teacher's wife and baby. The student was out of school for weeks. When he returned, the school psychologist recommended placing him in a program for emotionally disturbed students. The mother again insisted he remain in a regular classroom. On a day when the student had knocked down a classmate on the playground, a teacher accompanied him to the school bus. The student charged into her and knocked her down on the bus. The teacher received workers' compensation benefits of over $91,000, but sought additional benefits for serious and willful misconduct.

The state Workers' Compensation Appeals Board found that the school district engaged in "serious and willful misconduct" by failing to permanently remove the physically and verbally aggressive student from the teacher's classroom. It awarded her an additional $45,785. The Court of Appeal of California held that **the school district did not deliberately or consciously fail to take action for the teacher's safety**. It had been trying to place the student in a behavior-based placement since third grade, but the parents had repeatedly refused to consent. The district had found the student eligible for an emotionally disturbed program, put him on a daily contract, and suspended and counseled him several times. As a result, the court annulled the award of additional benefits. *Elk Grove Unified School Dist. v. Workers' Compensation Appeals Board*, No. C052945, 2007 WL 1169336 (Cal. Ct. App. 4/20/07).

◆   A Georgia school bus driver's family had a history of asthma, and one of her sisters had died at age 21 after a severe asthma attack. The driver was diagnosed with asthma after two years of work in the district. She suffered an asthma attack on her special needs school bus, and claimed that fumes and chemicals caused it. Doctors soon released her to work without restrictions, but she did not return. A workers' compensation panel physician and a pulmonologist released her to work without restrictions, but the driver did not feel safe driving special needs children. A clinical psychologist diagnosed her with adjustment disorder and depression and stated that she had too much anxiety about driving a bus to return to work. A school psychologist found inconsistent symptoms suggesting she had "a severe somatization disorder and/or malingering." The board discharged her for job abandonment. A state administrative law judge found the driver suffered a compensable injury. The state court of appeals affirmed the judgment for the driver. It held **a claimant is entitled to workers' compensation benefits for mental disability and psychic treatment arising out of an accident in which a compensable physical injury was suffered**. There was evidence that the driver's psychic problems were based on a real fear of her death from an asthma attack and her concern for special needs children on her bus. *DeKalb Board of Educ. v. Singleton*, 294 Ga.App. 96, 668 S.E.2d 767 (Ga. Ct. App. 2008).

◆ An Idaho behavioral counselor worked for a behavioral support division and traveled to different schools in Idaho Falls School District No. 91. She also spent two days each week at an alternative school in Bonneville County Joint School District No. 93. The school was attended by students from both school districts. The counselor went on a field trip with students and District 93 employees to a former ski lodge leased from the U.S. government. She was injured while helping to catch a student during a "trust fall" exercise. The counselor received workers' compensation benefits from District 91, but filed a personal injury lawsuit against District 93 in the state court system, claiming negligence. The court held she was a statutory employee of District 93, making the district immune from personal injury lawsuits. The counselor appealed.

The Supreme Court of Idaho held that **if the counselor was either a statutory employee or a "borrowed employee," District 93 was entitled to immunity** from personal injury damages. Since District 93 did not operate a "business" as defined in state law, it could not be the counselor's statutory employer. But the trial court had incorrectly held that the counselor was not a "borrowed employee," as it remained unclear whether District 91 or District 93 had the right to control her. The court remanded the case for a determination of whether the counselor was a borrowed employee. *Cordova v. Bonneville County Joint School Dist.*, 144 Idaho 637, 167 P.3d 775 (Idaho 2007).

◆ A disabled Washington student inflicted frequent injuries on students and staff. In one school year, he caused over 200 documented injuries. The student pushed his teacher as she tried to intervene during one of his attacks, knocking her unconscious. The next day, he bit an aide on her breast as she tried to distract him from other students. Despite these incidents, the student remained in his class with the same staff for most of the year. Both employees received workers' compensation benefits, but sought additional damages and sued the school district. The case reached the Supreme Court of Washington, which stated that **while workers' compensation is typically the exclusive remedy for an injured employee, a limited exception applies to employers who intentionally injure employees**. An employer's gross negligence or failure to observe safety laws and procedures does not constitute deliberate intent to injure. An employee had to show that an employer had actual knowledge injury was certain to occur before the employer could be liable in a tort case. The behavior of a child with special needs was far from predictable. The district had tried increasingly restrictive strategies to address his behavior. The employees did not show the district was certain its strategies would fail. There could be no liability for the district based on simple negligence. *Vallandigham v. Clover Park School Dist. No. 400*, 109 P.3d 805 (Wash. 2005).

♦   A Florida school bus attendant was injured when a wheelchair lift fell on him. He claimed that a maintenance worker negligently repaired or adjusted the lift twice in a four-month period before the accident. He sued the school board for negligence, arguing that he and the maintenance employee were involved in "unrelated work" under the workers' compensation law. The court held that the exception for unrelated work did not apply, and held for the board. The Supreme Court of Florida explained that **workers' compensation law created an exception to immunity for cases involving employees of the same employer when each was assigned primarily to "unrelated works."** The attendant and mechanics were both employed by the board, worked in the same facility and were involved in the same transportation services. The unrelated works exception applied only if an employee who caused injury was clearly engaged in works unrelated to the injured employee. The trial court had correctly held the employees had the common goal of providing safe transportation. *Taylor v. School Board of Brevard County*, 888 So.2d 1 (Fla. 2004).

♦   The Supreme Court of South Dakota upheld an administrative decision denying workers' compensation benefits to a school bus driver injured while snow skiing on a school field trip. She was receiving "down time" pay during the student activity and was free to do whatever she wanted when she accepted a free lift pass. Here, the driver's injury was not "work-related" because it did not arise out of her employment. She was not expected to supervise students after they left the bus. **The driver had "stepped aside from her employment purpose when she went skiing,"** and was not entitled to benefits. *Norton v. Deuel School Dist. #19-4*, 674 N.W.2d 518 (S.D. 2004).

CHAPTER TEN

Tenure and Due Process

I. STATE TENURE STATUTES

A. Tenure Status

1. Temporary and Probationary Assignments

In Kahn v. New York City Dep't of Educ., *below, New York's highest court held decisions to non-renew probationary employees in New York City schools were not open to challenge in an optional internal appeal procedure.*

In Bailey v. Blount County Board of Educ., *below, the Supreme Court of Tennessee held that prior to non-renewal, non-tenured, non-licensed employees are generally only entitled to notice of the charges against them, an explanation of the administration's evidence and an opportunity to respond in writing.*

◆ Two New York City probationary school employees were notified that they would not be rehired due to performance issues. Both sought review via an optional procedure from their collective bargaining agreement (CBA). One proceeding took four months, and the other took more than two years. In both cases, the city department of education (DOE) upheld the decisions. The employees filed separate state court actions against the DOE after their CBA challenges concluded. Their cases reached the New York Court of Appeals. It considered the cases together and noted the CBA provision and DOE bylaws gave probationary employees an opportunity for administrators to reconsider termination decisions. In both cases, the employees awaited the outcome of optional CBA procedures before pursuing state court actions. Since state law required the filing of such actions within four months, neither case was timely.

State law made a decision to terminate the employment of a probationary teacher final and binding on the effective date of termination, even if administrative review was available. A 1984 case established the right of DOE's chancellor to terminate a probationary contract at any time and for any reason other than actions taken in bad faith or for unconstitutional or unlawful reasons. Decisions not to grant tenure to probationary teachers were intended to be final, and the statute had no provision for review. As DOE internal review procedures under its bylaws and the CBA were optional and did not affect the finality of a termination decision, the court upheld the DOE's decisions. *Kahn v. New York City Dep't of Educ.*, 18 N.Y.3d 457 (N.Y. 2012).

◆ A Massachusetts probationary school nurse received notice that she would not be rehired near the end of her second year of work for a school district. The notice was sent a week before the June 15 statutory deadline for notification of the non-reemployment of a teacher without professional status. According to the nurse, she had been "dismissed" and should have received a notice of the intent to dismiss her, with an explanation of the grounds in sufficient detail to permit her to respond. She also claimed the right to receive certain documentation. Although the nurse sued the superintendent and school committee in a state superior court, the case was dismissed. She appealed to the Supreme Judicial Court of Massachusetts, arguing her non-renewal was a "dismissal" within the meaning of state law. The court stated that **teachers with no professional status serve on a year-to-year basis and are subject to the reappointment process each year**. Such teachers had no guarantee of employment beyond the current school year, unless June 15 passed without the required notice of nonreappointment from the school committee. The court held dismissal was not a non-renewal. Since the nurse was not "dismissed," she was not entitled to the safeguards she claimed. *Laurano v. Superintendent of Schools of Saugus*, 459 Mass. 1008, 945 N.E.2d 933 (Mass. 2011).

◆ A California district hired a high school baseball coach. A year later, the district employed him as a full-time teacher. He continued to serve as a teacher and coach for the next year and a half. After that time, the school never rehired him as a teacher. Five years after losing his full-time teaching job, the coach learned that he would be relieved of his coaching duties. His request to file a grievance was denied because he was not a member of the employee association representing teachers in the district. The coach sought a special order from a state court declaring that the district had unlawfully classified him as a temporary employee. But as he admitted receiving notice of the termination of his coaching duties before June 30, the court denied his request.

On appeal, the state court of appeal found that **except for substitutes, school boards are to classify as "temporary" those employees "employed to serve in a limited assignment supervising athletic activities of pupils."** Coaches were "temporary employees" under state law, and the court rejected a claim that the district had to classify the coach as a "probationary employee." He was employed in a limited assignment to supervise athletics, and the court found no legal duty to classify him as a "probationary employee." As the lower court held, the district provided the coach with adequate notice of termination and did not unlawfully classify him. *Neily v. Manhattan Beach Unified School Dist.*, 192 Cal.App.4th 187, 120 Cal.Rptr. 3d 857 (Cal. Ct. App. 2011).

◆ A non-licensed, non-tenured Tennessee high school teaching assistant (TA) had a one-year contract to supervise an in-school suspension program. A student filed a sexual harassment complaint against him. The next year, a teacher claimed the TA emailed her about her appearance in jeans, and she filed a sexual harassment complaint against him. The director of the school district suspended the TA for 10 days with pay, pending an investigation. A day after sending the TA notice of his hearing rights, the director sent him another letter advising him that he was dismissed as of that date for improper conduct. The TA's attorney appeared on his behalf at a personnel hearing. A school personnel hearing authority upheld the dismissal. Instead of appealing to the school board as specified by the district's policy, the TA appealed to the state court system.

The court awarded judgment to the school board and awarded the board attorneys' fees based on filing a frivolous case. On appeal, the Supreme Court of Tennessee held **Section 49-2-301 of the state code gave the director authority to non-renew an unlicensed staff member such as the TA before the end of his contract for insubordination, neglect of duty, incompetence, inefficiency, or improper conduct**. There was a clear difference in termination procedures for unlicensed employees and for those who held licenses. Neither Section 49-2-301 nor board policy conferred rights on the TA to a full hearing. He chose not to appeal to the school board after his hearing before the personnel authority, defeating his due process and related claims. But since the trial court had failed to consider any non-due process claims, they would have to be reconsidered. This included a wrongful discharge claim. The court held the trial court had erroneously assessed the TA attorneys' fees for filing a frivolous lawsuit. *Bailey v. Blount County Board of Educ.*, 303 S.W.3d 216 (Tenn. 2010).

◆ A Kentucky school board did not violate state law by passing over a special education teacher for promotion to a special education teacher/director position. It hired a qualified applicant who had emergency certification for the job. After a state trial court ruled for the school board, the Court of Appeals of Kentucky noted evidence that **the teacher was unqualified for the promotion**. A former employer "absolutely did not recommend him for employment," and he was under review by the state Professional Standards Board. *Hicks v. Magoffin County Board of Educ.*, 292 S.W.3d 335 (Ky. Ct. App. 2009).

◆ A New York school district hired a teacher to serve as an administrator under a three-year contract. Six months into the contract, the district decided to eliminate the position for financial reasons. The administrator sued for breach of contract, and a state court ruled in her favor. An appellate division court affirmed, and the case reached the New York Court of Appeals. On appeal, the school district argued that a breach of contract claim could not be maintained, as New York Education Law prohibits school districts from entering contracts that guarantee employment to non-tenured administrators for a specific term.

The court held state law allowed school districts to end probationary appointments at any time during the probationary period. The law did not prohibit a school board from entering into a durational, three-year contract of employment with a probationary school administrator. However, **absent an express waiver, a school district retained the right to discharge teachers during a probationary term**. Here, the language of the contract was too equivocal to establish a conscious waiver by the district. Thus, the judgment was reversed. *Consedine v. Portville Cent. School Dist.*, 12 N.Y.3d 286, 907 N.E.2d 684, 879 N.Y.S.2d 806 (N.Y. 2009).

◆ In April 2005, a South Dakota school board held an executive session to decide whether to renew the contracts of 34 teachers. When it reconvened in open session, the board voted to renew 30 of the contracts. Two probationary teachers were among the four who were not offered contracts. The superintendent sent them written notices of non-renewal before April 15. The probationary teachers claimed they were entitled to an affirmative vote of non-renewal by the board. They sued the school district in a state court, which held that the notices satisfied state law. On appeal, the Supreme Court of South Dakota held that **the superintendent or board had to give written notice of non-renewal by April 15, but was not required to give further process or a reason for non-renewal of the probationary teaching contracts**. Nothing in state law required an affirmative school board vote. The law authorized the board to renew the contracts by a vote or to non-renew them by refusing to vote. The board's refusal to vote to offer new contracts was within its statutory right to "not renew" the teachers' contracts. *Scheller v. Faulkton Area School Dist. #24-3*, 731 N.W.2d 914 (S.D. 2007).

◆ A California teacher completed a one-year contract under an emergency teaching permit and then received a professional clear teaching credential. The district classified him as a probationary employee. The teacher worked the full school year for the district. On May 23, he was sent a notice of non-reelection of employment for a third year. He sued the district, arguing that he had completed two years of service in a teaching position requiring certification qualifications, and that he had a right to notice of non-reelection of employment by March 15. The case reached the Court of Appeal of California. It stated that if a board does not give the required notice to a permanent employee by March 15, the employee is deemed reelected. **But notice applied only to those eligible to become permanent employees under tenure rules.** Here, the teacher was ineligible for permanent employment and could not insist on notice. The case was unlike *California Teachers Ass'n v. Governing Board of Golden Valley Unified School Dist.*, 98 Cal.App.4th 369, 119 Cal.Rptr.2d 642 (2002), where a teacher who served under an emergency credential was held to qualify as a probationary employee. That case did not involve a claim to permanent employment, so the court held for the district. *Culbertson v. San Gabriel Unified School Dist.*, 121 Cal.App.4th 1392, 18 Cal. Rptr.3d 234 (Cal. Ct. App. 2004).

2. Contract Renewal by Operation of Law

In McIntyre v. Sonoma Valley Unified School Dist., *below, a California court rejected a temporary teacher's claim to automatic elevation from temporary to probationary status based on her two consecutive years of temporary service.*

In Williams v. Lafayette Parish School Board, *533 So.2d 1359 (La. Ct. App. 1989), the Court of Appeal of Louisiana held voluntary resignation breaks the continuity of state tenure law. In* Brubaker v. Hardy, *5 Ohio St.2d 103, 214 N.E.2d 79 (Ohio 1966), the Supreme Court of Ohio held the acceptance of a teacher's resignation, and his subsequent acceptance of a one-year teaching contract, resulted in waiver of the right to a continuing employment contract.*

◆   A California school district hired a temporary teacher. It then released her and rehired her as a long-term temporary. It did so again the next year. After hiring the teacher for a third year, the district did not rehire her and gave her a timely non-renewal notice. She petitioned a state court to compel the district to reinstate her as a permanent tenured teacher. After the court denied the petition, she appealed. The Court of Appeal of California held that since substitute and temporary employees filled the short-range needs of school districts, they could generally be released in summary fashion. No statement of reasons or hearing was required to release a temporary teacher if proper statutory notice was given.

The court held **teachers hired on a temporary basis did not obtain employment rights**. If they did, districts would be in the untenable position of having to employ two teachers when a teacher on leave of absence returned. State Education Code Section 44920 allowed districts to hire certificated employees based on the leave or illness of another teacher. A district's use of the Section 44920 temporary classification did not depend upon a one-to-one match of employees on leave to temporary teachers. In this case, the district complied with the requirement that the number of temporary employees not exceed the number of probationary and permanent employees on leave. A district was not prevented from "hiring temporary teachers to replace teachers on leave on a year-to-year basis without elevating them to probationary status." As a result, the court held for the district. *McIntyre v. Sonoma Valley Unified School Dist.*, 206 Cal.App.4th 170, 141 Cal.Rptr.3d 540 (Cal. Ct. App. 2012).

◆   After teaching in a school district for 16 years, a Montana educator became an elementary school principal. She then served as principal of a district high school for four years. The district provided the educator no written notice when it reassigned her to an elementary teaching job. The reassignment increased her annual salary by $3,000 and decreased her work calendar by 20 days. After accepting the reassignment under protest, the educator appealed to the state superintendent of public instruction, who found the positions of teacher and principal were not comparable in reassignment cases not involving budgetary reasons. Appeal reached the Supreme Court of Montana, which noted that Section 20-4-203 of the state code applied to both teachers and principals. In reviewing relevant state laws, the court held a "principal" was a person holding a valid Montana teacher certificate and a principal's endorsement. **Any** reference to "teacher" under the tenure statute included a principal, and principal and teacher positions were "comparable" under state law. This was true even though no position was eliminated for financial reasons and the board had hired another person to take the educator's former position. There was no merit to her claim that the board had to provide her advance written notice of the reassignment and a hearing. *King v. Hays/Lodge Pole Public School Dist. #50*, 361 Mont. 415, 259 P.3d 772 (Mont. 2011).

◆   During a summer break, a New York school board voted to terminate the contract of a probationary teacher in 30 days. But the board did not provide him written notice until two days before the action was to take effect. The teacher sued the board in a state court for 28 days of pay, plus a name-clearing hearing and attorneys' fees based on violation of federal due process principles. The court held for the board, as did a state appellate division court. On appeal, the New York Court of Appeals observed that state Education Law Section 3019-a required school officials to give probationary teachers a 30-day written notice before the effective date of employment termination. **If a probationary teacher was being denied tenure, written notice had to be provided no later than 60 days before the probationary period expired.** While the law did not specify a remedy for failure to provide teachers required notices, the court had held in a 1993 case that a teacher was entitled to a day's pay for each day a termination notice was late. This was true here, even though the failure to comply occurred over the summer vacation. Ruling the teacher was entitled to 28 days of pay plus attorneys' fees, the court reversed the judgment. *Vetter v. Board of Educ., Ravena-Coeymans-Selkirk Central School Dist.*, 14 N.Y.3d 729 (N.Y. 2010).

◆   An Ohio school district's part-time Safe and Drug Free Schools coordinator position was funded entirely by grants. A licensed substitute teacher was hired for the job. She lacked an Ohio teacher's certificate and was unauthorized to teach full time. After seven years of part-time employment, the school board employed the coordinator full time under successive two-year contracts. The board then approved a five-year contract that did not specify it was contingent on funding. The state auditor declared the school district to be in a fiscal emergency, and the coordinator position was abolished based on declining enrollment and the loss of grant funding. The school board suspended the coordinator's contract prior to the 2005-06 school year. An arbitrator rejected her grievance, finding that her position was not within the bargaining unit. The coordinator petitioned the Supreme Court of Ohio, seeking her reinstatement.

The court found that **after three years of full-time employment, non-teaching school employees were deemed to be employed pursuant to a continuing contract**. The coordinator had been employed full time in a non-teaching position for three years when the board approved her five-year contract. She was a continuing contract employee under state law, and this status was not contingent on grant funding. As the coordinator had continuing contract status, the board of education was not authorized to abolish her position and lay her off. The court ordered the board to reinstate her. *State ex rel. Couch v. Trimble Local School Dist. Board of Educ.*, 120 Ohio St.3d 75, 896 N.E.2d 690 (Ohio 2008).

◆ The Colorado Teacher Employment Compensation, and Dismissal Act (TECDA) requires written notice to probationary teachers of a contract non-renewal by June 1. In April 2004, a school board held a meeting to discuss contract renewal for probationary teachers. It moved into an executive session, where it decided not to rehire a teacher for the 2004-05 school year. The district superintendent sent him a "letter of intent," stating that the board did not intend to offer him a teaching contract for the next year. The board did not ratify its decision in a public session until September 2004. The teacher sued, and his case reached the Supreme Court of Colorado. It held the vote in executive session violated the state Open Meetings Law and was not binding. **Failure to provide timely written notice to the teacher of a non-renewal vote resulted in automatic reemployment under the TECDA.** As the board did not advise the teacher of his non-renewal by June 1, he was automatically reemployed for 2004-05. *Hanover School Dist. No. 28 v. Barbour*, 171 P.3d 223 (Colo. 2007).

◆ An Indiana school hired a biology teacher under a one-year contract, even though he lacked a standard teaching license. The principal emailed him on May 7 of the school year that he would meet with him the next day to discuss his employment. The principal then orally notified the teacher his teaching contract would not be renewed. The teacher sued, claiming the law required him to be notified by May 1 or else his contract would automatically be renewed. The case reached the Court of Appeals of Indiana, which rejected the district's argument that the teacher's limited teaching license relieved it of the statutory notice requirements. There was no exception for teachers who held limited licenses. While non-permanent teachers were entitled to only minimal due process protections, school officials had to comply with statutory procedures when informing them about contract renewal. **Since the school district did not give the teacher the written notice he was due by May 1 of the school year, his contract was automatically renewed for the next year.** *Pike Township Educ. Foundation v. Rubenstein*, 831 N.E.2d 1239 (Ind. Ct. App. 2005).

◆ A veteran Louisiana teacher became a special education teacher at a youth correctional center under two probationary contracts. At the end of her second year, the center's principal recommended her contract not be renewed. The state board of education approved the recommendation, but did not state the reasons for the action, as required by law. The teacher sued the board, claiming it tried to circumvent the law by disguising her discharge as a non-renewal.

The case reached the Supreme Court of Louisiana, which explained that probationary teachers who do not receive written notification of discharge from their school board automatically become regular or permanent teachers if they have completed their three-year probationary terms. **The board had to state the valid reasons for a recommendation of discharge or dismissal at any time during a teacher's probationary period, even at the conclusion of a school year.** Here, the board violated state law by failing to provide the teacher with valid reasons for her contract non-renewal during a probationary period, and the court held in her favor. *Palmer v. Louisiana State Board of Elementary and Secondary Educ.*, 842 So.2d 363 (La. 2003).

3. Special Programs

States have separate laws for teachers in special programs such as California's regional occupational program. In Schnee v. Alameda Unified School Dist., *125 Cal.App.4th 555, 22 Cal.Rptr.3d 800 (Cal. Ct. App. 2004), the Court of Appeal of California held a reading specialist could not claim to be a probationary employee based on eight years of service as a specialist.*

But in Stockton Teachers Ass'n CTA/NEA v. Stockton Unified School Dist., *this page, a California court held teachers who were hired for a categorically funded program were properly deemed "probationary" teachers under state law, since no evidence indicated that the special project for which they were hired ended when they were discharged.*

According to the Supreme Court of Alabama, teachers who were employed under the federally funded Head Start program were entitled to state tenure law protections. They were deemed school board "employees" under state law, because local officials controlled their selection and work assignments.

◆   A California school district laid off teachers who served in a categorically funded project. Their teachers association sued, asserting they were improperly classified as "temporary employees" rather than "probationary employees" under Section 44909 of the state Education Code. When the case reached the state court of appeal, it found Section 44909 allows districts to hire credentialed employees for categorically funded projects by written agreement but does not state whether employees hired under them are "probationary" or "temporary."

Instead, **employees hired under Section 44909 could be terminated at the expiration of the specially funded project without regard to the other requirements of probationary employment**. California law specified that unless an employee was classified as permanent, substitute or temporary, he or she was to be classified as "probationary." The intent of the law was to limit the use of temporary employees so the rights of district teachers in secure employment would not be subordinated to administrative needs. In the court's view, Section 44909 was intended to allow districts to operate special programs without having to deal with a surplus of probationary or permanent employees when a specially funded program expired. Since there was no evidence that the employees in this case were discharged when a categorically funded project expired, the court held they had to be treated as probationary employees. *Stockton Teachers Ass'n CTA/NEA v. Stockton Unified School Dist.*, 203 Cal.App.4th 1552, 138 Cal.Rptr.3d 404 (Cal. Ct. App. 2012).

◆   An Alabama teacher and a teaching assistant were employed under the federally funded Head Start program. After being discharged, they attempted to contest the action pursuant to guidelines in the Head Start policy manual. After this failed, they sued the school board, asserting that they were school board employees entitled to the statutory protections applicable to city and county employees under the Alabama Fair Dismissal Act. The case reached the Supreme Court of Alabama, which explained that whether the teacher and assistant were considered "employees" of the school board depended upon the extent to which the board had a right to select and control them while they worked at Head Start. The board had delegated its authority to approve policies and procedures for Head Start operations in the county to a "policy council." Federal Head Start regulations state that there is a "partnership" between school boards and Head Start policy councils regarding the hiring and firing of Head Start personnel. Policy councils are encouraged to work with school boards to reach employment decisions. Here, the school board had control over the Head Start director's employment. His involvement with the policy council indicated that the board could influence or control the employment of other Head Start employees. Therefore, **the teacher and the assistant were employees**. *Peterson v. Lowndes County Board of Educ.*, 980 So.2d 975 (Ala. 2007).

◆   A California teacher taught agricultural maintenance in a school district's regular education program as a .57 full-time equivalent (FTE) employee. He also worked as a .43 FTE maintenance employee in a regional occupational program (ROP). After the district notified him that it was not going to rehire him for either position the following year, he sought a court order that the district had to reelect him for both positions. He claimed that he was a regular teacher who was "subsequently assigned" to the ROP position. A court agreed and ordered the district to reinstate the teacher to both jobs. The Court of Appeal of California upheld the decision concerning the .57 FTE position. However, **the period of time (.43 FTE) that the teacher spent in the ROP position did not count toward his attainment of permanent status** because he was "not assigned out from a regular teaching position into an ROP position," but was assigned to a second, concurrent position in the ROP. The court reversed the judgment concerning the .43 FTE ROP assignment, as this service did not count toward permanent status. *Reis v. Biggs Unified School Dist.*, 126 Cal.App.4th 809, 24 Cal.Rptr.3d 393 (Cal. Ct. App. 2005).

◆   Two Massachusetts teachers worked as public school teachers in the 1950s and 1960s, before leaving their jobs to raise families. Both held elementary education teaching certificates from the state education department. The teachers returned to work in the 1980s, taking jobs in a federally funded Chapter I supplemental instruction program. One worked in the program for 15 years and the other for eight years before they were laid off due to budget cuts. They claimed to have "professional teacher status," with the right to bump non-tenured teachers from elementary teaching positions. The district superintendent denied their requests, and after holding separate arbitration hearings, arbitrators issued a joint decision for the school committee. The arbitrators held that the teachers had no bumping rights because they were not "teachers" as defined by state law.

The teachers appealed to a state court, which vacated the arbitration award as a violation of public policy. The school committee appealed to the Supreme Judicial Court of Massachusetts, which noted the strong public policy in favor of arbitration. Courts may vacate arbitration awards only in limited circumstances. Here, the arbitrators had analyzed the teachers' conditions of employment and job functions in resolving whether they were "teachers" under the state professional teacher status provision. Accordingly, the decisions were not subject to judicial review. **The teachers had no bumping rights.** *Lyons v. School Committee of Dedham*, 440 Mass. 74, 794 N.E.2d 586 (Mass. 2003).

B. Tenure Rights

1. Reductions in Force

Under traditional tenure laws, a tenured teacher may not be laid off and bumped by a non-tenured teacher if the tenured teacher is properly certificated for the position. However, state legislatures are considering legislation to base teacher retention decisions on performance, rather than seniority. Florida and Colorado have already enacted such legislation.

California Education Code Section 44955 permits the retention of junior teachers during a reduction in force, via a practice referred to as "skipping."

◆ Los Angeles Unified School District laid off temporary and probationary teachers due to budgetary problems in consecutive school years. Three schools in the district employed large numbers of new teachers and lost up to two-thirds of their teachers, filling the vacancies with substitutes. Students and an interest group claimed the reduction in force (RIF) denied students equal educational opportunities. They sought a court order to prevent further layoffs. A state court granted the order, holding that high teacher turnover devastated educational opportunity and impacted student rights. A consent decree was agreed upon by the parties and submitted to the court for approval. The decree identified "target schools" that were likely to be negatively affected by teacher turnover. The district agreed to retain or "skip" teachers during RIFs at these schools and at the three initially identified schools. After a hearing, the court approved the consent decree over the objection of the United Teachers Los Angeles (UTLA).

The case reached the state court of appeal. It explained that **the retention of junior teachers in a RIF, known as "skipping," is permitted by Section 44955 of the California Education Code**. Skipping allowed schools to retain less-senior teachers who were certificated in relevant areas instead of retaining more senior teachers who lacked such certification. The court held a consent decree could not abrogate the rights of third parties such as the UTLA. UTLA members were prejudiced by the consent decree, and the trial court had not yet ruled on the students' claims. For these reasons, the court refused to approve the consent decree. It returned the case to the trial court. *Reed v. United Teachers Los Angeles*, 208 Cal.App.4th 322, 145 Cal.Rptr.3d 454 (Cal. Ct. App. 2012).

◆ A California school board resolved to skip teachers who held Bilingual Crosscultural Language and Development (BCLAD) certification who were expected to teach classes requiring BCLAD certification the next year. Under the resolution, those who had taught classes in a designated subject matter were "competent" under the skipping criteria of state Education Code Section 44955. The board also sought to retain teachers with credentials to teach special education classes who were currently teaching special education classes and expected to teach special education in the district for the next school year.

A district administrator considered only teachers who had taught bilingual classes the previous school year when selecting those available for skipping. Twelve teachers who received layoff notices requested a hearing. Their case reached the state court of appeal, which held **Section 44955 allows deviation** from the order of seniority if a district "demonstrates a specific need for a certificated employee with special training and experience which others with more seniority do not possess." Section 44955 did not allow dismissal of tenured teachers in violation of their seniority rights based on a previous year's teaching assignment. For this reason, the district was obligated to appoint the most senior qualified employees. *California Teachers' Ass'n v. Oxnard School Dist.*, No. B222673, 2011 WL 105869 (Cal. Ct. App. 1/13/11).

◆ A California school district reduced or discontinued five positions, including a full-time equivalent (FTE) psychologist position. Instead of rehiring two part-time psychologists for the new full-time job, the district hired a less senior full-time certificated school psychologist. A state court denied relief to the part-time employees, and they appealed. The Court of Appeal of California found that **state law permitted a school board to make assignments and reassignments in such a way that employees were retained to render services for which their seniority and qualifications made them fit**. State law did not compel the district to split positions in the event of layoffs. School districts had broad discretion to define job positions and establish employment requirements. The court found little reason why the district could not define the position as "full time," if it found the job duties could not be performed by two part-time employees. The district needed to employ a full-time psychologist for several reasons. As the part-time psychologists did not have the right to force the district to divide the duties of a full-time position to accommodate their wishes, the court affirmed the judgment. *Hildebrandt v. St. Helena Unified School Dist.*, 172 Cal.App.4th 334, 90 Cal.Rptr. 855 (Cal. Ct. App. 2009).

◆ A South Dakota computer science teacher had worked for a school district for 17 years. The district employed three other computer teachers, including one who had taught in the district for over 30 years. Another teacher had 10 years in the district, while another was in his first year there. The collective bargaining agreement (CBA) between the board and teachers had a two-part method for determining if seniority could be used. This included appropriate certification and the courses taught by a teacher in the preceding seven years. The school board determined that the 30-year veteran teacher could use her seniority only for the areas in which she had taught during the previous seven years. As a result, she was allowed to bump only into a computer science position.

The 30-year veteran could not bump the 10-year veteran, who also taught business classes. Nor could the 30-year veteran teacher satisfy the seniority requirements for the first-year teacher's assignments, as he taught technology modules that were heavily weighted on math and science. The computer science teacher was unable to bump the 10-year and first-year teachers for the same reasons. Her contract was not renewed, and her case reached the state supreme court. It held **the teacher lacked the certification and recent experience of the less-senior teachers whose positions she was trying to assume**. She could not partially bump other teachers by assuming parts of their jobs. The district had properly followed the CBA policy, and its action was upheld. *Hanson v. Vermillion School Dist. No. 13-1*, 727 N.W.2d 459 (S.D. 2007).

◆   A New York board of cooperative educational services (BOCES) provided student occupational programs in several districts. Teaching assistants (TAs) supplemented the services of classroom teachers. The BOCES laid off nine TAs due to declining student enrollment. Layoffs were not in accord with seniority. Five of the laid off TAs sued the BOCES in a state court, which allowed the state education commissioner to determine if TAs were "teachers" as defined by New York Education Law. The TAs claimed they could only be dismissed according to seniority under a tenure provision addressing the appointment of "teachers and members of the teaching staff." The BOCES asserted that TAs were like vocational teachers, without specific educational, certification, or licensure requirements. The commissioner disagreed and reinstated the TAs with back pay and benefits. The case reached the Court of Appeals of New York, which agreed with the commissioner that **the TAs should be included in the tenure system.** As the BOCES appeared to be going against its own policies, the court ruled that the TAs were entitled to be laid off by seniority. *Madison-Oneida Board of Cooperative Educ. Services v. Mills,* 4 N.Y.3d 51, 823 N.E.2d 1265, 790 N.Y.S.2d 619 (N.Y. 2004).

◆   An Ohio school district laid off a teacher with seven years of experience as part of a reduction in force. The board employed her the next year for 180 days as a substitute for a teacher on sick leave, paying her according to the minimum salary under its salary schedule for teachers with a bachelor's degree and zero years of teaching experience. The next school year, the board rehired the teacher for full-time work, crediting her with eight years of experience on the salary scale. The teacher sued the board in a state court, seeking the salary and benefits that would reflect nine years of teaching experience. Appeal reached the state supreme court, which held that state law confers certain "local privileges" upon long-term substitutes, including salary not less than the minimum on the current salary schedule. **School boards were required only to pay the minimum amount to substitutes** under the law. *State ex rel. Antonucci v. Youngstown City School Dist. Board of Educ.,* 87 Ohio St.3d 564, 722 N.E.2d 69 (Ohio 2000).

2. Other Substantive Rights

South Carolina's Teacher Employment and Dismissal Act allows certified education personnel to retain rights as teachers if they are employed as administrators. But the state's highest court held an administrator who was demoted did not retain her hearing rights under the act. A Minnesota school administrator whose position did not require state licensure was not deemed a "teacher" under state law and could not claim teacher tenure protections.

◆   A Minnesota school administrator served as a district activities director for three years. He was then hired as an interim middle school principal. Although the job posting required candidates to hold a state principal license (or be in the process of obtaining one), the state Department of Education never required the licensure of school activities directors. Near the end of his year as interim principal, the school board voted not to renew the administrator's contract. It did not hold a hearing or afford him any of the rights granted to continuing-contract employees under Section 122A.40 of Minnesota Statutes. After the administrator's grievance was denied, the case reached the Supreme Court of Minnesota. It explained that Section 122A.40 defined "teacher" as a "principal, supervisor, and classroom teacher and any other professional employee required to hold a license" from the state education department. **As the activities director position did not require state licensure, the administrator was not a "professional employee" who was required to hold a state license** when he held that job. It did not matter to the court that the job description required licensure. As a result, the court held the administrator was not a "teacher," and he was not entitled to a hearing or other statutory protections. *Emerson v. School Board of Independent School Dist. 199*, 809 N.W.2d 679 (Minn. 2012).

◆ South Carolina's Educational Accountability Act of 1998 allowed certified education personnel to retain their rights as teachers if they were employed as administrators under annual or multi-year contracts. But the law stated "no such rights are granted to the position or salary of administrator." An administrator who was demoted and suffered a salary reduction filed a federal court action against her school district, asserting she retained hearing rights under the state Teacher Employment and Dismissal Act. Finding no authority to interpret the state-law question, the court asked the Supreme Court of South Carolina whether an employee had rights under the Employment and Dismissal Act to a hearing to contest her demotion and salary reduction. Agreeing to review the question, the state supreme court noted a pre-1998 decision in which it held teachers had no right to an adversarial hearing upon transfer, reassignment or demotion. A second case held an assistant principal was entitled to a hearing after he lost his position, as distinguished from a simple wage loss.

The court found the legislature knew of these cases when it passed the 1998 legislation. It held the 1998 amendment contradicted its prior decisions by stating **"an administrator has no rights in her position or salary."** As the amendment rejected the notion that an administrator facing adverse action is entitled to a hearing, the court held the employee had no right to contest her demotion and salary reduction under the 1998 amendment. *Henry-Davenport v. School Dist. of Fairfield County*, 391 S.C. 85, 705 S.E.2d 26 (S.C. 2011).

◆ In three years of probationary service teaching high school social studies, a New York teacher earned satisfactory reviews and year-end reports. He was denied tenure and agreed to extend his probationary period another year. During his fourth year, the school assigned the teacher two unsatisfactory classroom reports and sent two letters to his file for "unbecoming conduct." His building principal assigned an unsatisfactory rating on his year-end report and an overall unsatisfactory rating. The New York City School Department denied the teacher certification of completion of his probationary period, resulting in termination of his service and preclusion from reemployment with other city high schools.

A state appellate division court noted evidence that **the principal who assigned the teacher an unsatisfactory rating did not make either of the required observations during his final years of work at the school**. City education department rules required at least one observation by the principal and pre-observation meetings with a teacher in danger of unsatisfactory ratings. In addition, the year-end report included unsatisfactory rankings in each category, even where unsupported by any evidence or contradicted by evidence in the report itself. The court found this was arbitrary. Evidence indicated that assistant principals at the school were pressured to give negative evaluations without performing actual observations. As these deficiencies undermined the integrity and fairness of the process, the court held for the teacher. *Kolmel v. City of New York*, 88 A.D.3d 527, 930 N.Y.S.2d 573 (N.Y. App. Div. 2011).

◆   A Wyoming school district hired a guidance counselor in 1990 under a contract describing her as a "qualified certified employee" without continuing contract status. She worked for the school district under a series of non-teaching contracts until 2003, when the district advised her that her position was being cut for budgetary reasons. She asked for a hearing, but the request was denied, as the district deemed her to have no contract or statutory rights. She sued, claiming protection under the Wyoming Teacher and Employment Law (WTEL). A state court held for the district, and the counselor appealed to the Supreme Court of Wyoming. According to the court, the WTEL defined a "teacher" as any person employed under contract by a school board as a "certified professional employee." The counselor argued that her professional certification required treating her as a "teacher," since she was a "certified professional employee." She noted that she instructed students in various skills.

The court held that the WTEL had to be read with other parts of the Wyoming Education Code. **While the WTEL required all teachers to be certified employees, not all certified professional employees were teachers.** Several Education Code provisions recognized a distinction between teachers and other certified professional employees. Instruction of non-academic skills and studies did not make the counselor a "teacher." *Luhm v. Board of Trustees of Hot Springs County School Dist. No. 1*, 206 P.3d 1290 (Wyo. 2009).

◆   Birmingham (Alabama) hired public school teachers for non-teaching duties under supplemental contracts to serve as coaches, football workers and support activity sponsors. Positions were not reserved for teachers and no teaching certification was required for them. In 2004, 2005 and 2006, the board failed to notify some teachers before the end of the school year of the non-renewal of supplemental contracts for the following school years. Teachers sued the board for improperly cancelling the contracts. The case reached the Supreme Court of Alabama, which found that state law defined "teacher" to include all persons regularly certified by the state as instructors, principals or supervisors in the public schools. **Coaches and other employees under supplemental contracts were not certified by the state to perform duties of an instructor, principal or supervisor.** For this reason, the court declined to afford state law protections to teachers performing supplemental duties independent of their teaching functions. As a result, the court ruled for the board. *Boone v. Birmingham Board of Educ.*, 45 So.3d 764 (Ala. 2009).

◆   A Mississippi school guidance counselor learned her contract would not be renewed at the end of her first year. She requested the factual basis for non-renewal and a hearing before the school board. The board upheld the action, and the counselor appealed to a state chancery court under the Education

Employment Procedures Act of 2001, Mississippi Code Sections 37-9-101 to 37-9-113. The court held that the act unconstitutionally conferred jurisdiction on chancery courts. The parties appealed to the Supreme Court of Mississippi.

The court held chancery court jurisdiction was limited. Several decisions prior to enactment of the 2001 act made it clear that school board and other agency decisions were "matters in equity," which the state constitution allowed chancery courts to hear. **The court held Mississippi Code Sections 37-9-111 allowed an aggrieved school employee to appeal a final board decision to a chancery court.** The scope of a chancery court's review was limited to determining if the board action was supported by substantial evidence, was arbitrary or capricious, beyond the board's authority, or in violation of the employee's statutory or constitutional rights. As the chancery court committed error by holding the Education Employment Procedures Act unconstitutional, the court reversed and remanded the case with instructions for the court to decide if the action complied with Mississippi Code Sections 37-9-101 to 37-9-113. *Lawrence County School Dist. v. Bowden*, 912 So.2d 898 (Miss. 2005).

◆ **An Alabama principal employed under a probationary contract was not entitled to an evaluation and 90 days' notice prior to termination of his contract.** The Alabama Court of Civil appeals held that the Teacher Accountability Act distinguished between contract principals and probationary principals. As the principal was not entitled to the statutory protections he claimed, the court affirmed a lower court judgment for the school board. *Holmes v. Macon County Board of Educ.*, 11 So.3d 205 (Ala. Ct. App. 2006).

C. State Regulatory Authority

A Florida school board that delegated its investigatory powers to an office of professional standards was bound to comply with an administrative law judge's order to comply with an investigation by the office. In the following case, an Ohio court rejected a school board's argument that an employee who did not disclose felonies on his job application was "statutorily unemployable."

◆ Upon applying for employment with an Ohio board of education in 2005, an employee admitted he had been convicted of disorderly conduct. A background check uncovered charges of telephone harassment and felonious assault. A meeting was held that "resolved the discrepancy," and the board hired the applicant. Two years later, the state enacted a law requiring school districts to conduct criminal background checks. Any person subject to a check who was convicted of (or pleaded guilty to) a described offense was to be released from employment or not hired. Those who met state rehabilitation standards were exempt from the requirement. Since telephone harassment and felonious assault were specified offenses in the law, the board discharged the employee. He appealed to the state civil service commission, which reinstated him with back pay. Appeal reached the state court of appeals, which noted the commission's finding that **the board knew about his criminal history for years but decided not to act on it**. In the court's view, the board ignored an exception allowing retention of an employee convicted of one of the listed offenses "if the person meets the rehabilitation standards adopted by the department of education." As it was not shown that the employee did not meet the department's rehabilitation standards, the court held in his favor. *Akron City School Dist. Board of Educ. v. Civil Service Comm'n*, No. 26026, 2012 WL 1207407 (4/11/12).

◆   A Florida teacher was investigated for possible misconduct with a student. An investigator for the school board's office of professional standards (OPS) directed the teacher to appear for an investigatory interview. When she advised him the interview would take place with no attorney, the teacher declined. Due to the teacher's refusal to appear before the OPS investigator, the superintendent recommended his suspension pending termination for misconduct, gross insubordination and violation of a school policy requiring employees to cooperate with the OPS. An administrative law judge (ALJ) found the teacher had been compelled to appear before the OPS investigator in the course of an official investigation. For that reason, **he was entitled to be accompanied by counsel at his own expense under Florida Statutes Section 120.62(2).** The board rejected the ALJ's decision and fired the teacher. A Florida District Court of Appeal agreed with the ALJ that the board had delegated its investigatory powers to the OPS. The court agreed with the ALJ that the teacher was ordered to appear before the OPS investigator in the course of an official investigation. As a result, the court reversed the board's decision. *Raven v. Manatee County School Board*, 32 So.3d 126 (Fla. Dist. Ct. App. 2009).

◆   An Alabama teacher was discharged after two students accused him of cursing at them and soaking their pants with water. Discharge was based on the most recent discipline and 11 others over the past four school years. At a hearing, the school board sought to prevent the teacher from offering any evidence about the underlying events for the 11 prior incidents documented in his file. The hearing officer allowed him to present evidence beyond what was in his personnel records, including the argument that many of the prior incidents were the result of bias. The hearing officer then reinstated the teacher and ordered nine of the 11 disciplinary actions expunged (erased) from the teacher's personnel file as either unwarranted or the result of personal bias.

The Supreme Court of Alabama held that a "hearing officer may consider the employment history of the teacher, including, but not limited to, matters occurring in previous years." **Hearing officers had discretion to accept testimony and exhibits, and the court found nothing in the Act to limit this discretion.** However, the Tenure Act did not grant hearing officers authority to alter prior disciplinary actions or expunge them from a teacher's employment records. The case was returned to the hearing officer to vacate the part of his order altering past disciplinary action and expunging the teacher's employment records. *Ex parte Webb*, 53 So.3d 121 (Ala. 2009).

◆   A Texas school counselor was accused of violating district policies and Section 261.101 of the Texas Family Code by failing to report suspected child abuse or neglect, and only minimally cooperating with a police investigation. After a hearing, a hearing examiner recommended non-renewal of his contract. The school board voted to accept the recommendation. Instead of appealing to the state commissioner of education under the Texas Term Contract Nonrenewal Act, the counselor sued the district in a state district court for retaliation. The case reached the Court of Appeals of Texas, which explained that the state Term Contract Renewal Act specified procedures for teachers employed under term contracts to obtain review of adverse decisions. **An aggrieved party had to first exhaust all administrative remedies if the subject matter of an action concerned the administration of school laws and involved questions of fact.**

The court held that the case involved questions of fact that must be appealed to administrative authorities before resort to the courts. It rejected the claim that the case was excused from exhaustion as a retaliation suit. The counselor was a term contract employee. The board had properly notified him of its non-renewal decision and his next step was to appeal to the commissioner. The court reversed the judgment, holding the counselor could not file a retaliation suit and had to comply with state administrative procedures. *Ysleta Independent School Dist. v. Griego*, 170 S.W.3d 792 (Tex. Ct. App. 2005).

II. DUE PROCESS REQUIREMENTS

The Fourteenth Amendment to the U.S. Constitution has a Due Process Clause that requires states to provide "due process of law" whenever a person is threatened with the taking of life, liberty or property. Since public employment is considered a "property interest," school districts are required to provide relevant statutory notices and hearings to comply with employee due process. State constitutions have similar due process provisions, and the Fifth Amendment has a Due Process Clause applicable at the federal level.

"Due process" rights arise from state laws, contracts and expectations. For example, a collective bargaining agreement creates a "property interest" in employment for the term of the contract. State tenure and continuing contract laws create property interests in the procedures described in the laws.

At a minimum, due process means that the government will give an individual notice and an opportunity to be heard when it threatens the individual's liberty or property interests. In a pair of landmark cases, the U.S. Supreme Court found pre-termination hearings are designed to be an "initial check" against a mistaken employment decision.

◆   A Wisconsin university hired a teacher for a fixed contract term of one year. At the end of the year, he was informed he would not be rehired. No hearing was provided and no reason was given for the decision. In dismissing the teacher's due process claims, the U.S. Supreme Court held no liberty interest was implicated because in declining to rehire him, the university made no charge such as incompetence or immorality. Such a charge would have made it difficult for the teacher to gain employment elsewhere and thus would have deprived him of liberty. **As no reason was given for the non-renewal, the teacher's liberty interest in future employment was not impaired and he was not entitled to a hearing on these grounds.** Because he had not acquired tenure, he had no property interest in continued employment. To be sure, the teacher had a property interest in employment during his one-year contract term, but upon its expiration his property interest ceased to exist. The Court held that **"to have a property interest in a benefit, a person clearly must have more than an abstract need or desire for it. He must have more than a unilateral expectation of it. He must, instead, have a legitimate claim of entitlement to it."** *Board of Regents v. Roth*, 408 U.S. 564, 92 S.Ct. 2701, 33 L.Ed.2d 548 (1972).

◆   A teacher worked at a Texas university for four years under one-year contracts. When he was not rehired for a fifth year, he brought suit contending that due process required a dismissal hearing. The Supreme Court held "a person's interest in a benefit is a 'property' interest for due process purposes if there are such rules and mutually explicit understandings that support his claim of entitlement to the benefit that he may invoke at a hearing." **Because the teacher had been employed at the university for four years, the Court felt that he might have a protectable property interest in continued employment.** The case was remanded to determine whether there was an unwritten "common law" of tenure at the university. If so, the teacher would be entitled to a dismissal hearing. *Perry v. Sindermann*, 408 U.S. 593, 92 S.Ct. 2694, 33 L.Ed.2d 570 (1972).

A. Property Interest

A school employee must have a liberty or property interest in employment to have procedural due process rights. A common source for creating a property interest arises from state tenure statutes. Notice and an opportunity to respond are the essential requirements of due process. In Ray v. Nash, *below, the U.S. Court of Appeals, Fifth Circuit, explained that a protected property interest is determined by reference to state law. A probationary contract itself creates no protected property interest in continued employment beyond its own terms.*

◆   An Iowa student was disruptive on his school bus and refused to exit when instructed. The driver approached the student, who got off the bus. Later, the student accused the driver of improperly touching him. His parents gave his account to a school board member and the police. Criminal assault charges were filed against the driver, who was a licensed educator who had also served the district as a teacher and coach. After a hearing, the school board voted for dismissal. A jury then acquitted him of assault, and he sued the board, parents and school officials. Appeal reached the U.S. Court of Appeals, Eighth Circuit.

The court found Iowa law afforded teachers fairly elaborate pretermination procedures, such as board hearings and the right to review personnel files and documentation to be presented at hearings. At pretermination hearings, teachers could cross-examine witnesses and present their own witnesses and evidence. State law provided for extensive post-termination review, with judicial review available. In this case, the employee did not appeal the termination decision as provided by law. Since an employee who does not request a hearing cannot sue for denial of due process, the court held the claim based on post-termination processes was properly dismissed. As for the pre-termination proceedings, the employee received a board hearing, and he did not explain how he was denied due process. **The court rejected the argument that a board hearing should have been delayed until after the criminal jury reached a verdict.** Due process did not require a delay between notice and the opportunity to respond. *Christiansen v. West Branch Community School Dist.*, 674 F.3d 927 (8th Cir. 2012).

♦   A Georgia school district and the union representing its bus drivers settled a dispute by written agreement that required the district to expand a grievance policy for classified employees. Classified employees with at least two years of continuous board service could appeal a recommendation for termination of employment to the board or its personnel committee. After the agreement was reached, a driver confronted some students on his bus. Students stated that he pushed students, yelled at them and read from a clipboard while the bus was in motion. A bus aide and the principal corroborated these statements. After an investigation, a series of meetings was held among the driver, his supervisor and other administrators, including a final meeting with the district superintendent.

Although the driver sought a hearing, the board declined one, declaring it had enough information for a decision. After the board voted for termination, he sued for due process violations and breach of the settlement agreement. A federal court held for the school board, and the driver appealed. The U.S. Court of Appeals, Eleventh Circuit, rejected his claim that denial of a hearing violated the settlement agreement. Nothing in the agreement required a hearing. It only allowed classified employees to "appeal" a recommendation for termination prior to final board action. The driver had received such an appeal. Nor did the agreement require the board to offer classified employees the same procedures it provided to certified teachers. **Finding the denial of an in-person hearing was not a due process violation, the court held for the board.** *Strickland v. Columbia County Board of Educ.*, 494 Fed.Appx. 998 (11th Cir. 2012).

♦   As a Texas teacher's probationary term neared completion, her education board notified her that it had decided not to renew her contract. She requested hearings to address the cause for non-renewal, but the board maintained that its decision was final and could not be further appealed. In a grievance proceeding against the school district, the teacher claimed her contract was not renewed in retaliation for a previous complaint regarding tutoring work she had performed for no compensation. But she abandoned the grievance and filed a state court action against the district. The case was removed to a federal court, which held the teacher had no due process interest in employment beyond the single-year term of her contract. On appeal, the Fifth Circuit explained that **a protected property interest is determined by reference to state law**. A probationary contract itself creates no protected property interest in continued employment beyond its own terms. In this case, the contract did not create tenure rights or any other expectation of continued employment. Since state law declared that probationary contracts may not be for a term of over one year and could be non-renewed if this was in the board's best interests, the teacher was not entitled to any hearing. Her contract could be terminated at the end of its term simply by giving her timely notice. *Ray v. Nash*, 438 Fed.Appx. 332 (5th Cir. 2011).

◆   An investigation determined that a Louisiana teacher had hit a special needs student on the head. After being suspended for two days without pay, the teacher complained that he was denied his rights under the state Teacher Bill of Rights law. As he was still in probationary status, the superintendent found no reason to provide him a hearing. But he invited the teacher to prepare a written rebuttal. The teacher took an extended sick leave, then resigned and sued the school board in a state court to recover two days of lost pay. The case reached the Court of Appeal of Louisiana, which agreed with the board that **the teacher was not entitled to a hearing, and had no viable due process claim**. Since the board had investigated the complaint and provided him an opportunity to explain his side of the incident, the court found he had been afforded all the process he was due. Loss of two days of pay did not require notice and hearing. *Monier v. St. Charles Parish School Board*, 65 So.3d 731 (La. Ct. App. 2011).

◆   A tenured Tennessee teacher was suspended for kissing a student and sending love notes to others. After a hearing, the board of education voted to suspend him, impose a three-year probationary period and require sensitivity training. Grounds for the suspension were insubordination, conduct unbecoming a teacher and unprofessional conduct. A state court affirmed the suspension, and appeal reached the Court of Appeals of Tennessee. The court held the teacher's right to due process was not violated when the board charged him with "conduct unbecoming to a member of the teaching profession" as well as "unprofessional conduct." **There was no deficiency of the notice to him under the state Teacher Tenure Act.** The teacher received a full set of charges. While "unprofessional conduct" was not a statutory ground for dismissal or suspension under the Tenured Teachers Act, the court found it was a ground for teacher discipline. Since the board did not violate his due process rights and he created an atmosphere that was harmful to student learning, the suspension was affirmed. *Taylor v. Clarksville Montgomery County School System*, No. M2009-02116-COA-R3-CV, 2010 WL 3245281 (Tenn. Ct. App. 8/17/10).

◆   After about two years of work at a Connecticut technical high school, an untenured teacher began posting profiles on MySpace.com. He used a profile called "Mr. Spiderman" to communicate with students for school and private discussions. A school guidance counselor learned of the teacher's MySpace profile and found pictures of naked men and "inappropriate comments" posted on it. After the counselor complained to the teacher about his profile, he took it down and created a new one. School officials viewed the profile and found it was nearly the same as the "Mr. Spiderman" profile. They placed the teacher on leave with pay and eventually informed him that his contract would not be renewed. The teacher sued, alleging Due Process Clause violations. The court found the teacher had no protected property interest in his employment, as he did not have tenure under the state Teacher Tenure Act. **The employment relationship was governed by the collective bargaining agreement, not the Teacher Tenure Act.** School officials complied with the collective bargaining agreement by providing timely written notice of the contract non-renewal, and there was no due process violation. The agreement did not require "just cause" to terminate an untenured teacher's contract. The court agreed with the officials that the teacher was disruptive. It was reasonable to expect him to maintain a professional, respectful association with his students and not communicate with them as if they were peers. Accordingly, the court upheld the non-renewal. *Spanierman v. Hughes*, 576 F.Supp.2d 292 (D. Conn. 2008).

◆ A Mississippi Junior ROTC instructor worked for a school district for three school years, left for a year, then returned to his job for a week. The U.S. Court of Appeals, Fifth Circuit, held that he had no protected property interest in employment. The school board never approved a recommendation by the principal to rehire the instructor. State law codified the procedures for hiring teachers and limited the role of principals to recommending candidates. **Any expectation for reemployment held by the instructor was based on statements allegedly made by the principal.** This was not enough to create a property interest in employment, and the district was entitled to judgment. *Watson v. North Panola School Dist.*, 188 Fed.Appx. 291 (5th Cir. 2006).

B. Notice

Due process requires the government to provide notice and an opportunity to be heard at a relevant time when a liberty or property interest is at stake. To determine the specific notices and timelines for a school employee, districts must look to relevant state laws and collective bargaining provisions.

◆ A Texas elementary school lost its "exemplary" rating due to low scores on the standardized Texas Assessment of Knowledge and Skills (TAKS). To improve TAKS scores, the principal developed an improvement plan. Instead of modifying individualized education programs (IEPs) through the admission, review and dismissal (ARD) committee process, she told her staff to contact affected parents and ask for their permission to modify IEPs. An assistant principal reported this, and the principal was placed on administrative leave. After an investigation, she resigned, and the state educator certification board filed a 36-count petition against her. Although the principal was charged with making changes to IEPs outside the ARD committee process and without notice to parents, she was not charged with failing to provide parents written notices. An administrative law judge held almost entirely for the principal, but found she did not give written notice of IEP changes to the affected parents.

Appeal reached the Court of Appeals of Texas. It found no reference in the petition to the single remaining sanction against the principal – failure to give written notice of program changes to the affected parents. According to the court, the notice to the principal did not comply with minimum standards of due process. In the court's opinion, a reasonable person who read the board's petition would have only concluded that the board was charging the principal with "total lack of notice or parental involvement." **As the violation at issue was not identified in the petition, the principal did not have an opportunity to present her side of the story and this amounted to a violation of her due process rights.** As a result, the sanction was vacated. *Barton v. State Board for Educator Certification*, 382 S.W.3d 405 (Tex. Ct. App. 2012).

◆   Virginia's state department of education received reports that some middle school students received improper help on a state assessment. Administrators at their school were placed on probationary status. They then refused to sign probationary contracts and sued the school board, superintendent and school board members in federal court for due process violations. After filing the lawsuit, the administrators signed standard contracts for the next school year. But they were later reassigned by the superintendent to teaching positions.

The U.S. Court of Appeals, Fourth Circuit, held Virginia law permitted the reassignment of a tenured administrator to a teaching position with a salary reduction, so long as there was written notice and an opportunity for an informal meeting before the demotion. Supreme Court cases have held **the only process guaranteed by the Constitution is notice and a hearing before employment termination or deprivation of a protected property right**. In this case, the administrators had written notice of the demotions and opportunities for a meeting prior to the proposed action. Administrators have protected property rights in employment once they attain continuing contract status, but the court found **there is no constitutional guarantee to a particular job**. As they did not show their property rights were violated, the court held for the board. *Hibbitts v. Buchanan County School Board*, 433 Fed.App. 203 (4th Cir. 2011).

◆   An Arkansas school district complied with state law when it discharged a teacher who was arrested in an ex-boyfriend's driveway with her minor child. She was allegedly under the influence of and in possession of chemical substances. The teacher did not appear at her termination hearing, and the board voted to discharge her. She claimed the board gave her a faulty notice, and she received a new hearing. The board again voted to fire the teacher. On appeal, **the Court of Appeals of Arkansas held that a subsequent hearing cures any notice defect from a prior hearing**. The board based its action on the record before it, and the teacher received ample opportunity to address the charges. The discharge was supported by a police report. While the teacher had been found competent in the classroom, her arrest with her child while intoxicated and stalking an ex-boyfriend justified her firing. *Harter v. Wonderview School Dist.*, No. CA 06-1254, 2007 WL 3276989 (Ark. Ct. App. 11/7/07).

◆   A Maryland school board did not violate the due process rights of an instructional assistant who was discharged for his inappropriate relationships with students. He invited student mentees to his house and individual lunches, causing suspicion of misconduct. The board placed the instructional assistant on leave with pay, contacted police and initiated an investigation. He had an opportunity to meet with investigators and respond to the charges. The assistant went through a grievance procedure and had two hearings. The case reached the U.S. Court of Appeals, Fourth Circuit, which found no U.S. Supreme Court case making detailed notices of possible discipline a formal requirement. The instructional assistant got a written suspension notice, alerting him that the charges against him were serious. **As he was on notice of serious consequences, he received all the process he was due.** *Curtis v. Montgomery County Public Schools*, 242 Fed.Appx. 109 (4th Cir. 2007).

◆   A Washington teacher fired for misconduct with a student was not denied due process protections at her discharge hearing, according to the state court of appeals. The district gave her proper notice of misconduct charges including sexual relations with the student, giving him alcohol and staying with him in a hotel. The notice complied with state law and nothing indicated the hearing officer improperly assigned the burden of proof to the district. **The teacher had no constitutional right to counsel, which is limited to cases in which a fundamental liberty interest is at stake.** *Powell v. Cascade School Dist. No. 228,* No. 22831-2-III, 124 Wash.App. 1055 (Wash. Ct. App. 2004).

◆   During a Nebraska teacher's third year of employment, her principal sent her a letter stating that he would not recommend renewing her contract due to classroom management problems. After an informal hearing, where the teacher appeared with her attorney, the board deliberated in a closed session, then recessed. The board held another closed session, then returned to open session to vote against renewal. When the teacher appealed, the Nebraska Supreme Court found the principal had evaluated her, provided a written growth plan for the year, and notified her of her classroom management problems. There was no state requirement that a probationary teacher receive notice that a performance deficiency is of such magnitude that failure to remedy it could lead to non-renewal. **The board complied with statutory observation and evaluation requirements, and state law notice and hearing requirements by providing written notices of both hearings.** State law did not require board deliberations in open session. The court affirmed the judgment. *McQuinn v. Douglas County School Dist. No. 66,* 259 Neb. 720, 612 N.W.2d 198 (Neb. 2000).

C. Hearing

1. Minimum Requirements

In 2011, Oklahoma legislators amended state law by deleting career teacher pretermination hearing procedures and removing a right to a "trial de novo" for career teachers facing removal. Under former law, teachers facing non-renewal could respond to a recommendation for dismissal or non-reemployment prior to any board vote. They could also petition for a new court trial within 10 days of notification of non-renewal or dismissal. The amended law deleted the word "probationary" from provisions for hearings by education boards after a recommendation for dismissal.

◆   A Georgia school paraprofessional was fired without a hearing after being attacked and injured by a student. Arguing she was a classified employee who could be discharged only for just cause, she sued her school district in a federal court. It held that she had adequate state remedies, and it dismissed the case. Next, the paraprofessional filed a state court action against the district, again asserting due process violations. While this action was pending, the school board granted her a hearing and she was reinstated to her job. In view of her reinstatement, the paraprofessional amended her state law complaint to reassert violations of the U.S. Constitution. The state court held for the school district, finding the prior federal action barred a subsequent action on the same subject matter between the same parties. Also, the action was moot. No constitutional claims could be viable in view of the adequate state-law procedures. On appeal, **the Court of Appeals of Georgia held an employer's failure to provide a hearing does not violate the Constitution if the state provides a procedural remedy**.

In this case, the paraprofessional was provided with due process in the form of the board hearing that was offered before she filed an amended state complaint. In due process cases, the focus is on whether adequate procedures were provided, not on whether a person took advantage of procedures and obtained a successful outcome. The court held for the school district. *Boatright v. Glynn County School Dist.*, 315 Ga.App. 468, 726 S.E.2d 591 (Ga. Ct. App. 2012).

◆   An Idaho teacher sought a day off to defend his final project in a master's degree in educational administration. The school principal refused to allow it. A grievance on behalf of the teacher was denied, and the teachers' association sued the district and its board in a state court for breach of contract. The Supreme Court of Idaho found that while the relevant master agreement seemed to give a principal the discretion to authorize professional leave, all contracts are subject to a "covenant of good faith and fair dealing." It was clear to the court that the contract required teachers to obtain the principal's written approval before taking paid professional leave. Nothing in the master agreement created an entitlement to take professional leave. Instead, the school district was vested with discretion to allow teachers two days of paid leave.

So long as this was done in good faith, the court found the principal had authority to deny a request for professional development leave. A reason stated for denying leave was that **the master's program was not pedagogical in nature but instead prepared teachers for administrative careers**. The principal and district could have interpreted the agreement in good faith as permitting leave only for activity within a teacher's particular academic area. As the agreement did not require the district to offer professional development leave to pursue a degree in a field unrelated to a teacher's academic area, the lower court had correctly awarded judgment to the district. *Potlatch Educ. Ass'n v. Potlatch School Dist. No. 285*, 148 Idaho 630, 226 P.3d 1277 (Idaho 2010).

◆   An untenured Tennessee teacher was suspended for 10 days without pay for making sexually inappropriate remarks to a female student. The next school year, two teachers complained that he emailed them inappropriate comments. The teacher hired a lawyer and requested a chance to be heard before any discipline was imposed. Instead, the director of schools for the district sent the teacher a letter discharging him as of the date of the letter and notifying him that he could request a hearing with a personnel hearing officer. The teacher requested a hearing, but the discharge decision was upheld. Appeal went before the Court of Appeals of Tennessee. It held **the state code required notice of the charges and an opportunity for a full and complete hearing prior to the dismissal of any non-tenured, licensed employee**. There was no opportunity for a hearing until after the teacher was dismissed, since the director's letter stated he was dismissed as of that date. But on further appeal, the Supreme Court of Tennessee found the teacher was allowed to respond in writing to the charges being investigated. As an untenured teacher, he was not specifically entitled to a post-dismissal hearing under state law. And the teacher waived his claim that he was dismissed prematurely. Although there was no due process violation, the case was returned to the trial court to review his remaining claims. *Bailey v. Blount County Board of Educ.*, 303 S.W.3d 216 (Tenn. 2010).

◆ The Supreme Court of North Carolina decided not to review lower court decisions that found a probationary teacher was not entitled to a school board hearing regarding her contract non-renewal. The school board did not make an arbitrary decision based on evidence that she hit students with a ruler and used profanity in her classroom. **State law required notice to probationary teachers of non-renewal decisions, but it did not provide them with rights to evidentiary hearings.** *Moore v. Charlotte-Mecklenburg Board of Educ.*, 185 N.C. App. 566, 649 S.E.2d 410 (N.C. Ct. App. 2007).

◆ The U.S. Court of Appeals, Fifth Circuit, upheld the firing of a bilingual education teacher who was accused of improperly helping students during an administration of the Texas Assessment of Knowledge and Skills reading test. Colleagues observed her making erasures on tests and making comments to students beyond the test script. After a hearing, the teacher was fired. She sued the school district for due process violations. The court held for the district, and she appealed to the Fifth Circuit. The court of appeals affirmed, noting that **she had received a trial-like hearing that satisfied due process requirements**. As the teacher had opportunities to address the school board before it made any decision, there was no merit to her due process claim. *Rodriguez v. Ysleta Independent School Dist.*, 217 Fed.Appx. 294 (5th Cir. 2007).

◆ A police officer employed by a Pennsylvania state university was arrested and charged with marijuana possession and distribution. State police notified the university of the arrest and charges, and the university immediately suspended the officer without pay pursuant to a state executive order requiring such action. Although the criminal charges were dismissed, university officials demoted the officer. The university did not inform him it had obtained his confession from police records, and he was unable to fully respond to damaging statements in the police reports. He sued university officials for failing to provide him with notice and an opportunity to be heard before his suspension without pay. The U.S. Supreme Court held that **the university did not violate due process by refusing to pay a suspended employee charged with a felony pending a hearing**. Any pre-suspension hearing would have been useless, since the filing of charges established an independent basis for believing that the officer had committed a felony. The Court noted that the officer faced a temporary suspension without pay and not employment termination. *Gilbert v. Homar*, 520 U.S. 924, 117 S.Ct. 1807, 138 L.Ed.2d 120 (1997).

◆ A security guard hired by a school board stated on his job application that he had never been convicted of a felony. Upon discovering that he had in fact been convicted of grand larceny, the board summarily dismissed him for dishonesty in filling out the job application. He was not afforded an opportunity to respond to the dishonesty charge or to challenge the dismissal until nine months later. In a second case, a school bus mechanic was fired because he had failed an eye examination. The mechanic appealed his dismissal after the fact because he had not been afforded a pre-termination hearing. The U.S. Supreme Court held that **the employees had a property right in their employment and were entitled to a pre-termination opportunity to respond to the charges**. The pre-termination hearing need not fully resolve the propriety of the discharge but should be a check against mistaken decisions. The employees were entitled to a pre-termination opportunity to respond and a full administrative hearing at a later time. *Cleveland Board of Educ. v. Loudermill*, 470 U.S. 532, 105 S.Ct. 1487, 84 L.Ed.2d 494 (1985).

2. Hearing Procedures

State tenure and dismissal laws determine the applicable hearing procedures for tenured teachers. The Court of Appeal of California has held that while school boards "are not expected to observe meticulously all of the rules of evidence applicable to a court trial, common sense and fair play dictate certain basic requirements for the conduct of any hearing."

◆ An Indiana special education aide claimed two 16-year-old students came to a party at his house without being invited and brought alcohol with them. The students stated that the aide offered them alcohol and sexually propositioned them. The aide claimed that he asked the students to leave several times and denied propositioning them or providing them with liquor or illegal drugs. School officials found that "he had engaged in improper conduct with the minors." The superintendent suspended him and barred him from school grounds. The aide claimed that the union representative did nothing to help him, and that he was never told of his hearing or grievance rights.

The board discharged the aide, who did not attend the board meeting, as he had been excluded from school grounds. The aide sued the school board in a federal court, which rejected the board's assertion that the meetings with the aide and the hearing satisfied his due process rights. **He was excluded from school grounds and reasonably believed he could not attend the meeting where his discharge was discussed.** He was never presented with the evidence against him, or allowed to cross-examine the two students or present his own evidence. The board did not allow the aide to respond to the charges of sexual impropriety and denied him due process of law. The aide's negligence and due process claims could proceed. *Badger v. Greater Clark County Schools*, No. 4:03-CV-0101 SEB-WGH, 2005 WL 645152 (S.D. Ind. 2005).

◆ A California school board employed a plumber for over 21 years. He was suspended pending an investigation of charges that he used paid sick leave on five days when he was doing plumbing work in a private home. The board held a hearing to consider discharge. It relied on videotapes of the employee apparently working in private homes on the days he called in sick. The person who made the videotapes did not attend the hearing. The videotapes had time lapses, and dates on them "skipped around." A human resources officer who introduced the videotapes had no knowledge of who made the tapes, did not know if they had been edited, and could not state whether their dates were accurate. The board found the tapes proved the employee was not ill on the days he called in sick, and it fired him for dishonesty, falsifying information, and contract violations. The case reached the state court of appeal, which noted that **while school boards "are not expected to observe meticulously all of the rules of evidence applicable to a court trial, common sense and fair play dictate certain basic requirements for the conduct of any hearing."** Here, the unauthenticated videotapes were not properly admitted as evidence and were irrelevant. A lower court had incorrectly allowed the board's request for a new hearing, and the court held for the employee. *Ashford v. Culver City Unified School Dist.*, 29 Cal.Rptr.3d 728 (Cal. Ct. App. 2005).

◆   An Alabama school board unanimously voted to fire an elementary teacher. She appealed to the state tenure commission for a hearing and asked the school to send all documents it intended to present at the hearing. It did so in a timely manner. While many documents were retrieved from the teacher's personnel file, some had been kept elsewhere. The teacher did not know before the request that the files outside her personnel file even existed. She argued that the board did not give her proper notice of those documents. The commission rejected her argument and ruled in the board's favor. A state court held that the board did not provide adequate notice of the grounds for dismissal, but the state civil appeals court found the notice sufficient and reversed the trial court's decision. The teacher appealed to the state supreme court.

The teacher claimed that the documents outside her personnel file were "illegally obtained," and that their admission at the hearing violated her due process rights. The court held that due process requires only notice and a hearing at a relevant time. **The board gave the teacher advance notice of all documents it intended to present and provided a hearing.** The court affirmed the judgment, finding that even if it accepted the teacher's argument that the board could not collect and use the information from outside her personnel file, she did not allege any injury from the retention of these documents. *Ex parte Jackson*, 881 So.2d 450 (Ala. 2003).

3.   Impartiality

◆   A teacher was investigated and then discharged for improperly touching a student. Among other things, the teacher was charged with inviting a female student, whom he coached, to sleep at his house. His conduct was found "predatory," and the district superintendent authorized an immediate dismissal. After three days of arbitration hearings, the district offered to settle the case. Attorneys met with the arbitrator, who then met privately with the teacher and his attorneys. She advised them that based on the evidence up to that point, she would uphold the dismissal. The teacher rejected a settlement offer. His request for a new arbitrator was refused, and the arbitrator upheld the dismissal based on conduct unbecoming a teacher. Appeal reached the Supreme Judicial Court of Massachusetts, where the teacher claimed the state Education Reform Act (ERA) of 1993 impermissibly delegated judicial functions to arbitrators. The court held **the ERA conferred the right to make dismissal decisions to a principal or superintendent, not to arbitrators**. Courts retained their powers as the final adjudicators of employment disputes. In the court's view, the superintendent's investigation was not unfair. And the teacher did not show misconduct or bias by the arbitrator. As the teacher's other arguments lacked merit, the court affirmed the judgment for the school district. *Atwater v. Commissioner of Educ.*, 460 Mass. 844, 957 N.E.2d 1060 (Mass. 2011).

◆ A California math teacher was hired under the assumption that he would learn the nationwide college preparatory mathematics (CPM) curriculum the district used. The teacher participated in CPM training sessions, but shortly after the start of the school year objected to using CPM materials and allegedly pursued a course of argumentative, rude and arrogant behavior with students, staff and supervisors. The principal placed the teacher on administrative leave, and the district held a dismissal hearing, appointing an attorney who represented the district to serve as hearing officer. The teacher noted that the attorney's wife worked for the district and claimed bias. The attorney declined to recuse himself. The board voted to discharge the teacher for dishonesty, unfitness for service and persistent refusal to obey administrative directions. The board decision was upheld by a state trial court. The state court of appeal upheld the dismissal. The teacher's due process claim was based on alleged bias by the hearing officer/attorney and superior court judge. Courts have held that **there must be more than an appearance of bias to establish a due process violation. There was no showing of any actual bias or dishonesty.** The district did not have to bring in a hearing officer from outside the area to avoid bias or prejudice. *Regan v. Governing Board of Sonora Union High School Dist.*, No. F037765, 2002 WL 31009412 (Cal. Ct. App. 2002).

◆ A Pennsylvania high school principal received satisfactory evaluations but was assigned areas of concern during his first three years of employment. The district superintendent issued him an unsatisfactory rating at the end of his fourth year, and the board voted to demote him. He petitioned the state secretary of education for review, arguing that a board member was married to a district secretary who had testified against him and that potential bias existed because of their relationship. The secretary held that the decision was justified and that while allowing the board member to participate in the voting was imprudent, it did not violate the school code. The secretary's *de novo* review of the case cured any potential for bias in the board proceedings. On appeal, the Supreme Court of Pennsylvania observed that although school board proceedings have an inherent potential for bias because of a board's dual prosecutorial and judicial roles, **independent review by the secretary ensured that the requirements of due process were satisfied**. Since the principal received all the process he was due, the court held for the school district. *Katruska v. Bethlehem Center School Dist.*, 767 A.2d 1051 (Pa. 2001).

CHAPTER ELEVEN

Labor Relations

I. PROFESSIONAL ASSOCIATIONS

A. State Law Provisions

In Wisconsin Educ. Ass'n Council v. Walker, *below, the U.S. Court of Appeals, Seventh Circuit, upheld Wisconsin Act 10, which significantly limited the collective bargaining rights of teachers and other public employees. In doing so, the court acknowledged arguments that the law had a political motive.*

California courts do not allow greater contract protections for probationary teachers than those created by law. In Board of Educ. of Round Valley Teachers Ass'n, *13 Cal.4th 269, 52 Cal.Rptr.2d 115, 914 P.2d 193 (1996), the Supreme Court of California held that parties cannot negotiate greater protections for probationary teachers than what is afforded by statute. A decision not to reelect a teacher cannot be collectively bargained.*

◆ Wisconsin's Act 10 of 2011 divided public employees into two classes – "general employees" and "public safety employees." Act 10 prohibited general employees from collective bargaining on issues other than base wages. It also imposed rigorous recertification requirements on their collective bargaining representatives and prohibited employers from deducting union dues from their paychecks. Public safety employees and their unions were not subject to these

411

restrictions. Seven of the state's largest public-sector unions sued state officials in a federal court, challenging Act 10 provisions. When the case reached the Seventh Circuit, it considered the challengers' claim that the act discriminated against public employees who did not endorse Governor Scott Walker in 2010.

The challengers claimed those who were now categorized as "public safety employees" were exempt from Act 10 restrictions in violation of the Equal Protection Clause. But the court found that members of some unions which had not supported Governor Walker were now within the Act's "public safety employee" definition. It held Act 10 created no barriers to speech. Since states are not obligated to aid unions in their political activities, the court held Act 10 did not violate the First Amendment. While members of the two categories of unions had different views, Wisconsin was free to distinguish between them. The court found no viewpoint discrimination and held there was a legitimate government objective for Act 10. As Wisconsin argued, the act provided public employers greater leverage in collective bargaining. The state could rationally believe that Act 10 might cause labor unrest that could not be tolerated from members of public safety unions. Justifications for the collective bargaining limitation also applied to the act's recertification requirement. As **the court found the act exhibited "a rational belief that public sector unions are too costly for the state,"** it upheld the challenged provisions. *Wisconsin Educ. Ass'n Council v. Walker*, 705 F.3d 640 (7th Cir. 2013).

◆   Due to neglect, a Montana teacher let his certificate lapse. In November of the school year, the district received notice of his expired certification and advised him he was no longer eligible to receive compensation under the state code. The teacher continued teaching as a non-certified substitute for one month, but was then discharged. Seven days later, he obtained a new certificate, with a validation date retroactive to one day after his old one lapsed. He filed a grievance for being discharged without just cause in violation of the collective bargaining agreement, but the school board rejected it.

The case reached the Supreme Court of Montana, which found the board's position conflicted with state law. When the contract was signed, the teacher held a valid certificate. The board had authority to employ him and he was a member of the bargaining unit at the time. The state law cited by the board did not provide for discharge. Instead, it required the cessation of further compensation under the employment contract, until the teacher registered a certificate. The court found significant questions regarding the status of the teacher's contract and the application of the collective bargaining agreement that should go before an arbitrator. **As the U.S. Supreme Court has explained, there is a presumption of arbitrability, unless it may be said with positive assurance that the arbitration clause does not cover the dispute.** Doubts are to be resolved in favor of arbitration. *Kalispell Educ. Ass'n v. Board of Trustees, Kalispell High School Dist. No. 5*, 361 Mont. 115, 255 P.3d 199 (Mont. 2011).

◆   A California school district refused to reelect a teacher after his second year as a probationary teacher, denying him tenure. His teachers' association filed a grievance, claiming retaliation for his participation in association activities. An arbitrator held the action came in retaliation for the teacher's exercise of rights protected by the collective bargaining agreement and the state Educational Employment Relations Act (EERA). The arbitrator ordered reinstatement of the teacher with lost wages and other relief. A state court held the district had an absolute right to decide whether or not to reelect a probationary teacher under state law. On appeal, the Court of Appeal of California noted that the association had filed its grievance under a collective bargaining provision repeating substantive rights and duties of the EERA. **For that reason, the arbitrator exceeded his powers by enforcing a collective bargaining provision that conflicted with the statutory scheme.** The state supreme court has held that parties cannot negotiate greater protections for probationary teachers than afforded by statute. A decision not to reelect a teacher cannot be collectively bargained. Since the association's interpretation would grant a probationary teacher a grievance procedure prohibited by state law, the decision could not be challenged as a breach of the collective bargaining agreement. *Sunnyvale Unified School Dist. v. Jacobs*, 171 Cal.App.4th 168, 89 Cal.Rptr.3d 546 (Cal. Ct. App. 2009).

B. Representation

Union members are entitled to representation during an "investigatory interview" under NLRB v. J. Weingarten, Inc., *420 U.S. 251 (1975). But in* SPEED Dist. 802 v. Warning, *below, Illinois' highest court held a probationary teacher was not entitled to union representation at remediation meetings under state law or the relevant collective bargaining agreement. Such meetings were intended to help correct performance deficiencies, not to impose discipline.*

◆ An employees' association accused a Florida school board of refusing to comply with the salary schedules of a collective bargaining agreement (CBA). In response, the board asserted the salaries described by the schedules were incorrect due to a mutual mistake. In a grievance filed under the CBA, the association sought a declaration that the board had violated the CBA.

The difference between the schedule that had been bargained for by the parties and the one attached to the CBA would have required the board to pay about $9 million more than it had budgeted for employee salaries during the three-year contract period. The arbitrator found that after the parties learned of the mistake, they executed a revised salary schedule. But association members had refused to ratify the revision. As a result, the arbitrator reformed the salary schedules to reflect the intent of the parties. When the case reached a Florida District Court of Appeal, it disagreed with the association's claim that the reformation of the CBA was an impermissible contract modification. It held none of the grounds for vacating an arbitration award were present. Instead, the court found the case was "a classic example of a mutual mistake." **When a mutual mistake exists, reformation of the document is appropriate to ensure that it expresses the true intentions of the parties.** The arbitrator's modification did not violate a "no-modification clause" of the CBA. The award was reinstated. *American Federation of State, County and Municipal Employees, Local 1184, AFL-CIO v. Miami-Dade County Public Schools*, 95 So.3d 388 (Fla. Dist. Ct. App. 2012).

◆   After a Florida teacher decided not to be a dues-paying union member, he sought to have the union represent him at a formal meeting called a conference-for-the-record. It declined, and he filed an unfair labor practice charge against the union. A hearing officer appointed by the state Public Employees Relations Commission recommended that the charge be upheld. Appeal reached the Florida District Court of Appeal, where the union argued that the relevant collective bargaining agreement (CBA) did not require it to represent non-union members. **The court held the union could not prefer dues-paying members over non-dues-paying members of the bargaining unit in matters of representation and contract negotiations.** Nor could the union in good faith negotiate, maintain or condone a CBA by which it knowingly created and perpetuated a discriminatory system that required employees to become dues-paying union members to obtain a benefit. The court held CBA language resulted in a discriminatory benefit to union members, and it found competent, substantial evidence supported the hearing officer's findings. Since the law was well established that labor organizations were prohibited from encouraging union membership by providing union members superior contract privileges, the teacher was entitled to his attorneys' fees and costs. *United Teachers of Dade v. School Dist. of Miami-Dade*, 68 So.3d 1003 (Fla. Dist. Ct. App. 2011).

◆   An Illinois teacher was placed on a corrective action plan. She asked for her union representative to sit in on remedial meetings with the principal. The principal refused, but the representative told him that *NLRB v. J. Weingarten, Inc.*, above, permitted union representatives at an "investigatory meeting" if an employee reasonably believed the meeting may involve disciplinary action. The representative was permitted to attend meetings but was not allowed to speak.

The principal later advised the teacher that her union representative could not attend the meetings. After the teacher earned poor ratings, she was advised that her contract would end with the school year. Her union filed a successful unfair labor practice charge with the Illinois Educational Labor Relations Board. Appeal reached the Supreme Court of Illinois, which held that **no right to union representation automatically attached to "post-observation conferences" such as remediation meetings**. The collective bargaining agreement (CBA) did not state a right to union representation at remediation meetings. Under the CBA, teachers were entitled to union representation "at any meeting leading to disciplinary action." Post-observation conferences were not disciplinary and were required by the state board. And the CBA gave supervisors discretion over evaluative conclusions and remediation decisions. While remediation meetings "had the potential of resulting in adverse action," the court held the CBA did not require representation. As neither the law nor the CBA assured a right to union representation, the judgment was reversed. *SPEED Dist. 802 v. Warning*, 242 Ill.2d 92, 950 N.E.2d 1069 (Ill. 2011).

◆   **The U.S. Supreme Court upheld a collective bargaining agreement between an Indiana school board and a teachers union which gave the union exclusive access to the school district's internal mail system.** A rival union claimed that the denial of access to the mail system violated the First Amendment and the Equal Protection Clause. The Supreme Court held that since the inter-school mail system was not a public forum generally available for use by the public, access to it could be reasonably restricted without violating either free speech or equal protection rights. The Court noted the special responsibilities of the exclusive bargaining representative and the fact that other channels of communication remained available to the rival union. *Perry Educ. Ass'n v. Perry Local Educators' Ass'n*, 460 U.S. 37, 103 S.Ct. 948, 74 L.Ed.2d 794 (1983).

◆ A Minnesota law required public employers to engage in official exchanges of views only with their professional employees' exclusive representatives on certain policy questions. By law, public employers were required to bargain only with the employees' exclusive bargaining representative. The statute gave professional employees rights to "meet and confer" with the employer on matters outside the scope of a collective bargaining agreement. Community college faculty members sued the state board for community colleges, claiming the law violated the First Amendment. The faculty members objected to the "meet and confer" provision, saying that rights of professional employees within the bargaining unit who were not union members were violated. The U.S. Supreme Court held the "meet and confer" provision did not violate the faculty members' constitutional rights. **There was no constitutional right to force public employers to listen to employees' views.** The fact that an academic setting was involved did not give the faculty members any special constitutional right to a voice in the employer's policy-making decisions. The state had a legitimate interest in ensuring that public employers heard one voice presenting the majority view of its professional employees on employment-related policy questions. *Minnesota Community College Ass'n v. Knight*, 465 U.S. 271, 104 S.Ct. 1058, 79 L.Ed.2d 299 (1984).

C. Agency Fees

Expenditures of employee associations fall into two categories: chargeable expenses, which relate directly to collective bargaining and representation; and nonchargeable expenditures, which include funding of political causes. The U.S. Supreme Court has held that employee financial support of collective bargaining representatives implicates the First Amendment.

◆ Detroit teachers elected a labor association to become their exclusive collective bargaining representative, and it instituted an agency shop agreement. A group of teachers filed a class action lawsuit, stating that they would not pay dues or agency fees because of their opposition to collective bargaining in the public sector. They disapproved of the union's political and social activities, which they claimed were unrelated to the collective bargaining process. The teachers argued that the agency shop agreement violated state law and the First and Fourteenth Amendments. The U.S. Supreme Court agreed with the teachers that **compelled agency fees should not be used to support political views and candidates that were unrelated to collective bargaining issues.** Because the state court had dismissed the case without a trial, the teachers had not received the opportunity to make specific allegations that their contributions were being used to support activities with which they disagreed. There was no evidentiary record, and the Court remanded the case. If the teachers could prove a First Amendment violation, they were entitled to relief in the form of an injunction or a *pro rata* refund of fees being used for such purposes. *Abood v. Detroit Board of Educ.*, 431 U.S. 209, 97 S.Ct. 1782, 52 L.Ed.2d 261 (1977).

◆ A school board and teachers' union agreed to deduct "proportionate share payments" from the paychecks of any nonunion employee. The deduction was fixed at 95% of the dues for union members, and no explanation was given as to how that figure was reached. This method of deduction was held to violate First Amendment freedom of speech protections. **To guard against the possibility of nonunion teachers' service fee payments being used for political purposes disagreeable to the nonmembers**, there must be an adequate accounting and explanation of the basis for the deduction. In case of a challenge, there must be an opportunity for a reasonably prompt decision by an impartial decisionmaker as to whether any part of the deduction has gone to fund political causes. Any amount reasonably in dispute had to be held in escrow during the challenge. *Chicago Teachers Union v. Hudson*, 475 U.S. 292, 106 S.Ct. 1066, 89 L.Ed.2d 232 (1986).

◆ Washington law permitted public employee unions to negotiate agency shop agreements. Unions could charge nonmembers who were in a collective bargaining unit an "agency fee" that was equivalent to full union membership dues. State voters approved an initiative that prohibited unions from spending the agency fees collected from union nonmembers for election-related purposes unless this was "affirmatively authorized" by the individual nonmember. The Washington Education Association (WEA) sent nonmembers biannual notices of their right to object to paying fees for expenditures that were spent on items unrelated to collective bargaining. The options included paying fees under objection and applying for a rebate. The state and a class of nonunion public school employees sued the WEA, claiming the union had used nonmember fees to make political expenditures without affirmative authorization. The state supreme court held that the affirmative authorization requirement violated the First Amendment. The U.S. Supreme Court held a state could require its public-sector unions to receive affirmative authorization from a nonmember before spending that nonmember's agency fees for election-related purposes. **As unions had no entitlement to the fees of nonmember employees**, the Court upheld the law requiring affirmative opt-in. *Davenport v. Washington Educ. Ass'n*, 551 U.S. 177, 127 S.Ct. 2372, 168 L.Ed.2d 71 (2007).

◆ The exclusive bargaining representative of the faculty at a state college entered into an agency-shop arrangement with the college requiring nonunion bargaining unit employees to pay a service or agency fee equivalent to a union member's dues. Employees who objected to particular uses by the unions of their service fee brought suit under 42 U.S.C. § 1983, claiming that using the fees for purposes other than negotiating and administering the collective bargaining agreement violated their First and Fourteenth Amendment rights. A federal court held that certain collective bargaining expenses were chargeable to the dissenting employees. The U.S. Supreme Court held **chargeable activities must be "germane" to collective bargaining activity and be justified by the policy interest of avoiding "free riders" who benefit from union efforts without paying for union services**. A local union could charge the objecting employees for their pro rata share of costs associated with chargeable activities of its state and national affiliates, even if those activities did not directly benefit the local bargaining unit. The local could even charge the dissenters for expenses incident to preparation for an illegal strike. However, lobbying activities and public relations efforts were not chargeable to objecting employees. The Court remanded the case. *Lehnert v. Ferris Faculty Ass'n*, 500 U.S. 507, 111 S.Ct. 1950, 114 L.Ed.2d 572 (1991).

D. Payroll Contributions

In 2009, both the U.S. Supreme Court and the U.S. Court of Appeals, Tenth Circuit, held states were not required to assist employee associations in the funding or expression of their political ideas though payroll deductions.

◆ The Michigan Campaign Finance Act (MCFA) prohibited a "public body" from using public resources to make a "contribution or expenditure" for political purposes. A school district administered a payroll deduction plan for school employees to contribute to the Michigan Education Association Political Action Committee (MEA-PAC). The district was to be paid in advance for its costs of administering the payroll deductions. Although the MEA insisted this insulated the district from making "expenditures" in violation of MCFA Section 57, the secretary of state held the arrangement was prohibited. The dispute eventually went before the state supreme court, which held the school district's administration of the payroll deduction plan violated Section 57. Through administration of a payroll deduction plan that remitted funds to a partisan political action committee, the school district made both a prohibited "contribution" and an "expenditure" under the MCFA. For this reason, **the court held the district's payroll deduction plan was prohibited**. *Michigan Educ. Ass'n v. Secretary of State*, 489 Mich. 194, 801 N.W.2d 35 (Mich. 2011).

◆ Idaho's Voluntary Contributions Act (VCA) amended the Right to Work Act in 2003 to permit all employees of the state and its political subdivisions to continue authorizing payroll deductions for general union dues. But they could not authorize payroll deductions for "political activities," which were defined as "electoral activities, independent expenditures, or expenditures made to any candidate, political party, political action committee or political issues committee in support of or against any ballot measure." The Idaho Education Association and Pocatello Education Association sued state officials in a federal court, asserting that the VCA violated employee rights. The court upheld the prohibition on political payroll deductions for state-level employees, since the state incurred costs to set up and maintain the payroll deduction program. But the court found the VCA prohibition was not valid at local levels. The U.S. Supreme Court held that **the government is not required to assist in the funding of political expression**. Both sides agreed that the state did not need to provide payroll deductions. Idaho was not obligated to assist unions with their political causes. Unions remained free to engage in political speech, but were "simply barred from enlisting the State" for that purpose. The VCA ban on political payroll deductions furthered a government interest in distinguishing between government operations and private speech. According to the Court, "Idaho does not suppress political speech but simply declines to promote it through public employer checkoffs for political activities." As the VCA ban on political deductions helped to separate public employment from political activities, the Court reversed the judgment. *Ysursa v. Pocatello Educ. Ass'n*, 555 U.S. 353, 129 S.Ct. 1093, 172 L.Ed.2d 770 (2009).

◆ Utah's Voluntary Contributions Act (VCA) ended voluntary payroll contributions to labor union political funds. The legislation prompted the Utah Education Association (UEA) and other public employee unions to file a federal court action, seeking to nullify the Act on First Amendment grounds. According to the unions, the VCA restricted member employee rights. The court agreed, as did a panel of the U.S. Court of Appeals, Tenth Circuit. After the U.S. Supreme Court upheld a similar Idaho statute in *Ysursa v. Pocatello Educ. Ass'n*, above, the Tenth Circuit held that **a state was not required to assist a union in the funding or expression of political ideas**. When a state declined to subsidize speech, it did not infringe upon individual First Amendment rights. The VCA had a rational basis that survived limited judicial scrutiny. Like the Idaho VCA, Utah's VCA did not suppress political speech, but simply declined to promote it through a system of public employee payroll deductions. *Utah Educ. Ass'n v. Shurtleff*, 565 F.3d 1226 (10th Cir. 2009).

II. COLLECTIVE BARGAINING AGREEMENTS

Federal labor law imposes a duty on employers to bargain with duly elected collective bargaining representatives over the terms and conditions of employment. School districts and employees become bound by the terms of their agreements, and failure to abide by them constitutes an unfair labor practice.

A. Compensation

◆ Although most Rhode Island public school teachers were employed under collective bargaining agreements (CBAs) specifying 12-step salary schedules, the Cumberland School Committee and its teachers had a 10-step schedule that reflected wages well below the state average. Seeking to address these issues, the committee and teachers association negotiated a three-year CBA for 2006-07, 2007-08 and 2008-09. A last-minute agreement was reached that left the parties with "very different understandings" of how a 10-step schedule would be implemented. Under the CBA, the salary schedule would go to 11 steps for 2006-07 and 10 steps for the next two years. As the 2007-08 school year began, the parties disagreed about implementation of the 11-step schedule. The matter was referred to an arbitrator. After four days of hearings, he denied the grievances, finding an agreement to move teachers horizontally on the step schedule for 2006-07 and then increase their pay by 4% for 2007-08.

A state court confirmed the award, and appeal reached the Supreme Court of Rhode Island. It held courts may not disturb arbitration awards unless there has been fraud, an abuse of authority, or manifest disregard for the law. In upholding the award, the court found the parties had never decided how to transition to a new salary scale for 2007-08. In fact, the parties did not see fit to include any written transitional rules. **Had the arbitrator adopted the association's view, some teachers would have received an exorbitant pay increase that was unintended by either party.** Under the deferential standard of review for arbitration awards, the court upheld the decision. *Cumberland Teachers Ass'n v. Cumberland School Committee*, 45 A.3d 1188 (R.I. 2012).

◆   Teachers at a North Dakota alternative high school worked under the same contract as traditional high school teachers in the district. Under the contract, the normal teaching workload for all teachers in the district included weekly student contact time of 1,500 minutes. High school classes lasted 50 minutes, and teachers at traditional high schools had a normal class schedule of five classes per day. The remaining 250 weekly contact minutes were filled by tutorial periods. But at the alternative high school, teachers had two daily 150-minute teaching blocks, for a total of 300 contact minutes per day and 1,500 minutes per week. Arguing they were working more than a "normal five" period day, the alternative school teachers sought extra pay.

Appeal reached the Supreme Court of North Dakota, which noted that **teachers at the alternative and traditional high schools both delivered 300 minutes of daily teaching time.** When the 1,250 minutes of weekly teaching time worked by traditional high school teachers was added to their 250 weekly tutorial period minutes, the result was the same 1,500 minutes of weekly contact time that the alternative high school teachers worked, but in a different format. The conduct of the parties in the past decade indicated their mutual understanding that alternative school teachers were fulfilling their normal contract role under this arrangement. As they were not due additional compensation, the court held for the school district. *Kalvoda v. Bismarck Public School Dist. #1*, 794 N.W.2d 454 (N.D. 2011).

◆   A California school district paid its teachers for working 185 days during the 2006-07 school year. This included 180 instructional days, two days before classes started and three staff development days when students did not attend school. Classified employees (including paraeducators, instructional assistants and special education assistants) were not paid for staff development days when no students attended school. The union representing the classified employees petitioned a state court for a special order, asserting the district violated state law by not paying them on staff development days when they did not work.

A state superior court denied the petition, and the union appealed to the Court of Appeal of California. It held a review of Education Code Section 45203 revealed that the classified employees were not entitled to the relief sought by the union. The section required payment of classified personnel on school days when pupils would otherwise have been in attendance but were not, and for which certificated teachers received regular pay. **Agreeing with the**

school district, the court held the staff development days were not "schooldays" during which pupils would otherwise have been in attendance. As the district argued, staff development days were in addition to, not in lieu of, the 180 days of instruction required by state law. *California School Employees Ass'n v. Torrance Unified School Dist.*, 182 Cal.App.4th 1040, 106 Cal.Rptr.3d 375 (Cal. Ct. App. 2010).

◆   A South Dakota school district and the association representing its teachers reached impasse in negotiations for a contract for the 2006-07 school year. The 2005-06 agreement stated that it would remain in effect until a new contract was approved, and it provided for implementation of contract terms under Section 3-18-8.2 of the state code. While contract negotiations were in progress, the district hired 15 new teachers for 2006-07 and paid them on the 2005-06 salary schedule. South Dakota law did not permit teacher strikes, and after impasse, the Section 3-18-8.2 provisions took effect. Under this law, the school board's last offer had to be implemented "as a minimum," and the offer became the relevant agreement between the parties. The board's last offer for 2006-07 had a new salary schedule that departed significantly from the 2005-06 schedule. Without notifying the teachers association, the district unilaterally declined to adjust the salaries of the 15 new teachers downward. When the association learned of this, it filed a grievance with the state department of labor (DOL).

The case reached the Supreme Court of South Dakota. It held **agreements imposed when an impasse is reached are legally binding on the parties**. The district's last salary offer was based on a formula that tied increases to teacher degrees and a pool of money referred to as the Average Daily Membership Advancement Pool. Statutory language did not require the district to honor individual teacher contracts that were more favorable than the last offer, as the district contended. To interpret the "as a minimum" language of Section 3-18-8.2 as the district urged would undermine the entire collective bargaining process. **Collective bargaining statutes did not allow districts to negotiate with individual members of the bargaining unit.** The case was returned to the lower court for an appropriate award of relief. *Spearfish Educ. Ass'n v. Spearfish School Dist. # 40-2*, 780 N.W.2d 481 (S.D. 2010).

◆   Washington's highest court rejected a lawsuit asserting that legislative funding formulas which allowed differing salaries among employees in various school districts violated the state constitution. **Local salary variations were permitted, since the legislature was aware of the relevant political and economic issues.** *Federal Way School Dist. No. 210 v. State of Washington*, 219 P.3d 941 (Wash. 2009).

◆   A Wisconsin school district hired a teacher in 2002 who qualified for salary at the BA +8 lane of the collective bargaining agreement (CBA). However, the district accidentally put her at the BA + 0 level, where she remained for three school years. At the end of the 2004-05 school year, the teacher finally realized she was being underpaid and submitted a formal request to change lanes for the 2005-06 school year. The change was approved and she was paid at the BA + 8 lane, but nothing was done to remedy the underpayment of her wages during the prior years. When the teacher sought back wages to reflect the BA + 8 pay rate for her first three years of employment, the district refused the request. She filed a formal grievance, and an arbitrator found her grievance timely under a CBA provision requiring employees to give written notice to their immediate supervisor 15 days after learning the facts upon which a grievance was based.

Among the arbitrator's findings was that initial placement on the incorrect pay lane did not trigger the grievance. The case reached the Supreme Court of Wisconsin, which held that **the arbitrator permissibly found that the teacher did not know she had a grievance with the district until it made the decision to deny her back wages.** The teacher was challenging the denial of back wages, not her initial placement in the BA + 0 lane. Since this construction of the CBA had a foundation in reason, the award had to be upheld. *Baldwin-Woodville Area School Dist. v. West Cent. Educ. Ass'n - Baldwin-Woodville Unit*, 317 Wis.2d 691, 766 N.W.2d 591 (Wis. 2009).

◆ A Nebraska school district designated a long-term certificated teacher as a "substitute" and assigned her to take the place of a teacher who had resigned. The substitute was the only applicant with proper certification for the job. But a school administrator wanted to avoid hiring her as a permanent employee, so he designated her a "long-term substitute" instead of offering her a probationary contract. Later, the district re-posted the position and hired one of the previous applicants for the job, who had by then obtained proper certification. The district then told the substitute her services were not needed. Her union filed a grievance on her behalf, but the district denied the grievance and took her name off its list of active substitute teachers. The union filed an action with the state Commission of Industrial Relations, which ordered the district to reimburse the substitute by the amount she would have otherwise received under the collective bargaining agreement. On appeal, the Supreme Court of Nebraska found that **the district improperly hired the teacher as a long-term substitute**, even though she was a certificated teacher replacing a teacher who had resigned and did not plan to return. The district unilaterally altered the wages of a bargaining unit member, which was prohibited. *South Sioux City Educ. Ass'n v. Dakota County School Dist. No. 22-0011*, 278 Neb. 572, 772 N.W.2d 564 (Neb. 2009).

◆ A California school district and a teachers association agreed to a collective bargaining agreement (CBA) provision "compressing" teacher salaries to keep its salary rates competitive. The former 27-step schedule was compressed into 24 steps. All teachers with 17 to 20 years of service were placed into step 17. New step 20 was renumbered step 17, and all subsequent steps were renumbered. As a result, steps for teachers with at least 17 years of service did not correspond to their years of experience. Some teachers were moved three steps back. Aggrieved teachers sought a state court order recognizing uniform credit for each year of teaching experience, and the case reached the Court of Appeal of California. It held the state Education Code mandates uniform teacher salary schedules when they are based on years of experience and training.

A "uniform salary schedule" was one in which teachers were compensated invariably according to seniority and education. **The step reassignment in this case caused non-uniform treatment of teachers with equal experience.** The salary schedule treated more experienced teachers as "second-class employees" by requiring them to work longer than others to obtain the same salary increases. This violated the Education Code requirement that salaries be commensurate with years of experience and training. And although parties could negotiate CBAs based on criteria other than a uniform allowance for years of training and experience, there were no such criteria in this case. *Adair v. Stockton Unified School Dist.*, 162 Cal.App.4th 1436, 77 Cal.Rptr. 62 (Cal. Ct. App. 2008).

◆ **A Texas school administrator who did not follow her school district's procedure for addressing wage and earnings grievances could not pursue a due process claim** in federal court. The U.S. Court of Appeals, Fifth Circuit, affirmed a judgment for the district, which cut the administrator's pay when it involuntarily transferred her from a regular high school to an alternative school. The district later notified her that the reduction was in error and paid her for back wages. The administrator could not show a due process violation, as she did not use the district's grievance procedure prior to filing suit. *Vicari v. Ysleta Independent School Dist.*, 291 Fed.Appx. 614 (5th Cir. 2008).

◆ A Nebraska school district and the association representing its teachers failed to reach a negotiated agreement for the 2002-03 school year. The parties disputed the inclusion of a deviation clause in the agreement that was part of their 2001-02 contract. The clause permitted the school board to deviate from the agreement if this was necessary to hire teachers for particular positions. The association petitioned the state Commission of Industrial Relations (CIR), which held for the association, finding that the deviation clause should be excluded. The Supreme Court of Nebraska then noted that **each district with a deviation clause had the ability to depart or deviate from the salary schedule**. Since this commonality among contracts was consistent with the definition of "deviation," the CIR had incorrectly struck down the deviation clause. The court reversed the judgment with instructions to include the clause in the parties' 2002-03 contract. *Hyannis Educ. Ass'n v. Grant County School Dist. No. 38-0011*, 274 Neb. 103, 736 N.W.2d 726 (Neb. 2007).

◆ The Waterloo (Iowa) Education Association (WEA) submitted a proposal to require extra pay for elementary teachers who taught over 300 minutes as part of their daily regular assignment. The district claimed the proposal was not a mandatory subject of bargaining. The state Public Employment Relations Board agreed, and the case reached the Supreme Court of Iowa. The court explained that the state Public Employment Relations Act required public employers and employee associations to negotiate in good faith over wages, hours, vacations, insurance, holidays, leaves of absence, overtime compensation, supplemental pay, seniority, transfers and the other listed mandatory collective bargaining topics. Here, **the compensation proposal was within the statutory definition of "wages," and it was a mandatory subject of collective bargaining**. The parties were required to bargain over the proposal. *Waterloo Educ. Ass'n v. Iowa Public Employment Relations Board*, 740 N.W.2d 418 (Iowa 2007).

♦ A Montana school superintendent agreed to pay a prospective teaching candidate $2,000 in moving expenses as an inducement. The school board later offered the candidate a teaching position. Two weeks later, the board voted to hire another teaching candidate who also sought moving expenses. However, her request was denied on grounds that this would exceed the salary specified in the collective bargaining agreement (CBA). The teachers' association filed an unfair labor practice charge with the state Board of Personnel Appeals (BOPA), which held the incentive was additional compensation and a condition of employment that was subject to mandatory collective bargaining. The Supreme Court of Montana affirmed the BOPA's decision. Terms and conditions offered by an employer to a non-employee may still be subject to mandatory bargaining if they "vitally affect" the terms and conditions of employment for current employees. The $2,000 inducement materially or significantly affected the terms and conditions of employment for association members. **The board circumvented the collective bargaining process by bargaining directly with and agreeing to pay the candidate compensation beyond what was stated in the CBA.** *Ekalaka Unified Board of Trustees v. Ekalaka Teachers' Ass'n, MEA-MFT, NEA*, 335 Mont. 149, 149 P.3d 902 (Mont. 2006).

♦ In 2000, Washington voters approved Initiative 732, which mandated an annual cost-of-living increase for all school employees. When the legislature responded to a significant budget deficit in 2002 by reducing "annual learning improvement days" from three to two, some educational employees lost about one-half of a percent of their annual pay. A coalition of teachers, districts and others challenged the reduction. The case reached the Supreme Court of Washington, which stated that learning improvement days were not part of the constitutionally mandated basic education. Thus, **the legislature's decision to fund only two learning improvement days rather than three did not result in a lower cost-of-living increase than was required by Initiative 732.** *Brown v. State of Washington*, 119 P.3d 341 (Wash. 2005).

B. Positions

In Sacco v. Cranston School Dep't, *below, Rhode Island's highest court held that supplemental contracts to coach extracurricular athletic teams were outside a district's collective bargaining regime. For additional cases involving coaching contracts, see Chapter 13, Section III of this volume.*

♦ Two Rhode Island high school teachers coached varsity athletic teams. After one served for nine years, and the other seven, they received unacceptable coaching evaluations. One teacher was placed on probation for a year, and the other lost his coaching duties. Both teachers disputed their evaluations and sought to file grievances under the collective bargaining agreement (CBA) between their school department and employees association. But the school department declined the requests, asserting that coaching duties were covered by separate, one-year contracts and not the CBA. Appeal reached the Supreme Court of Rhode Island, which held that extracurricular work traditionally performed by teachers is not "professional in nature." **Numerous cases from**

other states supported the supreme court's conclusion that teachers could not arbitrate disputes regarding their extracurricular positions under a CBA. For this reason, the court held for the school department. *Sacco v. Cranston School Dep't*, 53 A.3d 147 (R.I. 2012).

◆ A non-tenured New Jersey teacher/secretary worked under an individual contract that could be terminated by either party upon 60 days' notice. A month into her job, the district superintendent began receiving complaints about her. His classroom observation found she was "unsatisfactory" or "needed improvement" in 22 of 25 relevant areas. Her contract was terminated for "serious deficiencies" in performance, and she asked her union to file a grievance on her behalf. It did so, asserting the action was not supported by "just cause" under the collective bargaining agreement (CBA). The board sought to prevent arbitration and the case reached the Supreme Court of New Jersey. It found that **despite language recognizing employee rights to grievance procedures, the CBA recognized the existence and enforceability of individual employment contracts, like the employee's.** The CBA stated that grievances were inapplicable when the board decided not to renew a non-tenured employee's contract. Since the board had reserved its rights to terminate any non-tenured employee in the best interest of the school district, arbitration was rejected. *Northvale Board of Educ. v. Northvale Educ. Ass'n*, 192 N.J. 501, 933 A.2d 596 (N.J. 2007).

◆ An Ohio school board employed an unlicensed non-teacher as a girls' high school basketball coach for many years. A middle school teacher who was an assistant varsity coach and junior varsity head coach applied for the high school varsity coaching job. However, the high school's athletic director rehired the non-teacher coach. The middle school teacher grieved the board's decision, asserting that the collective bargaining agreement required the board to award a certificated employee a supplemental coaching contract over a non-teacher. An arbitrator determined that state law required the hiring of the teacher. The Court of Appeals of Ohio agreed with the arbitrator that **the board had to offer the position to the middle school teacher before it could give the job to the non-teacher.** There was no collective bargaining provision about the matter, so the parties were subject to state laws or local ordinances pertaining to wages, hours and terms and conditions of employment. State law allowed the board to hire a non-licensed coach only if it offered the job to licensed employees of the district and none accepted it. *Eastwood Local School Dist. Board of Educ. v. Eastwood Educ. Ass'n*, 172 Ohio App.3d 423, 875 N.E.2d 139 (Ohio Ct. App. 2007).

C. Unfair Labor Practices

"Terms and conditions of employment" are matters that must be negotiated through collective bargaining. Tennessee law defines the phrase as "those fundamental matters that affect a professional employee financially or the employee's employment relationship with the board." By contrast, inherently managerial subjects such as the school calendar cannot be bargained over.

A Tennessee court held a dress code had fundamentally affected teachers, and required mandatory bargaining. Polk County Board of Educ. v. Polk County

Educ. Ass'n, 139 S.W.3d 304 (Tenn. Ct. App. 2004). *And the South Dakota Supreme Court held the school calendar was a matter of general public interest that affected the community and was an inherently managerial subject that could not be negotiated over in collective bargaining.* West Cent. Educ. Ass'n v. West Cent. School Dist. 49-4, *655 N.W.2d 916 (S.D. 2002).*

◆ A Florida teacher drafted a sexual orientation harassment charge against his principal and school district for a security guard. After the principal learned of the complaint, she questioned the teacher about it. He said she retaliated against him by taking two groundless disciplinary actions and transferring him to another school. The teacher filed three unfair labor practice charges with the state public employee relations commission (PERC). Each of the charges was dismissed, and the case reached the Supreme Court of Florida. It held **Florida law prohibits public employers from interfering with, restraining or coercing their employees in the exercise of any right guaranteed by labor law**. This included discharging or discriminating against a public employee because he or she filed charges or provided testimony under the labor law. In the court's view, the PERC used an improper heightened standard when assessing the teacher's initial charge that protected conduct was a substantial or motivating factor in the employer's decision. Since he claimed to be engaged in protected activity, declared he was subjected to an adverse action, and alleged a causal link between the activity and adverse action, he could proceed with his case. *Koren v. School Board of Miami-Dade County*, 97 So.3d 215 (Fla. 2012).

◆ Connecticut special education teachers complained that their workloads were increased by 10 to 14 hours each week after a colleague quit. A district director of pupil personnel said there was no point in making a complaint through their union. She also suggested that the teachers maintain that the union president had approached them about making a complaint, not the reverse. The union filed a complaint against the school board with the State Board of Labor Relations (SBLR). The case reached the Supreme Court of Connecticut, which held that education boards cannot refuse to bargain in good faith with employee collective bargaining agents or representatives.

A unilateral change to an employment condition is an unlawful refusal to negotiate under state law. **To establish a unilateral change of a condition of employment, the court held the union had to show the practice was clearly enunciated and consistent, had endured over a reasonable time, and was an accepted practice by both parties.** There was evidence that in two earlier years, the teachers had even larger caseloads. As the teachers failed to show their caseloads were substantially increased after their colleague left work, the court held the board did not make a unilateral change to a fixed and definite employment practice. But the SBLR had correctly found the director's actions amounted to unlawful direct dealing with the teachers. An employer has a duty to collectively bargain with the chosen representative of its employees and cannot negotiate wages or other terms of employment with individual employees through direct dealing. *Board of Educ. of Region 16 v. State Board of Labor Relations*, 299 Conn. 63, 7 A.3d 371 (Conn. 2010).

◆   A Florida school district had to provide no-cost employee health insurance under three collective bargaining agreements (CBAs). Each CBA required the district to create an insurance committee to study and make recommendations about employee health, life, dental and vision insurance coverage. Due to state funding reductions, the Florida Department of Education advised the district it could face a $90 million shortfall. Without consulting the insurance committee, the board of education approved two insurance options that would require employees to pay monthly premiums. In an exchange of correspondence, the district's employee relations director noted that collective bargaining over the healthcare issues would "create an insurmountable stalemate." After the board approved plans over the association's objections, the association filed an unfair labor practices complaint with the state Public Employee Relations Committee.

Appeal reached the Florida District Court of Appeal. It found there had been no unmistakable waiver of rights by the association. The board-approved health plans were never discussed by the insurance committee. And the district rejected a request to collectively bargain the changes, predicting that collective bargaining would end in a stalemate. **The court held nothing in state labor law absolved the district of collective bargaining obligations "because the subject matter is contentious and complex."** There was also no showing that exigent circumstances justified the district's conduct. As a result, the court held for the association. *School Dist. of Polk County, Florida v. Polk County Educ. Ass'n,* 100 So.3d 11 (Fla. Dist. Ct. App. 2011).

◆   A Florida District Court of Appeal held a district improperly implemented a new policy that would require teachers to submit lesson plans via the Internet. It held the new policy would impact teacher workload and training. **An employer must bargain over the impact that a decision has on the terms or conditions of employment of the members of the bargaining unit.** This is known as "impact bargaining." Under the new policy, there would be a need for new training, and equipment would have to be provided. The policy would require equivalent schools to standardize the content required for electronic submission of lesson plans. There would be disciplinary consequences for noncompliance with the new policy, and the union asserted a financial impact on the bargaining unit. The court found the union satisfied requirements that the charge identify specific impacts on wages, hours or terms and conditions of employment. As the union had identified a negotiable effect on wages, hours and terms and conditions of employment that was "direct and substantial," the court held in its favor. *School Dist. of Indian River County, Florida v. Florida Public Employees Relations Comm'n,* 64 So.3d 723 (Fla. Dist. Ct. App. 2011).

◆   A Minnesota school district that had 24 approved vendors for its employee 403(b) retirement plans began using a single vendor. The district declined the employee association's demand to meet and negotiate over the issue, and the association sued, claiming the district's unilateral decision was an unfair labor practice under the state Public Employee Labor Relations Act (PELRA). The case reached the Court of Appeals of Minnesota, arguing that retirement benefits were within the PELRA's definition of "terms and conditions of employment" and thus a mandatory subject of negotiation. The court explained that "terms and conditions of employment" includes subjects such as hours of work, compensation and fringe benefits. But the PELRA excluded "retirement contributions or benefits" unrelated to health insurance coverage. While the court found the selection of a 403(b) plan vendor was a "fringe benefit," the PELRA excluded certain fringe benefits, and the exception for retirement contributions or benefits unambiguously covered the selection of vendors for 403(b) plans. The primary purpose of such plans was to help employees save for retirement. **The PELRA excluded the selection of 403(b) plan vendors as a subject of mandatory negotiation.** *Educ. Minnesota-Osseo v. Independent School Dist. No. 279, Osseo Area Schools*, 742 N.W.2d 199 (Minn. Ct. App. 2007). In 2008, the Minnesota Supreme Court declined to review the case.

◆ The New Jersey state health benefits plan was revised to increase the minimum weekly work hours required for employees to qualify for paid health insurance coverage. A local school board increased the minimum weekly hours for coverage from 20 hours to 32 to qualify for paid coverage. The union representing its teachers objected, but the parties did not refer to the elimination of health insurance benefits for part-time employees during negotiations for collective bargaining agreements (CBAs) until five years later, when a special education teacher who worked at least 20 hours per week complained that she was not receiving paid health insurance. But the new CBA for 2002-04 again did not resolve the issue of paid insurance benefits for part-time employees. An arbitrator held **the board committed a "continuing violation" of the CBA, based on the elimination of benefits for part-time employees without notice and without negotiating a change in the CBA**. The award required the board to provide paid health insurance benefits to the teacher and another certificated part-time employee who worked over 20 hours per week. On appeal, the state supreme court upheld the award. *Board of Educ. of Borough of Alpha, Warren County v. Alpha Educ. Ass'n*, 188 N.J. 595, 911 A.2d 903 (N.J. 2006).

III. GRIEVANCES AND ARBITRATION

A. Arbitrability

By including arbitration clauses in collective bargaining agreements, the parties agree to an arbitrator's interpretation of the agreement. If an arbitrator resolves a dispute concerning the interpretation of contract terms and the award draws its essence from the agreement, a court may not disturb the award.

◆ A Pennsylvania teacher was charged with improperly touching seventh-grade girls. After an evaluation that recommended he have no contact with students outside of structured classrooms, he was placed on an improvement plan. He defied the plan by meeting with students during lunch and in the classrooms of other teachers. He had physical contact with students and made death threats against school administrators. Since the teacher did not meet the terms of his improvement plan, the district prepared to terminate his contract. He was informed of his discharge for violating state law and the district sexual harassment policy, and for unprofessionalism toward administrators.

The case was submitted to an arbitrator. By the time an award was issued, the teacher had been suspended without pay for parts of two school years. Although the arbitrator found the teacher "guilty of grievous misconduct," he decided the teacher should return to work under the improvement plan. On appeal, the Commonwealth Court of Pennsylvania held **the arbitrator did not interpret the collective bargaining agreement** (CBA). Instead, he found the teacher guilty of violating a district policy. Since the arbitrator clearly went outside the CBA, the award was not rationally derived from the CBA. As the award violated a well-defined and established policy of protecting students from sexual harassment during school hours on school property, the award had to be vacated. *Bethel Park School Dist. v. Bethel Park Federation of Teachers, Local 1607*, 55 A.3d 154 (Pa. Commw. Ct. 2012).

◆ Massachusetts' highest court held an arbitrator did not exceed her authority by agreeing to arbitrate a school cafeteria manager's case. In the arbitration case, a school's decision to discharge the manager was upheld. On appeal, the Supreme Judicial Court of Massachusetts found the arbitrator did not exceed her authority by finding the matter was arbitrable. In arbitration, the manager's union did not dispute a claim by the school department that **she was a civil service employee who was bound by the relevant collective bargaining agreement**. And the union did not question arbitrability at the start of the case. *American Federation of State, County, and Municipal Employees, Council 93, AFL-CIO v. School Dep't of Burlington*, 462 Mass. 1009 (Mass. 2012).

◆ A New Jersey custodian disobeyed a supervisor's instruction to knock and announce himself before entering girls' changing areas on the night of a school dance recital. When challenged by a teacher for entering the classroom, he asked her, "What's the big deal?" An investigation was conducted by the state division of youth and family services. The division closed its case, and the board of education conducted its own investigation. It then voted to fire the custodian. A grievance was filed on his behalf. An arbitrator noted that the relevant collective bargaining contract required "just cause" to impose discipline. In the arbitrator's view, progressive/corrective discipline was an integral part of the just cause concept. As this was the custodian's first offense, the arbitrator imposed only a two-week unpaid suspension. Appeal reached the Supreme Court of New Jersey, which found **the lack of a contractual definition of "just cause" made it necessary for the arbitrator to attempt an interpretation of the term**. Finding the arbitrator's decision was fully compliant with the relevant contract, the court affirmed the arbitration award. *Linden Board of Educ. v. Linden Educ. Ass'n*, 202 N.J. 268, 997 A.2d 997 (N.J. 2010).

After the custodian's grievance was filed, but before it reached arbitration, the board approved a list of employees who would be offered contracts for the next school year. It did not include the custodian's name. Following the state supreme court's decision upholding the arbitration award, the board took the position that the non-renewal of his contract could no longer be challenged and he was not entitled to reinstatement. The custodian later died. His employees' association obtained a court order requiring the board to pay his estate $122,022 in back wages. On appeal, **a New Jersey appellate division court rejected the board's claim that the association had to file a separate grievance for the present matter**. In its efforts to vacate the arbitration award, the board never made this argument. The court held for the estate. *Linden Board of Educ. v. Linden Educ. Ass'n*, 2012 WL 611859 (N.J. Super. Ct. App. Div. 2/6/12).

◆   The Classified Employees Association (CEA) was the representative of many Alaska school district employees. No collective bargaining agreement (CBA) provision dealt with outsourcing, but the subject was much discussed in negotiations. While the CEA claimed the district gave assurances that work would not be outsourced, the CBA did not reflect this. During the term of the CBA, the district contracted for custodial services and maintenance for specified facilities. The CEA sought a grievance, then sued to compel the district to participate in the grievance proceeding. It claimed a state law prohibited outsourcing school custodial work. Agreeing with the district, the court held the CBA did not apply to disputes over decisions to privatize work.

On appeal, the Supreme Court of Alaska found a presumption in favor of arbitrability of disputes when parties intend arbitration. But **the court found no CBA provision on outsourcing, nor any management clause that could be misinterpreted or inequitably applied**. Alaska law required written collective bargaining agreements, foreclosing the CEA's claim that there had been an oral agreement not to outsource work. And state law did not provide for interest arbitration for the class of employees represented by the CEA. As the lower court had correctly found arbitration improper, and state law did not bar outsourcing, the judgment was affirmed. *Classified Employees Ass'n v. Matanuska-Susitna Borough School Dist.*, 204 P.3d 347 (Alaska 2009).

◆   A Massachusetts teacher was suspended for 10 days for closing a door on a student's arm. The union representing the teacher filed a grievance, claiming it was harmed in its representation of the teacher by the school committee's failure to provide the names of student witnesses to the incident. An arbitrator held that the school committee's blocking of student identification was not supported by any practice or policy, or by any law or the relevant collective bargaining agreement. The school committee appealed to a Massachusetts superior court, which held that the award did not require the committee to violate a law or public policy. On appeal, **the Appeals Court of Massachusetts affirmed the decision. The legislature had narrowly limited the grounds for vacating an arbitration award.** As the lower court had found, the school committee did not show that the arbitration award violated any law or public policy. *School Committee of Boston v. Boston Teachers Union*, No. 07-P-518, 71 Mass.App.Ct. 1121, 885 N.E.2d 173 (Table) (Mass. App. Ct. 2008).

◆   Soon after accepting employment as a non-tenured employee under a one-year contract, a New Jersey school custodian was accused of hitting a coworker. The school board held a disciplinary hearing the same day and fired him. The custodian's union filed a grievance, claiming the collective bargaining agreement (CBA) required arbitration. The board sued to restrain arbitration, based on the argument that the custodian's contract had a 14-day notice period for termination and was not subject to arbitration. A state court agreed and restrained arbitration. A New Jersey appellate court affirmed. But it emphasized that the custodian could still request reasons for the discharge and obtain a board hearing under the CBA The Supreme Court of New Jersey held that a CBA generally superseded an individual contract. **If individual contract provisions conflicted with a CBA and diminished rights granted under the CBA, the individual contract had to yield.** Here, the custodian's individual contract conflicted with and diminished his CBA rights. So the contract had to yield to the CBA. Also, state law adopted a presumption in favor of arbitration of public employee CBAs. The judgment was reversed with instructions to send the case to arbitration. *Mt. Holly Township Board of Educ. v. Mt. Holly Township Educ. Ass'n*, 972 A.2d 387 (N.J. 2009).

◆ A New Hampshire school district reassigned an elementary teacher to a middle school. He claimed this was based on his pro-union activity, and his union first filed a grievance, then arbitration. The association also filed an unfair labor practice complaint with the state public employee labor relations board (PELRB). The PELRB ordered the parties into arbitration, unless a party requested an additional hearing within 30 days of an arbitration decision. The arbitrator upheld the grievance and ordered the district to reassign the teacher to his former position. The district requested a new hearing before the PELRB, asserting the arbitration decision was improper and inconsistent with the collective bargaining agreement. The PELRB denied the request. The district appealed to the Supreme Court of New Hampshire, which **rejected the district's claim that the PELRB was obligated to consider an appeal from the arbitration award**. Once arbitration was concluded, the PELRB lacked authority to review the award unless there was a filing of a subsequent unfair labor practice complaint by the association alleging district failure to implement the award. As there had been no such filing, the arbitration award was final. *Appeal of Laconia School Dist.*, 840 A.2d 800 (N.H. 2004).

B. Procedures

Parties to a collective bargaining agreement are required to exhaust the remedies of their agreement. Court review of an arbitration award is extremely limited. In Wisconsin, an arbitration award may be overturned only if it is a "perverse misconstruction," a "manifest disregard of the law," is illegal, or violates a strong public policy. Pennsylvania courts may only vacate an award that has no foundation or does not flow from a collective bargaining agreement.

◆ New York City teachers were reprimanded by letter for separate incidents. According to the teachers, the city education department violated Education Law Section 3020-a procedures by placing the letters in their files. But the department asserted they had waived statutory procedures in the collective bargaining agreement that governed their employment. The teachers sued the department in the state court system. Appeal reached the New York Court of Appeals, which noted that Section 3020 protected tenured employees from discipline or removal except for just cause and in accordance with Section

3020-a. **But Section 3020 allowed "alternate disciplinary procedures contained in a collective bargaining agreement."** The court held a collective bargaining agreement could modify or waive the Section 3020-a procedures.

In this case, the collective bargaining agreement addressed procedures governing the placement of written reprimands in tenured teacher files. This constituted a limited waiver of Section 3020-a procedural rights by detailing the relevant due process and review procedures. The history of collective bargaining between the department and union indicated an awareness that the agreement was a substitute for Section 3020-a protections. Since the court found the union knowingly waived Section 3020-a procedures on behalf of the teachers, the letters were not subject to Section 3020-a, and the teachers were not entitled to have the letters removed from their files. *Hickey v. New York City Dep't of Educ.*, 17 N.Y.3d 729, 952 N.E.2d 993 (N.Y. 2011).

◆   The Court of Appeals of Michigan held a teacher who had been laid off, then passed over for rehiring, had to pursue arbitration under relevant collective bargaining agreement (CBA) procedures before filing a lawsuit. The teacher was laid off in 2004. In 2007, she was removed from the district's seniority list because she had been laid off for more than three years. She filed a grievance under the 2006-08 CBA, rather than a 2002-06 CBA that did not specify a time limit for how long a teacher could be on layoff and still maintain seniority. Instead of seeking arbitration, the teacher sued. The state court of appeals held **employees generally cannot sue employers unless there has been an exhaustion of CBA remedies**. In addition, the court rejected an argument that arbitration would have been futile. *Powell v. St. Ignace Area Schools*, Docket No. 295553, 2011 WL 711448 (Mich. Ct. App. 3/1/2011).

◆   An Ohio school cafeteria worker pled guilty in 1992 to fourth-degree felony endangerment of a child. She was placed on probation, but the conviction did not affect her employment. In 2007, Ohio enacted a law requiring background checks for school employees who did not require state licensure, such as the worker. She left work under a memorandum of understanding (MOU) by which the district would reemploy her if the disqualifying conditions were eliminated through expected changes in criminal background check laws. In 2009, the state education department adopted rules implementing the 2007 law. Child endangerment was not a "non-rehabilitative" offense unless a violation occurred within five years of a criminal background check. As the worker's conviction was 16 years old, she sought reinstatement. When the request was denied, she sued the board. The court found the new law and administrative rule altered the worker's status and triggered the MOU requirement that the board rehire her. **The court held the MOU provision was a waiver of the board's discretion to decide whether she had rehabilitated herself.** But the court held the special order requested by the worker (called a writ of mandamus) was not the proper way for her to resolve the dispute. It dismissed the case and held she could seek court relief under the new regulations. *State of Ohio v. Kent City School Dist. Board of Educ.*, No. 2010-P-0038, 2011 WL 379165 (Ohio Ct. App. 2/7/11).

◆   Pennsylvania's highest court reversed an appellate decision that would have reinstated an arbitration award for a maintenance employee who tested positive for use of marijuana shortly after a workplace injury. An arbitrator interpreted the district's drug-free workplace policy to prohibit drug usage only on school grounds. He found the employee's off-school conduct beyond the control of the school district. A trial court held the arbitrator exceeded his authority. The state supreme court vacated the decision and ordered the trial court to reconsider the case in view of *Westmoreland Intermediate Unit #7 v. Westmoreland Intermediate Unit #7 Classroom Assistants Educ. Support Personnel Ass'n, PSEA/NEA*, 939 A.2d 855 (Pa. 2007), this chapter. **Courts may only vacate an award that has no foundation or does not flow from a collective bargaining agreement.** *Loyalsock Township Area School Dist. v Loyalsock Custodial Maintenance, Secretarial and Aide Ass'n*, 957 A.2d 231 (Pa. 2008).

◆   A Wisconsin teacher was involved in a disciplinary grievance proceeding in which she provided a union-appointed attorney a copy of a student's IEP. The district reprimanded the teacher in writing for releasing the student record to an unauthorized third party without consent. The reprimand matter was submitted to an arbitrator, who found that the teacher could provide the IEP to her union attorney. The Court of Appeals of Wisconsin noted that the disclosure violated two school board policies intended to comply with state law and the federal Family Educational Rights and Privacy Act (FERPA). One policy prohibited the disclosure of personally identifiable student information from a school's education records without prior written consent from parents.

In ruling for the teacher, the court held **an arbitration award may be overturned only if it is a "perverse misconstruction" or "manifest disregard of the law," is illegal or violates a strong public policy**. A mistake of fact or law is not grounds for setting aside an award. The arbitrator did not make any finding that the teacher had violated state and federal privacy laws. There was a considerable discussion of FERPA, but this was to explore whether the teacher had violated the board's policy rather than the laws themselves. The court rejected the board's argument that the award violated a strong public policy favoring limited disclosure of student records, and affirmed the award. *Madison Metropolitan School Dist. v. Madison Teachers*, 308 Wis.2d 395, 746 N.W.2d 605 (Table) (Wis. Ct. App. 2008).

◆   A New Hampshire teacher had worked for the same school district since 1986. She remained seated and refused to participate in recitals of the Pledge of Allegiance by her class. In 2003, a new principal began work at the teacher's middle school, and he expressed displeasure with her non-participation. She said the principal and school district then began to retaliate against her. From 2004 to 2007, the teacher filed four grievances relating to her retaliation claims. She eventually sued the school district and principal in a federal district court for retaliating against her based on her refusal to participate in Pledge recitals.

The court held **employees may invoke rights independent of the collective bargaining process on their own behalf and not as members of a collective bargaining organization**. Significantly, the court held that "the mere existence of a collective bargaining agreement does not waive those separate statutory rights." A union-negotiated waiver of employee rights must be clear and unmistakable from the language of the CBA. Here, since the CBA contained no clear waiver of employee rights to pursue constitutional claims, the teacher's failure to appeal her grievances under the CBA did not bar the lawsuit. *Dunfey v. Seabrook School Dist.*, No. 07-cv-140-PB, 2008 WL 1848655 (D.N.H. 4/24/08).

◆ A Virginia superintendent suspended a principal without pay and advised him of his right to a hearing before the school board. The principal instead sought a hearing before a fact-finding panel under a state board grievance procedure, seeking immediate reinstatement. The superintendent informed the principal that suspension with pay was not grievable. The school board upheld the decision and demoted the principal to a teaching position, with a reduction in pay. He appealed to a Virginia circuit court, arguing that the suspension presented a grievable issue. The court held that the principal's suspension was grievable under the state board procedure and had to be timely resolved. But the state supreme court reversed, finding that **the principal's only recourse was the very process he had rejected when the superintendent offered him a hearing.** *Tazewell County School Board v. Brown*, 591 S.E.2d 671 (Va. 2004).

C. Standard of Review

A court may vacate an arbitration award on the basis of fraud, corruption or procedural irregularities, or if the arbitrator exceeds his or her powers. Arbitration awards may be vacated if they do not draw their essence from a collective bargaining agreement, are not based on a plausible interpretation of the agreement, disregard a contract provision or reach an irrational result.

◆ A New York school bus driver with no prior disciplinary incidents in nearly 10 years of work for her district tested positive for marijuana use. A collective bargaining agreement (CBA) provision called for progressive discipline, but the school board fired the driver instead, and she filed for arbitration. An arbitrator found the board violated the CBA and ordered her reinstated, but without back pay. He also ordered the driver to comply with follow-up drug and alcohol testing, and be evaluated by a substance abuse professional.

The board appealed to the state court system, and appeal reached the New York Supreme Court, Appellate Division. It held **arbitration awards may be vacated only where there is a violation of a strong public policy, or if the award is irrational or clearly exceeds a specific arbitrator power**. In this case, the CBA provided for progressive discipline, except in the most serious cases. No "zero tolerance policy concerning positive drug tests" was referenced in the CBA, as the board maintained. Instead, the CBA controlled the relationship between the parties. The arbitrator could have reasonably found the board had violated the CBA by refusing to consider disciplinary options and imposing discharge as if it were mandatory. The arbitration award was to be confirmed. *Shenendehowa Cent. School Dist. Board of Educ. v. Civil Service Employees Ass'n*, 90 A.D.3d 1114, 934 N.Y.S.2d 540 (N.Y. App. Div. 2011).

◆   A Massachusetts teacher had a record of discipline for directing profanity at students. In response to an armed services career day at his school, he organized a protest and intended to wave signs and hand out literature at the event. Although the teacher changed his plan, the principal later found him outside the school, staging a protest in which he was barefoot, in a costume and playing a bongo drum. The principal placed him on leave and later discharged him for insubordination, improper use of sick time and profanity. The teacher filed a grievance that was arbitrated under the collective bargaining agreement. An arbitrator found there had been no progressive discipline and that discharge was not commensurate with the teacher's violations. Appeal reached the Court of Appeals of Massachusetts, which found that **while arbitration awards are subject to limited court review, state law required that a court vacate an award if the arbitrator exceeded his or her powers**. In this case, the arbitrator made the award on the assumption that the collective bargaining agreement controlled. State tenure law was not mentioned, and there was no consideration for the best interests of students. As the arbitrator did not apply the tenure statute, the award had to be vacated. *School Committee of Chicopee v. Chicopee Educ. Ass'n*, 80 Mass. App. Ct. 357 (Mass. App. Ct. 2011).

◆   A Cambodian refugee began teaching in Massachusetts public schools in 1992. Her annual evaluations earned the highest ratings until 2002, when a new principal began evaluating teachers for English proficiency. He assigned her an unsatisfactory rating. Due to post-traumatic stress disorder, the teacher took a medical leave. During her leave, she failed two English fluency assessments. She claimed she was experiencing symptoms of post-traumatic stress disorder at the time. When the teacher advised the superintendent she could return to work, she was again told her English was insufficient. A review hearing was held in 2005, but the superintendent again found her insufficiently fluent in English. The school committee dismissed the teacher, but an arbitrator held reliance on the English fluency assessments alone violated due process. The case reached the Supreme Judicial Court of Massachusetts, which explained that **state law placed the burden upon the school committee to prove that "just cause" existed for her dismissal**. An arbitration decision may be vacated only if the arbitrator exceeded his powers or if the award required a person to commit an act prohibited by law. The court found nothing in state law or regulations required the superintendent to rely on the principal's assessment. And the teacher was not told her fluency was being observed or evaluated at the time. Medical evidence indicated her condition negatively affected her ability to demonstrate her English ability. As a lower court was not authorized to review this finding, the court reinstated the award in her favor. *School Committee of Lowell v. Robishaw*, 456 Mass. 653, 925 N.E.2d 803 (Mass. 2010).

◆   A New York teacher began exchanging emails and instant-messaging one of her students. Eventually, he reported the conversations to the principal, and the case was referred to a school investigatory office. When confronted, the teacher admitted making inappropriate communications. She entered therapy to cope with the situation. Later, the student discovered postings to an online journal by the teacher under an alias. They discussed the teacher's desire to be close to him and kiss him. At the conclusion of the investigation, the school department recommended employment termination. A hearing was held, and the teacher was found guilty of three charges. The hearing officer noted she was remorseful and that she had entered therapy. He found that she had learned her lesson about inappropriate relationships with students and believed she would not repeat the conduct. Rejecting the recommendation to discharge the teacher, the hearing officer imposed a 90-day unpaid suspension and assigned her to a different school. Appeal reached a state appellate division court. **The court held arbitration awards may only be vacated based on evidence of misconduct, bias, an excess of arbitrator authority, or a procedural defect.**

There was no basis for disturbing the hearing officer's decision. Arbitration awards may be vacated if they are contrary to public policy. The public policy must be "more than a general societal concern." The lower court had violated this rule by scrutinizing the facts. The court also held the penalty imposed was not so lenient as to be arbitrary and capricious. Since there was a rational basis for the hearing officer's decision, and a strong basis for concluding the teacher could be trusted again, the court reinstated the arbitration award. *City School Dist. of City of New York v. McGraham*, 905 N.Y.S.2d 86 (N.Y. App. Div. 2010).

◆ A Pennsylvania classroom assistant was found unconscious in a school lavatory. She later admitted wearing a narcotic Fentanyl patch. As she had no valid prescription for it, this was a misdemeanor. The school intermediate unit fired her, but an arbitrator found no "just cause" to do so under the Pennsylvania School Code. Her conduct did not rise to the level of "immorality," and she had a previously unblemished 23-year career. A Pennsylvania court reinstated the discharge. The case reached the Supreme Court of Pennsylvania, which held that broad judicial review of arbitration awards would undercut the value of arbitration. An award could be vacated if it violated a well-defined public policy. The court found the award was rationally derived from the collective bargaining agreement. It returned the case to the lower court for a determination of whether public policy precluded the award. *Westmoreland Intermediate Unit #7 v. Westmoreland Intermediate Unit #7 Classroom Assistants Educ. Support Personnel Ass'n, PSEA/NEA*, 939 A.2d 855 (Pa. 2007).

The case was returned to a lower court. It noted evidence of the assistant's "extensive history of abuse of pain pills." **While the arbitrator's attempts to rehabilitate the assistant were "admirable," immediate reinstatement to the classroom violated public policy.** Fentanyl is a controlled substance with effects more potent than heroin. To reinstate an employee charged with caring for children after being at work under the influence of this drug "defies logic and violates public policy." As an elementary classroom was "no place for a recovering addict," the court vacated the arbitration award for violating a dominant public policy to protect children. *Westmoreland Intermediate Unit #7 v. Westmoreland Intermediate Unit #7 Classroom Assistants Educ. Support Personnel Ass'n, PSEA/NEA*, 977 A.2d 1208 (Pa. Commw. Ct. 2009).

◆ An Alabama coach and tenured teacher taught physical education and was the cheerleading sponsor for a high school. Following a complaint from a parent whose child was removed from the cheerleading squad, an investigation revealed 14 grounds for discharge, many involving the improper use of funds. The coach allegedly violated school board fundraiser and cheerleader fund policies, resulting in the loss of almost $6,000 in cheerleading funds in one year. The board voted to discharge the coach, but she received a new hearing before a hearing officer under the Alabama Teacher Tenure Act. The hearing officer reversed the board's decision and ordered no discipline. The case reached the Supreme Court of Alabama, which held that the 2004 Tenure Act amendments did not strip school boards of their authority to discharge teachers. The discretion to determine good and just cause for discharge remained with local school officials. Also, **the hearing officer had improperly applied employment law standards from collective bargaining agreements** rather than applying the amended Teacher Tenure Act. The court ruled against the coach. *Ex Parte Wilson*, 984 So.2d 1161 (Ala. 2007).

◆ A Rhode Island school committee eliminated a longstanding practice of assigning high school English teachers a composition period for budgetary reasons. Instead of filling two newly vacated English teaching positions, the superintendent of schools hoped to eliminate the composition periods and redistribute English classes among remaining teachers. The school committee adopted the superintendent's plan and voted to eliminate the composition periods. A grievance was denied, and the case was put before an arbitrator.

After a hearing, the arbitrator upheld the union's claim that the composition period amounted to a past practice of the parties. Eliminating the practice thus violated a savings clause in the parties' agreement. The case reached the Supreme Court of Rhode Island, which explained that review of arbitration awards was limited in scope. Public policy favors the finality of arbitration awards, which may be overturned only if irrational or manifestly in disregard of the law. In this case, the arbitrator had found the school committee made its decision based on workload, and did not make an educational policy choice involving a management prerogative. **As the arbitrator had noted, workload decisions were "always subject to negotiation."** Since the arbitrator did not exceed his powers or manifestly disregard the law, the award was upheld. *North Providence School Committee v. North Providence Federation of Teachers, Local 920, American Federation of Teachers*, 945 A.2d 339 (R.I. 2008).

◆ A New Hampshire school district issued several teachers renewal letters requiring them to prepare improvement plans before the end of the 2003-04 school year. The teachers' association claimed the letters were a unilateral change to procedures in the collective bargaining agreement concerning teacher evaluation and performance reviews. The agreement specified that tenured teachers would be observed at least once a year and evaluated in writing. The association filed a complaint with the New Hampshire Public Employee Labor Relations Board (PELRB), which held that the district committed an unfair labor practice by using new procedures to communicate teacher deficiencies.

The district appealed to the Supreme Court of New Hampshire, which found that collective bargaining agreement procedures for evaluating teachers and communicating deficiencies were clear. When the district issued renewal letters with reservations and required improvement plans, it did not follow the procedures of the agreement. **The use of renewal letters with reservations and requirements for teacher improvement plans violated the collective bargaining agreement.** The district had no reserved right to implement different procedures for addressing teacher performance and evaluation than those specified in the agreement. The court upheld the PELRB's decision. *Appeal of White Mountain Regional School Dist.*, 908 A.2d 790 (N.H. 2006).

IV. STRIKES

The purpose of state legislation to prohibit or limit strikes by public employees is to protect the public and not to circumvent meaningful collective bargaining. Courts have upheld punitive actions taken against unlawfully striking teachers and their unions.

◆ A Massachusetts law prohibits public employees and unions from inducing, encouraging or condoning a strike, work stoppage, or slowdown, and from withholding services by public employees. This law requires public employers to petition the Commonwealth Relations Board (CRB) to investigate violations, and it governs relations between the Boston Teachers Union and the Boston School Committee. After a collective bargaining agreement expired in 2006, the parties unsuccessfully and acrimoniously negotiated for a new one. Union leaders announced a meeting to consider a one-day strike, and notified the school superintendent regarding a pending strike vote. Anticipating that union members would vote to strike, the school committee petitioned the CRB to investigate as specified by the law. After an investigation and hearing, the CRB found that a strike was about to occur. The union did not comply with the CRB's order to rescind and disavow the strike vote. A Massachusetts court enforced the CRB order and ordered the union to pay a $30,000 fine for contempt. On appeal, the Court of Appeals of Massachusetts held that **the union violated the law by encouraging and inducing a strike**. Any incidental limitation of First Amendment freedoms was justified. *Comwlth. Employment Relations Board v. Boston Teachers Union, Local 66, AFT, AFL-CIO*, 908 N.E.2d 772, 74 Mass. App. Ct. 500 (Mass. App. Ct. 2009).

◆ A Minnesota school district violated an agreement not to take action against teachers who participated in a lawful strike when it failed to rehire a probationary Spanish teacher who participated in the strike. The district and union resolved the dispute that led to a two-month teacher strike and agreed to a memorandum of understanding (MOU). The MOU bound the district not to take reprisal, punishment or other action against teachers due to lawful participation in the strike. The district later refused to renew the contracts of four of the five probationary teachers it employed, including the Spanish teacher. An arbitrator sustained a grievance in her favor, and the case reached the Court of Appeals of Minnesota. It found the district had agreed to include probationary teachers under the MOU. **State law placed a school district's right to select staff beyond the scope of collective bargaining, but the district had waived this right.** Having entered into an agreement that clearly stated it would not retaliate against strikers, the district could not rely on rights it had waived. *Independent School Dist. #182, Crosby-Ironton v. Educ. Minnesota Crosby Ironton, AFL-CIO, Local 1325*, No. A07-0745, 2008 WL 933495 (Minn. Ct. App. 4/8/08, Minn. review denied 6/18/08).

◆ Wisconsin education law prohibited strikes by teachers, and gave school boards sole authority over hiring and firing decisions. Boards were required to negotiate the terms and conditions of employment with collective bargaining representatives. When contract negotiations between teachers and a local school board became protracted, the teachers called a strike. The board attempted to end the strike, noting that it was in direct violation of state law.

When the teachers refused to return to work, the board held disciplinary hearings and fired the striking teachers. The teachers appealed to the Wisconsin courts, arguing that the board was not an impartial decisionmaker and that the discharges had violated their due process rights. The state supreme court held due process required an impartial decisionmaker. The board was not sufficiently impartial to make the decision to discharge the teachers. The board appealed to the U.S. Supreme Court, which found no evidence that the board could not make an impartial decision in determining to discharge the teachers. The fact that the board was involved in negotiations with the teachers did not support a claim of bias. **The board was the only body vested with statutory authority to employ and dismiss teachers, and participation in negotiations with the teachers was required by law.** This involvement prior to the decision to discharge the teachers was not a sufficient showing of bias to disqualify the board as a decisionmaker. *Hortonville Joint School Dist. No. 1 v. Hortonville Educ. Ass'n*, 426 U.S. 482, 96, S.Ct. 2308, 49 L.Ed.2d 1 (1976).

◆ The collective bargaining agreement between an Ohio school board and the union representing its bus drivers expired without a new agreement. The board contracted with a private company for transportation services and abolished its driver and mechanic job classifications. Union members declared a strike, but within days most of them notified the superintendent of their intention to return to work under their continuing contract rights. The company agreed to hire district drivers. Eight of the district's drivers retired, but four reported to work at the district's bus garage. The board assigned them to new positions for which their wages and daily work hours were reduced. The four drivers sought an order compelling the board to recognize their continuing contract rights. The case reached the state supreme court, which held that the drivers were entitled to the relief they requested. **State law did not authorize the board to lay them off by abolishing their positions and hiring nonpublic employees.** The contracting out of the drivers' jobs was invalid. The drivers were entitled to recognition as continuing contract employees of the board and could not be reclassified as general public employees. The court ordered the board to reinstate the drivers with back pay. *State ex rel. Boggs v. Springfield Local School Dist. Board of Educ.*, 757 N.E.2d 339 (Ohio 2001).

CHAPTER TWELVE

School Liability and Safety

I. NEGLIGENCE

Negligence is the failure to use reasonable or ordinary care under the circumstances. In order for a school district to be held liable for negligence, it must have a duty to the person claiming negligence. If a reasonably prudent person cannot foresee any danger of direct injury, there is no duty, and thus no negligence. A school district may be held liable for the acts or omissions of a negligent employee. A pattern of negligence showing a conscious disregard for safety may be "willful or wanton misconduct," a form of intentional conduct.

A. Elements

The elements of a negligence lawsuit are: 1) the existence of a **legal duty** *to conform conduct to a specific standard in order to protect others from unreasonable risks of injury, 2) a* **breach** *of that duty that is, 3) the direct* **cause of the injury**, *and 4)* **damages**. *In short, negligence consists of a duty of care, followed by a breach of that duty which causes injury and damages.*

Foreseeability of harm is also a prerequisite to liability in negligence cases. In A.W. v. Lancaster County School District 0001, 784 N.W.2d 907 (Neb. 2010), this chapter, the Supreme Court of Nebraska held that foreseeability questions are generally for juries to determine. It found questions of foreseeability are not "legal" questions, but involve common sense, common experience, and the application of community standards and behavioral norms. So juries, rather than judges, are typically entitled to consider questions of foreseeability.

◆   An Indiana parent claimed her son choked to death while eating lunch at his elementary school. In her state court negligence action, a jury returned a verdict of $5 million in her favor. Later, the court reduced it to $500,000 – the maximum allowed by the state Tort Claims Act. Appeal reached the Supreme Court of Indiana, where school officials argued the jury instruction "merely set forth a shortened version of the [parent's] contentions." It appeared to the court that the jury was asked to find the district negligent in one of five ways. This included failing to implement or monitor a system for providing health services and emergency care, failing to properly train staff, failing to assemble a first aid team, and failing to prepare for a medical emergency response. In the court's view, jury instructions must advise jurors of the elements of a negligence claim and make a "roadmap" for the decision. In this case, the language of the disputed instruction permitted jurors to make improper inferences that facts alleged by the parent were automatically deemed "negligence" if proven. This would create duties that were not recognized by state law. **Indiana public elementary schools had a duty only to exercise reasonable and ordinary care.** The case had to be returned to the trial court for a new trial on liability. *LaPorte Community School Corp. v. Rosales*, 963 N.E.2d 520 (Ind. 2012).

◆ During a P.E. class, a Nebraska student fell into a manhole on school grounds. Her parents contacted the principal, who had served at the school for 21 years but did not know the manhole was there. A school district supervisor knew of the manhole but did not know of any prior problems in his nine years of district service. The parents claimed the city and school district knew or should have known that the manhole cover presented a dangerous situation. They sued both entities in a state court for negligence. After the court held for the city and the district, the parents appealed. The state court of appeals held that **to impose liability on a property owner, it must be shown that the owner created, knew of or could have discovered a condition involving an unreasonable risk of harm to a lawful visitor**. To impose liability, it had to be shown that a property owner should have expected that a visitor would not have realized the danger or failed to protect him or herself from it, and that the owner did not use reasonable care to protect the visitor from danger. In trial court proceedings, it was shown that neither the city nor the district received any complaints about the manhole before the accident. The court held neither the city nor the district knew of a dangerous condition, created such a condition, or could have discovered such a danger with the use of reasonable care. *Bonifas v. City of Lexington*, No. A-10-623, 2011 WL 1522530 (Neb. Ct. App. 4/19/11).

◆ A Montana student submitted a list of resolutions with violent themes for a school assignment. Among the themes were to "get a drivers license so I can do those horrible things people like to read about in the paper," and "kill the tooth fairy." A teacher reported the list, and his parents were contacted. In a meeting, the principal stated that although the list was inappropriate, the student was "a normal kid." Meeting attendees felt the list was "a teenage attempt at black humor" that he knew was inappropriate, so no action was taken. While driving near the high school some 17 months later, the student intentionally ran over a jogger. Before doing so, he told a passenger he planned to run her over and commit necrophilia with her corpse. The jogger sued the district for negligence.

A Montana court found no "special relationship" between the district and the jogger so as to give rise to liability. The Supreme Court of Montana rejected the jogger's argument that she did not need a special relationship with the school district for it to have a duty of ordinary care to protect her from the student. She was not a "foreseeable plaintiff." **Foreseeability is of primary**

importance in establishing the existence of a legal duty of care. If a reasonably prudent person cannot foresee any danger of direct injury, there is no duty, and thus no negligence. It was not foreseeable that 17 months after writing the list, the student would deliberately run over a jogger, after school hours and off school grounds. The court affirmed the ruling for the district. *Emanuel v. Great Falls School Dist.*, 351 Mont. 56, 209 P.3d 244 (Mont. 2009).

B. Defenses

◆   An 11-year-old New York student fell from a banister at school while unsupervised and suffered serious injuries. When his parents sued the district for negligence, it asserted that he had assumed the risk of harm by engaging in horseplay when he slid down the banister. The case reached the Court of Appeals of New York, which found that **assumption of risk is typically raised in cases involving athletic and recreational activities.** Allowing the defense here would have unfortunate consequences and could not be used to nullify the district's duty. If assumption of risk was allowed, students would be deemed to consent in advance to the risks of their own misconduct. Children often act impulsively and without good judgment. This does not mean they consent to assume the resulting danger. If the student's injury was attributable to his own conduct, this could be handled by allocating comparative fault. The court returned the case to a lower court for more proceedings. *Trupia v. Lake George Cent. School Dist.*, 927 N.E.2d 547 (N.Y. 2010).

1. Immunity

Immunity protects school districts and their employees from liability in many cases. Sovereign or "governmental" immunity precludes district liability in cases where school employees are performing "discretionary duties" within the scope of their employment. State laws define the scope of school and official immunity in specific cases. "Discretionary" or "official" immunity protects school employees and officials from liability when they perform "discretionary" (as opposed to "ministerial") duties. A "ministerial act" leaves nothing to discretion and is a simple or definite duty. Public officials whose duties require them to exercise judgment or discretion are not personally liable for damages unless they act intentionally. Discretionary or official immunity ensures that public officials who are charged by law with duties calling for the exercise of judgment or discretion are not held personally liable for damages, if they act in the scope of their employment and not intentionally, wilfully or with malice.

◆   A tax-exempt organization leased space from a Delaware school district to hold a celebration. A high school assistant principal processed a facility request form without requiring any proof of insurance, since the organization had leased space for the event in previous years. At the event, a patron said her feet slipped out from under her when she stepped out of her car at the high school entrance. In a state court action against the school district and event sponsor, she asserted negligent failure to warn her of an underlying maintenance problem. While the patron claimed the sponsor's failure to purchase liability insurance amounted to a waiver of immunity, the court disagreed. She settled her claim against the sponsor and appealed a judgment for the district to the state supreme court.

On appeal, the patron claimed the failure of the district to require the sponsor to own a liability insurance policy resulted in a waiver of immunity. But the court found no statutory support for that position. **Immunity applied to any tort claim for "any damages by reason of negligence in the construction or maintenance of [public school] property."** State law intended to encourage participation in community activities. If school districts were to encourage use of their facilities for community activities, they required some assurance that such use would not embroil them in lawsuits. As the theories advanced by the patron did not block state law immunity, the court held for the school district. *Bantum v. New Castle County Vo-Tech Educ. Ass'n*, 21 A.3d 44 (Del. 2011).

◆   On a February day, an Indiana teacher took her students to a middle school for enrichment classes. She slipped and fell on a walkway. While there had been no precipitation for at least two days, a witness later described the area as "slick and wet looking." The teacher sued the district for negligence, and a jury awarded her $90,000. The Supreme Court of Indiana upheld the verdict. It held **the state tort claims act confers immunity on government units for injuries caused by temporary conditions on "a public thoroughfare" resulting from weather**. However, there is a common law duty to maintain roads and sidewalks in a reasonably safe condition. In this case, the school district claimed that the accident was due to normal thawing and freezing of a thin layer of ice. But because there had been no precipitation for a few days before the accident, the court found there was no "temporary conditions" immunity. *Gary Community School Corp. v. Roach-Walker*, 917 N.E.2d 1224 (Ind. 2009).

◆   A Kansas parent entered a school gymnasium to pick up his stepson. He then left the gym through double doors leading to a commons area. One of the doors came off a closing mechanism and fell on the parent's head. He sued the school district in the state court system for negligence. A trial court agreed with the district that the Kansas Tort Claims Act (KTCA) provided immunity. It applied the KTCA's "recreational use exception" to liability. After the state court of appeals affirmed the decision, the Supreme Court of Kansas agreed to hear the case. It held the legislative purpose of the KTCA was to immunize government entities to encourage them to build recreational facilities without fear of lawsuits. The court found that while the commons was not exclusively used for recreational purposes, it was an integral part of the gymnasium's use.

The commons was used to sell tickets and concessions during events and was not "incidentally connected to the gymnasium." And the court found the commons was necessarily connected to the gymnasium as a principal means of access and for purchasing tickets and concessions. **A school would be discouraged from opening a gymnasium for recreational use if liability was permitted in an area that was an integral part of its recreational usage.** Accordingly, the school district was immune from liability under the recreational use exception to the KTCA. *Poston v. Unified School Dist. No. 387, Altoona-Midway, Wilson County*, 189 P.3d 517 (Kan. 2008).

◆   An Illinois eighth-grader participated in an extracurricular tumbling class during lunch periods in his school gymnasium. The teacher who supervised the class had a physical education degree, but little mini-trampoline experience. After taking a forward flip off the mini-trampoline, the student seriously injured his neck and became quadriplegic. He and his mother sued the school board and teacher. They claimed that the teacher failed to provide any spotters and did not watch students while they used the mini-trampoline. The complaint also named the Chicago Youth Centers (CYC), which ran the tumbling class. The family asserted that use of a mini-trampoline was a hazardous recreational activity, and that the CYC and the teacher could not claim state law immunity because they acted willfully and wantonly. The trial court granted immunity to the teacher, the CYC and the board. Appeal reached the Supreme Court of Illinois. It held the Illinois Local Governmental and Governmental Employees Tort Immunity Act contained exceptions to immunity for hazardous recreational activities.

Trampolining was listed in the act as a hazardous recreational activity. The risk of spinal cord injuries from the improper use of a mini-trampoline was well known. Evidence indicated the CYC tumbling/trampoline program was not supervised by an experienced instructor and was not taught properly, as trained spotters and safety equipment were often not provided. Genuine issues of fact existed regarding whether the board, CYC and teacher were guilty of willful and wanton conduct, and the case required a trial. *Murray v. Chicago Youth Center*, 224 Ill.2d 213, 864 N.E.2d 176 (Ill. 2007).

2.   Comparative and Contributory Negligence

Under comparative negligence principles, courts may apportion negligence among parties by their degree of fault. For example, a jury may find a student who slipped on a bar of soap in a school locker room 40% negligent, and the district whose employee left out the bar of soap 60% negligent. If the damages were $10,000, the student would recover $6,000 from the district.

"Contributory negligence" is a defense barring any recovery by a plaintiff in a negligence case when the plaintiff is at fault in any part for the injury. In 1985, Indiana adopted a "modified comparative fault system." But in 2007, the state supreme court held contributory negligence principles still applied in school cases.

◆   A North Dakota teacher held a "60s Day" each year for her history class. She showed a student a video taken two years earlier in which a student rode a bicycle off the school auditorium stage and onto the floor at the event. After school, the student and a friend went to the auditorium to practice the stunt. Although the teacher tried to discourage them, they snuck in and tried it. The student was injured when he crashed and struck his head on the floor. In a state court, the student's father sued the school district and teacher for negligence.

The court held for the district, but the Supreme Court of North Dakota held the state's recreational use immunity statutes did not bar the case and returned it to the lower court. The teacher settled the claim against her prior to trial. A jury found other district employees were 30% at fault and the student 70% at fault. Although the jury found the student's father should get $285,000 for his medical expenses, he received no damages because the student's fault was greater than the district's. The case returned to the supreme court, where the parent claimed he was entitled to $85,500 in medical expenses. This represented the share of fault apportioned to district employees. The court found **the majority of courts have held a child's negligence is a factor in determining the extent of a parent's recovery against a third party for medical expenses**. North Dakota has a modified comparative fault statute under which recovery is barred if the claimant's fault was as great as the combined fault of all others contributing to injury. The negligence of an injured child was attributed to parents. As the right to recover medical expenses could be barred by the student's own negligence, the court affirmed the judgment for the school district. *M.M. v. Fargo Public School Dist. No. 1*, 815 N.W.2d 273 (N.D. 2012).

◆ A 13-year-old Indiana student blacked out during a basketball practice. Later, his mother told the coach he could walk through plays but could not run or perform strenuous activities. The student attended school for the next two days without incident. Although a doctor did not clear him to practice, he did so without restrictions at a practice two days after the blackout. During a running drill, the student collapsed and died. His parents sued the school district in the state court system. There, the district argued the student's own negligence was a contributing factor in his death. A jury returned a verdict for the parents, and the district appealed. The case reached the Supreme Court of Indiana, which held **a child between ages seven and 14 is required to exercise due care for his or her own safety**. Indiana law recognized a presumption that children between ages seven and 14 are incapable of contributory negligence. In this case, the district failed to overcome that legal presumption. *Clay City Consolidated School Corp. v. Timberman*, 918 N.E.2d 292 (Ind. 2009).

◆ A deaf Florida student left her school bus near her home on a two-lane residential street with a 25 mile-per-hour speed limit. The bus driver activated the bus' flashing lights and waited for her to cross the street. The driver heard a pickup truck speeding down the street and tried to signal the student. However, the pickup struck the student and knocked her to the ground. The pickup truck driver pleaded no contest to criminal conduct and was sentenced to five years in prison for reckless driving. The student's family sued the school board for negligence. In pre-trial activity, the bus driver said, "in my heart, yes, I feel like I hurt her a lot." A jury found the board 20% at fault for the student's injuries, the pickup driver 70% at fault, and the student 10% at fault. The family appealed to a Florida District Court of Appeal, arguing that the pickup driver acted intentionally (removing him from the negligence calculations), and that the school board should have been liable for a greater share of liability. The court of appeal affirmed, noting that **although the pickup driver had been fleeing police, he never intended to injure the student**. The percentage of fault had been properly calculated. *Petit-Dos v. School Board of Broward County*, 2 So.3d 1022 (Fla. Dist. Ct. App. 2009).

◆ A Washington student and her family sued a teacher, school district and principal for sexual abuse by the teacher. The claims included negligent supervision and hiring. The principal and district sought to have any potential damage award reduced in part based on the student's alleged consent to have sexual relations with the teacher. The case reached the Supreme Court of Washington. It noted that the state Tort Reform Act required comparing the fault of the parties in negligence cases. However, contributory fault did not apply in this case. **Washington schools have a "special relationship with students" and a duty to protect them from reasonably anticipated dangers.** Because of the vulnerability of students, they had no duty to protect themselves from sexual abuse by teachers. This result was consistent with cases from Indiana, South Carolina, Colorado, Oregon, and Pennsylvania. The school district could not rely on the defense of contributory negligence. *Christensen v. Royal School Dist. #160*, 156 Wash.2d 62, 124 P.3d 283 (Wash. 2005).

◆   An Indiana high school student helped an elementary school music teacher produce the play "Peter Pan." He had rock climbing experience, and he designed and built a pulley mechanism to allow the Peter Pan character to "fly." The teacher held a ladder for the student as he connected himself to the mechanism during a dress rehearsal for the play. When the student jumped from the ladder, the mechanism failed and he fell to the gym floor, suffering serious injuries. He and his mother sued the school district for negligence. A jury awarded him $200,000, but the state court of appeals held the jury instructions were improper. The student appealed. The Supreme Court of Indiana reinstated the jury's award. Although the jury instruction had been inaccurate, it did not prejudice the school. **Under contributory negligence principles, the school could not defend its negligence by asserting the student was negligent.** *Penn Harris Madison School Corp. v. Howard*, 861 N.E.2d 1190 (Ind. 2007).

II.   SCHOOL ATHLETICS

Student-athletes assume the inherent risks of sports participation. Absent a showing of gross negligence or intentional conduct by a coach, league or school, they may not recover damages. The cases in this section involve district or school board liability. For more cases attempting to hold coaches personally liable for student injuries, please see Chapter Thirteen, Section III.C.

A. Participants

1. Duty of Care

◆   The family of a Louisiana high school sophomore claimed two freshmen urinated on his locker. As the board maintained separate campuses for freshmen and upperclassmen, the family claimed the school board breached a legal duty by allowing the freshmen to be in the locker room. In a state court, the family sued the board for mental anguish, emotional distress and loss of consortium. After the case was dismissed, the family appealed to the Court of Appeal of Louisiana. In reviewing state supreme court precedents, the court held a school board owes its students a duty of reasonable supervision. Supervision must be reasonable, competent and appropriate to the student's age and circumstances.

Like many other courts, **the court held there was no duty to constantly supervise all students. A school board's duty did not make it the insurer of student safety.** To impose liability on a Louisiana school board for failure to adequately supervise student safety, there must be proof of negligent supervision and proof of a causal connection between the lack of supervision and the harm. In addition, the risk of an unreasonable injury must be foreseeable to the board and preventable through reasonable supervision. In this case, the incident was not foreseeable to the board. No prior locker room misconduct had occurred. No other student incidents gave the school board notice that closer locker room supervision was needed. Since board employees stated that this was the first time an inappropriate incident had occurred in the locker room, the court held for the board. *Creekbaum v. Livingston Parish School Board*, 80 So.2d 771 (La. Ct. App. 2011).

◆ An Iowa high school basketball player elbowed an opposing player on the court. The opponent suffered from postconcussion syndrome, and his family sued the player in a state court for assault and battery, adding a claim against the player's district for negligent supervision. The court awarded damages against the player but refused to award the opponent's family any punitive damages. It also dismissed the claims against the district. The Supreme Court of Iowa found no error in the compensatory damage award against the player. **Under Iowa law, school districts have a duty of reasonable care. But there was no foreseeable risk in this case.** The assaulting player had only committed one previous technical foul, and it was for using profanity. While he was regarded as an intense player, his school district was not held liable because it could not have foreseen he would commit a battery during a game. *Brokaw v. Winfield-Mt. Union Community School Dist.*, 788 N.W.2d 386 (Iowa 2010).

◆ A California community college baseball player was hit in the head by a pitch, possibly in retaliation for a pitch thrown by his teammate the previous inning. After being hit, the student staggered, felt dizzy, and was in pain. His manager told him to go to first base. The student did so, but complained to his first-base coach, who told him to stay in the game. Soon after that, the student was told to sit on the bench. He claimed no one tended to his injuries. The student sued the host college for breaching its duty of care by failing to supervise or control its pitcher and failing to provide umpires or medical care. The court dismissed the case, and appeal reached the Supreme Court of California. It noted that in sports, the doctrine of assumption of risk precludes liability for injuries deemed "inherent in a sport." **Athletic participants have a duty not to act recklessly or outside the bounds of the sport.** Coaches and instructors have a duty not to increase the risks inherent in sports participation. Being hit by a pitch is an inherent risk of baseball. Colleges are not liable for the actions of their student-athletes during competition. The failure to provide umpires did not increase risks inherent in the game. As the student's own coaches, not the host college, were responsible for removing him from the game, the court held for the community college. *Avila v. Citrus Community College Dist.*, 38 Cal.4th 148, 41 Cal.Rptr. 299, 131 P.3d 383 (Cal. 2006).

2. Governmental Immunity

Wisconsin's Supreme Court held a cheerleading spotter and his school district were entitled to immunity in an action by a cheerleader who was injured while practicing a stunt. Wisconsin Statues Section 895.525 had a legislative purpose to decrease uncertainty in recreational liability issues and helped to assure the continued availability of school recreational activities.

◆   A Wisconsin varsity basketball cheerleading squad practiced a stunt in their high school commons area without mats. A spotter failed to stop a cheerleader from falling backward and striking her head. The cheerleader sued the spotter and school district for negligence. Evidence indicated that the cheerleaders were practicing a stunt they had not previously performed together, and that the spotter was not positioned to prevent the injury. The cheerleading coach was working with others about 10 feet away at the time of the fall. The court held that the spotter and the school district were entitled to immunity, but the state court of appeals reversed the judgment against the spotter. On appeal to the state supreme court, the cheerleader argued that state law gave immunity only to athletes in "contact sports," and that cheerleading was neither a team nor a contact sport. However, the court held that cheerleading was a "contact sport."

The court found no evidence that the spotter was "reckless," which would defeat his claim to statutory immunity. He was simply standing in the wrong place. His conduct was characterized as "discretionary," not ministerial. In this case, the cheerleading squad operated under "spirit rules" that did not eliminate the coach's discretion. Spirit rules did not mandate a spotter for this exercise, and the coach had discretion to use mats. **The district was entitled to immunity.** *Noffke v. Bakke,* 315 Wis.2d 350, 760 N.W.3d 156 (Wis. 2009).

◆   An Illinois school district operated a summer football camp. A student was hurt when he tripped over a grass-concealed shot-put bumper on the route he was told to take. His parent sued the district in a state court for over $50,000 in damages for negligence and willful and wanton conduct. Applying a recreational immunity provision of Illinois law, the court dismissed the action against the district. Before the Appellate Court of Illinois, the parent argued that the football facility was educational and not recreational in nature. This would preclude a recreational immunity defense. **The appellate court noted that immunity depended upon the character of the property, not the activity performed.** The property was on school grounds and was being used for a summer camp – by inference an educational purpose. As the lower court did not fully explore the property's character, dismissal was improper. *Peters v. Herrin Community School Dist. No. 4,* 928 N.E.2d 1258 (Ill. App. Ct. 2010).

◆   A 17-year-old Mississippi student collapsed during football practice on a hot August day. Emergency responders were unable to revive him, and he later died at a hospital. His survivors sued the school district for negligence, and the case reached the Supreme Court of Mississippi. It noted the Mississippi Tort Claims Act (MTCA) is the exclusive remedy in a negligence action against a governmental entity or employee. The MTCA provides immunity to state and political subdivisions whose employees act in the course and scope of their employment while performing discretionary acts. **Acts are discretionary if they require officials to use their own judgment and discretion. Coaching is a discretionary act.** Nothing indicated that the district or its coaches violated any statute, ordinance or regulation, and the school district was entitled to immunity. *Covington County School Dist. v. Magee*, 29 So.3d 1 (Miss. 2010).

◆ An Ohio student injured his forehead and wrist during a pole vault at a high school track meet. He landed on improper padding near the landing pad that was later identified as in violation of National Federation of State High School Associations rules. The student's negligence case against the school district, coach and other officials reached the Court of Appeals of Ohio. It held the state recreational user statute did not apply, since the student was not a "recreational user." A trial court had committed error by finding he assumed the risk of injury in the inherent dangers of pole vaulting. The court held **the sponsor of a sporting event has a duty not to increase the risk of harm over and above any inherent risks of the sport**. It rejected the district's claim to immunity, as there was no discretionary, policy-making, planning or enforcement activity. But the coach was entitled to immunity under state law, as he did not act recklessly, with malice, or in bad faith. *Henney v. Shelby City School Dist.*, No. 2005 CA 0064, 2006 WL 747475 (Ohio Ct. App. 2006).

◆ A Maine high school wrestling team ran timed drills in school hallways in its warm-up routine. A wrestler was seriously injured after being bumped into a window by a teammate during a drill. The school had no policy prohibiting athletic training in school hallways at the time. The student sued the school district in the state court system for personal injury. A court held that the district and officials were protected by discretionary immunity. The Maine Supreme Judicial Court agreed and held **government entities are generally entitled to absolute immunity from suit in any tort action for damages**. An exception to this rule imposes liability on government entities for the negligent operation of a public building. Here, allowing relay races in the school hallway was not the "operation of a public building." To impose liability under the public building exception to immunity, the claim must implicate a building's physical structure. The district and officials were protected by discretionary immunity. *Lightfoot v. School Administrative Dist. No. 35*, 816 A.2d 63 (Me. 2003).

3. Assumption of Risk and Waiver

The New York Supreme Court, Appellate Division, recently restated the general rule that "by engaging in a sport or recreational activity, a participant consents to those commonly appreciated risks which are inherent in and arise out of the nature of the sport generally and flow from such participation."

◆ A New York student said he contracted herpes in a school wrestling match. He sued his school district, high school, wrestling opponent and the opponent's school in a state court for negligence. The case reached the New York Supreme Court, Appellate Division, which explained that **athletes consent to commonly**

appreciated risks inherent in the sport. Athletes indicate their consent to injury-causing events by participating in them when risks are known, apparent or reasonably foreseeable, and are not assumed, concealed or unreasonably increased risks. Wrestling involved close contact between athletes, and diseases transmitted through skin-to-skin contact could result. The wrestling coach had identified communicable diseases as an "inherent danger of the sport." Even the student's expert admitted that herpes may exist in 29.8% of high school wrestlers. And the lower court had found that the possibility of contracting communicable diseases such as herpes is well known to coaches and officials.

Contrary to the student's argument, school officials informed him of the specific risk of contracting herpes, as well as the general risk of contracting skin diseases through wrestling. He was instructed to shower after each practice, and to use strong soap and shampoo to limit the possibility of contracting skin diseases including staph, ringworm, impetigo and herpes simplex virus. The court rejected all the student's arguments and reversed the judgment. *Farrell v. Hochhauser,* 65 A.D.3d 663, 884 N.Y.S.2d 261 (N.Y. App. Div. 2009).

◆   An Indiana student-athlete who weighed over 250 pounds had "dry heaves" in a morning school football practice session. He stopped his activity for a minute, then told coaches he felt better. The student ate lunch during a team rest period. He spent time lying on the locker room floor. Near the end of the afternoon session, the student told a coach he did not feel well. The coach told him to get water, but he soon collapsed. The coaches took him to the locker room and placed him in a cool shower. He lost consciousness, and the coaches called for an ambulance. He died at a hospital the following day. His parents sued the school district in the state court system for negligence. After a trial, a jury returned a verdict for the school district. The parents appealed to the Court of Appeals of Indiana, which held that since school release forms excluded the word "negligence," the district was not released from negligence claims. **To negate a legal duty of care and avoid any finding of negligence, a participant must have "actual knowledge and appreciation of the specific risk involved and voluntarily acceptance of that risk."** The trial court should have granted the parents' request for a jury instruction stating that they had not released the district from negligence. The court reversed the judgment and returned the case to a lower court for a new trial. *Stowers v. Clinton Cent. School Corp.,* 855 N.E.2d 739 (Ind. Ct. App. 2006).

◆   A Massachusetts school district required a signed parental release for all students seeking to participate in extracurricular activities. For four years, the father of a high school cheerleader signed a release form before each season. During her fourth year, she was injured during a practice. When the cheerleader reached age 18, she sued the city in a state court for negligence. She added claims for negligent hiring and retention of the cheerleading coach. The court held for the city on the basis of the parental release, finding the father had released the city from any and all actions and claims. The cheerleader appealed to the Massachusetts Supreme Judicial Court, asserting the release was invalid. The court held that **enforcement of a parental release was consistent with Massachusetts law and public policy**. There was undisputed evidence that the father read and understood the release before signing it, and that the form was not misleading. It was not contrary to public policy to require parents to sign releases as a condition for student participation in extracurricular activities. To hold the release unenforceable would expose public schools to financial costs and risks that would lead to the reduction of extracurricular activities. *Sharon v. City of Newton*, 437 Mass. 99, 769 N.E.2d 738 (Mass. 2002).

B. Spectators, Employees and Parents

A Louisiana court has held that to impose liability on a public entity, the entity must know of "a particular vice or defect" that causes damage, yet fail to fix the defect after having a reasonable opportunity to do so. In Alabama litigation, numerous claims against county school boards have been barred by Article I, Section 14, an "absolute immunity" provision of the state constitution.

◆   A Texas parent with disabilities could not access bleacher seating at her son's junior varsity football game. She moved her wheelchair to an accessible area adjacent to the bleachers and watched the game through a chain-link fence. The parent claimed she had an obstructed view and had to hold on to the fence to keep from rolling backward. She did not ask for other seating, and her husband watched from the bleachers. The parent sued the school district in a federal court, claiming violation of the Americans with Disabilities Act (ADA).

In pretrial activity, the court granted the parent partial judgment. Appeal reached the U.S. Court of Appeals, Fifth Circuit, which found the stadium was built in 1968 and was an "existing structure" under the ADA. It disagreed with the claim that any separation of disabled persons from general public seating areas was discriminatory. Accessible seating was offered in the stadium. Much of the parent's argument focused on actual compliance with ADA rules, and she confused the standard for assessing newly constructed facilities with the one for existing facilities such as the stadium. **The school district only had to show its program as a whole was accessible to individuals with disabilities.** By her own admission, the parent was able to access the parking lot, move around the stadium, buy a ticket and concessions and see part of the game. As a result, the court held for the school district. *Greer v. Richardson Independent School Dist.*, 472 Fed.Appx. 287 (5th Cir. 2012).

◆   A North Carolina school board avoided liability for injuries to a six-year-old child who fell through a gap in the bleachers of a high school stadium. At the time of the incident, the bleachers were damp from condensation. The child slipped and fell through an 18-inch to 24-inch gap between the seats and the floorboard. He fell about 10 feet, struck his head on concrete, and suffered a fractured skull requiring surgery and the insertion of permanent metal plates and screws. In a state court action against the board, the child's family claimed the board breached a duty to ensure that the bleachers were reasonably safe for all users. After a trial court held for the school board, appeal reached the Court of Appeals of North Carolina. It held that to avoid liability for negligence, a property owner must exercise the degree of care that a reasonable and prudent person would exercise under similar conditions. **Liability for negligence may** be imposed when the owner of the premises could have foreseen that injury was probable under the circumstances. In this case, the court found evidence that the board of education had complied with the state building code and that the athletic director was unaware of any problems with the bleachers. This evidence, combined with the lack of notice of any prior problems with the bleachers, was sufficient to defeat the family's claims. The fact that the child slipped and was severely injured did not, by itself, prove negligence. As the trial court had correctly found for the board, the judgment was affirmed. *Davis v. Cumberland County Board of Educ.*, 720 S.E.2d 418 (N.C. Ct. App. 2011).

◆   The Supreme Court of Delaware denied a request for relief from a pretrial order that required a private cheerleading organization to defend and indemnify a school district for injuries to a spectator who was attending a cheerleading event at a district high school. The organization had leased the school gymnasium from the school district for a cheerleading competition. After the spectator fell from the bleachers, the organization claimed gross negligence by school staff who failed to install guard rails. In pretrial proceedings, a state trial court dismissed negligence claims against the school board and officials, but allowed the claims for gross or wanton negligence to proceed. As the court found no reason to allow an appeal at this stage of the case, **the organization had to provide legal defense to the school board and indemnify it for any loss.** *Diamond State Wildcats v. Boyle*, 986 A.2d 1164 (Table) (Del. 2010).

◆   A patron at an Alabama high school basketball game fell from the bleachers where he had been sitting, and was injured. He sued the school board for negligence and contract claims. A trial court held for the school board on the negligence claims, but allowed a breach-of-implied contract claim to survive. On appeal to the Supreme Court of Alabama, the patron argued that county education boards can be sued for an implied breach of contract for failing to provide safe premises for athletic contests. In contrast, the board argued that it was an agency of the state entitled to the same immunity as any state agency enjoyed. The court found that immunity was conferred by the Constitution, and it affirmed the judgment for the board. **Absolute immunity extended to all arms or agencies of the state, including county education boards.** *Ex parte Hale County Board of Educ.*, 14 So.3d 844 (Ala. 2009).

◆   An Alabama five-year-old fell from bleachers at a quarterfinal football playoff game held at a high school by the Alabama High School Athletic Association (AHSAA). The child fell through an opening in the seats and broke both her wrists. Her parents sued the school board for breach of an implied contract and breach of implied warranty of safe premises. The case reached the Supreme Court of Alabama, which stated that **Alabama county education boards are considered state agencies and are immune from tort actions.** The court agreed with the school board that the AHSAA sponsored and controlled the game, defeating any contract claim. The parents' claim was barred by an absolute immunity provision of the state constitution. *Ex Parte Jackson County Board of Educ.*, 4 So.3d 1099 (Ala. 2008).

III. OTHER SCHOOL ACTIVITIES

Courts have held schools liable for injuries during school events which resulted from the failure to provide a reasonably safe environment, failure to warn participants of known hazards (or to remove known dangers), failure to properly instruct participants in the activity, and failure to provide supervision adequate for the type of activity and the ages of the participants involved. Schools and their staff members are not liable for unforeseeable harms, as schools are not the insurers of student safety. The fact that each student is not personally supervised at all times does not itself constitute grounds for liability.

A. Physical Education Classes

1. Duty of Care

◆ A California school district was not liable for injuries to a student who was hit by a golf club swung by a classmate in their physical education class. According to the student, the teacher did not give a whistle command for the classmate to hit the ball, as was her usual practice. The student sued the school district for negligence. A state court found that the district did not breach its limited duty of care and held for the district. The student appealed to the Court of Appeal of California, which held that the lower court applied the wrong legal standard. **The Supreme Court of California has applied the "prudent person" standard of care to cases involving students injured during school hours.** This simply requires persons to avoid injuring others by using due care. As the lower court should have applied the prudent person standard, the court reversed the judgment and remanded the case. *Hemady v. Long Beach Unified School Dist.*, 143 Cal.App.4th 566, 49 Cal. Rptr.3d 464 (Cal. Ct. App. 2006). The Supreme Court of California denied review of this case in 2007.

◆ During a gym class, an Ohio eighth-grader with a history of mild asthma obtained his teacher's permission to retrieve his prescription inhaler from his locker. Minutes later, another teacher found the student on the locker room floor unconscious and not breathing. Despite the administration of medical treatment, he died. The student's estate sued the school board for wrongful death. A jury found for the board, and the Court of Appeals of Ohio affirmed. The trial court had heard a physician testify that the death of a student previously recognized as having "mild asthma" was "one in a million." **According to the physician, not even medical professionals could have foreseen the death.** The court rejected the estate's arguments and held for the board. *Spencer v. Lakeview School Dist.*, No. 2005-T-0083, 2006 WL 1816452 (Ohio Ct. App. 6/30/06).

◆ A New York student was playing football in a physical education class when a classmate threw a football tee that hit her in the eye. Her parents brought a negligence action against the school district in a state court. A state appellate division court held the district had a duty to adequately supervise and instruct students, and was liable for foreseeable injuries caused by their negligence. But **school districts are not insurers of student safety and will not be held liable**

for every spontaneous, thoughtless or careless act by which one student injures another. In affirming a judgment for the student, the court held that the trial court would have to determine if the injury causing conduct was reasonably foreseeable and preventable. *Oakes v. Massena Cent. School Dist.*, 19 A.D.3d 981, 797 N.Y.S.2d 640 (N.Y. App. Div. 2005).

2. Governmental Immunity

Although state laws grant varying degrees of immunity to school districts in negligence cases, the general rule is that government agencies and employees have immunity from civil liability based on "discretionary actions." An Illinois court held immunity is allowed for "policy decisions," which require the balancing of competing interests so that there must be a "judgment call."

◆   A Mississippi student slipped and fell headfirst down bleacher steps during a physical education (PE) class. He lost his front teeth and sprained a knee. The student sued the school district, claiming his PE instructor negligently told the class to "run the bleachers" in bad weather. The court held the district and its employees had immunity under the Mississippi Torts Claim Act (MTCA). On appeal to the state court of appeals, the student claimed the instructor breached his duty to teach and implement appropriate warm-up techniques. But the court noted the student had admitted he was walking down the bleachers at the time of his fall, making such instructions irrelevant. State governmental entities and employees who act in the course and scope of their employment are not liable for any claim involving a discretionary function. In this case, the district had guidelines for PE classes that only required instructors to use appropriate warm-up and cool-down methods. The guidelines left the particular types of techniques to the discretion of the instructor. **The court rejected the claim that a PE coach was not entitled to the discretionary immunity that athletic coaches enjoy.** Establishing and operating athletic activities was deemed an exercise of policy. Since the instructor acted in a discretionary manner, MTCA immunity provisions applied, and the judgment for the school district was affirmed. *Clein v. Rankin County School Dist.*, 78 So.3d 384 (Miss. Ct. App. 2012).

◆   An Illinois student was injured while adjusting a volleyball net crank in her high school gym. In her state court negligence case, a trial court held the school district's conduct was not "willful and wanton" and thus did not qualify for an exception to immunity. On appeal, the student argued that a warning label on the volleyball net crank put school employees on notice of a risk of injury. She said that allowing her to operate the crank without warning her of its potential dangers demonstrated utter indifference to and conscious disregard for her safety. She said the school knew the volleyball equipment was unsafe and/or defective and was aware of difficulties with the equipment. But the Appellate Court of Illinois held allegations of problems with the equipment did not demonstrate the school's "utter indifference and conscious disregard" for safety. **Under the state tort liability act, governmental entities were liable for a tort injury only if it was caused by "willful and wanton conduct."** The court explained that this meant more than "inadvertence, incompetence or lack of skill." Prior Illinois decisions had found willful and wanton conduct only where an entity knew of a dangerous condition and took no corrective action. In this case, the student did not claim the school knew of prior injuries caused by the crank that might have placed it on notice of a risk to safety. She only claimed the warning label itself was sufficient notice for this purpose. The court held for the school district, as there was no willful, wanton conduct. *Leja v. Community Unit School Dist. 300*, 979 N.E.2d 573 (Ill. App. Ct. 2012).

◆ After a Wisconsin student expressed fear about performing a beginning parallel bar exercise, her physical education teacher moved the bars to their lowest setting. Another student demonstrated the exercise, and the teacher positioned herself to spot the student. However, the teacher's attention was diverted by another student who asked a question. The student caught her leg on the bar and seriously injured her knee. She was the first student injured during the teacher's 32-year career. In the student's negligence action against the teacher and the school district, a state trial court held that the teacher deserved governmental immunity. On appeal, the Court of Appeals of Wisconsin held that **Wisconsin law immunizes government agencies and employees from liability for "discretionary actions."** There was no statute, rule or regulation specifying how the teacher should teach gymnastics. Since any directives she received did not eliminate her discretion, immunity protected her. *Krus v. Community Insurance Corp.*, 324 Wis.2d 306 (Wis. Ct. App. 2010).

B. Shop Class Injuries

1. Duty of Care

Schools are required to provide their students with a safe environment. Known shop class dangers must be minimized, and safety devices are to be in place and working. Failure to supervise, warn students of known dangers, or maintain safety devices can result in school liability.

◆ A Minnesota student amputated a finger in a wood shop class accident. He had experience using the saw, which was equipped with a blade guard. Before students could use the saw, they had to pass a test on a protocol for its use. The protocol stated that the best practice for cutting small strips of wood was to disengage the blade guard and use a push stick to guide the strips through the saw. On the day of the accident, the teacher instructed the student to cut small wood strips using a push stick with the blade guard disengaged. After watching the student cut some strips, he moved to another part of the room. The student then reached over the blade to remove a piece of scrap wood and lost a finger.

The student sued the teacher and school district for negligence. A state court denied the teacher's claim to official immunity, and the district's motion for statutory immunity. The case reached the Supreme Court of Minnesota, which explained that teachers did not forfeit official immunity because their conduct was "ministerial," if that conduct was established by a policy or protocol that was created though the exercise of discretionary judgment. Both the decision to establish a protocol and the protocol itself involved the exercise of professional judgment. **The teacher was entitled to common law official immunity because his liability was based on compliance with the protocol.** The court reversed the judgment against the teacher and held that the school district was entitled to vicarious immunity. *Anderson v. Anoka Hennepin Independent School Dist. 11*, 678 N.W.2d 651 (Minn. 2004).

2. Governmental Immunity

◆   An Ohio student lost fingers on his dominant hand when he tried to operate a jointer machine in his high school shop class. Prior to the accident, the teacher had demonstrated its use and instructed the students on safety issues. Neither the student nor the teacher could later say for sure what had happened. After the accident, the machine was taken out of operation and stored. The student sued the school board in a state court for negligence. An inspection of the machine about a year after the incident revealed that its guard was locked open. The court considered testimony from the teacher that it "would probably take five years" for the guard to remain in the open position. The teacher believed the guard was functioning properly, and he adjusted it weekly. The court denied the board's motion for state political subdivision immunity. On appeal, the Court of Appeals of Ohio held **employees of political subdivisions are immune from liability unless their actions or omissions are manifestly outside the scope of employment or their official duties.** A jury would have to decide whether the teacher's conduct was reckless, and consider inconsistencies in his statements. *Bolling v. North Olmsted City Schools Board of Educ.*, No. 90669, 2008 WL 4599670 (Ohio Ct. App. 10/16/08).

C. Field Trips

California Education Code Section 35330 creates "field trip immunity" for school districts. All persons making a field trip or excursion shall be deemed to have waived all claims against a school district, a charter school, or the state for injury, accident, illness, or death occurring during or by reason of the field trip or excursion. Under state law, adults and the parents or guardians of pupils taking out-of-state field trips must sign waivers of all claims.

◆   A 14-year-old Minnesota student suffered a permanent paraplegic injury when he lost control of his snowboard at a school-sponsored event at a ski area. In a state court negligence action against the school district and principal, his family alleged negligent supervision and negligent implementation of safety measures. The court held the case could not proceed because the student had assumed the risk of harm. On appeal, the state court of appeals held official immunity protected officials charged by law with duties that called for exercising judgment or discretion, except in cases of a willful or malicious wrong. To gain immunity in a tort case for negligence, the conduct had to call for a "discretionary decision" involving professional judgment. By contrast, "ministerial duties" are those that are "absolute, certain and imperative, involving merely execution of a specific duty arising from fixed and designated facts." In this case, the court found no specific and definite protocol that the principal was bound to follow in supervising the event. **Only basic principles guided the supervision of students, and the principal exercised "operational discretion."** The court held he was entitled to immunity, and as he had immunity, the district enjoyed vicarious immunity. *Motl v. Powder Ridge Ski Area*, No. A11-971, 2012 WL 426602 (Minn. Ct. App. 2/13/12).

◆ A federal district court rejected a student's claim that school officials discriminated against her by failing to appoint a teacher to accompany her to a science fair in California because she was then seven months pregnant. Evidence indicated that while the school usually sent a teacher with students who attended the science fair, **no one was willing to assume the responsibility for a pregnant student**. There was evidence that two past qualifiers for the science fair had gone to the event with their parents, and the student was not treated differently from them. *Dawson v. Pine Bluff School Dist.*, No. 5:10CV00213 JLH, 2011 WL 5508885 (E.D. Ark. 11/10/11).

◆ A California student with asthma went on a field trip to a science camp operated by her school district. When she suffered an asthma attack, camp counselors gave her an asthma inhaler and performed CPR until paramedics arrived. She died as she was being airlifted to a hospital. Her parents sued the school district for negligent failure to provide adequate medical staff and misrepresenting the level of medical staffing that would be available at the camp. A state court held for the district, as did the Court of Appeal of California. **It held the district was entitled to immunity because any person on a school field trip was deemed to have waived all claims against a school district,** charter school or the state for injury, accident, illness or death occurring "during or by reason of the field trip or excursion." The court held this broad grant of immunity was designed to encourage the use of field trips. *Sanchez v. San Diego County Office of Educ.*, 182 Cal.App.4th 1580, 106 Cal.Rptr.3d 750 (Cal. Ct. App. 2010).

D. Other Supervised Activities

1. Duty of Care

School districts have a duty to use reasonable care to supervise and protect students against hazards on school property that create an unreasonable risk of harm. Liability may also exist if supervision is absent or negligently performed.

◆ A 16-year-old Iowa student collapsed while listening to guest speeches as she stood at attention following an outdoor band performance. Two and a half years later, she sued the school district in a state court, claiming that the band director negligently failed to supply water and failed to recognize signs of heat stroke, heat exhaustion and/or dehydration. A state court held the action was untimely under the state's two-year statute of limitations. The Supreme Court of Iowa rejected the student's claim that she had up to a year after her eighteenth birthday to initiate a lawsuit. Iowa law provided that every action against a municipality must be filed within six months, or within two years if the person seeking damages filed a notice of a claim of loss. In this case, **the student had not filed a notice with the school district**. The court noted that the legislature had simplified the law by removing the notice requirement and provided that minors will now have one year from reaching majority to file complaints. *Rucker v. Humboldt Community School Dist.*, 737 N.W.2d 292 (Iowa 2007).

◆   A Montana high school freshman rode home from an out-of-town school basketball game on a pep band bus. The driver teased students by pumping the brakes and jarring the bus. The student asked for a restroom break, but the band instructor denied the request. Many students threw food and candy during the trip. As the bus neared the school, the band instructor announced that no one could leave the bus until it was cleaned up. The student told the instructor twice "you let me off this fucking bus." The driver pumped the brakes while stopping the bus, and the student wet himself. Eight days later, he was hospitalized with a life-threatening condition. He recovered, but was diagnosed with Type I diabetes and post-traumatic stress disorder (PTSD). The student and his parents sued the district, band instructor and driver for causing or accelerating his diabetes and PTSD. Appeal reached the Supreme Court of Montana. It held that **to impose liability on a school district for negligence, it must first be shown the district had a duty of care**. In this case, a trial court had erroneously found the district owed no duty to the student. But even his doctor could not establish that diabetes was a likely result of the bus trip or its aftermath. Since the family could not prove the district caused the injuries, the court held in its favor. *Hinkle v. Shepherd School Dist. #37*, 322 Mont. 80, 93 P.3d 1239 (Mont. 2004).

◆   A North Dakota school district operated a middle school in a building owned by the U.S. Bureau of Indian Affairs (BIA) that was mostly attended by American Indian students. The principal was a BIA employee who supervised both BIA and district staff. BIA teachers supervised the lunchroom under a plan created through a collective bargaining agreement. A BIA teacher tried to break up a fight between two students during her lunchroom supervision period and suffered a disabling, traumatic brain injury. The teacher sued the district for personal injury, alleging negligent failure to maintain a safe environment. When the case reached the state supreme court, it found no evidence of district control over the lunchroom, supervision plan or teacher. The teacher was a BIA employee performing her duties under the collective bargaining agreement. **As she did not show her relationship with the district imposed a legal duty to provide her with a safe working environment, the district was entitled to judgment.** *Azure v. Belcourt Public School Dist.*, 681 N.W.2d 816 (N.D. 2004).

2.   Governmental Immunity

As discussed in other areas in this chapter, state laws typically grant immunity to school districts and their employees based on the exercise of discretion. Alabama school officials were held immune from negligence claims based on allowing a third-grade student with attention deficit hyperactivity disorder to go to a school lavatory without supervision by her teacher.

◆ An Alabama parent advised her child's school about her attention deficit hyperactivity disorder, but the child was not assigned to a special education program. Nor did she receive additional monitoring. According to a state court complaint, the parent told the school that her child should not be allowed to wander around the school. But the student fell in a lavatory stall while trying to climb over a locked door. The court denied a request for immunity by the board and teacher, and school officials appealed to the Supreme Court of Alabama. A review of Article 1, Section 14, of the state constitution led the court to find it created an almost "invincible wall" of immunity. It was well-settled in Alabama law that local school boards were state agencies that had absolute immunity. School officials such as board members were entitled to state law immunity in their individual capacities. **As for the claims against the teacher, the court held it was within her discretion to decide when and how students would take lavatory breaks.** No school rule required teachers to go with students to the lavatory, and the student had gone there unsupervised many times. As the teacher and board members were entitled to immunity, the court held in their favor. *Ex Parte Montgomery County Board of Educ.*, 88 So.3d 837 (Ala. 2012).

◆ Two Connecticut teachers chaperoned an eighth-grade graduation dance held at a private facility. A student who had taken off her shoes to dance stepped on a shard of broken glass and seriously injured her foot. In a state court action against the school board and teachers, the student claimed negligent supervision of students at the dance. The case reached the Supreme Court of Connecticut, which noted that **state law shields municipalities from liability for negligent acts or omissions that require the exercise of judgment or discretion**. On the other hand, the government is generally liable for the "ministerial acts" of its agents. The court held the "hallmark of a discretionary act is that it requires the exercise of judgment." In this case, the court found that sponsoring a middle school graduation party was a discretionary act. An exception to discretionary immunity based on "imminent harm" did not apply. The student's injuries occurred at a voluntary event and because she had voluntarily removed her shoes. As both teachers were exercising their discretion, no exception to immunity applied. The court held for the board. *Coe v. Board of Educ. of Town of Watertown*, 301 Conn. 112, 19 A.3d 640 (Conn. 2011).

◆ An Idaho school district held a carnival to celebrate the last day of the school year. A contractor provided the activities. Participants in a "bungee run" wore harnesses tethered to a fixed object by a bungee cord. They raced over an inflated rubberized surface until the cord snapped them back. A student who was injured on the bungee run sued the district and contractor in a state court. The court found the district had immunity under the Idaho Tort Claims Act. On appeal, the Supreme Court of Idaho held the act generally made governmental entities liable for damages to the same extent that a private person would be under the circumstances. Schools generally have a duty to supervise student activities, including extracurricular and school-sponsored events, and a duty to protect students from reasonably foreseeable risks. The court found the student had stated valid claims based on allowing her to participate in an unreasonably hazardous activity, failing to supervise her, and failing to supervise the contractor. **The district court had correctly found the district was immune from liability for negligent supervision and failing to inspect equipment.** But the student should have been allowed to pursue a theory of direct liability for planning and sponsoring an unreasonably dangerous activity. *Sherer v. Pocatello School Dist. #25*, 143 Idaho 486, 148 P.3d 1232 (Idaho 2006).

IV. UNSUPERVISED ACCIDENTS

Schools are required to exercise reasonable care to maintain safe buildings, grounds and facilities. They can be found liable for negligently maintaining buildings or tolerating hazardous structures, fixtures or grounds.

A. On School Grounds

1. Duty of Care

◆   An Oklahoma middle school student said he broke his shoulder when a female student pushed him as they scrambled for a loose ball. In a state court action, the student's parent asserted negligent supervision and failure to train a substitute teacher who was inside her classroom instead of outside monitoring the playground. The school district argued it had immunity and that the student could not show that a breach of its duty of care was the cause of his injury. Agreeing with the district, the court held in its favor. On appeal to the Court of Civil Appeals of Oklahoma, the student argued that if an adult had been watching the students, he would not have been hurt. He added that the school had no written guidelines for playground supervision and had never trained the substitute. The court found some evidence that a school policy was violated when the substitute let students go outside while she remained inside. But it held a violation of a school policy did not by itself prove negligence.

It appeared that the female student had spontaneously run after the ball and could not have been stopped by a teacher in the immediate vicinity. **It was not foreseeable that a student would jump up and intentionally push a classmate down. Nor could a teacher stop such an unforeseen event.** As a result, the court held lack of supervision did not cause the injury. The lower court had properly held for the school district. *Provinsal v. Sperry Independent School Dist. No. 8 of Tulsa County*, 269 P.3d 51 (Okla. Ct. Civil App. 2011).

◆   A New York child fractured her clavicle and femur after falling off a slide on a playground maintained by a city and school district. According to the child's family, the playground used no protective ground cover and was grass and dirt. Other playgrounds operated by the city and district had protective ground cover such as pea stone to lessen injuries, as recommended by the U.S. Consumer Product Safety Commission (CPSC). The family sued the school district and city. After the trial court denied pretrial dismissal, a state appellate division court held that the school's expert witness established that lack of adequate ground cover was not the legal cause of the injuries. On appeal, the New York Court of Appeals held the expert had calculated the force of the child when she landed on the ground, relying on prior tests in which he had used rubber mats. By contrast, CPSC and similar guidelines were based on use of various ground covers. **The expert witness did not provide a scientific or mathematical foundation to substantiate his opinion that the type of ground cover did not cause injury.** So the court reinstated the claims. *Butler v. City of Gloversville*, 12 N.Y.3d 902, 885 N.Y.S.2d 245 (N.Y. 2009).

◆ A California student joined other children on school property who were picking oranges from a tree on the other side of the fence. He placed a bike next to the fence and poked the handlebar through the fence for stability. However, the bike slipped, and he fell and cut his arm on the fence. The student's parents sued the school district for negligence. A state superior court held for the district, and appeal reached the Court of Appeal of California. It noted that there were no prior complaints about the fence. The state Government Code made a public entity liable for injuries caused by dangerous conditions on public property. A "dangerous condition" is one that creates a substantial risk of injury when the property is used with due care, and in the manner intended. **The student could not show that he was using "due care" while using the fence.** The danger was obvious, and common sense would demonstrate that even a 9-year-old child could see the danger of injury created by attempting to use a bike as a ladder. The lower court had properly found the metal tines on the top of the fence were not a "dangerous condition of public property." The court affirmed the judgment. *Biscotti v. Yuba City Unified School Dist.*, 158 Cal.App.4th, 69 Cal.Rptr.3d 825 (Cal. Ct. App. 2007).

2. Governmental Immunity

◆ A Colorado student broke her arm when she fell from a "zip line" on her playground at recess. Her parents sued the school district for premises liability and negligent supervision. After the court dismissed the case, appeal reached the Court of Appeals of Colorado. It found the Colorado Government Immunity Act (CGIA) provided immunity to public entities for certain actions but waived immunity in cases involving injuries resulting from a "public facility located in any park or recreation area maintained by a public entity." In the court's opinion, **a school district is a "public entity" and a school playground is a "recreation area" under state law**. Playground equipment is visible and not secluded from the public. Man-made equipment was deemed a "facility" within the meaning of the CGIA. Since the public facility waiver applied to man-made objects such as playground equipment, the court reversed the judgment and held immunity did not apply to the parents' premises liability claim. On the other hand, the court held the negligent supervision claim had been properly dismissed and could not go forward. *Loveland v. St. Vrain Valley School Dist. RE-1J*, No. 11CA1019, 2012 WL 2581034 (Colo. Ct. App. 7/5/12).

◆ A New Jersey student was unable to hold her school district and a snow removal company liable for injuries to her knee after she fell on school grounds. A state court held **common law immunity was conferred upon public entities for snow removal activities**. It found evidence that the snow removal company had performed its duties. On appeal to a state appellate court, the student claimed state law immunity did not apply because the place she fell was a "finite, bounded area." The court held this theory would "destroy the common law immunity which has protected public entities against liability for their snow removal activities for over a quarter of a century." *Coehlo v. Newark Board of Educ.*, 2011 WL 4345822 (N.J. Super. Ct. App. Div. 9/19/11).

◆   A Kansas student fell on the driveway of a school shop. In a state court lawsuit against his school district, the student claimed the immunity provisions of the Kansas Tort Claims Act did not apply. But the court disagreed, and he appealed to the state court of appeals. According to the court, **one of the Act's exceptions is for snow, ice and other temporary and natural conditions on any public way or public place due to weather, unless the condition is affirmatively caused by government negligence**. The court rejected the student's argument that the driveway was not accessible to the public. There was evidence that although the driveway was not generally used by the public, it was accessible. A gate that barred cars approaching from one side of the area did not make the driveway inaccessible to the public, as the student claimed. According to the court, his interpretation of the act would encourage school officials to focus on the removal of snow and ice from seldom-traveled areas at the expense of high traffic areas. As the legislature could not have intended this consequence, the court held for the district. *Waters v. Unified School Dist. #428*, 258 P.3d 994 (Table) (Kan. Ct. App. 2011).

◆   At recess, a Massachusetts student chased a first-grader around an enclosed area and pushed him. The first-grader fell against the corner of a bench wall, suffering a severe injury. The principal directed that first-graders have recess in the enclosed area, despite its sharp-cornered concrete bench-walls. In a state negligence case, school officials claimed immunity under the Massachusetts Tort Claims Act (MTCA). The state appeals court explained that the MTCA prevents liability for claims asserting an act (or failure to act) to prevent or diminish harmful acts by a third person "not originally caused by the public employer." In this case, the principal had ordered that first-grade recess be held in the concrete courtyard. According to the court, the causal link between the decision to hold recess in the enclosure and the injury was "not so remote" as to hold that the principal's decision was not an "original cause" of the injury. **The principal's decision to hold recess in the courtyard was not a "policymaking decision," and it was not entitled to discretionary immunity.** *Gennari v. Reading Public Schools*, 933 N.E.2d 1027 (Mass. App. Ct. 2010).

B. Off School Grounds

1. Duty of Care

Courts have disagreed about the duty of a school to supervise students after they are dismissed from school. The age of the student plays a role in whether school liability exists. In a case involving an elementary student, New Jersey's Supreme Court held that "dismissal is part of the school day," creating a legal duty for schools to supervise dismissal. On the other hand, a Florida court recently found no duty to supervise high school students from unforeseen off-campus hazards. Courts in Louisiana and California have imposed a duty to supervise student safety at dismissal. And New York's highest court held that if a student is injured off school grounds, a school district could not be held liable because the district's duty of care only extended to its own boundaries.

◆ Nebraska's supreme court refused to hear an untimely appeal from a trial court decision finding a school district not liable for the death of a student who had an asthma attack after a group of juveniles assaulted her at a restaurant near their school. In a state court lawsuit, the student's family claimed she went to the restaurant while on a lunch break from her summer school class. Four or five juveniles then assaulted her. At least two of the assailants also attended the summer school. A pretrial order held **the district had no duty to supervise and protect the student off campus**. After a final order dismissing claims against the restaurant owner was entered, the family did not timely appeal. The supreme court held it could not review the case. *Wright v. Omaha Public School Dist.*, 280 Neb. 941, 791 N.W.2d 760 (Neb. 2010).

◆ Two female students in Idaho reported that two males were planning a Columbine-style attack at school. The principal confronted one of the male students, who said he was "going to have a school shooting" on a specified date. The two male students were warned about their threatening conduct, and they agreed not to make further statements. But one month later, the students were accused of threatening to shoot guns at a school dance. Two years after these incidents, one of the male students wrote threatening notes that were viewed by his locker partner. Although the threats were brought to the attention of the school resource officer and a vice principal, they were "dismissed." The same month as the notes were found, the student and a male accomplice murdered a female student at the house of her friend. When her parents sued the school district in a state trial court, it was found that the district owed no duty to protect the student off school grounds and after school hours. On appeal, the Supreme Court of Idaho affirmed the judgment. Nothing in the record convinced the court that the district knew that one of the male students would commit a murder based on information received about him some 30 months earlier. **As the murder was not foreseeable, the district had no duty to prevent it.** *Stoddart v. Pocatello School Dist. #25*, 239 P.3d 784 (Idaho 2010).

◆ Washington high school seniors bought six kegs of beer for an off-campus party at a remote location without adult supervision. At the party, three seniors confronted the only junior class member who attended. One of the seniors hit him on the forehead with a beer mug. Although the wound appeared minor, the junior collapsed and fell into a coma four months later. After surviving four years in a persistent vegetative state, the junior died. His estate sued the seniors who had bought the beer, the students who confronted him at the party, and the beer distributor that made the beer kegs available. The Court of Appeals of Washington held that **the non-assailant seniors could not be held liable for the attack on the junior without evidence that they knew the assailants had**

violent tendencies. A state law forbidding the purchase of alcohol by minors did not give rise to a duty of care because the law was not intended to protect against assaults. *Cameron v. Murray*, 214 P.3d 150 (Wash. Ct. App. 2009).

◆   The New York Court of Appeals held that a school district was not liable for injuries suffered by a tenth-grader who was struck by a vehicle while crossing a street off school property. The district was not responsible for any hazardous condition off school grounds where the student was injured. A school's duty to its students "is co-extensive with the school's physical custody and control over them ..., and **when a student is injured off school premises the school district cannot be held liable for the breach of a duty that generally extends only to the boundaries of the school property**." The accident in this case occurred after school and off school property, and the municipality that owned the road was responsible for warning of any hazards on it. *Hess v. West Seneca Cent. School Dist.*, 15 N.Y.3d 813 (N.Y. 2010).

◆   A nine-year-old New Jersey student was left quadriplegic after being struck by a car several blocks from school and about two hours after school dismissal. His family sued the car driver, the school principal and the board of education in a state court. They asserted that the district and principal breached their duty of reasonable supervision during dismissal. The complaint claimed the parents did not have advance notice on the day of the accident that it was an early-dismissal day. The family settled its claims against the car driver. But the court then held that the board's duty did not apply to an accident that occurred two hours after dismissal and several blocks from school. The case reached the Supreme Court of New Jersey, which explained that dangers to students continued at dismissal time because they were susceptible to numerous risks.

In the court's view, it was foreseeable that unsupervised young students leaving school grounds were vulnerable. A school's duty to exercise reasonable care for students was integral to the state's public education system. **"Dismissal is part of the school day." The school's duty of supervision did not disappear when the school bell rang.** The duty required school districts to create a reasonable dismissal supervision policy, provide notice to parents, and comply with the policy and with parental requests concerning dismissal. The court affirmed the decision of the appellate division court, and returned the case to the trial court. *Jerkins v. Anderson*, 191 N.J. 285, 922 A.2d 1279 (N.J. 2007).

◆   A Florida student died in an automobile crash after skipping class with several other eleventh-graders who simply walked to their cars and left school grounds. The car in which she was riding was driven at over 70 miles per hour. This occurred on wet roads in a residential area with a 35-mile-an-hour speed limit. The car crashed into a tree, killing the student. The student's estate sued the driver of the vehicle and the school board for negligence. A state trial court rejected the estate's argument that lax enforcement of truancy rules made the death foreseeable. A Florida District Court of Appeal found that even if the students were deemed habitually truant, there was no duty of the school board to protect them from unforeseen off-campus hazards. The primary purpose of Florida truancy laws was to promote academic success, not to enhance student safety. School attendance rules did not impose a duty of care on the district to protect students from off-campus traffic injuries. The court found **"the decision whether to have an open campus, a 'fortress,' or something in-between, is a policy decision that should be left to school professionals and not second-guessed by civil juries."** The court held for the school board. *Kazanjian v. School Board of Palm Beach County*, 967 So.2d 259 (Fla. Dist. Ct. App. 2007).

2. Governmental Immunity

In the next case, the Supreme Court of Alabama restated a general rule that an agent of the state is immune from civil liability for conduct based on the formulation of plans, policies or designs.

◆ An Alabama sixth-grade student told her teacher she was sick and wanted to go home. The teacher instructed her to telephone her mother, and she went to the office to do so. Later, an 18-year-old former student arrived at the office and identified himself as the student's brother. An instructional assistant who had been assigned to check students in and out from school allowed the student to leave with the former student. Staff members realized she had left school under false pretenses, and left school to search for her. After the former student sexually assaulted the student in a car, the student's family sued the school board, principal, instructional assistant, and secretary for negligence. A state trial court held the school board and the secretary were entitled to immunity.

But the court denied state-agent immunity to the teaching assistant and the principal. On appeal, **the Supreme Court of Alabama stated the general rule that an agent of the state is immune from civil liability for conduct based on the formulation of plans, policies or designs**. State agents are immune for claims based on the exercise of judgment in the discharge of duties imposed by statute, rule or regulation when educating students. The school's standard checkout procedure allowed students to leave with an older sibling, and the incident occurred while the principal and assistant were "discharging their official duties." The student did not show they acted "willfully, maliciously, fraudulently, in bad faith, or beyond their authority." The trial court should not have denied pretrial judgment to the principal and the teaching assistant. *In re T.W. v. Russell County Board of Educ.*, 965 So.2d 780 (Ala. 2007).

◆ The Court of Appeal of Florida held that a school board had sovereign immunity in a negligence lawsuit filed by a parent whose 13-year-old son was killed while walking home from school. The death occurred at an intersection with no crossing guard. The student was the fourth child to die in transit to or from the school in a seven-year period. The mother asserted that the decision to operate the school from 9:00 a.m. to 4:00 p.m. negligently exposed students to rush-hour traffic. **The court found the scheduling of school hours was a planning-level decision that deserved immunity.** The board did not create a hidden or dangerous condition for which there was no proper warning. Traffic hazards at the site were readily apparent, and the court held the school board had no authority over the regulation of traffic. *Orlando v. Broward County, Florida*, 920 So.2d 54 (Fla. Dist. Ct. App. 2005).

V. LIABILITY FOR INTENTIONAL CONDUCT

"Willful or wanton conduct" refers to intentional conduct. A finding of intentional, willful or wanton conduct typically defeats immunity. Courts have found school districts liable for intentional acts of third parties on or near school grounds. In such cases, a court must find the district should have foreseen the potential misconduct. For intentional misconduct cases involving coaches, please see Chapter Thirteen, Section III.C. For corporal punishment cases, see Chapter One, Section V. Additional cases involving sexual harassment and abuse appear in Section III.D. of Chapter Eight, and in Chapter One, Section I.

A. Employee Misconduct

1. Types of Misconduct

◆   The Urbana (Illinois) School District hired a teacher who had worked for McLean County (Illinois) schools. At an Urbana elementary school, he sexually abused two students. Parents of the victims sued the teacher, both districts and school officials. They said McLean administrators knew the teacher abused children after gaining their trust through "sexual grooming" behavior. McLean officials were accused of failing to record incidents, investigate reports or timely report abuse as mandated by law. Significantly, the parents claimed the teacher left McLean under a severance agreement that intentionally concealed his abuses and falsely indicated he had worked a full school year. A trial court found no willful and wanton conduct, and it dismissed the case.

Appeal reached the Supreme Court of Illinois. It held "willful and wanton conduct" is an aggravated form of negligence requiring "deliberate intention to harm or a conscious disregard for the plaintiff's welfare." **A duty was owed to the parents based on McLean's misstatement about the teacher's work history on an employment verification form.** Urbana officials were not told that the teacher was twice removed from his classroom for discipline and had left his job during the school year. The court held misrepresentations of misconduct created a duty based on the relationship between the parties and supported the willful and wanton conduct claims. And the parents showed injury was reasonably foreseeable and likely. By falsely stating the teacher had taught for the full school year, McLean implied that his severance had been routine. Urbana officials had no reason to suspect he had left due to misconduct. Courts in California, New Mexico and Texas have found injuries were reasonably foreseeable on similar facts. As injury was foreseeable and any "burden" of truthfully filling out employment forms was slight, the parents could pursue willful and wanton misconduct claims. *Doe-3 v. McLean County Unit Dist. No. 5 Board of Directors*, 973 N.E.2d 880 (Ill. 2012).

◆   A California student said a school counselor engaged him in sexual conduct both on and off school grounds. His negligence case reached the state supreme court. It held that prior California decisions found school districts and their employees have a "special relationship" with students. **School administrators must take reasonable measures to guard students against harassment and**

abuse from foreseeable sources, including teachers or counselors. If the student could show school administrators and employees knew (or should have known) that the counselor presented a danger, the district could be held liable for negligently hiring, retaining and supervising her. In *Dailey v. Los Angeles Unified School Dist.*, 2 Cal.3d 741, 87 Cal.Rptr. 376 (Cal. 1970), the court held school personnel may be held liable for the negligent failure to protect students. While the student could pursue the case, he would have to prove each element of a negligence claim and not rely on speculation. Even if an administrator knew that the counselor presented a danger to the student, most of the fault would likely lie with the counselor herself. *C.A. v. William S. Hart Union High School Dist.*, 138 Cal.Rptr.3d 1, 270 P.3d 699 (Cal. 2012).

◆   A Michigan teacher said a parent became upset with her during a disciplinary hearing and hit her in the stomach. She was pregnant at the time, and she reported the incident to police. Although the parent was prosecuted for assault with intent to do great bodily harm, a jury found him not guilty. He sued the teacher and school district for malicious prosecution, infliction of emotional distress and defamation. After a state court dismissed the action, the parent appealed to the Court of Appeals of Michigan. The court noted that the parent was criminally charged by a county prosecutor, not the teacher. **A person who has no active role in initiating a criminal prosecution cannot be held liable for malicious prosecution.** The teacher was not accused of lying to authorities, and she did not institute the charges. An important state policy encouraged citizens to report possible crimes. Governmental immunity protected the district and teacher. Since information available to the prosecutor would cause a reasonable person to believe the parent was guilty and there was no evidence of false testimony, the court affirmed the judgment. *Bradley v. Detroit Public Schools*, No. 292749, 2011 WL 255274 (Mich. Ct. App. 1/27/11).

◆   A Georgia teacher was accused of shoving a disabled student's head into a trash can and then pulling him out by his legs. The principal investigated and, after finding that the teacher and student had often engaged in horseplay prior to the incident, determined it was only horseplay. Although the teacher was counseled to end this type of conduct with students, the parents decided to sue. A federal court held the school district and officials were entitled to qualified immunity. The Eleventh Circuit affirmed the judgment, finding the trash can incident did not violate the student's rights. **Only intentional actions by officials that shock the conscience may be found to violate the Constitution.** As the lower court had found, the student did not suffer physical injury and there was no evidence that the teacher acted with malice or intent to harm him. *Mahone v. Ben Hill County School System*, 377 Fed.Appx. 913 (11th Cir. 2010).

◆   A Louisiana high school teacher twice assaulted a student who had volunteered to work with special education students. Others complained about him and criminal charges were filed. He pleaded guilty to simple battery, was fined small amounts and served 30 days in jail. After settling claims against the teacher in a state court civil action, the student pursued the school board for further damages. A jury found the board should pay her $45,000, and the board appealed to the Court of Appeal of Louisiana. The court held **the teacher was engaged in business so closely related to his teaching duties that the board was liable for his conduct**. The state supreme court has held employers should be held liable for employee misconduct if a wrongful act was rooted in employment, reasonably incidental to employment duties, occurred on the employer's premises and occurred during work hours. As the teacher's conduct met this test, and the damages were not excessive, the judgment was affirmed. *T.S. v. Rapides Parish School Board*, 11 So.3d 628 (La. Ct. App. 2009).

◆   An Arkansas student attended a band competition in Atlanta with his school band. He became ill and missed the entire competition while remaining in his hotel room. Shortly after the student returned home, his mother took him to a medical center. He suffered a cardiac arrest and died of a diabetic condition the next day. His mother sued the school district and officials for negligence and deliberate indifference to her son's medical needs. A federal court dismissed her constitutional claims, and the case went before the U.S. Court of Appeals, Eighth Circuit. It held the Due Process Clause does not confer affirmative rights to government aid. **School officials have no duty to care for students who participate in voluntary school-related activities such as school band trips.** *Lee v. Pine Bluff School Dist.*, 472 F.3d 1026 (8th Cir. 2007).

2. Governmental Immunity

Article 1, Section 14 of the Alabama Constitution provides that the state cannot be made a defendant in any court. In the opinion of the Supreme Court of Alabama, it is well settled that local education boards may claim immunity as agencies of the state, and are not considered part of local government units.

◆   A Missouri parent did not authorize H1-N1 vaccinations on a consent form from her son's school because she believed nasal mist should not be used due to his asthma. The student claimed that when he gave the nurse the form and told her his mother did not consent, the nurse said he needed the vaccine regardless of what his mother said. She then gave him the H1-NI vaccine. The parent sued the school board, nurse and the district's lead nurse, asserting constitutional rights violations and negligence. The case reached the U.S. Court of Appeals, Eighth Circuit, which found the claim against the lead nurse was not viable. **She was entitled to state law official and public duty immunity.** As for the claims against the board, a government entity may not be sued for negligence in a constitutional rights action filed under 42 U.S.C. § 1983. The court held the failure-to-train claims recited legal conclusions without stating sufficient facts to pursue the case. Any substantive due process claim required proof of "conscience-shocking behavior" by a school. Since the court found the complaint did not meet these rigorous standards, the lower court had properly dismissed the remaining claims. While the court noted it might have been inappropriate for the nurse to override the parental refusal to consent, it found this could not be deemed "conscience-shocking behavior." *B.A.B. v. Board of Educ. of City of St. Louis*, 698 F.3d 1037 (8th Cir. 2012).

◆   After an Alabama teacher claimed she was paddled by the superintendent, he read a statement at a press conference denying the incident had occurred. In a state court action, the teacher sued him, along with the education board and its members in their official capacities, for assault, battery, defamation, libel and slander. The court denied immunity to the board and board members. On appeal, the Supreme Court of Alabama explained that local school boards are agencies of the state and not of the local governmental units they serve. For that reason, **the board had absolute immunity and the claims against it were barred**. Claims against the board members in their official capacity also had to be dismissed. They enjoyed the same immunity as the board under the Alabama Constitution. *Ex Parte Boaz City Board of Educ.*, 82 So.3d 660 (Ala. 2011).

◆   Three Ohio students claimed a bus driver subjected them to discrimination, harassment and bullying. They also accused him of encouraging others to bully, intimidate and threaten them based on religion and national origin. Nine claims were asserted, including failure to train employees, simple negligence, violation of Title VI of the Civil Rights Act of 1964, infliction of emotional distress, vicarious liability and loss of consortium. The court dismissed a challenge by the families to the Political Subdivision Tort Liability Act. The Sixth Circuit had rejected a similar challenge in *Ellis v. Cleveland Municipal School Dist.*, 455 F.3d 690 (6th Cir. 2006). As for the negligence claims, **immunity under the Ohio Political Subdivision Tort Liability Act applies absent an exception**. None of the exceptions applied, so immunity barred the state law claims. There was no merit to the parents' argument that a political subdivision lost immunity based on claims of willful or wanton conduct. *Y.S. v. Board of Educ. of Mathews Local School Dist.*, 766 F.Supp.2d 839 (N.D. Ohio 2011).

◆   An Alabama fifth-grader repeatedly disrupted his class. An education board policy required the presence of a witness whenever corporal punishment was administered. When the student avoided his teacher's attempts to hit his palms with two taped-together rulers, she retrieved a paddle and hit him with it. She claimed this was the end of the incident. But the student claimed she kept hitting him, causing injury. He enrolled in another school and then sued the school board and teacher for negligence. A state court denied claims by both the education board and the teacher for judgment based on absolute immunity. On appeal, the Supreme Court of Alabama held the board had been wrongly denied immunity. It reversed that part of the judgment. But the board's policy required the presence of a witness whenever corporal punishment was administered. **The teacher's rationale for deviating from the policy was that she could not leave her other students alone to find a witness.** While this was supported by her statement and those of her supervisors, further inquiry by the trial court was necessary. *Ex Parte Monroe County Board of Educ.*, 48 So.3d 621 (Ala. 2010).

◆   A Tennessee alternative school student repeated grade nine at another school in the same system. His disciplinary record was not forwarded from the alternative school. At his new school, the student began harassing a female student. An assistant principal received repeated reports from the female, her parents and others about the male student, and told the male student to avoid contact with the female. But he later knocked her unconscious in a school hallway and broke her jaw. She was hospitalized and underwent surgery. Her father sued the male student, his mother, the assistant principal and the school board in a Tennessee court. The assistant principal was dismissed from the case, but the court found the assault was foreseeable and the school board negligent for failing to protect the female student. She received $75,000 for emotional distress, pain and suffering, and her parents won over $10,000 for medical costs. The state court of appeals rejected the board's claim to immunity under the doctrine of public duty. **School systems, teachers and administrators have a duty of reasonable care to supervise and protect students.** The board had a duty to protect students from foreseeable intentional acts of third parties such as the male student. *Dean v. Weakley County Board of Educ.*, No. W2007-00159-COA-R3-CV, 2008 WL 948882 (Tenn. Ct. App. 4/9/08).

◆   The parents of a 14-year-old South Carolina student learned a substitute had sexual relations with their child. The substitute was convicted of criminal sexual conduct with a minor. The parents sued the school district in a separate action, and a state court held for the district. On appeal, the Supreme Court of South Carolina affirmed the judgment on a claim for infliction of emotional distress. But it agreed with the parents that their claim for negligent supervision had been wrongly dismissed. The state Tort Claims Act precluded government liability for losses resulting from any responsibility or duty such as the supervision, protection, control, confinement, or custody of a student, except where the responsibility or duty was exercised in a "grossly negligent manner." Here, **the parents had alleged gross negligence by the district**. As a result, that claim had been improperly dismissed. The case had to be reconsidered. *Doe v. Greenville County School Dist.*, 375 S.C. 63, 651 S.E.2d 305 (S.C. 2007).

B. Student Misconduct

1. Types of Misconduct

In Dailey v. Los Angeles Unified School Dist., *2 Cal.3d 741, 87 Cal.Rptr. 376 (Cal. 1970), the Supreme Court of California held school authorities are to "supervise at all times the conduct of the children on school grounds and to enforce those rules and regulations necessary to their protection." The standard of care for supervising students is that which a "person of ordinary prudence" would exercise when performing comparable duties.*

◆   A North Carolina high school student accused her band teacher of making many sexual advances and inducing her into having sex with him. He was eventually arrested and pleaded guilty to taking indecent liberties with a child. In a state court, the student sued the board of education for negligent hiring, supervision and retention. She added emotional distress and state constitutional violations claims. The court dismissed the negligence and emotional distress claims, but it refused to dismiss the constitutional claims. On appeal, the Court of Appeals of North Carolina noted the lower court had based its constitutional rulings on *Craig v. New Hanover City Board of Educ.*, 363 N.C. 334, 687 S.E.2d

351 (N.C. 2009), Chapter Six, Section VII.C., of this volume. In *Craig*, the state supreme court stated that the existence of common law claims that were barred by governmental immunity did not also bar a party from asserting any available constitutional claims. But **the court held there was no state constitutional right to recover damages from local boards for injuries based on negligent supervision of employees.** As the student did not state a viable claim under the state constitution, she could not recover damages from the board. The judgment was reversed. *Doe v. Charlotte-Mecklenburg Board of Educ.*, 731 S.E.2d 245 (N.C. Ct. App. 2012).

◆   An Idaho student reported that a classmate bumped him on the head. On the school bus ride home, the classmate again hit his head. After the student began having daily headaches, his parents sued the school district and classmate's family in a state court. When the case reached the Supreme Court of Idaho, it held a government entity may be liable for wrongful actions of employees acting within the course and scope of their employment, in circumstances where a private entity would be liable under state law. Although the court noted the district's "duty to act affirmatively to prevent foreseeable harm to its students" while they are in district custody, it held this duty was "not an absolute mandate to prevent all harm." Instead, **a school was obligated to exercise due care and take reasonable precautions to protect students.** In this case, school staff only had knowledge about the student's first injury, and no facts supported a claim for failing to prevent it. **A school district's liability was limited to injuries caused by a person under district supervision.** No evidence showed the school staff members had been reckless, willful or wanton. *Mareci v. Coeur D'Alene School Dist. No. 271*, 150 Idaho 740, 250 P.3d 791 (Idaho 2011).

◆   A California student sued his school district for injuries caused by another student who beat him with a baseball bat off school grounds after school hours. According to the student, the district allowed his assailant to carry a bat around school during school hours, in view of teachers and administrators. He claimed the assailant threatened others with violence and had a history of violence and discipline at school. The district claimed discretionary immunity and argued it could not be held liable for an injury taking place off school grounds after school hours. The Court of Appeal of California agreed, finding **neither school districts nor their employees are liable for the conduct or safety of any student when not on school property, unless there is a specific undertaking by a school district** or a sponsored activity, which was not the case here. *Cortinez v. South Pasadena Unified School Dist.*, No. 2352046, 2010 WL 2352046 (Cal. Ct. App. 6/14/10).

◆   A 185-pound Louisiana student with autism began to hit himself on the head. His teacher was pushed into a wall while trying to keep a mat under him to prevent injury. During the 45-50 minute struggle, the teacher was "twisting and sliding the entire time" but was not hit, knocked down or bitten by the student. She reported injuries to her hand, knee and buttocks. Claiming entitlement to "assault pay" under a state law provision, the teacher sued the school board. A state trial court granted pretrial judgment to the board, but the

Court of Appeal of Louisiana held that a trial was required. **"Assault pay" is available to teachers injured or disabled while acting in an official capacity as a result of an assault or battery.** Under the assault pay provision, injured or disabled teachers receive sick pay with no reduction in pay or accrued sick leave days while disabled as the result of the assault or battery. A separate provision covers teachers who are injured as a result of "physical contact" while assisting students. Here, the facts would determine if the teacher's injuries resulted from an "assault" by the student. *Miller v. St. Tammany Parish School Board*, Nos. 2008 CA 2582-2583, 2009 WL 3135208 (La. Ct. App. 9/11/09).

◆   A California school district operated a free after-school program on a school playground. Between 200 and 300 children participated, with two adults typically present to supervise them. One day, only one supervisor was present to watch over 113 participants. A second-grade girl was led by an older girl to an unlocked shed on campus that was off-limits to program participants. The older girl forced a boy to have sexual contact with the second-grader. Both the boy and the second-grader later said the girl held them against their wills and threatened to hit them. The second-grader's mother sued the school district for negligent supervision, claiming the district and employees knew for some time that some of the children had been kissing and engaging in other inappropriate activity. The case reached the state court of appeal, which noted that the after-school program was voluntary. A question remained regarding whether the absence of a supervisor from her post contributed to the injury. As a result, the case required further fact-finding. **If the supervisor allowed dangerous conduct to go on, liability could be imposed.** *J.H. v. Los Angeles Unified School Dist.*, 183 Cal.App.4th 123, 107 Cal.Rptr.3d 182 (Cal. Ct. App. 2010).

◆   A 14-year-old California student with multiple disabilities functioned in her public school on a "borderline basis." During a lunch period, a male special needs student led her from the cafeteria to a hidden alcove under a stairway and sexually assaulted her. In the resulting negligence action against the district, a state court noted that the alcove was hidden from anyone on campus and was considered a "problem area." A "tardy sweep" of the campus should have been conducted six minutes after every lunch period. But the students were found about 14 minutes after the final check of the alcove. The court held for the school district, and the student appealed. The Court of Appeal of California held that **school officials had a special relationship to special needs students and had to adequately supervise them due to the foreseeability of harm.** School officials were on notice that the alcove was a problem area. As the district had an affirmative duty to protect the student based on a "special relationship" with her, it could be held liable. It also had potential liability for maintaining a dangerous condition of public property, since a chain would not keep out a child who could not appreciate danger. *Jennifer C. v. Los Angeles Unified School Dist.*, 168 Cal.App.4th 1320, 86 Cal.Rptr.3d 274 (Cal. Ct. App. 2008).

◆   A Washington school district declared a school safe for a student who had been named on a "2 kill list" written by two others. The student's parents wanted one of the list writers suspended for the rest of the school year, and they sued the school district for negligence. A trial court held for the school district, and the parents appealed to the state court of appeals. The court explained that a school district's **duty to use reasonable care only extends to risks of harm that are foreseeable.** It rejected the parents' claim that the list writer had to be expelled for the rest of the school year. The district had to consider his educational needs, and acted within its authority by first expelling the writer on an emergency basis, then suspending him, and ultimately reducing the suspension on the basis of a psychiatrist's report. **The district was not obligated to impose discipline to accommodate the student's family.** *Jachetta v. Warden Joint Consolidated School Dist.*, 142 Wash.App. 918, 176 P.3d 545 (Wash. Ct. App. 2008).

2. Governmental Immunity

◆   A Missouri student tried to bring a knife to his charter school. Juvenile authorities arrested him, and he was admitted to a psychiatric hospital. Charter school officials expelled the student, and his mother enrolled him in a Kansas City public school. District officials learned about the knife incident and the hospitalization. Due to his learning disability, the student was referred to the district's special education department, which prepared an individualized education program (IEP) for him. The IEP did not refer to the knife incident.

A year later, the student attacked a classmate with a box cutter and sliced his neck open. The classmate survived, and he later sued Kansas City's district superintendent in a state court. The court held the superintendent had immunity under the Paul D. Coverdell Teacher Protection Act. The act is a No Child Left Behind (NCLB) Act provision applying to efforts "to control, discipline, expel, or suspend a student or maintain order or control in the classroom or school" while "acting in conformity with the law." On appeal, **the Supreme Court of Missouri held the Coverdell Act was a permissible exercise of Congress' spending power**. By accepting funds and choosing not to enact a law rejecting teacher immunity, Missouri accepted Coverdell Act immunity. Although the classmate claimed the superintendent failed to comply with district policies by neglecting to notify staff of the student's criminal history and hospitalization, the court found the policies were not within the definition of "law." And the student was not in the district when he brought a knife to the charter school. As all the classmate's arguments failed, the decision for the superintendent was affirmed. *Dydell v. Taylor*, 332 S.W.3d 848 (Mo. 2011).

◆   A state appellate court held **the New York City Board of Education was entitled to immunity in an action filed by a teacher who was injured while trying to restrain a disruptive student**. Although the teacher claimed the failure of school officials to remove the child from her classroom was not protected by immunity, the court held placement decisions were within the board's discretion. It was thus entitled to immunity. *Rivera v. Board of Educ. of City of New York*, 82 A.D.3d 614, 919 N.Y.S.2d 154 (N.Y. App. Div. 2011).

◆   Parents of an Ohio student with Down syndrome claimed he was sexually assaulted at school by two boys. A state court complaint said the assault occurred in circumstances showing recklessness and "an extreme lack of teacher oversight" in a classroom. The parents claimed the school knew one of the attackers had a history of psychological problems and that dangerous students were recklessly placed in the class. The Court of Appeals of Ohio noted that school employees were accused of failing to monitor student behavior, which was within the scope of their official job duties. **An assault under circumstances of recklessness and lack of teacher oversight established potential district liability.** *E.F. v. Oberlin City School Dist.*, No. 09CA009640, 2010 WL 1227703 (Ohio Ct. App. 3/31/10).

◆   A Mississippi cheerleader claimed male students secretly videotaped her changing into a swimsuit at an off-campus party. Her mother sued the parents of the male students and obtained a restraining order against the boys. But the principal found no evidence of harassment. The mother claimed that the boys and their parents harassed the cheerleader at sporting events. She sued the school system for negligence. A state trial court found much of the testimony concerned off-campus conduct. It found the school system took reasonable steps to prevent the harassment and was immune from suit under the Mississippi Tort Claims Act (MTCA). On appeal, the Court of Appeals of Mississippi held **the school system was not responsible for any harassment the student suffered outside of school that was linked to the videotaping.** And the school system was immune from any liability under the MTCA. *Beacham v. City of Starkville School System*, 984 So.2d 1073 (Miss. Ct. App. 2008).

◆   A Nebraska student claimed that she was sexually assaulted by a classmate with a history of physical and/or sexual misconduct. Claiming school officials took no steps to restrain him, she sued the school district for negligence. A state court held the district was immunized from liability by the state Political Subdivisions Tort Claims Act (PSTCA). On appeal, the Supreme Court of Nebraska explained that the PSTCA eliminated in part the traditional immunity of school districts for the negligent acts of their employees. **Districts are now generally liable for wrongful acts to the same extent as a private individual in a similar case.** The complaint alleged that the district knew of specific behavior by the classmate that made violent conduct reasonably foreseeable. The court therefore rejected the district's sovereign immunity defense. *Doe v. Omaha Public School Dist.*, 273 Neb. 79, 724 N.W.2d 447 (Neb. 2007).

C. Parent Misconduct

1. Sign-Out Policies

◆   After a Kentucky child was picked up from school by an unauthorized individual, the parent sued the education board and superintendent for negligence. The case reached the Court of Appeals of Kentucky, which stated that immunity applied to the board if it was performing a "governmental function." Here, the board's after-school pick-up and drop-off policy directly furthered the education of students, which was a governmental function. So the board was entitled to immunity. According to the parent, the superintendent did not investigate, take disciplinary action or enact policies to prevent future incidents. But the court held these alleged failures did not strip the superintendent of immunity. **Nothing in the complaint alleged any failure by the superintendent to exercise personal discretion, in good faith and within the scope of his authority.** Both the school board and superintendent were entitled to immunity. *Breathitt County Board of Educ. v. Combs*, No. 2009-CA-000607-MR, 2010 WL 3515747 (Ky. Ct. App. 9/10/10).

◆   A Louisiana father gave his children's middle school documentation that he had their sole "provisional custody." He claimed that they could only be released to him. School policy allowed only the persons listed on a check out form to sign a student out of school. When the children's mother appeared at their school prior to a holiday break, the principal telephoned the father. He stated that under no circumstances could they be released to her, and that he would come to the school. But when the father arrived at school 20 minutes later, the principal had already released the children to the mother. The father sued the school board, principal and insurer. After the case was dismissed, the state court of appeal held that the father's claims for out-of-pocket expenses could proceed if the school officials owed him a duty to refrain from allowing the mother to check the children out of school. **Schools have a "duty to make the appropriate supervisory decisions concerning a student's departure from campus during regular school hours."** As the father asserted violation of the policy on checking-out students, and claimed the sole authority to do so, the principal had violated the policy and her duty to the children and father. *Peters v. Allen Parish School Board*, 996 So.2d 1230 (La. Ct. App. 2008).

◆   A Tennessee couple began divorce proceedings. The wife told school staff not to release the children to their father, but a staff member told her that would require a court order. The husband signed the children out of school early the next day, giving as a reason: "keeping promise by mother" for the daughter and "pay back" for the son. A staff member read the reasons for early dismissal on the sign-out sheet after the father left, and she told the principal. Police were called. They arrived at the father's house to find it ablaze. The father brandished a knife, and the police shot him to death. The children's bodies were found inside the house. Later, the mother sued the school board for negligence in the state court system. A trial court held for the board, and the mother appealed.

The state court of appeals held that the board was not liable for negligently violating its own sign-out policy. There was no evidence that staff knew of a dispute until the mother called the day before the murders. The trial court had correctly held that a **school has no legal duty to follow the instruction of one parent not to release a child to the other parent without a court order to this effect**. But failure to read the father's reasons for signing out the children was evidence of breach of the duty to exercise ordinary care for safety. The court rejected a claim that the board had no duty to examine the reason for signing out a child. The trial court was to further consider this claim. *Haney v. Bradley County Board of Educ.*, 160 S.W.3d 886 (Tenn. Ct. App. 2004).

◆   An Alaska father had legal custody of his son, and the child's mother had visitation during the Christmas and summer vacations. The father warned the principal that the mother would attempt an abduction. A state court stayed enforcement of the parties' custody order pending investigations in Alaska and Washington. Just before Christmas vacation, the mother arrived at school to pick up the student, accompanied by a police officer. The principal noted that the custody order provided by the father did not specify visitation terms. The mother produced her copy of a previous order granting her visitation rights. The principal called the father, who objected to releasing the student. However, the principal released the student to the mother after a discussion with the police officer. The mother refused to return the student to the father after the Christmas break, and he was unable to regain custody for over five months.

The father sued the school district and principal for interference with his custodial rights in the state court system. A trial court held the principal and district were entitled to qualified immunity. On appeal, the Supreme Court of Alaska held state law established official immunity for "discretionary actions," which require personal deliberation, decision and judgment. The court found **the principal was entitled to immunity, since he acted with deliberation and made a considered judgment**. *Pauley v. Anchorage School Dist.*, 31 P.3d 1284 (Alaska 2001).

2. Parental Liability

Section 316 of the Restatement of Torts (a legal encyclopedia) states there is no legal duty for parents to prevent harm by their children unless "they are in a position to exercise immediate control over their children to prevent some foreseeable harm." Parents have no duty "to take precautionary disciplinary measures or to regulate their children's behavior on an ongoing basis."

◆   A Minnesota teacher had several confrontations with a parent and obtained a restraining order against her. A school district lawyer determined the order did not prohibit the parent from entering the school. It only prevented her from coming near the teacher's classroom. Within three months, the teacher saw the parent in the school and called 911 to report a violation of the order. She then left school for the rest of the day. The district maintained that the parent had not violated the harassment order and suspended the teacher without pay for three days. Near the end of the school year, the teacher saw the parent, and left school for the day. She later sued the district and parent for negligence. A state court held the district was entitled to official immunity. The teacher won a judgment against the parent for $32,205 for assault, then appealed the decision for the school district. The state court of appeals found the teacher's whistleblowing was not a "report" under Minnesota law. Also, a state law requirement for schools to adopt anti-harassment policies did not apply to parents. **The parent's harassment did not violate any contractual obligation of the district**, and the judgment for the school district was affirmed. *Ellison-Harpole v. Special School Dist. No. 1*, No. A07-1070, 2008 WL 933537 (Minn. Ct. App. 4/8/08).

◆   An Illinois teacher claimed that a student charged her and threatened to stab her with scissors. She was able to disarm the student, who ran out of the room, kicked the door, and slammed it shut on her finger. The teacher sued the school district and the student's mother, claiming she knew of the student's arrest record, mental illness, conduct disorder, character, and history of outbursts. A federal court held the parent could not be held liable simply because she was the student's mother. Liability required proof that she did not adequately control or supervise her son. To state a claim for negligent supervision, the teacher had to show the parent knew of specific prior conduct that put her on notice that the assault was likely to occur, and had the opportunity to control her son. **Parents have a duty to exercise "reasonable care" to control their minor children and prevent them from intentionally harming others.** The court found no duty of parents to "take precautionary disciplinary measures or to regulate their children's behavior on an ongoing basis." Since parental liability may result only if parents are in position to exercise immediate control over their children to prevent some foreseeable harm, the court dismissed the teacher's claim. *Bland v. Candioto*, No. 3:05-CV-716RM, 2006 WL 2735501 (N.D. Ill. 2006).

◆   Under Louisiana law, parents are legally accountable for the acts of their children. An 11-year-old student with impulsivity and aggression problems pointed a toy gun at a teaching assistant (TA). The TA did not know the gun was a toy and claimed to be emotionally and mentally traumatized. The school board sued the student's mother, claiming that the student was negligent and that the mother was personally liable for his actions. A trial court held for the mother. On appeal, the state court of appeal held **Louisiana parents of minor children can be liable for harm caused by a child's conduct even where a parent is not personally negligent.** But the student could be deemed negligent only if a court found that he violated the applicable standard of care. Here, given the student's maturity level, lack of awareness of risks and his inclination to be impulsive and aggressive, he did not breach the standard. As the student was not negligent, his mother could not be held liable for his actions. *Lafayette Parish School Board v. Cormier*, 901 So. 2d 1197 (La. Ct. App. 2005).

D. Suicide

◆   A New Hampshire student with learning disabilities was having problems at his middle school. During his seventh-grade year, a teacher's aide overheard him say he "wanted to blow his brains out." A guidance counselor called the student's mother, and had the student sign a contract for safety, but she took no other action. Several weeks later, the mother claimed that a special education teacher made a false and knowing attempt to impose discipline on her son. The next day, the student was reported to the vice principal and suspended. After the suspension, the student returned home and hanged himself. The mother sued the school administrative unit, a teacher and the guidance counselor for negligence, infliction of emotional distress and wrongful death. A state trial court dismissed the case, and later the Supreme Court of New Hampshire affirmed this decision. **It rejected the mother's claim that the counselor and administrative unit had a special duty to prevent the suicide** and that the counselor voluntarily assumed a duty to prevent it. There was no intentional or malicious conduct in this case that might create a duty to prevent the suicide. *Mikell v. School Administrative Unit #33*, 972 A.2d 1050 (N.H. 2009).

◆   A Minnesota student killed himself after returning home from school. A suicide note and his mid-term grades were found next to his body. His family sued the school district, claiming the suicide was a foreseeable consequence of bullying and school negligence that the district had a duty to prevent. A court held for the district, as did the state court of appeals. While Minnesota schools have a duty to protect students, they are not liable for sudden, unanticipated misconduct. Here, the suicide was not foreseeable. School staff had no reason to know of the student's continuing problems with bullying, because he did not report them. As there was no foreseeable harm, there was no duty to protect him. The court rejected claims by the estate that the principal should have proactively intervened with the bullies. **There was no evidence that a school bullying policy would have prevented the tragedy.** *Jasperson v. Anoka-Hennepin Independent School Dist. No. 11*, No. A06-1904, 2007 WL 3153456 (Minn. Ct. App. 10/30/07).

◆   A student who formerly attended an Idaho high school committed suicide. His estate tried to hold the Idaho district liable because an essay he wrote for a class showed that he had contemplated suicide in the past. He also wrote that he had "turned his life around" and was currently happy. The state legislature had enacted a law providing that **neither a school district nor a teacher had a duty to warn of a student's suicidal tendencies "absent the teacher's knowledge of direct evidence of such suicidal tendencies."** The law stated that "direct evidence" included "unequivocal and unambiguous oral or written statements by a student" that would not cause doubts in a reasonable teacher. The legislature adopted the new provision specifically to narrow the duty of a teacher to warn of a student's suicidal tendencies. The student's words provided an opposite conclusion to the one urged by his parents. *Carrier v. Lake Pend Oreille School Dist. No. 84*, 142 Idaho 804, 134 P.3d 655 (Idaho 2006).

E. Defamation

As teachers are deemed "public officials," they must show a false statement has been published to a third party, with "actual malice" and damages in order to recover in a defamation case. The actual malice standard is difficult to meet. A person seeking recovery in a defamation suit must prove the publication has caused damage to his or her reputation. Privilege is a defense to certain defamation claims. Persons with a common interest in the subject matter of speech (such as a teacher's performance) may enjoy a privilege to discuss their common interest in protecting students. For defamation cases involving coaches, please see Chapter Thirteen, Section III.B. of this volume.

◆   A Washington high school newspaper reported on a controversy in the school's neighborhood involving two adult brothers. It described them as "infamous landlords" who had a "bad reputation amongst both locals and city officials." The newspaper reported that the brothers had accumulated 48 housing and building maintenance code violations "and have also been accused of racist renting policies." One of the brothers sued the school district in a state court for defamation. In seeking a pretrial judgment, the district submitted 11 media articles to the court describing "deplorable conditions" and numerous housing code violations at rental properties owned by the brothers. The articles reported that the brothers hired a property manager who had founded a white supremacist organization and been convicted of hate crimes. The court admitted the media articles into evidence and dismissed the brother's case.

On appeal, the Court of Appeals of Washington held the articles were relevant, as they shed light on key issues in dispute in the case. These included whether statements in the high school newspaper were false, whether the district knew (or should have known) they were false, and whether the brothers' reputations would not have been damaged if not for the statement. In affirming the judgment, the court noted that **courts in Texas and Massachusetts had found newspaper articles relevant in regard to reputation evidence**. Since the brothers could not show they had been falsely "accused of racist renting policies" or were defamed, the court of appeals held for the district. *Sisley v. Seattle School Dist. No. 1*, 169 Wash.App. 1035 (Wash. Ct. App. 2012).

◆ A Colorado college student who attended a two-year program to obtain her state teaching license was hired by a school district as a teacher-in-residence. She claimed her principal refused to sign a form she needed to obtain a state teaching license. A paraprofessional claimed the college student made threatening statements, and a police report was made. Although the student was arrested, criminal charges were later dropped. In a federal court action against the school district, she asserted that the action delayed her from attaining state teacher certification. In pretrial activity, the court noted a claim that she had not been formally observed. As this was required by the relevant collective bargaining agreement, the court held the student could pursue this aspect of her breach of contract claim. Other aspects of the contract and due process violations claims lacked merit and had to be dismissed. The court found good reason to allow a defamation claim to proceed. It had to be determined whether the statements of the assistant principal and the paraprofessional were true. And **it had to be determined if the statements were made with reckless disregard for their truth**. *Garland v. Board of Educ. of Denver Public School Dist. No. 1*, Civ. No. 11-cv-00396-REB-KMT, 2012 WL 1834478 (D. Colo. 5/21/12).

◆ An Indiana principal notified a parent that his access to the school where his three children attended would be restricted because he was a convicted sex offender. After the parent supplied proof that he was not a sex offender, the principal wrote him a formal apology. But the parent stated that school officials continued to treat him as a sex offender and spread this belief throughout the community. He and his wife sued the school board, school officials and the city, alleging slander, civil rights violations and other claims. The defendants sought to have the case dismissed, but a federal court refused to do so. The parents alleged intentional treatment different from other parents regarding the pick-up and drop-off of their children, without a rational basis. The parents also raised an issue of false allegations by the principal "accusing them of being on the run from Florida law enforcement." In pretrial activity, the court found the defamation claim was barred by the state Tort Claims Act. It noted that even were it to consider the claim, there was no publication of a false document. Moreover, **truth was a complete defense to any defamation claim**. Since the parents were unable to prove required elements of a claim for defamation, and their other claims failed, the school board, city and officials were entitled to judgment. *Luera v. FWCS Board of School Trustees*, No. 1:09-CV-136 JVB, 2011 WL 5835818 (N.D. Ind. 11/18/11).

◆ Most of the students attending a Minnesota charter school were Somali Muslims. The American Civil Liberties Union of Minnesota (ACLU) sued the charter school, its directors and state education officials in a federal court to halt the school's allegedly religious practices. The school filed five counterclaims against the ACLU, including defamation and interference with its business relationships with the parents of students. These claims were based on comments made by the ACLU outside of the litigation. The court found that charter schools were a part of the state system of public education. **Established law prohibited government bodies from suing for libel, defeating the defamation claim.** Since the claim for interference with business relationships only duplicated the defamation claim, the ACLU was entitled to dismissal of both claims. *American Civil Liberties Union of Minnesota v. Tarek Ibn Ziyad Academy*, No. 09-138, 2009 WL 4823378 (D. Minn. 12/9/09).

After two more years of pretrial activity, the academy agreed to dismiss the case. The court approved of a settlement agreement by which the school would be liable for a $267,500 payment to the ACLU. This was to be paid by Islamic Relief. *American Civil Liberties Union of Minnesota v. Tarek Ibn Ziyad Academy*, Civil No. 09-138 (DWF/JJG), 2011 WL 4537962 (D. Minn. 9/29/11).

◆ A South Carolina special education teacher formed a close bond with a student and let him use her car, unaware that he did not have a license. She also gave him school computer passwords and wrote him excuses from his classes. The principal fired her after learning of this. She was also arrested and charged with contributing to the delinquency of a minor. Later, the principal told a staff member that the teacher had "cleaned [them] out," referring to the fact that when she left, she took a great deal of equipment that she had purchased. The teacher sued the principal for defamation and other claims. The state court of appeals held that she could pursue the defamation claim against the principal because **she was accused of a crime involving moral turpitude.** *McBride v. School Dist. of Greenville County*, 698 S.E.2d 845 (S.C. Ct. App. 2010).

◆ A West Virginia school employee learned he would be transferred due to declining enrollment. He accused the school board treasurer and superintendent of being "thieves," and implied that another board member lived with "his mistress." After requesting a hearing, the employee wrote "this is the night to expose the cockroaches." He claimed that funds for the school golf team were "stolen" for team travel, although this claim had been investigated and no impropriety found. At his hearing, the employee reasserted his accusations against board members and the superintendent, never reaching the substance of his own transfer. The superintendent said he would recommend employment termination for insubordination. The employee responded with more epithets, and the board voted to fire him for insubordination. After a grievance board upheld the action, a state court ordered him reinstated. On appeal, the Supreme

Court of Appeals of West Virginia held a school board's need to conduct its affairs far outweighed any right to make personal and potentially unfounded and damaging remarks against school officials. **Statements that are knowingly false, or made with reckless disregard of whether they are true, are unprotected** by the First Amendment. The employee's speech was not protected, and the decision in his favor was reversed. *Alderman v. Pocahontas County Board of Educ.*, 223 W.Va. 431, 675 S.E.2d 907 (W.Va. 2009).

◆   A Maine student left a ham sandwich on a cafeteria table where Somali Muslim students were sitting. The school suspended the student for 10 days and classified the incident as a hate crime/bias offense. A reporter contacted the superintendent and quoted him as saying that work had to be done to bring the community together. A user of a website platform called "Associated Content" posted an Internet article that mischaracterized facts and described the response to the incident by a Somali community center as an "anti-ham response plan."

Fox Network staff members retrieved the user's contrived article, read the reporter's original article, and based a three-hour cablecast on the incident. Two Fox co-hosts repeatedly ridiculed the superintendent and attributed a contrived anti-Somali statement to him. Fox later issued a retraction and apology, but the superintendent sued one of the cohosts and others for defamation. A federal court held the statements were protected, and appeal went to the U.S. Court of Appeals, First Circuit. It held discussions of public officials deserved "breathing space" under the Constitution. **A conditional privilege of free speech may only be overcome by clear and convincing evidence that a speaker made a defamatory statement with actual knowledge of its falsity.** Courts describe this as the "actual malice" standard. While some statements were defamatory, they did not meet the actual malice standard. The "anti-ham response plan" statement was not defamatory, and it was not suggested that the co-hosts knew the Associated Content posting was false. While the cohosts carelessly relied on the Associated Content posting, this was negligence, not actual malice. *Levesque v. Doocy*, 560 F.3d 82 (1st Cir. 2009).

◆   A Nevada school administrator obtained an evaluation of courses offered by a distance learning software seller and found that they did not comply with salary enhancement provisions of the relevant collective bargaining agreement. The seller demanded recognition of its classes and threatened legal action. The administrator wrote to the seller that its courses were not "credit bearing toward any degree" offered by three universities. She noted that some courses could be completed in three to five hours and that tests could be passed without reading the material. According to the letter, no safeguards assured a candidate actually took the test. The administrator then emailed three different teachers to explain that the seller's courses were not credit-bearing toward a degree. She said some courses were not eligible for elective credit at the universities offering them.

The seller sued the district for defamation and related claims in a state court. A jury found some of the administrator's comments were defamatory and awarded the seller over $340,000. On appeal, the Supreme Court of Nevada explained that **an absolute privilege protected the administrator's letter because the seller had already demanded that the district recognize its**

courses and threatened legal action if it did not. This privilege extended to non-lawyers as well as lawyers. The administrator's writings did not impugn the seller's fitness for trade. The communications concerned the fitness of the seller's products, and she had no intent to harm the seller's business interests. As she did not show reckless disregard for the truth, the judgment was reversed. *Clark County School Dist. v. Virtual Educ. Software*, 213 P.3d 496 (Nev. 2009).

◆ A California high school principal served with distinction at several inner city schools before being assigned to Jefferson High School in Los Angeles. Jefferson significantly improved its traditionally low-achievement standing, but a series of violent disturbances occurred that resulted in several student injuries and arrests. The superintendent of schools was quoted in the media as saying "stronger leadership was needed at Jefferson," and that the principal had "retirement plans that did not fit with the district's needs." The principal was removed from the school and reassigned to a "desk job." He retired six months later and sued the school district and two superintendents in a state court for defamation and invasion of privacy. The case reached the state court of appeal. It held **the superintendent "had an official duty to communicate with the press about matters of public concern."** His duty was to inform the public about how the district would respond to the violence, and these statements were privileged. The principal's leadership was a subject of legitimate public concern, and none of the statements divulged private information. The superintendent's statements were privileged in his capacity as chief executive officer for the district. The court upheld the judgment and held the school officials were entitled to their attorneys' fees. *Morrow v. Los Angeles Unified School Dist.*, 149 Cal.App.4th 1424, 57 Cal.Rptr.3d 885 (Cal. Ct. App. 2007).

VI. SCHOOL BUS ACCIDENTS

Florida state regulations place the burden on parents to ensure the safe travel of students to and from home, when they are not in school custody. But the Court of Appeal of California has stated that a school district's duty of care to its students is based on a special relationship between the students and the district. The fact that an injury occurs off-campus may not be determinative.

A. Duty of Care

◆ A Louisiana high school student was struck and killed by a school bus as she fought with another student near their school. In a state court action for negligence, the student's mother said school employees did not supervise students, failed to timely respond to the fight and did not adequately staff the area. Eight school board employees avoided liability by asserting that no cause of action existed against them under Louisiana Statutes Section 17:439(A). This section precluded claims against school employees based on "any statement made or action taken" within the course and scope of an employee's duties and within specific guidelines for employee behavior set by a school board. As for the bus driver, the trial court held there could be no direct claim against him under Section 17:439(D). The state court of appeal reversed this ruling. Appeal reached the Supreme Court of Louisiana. It held that **persons are liable for acts of omission and acts of commission** under Civil Code Article 2315.

The court reversed the decision regarding school employees other than the drivers, ruling that a determination had to be made regarding whether their statements or actions were covered under Section 17:439(A). A lower court had correctly held the driver was subject to a direct action to the extent of his insurance coverage or self-insurance. The case was returned to the court of appeal to consider whether employee statements or actions were "within the course and scope" of their duties and whether they were within specific guidelines for employee behavior established by the school board. *Credit v. Richland Parish School Board*, 85 So.3d 669 (La. 2012).

◆ A Mississippi motorist pulled her car out of a driveway onto a public road. Her car was struck by a school bus. In a state court negligence action against the school district, a trial judge awarded $800,000 to the motorist but held she was 75% at fault, reducing the judgment against the district to $200,000. The school district appealed to the Supreme Court of Mississippi. According to the district, state law required school boards and other local entities to set reasonable and safe speed limits "upon the basis of an engineering and traffic investigation." There was evidence that in 2001, a district employee had posted two signs declaring a 30-mile-per-hour speed limit on the road without an engineering and traffic investigation. When the school district sought judgment based on the lack of a statutorily required investigation, the trial court refused to grant it, finding the speed limit had been in place since 2001 and was accepted through "implied dedication." The supreme court found no support for this ruling. Since the speed limit signs in place at the time of the accident were not valid, **the court held the motorist did not show the bus driver violated any statute or ordinance**. This undercut the trial court's finding of negligence by the school district and required that the case return to the trial court for further proceedings. *Wayne County School Dist. v. Worsham*, 83 So.3d 380 (Miss. 2012).

◆ A six-year-old California student took the bus irregularly, due to his parents' schedules. About a month after starting school, he got on his bus, but soon told the driver that he saw his father's car. The driver grabbed him by the arm and asked if he was sure, and he said he was. When the student left the bus, he could not find his father and began walking with other students. He was later struck by a car as he tried to cross a busy street. In a state court, the family sued the school district, bus driver and car driver for personal injuries. The case reached the Court of Appeal of California, which recited the general rule in the state that **"a school district owes a duty of care to its students because a special relationship exists between the students and the district."**

Once a district agreed to provide transportation for its students, it had a duty to exercise reasonable care. It rejected the district's claim that "transportation" occurred only while a bus was moving. The district had undertaken a duty of care to its students after dismissal. During bus loading, students were still on school premises, and under school supervision. So the fact that the injury took place later and off-campus did not decide the case. The lower court should have considered whether there had been a duty of supervision, and whether the duty was breached. Once the child was on the bus, the district had a duty to exercise ordinary care over him. The case was returned to the superior court to consider questions such as the foreseeability of harm and whether the bus driver should have done more to help the student. *Eric M. v. Cajon Valley Union School Dist.*, 174 Cal.App.4th 285, 95 Cal.Rptr.3d 428 (Cal. Ct. App. 2009).

◆   A Florida middle school student was killed while crossing a street to get to her bus stop. She was using the stop because of problems she had with other students at the stop on her side of the road. Her school counselor told her to use the stop across the street. Her family sued the board in a state court. Appeal reached the state court of appeal. It found that if a student was harmed before reaching a designated bus stop (or after leaving one), the student was outside the board's duty of care. Florida regulations placed the burden on parents to ensure the safe travel of students to and from home, when they were not in school custody. **Since the student was under the exclusive control of her parents while she walked to the bus stop, the school district had no duty to ensure her safe arrival.** The court affirmed the judgment for the board. *Francis v. School Board of Palm Beach County*, 29 So.3d 441 (Fla. Dist. Ct. App. 2010).

◆   A nine-year-old North Carolina student was seated on a school bus next to another student who was poking holes in paper with a pencil. The driver told the other student to put the pencil away and told the student to turn around in the seat and stay out of the aisle. When the bus went over a dip in the road, the driver heard a scream. The student's left eye was punctured by the other student's pencil, causing a serious injury. In a State Tort Claims Act proceeding before the North Carolina Industrial Commission, the student's parents claimed the bus driver's failure to supervise the other student was the cause of the eye injury. The commission found the student's injuries resulted from the driver's negligence and awarded the student $150,000 in damages. The state court of appeals upheld the award. **Evidence supported the commission's finding that the driver had a duty of care to enforce school safety policies but failed to do so.** And this failure was the legal cause of the student's eye injury. *Lucas v. Rockingham County Schools,* 692 S.E.2d 890 (N.C. Ct. App. 2010).

B. Governmental Immunity

◆   A Texas student was assaulted by a classmate on a school bus. He sued the school district for negligence in a state court. Appeal reached the state court of appeals, which sought to determine whether the school district had waived its immunity under the Texas Tort Claims Act. State law immunity protects Texas state political subdivisions from suit absent an express statutory waiver. **An exception to immunity applies to the operation or use of a motor-driven vehicle if the employee would be personally liable under state law.**
According to the student, his injury "arose from" the operation or use of a motor-driven vehicle. He said that at the time of the assault, the driver allowed students on the bus to stand up, and that the driver failed to stop the bus or to take other action while the assault was taking place. The court held there has to

be some nexus between an injury and operation or use of a motor vehicle to create liability. When an injury occurs on a school bus and the "bus is only the setting for the injury," immunity is not waived. Each of the student's claims related to supervisory responsibilities that were independent of the operation or use of the bus. Allowing students to stand up related to the control of passengers and not to the operation or use of the bus. As a result, the court affirmed the judgment finding no waiver of immunity. *Simon v. Blanco Independent School Dist.*, No. 03-10-00122-CV, 2011 WL 255540 (Tex. Ct. App. 1/18/11).

◆   According to a complaint filed in the Alabama state court system, a school bus was involved in an accident with a stationary vehicle. Several students on the bus were injured. Among the claims were negligent entrustment against the board of education, negligence and wantonness against the bus driver, and loss of services against the board and driver. A county court dismissed case based on Article I, Section 14, an immunity provision of the state constitution. Appeal reached the Supreme Court of Alabama, which held **city boards of education have absolute immunity from civil actions**. Like county school boards, Alabama city education boards are considered agencies of the state and not municipal subdivisions. No mention is made in state laws of any ability to sue a city education board. Since no legislation allowed a tort action against a city education board, the board was a local agency of the state with immunity from tort actions. *Ex Parte Phenix City Board of Educ.*, 67 So.3d 56 (Ala. 2011).

◆   A disabled Ohio student rode a bus with three middle school boys with special needs. An aide on the afternoon route saw a male student with his hand up the student's dress. They were immediately separated. When questioned, the female student said the male student had sexually molested her each day on the afternoon route. The parents claimed that the assaulting student had serious behavior problems and exhibited physical and verbal aggression. They sued the school board and officials in the state court system, asserting negligence and related claims. A trial court denied the board's motion for state law immunity.

The case reached the Supreme Court of Ohio, which noted that state law barred immunity for injuries arising from the "operation of any motor vehicle," but did not define the term "operation." According to the family, the term meant all the essential functions that a driver is trained or required to do by law, not just driving. A dictionary definition of "operate" is to "control or direct the functioning of." This suggested to the court that the term is limited to driving the vehicle itself. **The court held the exception to immunity for negligent operation of a motor vehicle applied only to negligence in driving the vehicle.** It held for the school board. *Doe v. Marlington Local School Dist. Board of Educ.*, 122 Ohio St.3d 124, 907 N.E.2d 706 (Ohio 2009).

◆   A Texas pre-kindergartner fell asleep on her school bus and was locked inside it for a full afternoon. After arriving at school, the driver and bus monitor failed to check the bus before locking it. The child's parents sued the school district for negligence. The district claimed sovereign immunity, and the case reached the Court of Appeals of Texas. It explained that the Texas Code waives immunity for property damage, personal injury and death that "arises from the operation or use of a motor-driven vehicle." The court noted that in an earlier case, **the Supreme Court of Texas had found that the unloading of a school bus was part of the transportation process**. Here, the family's claim was based on the "use of the bus." Since the locking of bus doors was distinguished from negligent supervision, sovereign immunity was waived. *Elgin Independent School Dist. v. R.N.*, 191 S.W.3d 263 (Tex. Ct. App. 2006).

VII. SCHOOL SECURITY

In Hood v. Suffolk City School Board, *below, the U.S. Court of Appeals, Fourth Circuit, rejected a Virginia teacher's claim to a constitutional right to a safe workplace. The* Hood *court noted this type of claim had been rejected 20 years ago by the U.S. Supreme Court in* Collins v. City of Harker Heights, *503 U.S. 115 (1992). In that case, the Court refused to find government employers have a duty under the Due Process Clause to provide safe workplaces.*

State legislatures have enacted laws regarding school safety, but most of the lawsuits arising from breaches of school security remain rooted in negligence principles. School districts owe their students a duty of reasonable care, and schools have a well-established duty to supervise and protect their students.

A. Duty of Care

◆ A Virginia teacher complained of a wet, moldy classroom and said it caused a rash and irritated her eyes. The teacher said that by her second week of teaching, she had serious allergic reactions. Efforts were made to clean the room more often. A dehumidifier was provided, and air testing was conducted. After the teacher obtained a physician's note instructing her not to return to work, an administrator told the teacher to pursue a workers' compensation claim. When the teacher sought to be transferred, the school board denied her request. She sued the board in a state court. After the board removed the case to a federal court, the teacher amended her complaint to assert violation of a liberty interest in bodily integrity and a deprivation of her due process rights. She accused the board of deliberate acts such as intentionally concealing mold. Her case reached the U.S. Court of Appeals, Fourth Circuit, which held **federal courts have recognized a liberty interest in bodily integrity in limited circumstances**, such as the sexual molestation of a child. Despite her claim to a constitutional interest in bodily integrity, the court held the teacher was in truth claiming a right to be free from a dangerous condition in the workplace. This theory was rejected by the U.S. Supreme Court in 1992. As there was no right to be free from an unreasonable risk of harm in the workplace, the court held for the board. *Hood v. Suffolk City School Board*, 469 Fed.Appx. 154 (4th Cir. 2012).

◆ New York's highest court denied an appeal by a student who sought to hold school officials liable for injuries he suffered in a hallway fight at school. According to the student, officials violated their duty of supervision and did not comply with a school safety plan requiring staff hallway patrols. In prior court activity, a state appellate division court held the evidence demonstrated that the supervision provided was sufficient and that **the attack was sudden and spontaneous, and could not have been prevented by more supervision**. In addition, a witness testified that employees who were designated to keep the halls clear were doing their jobs at the time of the fight. *Espino v. New York City Board of Educ.*, 17 N.Y.3d 709, 930 N.Y.S.2d 554 (Table) (N.Y. 2011).

◆   An Iowa student used a BB gun to shoot a classmate on a sidewalk outside their high school at dismissal time. Law officers arrested the student and two other boys later in the day when they used the same BB gun during a theft. Although the student claimed the shooting was accidental, he was placed in juvenile detention and expelled. In a negligence case by the classmate's mother, a jury returned a verdict for the district and officials. On appeal, the Court of Appeals of Iowa noted that **schools must exercise the same care as a parent of ordinary prudence would in comparable circumstances**. In the month before the shooting, the student had been involved in three fights at school. The school had responded with a student responsibility plan and placed him on "full escort" at all times. In addition, the student was suspended and recommended for alternative placement the next year. The court found evidence from which the jury could find the school had responded appropriately and followed district disciplinary policies. Moreover, the fights may have been provoked and were "mutual" in nature. The court held for the district and officials. *Herrig v. Dubuque Community School Dist.*, 772 N.W.2d 15 (Iowa Ct. App. 2009).

◆   In 2005, an Oregon school district adopted a policy that any employee having a firearm in school or at a school event would face discipline up to and including termination. A teacher had an ex-husband whom she feared might turn violent. She sought to bring a handgun to school, asserting that she was licensed to carry a concealed weapon and that she needed it for self-defense. The district's human resources department warned her that she could be fired for bringing the gun to school, and she sued. She claimed that the policy was illegal because **Oregon law states that only the legislature can "regulate" firearms or pass ordinances concerning them**. A court dismissed her claim, holding that the law didn't apply to workplace policies, and the Oregon Court of Appeals affirmed. The state law was only intended to prevent cities and counties from creating a patchwork of conflicting laws concerning firearms. It was not intended to reach as far as internal employment policies. *Doe v. Medford School Dist. 549C*, 221 P.3d 787 (Or. Ct. App. 2009).

B. Governmental Immunity

Public school officers and employees enjoy qualified immunity if they are performing discretionary acts involving the exercise of judgment or personal deliberation. It is further required that the government official or employee be acting in good faith and within the scope of their authority.

◆   A Minnesota kindergartner said that he did not want to go outside with his class for recess. He stayed in a supervised detention room in the school office, but an aide instructed him to use a lavatory down the hallway instead of the one in the detention area. While in the lavatory, the kindergartner was sexually assaulted by a recent high school graduate who had been inside the school several times in the days before the assault to do janitorial work. On the day of the assault, he entered the school through a side door without signing in and obtaining a visitor badge. The kindergartner's mother sued the school district for negligent supervision and failure to have and enforce a specific policy on school security. A court denied pretrial judgment on the negligent supervision claim, and the Court of Appeals of Minnesota agreed that a trial was required on that issue. The aide had let the kindergartner go unaccompanied to a restroom outside a detention room equipped with its own lavatory, and the graduate somehow got in the school building without signing in and wearing a badge. But **the school district was entitled to immunity for not having a specific policy to protect elementary children from intruders**. These decisions took place at the planning level and involved the evaluation of financial, political, economic and social factors. *Doe v. Independent School Dist. No. 2154*, No. A09-2235, 2010 WL 3545585 (Minn. Ct. App. 9/14/10).

◆ A Georgia student was severely beaten by a classmate after they left their classroom. The principal and vice principal found the student unconscious and bleeding profusely in the hallway. According to the student's parents, the school's only effort to assist him was taking him to the school clinic, where a nurse cleaned his wounds. They claimed he was placed in an intensive care unit for traumatic brain injury due to the lack of immediate treatment. The parents filed a negligence action against the district, asserting that the school knew of the classmate's extensive history of violence and that a teacher ignored his threats against the student. The court awarded judgment to the district, and the parents appealed. The Supreme Court of Georgia found a state constitutional provision requires schools to prepare safety plans to address violence in schools, and to provide a safe environment. But qualified immunity protects officials for their discretionary actions taken within the scope of their official authority. **Public officials and employees may be held personally liable only for ministerial acts that are negligently performed, and for those acts performed with malice or intent to injure.** School officials had exercised discretion in how they created a school safety plan. Their alleged malice in not providing the student immediate medical care did not deprive them of immunity. *Murphy v. Bajjani*, 282 Ga. 197, 647 S.E.2d 54 (Ga. 2007).

C. Building and Grounds

1. Visitors and Intruders

◆ A Nebraska school policy required visitors to check in at the main office of the school. However, an intruder entered the school without being observed by school secretaries. Teachers asked the intruder if they could help him, but he ignored them. One teacher directed him to a restroom and told him to report to the office after he was finished. Another teacher reported him to the office, but she did not continue observing him. After the teachers lost sight of the intruder, he went to another restroom and sexually assaulted a five-year-old student. The student's mother sued the school district for negligence. A state court awarded pretrial judgment to the district, but on appeal, the Supreme Court of Nebraska stated that a trial was required. In this case, the district owed the student a duty of reasonable care. Whether the assault was reasonably foreseeable was a fact-specific inquiry for a jury. **As the teachers had permitted the intruder to evade them, reasonable minds could differ as to whether the assault was foreseeable.** It had been improper for the lower court to award judgment to the district, and the case was returned to it for further proceedings. *A.W. v. Lancaster County School District 0001*, 784 N.W.2d 907 (Neb. 2010).

◆   Washington school employees identified a former student as the person who broke into a junior high school and damaged it, based on their review of surveillance camera video. After police arrested him and charged him with criminal conduct, fingerprint analysis showed he was not the offender. By the time the fingerprint analysis exonerated him, the former student had spent 19 days in jail. He sued the school district in the state court system for malicious prosecution. The state court of appeals held the former student did not satisfy the legal requirements for a malicious prosecution claim. **He had to show more than just a mistake by proving "evil intent," but he failed to do so.** *Hubbard v. Eastmont School Dist. No. 206*, 152 Wash.App. 1040 (Wash. Ct. App. 2009).

◆   A Kansas jogger was approached by a municipal police officer because her dog was running loose on school grounds. She had an unloaded handgun with her. A state court acquitted the jogger of a criminal charge of possessing a firearm on school property, since there were no classes in session and no school-sponsored activities at the time. The Court of Appeals of Kansas noted **state law declared that possession of a firearm by any person (other than a law enforcement officer) in or on any school property or grounds was a criminal offense.** None of the exceptions to the law applied here. Whether school was in session was irrelevant, and the court reversed the judgment. *State of Kansas v. Toler*, 41 Kan.App.2d 986, 206 P.3d 548 (Kan. Ct. App. 2009).

2. Building Entry Policies

Doe v. Covington County School Dist., *675 F.3d 849 (5th Cir. 2012), below, considered school liability for alleged constitutional violations under* DeShaney v. Winnebago County Dep't of Social Services, *489 U.S. 189 (1989). In* DeShaney, *the Supreme Court held a child had no constitutional right to be protected by a government agency from harm by a third party.*

◆   A Mississippi adult was able to sign a young child out of school six different times by falsely indicating he was her parent. He sexually molested her and returned her to school. After the child's parents learned of this, they sued the school district in a federal court. Among their claims was that the school's check-out policy violated the Constitution by allowing employees to release a child without first verifying the signer's identity or authority to sign out the child. A federal court held constitutional liability was foreclosed under *DeShaney v. Winnebago County Dep't of Social Services*, 489 U.S. 189 (1989). Appeal reached the Fifth Circuit, where a three-judge panel held for the family. A majority of judges of the Fifth Circuit voted to rehear the case and found a constitutional claim could proceed only if the district had a duty to protect the student from a private party. This required a special relationship between the student and district. But state compulsory attendance laws did not create a special relationship between schools and their students. The court held **public schools have no special relationship with students that would require protection from harm by private actors such as the adult in this case.** The parents raised other arguments, but the court rejected them. It held the student's young age was not a relevant factor under the special relationship analysis. Carelessness by school employees did not mean they knew that the adult was unauthorized to sign out the child. And the parents did not claim the district was deliberately indifferent to a known danger. The court held for the district. *Doe v. Covington County School Dist.*, 675 F.3d 849 (5th Cir. 2012).

◆ After a sex offender entered a Texas school and exposed himself to a child, the district implemented a regulation requiring every visitor to produce a state-issued photo identification as a condition of entering secure areas where students were present. Under the regulation, pictures were taken of visitor identification cards but no other information was taken. The system enabled schools to check visitor names and birth dates to determine if they were listed on national registered sex-offender databases. A parent refused to allow her child's school to either scan her driver's license or permit manual entry of her information. As a result, she was denied access to areas of the school. She and her husband sued, challenging the policy as a violation of their constitutional rights. A federal court held for the district, and the Fifth Circuit affirmed. **The regulation addressed a compelling state interest and was not overly intrusive.** The system took only the minimal information needed to determine sex offender status. *Meadows v. Lake Travis Independent School Dist.*, 397 Fed.Appx. 1 (5th Cir. 2010).

◆ A Chicago third-grader had conflicts with another girl at school. The other girl's mother and a companion threatened the student's mother at her home. The school principal set up a meeting between the families. Near the end of a school day, the other girl's parent and an adult cousin fought the student's mother and grandmother in a school office. The principal called police and swore out criminal complaints for disorderly conduct against all four adults. Criminal charges were dismissed, and the principal later said he had made a mistake and should have only had two of the women arrested. The parent and grandparent sued. The U.S. Court of Appeals, Seventh Circuit, noted the issue was not whether a parent or grandparent had actually committed disorderly conduct. **It was only necessary to show a reasonable person in the principal's position had probable cause to believe there was disorderly conduct.** The principal entered a chaotic situation and could easily have viewed the mother to be an equal participant in the fight. Each of the family's civil rights claims failed. *Stokes v. Board of Educ. of City of Chicago*, 599 F.3d 617 (7th Cir. 2010).

CHAPTER THIRTEEN

Interscholastic Athletics

I. HIGH SCHOOL ATHLETICS

A. Eligibility Rules and Restrictions

Courts do not generally interfere in a voluntary state athletic association's student-athlete eligibility rulings, unless a member's financial or property rights are involved or there is evidence of a serious mistake or wrongdoing. As the Supreme Court of Oklahoma has held, participation in interscholastic athletics is not a right but a privilege subject to state eligibility rules.

1. Transfer Students

◆ Parents of a Virginia student-athlete were unable to convince the Fourth Circuit Court of Appeals that the state high school league's transfer rule violated their child's constitutional rights. The court affirmed the judgment of a lower court and held it properly dismissed two procedural claims by the parents. It also held their claims under the Due Process Clause were properly dismissed. **While parents have constitutional rights to control the education of their children, they lack rights to control individual aspects of their children's education,** such as participation in interscholastic sports and other activities. *Bailey v. Virginia High School League*, 488 Fed.Appx. 714 (4th Cir. 2012).

◆   Bylaw 13 of the Kentucky High School Athletic Association (KHSAA) limited the merit-based scholarship assistance that a student could receive while remaining eligible for KHSAA-sanctioned high school athletics. Kentucky private school students challenged Bylaw 13 in a federal court, and the case reached the U.S. Court of Appeals, Sixth Circuit. It found the bylaw intended to prevent the recruitment of student-athletes by member schools. It did so by limiting merit-based financial aid to 25% of the cost of tuition and banning students from accepting financial aid from a source that was not under the custody and control of a member school or its governing board. **The court rejected a claim that the grouping of Catholic schools into a class in the bylaw was discrimination.** The classification placed Catholic schools into a broader category of private schools that treated schools alike in relevant ways.

No religious discrimination was found, as the bylaw applied in the same way to all non-public schools regardless of a religious affiliation. Although the U.S. Supreme Court has recognized a fundamental right of parents to direct and control the education of their children, this right "does not extend to a right to demand that their children be allowed to participate without restrictions in extracurricular sports" in the school selected by parents. The bylaw had a legitimate purpose to prevent and deter recruiting by not allowing member schools to "pay" student-athletes to play at a school through financial aid. *Seger v. Kentucky High School Athletic Ass'n*, 453 Fed.Appx. 630 (6th Cir. 2011).

◆   A Minnesota student said he was falsely accused of putting drugs in a meal that a class was making. He was suspended from interscholastic activities and transferred to a charter school. After transferring, the student learned he could appeal the athletic eligibility ruling and sought to appeal. But the appeal was denied, and because the charter school did not offer any interscholastic sports, he was unable to continue wrestling. In a state court action, the student claimed he was denied due process because he was not offered a hearing before he transferred. When the case reached the state court of appeals, it held the student would not be eligible to participate in league activities even if it ruled in his favor on the hearing issue. **A state high school athletic league rule declared transfer students ineligible for interscholastic sports for one year after a transfer**, making the case moot. *C.I.H. v. Anoka-Hennepin Public Schools, ISD No. 12*, No. A11-2158, 2012 WL 2369000 (Minn. Ct. App. 6/25/12).

◆   An Indiana student hoped to get a college basketball scholarship. Her AAU coach suggested that she transfer to a high school where he coached to improve her recruiting chances. Near this time, the student's family experienced severe setbacks, including the incarceration of her father, foreclosure on the family's house and a reduction in her mother's work hours. The AAU coach worked at a high school in a city where the student's extended family lived. But the student's high school refused to approve her transfer request, contending it was "for primarily athletic reasons" in violation of state athletic association Rule 19-4. It also asserted undue influence by the AAU coach, in violation of association Rule 20-1. After review by the athletic association, the transfer was found to violate both rules. Appeal reached the Supreme Court of Indiana, which found the association's decisions were entitled to deference. Numerous statements by the student and her family supported the conclusion that the family planned to move before the foreclosure. Witnesses confirmed recruiting efforts by the AAU coach. **The association had considered the evidence from the witnesses and assessed their credibility, finding the transfer was primarily for athletic reasons.** Substantial evidence supported the association's findings, and the court reversed a lower court order that found for the student. *Indiana High School Athletic Ass'n v. Watson*, 938 N.E.2d 672 (Ind. 2010).

◆   A Louisiana student transferred to a different public high school. He asked the Louisiana High School Athletic Association (LHSAA) to rule on his eligibility. The LHSAA determined there had not been a bona fide change of residence under its "transfer rule" and that he was ineligible to play football during his first year at the new school. His parents sued the LHSAA in a state court for an order allowing him to compete in varsity athletics at his new school. The case was dismissed on a technicality, and by the time an appeal reached the state court of appeal the student had graduated from high school. For this reason, the court held the claim for an order against the LHSAA requiring the association to allow his participation in sports was moot. As for the student's challenge to the transfer rule and the LHSAA's eligibility ruling, the court found **LHSAA actions were "internal affairs of a voluntary association."**

According to the court, an amateur organization conducting sports competitions maintained exclusive authority over a specific class of amateur athletes. While the lower court had incorrectly declined to consider claims for damages for alleged deprivation of constitutional rights, the court of appeal rejected the constitutional issues. LHSAA investigations and the enforcement of its rules were not "state action." As the student had no due process right to interscholastic athletic participation and did not advance a valid equal protection claim, the court affirmed the judgment on those claims. *Menard v. Louisiana High School Athletic Ass'n*, 30 So.3d 790 (La. Ct. App. 2009).

◆   An Oklahoma student athlete's parent made a negative comment about the basketball coach after a game and later refused to discuss the incident with the district superintendent. The parents were then barred from school property. The student quit the team and two months later transferred to a different school. The Oklahoma Secondary School Activities Association (OSSAA) denied the student's request for a waiver from its transfer rule, which bars transfer students from playing varsity sports for one year unless the OSSAA grants a waiver. A state court granted the family's petition for relief from the OSSAA ruling. On appeal, the Supreme Court of Oklahoma noted that OSSAA rules explicitly bar hardship waivers when circumstances indicate discontent with the school in which eligibility has been established. **Participation in interscholastic athletics is not a right but a privilege subject to OSSAA eligibility rules.** Courts do not generally interfere in a voluntary association's internal affairs unless a member's financial or property rights are involved or there is evidence of a serious mistake or wrongdoing. No such mistake had occurred here, and the lower court committed error in ruling otherwise. *Morgan v. Oklahoma Secondary School Activities Ass'n*, 207 P.3d 362 (Okla. 2009).

◆   The U.S. Court of Appeals, Eleventh Circuit, affirmed a court ruling against a Georgia high school football coach and former players who alleged harm when the state high school association forfeited their games for a season. The association found that **the school improperly included a nonresident player on the team**. The lower court rejected student claims based on lost opportunities to receive college scholarships. Students have no constitutional right to participate in athletics. As the coach was not discharged or demoted, his constitutional rights were also not violated. *Stewart v. Bibb County Board of Educ.*, 195 Fed.Appx. 927 (11th Cir. 2006).

◆   A Kansas parent claimed that a public high school athletic director recruited his son extensively. The student decided to transfer. He sent the athletic director a "limited eligibility transfer form" that would allow him to remain eligible for non-varsity sports after a transfer. The director refused to sign the eligibility form, asserting that the transfer was athletically motivated. The state athletic association approved the denial, relying on statements by school officials, who declared that the parent considered his son's athletic opportunities when making the transfer decision. The parent claimed the transfer was not motivated by athletics, and he sued. A federal court noted that the student would miss only 18 weeks of basketball eligibility and could still practice with the football team if it did not issue an order. The board had a legitimate basis for denying the eligibility request. **As there is no recognized property interest in playing non-varsity sports, the court found no equal protection violation.** *Love v. Kansas State High School Activities Ass'n*, No. 04-1319-JTM, 2004 WL 2357879 (D. Kan. 10/15/04).

2. Other Rules

State athletic associations have broad powers to interpret their own rules. The Supreme Court of Appeals of West Virginia held a dispute regarding the participation of student-athletes had to be resolved by the state athletic association and was beyond court review. Decisions by game officials were not reviewable by a court. Many courts have found no constitutional interest to participate in interscholastic athletics or other extracurricular activities.

◆   With 14 seconds left in a West Virginia high school football playoff game, players threw punches at each other. Others from the sideline joined in. Faced with a near riot, police used pepper spray to gain control of the field and ordered the officials into their locker room for safety. The game was called. Four players from each team were ejected for unsportsmanlike conduct. After the game, officials reviewed their cards and noted that a wrong jersey number had been recorded for one ejected player. A report concerning the game was sent to the state athletic association within 24 hours, listing the correct jersey numbers of ejected players. Four players from the winning team were suspended from the next game, which was a semifinal playoff game. But they won a temporary order from a state court, asserting officials had misidentified them and suspended them after the game had ended. As a result of the court order, the suspended players played in the semifinal game, and their team won.

After a hearing, the court found officials violated state athletic association rules by ejecting the players after the game had ended. On appeal, the Supreme Court of Appeals of West Virginia prohibited the trial court from enforcing the order. It held **a dispute regarding the participation of the ejected players had to be resolved by the state athletic association and was beyond court review**. The association then announced that the school could not play in the championship game. Weeks later, the supreme court of appeals held officials complied with state rules by filing an initial report within 24 hours. The association's suspension powers were not limited to on-field ejections and the courts were not to review rulings by officials. *West Virginia Secondary School Activity Comm'n v. Webster*, 228 W.Va. 75, 717 S.E.2d 859 (W.Va. 2011).

◆ West Virginia state athletic association rules imposed a two-game suspension on any student-athlete who was ejected from a basketball game. After being ejected from a game, a student-athlete had physical contact with a referee, triggering another rules violation. He sued the West Virginia Secondary Schools Activities Commission (SSAC), seeking an order to prevent enforcement of the two-game suspension. Meanwhile, his school suspended him for four games. By the time the court held a hearing, the parties had reached an agreement by which he would miss three games. Despite the agreement, the court proceeded to consider an SSAC rule regarding the forfeiture of games involving suspended players. The court struck down the rule and another SSAC rule based on its lack of provisions for administrative review.

The SSAC appealed to the Supreme Court of Appeals of West Virginia, which reversed the decision for the student. **The lower court's attempt to declare an SSAC rule on multi-game suspensions unconstitutional was improper.** The SSAC was not a state actor, and no due process right was implicated. *Mayo v. West Virginia Secondary Schools Activities Comm'n*, 223 W.Va. 88, 672 S.E.2d 224 (W.Va. 2008).

◆ A Delaware student played varsity basketball and remained in the school district when his mother moved to Georgia. She executed a power of attorney authorizing the basketball coach and a lawyer to make decisions regarding her son. After the lawyer came to the school for a copy of the student's transcript, the school investigated his relationship with the student. The principal concluded that the power of attorney was insufficient and that the student was not a resident. The principal informed the Delaware Interscholastic Athletic Association (DIAA) that the school had used an ineligible player, and stated that the school planned to forfeit all the games in which the student participated. He asked the DIAA to waive the forfeiture penalties. The DIAA denied the waiver request, and the state education board (SBE) upheld that decision. A court issued a letter opinion explaining that **Delaware law vested the DIAA with the power to decide all controversies involving its rules, regulations and waivers**. State law provided for appeals of DIAA decisions to the SBE, but declared that "the decision of the SBE shall be final and not subject to further appeal." *Cape Henlopen School Dist. v. Delaware Interscholastic Athletic Ass'n.*, No. 08A-01-003 ESB, 2009 WL 388944 (Del. Super. 1/28/09).

B. Athletic and Extracurricular Suspensions

In addition to refusing to recognize any constitutional right to participate in interscholastic athletics or other extracurricular activities, the courts have rejected the argument that the possibility of obtaining a college athletic scholarship is an interest protected by any constitutional provision. Students also lack rights to attend or play sports at a particular school.

◆   A Minnesota student-athlete was accused of holding a baseball teammate down while another team member put his genitals in his face. School officials suspended the student pending further investigation. An investigation found it likely that the student engaged in "sexual assault, bullying and hazing," and the school sought to discipline him under its anti-bullying and anti-hazing policy.

After studying at home for the rest of the school year, the student accepted a transfer to another school for his senior year. His parents filed a federal district court action against the school district. While the student challenged the initial five-day suspension, the court addressed only the transfer. It held that a transfer to a different high school did not deprive him of any property interest. While it might be a hardship to the student, state law declared attendance at a particular school a privilege. Federal courts have generally held that an alternative school placement implicates no due process rights. Under state high school association rules, the student would be excluded from varsity sports during his senior year due to the transfer. While the court agreed that this was a hardship, it did not violate his constitutional due process rights, since this was the result of the association's rule. **Courts have rejected claims that students have a property interest in varsity sports.** Since students had no right to attend a particular school, there was no right to play sports at a particular school. The court found no constitutional requirement that the student be allowed to stay at his school and repair his reputation. As there was no constitutional violation, the court denied his request for relief. *J.K. v. Minneapolis Public Schools (Special School Dist. No. 1)*, 849 F.Supp.2d 865 (D. Minn. 2011).

◆   Upset that his son was not playing a particular position, a parent approached a coach during a high school baseball game. A harsh exchange of words followed, and school officials banned the parent from all athletic events for one year. The parent sued the school board in a federal court for constitutional rights violations. After the court denied him temporary relief, he filed a notice of dismissal. The school district opposed dismissal because it appeared that the parent had filed a complaint with the Ohio Civil Rights Commission. Under federal rules, this meant he lost the right to voluntary dismissal. **The court exercised its discretion to dismiss the case, even though he would simply be pursuing his claims with the state.** *Pennington v. Lake Local Schools Board of Educ.*, 257 F.R.D. 629 (N.D. Ohio 2009).

◆   A Kentucky high school student admitted to the school principal that he had been drinking alcohol before coming to a school dance. The school board excluded him from playing basketball and all other extracurricular activities. He sued the board and principal, asserting that the discipline was arbitrary and capricious. He further alleged bias and due process violations. A court dismissed the complaint, and the student appealed. The Court of Appeals of Kentucky noted that students have no fundamental or vested property right to participate in interscholastic athletics. For that reason, the student's constitutional claims were properly dismissed. **A school board may suspend or expel a student for violating lawful school regulations.** However, the student claimed that the board acted arbitrarily and capriciously in denying his opportunity to participate in interscholastic athletics. The court held that he stated a viable claim for arbitrary and capricious action by the board and principal. The case required a trial. *Critchelow v. Breckinridge County Board of Educ.*, No. 2005-CA-001194-MR, 2006 WL 3456658 (Ky. Ct. App. 2006).

◆ A Washington school staff member saw a beer container in a student-athlete's car, and a search yielded an empty beer carton, cigars and tobacco. The school suspended the student for 10 days for violating a school policy against drinking alcohol as a member of the football team. An athletic board suspended him from one football game and five wrestling matches. He had to forfeit his football letter and individual honors and was recommended for alcohol evaluation and treatment. The principal upheld both the academic and athletic sanctions pursuant to an informal conference, as did a district hearing officer and the school board. When the student sued, a state court held for the district.

The state court of appeals held that **interscholastic sports participation is a privilege, not a constitutionally protected property or liberty interest**. The district provided the student with more process than required under the circumstances by applying the state law procedures for short-term academic suspensions. It was not required to provide him with the kind of protections he would receive for an expulsion. The judgment for the district was affirmed. *Taylor v. Enumclaw School Dist. No. 216*, 133 P.3d 492 (Wash. Ct. App. 2006).

C. Drug Testing

Drug testing by urinalysis has been deemed a Fourth Amendment "search." Testing limited to interscholastic sports participants has met with widespread court approval. Courts have held student-athletes to a higher standard of conduct than other students in drug-testing cases, due to the representative role they play and their reduced expectations of privacy. For drug search cases involving broader student populations, see Chapter Two, Section II.B.

◆ A Wyoming school board grew concerned over pervasive student drug and alcohol use. It adopted a policy requiring extracurricular participants in grades 7-12 to consent to random testing for drugs and alcohol. A group of students and parents brought a state court challenge to the policy under the state and U.S. Constitutions. Appeal reached the Supreme Court of Wyoming, where the families conceded that the policy did not violate the Fourth Amendment. While they contended the Wyoming Constitution afforded greater privacy protections than the Fourth Amendment, the court disagreed. An extensive review of state and federal cases on student testing programs for extracurricular participants led the court to find most courts reviewing random substance testing of students in extracurricular activities applied some version of the "reasonableness test." Similar student testing programs had been upheld in *Joye v. Hunterdon Cent. Regional High School Board of Educ.*, 176 N.J. 568 (N.J. 2003) and *Linke v. Northwestern School Corp.*, 763 N.E.2d 972 (Ind. 2002).

The random testing program disapproved in *York v. Wahkiakum School Dist. No. 200*, this chapter involved a state constitutional provision that was markedly different from the Fourth Amendment. By contrast, the Wyoming Supreme Court held Article One, Section Four of the Wyoming Constitution had similar language to the Fourth Amendment. The court held the testing policy was less intrusive than the one upheld by the Supreme Court in *Vernonia School Dist. 47J v. Acton*, this chapter. **Deterring drug and alcohol abuse by students is an important and legitimate concern.** While the families raised due process and equal protection claims, the court held them meritless. *Hageman v. Goshen County School Dist. No. 1*, 256 P.3d 487 (Wyo. 2011).

◆ A California school board expanded a random drug-testing program that had been previously limited to student-athletes. Although the superintendent said he had little reason to suspect students involved in competitive recreational activities (CRAs) used substances at a higher rate than others, he wanted to test as many students as possible. When the policy was approved, it covered 56.8% of high school students in the district, applying to CRAs such as choir, band, science bowl, "tri-mathalon," mock trial and the Future Farmers of America.

Parents of two honor roll students sued the school district in a state superior court for violation of their privacy rights under the state constitution. The court granted the students' request for a preliminary order halting the testing. Appeal went to the state court of appeal. It found the district offered "vague and shifting justifications" for testing CRA participants, and held the policy intruded upon privacy interests protected by the state constitution. **"Unlike the federal Constitution, the California Constitution contains an explicit guarantee of the right to privacy."** CRA participants did not have reduced expectations of privacy in comparison to others. Some CRAs were curricular and some fulfilled college admissions requirements. The court held the superior court did not abuse its discretion in finding the students were entitled to an injunction. They were likely to prevail in further activity by showing a sufficient expectation of privacy to pursue state constitutional claims. *Brown v. Shasta Union High School Dist.*, No. C061972, 2010 WL 3442147 (Cal. Ct. App. 9/2/10).

◆ After a 2000 survey indicated that 50% of student-athletes in a Washington school district self-identified as drug and/or alcohol users, the district began a random testing program. Participants had to agree to be tested for drug use as a condition of playing extracurricular sports. Drug test results under the program were not sent to law enforcement agencies. Students who tested positive were suspended from sports, but not from school. Parents of several students who played high school sports sued the school district, asserting the policy violated the state constitution. A state court upheld the policy, and the parents appealed.

The Supreme Court of Washington found "stark differences" between the Fourth Amendment and the Washington Constitution, which prohibits a search of a person "without authority of law." Under *New Jersey v. T.L.O.*, 469 U.S.

325 (1985), school officials may search students based on reasonable grounds for suspecting the search will turn up evidence of a violation of school rules. In *Vernonia School Dist. 47J v. Acton*, below, the Supreme Court upheld a random, suspicionless drug-testing program for student-athletes. The Washington court found the Supreme Court "never adequately explained why individual suspicion was needed in *T.L.O.* but not in *Acton*." **The state constitution provided greater protection than the Fourth Amendment**, and as students had a fundamental privacy interest in their bodily functions, the judgment was reversed. *York v. Wahkiakum School Dist. No. 200*, 178 P.3d 995 (Wash. 2008).

◆ An Oregon school district responded to increased student drug use by instituting a random drug-testing policy for all students wishing to participate in varsity athletics. Students who refused testing were suspended from sports for the rest of the season. A seventh-grader refused to sign a consent form and was suspended from sports for the season. His parents sued the district, arguing the policy violated the Fourth Amendment and the Oregon Constitution. The U.S. Supreme Court stated that the reasonableness of a student search under the Fourth Amendment is determined by balancing the interests of the government and individual. **Students have a lesser expectation of privacy than the general populace, and student-athletes have an even lower expectation of privacy.** This invasion of privacy was no worse than what is typically encountered in public restrooms. Positive test results were disclosed to only a few school employees. As the insignificant privacy invasion was outweighed by the district's important interest in addressing drug use by students who risked physical harm while playing sports, the Court held for the school district. *Vernonia School Dist. 47J v. Acton*, 515 U.S. 646, 115 S.Ct. 2386, 132 L.Ed.2d 564 (1995).

◆ The Supreme Court held that an Oklahoma school district with no discernible drug problem could test all students seeking to participate in extracurricular activities. **The Court found no reason to limit random drug testing to student-athletes**, extending *Vernonia* to cover all extracurricular activities participants. See Chapter Two, Section II.B. *Board of Educ. of Independent School Dist. 92 of Pottawatomie County v. Earls*, 536 U.S. 822, 122 S.Ct. 2559, 153 L.Ed.2d 735 (2002).

◆ A Pennsylvania school district required students who sought to participate in extracurricular activities or obtain a school parking permit to agree to random urinalysis testing. The policy was intended to deter drug use, prevent physical harm and require students to serve as role models for their peers. Two students sued the district for violating Article I, Section 8 of the Pennsylvania Constitution, which prohibits unreasonable searches and seizures. The court held for the district, but the Commonwealth Court of Pennsylvania reversed.

On appeal, the Supreme Court of Pennsylvania said Article I, Section 8 recognized stronger privacy interests than those recognized by the Fourth Amendment. And here, the policy was not a trivial incursion on student privacy. Students had a reasonable expectation that their excretory functions would only be modestly diminished at school. The district suggested no specialized need to test students for drugs and alcohol based on an existing problem, and there was no showing the group targeted for testing presented a drug problem. The policy unconstitutionally authorized a direct invasion on student privacy, with no suspicion that targeted students used drugs or alcohol in greater numbers than those who were exempt. The court held that **random testing of all students in extracurricular activities was unreasonable**, and it affirmed the judgment. *Theodore v. Delaware Valley School Dist.*, 575 Pa. 321, 836 A.2d 76 (Pa. 2003).

◆ A New Jersey school district implemented a random drug-and alcohol-testing program for all interscholastic sports participants. It later accepted a task force recommendation to expand the testing to extracurricular participants and school parking permit holders. A lawsuit challenging the policy reached the Supreme Court of New Jersey, which embraced U.S. Supreme Court language approving of minimally obtrusive drug testing to address the nationwide drug epidemic. The testing program was justified by the special need to maintain school order and safety. **Extracurricular activities participants and those seeking parking privileges subjected themselves to additional regulation that did not apply to all students.** The court rejected the parents' invitation to interpret the state constitution as providing greater protection of individual rights than the Fourth Amendment. *Joye v. Hunterdon Cent. Regional High School Board of Educ.*, 176 N.J. 568, 826 A.2d 624 (N.J. 2003).

D. Speech Claims

In Doe v. Banos, *this chapter, a New Jersey school district did not violate any speech rights by requiring consent to a "24/7" policy banning underage drinking and drugs as a condition for extracurricular participation.*

◆ A Texas cheerleader claimed two African-American students sexually assaulted her at an off-campus party. Although the two were arrested, a grand jury failed to indict them. The students returned to their regular classes, and one of them remained on the varsity basketball team. At a school basketball game, the cheerleader refused to cheer for the player and was eventually removed from the cheerleading squad. In a federal case against the school district and officials, she asserted speech, equal protection and due process claims. The court dismissed the case, and the Fifth Circuit Court of Appeals affirmed the decision.

While appeal was pending, the lower court found the claims were "patently frivolous, unreasonable, vexatious and utterly without foundation," justifying an award of attorneys' fees. On review, the Fifth Circuit held defendants in civil rights actions can recover attorneys' fees when the claims lack a basis in fact or rely on a meritless legal theory. Although her equal protection and due process claims lacked merit, **the cheerleader alleged the essential elements of a First Amendment claim. Since her "silent protest" had at least some merit, the court held the claim was not frivolous.** But the court agreed with the district court's findings that the equal protection and due process claims were frivolous. The district court was ordered to recalculate the attorneys' fees award. *Doe v. Silsbee Independent School Dist.*, 440 Fed.Appx. 421 (5th Cir. 2011).

◆   An Indiana school suspended two student-athletes from extracurricular activities after they posted suggestive pictures of themselves on Internet pages. A federal court held that the students' conduct was entitled to protection. While juvenile and silly, the images were an attempt at humor. Entertainment, even of a questionable nature, communicates ideas and deserves First Amendment protection. In the court's view, "petty disagreements among players" amounted to weak evidence of actual disruption. The court held the school's code of conduct provision on out-of-school conduct was unconstitutional. Language regarding the bringing of "discredit or dishonor upon the student or the school" reached "a substantial amount of protected conduct, and was too broad and subjective to pass constitutional standards. **But the principal was entitled to qualified immunity in this case, as the developing law on off-campus student Internet speech remained very unclear.** *T.V. v. Smith-Green Community School Corp.*, 807 F.Supp.2d 767 (N.D. Ind. 2011).

◆   A New Jersey school district required any student wishing to participate in extracurricular activities to sign an activities permission form that was also signed by a parent. The form acknowledged that a student understood that drug and alcohol use was prohibited 24 hours a day, seven days a week and 365 days a year. The parent of a student who wished to play on her school lacrosse team submitted a signed student activities permission form. But she crossed out some of the language on the form pertaining to the "24/7" policy. After the board rejected the modified form, the parent agreed to submit an unmodified form, but he sent it with a letter stating that he had "filled out the form under duress." The board declared the form invalid, and the student was excluded from lacrosse.

In a federal district court, the parent sued the board for First Amendment violations. The court denied his motion for a preliminary order that would have prevented exclusion of his child from the lacrosse team. On appeal to the U.S. Court of Appeals, Third Circuit, he argued he was being censored or compelled to make a statement against his wishes. According to the court, **predicating participation in extracurricular activities on an unconditional consent to the student participation form did not violate the parent's rights.** There was no First Amendment right to sign a school permission form "under duress" while dictating that the school allow a student's extracurricular participation. There was no evidence that the parent was otherwise inhibited from criticizing the "24/7" policy. Instead, the board had offered him opportunities to exercise his speech rights. As the lower court had correctly held against the student, the court affirmed the judgment. *Doe v. Banos*, 406 Fed.Appx. 185 (3d Cir. 2010).

◆   Boys varsity basketball players at an Oregon high school claimed their head coach used abusive tactics, intimidated them, yelled and used profanity. After a game, the coach told them he would resign if they wanted it. The players drafted a petition requesting his resignation, and all but two players signed it. After the coach brought the petition to his principal, the school's athletic director and principal met with the team and told them they would have to board the team bus for a game that evening or forfeit their privilege to play in the game. Eight of them did not board the bus. The principal permanently suspended players who refused to board the bus from the team. They sued the coach, principal, and school district for speech rights violations. A federal court upheld the discipline, finding their speech and conduct were not constitutionally protected.

On appeal, the Ninth Circuit found the petition and grievances were "a form of pure speech." The students could not be disciplined unless there was a reasonable forecast of substantial disruption or material interference. The First Amendment protected the petition and the complaints to school administrators. However, the boycott of the game substantially disrupted and materially interfered with a school activity. **If students decide not to participate in an extracurricular activity on the day it is scheduled to take place, "their conduct will inevitably disrupt or interfere with the activity."** This was true even if the event was not cancelled. The case was remanded for further proceedings. *Pinard v. Clatskanie School Dist. 6J*, 446 F.3d 964 (9th Cir. 2006).

II. DISCRIMINATION AND EQUITY

Federal civil rights laws forbid discrimination based on sex, race or disability in federally funded school athletic programs. All public school entities must also comply with the Equal Protection Clause.

A. Gender Equity and Gender Discrimination

Title IX of the Education Amendments of 1972, 20 U.S.C. § 1681(a), prohibits sex discrimination and exclusion from participation in any educational program on the basis of sex by any program or activity receiving federal funding. Federal regulations at 34 C.F.R. Part 106.41 provide guidance on equal athletic opportunities for members of both sexes. In determining whether equal opportunities exist, the U.S. Department of Education's Office for Civil Rights (OCR) considers several factors including: 1) whether selection of sports and levels of competition accommodate both sexes; 2) the provision of equipment or supplies; 3) the scheduling of games and practices; 4) travel and per diem allowances; 5) coaching and tutoring opportunities; 6) coaching and tutoring assignments and compensation; 7) provision of locker rooms, practice and competitive facilities; 8) provision of medical and training facilities and services; and publicity. See 34 C.F.R. Part 106.41(c).

◆   A group of Indiana student-athletes claimed only about half of girls' varsity basketball games in their district were scheduled on Fridays, while 95% of high school boys' games were on Fridays. They added that boys enjoyed the support of school bands, cheerleaders and dance teams while girls did not. The girls said they struggled to complete homework and study because weeknight games kept them at school late. They also said the placement of their games in "non-primetime" made them feel they were less important than the male students.

The girls filed a federal action against their school district for violations of Title IX and the Equal Protection Clause. After the court dismissed the case, the students appealed to the U.S. Court of Appeals, Seventh Circuit. It noted that Title IX bans athletic programs from "denying equivalence in benefits, such as equipment, facilities, coaching, scheduling and publicity." **Among the factors** used to assess equal athletic opportunity is the "scheduling of games and practice time." The court found the district's only response to the scheduling disparity was that it was not substantial enough to establish a Title IX violation. In the court's view, **a jury or judge could find the disparity in scheduling was substantial enough to deny equal opportunity to the girls.** A jury or trial court might also find the district had not done enough to remedy the harmful effects of this disparity. As a result, the court reversed the judgment. *Parker v. Franklin County Community School Corp.*, 667 F.3d 910 (7th Cir. 2012).

◆ Members of a Michigan middle school basketball team engaged in locker room horseplay that escalated during the course of the season. Eighth-graders on the team victimized seventh-grade team members in "games" with sexually violent overtones. One involved "turning off all the lights in the locker room, then 'humping and gyrating on the seventh graders.'" Eventually, some eighth-graders grabbed a seventh-grader, forced him to the floor, "pulled his pants down and anally penetrated him with a marker." The incidents were not met with a speedy response by school administrators, and the seventh-graders soon stopped going to the school. In a federal court, the seventh-graders sued the board of education for sexual harassment and assault by the eighth-graders. A jury returned twin $100,000 verdicts for the seventh-graders on their Title IX claims. Although the board challenged the verdicts after the trial, the court upheld them. Appeal reached the U.S. Court of Appeals, Sixth Circuit. It held **a jury could have reasonably viewed the marker incident as "not just horseplay gone awry, but rather as a serious incident of sexual assault."** A jury could have reasonably expected the school would impose more punishment than 11-day school suspensions and a month of team suspension on the eighth-graders. *Mathis v. Wayne County Board of Educ.*, 496 Fed.Appx. 513 (6th Cir. 2012).

◆ As the only female on her school's freshman football team, a Wisconsin student claimed discrimination by her head coach. She said he denied her access to the girls' locker room and kept snacks and practice schedules in the boys' locker room. After her mother complained to school officials that the coach was not letting her child obtain her equipment, the student practiced without pads and injured a shoulder and clavicle. She sued the school district and coach in a federal district court, which held that **to impose Title IX liability on a federal funding recipient, the institution must have actual notice of discrimination by employees and "deliberate indifference" to the discrimination.** There was evidence that when other players came to practice without equipment, the usual response was to find appropriate gear. In addition, the student made out a valid equal protection claim against the coach. A state law claim against him for disregarding a known danger deserved further consideration. But the student did not show the district had notice of discriminatory acts such as denial of access to the girls' locker room. As the district had no actual notice of discrimination, the Title IX claim against it was dismissed. The student claimed only that no official stopped her from harming herself by practicing without pads, and this did not support her due process claim against the district. *Elborough v. Evansville Community School Dist.*, 636 F.Supp.2d 812 (W.D. Wis. 2009).

◆   California high school girls sued their school district in a federal court for Title IX violations. They produced evidence that the difference between their enrollment numbers and the percentage of girls participating in sports was from 6.7 to 10.3 % in recent school years. The court found a 6.7% difference represented 47 girls, or at least one competitive team. Thus, the district failed the substantial proportionality inquiry of Title IX regulations. It was also found that female athletic participation rates at the school were not expanding. As a result, the district failed the second part of the regulatory test. Finally, the district failed the third part of the test because it discontinued a viable field hockey program twice due to its inability to retain a coach. **Student interest and ability, not the ability to retain a coach, determined whether the test was met.** As the district failed each part of the Title IX regulatory compliance test, the court found the district was not in compliance with Title IX. *Ollier v. Sweetwater Union High School Dist.*, 604 F.Supp.2d 1264 (S.D. Cal. 2009).

◆   Two female Tennessee students enrolled in a weightlifting/conditioning class along with 35 boys. The principal removed the girls from the class out of concern for inappropriate behavior by males, and a staff member told them to report to the guidance office to work as helpers. One student objected. A state official contacted the district's director of schools, and within a few days the principal permitted the student to return to the class. She sued the school board and officials in a federal court for violating the Equal Protection Clause and Title IX, claiming $1 million in damages. After the court dismissed the action, the U.S. Court of Appeals, Sixth Circuit, affirmed. **The principal was not executing an official policy of the board at the time he ordered her removal, and did not act as a board policy-maker.** Here, the board took immediate corrective action on her behalf as soon as the director of schools learned about the incident. As the board had no prior notice of the student's claim, it could not be found deliberately indifferent to known acts of discrimination. *Phillips v. Anderson County Board of Educ.*, 259 Fed.Appx. 842 (6th Cir. 2008).

◆   The Michigan High School Athletic Association (MHSAA) scheduled girls' basketball, volleyball and soccer seasons during non-traditional seasons throughout the state. Female student-athletes sued the MHSAA for violating the Equal Protection Clause, Title IX and the state Civil Rights Act. A federal court found psychological harm was done to female athletes. The scheduling created many disadvantages, such as lost scholarships and the inability to participate in "March Madness" events and tournaments. The court prohibited the MHSAA from continuing to schedule girls' sports in disadvantageous seasons. The Sixth Circuit then held that **competition in non-traditional seasons harmed girls, particularly by sending them a message that they were "second class" or were less valued than boys**. The MHSAA's evidence did not establish that separate seasons for boys and girls maximized opportunities for their participation. Female athletes were always required to play in disadvantageous seasons. The scheduling differences were properly found to be discriminatory, as boys' and girls' schedules were separate and treated unequally. *Communities for Equity v. Michigan High School Athletic Ass'n*, 459 F.3d 676 (6th Cir. 2006).

◆   A Wisconsin boy wanted to participate on the girls' gymnastics team at his high school. He filed a state court action against the Wisconsin Interscholastic Athletic Association (WIAA), challenging a rule prohibiting all interscholastic activity involving boys and girls competing against each other, except as permitted by law and board of control interpretations. The court denied any relief, noting that the WIAA is a private, voluntary association. As the WIAA was not a public entity, no equal protection suit could be brought against it. The WIAA received no federal funds and could not be sued under Title IX. The student appealed to the Court of Appeals of Wisconsin, which found that **he failed to offer any evidence that the WIAA was engaged in action traditionally reserved to the state**. His equal protection and Title IX claims could not succeed. The court affirmed the judgment for the WIAA. *Bukowski v. Wisconsin Interscholastic Ass'n*, 726 N.W.2d 356 (Table) (Wis. Ct. App. 2006).

◆   A male Rhode Island high school student desired to compete as a member of his school's girls' field hockey team. However, the regulations of the Rhode Island Interscholastic League forbade boys from participating on girls' athletic teams. A federal court denied his request for an injunction based on the Fourteenth Amendment's Equal Protection Clause. He then sued the league, seeking an injunction based on the state constitution's equal protection provisions. The trial court granted the injunction, but the Rhode Island Supreme Court vacated the injunction. Gender classifications under the state constitution need only serve important governmental objectives and be substantially related to the achievement of those objectives. **Safety concerns and physical differences between the sexes justified the rule.** *Kleczek v. Rhode Island Interscholastic League*, 612 A.2d 734 (R.I. 1992).

B. Race Discrimination

Title VI of the Civil Rights Act of 1964 prohibits intentional race discrimination in any program that receives federal funds. Title VI is based on the Equal Protection Clause, and many discrimination complaints allege violations of Title VI, the Equal Protection Clause, and analogous state laws.

◆   An African-American student starred in football for two years at a public high school before transferring to a religious school. His mother said the transfer was for academic and religious reasons. After the transfer, the student was not allowed to participate in interscholastic sports for one year. In a federal district court action, the student and his mother claimed equal protection and related violations by school officials and the Mississippi High School Athletics Association (MHSAA). They said two Caucasian students who transferred from the same high school to the private school were not required to sit out for a year.

Regarding the student's due process claim, the court held a year of interscholastic athletics amounted to a mere expectation, not an entitlement. In prior cases, the Fifth Circuit had "left no room for a lower court to hold that participation in sports is a liberty interest, since it has held that **participation in athletics falls completely outside the protection of due process**." MHSAA's transfer rule did not violate the Equal Protection Clause, but the court was unwilling to dismiss the claim that the MHSAA treated Caucasian students more favorably due to their race. The same was true of an equal protection claim against the public school, its athletic director and the MHSAA. A claim against the MHSAA, school district and school officials under 42 U.S.C. § 1981 could proceed, but claims against the private school and its officials could not. *E.C. v. Mississippi High School Athletics Ass'n*, 868 F.Supp.2d 563 (S.D. Miss. 2012).

◆   An African-American Illinois student was disciplined for wearing his pants too low. Later, he was disciplined for not following instructions to leave an area where some students were fighting. He moved outside the district, and his father presented administrators with false documents showing that the family still lived in the district. The family moved back into the district, and the student was allowed to play football his senior year. But the family sued for constitutional rights violations. **A federal court found no evidence that other students were disciplined for wearing their pants too low.** Caucasian students who were involved in the fight were disciplined, and 12 Caucasian students were placed on disciplinary probation in the same school year. The student apparently received the same treatment as others, and the court held for the district. *Bryant v. Board of Educ., Dist. 228*, No. 06 C 5697, 2008 WL 1702162 (N.D. Ill. 2008).

◆   The U.S. Court of Appeals, Eleventh Circuit, held that a lower court properly ruled against an Alabama student who filed an equal protection lawsuit based on his expulsion for striking two football coaches who removed him from a football game. **The claims failed because the student was unable to show that he was treated any differently than others.** He was not "similarly situated" to two other students who were not expelled, as their conduct involved horseplay and lesser misconduct. *Davis v. Houston County, Alabama Board of Educ.*, 291 Fed.Appx. 251 (11th Cir. 2008).

◆   Thirteen suburban Chicago school districts withdrew from the South Inter-Conference Association after over 30 years of membership. They formed two new athletic conferences, excluding two school districts in Thornton, Illinois that served mostly African-American students. The Thornton districts alleged a racially motivated conspiracy among the 13 districts, resulting in three racially segregated conferences. They joined several Thornton parents and students in a federal court action against the 13 districts. The Thornton parties **included a racially charged statement by a board member of one of the 13 districts accusing African-Americans of ruining neighborhoods in Chicago's south suburbs**. They also referenced apartheid, white flight and a racial Mason-Dixon line. Rejecting a claim by the Thornton parties that a reference to *Brown v. Board of Educ.* stated the grounds of their lawsuit, the court found there was no basis for any of the statements. As a result, the court struck them from the complaint. The lengthy statement by the board member was redundant and served no purpose but to scandalize the conduct of the 13 districts. His remarks might be inadmissible hearsay and had to be stricken. *Board of Educ. of Thornton Township High School Dist. 205 v. Board of Educ. of Argo Community High School Dist. 217*, No. 06 C 2005, 2006 WL 1896068 (N.D. Ill. 2006).

◆   A Mississippi student's parent claimed that the school's head football coach called her son "nigger" and "fat black ass" during team practices. A teammate allegedly repeated these epithets and hit the student's helmet with rocks during a practice. Coaches and the school principal allegedly took no action. The parent sued the school district, coaching staff and school officials in a federal district court, alleging deprivation of her son's civil rights. The court dismissed the claims, and the parent appealed to the U.S. Court of Appeals, Fifth Circuit. It found the teammate was not a "state actor" and thus could not be liable for civil rights violations. The Due Process Clause did not require coaches to protect a student from teammates. While the conduct of the school officials was found "morally reprehensible," the teammate's actions could not be attributed to them. **Use of racial epithets, without evidence of harassment or other deprivation of established rights, did not constitute an equal protection violation.** The school had investigated the incident, and while its response may have been inadequate, it was not shown that its inaction violated equal protection rights. *Priester v. Lowndes County,* 354 F.3d 414 (5th Cir. 2004).

The case returned to the district court, which found that the student should have a trial on his discrimination claims against the district. *Priester v. Starkville School Dist.,* No. 1: 03CV90, 2005 WL 2347285 (N.D. Miss. 2005).

C. Students with Disabilities

In PGA Tour v. Martin, *532 S.Ct. 661 (U.S. 2001), the Supreme Court held the Americans with Disabilities Act (ADA) requires an individualized inquiry to determine whether a modification is reasonable and necessary for an individual and whether it would fundamentally alter the nature of the competition.*

◆   As a third-grader, a Virginia student was identified as having a disability in reading and writing with an auditory processing deficit. He had average grades, but his parents agreed with the school's recommendation that he repeat grade three. In his freshman year of high school, the student learned he might not be eligible to play high school sports during his senior year because he would turn 19 on July 31 in the summer before that year. After playing football, basketball and baseball as an underclassman, he applied for a waiver from an age rule that bars students from playing in Virginia High School League (VHSL)-sponsored sports if they reached age 19 on or before August 1 of the school year. After a waiver was denied, the student filed a federal court action against the VHSL.

The court noted that VHSL regulations permit consideration of waivers for students with a delay or interruption in their education "due to a significant disability." But the rules stated that a waiver will not be considered if a student repeats a grade after making grades that were satisfactory for promotion. The courts "have rejected the notion that students have a constitutionally protected interest in participating in interscholastic athletics." The parents chose to have the student repeat third grade to improve his chances of academic success, even though his grades allowed promotion. He knew of his eligibility problem since his freshman year and the court denied him relief. *Sisson v. Virginia High School League,* No. 7:10CV00530, 2010 WL 5173264 (W.D. Va. 12/14/10).

◆   A 19-year-old Mississippi senior with learning disabilities who transferred to another school sought a temporary restraining order that would allow him to play basketball. He sued the state athletic association under the ADA, the IDEA and the Constitution. A federal court found no justification for disrupting the status quo. **The state high school athletic association had found that the transfer was made for athletic reasons**, and he failed to show a substantial likelihood of success on the merits of his claims. The student essentially argued that if he was not allowed to play varsity basketball, he would be less likely to get a professional contract. This could be remedied by an award of money damages, undercutting the claim that he would be irreparably injured in the absence of a court order. On appeal, the U.S. Court of Appeals, Fifth Circuit, rejected the student's arguments as financial in nature. *Newsome v. Mississippi High School Activities Ass'n*, 326 Fed.Appx. 878 (5th Cir. 2009).

◆   A Colorado student was diagnosed with attention deficit disorder (ADD) at age eight. By middle school, his special education program had ended, and by high school, his academic modifications were limited to additional time for tests and homework, and the provision of class notes. He missed several weeks of school in ninth grade due to a sinus infection, and repeated grade nine. When the student reached grade 12, state athletic association rules barred him from playing football, as he was in his ninth consecutive semester of high school attendance. The association denied his request for a hardship waiver, and he sought a court order to declare its eight-semester rule violated state law. The court denied his request for preliminary relief. On appeal, the Court of Appeals of Colorado found evidence that he repeated grade nine because of his parents' divorce, problems adjusting to a new school, and his sinus infection. **A single failed year of school was a temporary and short-term event that did not render the student "disabled" under state law or the ADA.** *Tesmer v. Colorado High School Activities Ass'n*, 140 P.3d 249 (Colo. Ct. App. 2006).

III. ISSUES IN COACHING

A. Employment

A property interest in a coaching assignment is limited to the term of the supplemental contract and severable from teaching contracts. In Boone v. Birmingham Board of Educ., *45 So.3d 764 (Ala. 2009), the court held coaching duties lack the statutory protections afforded to regular teaching assignments.*

◆   A full-time safety and security assistant at a Virginia high school also served as a part-time golf coach, for which he was paid an annual stipend. When the employee learned he would no longer receive overtime pay, he filed a federal district court action against the board, asserting violation of the Fair Labor Standards Act (FLSA). The court held the employee was a "volunteer" as to his coaching duties, and he appealed. On appeal, the U.S. Court of Appeals, Fourth Circuit, explained that the FLSA generally requires compensation of employees at a rate of one and one-half times their normal hourly rate for hours worked over 40 a week. **Under an FLSA regulation, a "volunteer" designation applies to public employees when they perform services that are not the same as the ones they are employed to perform.**

To be deemed a "volunteer," an employee may receive only a nominal fee or no money for performing different services. The court held that paying a stipend plus expenses to the employee did not mean he was not a "volunteer" under the FLSA. He was motivated in significant part by "humanitarian and charitable instincts," and could not rely on the Virginia Code to overcome FLSA language. A policy of allowing coaches to take paid leave time to coach during the regular workday did not mean they were entitled to overtime pay. This would make coaching "highly impractical" and discourage school employees from performing volunteer work. As none of the employee's arguments had merit, the court held he was properly deemed a volunteer as to his coaching duties. *Purdham v. Fairfax County School Board*, 637 F.3d 421 (4th Cir. 2011).

◆ A Texas high school administrator served as athletic director and director of extracurricular activities. He learned that a high school football player might be in violation of a state University Interscholastic League (UIL) residency rule. The administrator discussed the problem with other school officials. With district approval, he submitted a written report to the UIL, and the football team was barred from playoff games. About five weeks later, the district reassigned the administrator to an athletic trainer position. After a hearing, the district reinstated him to the extracurricular activities job. But he was not reinstated as an athletic director, and he sued the district under the Texas Whistleblower's Act. On appeal, the Supreme Court of Texas held **the elements of the state Whistleblower Act could be considered in order to determine both a court's jurisdiction and any liability issues**. It returned the case to the lower court for a determination of whether the administrator had stated a Whistleblower violation. *Galveston Independent School Dist. v. Jaco*, 303 S.W.3d 699 (Tex. 2010).

Upon its third review of the case, the court of appeals explained that the Whistleblower Act pertained to the good faith reporting by a public employee of a "violation of law" by the employing governmental entity. **Agreeing with the school district, the court found there was no "violation of law" asserted in this case. No state law required the UIL to have a residency rule.** *Galveston Independent School Dist. v. Jaco*, 331 S.W.3d 182 (Tex. Ct. App. 2011).

◆ Many complaints were made about an Iowa high school basketball coach's threatening and intimidating treatment of players and his use of profanity. In the coach's fourth season, 15 families wrote letters, complaining that he told injured players not to see their doctors, ignored athletic association rules, set a poor example for ethical behavior, and created a negative environment that damaged student self-esteem and confidence. The district superintendent specifically forbade the coach from correcting players outside the presence of an assistant coach, counselor or parent. In a basketball game held the next year, the coach and a player met briefly in a hallway with no other adult present. Administrators ruled that the coach had violated the directive. The school fired the coach, and the Supreme Court of Iowa noted that **the school board had appropriately considered the coach's entire history, as well as the final incident, when**

voting to terminate his coaching contract. The coach had been informed throughout his career about the need to respect his players, and the court held just cause existed for terminating his contract. *Board of Directors of Ames Community School Dist. v. Cullinan*, 745 N.W.2d 487 (Iowa 2008).

◆   A Tennessee teacher was employed as a varsity basketball coach under a separate contract from his regular teaching contract. He became embattled due to complaints about his conduct, and the school principal and the district's director of schools removed him from his coaching duties. While he retained his tenured teaching status, another teacher was named head basketball coach. The teacher's collective bargaining organization filed a grievance on his behalf. The arbitrator found the master contract covered teaching assignments, and that the coaching assignment had to comply with it since the position was a "professional advantage." The case reached the Supreme Court of Tennessee, which held that the teacher's coaching assignment was not protected by the parties' contract covering his regular employment as a teacher. Instead, he had a year-to-year coaching appointment. **His education association was precluded from representing teachers in their capacities as non-licensed coaches,** and the arbitrator had incorrectly found a master teachers contract governed the renewal of the coaching contract. But as the board had approved of the arbitrator's recommendations, it could not avoid paying for additional duties during the final year of the teaching contract. *Lawrence County Educ. Ass'n v. Lawrence County Board of Educ.*, 244 S.W.3d 302 (Tenn. 2007).

◆   An Alabama teacher/coach discovered that the girls' team at his school did not receive the same funding or access to equipment and facilities as boys' teams. He claimed that his job was made difficult by lack of funding and that the district did not respond to his complaints. Eventually, the teacher was removed as girls' coach. He sued the school board, claiming the loss of his supplemental coaching contracts constituted unlawful retaliation in violation of Title IX. The court dismissed the case, which later reached the U.S. Supreme Court. It held **Title IX covers retaliation against a person who complains about sex bias.** "Retaliation is, by definition an intentional act," and is a form of discrimination. Without finding bias had occurred, the Court held the teacher was entitled to attempt to show that the board was liable. A private right of action for retaliation was available under Title IX. Title IX does not require the victim of retaliation to also be the victim of discrimination. Teachers and coaches are often in the best position to vindicate the rights of students by identifying discrimination and notifying administrators. A reasonable school board would realize it could not cover up Title IX violations by retaliating against teachers. The Court held for the coach. *Jackson v. Birmingham Board of Educ.*, 544 U.S. 167, 125 S.Ct. 1497, 161 L.Ed.2d 361 (2005).

◆   An inner-city Alabama high school basketball coach was a tenured science teacher with 20 years of teaching experience. Before the start of the 2004-05 basketball season, he agreed with players to use a "one-minute drill" or "circle" as a form of discipline in practices. The "drill" consisted of the team encircling the rules violator, then hitting or kicking him for up to one minute. The coach looked on and timed the hitting with a stopwatch. The punishment was used 11 times in a six-week period. After the media reported a player's injuries, the school district placed the coach on administrative leave. A hearing officer found the coach engaged in serious misconduct but did not recommend canceling his contract. Instead, the coach was barred from coaching for four years, suspended without pay for 30 days, and ordered to apologize to all players and parents.

The case reached the Supreme Court of Alabama, which noted that at his hearing, the coach acknowledged his mistake and promised it would never happen again. Players uniformly stated that he was a positive influence in their lives. **The Alabama Teacher Tenure Act permitted consideration of a teacher's employment history, including matters occurring in previous years.** The coach had no prior disciplinary record, and parents and students expressed a strong and almost unanimous desire for him to remain. The coach had been able to improve grades and make college a realistic goal for his players. The hearing officer had attempted to balance a number of vital concerns. That decision was upheld. *Ex Parte Dunn*, 962 So.2d 814 (Ala. 2007).

B. Defamation

Many courts have found that coaches and teachers are "public officials" in defamation cases. This means that to prevail in a defamation case, they must show that defamatory statements were made with "actual malice." But in O'Connor v. Burningham, 165 P.3d 1214 (Utah 2007), the Supreme Court of Utah held a high school basketball coach did not enjoy "public official" status.

◆   Several parents of players on a Utah high school basketball team accused their coach of giving preferential treatment to the team's star player. They also criticized his demeanor and questioned his use of team funds. Eventually, the school dismissed the coach from his head coaching duties, and he sued the parents for defamation. A state trial court found he was a "public official," which meant he had to show they made their statements with "actual malice" to prevail on his defamation claims. The Supreme Court of Utah explained that **persons who are deemed to be public officials or public figures "surrender a sizeable measure of their right to recover damages from those who defame them."** Statements directed at public officials or public figures require proof that a speaker had actual malice. But the coach did not occupy a position with such "apparent importance" that he had "public official" status. Despite the increasing popularity of athletics, the court rejected the parents' claim that coaches should be treated as public officials. Unlike those in "policy-making positions," Utah teachers and coaches did not surrender their ability to protect their reputations by accepting their jobs. But the court held the parents could be entitled to a conditional privilege based on family relationships. The case was returned to the district court, which was to decide if their statements were defamatory. *O'Connor v. Burningham*, 165 P.3d 1214 (Utah 2007).

◆   Michigan High School Athletic Association rules required transfer students to sit out of interscholastic athletic competition for two semesters if a transfer was "athletically motivated." A star student-athlete told his football coach and others he was considering a transfer because "the program was in disarray." The student's mother told the principal the transfer was academically motivated, but the principal filed a complaint with the state athletic association, asserting the transfer was athletically motivated. Newspapers interviewed school officials, then published articles speculating that the transfer was athletically motivated. The student sued the school district, principal, coach and the district athletic director for defamation and other claims. The case reached the Court of Appeals of Michigan, which held **the principal, coach and athletic director were entitled to speak to reporters who were already aware of the story.** The trial court had properly dismissed defamation and invasion of privacy claims based on immunity. Statements to the association were limited to furthering the district's interest and were made in a proper manner. And the statements to the reporters were not defamation, as there was no evidence that they caused harm. The student himself openly spoke about his transfer. *Cassise v. Walled Lake Consolidated Schools*, No. 257299, 2006 WL 445960 (Mich. Ct. App. 2006).

◆   A Louisiana student and her mother were spectators at a game. She claimed a coach physically and verbally threatened them and called the police to have them removed from the gym. The student sued the school board and coach in a federal court, claiming "threatening and abusive language is actionable" in actions for federal civil rights violations under 42 U.S.C. § 1983. The coach moved for dismissal, asserting there was no viable Section 1983 claim, and that she was also entitled to qualified immunity. The court agreed with the coach, stating that **the Due Process Clause "does not transform every tort committed by a state actor into a constitutional violation."** Even in a state custodial situation, "the use of words, no matter how violent, does not comprise a Section 1983 violation." The court rejected the student's claim alleging harm to her reputation. The conduct she alleged did not raise a valid constitutional claim. Any harm to reputation was not a deprivation of a constitutional liberty or property interest recognized by state or federal law. *Paige v. Tangipahoa Parish School Board*, No. 04-354, 2005 WL 943636 (E.D. La. 2005).

◆   A Minnesota school district decided not to rehire a varsity football coach. A newspaper published articles quoting sources who said the coach was "known for his temper, inappropriate comments and foul language, which people claim he uses to intimidate players." While news accounts did not identify the source of these comments, one statement was attributed to a former assistant coach. The head coach sued the school district for defamation, breach of contract and other claims. A court twice denied motions by the coach to identify staff members who allegedly defamed him, then held for the district and employees.

The case reached the state supreme court, which said a defamation claim requires proof of: (1) a false and defamatory statement (2) in an unprivileged publication to a third party that (3) harmed the plaintiff's reputation in the community. **Public officials must also show the statement was made with "actual malice." In Minnesota, public school teachers and coaches are deemed public officials.** Since the speaker was anonymous, the court held his or her identity would necessarily lead to relevant evidence on the issue of actual malice. The district court had found the statements, if false, were defamatory.

The court reversed, finding that if any school employee was the source of the statements, there was probable cause to believe the speaker had relevant information. *Weinberger v. Maplewood Review*, 668 N.W.2d 667 (Minn. 2003).

C. Liability

In Kahn v. East Side Union High School Dist., *31 Cal.4th 990 (Cal. 2003), the Supreme Court of California held a school district generally has no duty to protect a student from the inherent risks in a sport. But sports instructors and coaches have a duty not to increase the risks of sports participation beyond what is inherent in the sport. For additional cases involving school district liability in the context of school athletics, see Chapter Twelve, Section II.*

◆   Parents of a Kentucky student-athlete claimed he had been the victim of a serious assault with a broomstick as part of a longstanding pattern of hazing at his school. In a state court action against the school district and school officials, the parents claimed the school board, superintendent and football coaches all knew about the hazing but did nothing to prevent it. The board, superintendent and coaches sought dismissal but were denied it because the district had purchased insurance. The board appealed to the Court of Appeals of Kentucky.

The court explained that the doctrine of governmental immunity arose in part from the separation of powers. In further court proceedings, the school board would have governmental immunity. As for the claim to immunity by the school officials, the lower court had yet to analyze the issue. **Immunity was available for officials and employees who were performing discretionary acts, in good faith and within the scope of their authority.** Supervision of students was a "discretionary" duty. On the other hand, the failure of teachers to supervise students in the face of known and recognized behavior was not discretionary and not protected by immunity. As the pretrial fact-finding process of discovery had not been conducted in this case, the court held it could not yet review the claims to immunity by the superintendent and coaches or determine whether the superintendent had acted in good faith. It vacated the order pertaining to the officials and returned the case to the trial court. *Jenkins Independent Schools v. Doe*, 379 S.W.3d 808 (Ky. Ct. App. 2012).

◆   An Arkansas student made the basketball team at his high school. Another tryout was then held so students who had played football could try out after the football season ended. In a federal court complaint against the state education department, the parent said her son's removal from the team after being chosen for it violated their equal protection and due process rights. Accepting the argument of education department officials, **the court held there is no constitutionally protected right to interscholastic athletic participation**.

According to the court, property interests are not created by the Constitution. They are instead created by existing rules or understandings that stem from state law. In fact, **"the vast majority of courts to consider this issue nationwide" have found that a student has no constitutional right to participate in extracurricular athletics**. These included courts in Texas, Pennsylvania, Utah, Louisiana and Tennessee. As the state of Arkansas had created no property interest in high school athletics, the court held there was no due process right to interscholastic sports competition. In addition, there was no parental right to have children compete in interscholastic sports, defeating the parent's due process claim on her behalf. An equal protection claim failed, as the court found a rational basis existed for granting the football players an additional tryout opportunity. Eighth Circuit authority established that courts should not intervene in matters of school policy. As a result, the court dismissed the family's constitutional claims. *Bloodman v. Kimbrell*, No. 4:11CV00818 JMM, 2012 WL 3560381 (E.D. Ark. 8/17/12).

◆   A Tennessee cheerleading sponsor worked in a school cafeteria and was not a certified teacher. She supervised the cheerleading squad for over two years without incident. A cheerleader then broke her arm during a practice. At the time of the injury, the sponsor had left the practice for other duties. The cheerleader sued the school board and sponsor for negligence. After a court awarded pretrial judgment to the board and sponsor, the cheerleader appealed. The Court of Appeals of Tennessee held that **the cheerleader failed to show that the sponsor's experience was inadequate or fell below an established standard of care.** Thus, the negligent hiring claim failed. But there was a dispute concerning the sponsor's level of supervision over the squad. While she said she told the squad not to perform stunts in her absence, the cheerleader said there was no such warning. A trial was required on that issue. *Britt v. Maury County Board of Educ.*, No. M2006-01921-COA-R3-CV, 2008 WL 4427190 (Tenn. Ct. App. 9/29/08).

◆   A Pennsylvania junior high school wrestling coach directed a 152-pound wrestler to "live wrestle" a 240-pound teammate during a practice. "Live wrestling" simulated actual competitive conditions, with both wrestlers giving their best efforts. Pennsylvania Interscholastic Athletic Association (PIAA) rules limited wrestling to competitors in their own weight class or one class above. The teammate was three PIAA weight classes above the wrestler, and he injured the wrestler's leg when he collapsed on him. The wrestler sued the school district and employees in a federal court, which held for the district. The wrestler appealed to the U.S. Court of Appeals, Third Circuit, which explained that **to hold the coach liable for a constitutional violation, it had to be shown that he deprived the wrestler of a federal right in a way that was foreseeable and fairly direct.** In this case, the coach had paired mismatched wrestlers simply because there was no partner for the teammate. The coach apparently had done this previously. As there was at least circumstantial evidence of deliberate indifference to the wrestler's rights, the court returned the case to the lower court. However, the claims against the school district failed. *Patrick v. Great Valley School Dist.*, 296 Fed.Appx. 258 (3d Cir. 2008).

◆   A Michigan middle school wrestling coach injured a student when he performed a maneuver in practice without prior warning. The student sued, and a state court denied pretrial judgment to the coach, finding that he was grossly negligent in performing the maneuver without prior notice. The case reached the Supreme Court of Michigan, which held that even if the coach had grabbed the student from behind and took him to the mat as alleged, this did not produce injury. **The injury occurred when the coach and student were engaged in wrestling activity.** The student testified that after he completed a body roll, he did what he had been coached to do – brace his arm and try to escape. This was what caused the injury. As the lack of adequate notice of the initial maneuver was not a basis for injury, the court reversed the judgment. *Jefferson Middle School v. Nadeau*, 477 Mich. 1109, 729 N.W.2d 840 (Mich. 2007).

◆   A Texas cross country coach had his team warm up on the paved shoulder of a two-lane state highway. He followed the team in his personal vehicle. The warmup took place about 7:00 a.m., in low-light conditions. After warming up, the team gathered on the shoulder of the eastbound lane of the highway. The coach parked on the westbound shoulder and activated his emergency flashers. An oncoming vehicle drove onto the eastbound shoulder, striking and killing a team member. The team member's parent sued the school board and coach in a state court, which held the board and coach were entitled to immunity under the Texas Tort Claims Act. The state court of appeals affirmed the judgment. Government units can be liable for property damage, personal injury and death in cases involving the use or operation of a motor vehicle. But the activation of the emergency flashers on the coach's car did not create a waiver of immunity under the Act. Even if it did, there was no evidence that the death arose from this use. The student was killed by the vehicle that struck him. **The coach's actions were supervisory in nature and did not involve the operation or use of a motor vehicle.** *Morales v. Barnette*, 219 S.W.3d 477 (Tex. Ct. App. 2007).

◆   Four Tennessee student-athletes claimed their varsity football head coach humiliated and degraded them, used inappropriate language, and required them to participate in a year-round conditioning program that violated school rules. They claimed he hit a player in the helmet and threw away college recruiting letters that were sent to "disfavored players." One of them typed a petition that said "I hate Coach Euverard and I don't want to play for him." Eighteen players signed the petition. When the coach learned of this, he summoned players into his office one by one to interview them. Players who signed the petition were allowed to stay on the team if they apologized and said they wanted to play for the head coach. Four players who did not apologize and accept the coach were taken off the team. They sued the coach, school board and other officials for First Amendment violations. The U.S. Court of Appeals, Sixth Circuit, held **the petition was reasonably likely to cause substantial disruption to the team and therefore was not protected**. There was no First Amendment violation as the players had implicitly agreed to accept their coach's authority by turning out for the team. *Lowery v. Euverard*, 497 F.3d 584 (6th Cir. 2007).

◆   An Ohio student was injured when a batted ball ricocheted off an L-screen that had been placed in front of him for protection. He sued the school district and coach for negligence, claiming that the coach failed to properly supervise the batting cage and did not provide protective helmets for pitchers. The complaint did not allege malice, bad faith or reckless conduct or claim damages from the coach individually. The case reached the state supreme court, which held teachers and coaches have wide discretion to determine what supervision is necessary for student safety. The coach's decisions reflected his discretion. He instructed pitchers regarding the L-screen as well as general guidance on game preparations. **The coach's direction represented the exercise of his judgment and discretion in the use of equipment or facilities in connection with his position.** As the injury resulted from the coach's judgment or discretion, the district could claim immunity. *Elston v. Howland Local Schools,* 113 Ohio St.3d 314, 865 N.E.2d 845 (Ohio 2007).

◆ A Texas basketball coach and an athletic trainer were blamed for the death of a student who collapsed after completing a two-mile run with her team. The student's parents claimed the coach and trainer failed to perform CPR or to give her other necessary medical attention. They sued the district, coach and trainer in a federal district court. **The court held that to show a school employee has violated a constitutional interest in bodily integrity, there must be proof of deliberate indifference toward the victim.** The family had alleged only negligence, not deliberate indifference. The coach attended to the student about five minutes after she finished running, and the trainer saw her about 12 minutes later. As this was not "conscious disregard" for her health and safety, they had qualified immunity. The district was entitled to immunity as well. *Livingston v. DeSoto Independent School Dist.,* 391 F.Supp.2d 463 (N.D. Tex. 2005).

◆ A Nebraska high school football player was struck on his head during a game. He felt dizzy and disoriented, but stayed in the game a few plays before taking himself out. Coaches observed he was short of breath but attributed this to hyperventilation. As the student made normal eye contact and had normal speech and movement, no medical attention was sought. The student later asked to return to the game, and coaches allowed him to do so. He suffered a headache the entire weekend, but coaches denied he said anything about it and allowed him to practice with the team. The next week student suffered a closed-head traumatic brain injury. He later sued the school district in a state court for personal injuries. After the court dismissed the case, the Nebraska Supreme Court held it should not have discredited expert testimony declaring that Nebraska **high school coaches should know that headache, dizziness and disorientation are symptomatic of a concussion.** The case then returned to the trial court. It heard testimony that little training or literature was available to coaches about head injury at the time of the injury. The court dismissed the case, finding the coaching staff complied with the duty of care required of a reasonably prudent person with a state coaching endorsement. The supreme court later affirmed this decision. *Cerny v. Cedar Bluffs Junior/Senior Public School,* 268 Neb. 958, 679 N.W.2d 198 (Neb. 2004).

CHAPTER FOURTEEN

School Operations

I. BUDGET AND FINANCE

A. Educational Finance and Equal Opportunity

Education is not a fundamental right under the U.S. Constitution. However, state constitutional education clauses require states to provide an "adequate," "sound basic" or "thorough and efficient" system of public schools.

The U.S. Supreme Court effectively eliminated educational financing claims based on the Equal Protection Clause of the U.S. Constitution by holding education is not a fundamental right in San Antonio School Dist. v. Rodriguez, *411 U.S. 1 (1973). State courts continue to consider financial equity and educational adequacy claims under state constitutions. Typical state court challenges to school financing systems involve differing local tax bases that result in disparities among school district revenues.*

◆ In *King v. State of Iowa*, the Supreme Court of Iowa held a lawsuit about educational standards presented a political question. It followed *Bonner v. Daniels*, 907 N.E.2d 516 (Ind. 2009), in which the Indiana Supreme Court found no state constitutional duty to achieve a particular standard of educational quality. In reviewing the case, the court found the Iowa, California, Indiana and Nevada constitutions have similar education clauses. Unlike the constitutions of most other states, Iowa's education clause did not mandate free public schools. The court found the clause did not require an education system to be adequate, efficient, quality, thorough or uniform, as most states do. Examination of the Iowa 1857 constitutional convention debates led the court to conclude that **there was no judicially enforceable right to a free public education with certain minimum standards of quality**. The court found the educational system assured every Iowa student roughly the same amount of funding for his or her education. Finally, the court held the challengers' attempt to make out a claim under state law could not succeed, since the law contained only policy pronouncements and did not create a cause of action. The lawsuit was properly dismissed. *King v. State of Iowa*, 818 N.W.2d 1 (Iowa 2012).

◆ Washington parents sued the state for violating Article IX, Section 1, of the state constitution. The section makes it the paramount duty of the state to amply provide for the education of all resident children. A trial court found the state did not meet its constitutional duty. On appeal, the Supreme Court of Washington reviewed *Seattle School Dist. No. 1 v. State*, 90 Wash.2d 476, 585 P.2d 71 (Wash. 1978). In that case, the court held the state did not meet its constitutional duty to provide a basic program of education. While the *Seattle* decision directed the legislature to fulfill its duty, it did not detail a funding structure. Legislative responses to fund basic education after 1977 focused on rectifying over-reliance on local levy funding. The court noted that current K-12 funding had suffered massive cuts in the state operating budget.

Substantial evidence supported the trial court's conclusion that the state did not adequately fund education. **Nothing in the constitution required the state to guarantee educational outcomes.** Instead, "education" was defined in terms of broad educational opportunities. The constitutional term "education" meant the opportunity to obtain knowledge and skills as described in the *Seattle* case and later legislation. While the legislature had broad discretion to discharge its constitutional duties, any reduction of programs from the basic education program had to be accompanied by an educational policy rationale. No part of the basic education program could be eliminated for budgetary reasons or expediency. In affirming the conclusion that the state failed to meet its constitutional funding obligations, the court found it inappropriate to order the legislature to set the cost of basic education and to provide the needed funding. Instead, the court would retain authority to monitor state compliance. *McCleary v. State of Washington*, 173 Wash.2d 477, 269 P.3d 227 (Wash. 2012).

◆ **A lawsuit challenging New York's funding of districts outside New York City was allowed to proceed.** State officials argued the case was not ripe for review because 2007 legislation in response to prior school funding litigation had not yet taken full effect. The state's highest court held school funding is appropriate for court review in *Campaign for Fiscal Equity v. State of New York*, 8 N.Y.3d 14 (N.Y. 2006). A state appellate division court held the trial court correctly refused to dismiss the case. *Hussein v. State of New York*, 81 A.D.3d 132, 914 N.Y.S.2d 464 (N.Y. App. Div. 2011).

◆ Non-profit corporations, students and parents sued Florida legislators and educators, claiming that public schools were not safe and secure, graduation rates were low, student promotion and retention policies were not effective, and achievement tests revealed numerous inadequacies. When the court refused to dismiss the case, state officials appealed. **The court of appeal noted that because this was a non-final trial court order, the relief sought could only be obtained in emergencies.** It asked the state supreme court to decide whether the Florida Constitution had judicially ascertainable standards to determine the adequacy, efficiency, safety, security and high qualify of public education on a statewide basis in a manner allowing a court to declare whether the state had complied with the constitutional mandate. There was no emergency here. *Haridopolos v. Citizens for Strong Schools*, 81 So.3d 465 (Fla. Dist. Ct. App. 2011). In 2012, the state supreme court declined to review the question presented by the court of appeals.

◆ Two groups challenged Colorado's public school funding system in the state court system. One group consisted of parents of students attending eight different school districts. The other was made up of 14 school districts. They asserted that the system was underfunded by at least $500 million in 2001-02 and that state officials allocated funds irrationally and arbitrarily in violation of the state constitution. They claimed that the state did not provide an adequate education to students with disabilities, those from lower socio-economic backgrounds, ethnic and racial minorities, and non-English speaking students. A state court held that the case posed a political question for the legislature to decide. But the Supreme Court of Colorado returned the case to the trial court so **the parents and districts could try to prove the state's current public school financing system was not rationally related to the constitutional mandate to provide a "thorough and uniform" system of public education.** If the court found the current system of public school finance was irrational and thus unconstitutional, the legislature would be given time to change the system. *Lobato v. State*, 218 P.3d 358 (Colo. 2009).

◆ Missouri school districts, advocacy groups and taxpayers challenged the state's school funding formula in 2004. The focus of the case shifted to Senate Bill Number 287, enacted in 2005. S.B. 287 revised the state funding formula by attempting to remedy inequities resulting from the system's reliance on a combination of state and local funding. Schools with greater "local effort" contributions received less state assistance. The case reached the Supreme Court of Missouri, which noted that **Section 1(a) of the Missouri Constitution concerning the "diffusion of knowledge" did not create a free-standing**

duty to provide certain schools with funding. The challengers were improperly attempting to read the 25% requirement of Section 3(b) as a separate funding duty in Section 1(a). Section 3(b) provided a minimum level of funding for schools and declared that the legislature "may" provide additional funding to account for deficiencies. Thus, the court found no merit to the claim that S.B. 287 created an unconstitutional funding formula.

There was no expressed right to equitable education funding in the constitution's provision for free public schools. S.B. 287 was justified by a clearly legitimate end. School funding was achieved through state and local resources, with state funding going disproportionately to districts with fewer local resources. Since none of the challengers' additional arguments had merit, the court affirmed the judgment for the state. *Committee For Educational Equality v. State of Missouri*, 294 S.W.2d 477 (Mo. 2009).

◆ A group of Indiana students sought a court ruling that the state was not satisfying its duty to provide a quality education for all public school students under the Indiana Constitution's Education Clause. The case reached the Supreme Court of Indiana, which explained that the General Assembly had two duties under the Education Clause. The first was to encourage moral, intellectual, scientific and agricultural improvement, and the second was to "provide for a general and uniform system of open common schools without tuition." But the Education Clause spoke only of a general duty to provide a system of common schools. **There was no requirement to attain any standard of educational quality.** Terms like "general and uniform," and "equally open to all" did not prescribe standards. Since there was no affirmative duty for a particular educational standard, the students' challenge failed. *Bonner v. Daniels*, 907 N.E.2d 516 (Ind. 2009).

◆ Educational adequacy and funding appeals reached the Supreme Court of New Hampshire in 1993, 1998, and 2002, when the court held the state had a duty of accountability in *Claremont School Dist. v. Governor*, 794 A.2d 744 (N.H. 2002). In 2005, the legislature mandated student opportunities to acquire skills in core subjects including reading, writing, science and math. Two school district administrative units and an organization representing 19 others filed an action in response to H.B. 616, which governed state education funding and allocation. A state superior court declared H.B. 616 unconstitutional. The Supreme Court of New Hampshire agreed, ruling that **H.B. 616 did not fulfill the state's duty to define and determine the cost of a constitutionally adequate education, failed to satisfy accountability requirements and created a non-uniform tax rate** in violation of the state constitution. *Londonderry School Dist. SAU #12 v. State*, 907 A.2d 988 (N.H. 2006).

The legislature then enacted Chapter 270, which paved the way for the state to determine the cost of an adequate education by creating a joint legislative oversight committee for further study. The administrative units claimed there were still infirmities in the law, such as failure to meet accountability requirements and an insufficient universal cost of education for each student. State officials argued that Chapter 270 represented sufficient steps toward satisfying the constitutional duty to provide adequate education to each child.

The court agreed, finding the education funding plan from H.B. 616 was no longer in effect. Because the legislature had acted in good faith to address the previously identified constitutional infirmities in prior legislation, the court dismissed the case. *Londonderry School Dist. SAU #12 v. State of New Hampshire*, 157 N.H. 734, 958 A.2d 930 (N.H. 2008).

◆ In 2002, the Supreme Court of Arkansas held that the state's school funding effort was insufficient. The General Assembly responded with Act 57 and Act 108. Act 57 described the General Assembly's continuing duty to assess what constitutes an "adequate education." The court ruled that legislative inaction had violated school funding requirements. But it refused to order the General Assembly to appropriate a specific increase in funding amounts. Instead, it was up to the General Assembly to determine whether, after correcting for constitutional infirmities, more funds should be appropriated. *Lake View School Dist. No. 25 v. Huckabee*, 364 Ark. 398, 220 S.W.3d 645 (Ark. 2006).

The supreme court later reviewed a special masters' report that found the General Assembly had enacted a comprehensive system for accounting and accountability for state oversight of school expenditures. A 2007 act authorized the state to assure the state's basic, per-student foundation funding was being met. An additional $50 million had been appropriated for school facilities in 2006. Categorical funding and teacher salaries were increased. The court held that **the General Assembly had taken necessary steps to assure that public school students were being provided with an adequate education and substantially equal educational opportunities**. *Lake View School Dist. No. 25 v. Huckabee*, 370 Ark. 139, 257 S.W.3d 879 (Ark. 2007).

◆ An association of Idaho school districts, superintendents and students sued the state, asserting that state funding levels and the funding method violated the Idaho Constitution. The case reached the Supreme Court of Idaho, which reviewed district court findings of myriad structural problems and fire hazards. The court rejected the state's attempts to "refocus this litigation into small, district-by-district battles" instead of addressing the larger issue of the legislature's constitutional duty toward public education in Idaho. Overwhelming evidence compiled by the lower court documented serious facility and funding problems in the state's public education system.

The state itself had documented facilities deficiencies in a 1993 assessment concluding that 57% of all Idaho school buildings had serious safety concerns. A 1999 report found the situation had further deteriorated. The "glaring gap" in the funding system was the lack of a mechanism to quickly deal with major, costly and potentially catastrophic conditions in low-population districts with low tax bases in economically depressed areas. The "list of safety concerns and difficulties in getting funds for repairs or replacements is distressingly long." **The funding system was inadequate to meet the state constitutional mandate for a thorough system of education in a safe environment.** While the legislature failed in its constitutional mandate, an appropriate remedy was a task for the legislature, not the court. *Idaho Schools for Equal Educational Opportunity v. State of Idaho*, 129 P.3d 1199 (Idaho 2005).

◆ In 1997, the Supreme Court of Vermont held that the state was denying students equal educational opportunities. The legislature responded with Act 60, also known as the Equal Educational Opportunity Act of 1997. A group of students asserted that nondiscretionary expenditures on special education, transportation and facilities resulted in less funding for instruction and curriculum. They claimed that their high school was in poor condition and offered such a limited curriculum that many students had taken all course offerings and had to take gym classes to fill their senior year schedules. Taxpayers claimed that Act 60 required them to pay disproportionately high state and local education taxes when compared to taxpayers in other Vermont towns. The students and taxpayers sued the state for equal protection violations. A trial court dismissed the case, ruling that recent legislation had remedied the claims. The taxpayers and students appealed to the state supreme court, which held that the trial court had improperly dismissed the case. The court found the allegations of the taxpayers and students sufficient to proceed with the case. **As they alleged that recent legislation caused the same fundamental violations as Act 60, the case was remanded for further proceedings.** *Brigham v. State*, 889 A.2d 715 (Vt. 2005).

◆ The Montana Legislature created the state's current educational funding system in 1993. House Bill (H.B.) 667 addressed a 1989 Montana Supreme Court decision concluding that the spending disparities among the state's school districts denied students equal educational opportunity under the state constitution. H.B. 667 addressed inequities by relying on a regression analysis to address the financial disparities among districts. The bill created a general fund with built-in maximum and minimum amounts computed by a statutory formula. A coalition of schools, school districts, parents and educational associations sued, alleging that H.B. 667 violated two provisions of the state constitution. The coalition stated that most districts were at or over their maximum budgets. Some districts said they could not provide a quality education unless they could spend more than their general fund maximum. The case reached the Supreme Court of Montana, which found that **the current system was constitutionally deficient**, based on evidence of budgeting at or near the maximum budget authority, growing accreditation problems, the cutting of programs, teacher flight to other states, deterioration of buildings, and increased competition between special and general education programs for general fund dollars. *Columbia Falls Elementary School Dist. No. 6 v. State of Montana*, 326 Mont. 304, 109 P.3d 257 (Mont. 2005).

◆ Forty-seven Texas school districts claimed that state control of the levy, assessment and disbursement of revenue resulted in a statewide property tax. Other districts claimed that funding for school operations and facilities was unconstitutional because children in property-poor districts did not have substantially equal access to revenue. The state supreme court noted that over half the annual cost of public education in the state was funded by ad valorem taxes imposed by independent school districts on local property.

The legislature's decision to rely heavily on local property taxes did not in itself violate the Texas Constitution, but the disparity between districts in size and wealth made it difficult to achieve efficient education funding. Some districts had to pay disproportionately high property taxes. School maintenance and operations were funded by a separate tax capped at $1.50 per $100 of valuation. Revenue disparities among districts were reduced by supplementing property-poor district tax revenue with state funds. **The court held the school financing system did not violate the efficiency requirement of the state constitution.** But state control of local taxation for education amounted to an unconstitutional state property tax. The number of districts taxing at the maximum "maintenance and operations" rate had risen from 2% of districts to 48%, and 67% of districts were taxing at or above $1.45. The state controlled more than $1 billion in local tax revenues recaptured from 134 districts. Recapture had doubled in less than a decade, and the number of districts and amount of revenue subject to recapture had almost tripled since 1994. Districts had lost any meaningful discretion to tax below maximum rates and still provide students with an accredited education. Districts were forced by educational requirements and economic necessities to tax at the valuation cap. This violated the state constitutional prohibition on a state property tax. As removing the cap would increase the disparity among districts, the court held that it had to be raised, or the system had to be changed by June 1, 2006. *Neeley v. West Orange-Cove Consolidated Independent School Dist.*, 176 S.W.3d 746 (Tex. 2005).

B. Property Taxes and Other Local Funding Issues

Courts usually refrain from intervening in state and local tax or funding questions. For example, the Supreme Court of North Carolina held that the legislature, not the judiciary, was vested with budgetary responsibilities.

◆ The Illinois education funding system was designed to assure that a combination of state financial aid and local resources provided each student with funding equal to (or more than) a prescribed "Foundation Level." State law categorized school districts as "flat grant districts," "foundation level districts," or "alternative formula districts." Two taxpayers claimed the state education funding system imposed substantially greater burdens on taxpayers residing in property-poor districts than on taxpayers residing in property-rich districts.

When the case reached the Supreme Court of Illinois, it rejected the taxpayers' claim that they were required to pay higher taxes as a direct result of enforcement of the education funding statute. In the court's view, the education funding statute was not a taxing statute. While the statute set a formula for determining state aid for school districts, it did not require districts to set a particular tax rate. It was entirely within the discretion of the districts to set the actual property tax rate. **Contrary to the taxpayers' claims, school districts, not state officials, set the amount of local property taxes.** The supreme court did not find that recent education statutes regarding school district performance were sufficient to confer standing on the taxpayers to pursue their action. Since local school districts had the ability to set their property tax rates, the court affirmed a lower court decision to dismiss the case for lack of taxpayer standing. *Carr v. Koch*, 981 N.E.2d 326 (Ill. 2012).

◆ **A Nebraska taxpayer could not pursue an action claiming that a general fund levy and a special building fund levy imposed by a learning community were unconstitutional.** When the case reached the Supreme Court of Nebraska, it held the taxpayer could not rely on a state law created to challenge taxes that were either "illegal" or "unauthorized" due to fraudulent conduct by officials. Instead, the taxpayer's recourse was to challenge the levies during the years they were imposed, which he failed to do. A law creating a means of challenging taxes already paid had been repealed in 1992. *Trumble v. Sarpy County Board*, 283 Neb. 486 (Neb. 2012).

◆ The Nebraska Court of Appeals upheld a taxpayer action under the state Budget Act to correct a material error in a school district budget statement. In seeking approval of a $3.865 million bond issue, the district had misstated its bond funding balance by about $75,000. **The court upheld a trial court order requiring the district to adjust its mill levy.** *Cook v. Nebraska Unified School Dist. No. 1*, No. A.11-720, 2012 WL 1432315 (Neb. Ct. App. 4/24/12).

◆ Due to budget difficulties, the state of California did not pay school districts for the costs of many new education programs that were mandated by the legislature. Instead, it sought to satisfy state constitutional requirements by paying $1,000 for each mandate and deferring the remaining costs for an indefinite time period. The California School Boards Association and a number of school districts challenged the practice of nominally funding and deferring full payment for state-imposed mandates. In addition to seeking a declaration that nominal funding was unconstitutional, the districts sought reimbursement of over $900 million in unpaid costs of complying with state mandates. After a hearing, a state trial court held that **the state's deferral practice violated the California Constitution and several applicable laws.** But the court declined the request to reimburse the districts, finding this would violate separation of powers principles. The Court of Appeal of California agreed in part, but it held that no injunctive relief should have been ordered. Like the lower court, it refused to order the state to pay almost $1 billion in deferred costs claimed by the school districts. The separation of powers doctrine prevents courts from ordering the legislature to appropriate funds. *California School Boards Ass'n v. State of California*, 192 Cal.App.4th 770 (Cal. Ct. App. 2011).

◆ Beaufort County (North Carolina) Commissioners allocated $2.7 million less than the county school board requested for fiscal year 2006-07. After mediation failed, the board sued the commission. A jury found that the board needed an additional $766,000. The court ordered the commissioners to appropriate this amount. Appeal reached the Supreme Court of North Carolina, where the commission argued that allowing the court system to decide public education funding levels impermissibly delegated a legislative duty under the state constitution. But the court disagreed, finding that the separation of powers clause of the North Carolina Constitution did not prevent the General Assembly from seeking assistance, "within proper limits," from other government branches – like determining the annual cost of education in the county. Fact-finding of this kind was within the historic and proper role of the judiciary.

The legislature, not the judiciary, allocated budgetary responsibility to local entities and required judgments against a county commission if school board costs exceeded the allocation. The court found the trial court had improperly instructed the jury regarding the term "needed" in the context of funding under Section 431(c). The case was returned to the lower court for a new trial. The jury was to be instructed that Section 431(c) required the county commission to appropriate the amount legally necessary to support a system of free public schools. In addition, the jury was to be instructed to consider state educational goals and policies, the board's budgetary request, the financial resources of the county, and county fiscal policies. *Beaufort County Board of Educ. v. Beaufort County Board of Commissioners*, 681 S.E.2d 278 (N.C. 2009).

◆   A Missouri land developer bought a parcel of land. It learned that Central School District owned and taxed it, despite the fact that it was surrounded by property included in the Farmington School District. It sought an order that the land was within the Farmington district, but a state trial court agreed with Central School District that the parcel was within its boundaries even though it was non-contiguous with the rest of the district. On appeal, the Supreme Court of Missouri held that the trial court did not err by relying on an assessor's map rather than on school district records. **State law and a state constitutional provision referring to contiguous boundaries for school districts applied to reorganization plans and boundary changes and did not require contiguity in other cases.** *MC Development Co. v. Cent. R-3 School Dist. of St. Francois County*, 299 S.W.3d 600 (Mo. 2009).

◆   The Supreme Court of South Dakota permitted a group of school districts to proceed with an action asserting underfunding of K-12 public education in the state. In prior challenges involving tax levies, the court had held that school districts lacked standing. But in this case, the districts asserted that the entire state public school system was under-funded. **The court held that the districts were designated by the South Dakota Constitution as the trustees of school trust funds, fines and taxes earmarked for education.** Based on this constitutionally defined status, the school districts could pursue the action. *Olson v. Guindon*, 771. N.W.2d 318 (S.D. 2009).

◆   After Iowa legislators authorized a local sales tax option in 1998, school districts in Polk County, including the Des Moines School District, adopted a local sales tax referendum. The school board proposed a 10-year plan to improve school facilities. It noted that the cost of improvements exceeded revenue projections from the sales tax and stated that the plan was subject to modification. By 2004, the Des Moines board found that local option sales tax revenues were short of projections. The district faced higher building costs and lower enrollment. The board modified the 10-year plan by closing four elementary schools and selling a central facility. It spent funds on facilities that were not part of the original plan and hired a firm to create a management plan.

Taxpayers sued the school board, challenging the modification of the original plan. A state trial court agreed with the board that the proper remedy was an appeal to the state department of education. The Supreme Court of Iowa then stated that school boards are authorized by state regulations to determine the number of schools to operate, and they are required to provide public notice and encourage public consideration when closing a school. Here, the board's decision did not jeopardize any student's right to attend a public school – it only meant that some students would be attending different schools. **This was a "legislative decision" that only a school board could make, and it was not subject to review by a court.** As the lower court held, the taxpayers could appeal to the education department. *Wallace v. Des Moines Independent Community School Dist. Board of Directors*, 754 N.W.2d 854 (Iowa 2008).

◆ The Cobb County (Georgia) School Board improperly bought laptop computers for its middle and high school students with proceeds from a special purpose local option sales tax (SPLOST) that had been authorized for certain capital outlay projects such as technology and information systems hardware and software, and technology infrastructure. A taxpayer sued the board, arguing that the laptop purchase was an abuse of discretion. The case reached the Supreme Court of Georgia, which noted that **state law limited the use of SPLOST proceeds for the exclusive purpose or purposes specified in the resolution or ordinance calling for the imposition of the measure**. In this case, the board resolution authorizing the SPLOST stated that the funds would be used on designated capital outlay projects, such as "system-wide technology improvements." The board could not use SPLOST proceeds for an entirely different purpose. The court ruled for the taxpayer. *Johnstone v. Thompson*, 631 S.E.2d 650 (Ga. 2006).

C. Federal Funding

Federal funding in education is within the jurisdiction of the Secretary of the U.S. Department of Education. Like other questions of budget and finance, the courts do not closely scrutinize these decisions.

◆ The Federal Impact Aid Act provides funding to school districts whose financial conditions are adversely affected by a federal presence, such as a large tract of tax-exempt land. States may not offset Impact Aid by reducing aid to school districts, but may reduce funding to equalize per-pupil expenditures among districts. The Act instructed the U.S. Education Secretary to calculate a disparity in per-pupil expenditures among school districts in a state. When doing so, the Secretary disregarded districts with per-pupil expenditures above the 95th percentile or below the fifth percentile of such expenditures in the state. New Mexico excluded 23 of its 89 districts for determining the equalization formula under the Impact Aid Program.

Two school districts challenged the calculation, as they stood to lose state funding due to an offset of Federal Impact Aid. **The case reached the U.S. Supreme Court, which found strong indications that Congress intended to leave the Secretary free to decide whether a state aid program equalized expenditures.** The alternative urged by the districts would permit gross disparities in district expenditures. The Secretary's method complied with the

Impact Aid Act by comparing per-pupil expenditures made by the state's highest and lowest spending districts. The Court upheld the calculation by the Secretary of Education. *Zuni Public School Dist. No. 89 v. Dep't of Educ.*, 550 U.S. 81, 127 S.Ct. 1534, 167 L.Ed.2d 449 (2007).

◆ **The U.S. Supreme Court held that the Secretary of Education has the authority to demand a refund of misused funds granted to states under Title I** of the Elementary and Secondary Education Act of 1965. Title I provides funding for local educational agencies to prepare economically underprivileged children for school. Recipient states must provide assurances to the secretary that local educational agencies will spend the funds only on qualifying programs. After federal auditors determined that the states of New Jersey and Pennsylvania had misapplied funds, the secretary ordered them to refund the amount of misapplied funds. Both states appealed to the U.S. Supreme Court, arguing that the secretary exceeded his statutory authority in ordering the refunds. The Supreme Court held that Title I, as originally enacted, gave the federal government a right to demand repayment once liability was established. The 1978 amendments to Title I were designed merely to clarify the secretary's legal authority and responsibility to audit recipient state programs and to specify the procedures to be used in the collection of any debts. *Bell v. New Jersey*, 461 U.S. 773, 103 S.Ct. 2187, 76 L.Ed.2d 312 (1983).

◆ The Supreme Court held that the 1978 Title I amendments' new, relaxed standards concerning local schools' eligibility to receive Title I funds could not be applied retroactively. *Bennett v. New Jersey*, 470 U.S. 632 (1985).

In a companion case, the Court held that the state of Kentucky's lack of bad faith was irrelevant in assessing its liability to repay misused Title I funds. *Bennett v. Kentucky Dep't of Educ.*, 470 U.S. 656 (1985).

D. School Expenditures and State Appropriations

In Federal Way School Dist. No. 210 v. State of Washington, *219 P.3d 941 (Wash. 2009), the Supreme Court of Washington rejected a lawsuit asserting that legislative funding formulas which allowed differing salaries among employees in various school districts violated the state constitution. The court held local variations were permitted and that the legislature was aware of the relevant political and economic issues.*

◆ A group of Kansas parents and students challenged aspects of the state's legislative responses to *Montoy v. State of Kansas*, this chapter. In a federal court, they asserted equal protection, due process and speech rights violations. The case reached the U.S. Court of Appeals, Tenth Circuit. In its current form, the Kansas School District Finance and Quality Performance Act sought to ensure equal per-pupil funding across all school districts by use of a complex formula. The formula set a "base state aid per pupil" figure to determine the state's financial aid. This amount was adjusted to actual enrollment numbers and used weighting factors that considered special and bilingual education populations and other variables. Each district was to levy a property tax at a specific rate, which was deemed the "local effort." If this amount was insufficient to generate the state aid under a statutory formula, the state made up the difference. Under the act, districts could also levy additional property taxes – described as the local option budget (LOB). **The challengers claimed a cap on the LOB had forced their school district to cut its budget by $20 million in a two-year period.**

There had been teacher layoffs, increased class sizes and school closures. While the district court had found the parents and students had no standing, the appeals court held this ruling was based on the finding that declaring the LOB unconstitutional would result in the invalidation of the entire act. The court of appeals vacated the ruling on the severability of the LOB issue and returned the case to the district court. *Petrella v. Brownback*, 697 F.3d 1285 (10th Cir. 2012).

◆   A Missouri student claimed she was a resident of the St. Louis School District. She said the district was no longer accredited, allowing her to transfer to a public school of her choice in another district of the same or an adjoining county under Missouri Code Section 167.131. But when the student sought to enroll in a school in the Webster Grove School District, it refused to let her do so. A state court denied Webster Grove's request for a hearing and ordered the district to enroll the student. On appeal, the Supreme Court of Missouri agreed with Webster Grove that the lower court judgment was unsupported by evidence. As the district had disputed several issues, pretrial judgment without a hearing was improper. As a result, the case was sent back to the lower court for more activity. One of the defenses asserted by the district was that Section 167.131 violated the Hancock Amendment to the state constitution because it required a new activity or service without full state financing. **But the court observed that the Hancock Amendment gave "any taxpayer" standing to enforce rights under the amendment.** As the district was not a taxpayer, it lacked standing to raise this defense. When the case returned to the lower court, the district could not raise a Hancock Amendment defense. *King-Willmann v. Webster Groves School Dist.*, 316 S.W.3d 414 (Mo. 2012).

◆   An alliance of Washington school districts sued the state, claiming that its partial special education funding method violated the state constitution. The alliance claimed districts were forced to use special excess levies for adequate funding in a way that violated the state constitution. The court noted that the state funded special education through three mechanisms. A Basic Education Allotment (BEA) provided districts funding based on the average annual full-time equivalent enrollment of all students in the district, whether they were in special education or not. Second, the state provided excess special education funding at 0.9309 times the BEA for special education students. Third, a "safety net" provided additional funds for districts with demonstrated needs beyond the amounts provided by the BEA and excess special education funding. In presenting its case to the court, the alliance did not include BEA funds in its analysis. The court found it was improper to exclude BEA funds.

Appeal reached the Supreme Court of Washington, which held that the BEA was to be included in any evaluation of special education funding adequacy. While the alliance argued that school districts had to pay an unfunded deficit of $112 million for special education services with local funds, the court found this deficit did not include district BEA funds. Quoting the superior court, the supreme court found the alliance was seeking to "decouple special education from BEA funding." But state law did not support any such distinction. For this reason, **the lower court had correctly included the BEA in calculations to determine the adequacy of special education funding**. Any perceived special education deficit disappeared when the BEA was included in calculations. *School Districts' Alliance for Adequate Funding of Special Educ. v. State of Washington*, 244 P.3d 1 (Wash. 2010).

◆   Parents of students attending English language learner (ELL) programs in Nogales (Arizona) Unified School District sued the district for violating the Equal Educational Opportunities Act (EEOA). The EEOA requires states to take appropriate action to overcome language barriers in schools. In 2000, the court held that Arizona's funding to ELL students was arbitrary and unrelated to the actual cost of ELL instruction in Nogales. The order was later extended to the entire state. Over the next eight years, the court issued more orders, found the state in contempt and fined it from $500,000 to $2 million a day. After fines grew to over $20 million in 2006, the legislature passed HB 2064. HB 2064 increased ELL incremental funding and created new funds to cover additional ELL costs, but permitted state funds to be offset by available federal funds. The case reached the Supreme Court, which held that **the lower courts should have determined whether enforcement of the 2000 order was supported by ongoing EEOA violations**. The EEOA gave state and local authorities substantial latitude to take appropriate action to overcome language barriers.

By focusing on Arizona's incremental funding, the Ninth Circuit improperly substituted its judgment for that of state and local officials. The Court reversed and instructed the lower courts to consider the factors that might justify relief. Factors included: 1) Arizona's new "structured English immersion" ELL instruction mandate; 2) evidence of student progress; 3) structural and management reforms in Nogales schools; and 4) an overall increase in Arizona's school funding since 2000. The lower court was to vacate its order extending relief beyond Nogales, unless it found a statewide EEOA violation. *Horne v. Flores*, 557 U.S. 433, 129 S.Ct. 2579, 174 L.Ed.2d 406 (2009).

◆   The Florida Legislature approved an amendment to the state constitution that modified a 2002 citizen initiative limiting public school class sizes. The proposal revised the class size requirements of the 2002 initiative, setting an average maximum number of students rather than just setting a maximum number of students. The ballot title and summary for the proposed 2010 amendment explained that 2002 limits on the maximum number of students assigned to each teacher in public school classrooms would become limits on the average number of students assigned per class to each teacher.

The Florida Education Association sued state officials, asserting the 2010 proposal violated state constitutional and statutory requirements for accuracy and clarity. It argued that the proposal would substantially reduce the state's constitutional obligation to fund class size restrictions and claimed that the ballot summary was defective because it did not state the amendment's chief purpose. The case reached the Supreme Court of Florida, which found that **the**

constitutional obligation of the state to provide "sufficient funds" for class sizes remained unchanged under the 2010 measure. There would be the same right to state provision of sufficient funds for mandated class sizes. The 2010 proposal had a stated purpose of establishing maximum class sizes, and the ballot summary was not misleading. The measure could appear on the November 2010 ballot. *Florida Educ. Ass'n v. Florida Dep't of State*, 48 So.2d 694 (Fla. 2010).

◆   Two education proposals were placed on the ballot for Florida voters in 2008. One would have eliminated restrictions on the use of state funds to aid religion. The other would have required school districts to spend at least 65% of their funding on classroom instruction. It also would have said the state's duty to provide for public education was not limited to free public schools. The proposals were submitted by the state Taxation Budget Reform Commission (TBRC). Opponents sought a state court order to prevent the items from going before voters. A Florida court awarded judgment to the state, and the opponents appealed. The Supreme Court of Florida held **the TBRC's duties were limited to dealing with the state budgetary process**. The proposal titled "Religious Freedom" clearly did not address taxation or the state budgetary process. Thus, the proposal for public funding of education was a subject for which the TBRC had exceeded its constitutional authority. The court ordered the secretary of state to prevent either of the constitutional amendments from appearing on the November 2008 ballot. *Ford v. Browning*, 992 So.2d 132 (Fla. 2008).

◆   In January 2005, the Supreme Court of Kansas held that the state's public school finance system violated the Kansas Constitution. The legislature enacted 2005 H.B. 2247, which increased school funding by $142 million for the 2005-06 school year and authorized a study to find the cost of delivering a K-12 curriculum and required programs. In June 2005, the state supreme court held that H.B. 2247 was unconstitutional because it was not based on actual cost considerations. The court also held that H.B. 2247 exacerbated existing funding inequities. Under-funding by the state forced some districts to use their local option budgets to fund the state's constitutional obligation.

A legislative division of post-audit (LPA) cost study was insufficient to determine the actual costs of providing a constitutionally suitable education. The governor called a special legislative session, which resulted in the passage of S.B. 3. This authorized an additional $147 million for the 2005-06 school year. The court then found that S.B. 3 complied with its order and approved the finance formula for interim purposes. In January 2006, the legislature enacted S.B. 549, containing vast changes to the school finance formula. The case returned to the state supreme court, which held that S.B. 549 created additional at-risk weightings for districts with high numbers of at-risk students and students who were not proficient in reading or math. **More districts with lower assessed valuation per pupil would now receive supplemental aid on local option budgets, bringing them up to par with other districts.** As the 2005 and 2006 acts substantially complied with the prior court orders, the case was dismissed. *Montoy v. State of Kansas*, 138 P.3d 755 (Kan. 2006).

E. Student Fees and Tuition

1. Transportation Fees

In the next case, the Supreme Court held the Equal Protection Clause does not require free transportation in public schools. Its rationale was rooted in the lack of a fundamental right to education under the U.S. Constitution.

◆ North Dakota statutes authorized thinly populated school districts to reorganize into larger districts for efficiency. Reorganized districts had to provide for student transportation to and from their homes. School districts choosing not to reorganize were authorized by statute to charge students a portion of their costs for transportation. The parents of a nine-year-old student refused to sign a transportation contract with the school district. The family was near or at the poverty level. Claiming inability to pay the fee, the family made private transportation arrangements that were more costly than the school's fee.

The parents sued the district for an order to prevent it from collecting the fee on grounds that it violated the state constitution and the Equal Protection Clause. After losing at the trial court level, the parents appealed to the North Dakota Supreme Court, which upheld the decision. On appeal to the U.S. Supreme Court, the parents claimed that the user fee for bus service deprived poor people of minimum access to education and placed an unconstitutional obstacle on education for poor students. The Court noted that the student continued to attend school during the time she claimed she was denied access to the school bus. **The Equal Protection Clause does not require free transportation.** Education is not a fundamental right under the U.S. Constitution. The Court upheld the statute, as it bore a reasonable relationship to the state's legitimate objective of encouraging school districts to provide bus service. The statute did not directly impose a bus fee requirement. It did not discriminate against any class or interfere with any constitutional rights. *Kadrmas v. Dickinson Public Schools*, 487 U.S. 450, 108 S.Ct. 2481, 101 L.Ed.2d 399 (1988).

2. Tuition and Other Fees

The Supreme Court of Indiana held that a mandatory fee imposed by a school district on all its students, was a "charge for attending a public school and obtaining a public education" in violation of the Indiana Constitution.

◆ A group of St. Louis parents enrolled their children in schools within the Clayton School District. They signed agreements obligating themselves to pay the tuition. After the parents took this action, the transitional school district of St. Louis lost its state accreditation. The parents asked Clayton to charge the transitional school district for their children's tuition because Missouri law required unaccredited districts to pay tuition for students attending accredited schools in adjoining districts. When Clayton rejected the parents' claim, they sued. A state court held for the school districts, and the parents appealed. The case reached the Supreme Court of Missouri, which noted that the unaccredited district was obligated to pay tuition for students attending accredited schools in other districts. But it rejected the parents' claim to a right to restitution for tuition they already paid. The contracts were valid, and the parents had no right to restitution. **The parents had contractually obligated themselves to pay Clayton for tuition, and there was no requirement for Clayton to seek payment from the transitional school district.** *Turner v. School Dist. of Clayton*, 318 S.W.3d 660 (Mo. 2010).

♦   An Indiana school district charged each of its students a mandatory $20 fee to address a $2.3 million budget deficit for 2002 that was projected to increase to $5.5 million in 2003. The district deposited the fees in its general fund with state funds and local property tax receipts to help pay the salaries of nurses, media specialists, counselors and a student services coordinator. The district also used the fees to pay for alternative education, a police liaison program, and for athletic, drama and music programs. The parents of students who qualified for reduced or free school lunch and textbook programs filed a class action against the school district, asserting that the fee violated the state constitution.

The case reached the Supreme Court of Indiana, which noted that Article 8, Section 1 does not provide for a system of "free schools," as many state constitutions do. Instead, it provides for "a general and uniform system of Common Schools, wherein tuition shall be without charge, and equally open to all." But without a specific statutory authority, fees or charges could not be directly or indirectly assessed against students or parents for public education cost items. Here, the fee was imposed on all students and was deposited into the district's general fund to offset the cost of non-instructional staff salaries, a police liaison program, alternative education program, and music and drama programs. **A mandatory fee, imposed generally on all students, was a "charge for attending a public school and obtaining a public education" in violation of Article 8, Section 1.** *Nagy v. Evansville-Vanderburgh School Corp.*, 844 N.E.2d 481 (Ind. 2006).

♦   As a result of increased enrollment, a Pennsylvania school board approved a program providing for a district-financed tuition scholarship for any student legally residing in the district for attendance at any private school or non-district public school. A group of resident taxpayers filed a declaratory judgment action against the district in the state court system challenging the program. The trial court agreed with the taxpayers and granted their motion for judgment on the pleadings, ruling that the district lacked authority to implement the plan. On appeal, the Commonwealth Court of Pennsylvania held school districts have no powers except those authorized by express statutory grant and necessary implication. **State law did not expressly authorize reimbursement of tuition and fees.** If a district found its financing insufficient, its options were to either obtain a court order or follow procedures set by the secretary of education. The legislature did not authorize tuition payments to parents in this case, and there was no implied authority for the district plan. A statewide program resembling the plan was struck down by the U.S. Supreme Court in *Sloan v. Lemon*, 413 U.S. 825 (1973). The district had clearly acted outside the scope of its statutory authority, and the court affirmed the trial court order. *Giacomucci v. Southeast Delco School Dist.*, 742 A.2d 1165 (Pa. Commw. Ct. 1999).

F. Private Contractors

In Ry-Tan Construction v. Washington Elementary School Dist. No. 6, *111 P.3d 1019 (Ariz. 2005), the Supreme Court of Arizona held that a public agency accepting a bid is not bound until a formal contract exists. Nothing in state law prohibited a public entity from withdrawing a bid after acceptance of the bid, but prior to the award of a contract.*

In Martin Engineering v. Lexington County School Dist. One, *365 S.C. 1, 615 S.E.2d 110 (S.C. 2005), the Supreme Court of South Carolina found a state code provision allowed correction or withdrawal of an erroneous bid before or after an award. Awards or contracts could be cancelled if there was a mistake.*

◆   A Virginia county school board used a "best value procurement method" in soliciting bids for janitorial services. This allowed it to consider factors such as experience and expertise rather than only price. After the board awarded the contract, a disappointed bidder protested, noting it had 36 years of janitorial service and had bid the lowest price. The board confirmed its selection, and the disappointed bidder sued it in a state court. The court held for the board, finding the "best value" method was permitted. On appeal, the Supreme Court of Virginia found state law required public bodies to determine whether the low bidder for a contract was responsible. If a low bidder was found not responsible, other bidders were entitled to notice and an opportunity to submit a rebuttal.

A public body then had to issue a written determination of responsibility that addressed the bidder's rebuttal. In this case, the board did not notify the disappointed bidder that it was "not responsible." The statute did not permit the board to substitute a "best value" concept for competitive sealed bidding in which the contract went to the lowest responsible bidder. **In addition to identifying statutory violations, the court found the bidder complained that the board relied on factors that were not stated in the bidding criteria** and did not fully credit its experience. Finding merit to the bidder's claim, the court returned the case to the trial court. *Professional Building Maintenance Corp. v. School Board of County of Spotsylvania*, 725 S.E.2d 543 (Va. 2012).

◆   The Supreme Court of Georgia held a school district did not breach a contract for construction management services that had been approved by local voters in an educational local option sales tax referendum. A state trial court had previously held the contract was void as a multi-year contract under state code Section 20-2-506(b). But the supreme court held the section did not apply unless a district entered into a multi-year acquisitional contract without voter approval. **Since voters had approved a sales tax for the relevant services, the school district was entitled to judgment.** *Greene County School Dist. v. Circle Y. Construction, Inc.*, 291 Ga. 111 (Ga. 2012).

◆   A Texas open enrollment charter school contracted with a construction company to build school facilities. When the company sued the school for breach of contract, the school claimed immunity under the Texas Tort Claims Act. A court held that the school was not a governmental unit. On appeal to the Supreme Court of Texas, the school argued that it was entitled to status as a government unit under catch-all language of the Tort Claims Act. The court agreed, noting that **the Tort Claims Act covered any institution, agency or organ of the government**. Open enrollment charter schools were held "part of the public school system of this state." Charter schools were created in accordance with the laws of the state and had primary responsibility for implementing the state's system of public education, along with traditional public schools. The school was entitled to pursue its claim to immunity. *LTTS Charter School v. C2 Construction, Inc.*, 342 S.W.3d 73 (Tex. 2011).

◆   The Los Angeles Unified School District contracted to build an elementary school, but later terminated the contract for material breach and default. It sought proposals from other contractors to complete the school and offered prospective bidders copies of a 108-page correction list that detailed defective, incomplete or missing work by the original contractor. A new contractor then submitted a bid to complete the school and repair deficiencies. It later found additional problems and sought more money. The district rejected its claim for extra compensation for "latent defects" but agreed to pay the contractor $1 million beyond the contract amount with a reservation of rights. It then sued the contractor and its insurer to recover the additional amount paid. After the court held for the school district, the Supreme Court of California held that **contractors cannot avoid obligations or seek additional compensation because of unanticipated difficulties**. But they may recover for extra work or expenses made necessary because conditions were not as represented by the public entity. A contractor does not have to show active misrepresentation or fraudulent concealment to recover expenses from a public entity that fails to disclose material information affecting the cost of performing a contract. The court returned the case to the trial court. *Los Angeles Unified School Dist. v. Great American Insurance Co.*, 49 Cal.4th 739 (Cal. 2010).

◆   A 2007 legislative amendment placed private contractor employees under Florida Statutes Section 1012.467. This provision required criminal background screening for all non-instructional contractors with permission to be on school grounds when students were present. Those convicted of child abuse and certain other charges were denied access to public school grounds when students were present. An employee of a private contractor pleaded no contest to a child abuse charge in 1996. He underwent a criminal background screen as required by the new law and was notified he would no longer have access to school property due to his 1996 no-contest plea. As a result, the contractor fired the employee. A state court enjoined the school board from barring him from school property. On appeal, the employee argued that the 2007 amendment retroactively converted his no-contest plea to a conviction, depriving him of a vested right to enter school property. The Florida District Court of Appeal found that the school board never terminated the relationship or demanded that the contractor fire him. He had no vested right to go onto school grounds. **Since the employee failed to show the board had divested him of any right, the court reversed the judgment.** *School Board of Miami-Dade County, Florida v. Carralero*, 992 So.2d 353 (Fla. Dist. Ct. App. 2008).

◆ A disappointed bidder claimed a Georgia school board had to accept its bid because of an immaterial defect by the low bidder on a construction project. The invitation for bids disallowed changes without board approval, but reserved the board's right to reject bids and waive "technicalities and informalities" in its best interest. The low bidder did not initially provide a subcontractor list, as required by the project specifications. It provided the list within two hours of the opening of bids, and the board accepted it. The contractor that submitted the next-lowest bid sought a court order declaring it the winner. The court denied its request for relief. The supreme court accepted the contractor's appeal and held that state law did not require every statement in an invitation for bids to be met precisely and without deviation. **The district retained statutory powers to waive technicalities.** There was no law, regulation or ordinance requiring all project subcontractors to be listed on public bids. The trial court did not commit error by concluding that the list of subcontractors was immaterial and could be waived. The supreme court affirmed the judgment. *R.D. Brown Contractors v. Board of Educ. of Columbia County*, 626 S.E.2d 471 (Ga. 2006).

G. Insurance Cases

State education laws require school employers to defend employees who cause harm while acting "in the course and scope of their employment" and "without malice." A Utah teacher who was acquitted of criminal charges had a right to reimbursement from her employer for her criminal defense costs.

◆ A New Jersey student accused a teacher of making sexual comments and sued the teacher, his board of education, school administrators and other school staff. A demand to defend the lawsuit was made on the teacher's behalf by the New Jersey Education Association (NJEA). But the board refused the demand, and the teacher obtained coverage through the NJEA's insurer. Later, the lawsuit was settled for $27,500 with no finding of liability by the teacher. NJEA's insurer paid the settlement amount with related attorneys' fees. The teacher and the NJEA's insurer sought reimbursement from the education board of $59,023.

An administrative law judge (ALJ) held for the teacher and NJEA's insurer, relying on a policy subrogation clause. On appeal, the board argued the teacher did not suffer financial loss and that his claim was barred by an anti-subrogation provision in the state Tort Claims Act (TCA). **The court held the case involved only a subrogation claim based on successful defense of the teacher's lawsuit.** As that action arose out of a contract, the TCA was not implicated. State law required education boards to defend and indemnify their employees for any act or omission arising out of and in the performance of their duties. Like the ALJ, the court rejected the board's defenses and it affirmed the decision. *Waters v. Board of Educ. of Township of Toms River*, No. 56-3/10, 2011 WL 6412143 (N.J. Super. Ct. App. Div. 12/22/11).

◆ A Utah teacher began a sexual relationship with a seventh-grader that lasted until the student was a high school senior. The student exposed the relationship after leaving school. An investigation revealed that the misconduct occurred mostly on school grounds, during school hours, and when the teacher was in control of the student. The teacher resigned, and her teaching license was revoked. But a criminal prosecution was dismissed. Certain evidence was excluded from the trial, including the teacher's journal, which was held to have been illegally seized. After the acquittal, the teacher sought reimbursement from the school district for her criminal defense costs and fees. The case reached the Supreme Court of Utah, which held that the reimbursement statute applied because the teacher was acquitted. **Even though the teacher admitted the improper relationship, an employee's right to reimbursement attaches upon an acquittal** or the dismissal of a criminal information. Since the teacher was acquitted, her right to reimbursement could not be defeated. *Acor v. Salt Lake City School Dist.*, 247 P.3d 404 (Utah 2011).

◆ A Maine wrestling coach rented several motel rooms for his team, which was participating in a tournament. He signed a form in which he agreed to pay all charges incurred, abide by rules and assume the risks of injury. Nothing in the rental contract addressed liability to the motel's insurer. During their stay, students in one room made a makeshift sauna to help a teammate "make weight" for the next day's match. They turned on the shower, blocked the vents and used a hair dryer, and the motel's sprinkler system activated as a result. After paying the motel nearly $11,000 to repair the damages caused by the students, the insurer sued the school district to recover for the loss. The Supreme Judicial Court of Maine noted that **the Maine Tort Claims Act effectively barred any tort claims against the district, including claims of negligence**. It found no express or implied provision in the document signed by the coach that would create contractual liability for the district. As a result, the insurer could not pursue the school district for any damages. *Middlesex Mutual Assurance Co. v. Maine School Administrative Dist. No. 43*, 26 A.3d 846 (Me. 2011).

◆ A due process hearing officer held that a Virginia school board violated the IDEA and ordered the board to reimburse a family for almost $118,000 in education costs and attorneys' fees. After a federal court approved the award, the Fourth Circuit affirmed. When attorneys' fees for the family were calculated, it was discovered that the board had expended almost $192,000 to fight the case. It sought coverage from the Virginia Commonwealth Division of Risk Management plan. When the plan denied coverage, the board sued. The plan argued that the IDEA due process hearing did not involve a "claim" and that the reimbursement of education costs was not "damages" under plan language. The Supreme Court of Virginia found that **the family had made a "claim" as defined by the plan and that the amount the board was ordered to pay was not excluded from coverage**. As the duty to defend is broader than the duty to provide coverage, the plan was necessarily liable for defending the case. This meant the plan had to pay the school board's legal fees. *School Board of City of Newport News v. Comwlth. of Virginia*, 689 S.E.2d 731 (Va. 2010).

◆ A Michigan school district's insurer sued the district to enforce its rights under state law with respect to the provision of nursing services to a student. It sought reimbursement for services it believed the district was providing and it was paying for. But the court of appeals noted that the student's IEPs did not specify the services in dispute, and the services being provided by the district were not being paid for by the insurer. Further, **the insurer had no right to try to determine, through a lawsuit, whether the district should be providing nursing services to the student**. *Progressive Michigan Insurance Co. v. Calhoun Intermediate School Dist.*, No. 290564, 2010 WL 2680112 (Mich. Ct. App. 7/6/10).

◆ A Maryland high school vice principal was accused of assaulting a student who was in his office discussing a report of harassment by another student. The vice principal claimed he showed the student a small knife he kept in his drawer and asked him how he would feel if someone he had picked on brought a knife to school. He told the student that this was "where harassment could lead." But the student claimed the vice principal shut the door and brandished the knife in front of him. He filed an assault action against the vice principal, who asked the board of education to defend him. The board was a self-insuring member of the Maryland Association of Boards of Education Group Insurance Pool. Asserting that an assault was intentional and malicious conduct that was excluded from coverage, the board refused to defend the vice principal. He obtained defense under his educators employment liability policy.

After a jury found that the vice principal did not commit assault, the educators liability insurer sought reimbursement from the board. The Court of Appeals of Maryland noted that **state law required a board to defend an employee who was both "acting in the scope of his employment" and "without malice."** Here, the vice principal won his case. The court found nothing in state law that would relieve a school board of its statutory duty based on the type of insurance coverage it had purchased. As the vice principal's response to the student's complaint asserted he was acting in pursuit of his duties, in the scope of his employment and without malice, the education board had a duty to defend him in the student's action. *Board of Educ. of Worcester County v. Horace Mann Insurance Co.*, 408 Md. 278, 969 A.2d 305 (Md. 2009).

◆ A Pennsylvania school hired a contractor to renovate an elementary school. The contract included a liquidated damages clause for work delays, and a performance bond was acquired from a surety to cover default by the contractor. The terms of the bond made the surety responsible for any remaining work after default, and made it eligible for any contract balance. Near completion of the project, the school district claimed that the contractor's work was untimely and deficient. It declared the contractor in default and withheld its final payment, also refusing to pay the balance to the surety. The contractor sued the school district, and the district counter-claimed against the contractor.

The district agreed to release all claims against the contractor and pay it $430,000. However, the district refused to release its claims against the surety, claiming it reserved all rights under the performance bond. The settlement was placed into the record before a judge, with no mention of the surety's rights or duties. The court held that the release of the contractor also discharged the surety. The case reached the Supreme Court of Pennsylvania, where the surety argued that it stood in the shoes of the contractor, and had no remaining liability after a settlement. The district argued that the release did not fully resolve all issues relating to the contractor's default. The court noted that **the district sought to have it both ways by releasing the contractor, then claiming additional rights against the surety**. However, the district was only entitled to performance by either the contractor or the surety. *Kiski Area School Dist. v. Mid-State Surety Corp.*, 600 Pa. 444, 967 A.2d 368 (Pa. 2008).

◆ A Missouri school district assigned a substitute to an elementary school classroom. He grabbed a student by the neck and lifted him off the ground. The teacher later pleaded guilty in state criminal court proceedings to third degree criminal assault and endangering the welfare of a child. The family accepted $20,000 in settlement of negligence claims against the district and board members, and agreed to settle claims against the teacher for $100,000. The agreement provided that any judgment would be sought from the district's insurer. The district had liability coverage through the Missouri United School Insurance Council (MUSIC), a pool of self-insuring school districts. After MUSIC declined to pay the judgment, the family sued for coverage.

A state trial court awarded pretrial judgment to MUSIC. The case eventually reached the Supreme Court of Missouri, which affirmed the judgment for MUSIC. It held that **the assault was an intentional act, and not a covered "occurrence" under the policy**. *Todd v. Missouri United School Insurance Council*, No. 223 S.W.3d 156 (Mo. 2007).

◆ The family of an Illinois student with disabilities sued their school district for violating the Individuals with Disabilities Education Act (IDEA), Section 504 of the Rehabilitation Act, and the Americans with Disabilities Act (ADA). The district's insurer paid the district $50,000 under a supplementary payments provision of its policy that limited coverage for defense costs to $50,000 for non-monetary claims involving disputes in special education. The insurer denied responsibility for further defense costs, relying on a policy exclusion precluding coverage for relief "other than monetary damages." It asserted that the family's suit was limited to the special education placement and did not seek damages. A federal court and the Seventh Circuit Court of Appeals held for the district. The family appealed the IDEA claims to the U.S. Supreme Court. The Court declined the case, but the appeal cost the district $9,901 in legal costs and fees.

The school district filed a separate action against the insurer in a state court to recover its additional defense costs. The case reached the Appellate Court of Illinois, which noted that the ADA, Section 504 and IDEA claims sought reimbursement for the cost of obtaining independent educational evaluations and services. The family would have been entitled to payment from the district had these claims succeeded. **The claims for reimbursement sought monetary damages as contemplated by the policy, and the insurer was required to defend the district.** The court affirmed the judgment for defense costs arising under the ADA and Section 504, and it reversed the judgment denying defense of the IDEA claims. The district would be entitled to the additional costs of defending the Supreme Court appeal, as it involved an IDEA claim. *General Star Indemnity Co. v. Lake Bluff School Dist. No. 65*, 819 N.E.2d 784 (Ill. App. Ct. 2004).

II. DESEGREGATION

In Brown v. Board of Educ., *347 U.S. 483 (1954), the U.S. Supreme Court declared unconstitutional "separate but equal" systems of segregation in public schools. Fourteen years after its landmark decision in* Brown, *the Court responded to widespread resistance by school districts to federal desegregation orders by ruling that segregation must be eliminated "root and branch."* Green v. County School Board of New Kent County, *391 U.S. 430 (1968).*

Courts rely on the factors identified in Green v. County School Board of New Kent County *to determine if a district should be declared unitary and released from federal court supervision. They also consider more recent cases such as* Board of Educ. of Oklahoma City Public Schools v. Dowell, *498 U.S. 237 (1991), and* Freeman v. Pitts, *503 U.S. 467 (1992).*

By 1992, the Court declared that formerly segregated, dual school districts could be released from federal court supervision upon a demonstration of good-faith compliance with a desegregation decree, where the "vestiges of past discrimination have been eliminated to the extent practicable." Freeman v. Pitts, *503 U.S. 467 (1992).* **In a 1991 Oklahoma case, the Supreme Court held that the supervision of local school districts by the federal courts was meant as a temporary means to remedy past discrimination.** *It returned the case to a lower court with instructions to determine whether a school district that achieved unitary status in 1977 had complied with constitutional requirements when it later adopted a student reassignment plan.* Board of Educ. of Oklahoma City Public Schools v. Dowell, *498 U.S. 237 (1991).*

The test from Freeman *and* Dowell *for releasing a school system from federal court supervision is whether there has been compliance with the decree, whether retention of the case by the court is necessary or practicable to achieve compliance with the decree, and whether the school district has demonstrated a good-faith commitment to the desegregation decree to the public and to minority parents and students. The* Freeman *decision is also important for approving the concept of the withdrawal of federal court supervision in stages as partial unitary status is achieved with respect to specific programs and areas including school facilities, faculty and staff assignments, extracurricular activities, transportation and student assignments.*

A. Release from Federal Court Supervision

◆   Federal court oversight of Shelby County (Tennessee) public schools began in 1963 with a class action alleging racial segregation. Over the years, the federal district court issued many orders requiring elimination of all vestiges of state-imposed segregation in accordance with *Brown v. Board of Educ.* In 2006, the school board and a class of students sought to end the lawsuit. After two fairness hearings, the court found that the goals of the desegregation plan had not been met. It refused to dismiss court oversight regarding student assignment, faculty integration and extracurricular activities, and it set "racial ratios" for student and faculty members to be met by 2012. A target for the end of court supervision was set for 2015. The school board and the U.S. government appealed to the Sixth Circuit. The court noted that a **"unitary"**

school system is one having unitary assignment of students, faculty and staff, and unitary school facilities, resources, transportation and extracurricular activities. If a school district complies in good faith with a desegregation decree, and eliminates the vestiges of past discrimination to the extent practicable, the system is entitled to be released from supervision.

Student assignment remained racially imbalanced in Shelby County schools, but the court found this was due to demographic factors. Political and social decisions beyond the board's control affected the district's racial balance. These influences were unrelated to the prior constitutional violation and were outside a court's power to resolve. The lower court had incorrectly found the board out of compliance with the decree based on variations in teacher ratio in some schools. Race-based hiring as ordered by the district court was unconstitutional. As the district court had denied the request for unitary status for extracurricular activities without explanation, the court rejected this part of the order, and reversed the judgment with instructions to dismiss the case. *Robinson v. Shelby County Board of Educ.*, 566 F.3d 642 (6th Cir. 2009).

◆ Little Rock (Arkansas) School District (LRSD) was in desegregation litigation since 1956. In 1989, a federal court approved an interdistrict settlement plan that allowed court supervision of remedial desegregation by LRSD and two neighboring districts. The parties agreed in 1998 that if LRSD substantially complied with a revised desegregation plan, the district would be declared unitary after the 2000-01 school year. In 2002, the court granted LRSD "partial unitary status" based on compliance with all plan provisions except those governing academic programs for improving African-American student achievement. The court imposed a compliance remedy upon LRSD. In 2004, the U.S. Court of Appeals, Eighth Circuit, affirmed the finding of substantial compliance. When LRSD asked to be declared unitary, a federal court held that it was still not in compliance with the academic assessment provisions. The Eighth Circuit rejected LRSD's claim that this was an error.

The case returned to the lower court, which found that **the LRSD acted in good faith to implement the program assessment process as required** by the 1998 revised plan. After the court declared the LRSD system unitary, a group of intervenors appealed. The Eighth Circuit expressed complete agreement with the lower court that LRSD substantially complied with its desegregation obligations. No evidence supported the current appeal. *Little Rock School Dist. v. North Little Rock School Dist.*, 561 F.3d 746 (8th Cir. 2009).

◆ In 1969, a Mississippi federal court divided a school district into three attendance zones and required the transportation of students in non-segregated, nondiscriminatory ways. The district also had to select locations for school construction and consolidate its schools to prevent recurrence of a dual system. In 2004, the district sought a declaration of full unitary status which, if granted, would end federal court oversight. The U.S. Government and private parties agreed that many areas of operation were unitary. But they alleged that the district did not act in good faith with court orders regarding facilities and a magnet high school that was still 98.5% African-American. The court held that the district was unitary and dissolved all its desegregation orders.

The case reached the Fifth Circuit, which held that the magnet program at the high school had been in operation long enough for the court to make informed findings about it. The district's good-faith compliance was seen in the expenditure of considerable resources for renovating the high school and implementing the magnet program. It had implemented minority recruitment, set up a biracial advisory committee, and fulfilled its reporting obligations. Racial imbalance in schools, by itself, does not create a constitutional violation. **While the magnet high school had failed to draw white students, there was evidence that this was primarily due to demographic and cultural factors.** The school district had achieved unitary status in all of its operations, and further judicial oversight was neither required nor desirable. *Anderson v. School Board of Madison County*, 517 F.3d 292 (5th Cir. 2008).

◆ In 1964, a federal court required all Alabama school districts to desegregate. In 1970, the court ordered the Roanoke City Board of Education to implement a desegregation plan proposed by the federal government. By 1997, the court ordered the parties to consider whether the Roanoke school system had achieved unitary status in several areas. In 1998, the court approved a consent decree which found the Roanoke schools had achieved unitary status in student assignment, facilities and transportation. These functions were returned to local control. The board agreed to take action in other identified areas to eliminate any remaining vestiges of segregation. These included faculty hiring and assignment, student assignment and instruction, special education, extracurricular activities, student discipline and graduation rates. During the 2006-07 school year, the board sought a declaration of unitary status and termination of the lawsuit.

A federal court found that the board had made considerable efforts to recruit and hire minority applicants for faculty positions, and had encouraged student assignment on a nondiscriminatory basis through special programs and courses. It had taken reasonable steps to ensure equal participation opportunities in extracurricular activities. Student discipline had been addressed through cultural diversity training, activities and workshops. The board hired a consultant to work with repeat offenders, significantly reducing disciplinary problems. The district dropout rate was 4% lower than the statewide average. African-American student participation in a high school math club and local chapter of the National Honor Society was increasing. **The city board and its members had met standards entitling the district to a declaration of unitary status.** *Lee v. Roanoke City Board of Educ.*, Civil Action No. 3:70cv855-MHT, 2007 WL 1196482 (M.D. Ala. 4/23/07).

◆ In 1969, a Georgia school system was ordered to close all legally recognized black schools. The system complied. In 1983, a plaintiff class contended that the school system improperly limited minority transfers to a predominantly white school and that the proposed expansion of a white high school would perpetuate segregation. The court ruled that the school system had achieved unitary status and did not have a discriminatory intent in deciding to expand the high school. The U.S. Court of Appeals, Eleventh Circuit, stated that the system had not discharged its duty in the areas of student assignment, transportation, and extracurricular activities by closing all legally recognized black schools in response to the 1969 order. The system would not achieve unitary status until it maintained at least three years of racial equality in the six categories set out in *Green*: student assignment, faculty, staff, transportation, extracurricular activities, and facilities. The U.S. Supreme Court, however, held on appeal that the *Green* framework did not need to be applied as construed by the court of appeals. **Through relinquishing control in areas deemed to be unitary, a court and school district may more effectively concentrate on the areas in need of further attention.** The Court held that the "incremental" approach was constitutional, and that a court may declare that it will order no further remedy in any area that is found to be unitary. The order of the court of appeals was reversed, and the case was remanded to the district court. *Freeman v. Pitts,* 503 U.S. 467 (1992).

The case returned to the district court, which found the evidence did not demonstrate a pattern of discrimination or absence of good faith by the school district. It therefore granted the district's motion to be released from federal court jurisdiction. *Mills v. Freeman,* 942 F.Supp. 1449 (N.D. Ga. 1996).

B. Liability Issues

Courts reviewing the actions of government officials in desegregation cases may find liability for civil rights violations where actions by the officials foreseeably perpetuate racial segregation in schools. Relief for constitutional violations may be apportioned among state and local school agencies.

1. Government Liability

◆ Illinois residents petitioned the state board of education to detach land from Joliet Township High School District and annex it to Lincoln Way Community High School District. Joliet objected to the petition, arguing that the state law under which the petition was filed violated the federal Equal Educational Opportunities Act (EEOA). According to Joliet, the state school code forbade state education department hearing officers from considering EEOA issues when ruling on school district detachment and annexation petitions.

The hearing officer found the conditions of the code were met and recommended granting the petition. Appeal reached the Supreme Court of Illinois, which explained that the Supremacy Clause of the U.S. Constitution declares the laws of the U.S. to be the supreme law of the land. Any state law that conflicts with a federal law is preempted by the Supremacy Clause and is unconstitutional. The court found the parties were in agreement that the EEOA claim should be heard, but were in disagreement over what court or agency should consider it. **The EEOA was a remedial statute designed to specify appropriate remedies for the orderly removal of vestiges of the dual system of racially segregated schools.** It was clear that Congress intended the states and their educational agencies to refrain from discrimination. As the courts of Illinois had an obligation to review and enforce the EEOA, the court held the proper means for redress of an EEOA violation was an original action in a state court. Joliet's EEOA claim could be fully litigated in the state court system, avoiding a court ruling that would invalidate the state law. *Board of Educ., Joliet Township High School Dist. No. 204 v. Board of Educ., Lincoln Way Community High School Dist. No. 210*, 231 Ill.2d 184, 897 N.E.2d 756 (Ill. 2008).

◆ A Georgia school district relied on ability grouping since the end of *de jure* school segregation. Teachers grouped elementary school students based on their perceived abilities and their actual performance. The local NAACP branch and several African-American families sued the district, asserting that the practice violated the Equal Protection Clause of the Fourteenth Amendment and Title VI of the Civil Rights Act of 1964. A federal court held that many areas of school operations had racial imbalances, but attributed them to demographics and other "external factors." Although disproportionate numbers of low-income children, most of them African-American, were put in lower ability groups and stayed there throughout their academic careers, there was no federal law violation. The court attributed this to an "impoverished environment," not discrimination. The case reached the Eleventh Circuit which held that **a school district's obligation is only to eliminate the vestiges of past discrimination "to the extent practicable."** Here, the record supported the finding that the imbalances in the ability grouping program did not result from intentional discrimination, but from poverty. The Eleventh Circuit upheld the lower court decision. *Holton v. City of Thomasville School Dist.*, 490 F.3d 1257 (11th Cir. 2007).

2. Inter-District Remedies

◆ The U.S. Supreme Court affirmed an intra-district school desegregation plan that included busing in *Columbus Board of Educ. v. Penick*, 443 U.S. 449 (1979). However, in the landmark Detroit school busing case, the Court rejected a plan that would have required multi-district, inter-district busing. It said there was no evidence that suburban districts outside Detroit, which were included in the plan, operated segregated school systems or affected segregation in other districts. The Court held that **absent some inter-district constitutional violations with inter-district effects, racial segregation existing in one district could not be remedied by inter-district solutions**. *Milliken v. Bradley*, 418 U.S. 717, 94 S.Ct. 3112, 41 L.Ed.2d 1069 (1974).

◆ In 1985, the Englewood Cliffs Board of Education petitioned the New Jersey state education commissioner to sever a longstanding agreement with the city of Englewood Board of Education, under which Englewood Cliffs students attended one of Englewood's high schools. Englewood opposed the petition, seeking to prevent further racial imbalance that would result from termination of the agreement. It also joined as a party to the action the Board of Education of Tenafly, a wealthy community that in 1982 began accepting nonresident students to Tenafly High School on a tuition-paying basis. An administrative law judge (ALJ) held that the Tenafly policy enticed white and Asian students from Englewood, exacerbating Englewood's racial imbalance. The ALJ held that state education officials had a constitutional and statutory responsibility to prevent segregation and ordered the Tenafly Board to stop accepting tuition-paying students from both Englewood and Englewood Cliffs. The case reached the state supreme court, which held that **the state board and commissioner had an affirmative duty to take action to remedy racial imbalances at the high school**. The school had gone from 65.8% black and Hispanic in 1982-83 to 84% in 1987-88. The first step in achieving a racial balance that would effectuate state policy was to enjoin all other districts, including Tenafly, from accepting Englewood and Englewood Cliffs students into their schools. The state board had improperly and perhaps unintentionally allocated the responsibility for addressing racial imbalances to the Englewood Board. The court rejected compulsory regionalization, and the commissioner and state board retained ultimate responsibility for addressing racial imbalance at the school. *Board of Educ. of Borough of Englewood Cliffs v. Board of Educ. of City of Englewood*, 170 N.J. 323, 788 A.2d 729 (N.J. 2002).

3. Budget Issues

◆ An Arkansas taxpayer and 14 school districts sued the governor for diverting equalization funds, (later known as "foundation funds") to satisfy court-ordered desegregation costs in Pulaski County, and to provide additional base funding for districts that did not meet other funding standards. They claimed the diversion violated Amendment 74 to the Arkansas Constitution, which assessed a uniform rate of taxation (URT) of 25 mills for each school district on the value of property "solely for the maintenance and operation of the schools." A claim was added that the state unlawfully retained and diverted Amendment 74 property taxes and funds allocated to the state Educational Excellence Trust Fund. A court held for the state officials, and the challengers appealed to the Supreme Court of Arkansas.

The court found that Amendment 74 set a URT of 25 mills for each district on the assessed value of property "solely for the maintenance and operation of the schools." But URT funds only partially funded the basic foundation for any given year. **The court rejected the argument that the state could not reduce its Amendment 74 funding based on increased tax revenues resulting from increasing property values.** Amendment 74 did not place limits on how the General Assembly appropriated these funds, once it established what was needed to provide all students with substantially equal educational opportunities. Amendment 74 permitted variances in school district revenues above the base rate of 25 mills to enhance curriculums, facilities and equipment. There was no retention of URT funds by the state when the growth in URT revenues resulted in a corresponding reduction in state funding. The 25 mill URT set the amount of state foundation aid. Since none of the challengers' other theories had merit, the court affirmed the judgment for the state. *Fort Smith School Dist. v. Beebe*, 2009 Ark. 333 (Ark. 2009).

◆ Two sparsely populated school districts in the Texas panhandle served fewer than 130 students each, and they depended on transfer students to be viable. "Virtually all" of the students in one district were transfer students. Texas law permits any eligible child to transfer if the receiving district and the parents agree. A 1970 federal court order required the state and the Texas Education Agency (TEA) to desegregate schools. A 1973 court order forbade the TEA from funding or supporting student transfers when the effect in either a sending or receiving school or district would be to reduce or impede school desegregation. The TEA began to track student transfers under an automated system. Both of the panhandle districts failed to report student transfers into TEA's transfer monitoring system. The TEA later informed the districts it would withhold funds for the following year for failing to report the transfers. After unsuccessfully challenging the actions within the TEA, the districts sought to intervene in the federal desegregation case. The court held that its 1973 order applied statewide because it was meant to eliminate the vestiges of race discrimination from Texas' former dual school system. But, as the panhandle districts received a state "sparsity adjustment," they did not receive any additional funds due to the transfers, and the TEA sanctions were disallowed.

On appeal, the U.S. Court of Appeals, Fifth Circuit, agreed with the districts that the 1973 order exceeded the lower court's authority. **The districts had never been subject to a desegregation order, and it was not shown that any of the transfers in this case were approved based on an intent to discriminate.** No state law provided for the sanctions, and the TEA's power to impose them arose solely from the 1973 court order. As the districts had never been found to have discriminated against students based on their race, the TEA could not sanction them. There must be a constitutional violation to sanction a school system. Accordingly, the judgment was reversed. *Samnorwood Independent School Dist. v. Texas Educ. Agency*, 533 F.3d 258 (5th Cir. 2008).

◆ In 1971, a federal district court entered Order 5281, requiring the desegregation of Texas school districts that had taken no steps to comply with *Brown v. Board of Educ.* Order 5281 prohibited the Texas Education Agency (TEA) from allowing student transfers that reduced or impeded desegregation, or that perpetuated discrimination. Hearne Independent School District (HISD) was not a party to Order 5281, but had been the defendant in another desegregation case. Its total student enrollment dropped from near 1,700 in 1991 to under 1,200 in 2004. Mumford Independent School District (MISD) grew from 57 students to over 400 during the same years, largely by receiving students from HISD of Hispanic or African-American descent. HISD and MISD remained "majority-minority" both before and after the transfers.

The U.S. government and HISD claimed the transfers violated Order 5281 and sued to halt them. A court prohibited further transfers of white students to MISD. On appeal, the Fifth Circuit noted that the racial composition of Texas schools had changed since 1971. **During the past decade, HISD had lost students of all races** via transfers, dropouts and changes of residence. The TEA had a "liberal transfer policy" in which state funding followed students across district lines. The lower court had rejected the TEA's balancing approach and ordered the TEA to cease all funding for the transfer of white students, including those who had attended MISD schools for their entire school careers. Small changes in the racial composition of a district due to student transfers did not justify mandatory inter-district desegregation remedies. The TEA's funding of transfers had no significant net racial impact upon either district. The district court order was vacated. *U.S. v. State of Texas*, 457 F.3d 472 (5th Cir. 2006).

◆ In 1977, the Kansas City, Missouri, School District (KCMSD), its school board and a group of resident students sued the state of Missouri and a number of suburban Kansas City school districts, claiming the state had caused and perpetuated racial segregation in Kansas City schools. A court held that the state and KCMSD were liable for an intra-district constitutional violation. The defendants were ordered to eliminate all vestiges of state-imposed segregation.

The U.S. Supreme Court held that the lower court's remedial plan had been based on a budget that exceeded KCMSD's authority to tax. The evidence did not substantiate the theory that continuing lack of academic achievement in the district was the result of past segregation. The lower court had exceeded its authority by ordering the construction of a superior school system to attract white students from suburban and private schools. Its mandate was to remove the racial identity of KCMSD schools, and an inter-district remedy went beyond the intra-district violation. **The magnet district concept of KCMSD schools could not be supported by the existence of white flight.** The lower court orders for state contribution to salary increases, quality education programs and capital improvements were reversed. *Missouri v. Jenkins*, 515 U.S. 70 (1995).

III. SCHOOL DISTRICT OPERATIONS

School district powers are created by state laws, and actions exceeding statutory authority may be set aside by a reviewing court. If state law provides, school district territories may be altered by annexation and detachment where economics or demographics make such action necessary.

A. School Closing and District Dissolution Issues

◆ A West Virginia parent who was denied a trial court order compelling state and local officials to halt a school consolidation project lost his appeal to the state's highest court. He asserted there were health and safety concerns at a construction site. After a state circuit court denied the requested order, the Supreme Court of Appeals of West Virginia noted that the construction was already substantially under way and that the board had already committed $3.2 million to contracts and stood to lose another $8.6 million in grants if the construction project was halted. Moreover, **there had already been public hearings on the matter and all the necessary procedural steps had been completed.** At a public meeting, the state board of education had approved the project. The lower court had properly refused to issue the special order sought by the parent. *Christini v. Board of Educ. of West Virginia*, No. 11-1060, 2012 WL 4054121 (W. Va. 9/4/12).

◆ New Hampshire's highest court denied a taxpayer challenge to a school district plan to build and renovate two elementary schools. A pair of taxpayers noted the lot sizes of the schools did not meet state administrative requirements. A state court allowed the school district to intervene in the lawsuit, and it argued that the taxpayers had no legal interest in enforcing the state administrative rule on lot size. In the meantime, the taxpayers raised a new claim that waiver of the minimum lot size violated a state duty to provide a constitutionally adequate education. After the court dismissed the case, the state supreme court affirmed the decision. It noted recent court cases finding that **taxpayers are required to demonstrate that their rights are impaired in order to obtain relief from a court**. It was not enough for the taxpayers to simply allege that they paid taxes in the district. Since they could not show they had any personal rights that were impaired by the lot size waiver, the judgment was affirmed. *Baer v. New Hampshire Dep't of Educ.*, 160 N.H. 727, 8 A.3d 48 (N.H. 2010).

◆   The Beaumont Texas board of school trustees announced a $388.6 million bond issue "for the purpose of acquiring, constructing, renovating, improving and equipping new and existing school buildings and school facilities." Voters approved of the bond issue, and the district began to define projects at various sites. When it became apparent that a particular school would be demolished, the Beaumont Heritage Society sued the district and school officials, claiming the board lacked the authority to demolish the school. At a hearing, the district superintendent testified that no middle school buildings would be retained.

According to the society, school officials had represented prior to the bond issue that the school would not be demolished. The court enjoined demolition of the school pending a full trial. School officials appealed to the Court of Appeals of Texas, which noted that contractors were apparently prepared to tear down the middle school buildings. If the society's evidence was true, school officials had made public misrepresentations prior to the bond issue. The district did not offer any board minutes reflecting a vote to demolish the school. But the superintendent had testified at the lower court hearing that no buildings at the school would be retained. **While school trustees are vested with the duty to manage school property, state law restricted expenditures of public funds to their authorized purposes.** The trial court did not abuse its discretion in halting the demolition pending a trial to consider whether the district's use of bond funds was authorized. *Thomas v. Beaumont Heritage Society*, 296 S.W.2d 350 (Tex. Ct. App. 2009).

◆   Act 60 of a 2003 Extraordinary Session of the Arkansas General Assembly required school districts with average daily memberships of fewer than 350 students to consolidate with – or be annexed by – other school districts. After Lake View School District was consolidated with another district, a group of challengers sued state officials in a federal court, which dismissed the case. Appeal went to the Eighth Circuit, which held that **the state had a legitimate interest in consolidating school districts to achieve economies of scale and other efficiencies.** *Friends of Lake View School Dist. v. Beebe*, 578 F.3d 753 (8th Cir. 2009).

◆   An Iowa school district closed five schools and the state board of education affirmed the decision. A group of taxpayers sought review, asserting that the board did not comply with its own regulations. After the court upheld the decision, appeal reached the state supreme court. Among the court's findings was that the school district considered revenue forecasts and discussed a staff report with strategic options for dealing with protected revenue shortfalls and cost increases. It considered other options and held meetings to solicit public input on its plans. According to the taxpayers, the district action had to be set aside because of failure to comply with two state board rules describing procedural steps for districts to follow when closing schools. They claimed public participation was limited because of insufficient notice. The court held that while the legislature had authorized the board to adopt rules for many specific subjects, there was no express legislative authorization of rules prescribing the procedures for closing schools. Instead, **the legislature's failure to grant the board such authority fit within the grant of exclusive jurisdiction to school districts in school matters**. The district's decision to close some of its schools clearly entailed discretion. The court ruled for the district. *Wallace v. Iowa State Board of Educ.*, 770 N.W.2d 344 (Iowa 2009).

B. Redistricting and Zoning

◆   A Kansas city planning commission held a hearing to consider a school district's application for a special use permit for a lighted softball complex and stadium. An adjacent property owner objected, and the planning commission voted to deny the application due to the frequency of stadium use and its impact on surrounding properties. After hearing from interested parties, the city council voted 5-3 to return the application to the planning commission for further review and examination of specific items. The planning commission again voted to deny the special use permit, but the city council voted 5-4 to grant it with modifications, with the mayor casting the tie-breaking vote. The objecting property owner sued, claiming violations of Kansas law. A court held that state law did not permit the city council to override the planning commission by a simple majority vote. It reversed the city's action. The city then appealed to the Supreme Court of Kansas, meanwhile voting 6-2 to ratify its action granting the special use permit.

The supreme court held that state law said nothing about a two-thirds majority by a city after a proposal was returned to a planning commission, then resubmitted. As the trial court had incorrectly interpreted the statute to require a two-thirds majority vote after the city returned the case to the planning commission, the court reversed the judgment. **The final authority in zoning matters rested with the agency with legislative power.** The court rejected the property owner's additional arguments, finding that he had received a fair, open and impartial opportunity to contest the application. *Manly v. City of Shawnee*, 287 Kan. 63, 194 P.3d 1 (Kan. 2008).

◆   A New York school district provided special education services at private, religious schools to students with disabilities who were members of the Satmar Hasidic group. The group's religious beliefs include segregation of school-age boys and girls and separation from mainstream society. A U.S. Supreme Court decision in 1985 prohibited the state from paying public school teachers for teaching on parochial school grounds. The state legislature passed a statute establishing a separate school district entirely within the Hasidic community to provide special education services. The New York Court of Appeals held that the statute endorsed religion in violation of the Establishment Clause.

The U.S. Supreme Court agreed to review the case. It held that a state may not delegate authority to a group chosen by religion. Although the statute did not expressly identify the Hasidim as recipients of governmental authority, it had clearly been passed to benefit them. The result was a purposeful and forbidden fusion of governmental and religious functions. **The creation of a school district for the religious community violated the Establishment Clause.** The Court held that the legislation extended a special franchise to the Hasidim that violated the constitutional requirement of religious neutrality by the government. *Board of Educ. of Kiryas Joel Village School Dist. v. Grumet,* 512 U.S. 687 (1994).

The legislature passed new legislation allowing municipalities to establish their own school districts upon the satisfaction of several criteria. Noting that these criteria would restore a Hasidic school district, the taxpayers renewed their challenge. The case reached the state's highest court, which held that **despite the neutral criteria of the amendments, the Hasidic village was the only municipality that could ever avail itself of the amendments.** As no other district could be eligible for redistricting under the law, it impermissibly favored the Satmar sect, and the court held for the taxpayers. *Grumet v. Cuomo,* 90 N.Y.2d 57, 659 N.Y.S.2d 173, 681 N.E.2d 340 (N.Y. 1997).

The legislature amended the law again in 1997, in an attempt to conform with the court of appeals' decision. The case again reached the New York Court of Appeals. Despite the law's facial neutrality with respect to religion, it only benefited Kiryas Joel residents, and its potential benefit extended to only one other district in the state. **Since other religious groups would be unable to benefit from the law in the manner enjoyed by the Satmar sect of Kiryas Joel, the law was not neutral in effect** and violated the Establishment Clause. *Grumet v. Pataki,* 93 N.Y.2d 677, 720 N.E.2d 66 (N.Y. 1999).

IV. SCHOOL BOARDS

A. Membership

1. Appointments, Elections, Residency and Recall

◆ A Washington school board voted to reschedule a school makeup day in violation of a collective bargaining provision. Many teachers did not report for work and those who did received no pay. The board found some substitutes, but it resorted to hiring jugglers and clowns to keep students occupied for the day. An arbitrator held that the board violated the bargaining agreement by unilaterally changing the makeup day, and that board members had "knowingly and willfully" violated contract rights by withholding pay. The incident cost the district almost $75,000. Three district residents filed recall petitions against two board members. The case reached the Supreme Court of Washington, which ruled that to be legally sufficient, **the recall petitions needed only "state with specificity substantial conduct clearly amounting to misfeasance, malfeasance or violation of the oath of office."** Here, the petition alleged that the board members knowingly and willingly broke a collective bargaining agreement and thereby unnecessarily caused substantial financial harm. As the charges against the board members were legally sufficient, the petitioners could continue seeking a special election to recall the members from office. *In re Recall of Young*, 100 P.3d 307 (Wash. 2004).

◆   Section Two of the federal Voting Rights Act of 1965 bars states and their political subdivisions from maintaining discriminatory voting practices, standards or procedures. Section Five of the act is limited to "covered jurisdictions." It bans the passing of new discriminatory laws as soon as old ones are struck down by freezing election procedures in covered jurisdictions unless the changes are nondiscriminatory. A Louisiana school board covered under Section 5 addressed population disparities revealed in the 1990 census by adopting a plan preserving a white majority in each of its 12 single-member districts. The board rejected a proposal by the local NAACP that would have created two districts with a majority of African-American voters. The board complied with Section 5 procedures by obtaining pre-clearance from a District of Columbia federal court. The U.S. Attorney General's office appealed to the U.S. Supreme Court, where it joined with the NAACP in arguing that a change in voting practices that violates Section 2 also constitutes an independent reason to deny pre-clearance under Section 5. The Court held that the sections addressed different voting policy concerns. Nothing in the statute justified presuming that a violation of Section 2 was sufficient for denying pre-clearance under Section 5. However, some of the evidence presented in support of a Section 2 claim might be relevant in a Section 5 proceeding. **As the district court had failed to consider evidence of the dilutive impact of the board's redistricting plan, the Court vacated the judgment and remanded the case.** *Reno v. Bossier Parish School Board,* 520 U.S. 471, 117 S.Ct. 1491, 137 L.Ed.2d 730 (1997). On remand, the district court again granted pre-clearance to the board, and the Attorney General obtained Supreme Court review. The Court held that Section Five does not prohibit pre-clearance of a redistricting plan enacted with a discriminatory but non-retrogressive purpose. Accordingly, the Court affirmed the judgment. *Reno v. Bossier Parish School Board,* 528 U.S. 320, 120 S.Ct. 866, 145 L.Ed.2d 845 (2000).

◆   Texas is a covered jurisdiction under Section 5 of the Voting Rights Act of 1965. The Texas legislature enacted a comprehensive statutory scheme for holding local school boards accountable to the state for student achievement. The law contained 10 possible sanctions on districts for failing to meet legislative standards governing the assessment of academic skills, development of academic performance indicators, determination of accreditation status and the imposition of accreditation sanctions. The law's most drastic sanctions – appointment of a master or a management team to oversee district operations – required the exhaustion of the lesser sanctions first. In compliance with Section 5, Texas requested administrative pre-clearance for the amendments. The attorney general approved most of the sanctions as not affecting voting but found the appointment of a master or management team could result in a Section 5 violation.

Texas appealed to the U.S. District Court for the District of Columbia, which held that the claim was not ripe for adjudication. The U.S. Supreme

Court agreed to review the case, and it stated the general rule that **a claim is not ripe for adjudication if it rests upon contingent future events that may not actually occur**. Texas had not identified any district that might become subject to the appointment of a master or management team and was not required to implement the sanctions until one of the remedies already approved by the attorney general had been exhausted. Because the issue was speculative and unfit for judicial review, the Court affirmed the judgment. *Texas v. U.S.*, 523 U.S. 296, 118 S.Ct. 1257, 140 L.Ed.2d 406 (1998).

2. Misconduct, Conflict of Interest and Nepotism

New York's highest court held that school board members who testified in an employee disciplinary process should have disqualified themselves from acting upon recommendations by a hearing officer to discharge the employee.

◆   A New York school district business manager was charged with failing to follow directives from a supervisor. He was accused of speaking to the board president to gain support for a candidate for treasurer and a plan to restructure positions. At a disciplinary hearing before the board, the board president and another board member testified about their personal knowledge of documents regarding an error in the budget as well as information provided by the business manager's supervisor. A hearing officer found the charges against the business manager were supported and recommended termination. The board adopted the recommendation and voted for discharge, with the board president and the other board member who had testified participating in the vote. The business manager then obtained a court order to annul the action. On appeal, the Court of Appeals of New York held **board members who are personally or extensively involved in a disciplinary process should disqualify themselves from reviewing and acting upon the recommendations of a hearing officer**. In this case, the two board members who testified at the hearing were extensively involved in the disciplinary process. As the lower court had properly held for the business manager, the judgment was affirmed. *Baker v. Poughkeepsie City School Dist.*, 18 N.Y.3d 714, 968 N.E.2d 943 (N.Y. 2012).

◆   A Texas school district's chief financial officer claimed his school board retaliated against him for endorsing an insurance bidder. Soon, another district employee initiated a grievance contending the officer had lied to the board. The officer resigned, with the understanding he would be offered a new position. He taped conversations between an employee and a former board member, and he confirmed his suspicion of bidding irregularities. He also confirmed his suspicion that district employees routinely filed grievances for career advancement and that the board prompted employees to file grievances to further its objectives. The officer approached the FBI and accused the board of improprieties and manipulating the bidding process. After he filed an unsuccessful grievance, his contract was not renewed and he was denied an expected reassignment. In a federal court, the officer sued individual board members under several theories.

After the court denied claims by the board members for qualified immunity, they appealed to the U.S. Court of Appeals, Fifth Circuit. The court found no error in the trial court's finding that the board could take "adverse employment action" in the absence of a formal vote. Fifth Circuit precedent established that **informal decisions such as the claimed agreement among board members in this case were sufficient to proceed with a constitutional claim**. As the lower court had properly denied qualified immunity to the board members at this stage of the case, the Fifth Circuit affirmed the judgment against them. *Juarez v. Aguilar*, 666 F.3d 325 (5th Cir. 2011).

◆   A New Jersey school board member resigned from office prior to the filing of a due process hearing request regarding his autistic son. He later reached an agreement with the board and again successfully ran for office. The day before his term began, he signed a settlement agreement with the board. The next year, the board member and his wife requested enforcement of the agreement. They claimed that the board breached the settlement by placing his son in an "abusive environment" due to lack of support by staff. The petition sought compensatory education, extended, at-home day services, attorneys' fees, costs and other relief. An administrative law judge found that the board member's conduct was allowed under the state School Ethics Act, N.J.S.A. Section 18A:12-24(j). But the commissioner rejected this finding and ordered his removal.

The case reached the Supreme Court of New Jersey, which found that **board members should not be removed from office simply because they were pursuing a claim against a school district involving an individual or immediate family interest**. Disqualifying conflicts of interest should be identified by type. That said, the claim in this case sought monetary relief, and the IDEA offered less adversarial options. A demand for substantial monetary relief could not be reconciled with continued service as a board member. The commissioner had engaged in the correct analysis. In the future, a case-by-case analysis was appropriate to consider claims involving a board member who has filed a claim against his or her own board of education. *Board of Educ. of City of Sea Isle City v. Kennedy*, 951 A.2d 987 (N.J. 2008).

B. School Board Powers and Duties

In 2009, North Carolina's highest court found that no state law required a rapidly growing school district to obtain parental consent before it assigned over 20,000 students to mandatory year-round schools.

◆   A California parent wanted to expand a middle school "Rainbow Day" into a general anti-bullying event. The school board rejected her request to place the matter on its meeting agenda, and the parent asked a state superior court for a special order called a "writ of mandate." The court denied the request, and the parent appealed to the Court of Appeal of California. It explained that a writ of mandate may be issued by a court to "compel the performance of a duty that is purely ministerial in character." **If an entity had some discretionary power or the ability to exercise judgment, a writ of mandate was unavailable.** In this case, the court found state law imposed a duty on school boards to permit a member of the public to place items on their agendas. But this duty was mixed with discretionary power, and not purely ministerial power, as the parent argued. The court found it was not an abuse of discretion for the board to determine it did not direct the specific activities at individual schools. There was evidence that "isolated student club activity" was not sufficiently related to school district business to merit board consideration. As the board had some discretion, the court held a writ of mandate could not be issued. *Mooney v. Garcia*, 207 Cal.App.4th 229, 143 Cal.Rptr.3d 195 (Cal. Ct. App. 2012).

◆   Section 10-223e of Connecticut's General Statutes permits the state to reconstitute local education boards when a district or school is "low achieving." Reconstitution of a local board requires board members to complete training mandated by the state board of education. A district in Bridgeport was deemed low-achieving for seven years. Although not all Bridgeport board members had completed relevant training, a majority voted to request reconstitution. The remaining board members were not informed of this. The state board of education authorized reconstitution and appointed a new local board. As a result, all nine local board members lost their positions. Three state court complaints were filed against state education officials, asserting violations of state law and the Connecticut Constitution. The Supreme Court of Connecticut consolidated the cases. It held Section 10-223e language supported the view that the state board lacked power to reconstitute a local board until the board members completed the mandatory training described in the statute. **The court held the local board could not waive the mandatory training requirement.** The court returned the cases to a lower court. A special election would be authorized to elect a new board that would resume control of the school district. *Pereira v. State Board of Educ.*, 304 Conn. 1, 37 A.3d 625 (Conn. 2012).

◆   On behalf of herself and others, an Alabama teacher sued the state department of education, its superintendent and officers who had been appointed to manage the fiscal operations of a local school district. **She claimed that her statutory pay increase had been miscalculated.** A court ruled in her favor, and the defendants appealed. The Supreme Court of Alabama held that although Article I, Section 14, of the Alabama Constitution gave the board of education immunity, Section 14 immunity does not extend to all officers of the state who act in an official capacity. Since Section 14 immunity does not prevent a court from compelling officials to perform ministerial acts, the teacher could seek relief from the board members in their official capacities. The board members had a statutory duty to pay the appropriate statutory salary increase. Since the trial court order was unclear regarding the amount of salary due, the case was returned to a lower court so it could make this calculation. *Ex parte Bessemer Board of Educ.*, 68 So.3d 782 (Ala. 2011).

◆   A Wisconsin school district received eight open-enrollment applications from resident students who wished to enroll in other districts in 2009. At the time, more than 10% of its resident students attended nonresident districts. It denied the applications, citing a state statute that allowed only 10% of a district's resident student population to enroll in other districts if the resident board chose to apply a statutory cap. As an additional reason for denying the applications, the district claimed financial hardship. When the students' parents requested administrative review, the state education superintendent agreed with them that the limit on the percentage of a district's residents transferring to other districts did not apply after the 2005-06 school year. The superintendent also held that any authority to deny applications based on undue financial burden were limited to cases of eligible students with disabilities.

On appeal, the Court of Appeals of Wisconsin noted that the statute in question provided no authority to limit transfers or open enrollment by percentage of students after the 2005-06 school year. As for the financial burden claim, the court agreed with the state superintendent's finding that only the cost of special education or related services required in an individualized education program could serve as a possible basis for denying an open enrollment application due to an undue financial burden. None of the students in this case had a disability requiring an individualized education program. **No state law provisions restricted student transfers based on the overall financial health of the resident district.** The court affirmed the superintendent's order. *School Dist. of Stockbridge v. Evers*, 792 N.W.2d 615 (Wis. Ct. App. 2010).

◆   South Carolina lawmakers consolidated eight school districts in Charleston County into a unified county district. The eight districts remained in existence as "constituent districts" of the unified district, with authority to control their own matters. The unified district set up a magnet school for gifted children within constituent District 20. Most of the school openings were reserved for District 20 residents, their siblings, and students who would otherwise attend low-performing schools. The remaining seats were allocated districtwide. District 20 adopted a motion to give priority for all magnet school seats to qualified students residing within District 20. The magnet school principal appealed to the unified district, asserting that District 20 had no authority to set school attendance guidelines. The unified district's board nullified the District 20 decision. Later, the state court of appeals found District 20 had incorrectly interpreted the law. As the magnet school's attendance zone was districtwide, the authority of constituent districts was not implicated. **The Act gave the unified district authority to provide a program for gifted children.** The court held District 20 lacked authority to set the magnet school's attendance guidelines. *Stewart v. Charleston County School Dist.*, 386 S.C. 373, 688 S.E.2d 579 (S.C. Ct. App. 2009).

◆   A Virginia court approved a sex offender's application to go onto school property to observe his stepson's activities, and to pick him up, drop him off and go to conferences. The court granted the offender conditional rights to be present on school property. It also terminated his duty to re-register every 90 days as a sex offender, instead requiring him to annually register with the state police as a convicted sex offender. The Commonwealth of Virginia and school officials objected to the order, and appealed to the Supreme Court of Virginia. According to the court, **the order lifting the ban on the sex offender violated the school district's constitutional authority to supervise students**. Thus, the court reversed the judgment and returned for a determination of whether and under what circumstances, the ban might be lifted in whole or in part. *Comwlth. v. Doe*, 278 Va. 223, 682 S.E.2d 906 (Va. 2009).

◆ Wake County (North Carolina) responded to fast growth and overcrowding in its schools by adopting multi-track, year-round calendars at some middle and elementary schools. After public hearings to discuss converting more schools to year-round calendars, the board involuntarily assigned over 20,000 students to year-round schools. Parents who opposed the assignments sued the board in a state court. The case reached the Supreme Court of North Carolina, which held state law authorized local boards to determine school calendars and class sizes. The statute did not classify calendars as "traditional," or "year-round," and did not declare a preference for any calendar. **Boards could devise calendars to achieve their educational goals, and calendar flexibility was encouraged to meet state-mandated performance standards.** Year-round schools were a legitimate option, and the court found no restriction on their use. While the law contemplated consultation between local boards and parents in the development of school calendars, there was no requirement for parental consent. *Wake Cares v. Wake County Board of Educ.*, 675 S.E.2d 345 (N.C. 2009).

◆ The Supreme Court of Georgia upheld a decision refusing to allow a would-be speaker to require a school board to place him on a meeting agenda. The speaker twice requested to be placed on a school board meeting agenda. Board policy vested the authority to grant or deny such requests with the superintendent, subject to a majority vote by the board to change the agenda and add persons wanting to address a meeting. The superintended denied the speaker's requests, and the board did not vote to add him to the agenda. A state superior court granted his request for a hearing but then dismissed the complaint. The Supreme Court of Georgia found no error by the lower court. The court explained that such relief is granted when a person has a clear legal right to compel a public officer to perform a required duty, and there is no other adequate legal remedy. However, **courts generally do not compel officials to follow a course of conduct, perform a discretionary act or undo a past act**. As the setting of a board agenda was a discretionary act, such relief was unavailable. *James v. Montgomery County Board of Educ.*, 283 Ga. 517, 661 S.E.2d 535 (Ga. 2008).

◆ A Montana citizen sued a school district in the state court system, asserting a right to participate in the selection of a new superintendent. She claimed that the school board failed to notify her of votes and decisions leading to the hiring. A state court dismissed the case, and the Supreme Court of Montana affirmed. It noted that the state constitution grants the right to a reasonable opportunity for citizen participation in the operation of government, and the right to examine documents or observe the deliberations of public bodies and agencies. **In order to satisfy the requirement of standing to bring suit, the citizen had to clearly allege a past, present or threatened injury to a property or civil right.** She further had to claim an injury that was distinguishable from injury to the public at large. The court rejected her claim that being an informed and interested citizen conferred standing. She had no personal stake or interest in the hiring of a new superintendent. *Fleenor v. Darby School Dist.*, 331 Mont. 124, 128 P.3d 1048 (Mont. 2006).

◆   The Salt Lake City School Board considered school facilities usage, school boundaries and school closings for over four years. It closed two elementary schools in one part of the city and planned to build new schools in another area that it identified as underserved. Parents who objected to the actions claimed that the board acted arbitrarily and failed to consider its own policy in closing the schools. A state court held a trial, where the opponents claimed that the board violated a policy requiring it to follow several factors in making school closing decisions. The factors included keeping neighborhood schools as close as possible to students and communities. The court found the opponents did not show the board ignored its policy, or act arbitrarily and capriciously in closing the schools. On appeal, the Supreme Court of Utah accepted the trial court's determination that the board had considered its policy. Meeting minutes, instructions to subcommittees and other documents were "replete with discussion of the factors" contained in the policy. **The board had thoroughly discussed the policy factors when it made the closure decisions.** *Save Our Schools v. Board of Educ. of Salt Lake City*, 122 P.3d 611 (Utah 2005).

◆   The Bedford New Hampshire School District (BSD) contracted with the Manchester School District (MSD) to educate its high school students. In 2001, MSD notified BSD and several other districts that it would terminate their 20-year tuition contracts at the end of the 2002-03 school year. BSD and MSD then negotiated a three-year tuition contract that included a per-pupil tuition payment. The payment had an operating expense component and a capital expense component. At BSD's annual meeting in 2004, BSD voters approved a $1.8 million deficit appropriation to fund the capital component of the tuition contract. Voters approved a general budget to fund the entire tuition payment for the 2004-05 school year. This included a $4.4 million appropriation for the capital component. Two taxpayers sued BSD and MSD in a state court, challenging the validity of the three-year contract and the votes.

   The taxpayers sought an order barring payment of the capital component of the tuition payment and restoration of amounts of capital expenses already paid. The state supreme court found nothing in the law at issue required voter approval before a contract could be made. The taxpayers misapprehended the nature of school districts. **The authority to appropriate money rested with the school board and its voters at a district meeting.** The board had authority to make necessary contracts such as the tuition payment contract. BSD voters had been informed of the contract and its financial consequences before approving of the deficit appropriations. The court ruled against the taxpayers. *Foote v. Manchester School Dist.*, 152 N.H. 599, 883 A.2d 283 (N.H. 2005).

◆   An Ohio trial court held that parents have no constitutional right to attend school activities or be present on school grounds. School authorities may exclude parents from school activities and property without a hearing. Ohio school boards may govern school activities and property without adopting formal rules on all aspects of governance, subject to the "abuse of discretion standard." There was no abuse of discretion in a case involving the parent of a middle school student who was banned from school activities for three months after a "verbal altercation" with her daughter's volleyball coach at a neighboring school. The right to a free public education belongs to students, not their parents. **Parents had a liberty interest in the education and upbringing of their children, but this did not create a constitutional right for them to attend school activities or be present on school property.** As the parent had no constitutional liberty interest in being on school grounds or attending school activities, the board could exclude her from them without a hearing. *Nichols v. Western Local Board of Educ.*, 805 N.E.2d 206 (Ohio Common Pleas 2003).

C. Open Meeting Laws

◆   A Virginia citizen claimed an education board violated the state Freedom of Information Act (FOIA) by discussing an elementary school closure through an exchange of emails. She claimed the board then voted to close the school at a public meeting and denied her access to records regarding the closure. In response, the board provided some copies of the emails but denied any FOIA violation. A state circuit court ordered further disclosure of emails. But it held the exchange of emails did not constitute a "meeting" of the board. After the court denied the request for an order to annul the board action, appeal went to the Supreme Court of Virginia. It held the FOIA defined a "meeting" as "an informal assemblage of as many as three members" or a quorum of the board, if less than three members, of any public body. The court found the term "assemble" had an inherent "quality of simultaneity" that might be present in a chat room or with instant messaging, but not typically when an email was sent.

It appeared to the court that the legislature believed some electronic communications might be deemed "a meeting" while others would not. The dispositive inquiry was how the email was used. **The court found the emails between board members were "in the nature of an ongoing discussion involving multiple participants."** It rejected the claim that the emails created a meeting of at least three members. As a result, the court affirmed the judgment that the board did not conduct an improper closed meeting in violation of the notice and open meeting requirements of the FOIA. *Hill v. Fairfax County School Board*, 727 S.E.2d 75 (Va. 2012).

◆   In advance of a scheduled Massachusetts school committee meeting, the chair of the committee emailed the four other committee members regarding the superintendent's job performance. Two committee members emailed their responses only to the chair, while another sent his views to all the members. The fourth member did not respond. At the meeting, the board went into executive session to "discuss collective bargaining," though in fact they discussed the superintendent's evaluation. A newspaper reporter complained to the district attorney about the superintendent's evaluation process, and the committee's failure to release the evaluation. The district attorney found that the school committee violated the open meeting law by conducting the evaluation outside of public view. The case reached the Supreme Judicial Court of Massachusetts.

The court explained that the committee's reason for going into executive session was improper under the open meeting law because it was inaccurate. The superintendent was not covered by collective bargaining. Evidence showed the committee discussed the superintendent's professional competence, which should have been discussed in open session. And the emails had the effect of circumventing the open meeting law. **As the emails were a "deliberation" that violated the letter and spirit of the open meeting law, they had to be made available to the public.** *Dist. Attorney for the Northern Dist. v. School Committee of Wayland*, 455 Mass. 561, 918 N.E.2d 796 (Mass. 2009).

◆   A group of Nebraska residents claimed their school board violated the state Open Meetings Act (OMA) by holding secret meetings prior to resolving to issue construction bonds for a new building. They said the construction issues were fully discussed in the secret meetings and then approved in a public meeting. But they did not file any action against the school board. Instead, they waited to see if the bond issue would pass in the election. After electors voted for the bonds, the residents sued, alleging OMA violations. A court held for the board, and the Supreme Court of Nebraska affirmed. Here, the residents' lawsuit was simply an election contest in the guise of an OMA action. They did not file suit within the time period specified by the election contest statutes. **An election contest was the exclusive remedy once an election has been held.** For this reason, the district court had properly dismissed the action. *Pierce v. Drobny*, 279 Neb. 251, 777 N.W.2d 322 (Neb. 2010).

◆   A Maine school committee went into executive session to discuss the handling of a budget shortfall by senior staff members. Some notes were taken, and the superintendent wrote a memorandum presenting her management philosophy. A newspaper publisher sought all notes, minutes, transcripts or other documents reflecting discussions during the closed session. The school committee denied the publisher's request under the state Freedom of Access Act (FOAA), and the publisher sued to obtain the records. The case reached the Supreme Judicial Court of Maine, which noted that the FOAA allows executive sessions in employment-related cases, such as assignments, duties, promotions, demotions, evaluations and discipline. **An executive session may be held only if public discussion could be reasonably expected to cause damage to an individual's reputation or rights to privacy.** In this case, the finance questions raised in the meeting were limited, and the school attorney said they should not be answered. The court found the executive session did not violate the FOAA, and the documents and notes used there were not public records. *Blethen Maine Newspapers v. Portland School Committee*, 947 A.2d 479 (Me. 2008).

◆   A Wisconsin school board held two closed meetings to discuss an administrator's employment, then voted in open session not to renew her contract. It did not provide her with the four months' notice of non-renewal, which administrators are to receive under state statute. The board maintained that she did not qualify as an "administrator" under this law because not all her duties were administrative. The administrator sued the school district, seeking the protection of the statute, including salary and other benefits. In the pretrial information-gathering process known as discovery, the administrator sought information from the closed board meetings. The court ordered the district to provide the information. The Supreme Court of Wisconsin held that **under state discovery rules, parties may have access to another party's information**

unless a privilege applies, so long as it is relevant to the subject matter of the lawsuit. The fact that the information might not be admissible at a trial was not grounds for objection, so long as the request for information was reasonably calculated to reveal admissible evidence. The mere fact that the information sought by the administrator related to a closed session did not mean it was privileged. *Sands v. Whitnall School Dist.*, 754 N.W.2d 439 (Wis. 2008).

◆   A Pennsylvania student fired a soft pellet gun at his girlfriend from his car. He was suspended with a recommendation for a one-year expulsion. The superintendent agreed to modify an expulsion recommendation with several conditions, including 50 hours of community service, counseling, and compliance with behavior and academic requirements. The school board voted two weeks later in an open session to ratify the reduced sanctions. The student appealed, arguing that a soft pellet gun was not a "weapon" and that the shooting of a toy gun at a student was not a terroristic threat. He also claimed that the board violated the state Sunshine Act by taking official action in private.

The Commonwealth Court of Pennsylvania noted that the state Public School Code defined "weapons" to include knives, guns and "any other tool, instrument or implement capable of inflicting serious bodily injury." Another court had applied the definition of "weapon" from the state Crimes Code to a student using a carbon dioxide-powered paintball. A pellet gun, like a paintball gun, could inflict serious injury to an eye. It was permissible to find it was a "weapon" under the code. **Even if the board had violated the Sunshine Act, its later vote in open session to modify the expulsion cured any violation.** *Picone v. Bangor Area School Dist.*, 936 A.2d 556 (Pa. Commw. Ct. 2007).

◆   A Colorado school board met in an executive session, where no minutes were taken and discussions were not disclosed. The board decided not to rehire a probationary teacher for the 2004-05 school year. The district superintendent sent him a "letter of intent," stating that the board did not intend to offer him a teaching contract for the next year. The board met twice in May 2005 and voted to renew all probationary teacher contracts, except that of the teacher. It failed to provide him with a non-renewal notice by June 1, as required by the Colorado Teacher Employment Compensation, and Dismissal Act (TECDA).

The teacher sued the district. Meanwhile, the board voted in public session that it would not rehire the teacher for 2004-05 or a later year. The board sent notices of the action to the teacher. The case reached the Supreme Court of Colorado, which held that **the vote to non-renew the teacher's contract in an executive session violated the state Open Meetings Law**. It was therefore not binding. No final policy decisions, including the non-renewal of a teacher's contract, may be made by a board in executive session. The superintendent's "letter of intent" had no effect. The TECDA required each school board to provide timely, written notice of a teacher termination. The failure to provide timely written notice to the teacher resulted in his automatic reemployment. While he was automatically reemployed for 2004-05, he was not entitled to reinstatement because he received timely notice of the open board meeting decision. *Hanover School Dist. No. 28 v. Barbour*, 171 P.3d 223 (Colo. 2007).

◆ A Washington school board held a meeting for the public to evaluate candidates for an open board position. A citizen sought handouts provided by candidates at the meeting, an audiotape of the meeting and letters of interest from the candidates. The district made an audiotape and the letters available, but said it did not have any copies of the candidates' handouts. The citizen claimed the audiotape did not work in his car stereo and refused to listen to it on a district system. He sued the district under the state Public Disclosure Act (PDA). A court held for the district, and the citizen appealed to the Court of Appeals of Washington. The court held **the PDA did not require an agency to explain, conduct research on, or create documents that did not exist and were not in its possession**. A document that is not possessed by an agency is not, by definition, a public document. While the PDA required an agency to give the fullest assistance to persons seeking to review public records, the law did not specify a format for audiotapes. The district had complied with the PDA. *Boss v. Peninsula School Dist.*, 125 Wash. 1024 (Wash. Ct. App. 2005).

◆ Some New York citizens attempted to videotape a school board meeting. When the board instructed them to discontinue the taping, they protested, and they were allowed to record the proceedings. Later, the board adopted a new resolution to reserve the right to allow or disallow videotaping of its meetings. After the board denied further efforts to videotape meetings, the citizens sued for violation of the New York Open Meetings Law. A state court dismissed the case, and appeal reached a New York appellate division court. It rejected the board's claim that videotaping meetings would make them "less open" by stifling shy citizens. **Although the Open Meetings Law did not explicitly compel the board to allow videotaping of its meetings, a liberal interpretation of the law allowed citizens the right to record them.** Because the board could not ban the tape recording of its meetings, the court reversed the judgment. *Csorny v. Shoreham-Wading River Cent. School Dist.*, 2003 N.Y. Slip. Op. 14079, 2002 WL 32092581 (N.Y. App. Div. 2003).

◆ The Washington Court of Appeals held that the state Open Public Meeting Act (OPMA) **applied not only to school board meetings, but to deliberations, discussions, and other communications**. Courts in other states have applied open meetings acts to telephonic communications, emails, individual meetings between superintendents and board members, and serial electronic communications among a quorum of board members. Email exchanges could be "meetings" if certain statutory factors were present. The OPMA would not be violated if less than a majority of board members was involved in the exchange of emails and the participants did not collectively intend to transact official business. Passive receipt of an email did not qualify as a "meeting." There had to be "action," as defined by OPMA. There was evidence in this case that some emails between board members related to board business, that some board members had knowledge that the OPMA might be implicated, and that there was an active exchange of emails. The case required a trial. *Wood v. Battle Ground School Dist.*, 27 P.3d 1208 (Wash. Ct. App. 2001).

CHAPTER FIFTEEN

Private Schools

I. PRIVATE SCHOOL EMPLOYMENT

Courts have held that the Free Exercise and Establishment Clauses of the First Amendment require limiting anti-discrimination laws to insulate the relationship between religious organizations and their ministerial employees.

In Hosanna-Tabor Evangelical Lutheran Church and School v. E.E.O.C., *this chapter, the U.S. Supreme Court upheld the right of religious institutions "to select and control who will minister to the faithful." The Court barred actions "brought on behalf of ministers against their churches, claiming termination in violation of employment discrimination laws." It employed a facts and circumstances test for determining who is a "ministerial employee."*

In Hollins v. Methodist Healthcare, Inc., *474 F.3d 223, 225 (6th Cir. 2007), the court held the ministerial exception balances government interests in preventing discrimination and the rights of religious institutions to be free from judicial interference in the selection of their ministerial employees. But in* E.E.O.C. v. Roman Catholic Diocese of Raleigh, N.C., *213 F.3d 795, 801 (4th Cir. 2000), the Fourth Circuit observed that courts have consistently held that judicial intervention in disputes involving employees whose primary duties are secular does not violate the First Amendment's guarantee of religious freedom.*

A. Employment Discrimination

◆ A Michigan Lutheran school teacher received a certificate of admission into the teaching ministry and became a "called" teacher who could be fired only for cause. She spent six hours and 15 minutes of her seven-hour workday teaching secular subjects using secular textbooks. She did have some religious duties – such as teaching a religion class and leading a chapel service twice a year. She was diagnosed with narcolepsy. When the school later fired her, she sued it for violating the Americans with Disabilities Act (ADA). A federal court dismissed her lawsuit, finding the teacher was a ministerial employee, but the Sixth Circuit reversed, stating she was not. The case reached the U.S. Supreme Court, which noted that a ministerial exception to employment discrimination laws is rooted in the First Amendment. A court order requiring a church to accept or retain a minister, or imposing liability for failing to do so, would intrude upon internal church governance and deprive churches of the power to select those who would carry out their mission. **The Court held the teacher qualified for ministerial status and thus could not sue under the ADA.** *Hosanna-Tabor Evangelical Lutheran Church and School v. E.E.O.C.,* 132 S.Ct. 694, 181 L.Ed.2d 650 (U.S. 2012).

◆ An unmarried Ohio Catholic school technology coordinator who was not a Catholic oversaw her school's computer systems and instructed students on computer use. She became pregnant through artificial insemination and asked for maternity leave. Religious officials advised the employee that her out-of-wedlock pregnancy was grounds for termination for violation of the philosophy and teachings of the Roman Catholic Church. In a federal court action against the school, the employee asserted pregnancy discrimination under federal and state law, and breach of contract. After release of the Supreme Court's decision in *Hosanna-Tabor Evangelical Lutheran Church and School v. E.E.O.C.,* above, the court considered the employee's claim that she was not a "minister." As a non-Catholic, she noted she could not even teach Catholic doctrine. In response, the school claimed she was a minister based on her "role as a Catholic role model," and her "teaching and interacting with impressionable students."

The court agreed with the employee that her duties showed she was not a minister under the ministerial exception. **It was not enough to generally call her a "role model," or find that she was a "minister" solely by virtue of her**

affiliation with a religious school. Since the court held the employee was not a minister and she had raised plausible claims of pregnancy discrimination and breach of contract, it refused to dismiss the case. *Dias v. Archdiocese of Cincinnati*, No. 1:11–CV–00251, 2012 WL 1068165 (S.D. Ohio 3/29/12).

◆   A Wisconsin first-grade teacher claimed a Catholic school dismissed her on the basis of her age. She complained to the state Labor and Industry Review Commission (LIRC), which denied the school's request to dismiss the case on the basis of a "ministerial exception" rooted in the First Amendment. Appeal reached the Supreme Court of Wisconsin, which found the case arose under the state Fair Employment Act (FEA). According to the school, the teacher occupied a "ministerial" position, barring her claim. The court held **the ministerial exception precluded employment discrimination claims "for employees whose positions were important and closely linked to the religious mission of a religious organization."** In this case, the school was committed to the Catholic faith and worldview, and the teacher's position was important and closely linked to that mission. The school was considered a ministry of the Catholic Church. The teacher led prayers with students, helped celebrate religious holidays, served as a catechist and taught Catholic doctrine and practice. Her FEA age discrimination claim unconstitutionally infringed upon the school's right to religious freedom under the Wisconsin Constitution. The court reversed the lower court judgments. *Coulee Catholic Schools v. Industry Review Comm'n*, 320 Wis.2d 275, 768 N.W.2d 868 (Wis. 2009).

◆   The U.S. Supreme Court held that the Mormon Church could discriminate on the basis of religion in hiring for a nonreligious job. The case involved an employee who worked at a church-operated gymnasium for 16 years. After being discharged for failing to meet religious requirements, he sued the church, alleging religious bias in violation of Title VII. The Supreme Court noted that Title VII does not apply to a religious corporation, association or educational institution "with respect to the employment of individuals of a particular religion to perform work connected with the carrying on by such [an organization] of its activities." **The Court upheld the right of nonprofit religious employers to impose religious conditions for employment in nonreligious positions** involving nonprofit activities. *Corp. of the Presiding Bishop of the Church of Jesus Christ of Latter-Day Saints v. Amos*, 483 U.S. 327, 107 S.Ct. 2862, 97 L.Ed.2d 273 (1987).

◆   A Michigan teacher worked as a church's director of religious education for eight years. After obtaining a master's degree in teaching, she became a teacher of math and religion courses. Her duties included planning Masses for several grades and assisting an elementary teacher with student liturgies. After a series of employment incidents that did not involve religion, the school discharged her. She sued the Catholic Diocese of Lansing under state laws including the Whistleblowers' Protection and Civil Rights Acts. A state court dismissed the whistleblower claim, but not the civil rights claim. The state court of appeals explained that **the ministerial exception barred any claim that would limit a religious institution's right to select an individual to perform spiritual**

functions. It returned the case to the trial court to resolve questions about the teacher's job duties. If they were primarily religious, she could not pursue her civil rights action further. But if they were not ministerial in nature, her civil rights claim could proceed. *Weishuhn v. Catholic Diocese of Lansing*, 279 Mich.App. 150, 756 N.W.2d 483 (Mich. Ct. App. 2008).

When the case returned to the trial court, it found the ministerial exception applied, requiring dismissal of the Civil Rights Act (CRA) and Whistleblower Protection Act (WPA) claims. The court of appeals affirmed the ruling that the teacher was primarily engaged in religious duties. As she was in a primarily religious position, she was a ministerial employee, and the school was entitled to judgment on the CRA and WPA claims. *Weishuhn v. Catholic Diocese of Lansing*, 287 Mich.App. 211, 787 N.W.2d 513 (Mich. Ct. App. 2010).

◆   **A Florida District Court of Appeal applied the ministerial exception to a state whistleblower claim by a principal of a Catholic school.** She asserted that when she complained to the Archdiocese about a supervisor's assault and battery, the Archdiocese retaliated against her by discharging her. The court held that the ministerial exception had been applied to federal claims under the ADA, the Age Discrimination in Employment Act, and the common law. As a result, the court found no reason why the ministerial exception should not apply to a state whistleblower claim. *Archdiocese of Miami v. Minagorri*, 954 So.2d 640 (Fla. Dist. Ct. App. 2007). The Supreme Court of Florida denied further review, as did the U.S. Supreme Court.

◆   A guitar instructor taught music part-time at a Florida Episcopal school. When the school learned he had been arrested on a domestic violence charge, it fired him. The school said he reacted by menacing and threatening to create bad publicity. The teacher filed a discrimination charge with the state Commission on Human Relations, alleging he was fired because of his Hindu faith, gender, unmarried status, and because he had a preschool-age child. At the hearing, the administrative law judge (ALJ) dismissed the religion-based charge because Florida does not allow such claims against religious institutions. The ALJ heard evidence on the other charges and found the instructor's arrest was a valid reason to fire him. The Eleventh Circuit upheld that decision. **The ALJ properly found that the termination was based on the teacher's domestic abuse arrest.** His threatening behavior confirmed the school's judgment. *Cataldo v. St. James Episcopal School*, 213 Fed.Appx. 966 (11th Cir. 2007).

◆   A teacher chaired the theology department at a Minnesota Lutheran school. His duties included counseling, and he was responsible for ensuring students followed the beliefs and doctrines of the synod – an advisory body of Lutheran congregations and ministers. After 22 years at the school, the teacher admitted he was gay, but said that he was not in a homosexual relationship and had never lived a gay lifestyle. The bishop and the school principal told the teacher he should remain "closeted" and celibate. When the school found a replacement, the teacher resigned. He sued the school, alleging discrimination based on sexual orientation in violation of the Minnesota Human Rights Act. The case reached the Court of Appeals of Minnesota. The teacher contended that although part of his job entailed pastoral duties, he was also a secular teacher, and the court could apply neutral principles of law to decide his case. The court ruled against the teacher because **the lawfulness of a discharge based on sexual orientation would have required it to delve into church doctrine** in violation of the Establishment Clause. There was no evidence that the teacher's position could be split into secular and nonsecular parts. *Doe v. Lutheran High School of Greater Minneapolis*, 702 N.W.2d 322 (Minn. Ct. App. 2005).

B. Labor Relations

The courts have ruled that "pervasively religious" schools may be able to avoid any obligation to bargain with employees under the National Labor Relations Act (NLRA). This exception to the NLRA's coverage is based upon First Amendment religious freedom considerations. Managerial employees are not protected by the NLRA.

◆   A New York religious academy granted tenure to a teacher in 1996. His annual salary during the seven years up to the 2006-2007 school year averaged more than $100,000. In 2007, the academy discharged the teacher. The parties agreed to arbitrate the matter of his employment termination in accordance with Jewish law. An arbitration panel found the academy had granted the teacher tenure and had wrongfully discharged him without just cause. The panel directed the academy to reinstate him to his teaching position at an annual salary of $100,000 with back wages and contributions to his pension plan. The academy petitioned a state court to vacate the arbitration award, arguing that the award would create a new contract. After the court vacated the award, a New York Appellate Division court reversed. **The arbitration award did not violate a strong public policy,** and the academy didn't show that it was irrational or that it exceeded the arbitrator's powers. As the teacher demonstrated that he could only be discharged for cause, he could enforce the award. *Brisman v. Hebrew Academy of Five Towns & Rockaway*, 70 A.D.3d 935, 895 N.Y.2d 482 (N.Y App. Div. 2010).

◆   A private New Hampshire day school had long-running contracts with three school districts. Two of its teachers filed unfair labor practice charges against the school with the state Public Employee Labor Relations Board. The National Education Association asked the state board to decide whether the school was considered a public employer. The board declared that the school was a "quasi-public corporation" and held that it had authority to decide the complaint. The school appealed to the Supreme Court of New Hampshire, which noted that the National Labor Relations Board **(NLRB) has jurisdiction over labor disputes at nonprofit educational institutions and private nonprofit secondary schools** with gross annual revenues high enough to qualify. The contract between the school and the school districts did not exempt the school from NLRB authority as a "political subdivision." Thus, the state board did not have jurisdiction to decide the complaint. *In re Pinkerton Academy*, 155 N.H. 1, 920 A.2d 1168 (N.H. 2007).

◆ The right of employees of a Catholic school system to form a collective bargaining unit was successfully challenged in a case decided by the U.S. Supreme Court. In this case, the unions were certified by the National Labor Relations Board (NLRB) as bargaining units but the diocese refused to bargain with them. The Court said that the religion clauses of the U.S. Constitution, which require religious organizations to finance their educational systems without governmental aid, also free the religious organizations of the inhibiting effect and impact of unionization of their teachers. The Court agreed with the employers' contention that **the threshold act of certification of the union would necessarily alter and infringe upon the religious character of parochial schools**. This would mean that the bishop would no longer be the sole repository of authority as required by church law. Instead, he would have to share some decisionmaking with the union. The Court held this violated the religion clauses of the U.S. Constitution. *NLRB v. Catholic Bishop of Chicago*, 440 U.S. 490, 99 S.Ct. 1313, 59 L.Ed.2d 533 (1979).

◆ In *NLRB v. Yeshiva Univ.*, the U.S. Supreme Court held that in certain circumstances, **faculty members at private educational institutions could be considered managerial employees**. The ruling was based on the conclusion that Yeshiva's faculty decided school curriculum, standards, tuition rates and admissions. The Court's decision applied only to schools that were "like Yeshiva" and not to schools where the faculty exercised less control. Schools where faculty members do not exercise binding managerial discretion do not fall within the scope of the managerial employee exclusion. *NLRB v. Yeshiva Univ.*, 444 U.S. 672, 100 S.Ct. 856, 63 L.Ed.2d 115 (1980).

◆ A Roman Catholic secondary school in New York City employed lay and religiously affiliated faculty and taught both secular and religious subjects. After a union began representing the lay faculty, the school administration and the union met repeatedly to negotiate the terms of a collective bargaining agreement. When those efforts failed, the union struck. The school discharged the striking workers and ended negotiations. The state Employment Relations Board cited the school for violating the state Labor Relations Act. It charged the school with refusing to bargain in good faith and with improperly discharging and failing to reinstate striking employees. The Court of Appeals of New York held that the Labor Relations Act did not implicate religious conduct or beliefs, and it did not restrict or burden religious belief or activities. The Establishment Clause argument failed because the state board's supervision over collective bargaining with respect to secular terms and conditions of employment was neither comprehensive nor continuing and did not entangle the state with religion. Here, **the government was not forcing the parties to agree on specific terms but instead to bargain in good faith on secular subjects**. *New York State Employment Relations Board v. Christ the King Regional High School*, 90 N.Y.2d 244, 660 N.Y.S.2d 359, 682 N.E.2d 960 (N.Y. 1997).

◆ Two teachers at a Pennsylvania Catholic elementary and secondary school attempted to organize a teachers union. Through an association of Catholic teachers, they petitioned the Pennsylvania Labor Relations Board (PLRB) to compel an election. The teachers were fired, and the association filed a second petition that was dismissed on the grounds that the school was not a public employer and the teachers were not public employees under the Public Employee Relations Act (PERA). The case reached the state supreme court, which found the NLRA does not apply to lay teachers employed at church-operated schools. However, the NLRA and the PERA do not have the same scope. The PERA defines a public employee as any individual employed by a public employer but excludes employees at church facilities "when utilized primarily for religious purposes." **As the school was operated primarily for religious purposes, the teachers were excluded under the PERA.** *Ass'n of Catholic Teachers v. PLRB*, 692 A.2d 1039 (Pa. 1997).

C. Termination from Employment

◆   A Louisiana Christian School hired a principal for its elementary/pre-school division under a contract requiring the submission of all employment-related disputes to Bible-based mediation or arbitration by the Institute for Christian Conciliation (ICC). The school discharged the principal before the end of the school year and paid her salary and benefits through the end of the year. She sued for breach of contract, gender discrimination, sexual harassment and retaliation. A court granted the school's motion to compel arbitration. According to ICC rules, arbitration was conducted under the Montana Uniform Arbitration Act. After a hearing, an arbitrator held the school breached its contract with the principal, violating the law and Matthew 18, and awarded the principal over $150,000 in damages. However, the arbitrator found no evidence of gender discrimination, sexual harassment or retaliation.

The principal then sued in a Louisiana federal court, seeking confirmation of the award. The court affirmed the award, finding that Montana law applied. The school appealed to the Fifth Circuit, which held that **the Federal Arbitration Act did not bar parties from structuring their contracts, or preempt state laws on arbitration**. However, while Montana law applied to the arbitration, the contract itself was properly interpreted under Louisiana law. The court vacated the judgment and remanded the case for further proceedings. *Prescott v. Northlake Christian School*, 369 F.3d 491 (5th Cir. 2004).

◆   A teacher contracted with a Nebraska Catholic high school for a year. The contract reserved the school's right to terminate the contract immediately in the event of overt conduct in violation of Catholic Church doctrine, or any other conduct which reflected grave discredit upon the school. Three months later, the teacher sought to be released from his contract to obtain a public school teaching position. The school refused his request and informed him that unless he reaffirmed his commitment to the contract, it would withhold $1,000 in pay and cancel his benefits. When the teacher did not reassert his commitment, the school withheld his pay and canceled his benefits. He petitioned a Nebraska trial court for a declaration that the school constructively terminated his contract. The court held that it lacked jurisdiction to review the terms of the contract because it would be an impermissible inquiry into church doctrine in violation of the First Amendment.

The Nebraska Court of Appeals affirmed the judgment, focusing on the contract clause permitting the school to immediately terminate a teacher for violating a doctrine of the Roman Catholic Church. **An analysis of whether the contract was unconscionable would require it to examine Roman Catholic doctrine.** This was held to be an impermissible inquiry by the court under the First Amendment. *Parizek v. Roncalli Catholic High School of Omaha*, 11 Neb. App. 482, 655 N.W.2d 404 (Neb. App. 2002).

II.   STATE AND FEDERAL REGULATION

Private schools must meet state accreditation and compulsory attendance standards. All public and private school teachers are mandatory child abuse reporters. More cases on abuse reporting appear in Chapter Seven, Section V.

A.   Sex Abuse and Mandatory Reporting

State laws require all educators and caregivers to timely report suspected child abuse or neglect. The laws provide incentives for reporting by offering immunity for good-faith reporters and imposing criminal penalties for failure to make timely reports. New York and Minnesota require mandated reporters who work for a school to report suspected child abuse or maltreatment themselves, and not through another school employee. New York's highest court has stated that teachers and other state-mandated reporters "ought to err on the side of caution and make a report" if they reasonably suspect child abuse or neglect.

◆   A teacher at the Missouri Military Academy observed bruises on a cadet's arms and insisted that school officials make a report of evidence of physical abuse to the state Division of Family Services. The academy fired him the same day. He sued for wrongful discharge and breach of contract. A court dismissed the wrongful discharge and emotional distress claims, but held a trial on the breach of contract claim and awarded the teacher $13,300 in damages. Appeal reached the Supreme Court of Missouri, which ruled that **a teacher under contract can sue for wrongful discharge just as "at-will" employees can if the termination violates a clear mandate of public policy.** Allowing contract employees to pursue wrongful discharge claims put them on the same footing as "at-will" employees. The teacher was under a clear statutory mandate to report suspected abuse of a child. He could pursue his wrongful discharge claim, and the judgment in his favor for breach of contract was affirmed. *Keveney v. Missouri Military Academy*, 304 S.W.3d 98 (Mo. 2010).

◆   Parents of a District of Columbia preschooler called her private school, claiming four other preschoolers sexually assaulted her in a school bathroom. Her parents had already taken her to the hospital and called the police and the Child and Family Services Agency (CFSA). The principal and vice principal investigated. After interviewing the other children and their parents, they decided the story was not credible. Neither reported the incident to the police or the CFSA – but the principal gave his written report of the school's investigation to the detective assigned to the case. The District of Columbia later charged both principals with violating the mandatory reporting statute. A judge found both administrators guilty of a misdemeanor, but the court of appeals vacated their convictions. **The mandatory reporting statute did not require them to report suspected sexual abuse involving only students.** *Hargrove v. District of Columbia*, 5 A.3d 632 (D.C. 2010).

◆   A Delaware student alleged that a priest who served as a teacher and later a principal sexually molested him from the time he was eight years old until he was 17. The student sued in 2004, alleging that the last incident of molestation occurred in 1985. He claimed that he told his parents only about the last incident and that they reported it to church officials in 1985. The officials allegedly agreed to deny the priest the opportunity to be near minors. The church sought to dismiss the case, claiming that the action was untimely under Delaware's two-year statute of limitations for personal injury claims, and the state's three-year limitation period for breach of contract claims. The student claimed his delay in filing his claims was excused because he suppressed any memory of the abuse until less than two years before he filed his lawsuit.

The court noted that **Delaware recognizes "the discovery rule exception" in cases involving child abuse.** This exception delays the start of the limitations period based on suppressed memories of sexual abuse. In this case, the student presented expert testimony indicating he had suppressed memories of the abuse. Although he could not rely on the discovery rule exception with respect to the incident he reported to his parents in 1985, he could rely on the exception with respect to 900 other alleged incidents of sexual abuse. Those claims were not barred by the statute of limitations. The court also found enough evidence to create a factual issue as to whether the church breached a contract with the parents by affirmatively concealing alleged molestations. A trial was required. *Eden v. Oblates of St. Francis de Sales*, No. 04C-01-069 CLS, 2006 WL 3512482 (Del. Super. Ct. 2006).

◆   An Ohio high school student received counseling from a psychologist at her private school for about a year. Sometime during the year, the psychologist made a report to the Cuyahoga County Department of Family Services that she believed the student's father had abused her. The report was investigated and the allegation of abuse deemed unsubstantiated. The father sued the psychologist, claiming she was required to act in good faith when filing the report. An Ohio trial court granted pretrial judgment to the psychologist, and the father appealed. He also appealed the court's failure to allow him access to certain material relating to the report and investigation. The court affirmed the judgment, holding that **the psychologist – statutorily obligated to report suspected child abuse – was entitled to immunity**. Under state child abuse reporting law, if an individual is subject to the mandatory reporting statute, that individual is granted immunity from liability when making a report. There was no statutory requirement that a report be made in good faith, despite the father's assertion to the contrary. As for his contention that he was denied investigation materials, the court held that they were confidential and privileged. *Liedtke v. Carrington*, 763 N.E.2d 213 (Ohio Ct. App. 2001).

B. Accreditation

◆   A University of California (UC) admission policy evaluated in-state applicants' qualifications by reviewing their high school courses – and only approving those it found college preparatory. A Protestant schools' association, a member school and five of the school's students claimed the practice violated the First Amendment's religious and free speech clauses as well as the Fourteenth Amendment's Equal Protection Clause. The case reached the Ninth Circuit, which upheld the policy as constitutional. It noted that **UC's policy did not prohibit high schools from teaching whatever and however they chose**. And UC approved some courses with religious content and viewpoints that used religious textbooks. Further, the court found no evidence that UC treated students from religious private schools worse than other applicants. *Ass'n of Christian Schools Int'l v. Stearns*, 362 Fed.Appx. 640 (9th Cir. 2010).

◆   The Ohio superintendent of public instruction registered Golden Christian Academy in the Ohio Pilot Project Scholarship Program. As a condition of registration, Golden signed an "assurance of compliance" stating that the school would meet all applicable state minimum standards for nonpublic schools and that all employees who worked with voucher students would pass criminal background investigations. The superintendent informed the school that she intended to revoke its registration for failure to meet the assurance of compliance. After the superintendent revoked Golden's registration, Golden appealed, arguing she had no authority to revoke the school's registration and that it complied with the assurance of compliance. The court of appeals noted that the statue was unclear about the superintendent's authority. However, **it would be illogical for the statute to grant the superintendent the power to register a school for the voucher program but not to revoke its registration**. The court held that the superintendent could revoke Golden's registration. *Golden Christian Academy v. Zelman*, 760 N.E.2d 889 (Ohio Ct. App. 2001).

C. Taxation

1. Federal Income Taxation

◆   Section 501(c)(3) of the Internal Revenue Code provides that "corporations ... organized and operated exclusively for religious, charitable ... or educational purposes" are entitled to tax-exempt status. The Internal Revenue Service (IRS) routinely granted tax exemptions under Section 501(c)(3) to private schools regardless of whether they had racially discriminatory admissions policies. In 1970, however, **the IRS concluded that it could no longer grant tax-exempt status to racially discriminatory private schools** because such schools were not "charitable" within the meaning of Section 501(c)(3). Two private colleges whose racial admissions policies were rooted in their interpretations of the Bible sued to prevent the IRS from interpreting the federal tax laws in this manner. The U.S. Supreme Court rejected the challenge and upheld the IRS's interpretation. The Court's ruling was based on what it perceived as the strong public policy against racial discrimination in education. Because the colleges were operating in violation of that public policy, the colleges could not be considered "charitable" under Section 501(c)(3). Thus, they were ineligible for tax exemptions. The Court held that the denial of an exemption did not impermissibly burden the colleges' alleged religious freedom interest in practicing racial discrimination. *Bob Jones Univ. v. U.S.* (1983).

◆ Parents of African-American public schoolchildren sought a federal court order requiring the IRS to adopt more stringent standards for determining whether private schools had racially discriminatory admissions policies. The parents claimed IRS standards were too lax and that certain private schools were practicing racial discrimination and were still obtaining tax exemptions. **The Supreme Court dismissed the parents' claims, ruling they had shown no injury to themselves as a result of the allegedly lax IRS standards.** None of their children had sought enrollment at the private schools involved, and the abstract stigma attached to living in a community with racially discriminatory private schools was also insufficient to show actual injury. Further, the parents' theory that denial of exempt status to such schools would result in greater white student enrollment in area public schools, and hence result in a greater degree of public school integration, was only speculation. *Allen v. Wright*, 468 U.S. 737, 104 S.Ct. 3315, 82 L.Ed.2d 556 (1984).

2. State and Local Taxation

◆ Arizona taxpayers sued to challenge a state tax credit for donations to school tuition organizations (STOs) that use the donations to fund scholarships for private school students. The case reached the Supreme Court on the issue of whether the taxpayers had standing to raise their claim. The Court stated that the taxpayers had to demonstrate a threat of direct harm that religion will be established by the government, such as in the case of mandatory prayer in public schools. In other words, the taxpayers had to show they suffered an "injury in fact." In ruling that **the taxpayers lacked standing to sue**, the Court noted that even if the STO tax credits were worth $50 million annually, any particular injury "would require speculation that Arizona lawmakers react to revenue shortfalls by increasing [their] tax liability." The STOs were funded by private contributors without state intervention. Since the state was not involved in the process, the taxpayers could not sue. *Arizona Christian School Tuition Organization v. Winn*, 131 S.Ct. 1436, 179 L.Ed.2d 523 (U.S. 2011).

◆ Prior to *Winn*, above, the Supreme Court held that the Tax Injunction Act (TIA) prevented federal courts from enjoining, suspending or restraining "the assessment, levy or collection of any tax under State law where a plain, speedy and efficient remedy may be had in the courts of such State." It did not immunize all aspects of state tax administration from court review. It only prevented federal courts from interfering with state tax collections. The "decades-long understanding" of courts was that **the TIA did not bar a third-party constitutional challenge to tax benefits such as this action.** *Hibbs v. Winn*, 542 U.S. 88, 124 S.Ct. 2276, 159 L.Ed.2d 172 (2004).

◆   A Maine nonprofit corporation operated a summer camp for children of the Christian Science faith. Activities included supervised prayer, meditation and church services. Weekly tuition was roughly $400. A Maine statute exempted charitable institutions from real estate and personal property taxes. However, institutions operated primarily for the benefit of nonresidents were only entitled to a more limited tax benefit, and then only if the weekly charge for services did not exceed $30 per person. Because most of the campers were not Maine residents and weekly tuition was over $30, the corporation was ineligible for the state tax exemption. It petitioned the town for a refund of the taxes it had paid, arguing the exemption violated the Commerce Clause of the U.S. Constitution. The U.S. Supreme Court found the camp was engaged in commerce not only as a purchaser but as a provider of goods and services. **A real estate tax, like any other tax, could impermissibly burden interstate commerce.** If the exemption applied to for-profit entities, there would be no question of a Commerce Clause violation. The Court found no reason why an entity's nonprofit status should exclude it from Commerce Clause coverage. Nonprofit institutions are subject to other laws regulating commerce and federal antitrust laws. *Camps Newfound/Owatonna, Inc. v. Town of Harrison, Maine*, 520 U.S. 564, 117 S.Ct. 1590, 137 L.Ed.2d 852 (1997).

◆   A New York school board developed a tax plan that would close one school and spend less so services to private schools could be improved and money could be freed up for religious school tuition. The board had four Orthodox Jews who were members and two other members who shared their aims. Five parents of public school students sued, alleging that the "Orthodox Majority" had tried to convert the school board "into an Orthodox ruling committee." A federal court and the Second Circuit ruled that the tax plan did not violate the Constitution because **all parents, whether religious or not, received the same tax breaks**. It did not matter that a large number of Orthodox Jewish taxpayers freely chose to spend their tax savings from the plan on religious education for their children. *Incantalupo v. Laurence Union Free School Dist. No. 15*, 380 Fed.Appx. 59 (2d Cir. 2010).

◆   Burr and Burton Academy is a Vermont private high school operated by Burr and Burton Seminary, a nonprofit corporation. In 1996, Burr and Burton constructed "Head House" as a residence for the academy's headmaster. Traditionally, housing had been part of the headmaster's compensation package. In April 1997, the town of Manchester appraised Head House at $290,000 and decided it was subject to applicable property taxes. The next year, the town added a Burr and Burton student dormitory to the taxable property list. However, the dormitory property had been placed on the real estate market in 1994 and had been leased to various tenants until being sold in 1999. Burr and Burton challenged the appraisals, asserting that the properties fell within a state property tax exemption for property owned by educational institutions.

    The case reached the state supreme court, which held that Head House qualified for the property tax exemption because it served an educational purpose. During the 1998-99 academic year, Head House held 11 school-related events. **Residences for headmasters and faculty serve an educational**

purpose. The fact that Head House was part of a compensation package did not prevent it from qualifying for the exemption. However, the dormitory property was ineligible for the exemption. It had not been used for any educational purpose since 1994. As the dormitory property had been used for commercial purposes, the academy was required to pay the assessed property taxes. *Burr and Burton Seminary v. Town of Manchester*, 782 A.2d 1149 (Vt. 2001).

◆   In a companion case to *Burr and Burton Seminary v. Town of Manchester,* the Berkshire School sought a tax exemption for a 212-acre parcel of land. The land had been donated to the school, which intended to use the property for a student mountain program and environmental science classes. The town of Reading appraised the undeveloped land at $250,000 and assessed taxes against Berkshire. Berkshire grieved the appraisal, asserting that under the language of 32 Vt. Stat. Ann. § 3802(4), mere ownership was sufficient for the exemption. A state court agreed, but the Vermont Supreme Court reversed under *Burr and Burton Seminary*. It reiterated the holding that an educational use requirement was implicit in the statutory language. **Even though the land was not being used for any purpose – educational, commercial or otherwise – nonuse would not qualify for exemption** under the statute. If Berkshire used the land for educational purposes in the future, the issue of exemption could be raised again. *Berkshire School v. Town of Reading*, 781 A.2d 282 (Vt. 2001).

◆   Pennsylvania's Institutions of Purely Public Charity Act exempts qualifying entities from real estate taxes. A private school in Pottstown was founded as an all-boys school. In 1996, the Pottstown School District and the local borough petitioned the county board of assessment appeals to remove the school's real estate tax exemption. They claimed that the school's policy of denying female students admission demonstrated it did not benefit a substantial and indefinite class of persons. The board affirmed the school's tax-exempt status, and the school district appealed to a state court. Meanwhile, the school amended its admittance policy to include females.

The Pennsylvania Commonwealth Court held that based on state court precedents, the school's exclusion of females did not undermine its status as a purely public charity under the state constitution. **Pennsylvania courts have long held that single-sex schools are considered purely public charities.** If the legislature had intended to exclude this type of school from the statute, it would have done so. The school was exempt from real estate taxation as a purely public charity. *Pottstown School Dist. v. Hill School*, 786 A.2d 312 (Pa. Commw. Ct. 2001).

D. Zoning and Local Regulation

◆   A Catholic high school in San Diego sought to modernize its 84-year-old campus – including its science labs and art studios as well as the school library and computer lab. It also sought to build a 20,500-square foot classroom building and a two-level, 104-space parking garage. It wanted to demolish two buildings on its property, but neighbors considered them an important part of the neighborhood and formed a protest group. After an extensive review process lasting more than a year, the city planning commission decided to grant the permits needed for the project. The neighbors appealed to the city council, which then denied the necessary permits. The school sued the city in federal court, asserting a violation of the Religious Land Use and Institutionalized Persons Act of 2000. That law bars the government from imposing or implementing a land use regulation in a way "that imposes a substantial burden on the religious exercise" of people and institutions. The school sought pretrial judgment, but the court held that a trial was required. **A jury could find that the denial of permits did not constitute a "substantial burden" on the students' religious rights.** *Academy of Our Lady of Peace v. City of San Diego*, No. 09cv962-WQH-AJB, 2010 WL 1329014 (S.D. Cal. 4/1/10).

◆   A Florida church claimed that attempted inspections of its school violated its religious free exercise and Fourth Amendment rights. Under Florida law, the state department of health (DOH) conducted periodic, unscheduled inspections of school and food service facilities. While a DOH inspector was inspecting a Baptist school located on the same property as the church, he noticed a playground. He stepped out of the kitchen to inspect the playground, but the pastor of the church stopped him, saying it belonged to the church and was outside his authority to inspect. The church later sued the DOH, its inspectors, and sheriff's officers who assisted them in attempting to inspect the property. The court dismissed the case, and the Eleventh Circuit affirmed. The attempted inspections did not violate the church's right to free exercise of religion under the state or federal constitutions or the Florida Religious Freedom Restoration Act. **The church did not show that the DOH's entry on its property was unlawful,** and there was no unreasonable search. *Youngblood v. Florida Dep't of Health*, 224 Fed.Appx. 909 (11th Cir. 2007).

◆   The U.S. Court of Appeals, Second Circuit, affirmed a judgment for a New York private school under the Religious Land Use and Institutionalized Persons Act (RLUIPA). The school was so short of space that groups were being taught in halls and even closets. It sought to renovate two buildings and build a new one, but a village zoning board rejected its request for a special permit. The case reached the Second Circuit, which held that **denying the permit substantially burdened the school's religious exercise by confining it to inadequate facilities**. The zoning board had no compelling government interest in denying the permit. It appeared that the board refused to grant the permit because of pressure created by vocal neighbors who opposed the expansion project. *Westchester Day School v. Village of Mamaroneck*, 504 F.3d 338 (2d Cir. 2007).

◆   Georgia's highest court held that increased traffic was a sufficient reason to deny an application for a conditional use permit by a private school seeking to build a football stadium near a residential area. The school's application for a 1,500-seat stadium was part of a plan to construct several new buildings. The expansion was opposed by residents in the adjoining neighborhood. The city planning commission approved most of the project, but it rejected the application for a permit to construct the stadium. The Supreme Court of Georgia held that local government decisions must be upheld if there is any support for them. A school study indicated there were two high school stadiums within a mile of the area. There was already congestion from the existing stadiums, so denial of the conditional use permit was not an abuse of discretion. **Traffic congestion was a valid consideration for the regulation of land use.** *City of Roswell v. Fellowship Christian School*, 281 Ga. 767, 642 S.E.2d 824 (Ga. 2007).

◆   Under California law, a joint powers authority (JPA) can issue tax-exempt revenue bonds for public benefit construction projects. About 350 California cities planned to issue tax-exempt bonds to benefit three Christian schools, including a prep school that planned to use bond proceeds to build classrooms, sports facilities and administrative offices. The JPA brought a validation lawsuit in state court, inviting any interested party to make objections before it issued the bonds. No party objected, but the court asked for a state attorney general's opinion. His opinion was that the tax exemptions might violate the separation of church and state principle of both the state and federal constitutions. The case reached the Supreme Court of California, which noted that **bond proceeds could not be used for religious projects**. It was unclear whether the program only "incidentally" benefited religion. The case was returned to the trial court with instructions for determining whether the Christian schools provided a broad curriculum of secular subjects taught in a religiously neutral way. *California Statewide Communities Development Authority v. All Persons Interested in Matter of Validity of a Purchase Agreement*, 40 Cal.4th 788, 152 P.3d 1070 (Cal. 2007).

III. PRIVATE SCHOOL STUDENT RIGHTS

Private school students do not enjoy the constitutional protections that the courts have recognized for public school students. Generally, courts have demonstrated a reluctance to interfere with private school academic and disciplinary policies. Federal discrimination and civil rights statutes also only provide limited protection. For example, civil rights cases attempting to assert private school liability under a constitutional theory or federal statutory right pursuant to 42 U.S.C. § 1983 require a determination that the school is a state actor. Although a private school may become a state actor based on performance of duties normally associated with government entities or close cooperation with the government, the U.S. Supreme Court in Rendell-Baker v. Kohn, *457 U.S. 830 (1982), limited the circumstances in which an ostensibly private institution can be found to be acting "under the color of state law."*

A. Admissions and Other School Policies

Although the U.S. Supreme Court has applied 42 U.S.C. § 1981 to private schools to prohibit race discrimination, the Court noted that its holding did not extend to religious schools that practiced racial exclusion on religious grounds. Title VI of the Civil Rights Act of 1964 (42 U.S.C. § 2000d) prohibits discrimination on the basis of race, color, or national origin but only applies to "programs or activities" receiving federal financial assistance. In the context of sex discrimination, Title IX applies to recipients of federal funding but also provides a specific exclusion which allows private undergraduate institutions to discriminate on the basis of sex in admissions (20 U.S.C. § 1681(a)(1)).

♦   A non-native Hawaiian student unsuccessfully applied to the Kamehameha Schools, a private K-12 educational institution created via a charitable trust and dedicated to the education of native Hawaiians. The school admits non-native Hawaiians only if openings remain after all qualified applicants of Hawaiian ancestry have been accepted. It conceded that he probably would have been admitted if he was of Hawaiian ancestry. The applicant claimed he was denied admission on the basis of his race, in violation of 42 U.S.C. § 1981. A federal court upheld the schools' admissions policy, and the Ninth Circuit affirmed. The school admittedly considered the race of applicants when making admissions decisions. But **the policy constituted a valid affirmative action plan**. The policy responded to a significant imbalance in the educational achievement levels of native Hawaiians as compared to other ethnic groups. Non-native Hawaiians did not lack adequate educational opportunities. The policy did no more than was necessary to correct the imbalance suffered by native Hawaiians. The preference would be applied only until the effects of past discrimination were remedied. *Doe v. Kamehameha Schools*, 470 F.3d 827 (9th Cir. 2006).

The case returned to the district court, where the student argued that he should be allowed to proceed anonymously with the case in view of "hundreds" of comments criticizing him on websites. The court refused, finding only a handful of comments, none of which showed an objective risk of severe retaliation. The Ninth Circuit again affirmed. *Doe v. Kamehameha Schools/Bernice Pauahi Bishop Estate,* 596 F.3d 1036 (9th Cir. 2010).

♦   Classmates of a Los Angeles college prep school student posted death threats and insults based on his sexual orientation on websites, and admitted making the threatening postings. Some threats had been made from school computers. The student's family moved. Later, the school paper published a story which reported that several of the website posts had called him a "faggot." When the newspaper revealed the family's new address and the name of his new school, the newspaper faculty advisor approved the story. The student and his ▌arents sued the school for violation of state hate crimes laws. The school enrollment contract had an arbitration agreement, so the case was arbitrated.

According to the arbitrator, the school could not be held responsible for the student postings, even though some of them had used school computers. This ruling was based on **a federal law for the Protection for Private Blocking and Screening of Offensive Material**. The law prohibits providers of interactive computer services from being treated as "the publisher or speaker of any information provided by another information content provider." Under the arbitration agreement, the prevailing party could obtain its costs and legal fees from the losing party. Applying these rules, the arbitrator ordered the parents to pay the school over $521,000 for its arbitration costs and attorneys' fees, but the state court of appeal overturned the award of costs and fees. *D.C. v. Harvard-Westlake School*, 176 Cal.App.4th 836, 98 Cal.Rptr. 300 (Cal. Ct. App. 2009).

◆ A small Kentucky Christian high school accepted students through renewable one-year contracts. A student performed well academically in her first year, but was later suspended or expelled for her negative attitude toward the school and her frequent tardiness. Several students reported that she engaged in sexual conduct with another female student, and the school refused to renew her contract for her senior year. The student sued the school and its headmaster for denial of due process, breach of contract, libel, slander and invasion of privacy. A court held for the school and headmaster, and the student appealed to the Kentucky Court of Appeals.

According to the court, the school did not violate the student's constitutional or contractual due process rights. The law pertaining to due process in private schools differs significantly from public school cases. **The relationship between a private school and its students is contractual in nature.** The court rejected the student's claim to the same due process rights afforded public school students. She received all the process she was due when she met with the headmaster and was allowed to respond and defend her actions. The headmaster's investigations into her conduct did not amount to defamation or invasion of privacy. The allegations were reported by students, and he did nothing more than question them. As a result, the lower court had properly held for the school and the headmaster. *Bentley v. Trinity Christian Academy*, 2009 WL 1491351 (Ky. Ct. App. 2009).

◆ The U.S. Supreme Court relied on 42 U.S.C. § 1981 to declare that black students could not be excluded from all-white elementary schools. Parents of black students sought to contract with private nonreligious schools for educational services advertised and offered to members of the general public. The students were denied admission because of their race. The Supreme Court recognized that **while parents have a First Amendment right to send their children to educational institutions that promote racial segregation, institutions are not protected by the same principle**. The school's argument that Section 1981 does not govern private acts of racial discrimination was rejected. However, the Court observed that its holding did not extend to religious schools that practiced racial exclusion on religious grounds. *Runyon v. McCrary*, 427 U.S. 160, 96 S.Ct. 2586, 49 L.Ed.2d 415 (1976).

B. Athletics and Extracurricular Activities

◆ Bylaw 13 of the Kentucky High School Athletic Association (KHSAA) limited the amount and type of merit-based scholarship assistance a student could receive while remaining eligible for KHSAA-sanctioned high school athletics. A group of private school students sued, claiming that the bylaw forced them to forgo financial aid. A federal district court dismissed the federal claims, and the Sixth Circuit affirmed. Bylaw 13 was intended to prevent and deter the recruitment of student-athletes by member schools. This was done by limiting merit-based financial aid to 25% of the cost of tuition. Also, no student could accept financial aid from a funding source that was not under the custody and control of a member school or its governing board. Bylaw 13 was neutral and of general applicability, and it only restricted the amount and type of financial aid received by a student who retained KHSAA athletic eligibility. **There was no religious discrimination, as the bylaw applied in the same way to all non-public schools, regardless of religious affiliation.** *Seger v. Kentucky High School Athletic Ass'n*, 453 Fed.Appx. 630 (6th Cir. 2011).

◆   Three days before a state basketball tournament, the New Jersey State Interscholastic Athletic Association banned a private school team because the coach held practices out of season. The school sued, alleging that the association's undercover investigator violated its privacy rights. Its coach admitted that he inadvertently broke the out-of-season rule. The school asked a federal court to issue an injunction allowing its team to compete in the tournament. The court refused, finding that the school was not likely to win the lawsuit. The school argued that its students would lose an "irreplaceable opportunity to gain college scholarships" by competing on a huge stage before an audience that would include many college coaches, scouts and recruiters. But **the judge quoted courts that found this link to scholarships speculative – and not the kind of harm a court order is intended to remedy.** *St. Patrick High School v. New Jersey Interscholastic Athletic Associations*, No. 10-cv-948 (DMC), 2010 WL 715826 (D.N.J. 3/1/10).

◆   The University Interscholastic League (UIL) is an association of public schools and open-enrollment charter schools that organizes Texas interscholastic and academic competition. Private schools may apply for UIL membership, but the association has narrow, specific qualifications, and only two non-public schools were UIL members. A UIL rule excluded any private school whose right to participate in a league similar to the UIL had been suspended or revoked for violating rules or codes. A Christian college prep school applied for UIL membership after being disqualified from the Texas Association of Private and Parochial Schools (TAPPS). Because the school was eligible for organizations similar to the UIL, its application for UIL membership was denied. The school and the parents of a student attending there sued the UIL, asserting constitutional rights violations.

A court dismissed the case, and the Fifth Circuit affirmed. The UIL rule did not burden the religious free exercise rights of the family. **Parental rights in education extend to the choice of a public, private, or home school, but not to a particular component of that education, such as participation in interscholastic athletics.** UIL rules did not violate equal protection principles. Distinctions drawn in the rules between large and small schools, and between public and private schools were rationally related to the state's interest in reducing unfair competition in the UIL. *Cornerstone Christian Schools v. Univ. Interscholastic League*, 563 F.3d 127 (5th Cir. 2009).

◆   A Massachusetts student transferred to a public school from a prep school in order to repeat her freshman year of high school. She joined the public school's swim team. During the next two years, the student proved to be one of the fastest swimmers in Massachusetts. Prior to her senior year, the Massachusetts Interscholastic Athletic Association (MIAA) deemed her ineligible to compete, based on its "fifth year student rule." The student sued, seeking an order that would allow her to compete as a high school senior on the prep school's swim team. The case reached the Massachusetts Supreme Judicial Court, which noted that the lower court had properly awarded judgment to the MIAA on the student's constitutional rights violation claims.

Any right to education she possessed did not extend to participation in extracurricular activities. Moreover, the student had chosen not to participate on any school's swim team as a freshman and had received the full benefit of her four years of varsity sports eligibility under MIAA rules. **She was not treated differently from other swimmers based on her participation in a private swim club during her first freshman year.** And she failed to show she was similarly situated to other swimmers who were granted MIAA waivers. *Mancuso v. Massachusetts Interscholastic Athletic Ass'n,* 453 Mass. 116, 900 N.E.2d 518 (Mass. 2009).

◆ The Ohio High School Athletic Association (OHSAA) was denied an appeal regarding the application of a transfer bylaw to a student who had already graduated by the time his case reached a state appeals court. The case involved a private school student who was a member of his school bowling team for three years. He transferred to a public school for one term and then returned to the private school. A court held that the OHSAA could not exclude the student from the private school team. The coach would decide if he would compete. As no harm would result from the student's participation, the OHSAA was not entitled to an order. **On appeal, the Court of Appeals of Ohio held the case was moot because of the student's graduation.** *Dankoff v. Ohio High School Athletic Ass,n,* No. 24076, 2008 WL 4150285 (Ohio Ct. App. 9/10/08).

◆ The Tennessee Secondary Schools Athletic Association (TSSAA) is made up of about 290 public schools and 55 private schools. It barred member schools from using "undue influence" in recruiting middle school students for athletics. The football coach of Brentwood Academy, a TSSAA member, wrote letters to eighth-grade boys who had enrolled at the academy, inviting them to practice with the team. He then made follow-up calls to their families. The coach also supplied two students with free tickets to Brentwood football games. Public high school coaches reported the coach's conduct, and the TSSAA fined Brentwood $3,000 for violating recruiting rules and excluded the school from football and basketball tournaments for one school year. Brentwood sued. A court held that the TSSAA was a state actor which violated Brentwood's First Amendment rights. The Sixth Circuit reversed, and the U.S. Supreme Court held that the TSSAA had a public character and was a state actor. *Brentwood Academy v. Tennessee Secondary School Athletic Ass'n,* 531 U.S. 288, 121 S.Ct. 924, 148 L.Ed.2d 807 (2001). The case returned to the district court, which again ruled for Brentwood. On appeal, the Sixth Circuit found that the TSSAA recruiting rule violated the First Amendment. It also found that the TSSAA violated Brentwood's due process rights. The Supreme Court again accepted review. It held that **enforcement of the TSSAA recruitment rule did not abridge the academy's free speech or due process rights.** Brentwood was afforded extensive notices and procedures, including an investigation, a hearing and an appeal. There was no free speech violation, as the rule did not forbid true communications about sports. Instead, it forbade the recruitment of middle school students. Brentwood made a voluntary decision to join the TSSAA and follow its recruitment rule. *Tennessee Secondary Schools Athletic Ass'n v. Brentwood Academy*, 551 U.S. 291, 127 S.Ct. 2489, 168 L.Ed.2d 166 (2007).

C. Breach of Contract

1.   Educational Programs

◆   Former students of a New York law school filed a class action against the school and its officials, claiming it published misleading and deceptive information about its graduation rates and the salaries earned by its graduates. They claimed the misrepresentations resulted in inflated tuition rates. Although the case was based on state law claims of fraud, misrepresentation and violation of the New York General Business Law, the university removed the case to a federal court under the federal Class Action Fairness Act of 2005. Noting that the case involved only state law, the students asked the court to return the case to a state court. The court explained that **under the Class Action Fairness Act, the case had to be returned to a state court if two-thirds or more of the proposed class members were New York residents**. Since the students produced evidence that strongly suggested more than two-thirds of the proposed class of law school graduates still lived in New York, the court held the case should return to the state court. Other factors indicated this was the correct course, including the fact that the claims arose under New York law. *Richins v. Hofstra Univ.*, No. CV 12–1110, 2012 WL 6163090 (E.D.N.Y. 12/10/12).

◆   A federal court dismissed an action by 350 parents and children against people and entities accused of offering students sham services at "gulags" that were supposed to help troubled teens. The parents claimed the services were a sham and students were subjected to horrific treatment that was then covered up. They sued under the Racketeer Influenced and Corrupt Organizations Act of 1984, and they added state fraud claims. **The court dismissed the case, as the parents did not specify how they might have been harmed by the use or investment of racketeering income.** *Wood v. World Wide Ass'n of Specialty Programs and Schools, Inc.*, No. 2:06-CV-708, 2011 WL 3328931 (D. Utah 8/2/11).

◆   Parents sued a Kansas military school in which their children were enrolled for negligent supervision, intentional failure to supervise, intentional infliction of emotional distress, breach of contract and related claims. They added a claim in their own capacities for breach of fiduciary duty. The school claimed an arbitration clause directed any disagreement of the parties into arbitration under the rules of the American Arbitration Association. The court noted that **the enrollment contracts did not indicate that personal injury claims were included in either of the arbitration clauses**. It denied the school's motion to enforce the arbitration and forum selection clauses with respect to the personal injury claims of the students. On the other hand, the parents had signed the contracts and were bound by the arbitration and forum selection clauses, and the court held for the school on their claims. *Bizilj v. St. John's Military School*, No. 08-CV-2036-CM, 2008 WL 4394713 (D. Kan. 9/24/08).

2. Tuition

◆ Parents of an Indianapolis private high school student stopped paying his tuition bill during his senior year. Later, the school sent transcripts to colleges and universities noting that his grades were "incomplete." In a federal court, the student claimed the school acted unlawfully by sending the transcripts. The court found the school's policy was to issue incomplete grades to any student whose tuition was in arrears. The school had already won a state court judgment against the family for unpaid tuition. **The court held the claims were untimely and that the private school could not be sued under federal laws applicable to those acting "under color of state law"** when they released his transcripts. Appeal regarding the federal claims reached the U.S. Court of Appeals, Seventh Circuit. It held the lower court had correctly dismissed the claims as untimely and for lack of any state action. The court found no evidence that the school "acted in concert" with public university officials or any state actors by releasing the transcripts. Many of the claims were found "clearly frivolous," and the court warned the family that further pursuit of them could warrant sanctions. *Mackall v. Cathedral Trustees, Inc.*, 465 Fed.Appx. 549 (7th Cir. 2012).

◆ A Maryland private school's re-enrollment contract specified that cancellation of a student's re-enrollment had to be in writing and delivered by May 31. Otherwise, the agreement held parents liable for charges for the entire academic year, plus any cost for collecting tuition from them. Parents paid the school a nonrefundable $1,000 deposit and agreed to pay the remaining $13,500 tuition in two installments. But in July – 44 days after the contract deadline – the parents tried to cancel their daughter's enrollment and asked for their deposit back. The school refused and informed the parents that they had to pay the full year's tuition. When they refused, the school sued them for breach of contract. The Court of Appeals of Maryland held that **the school did not have to mitigate its damages by trying to find another student** since the exact damages were already stated in the contract. Courts in Ohio, Arkansas, Kentucky and North Carolina have held that private schools in similar circumstances had no duty to mitigate damages caused by a breach of contract. The amount of damages based on the actual loss to the school was irrelevant, because the time to determine a liquidated damages clause is when the contract is formed. *Barrie School v. Patch*, 401 Md. 497, 933 A.2d 382 (Md. 2007).

◆ A Georgia private school enrollment contract made parents who withdrew their child liable for a full year's tuition. The only exception to this rule was if the parents notified the school they were moving more than 35 miles away. Less than two months after signing a tuition contract, two parents notified the school they were withdrawing their daughter and enrolling her at a different school. When they refused to pay tuition, the school brought a successful action against them in a state court. On appeal, the Court of Appeals of Georgia affirmed the judgment. **Liquidated damages provisions are valid if the damage resulting**

from a breach of contract is hard to accurately estimate and the amount is a reasonable estimate of the loss. The parents admitted it would be hard to establish the exact amount it would cost the school if it lost one student. The school's final enrollment and budget were unknown at the time, so the school could not accurately estimate the financial impact of one student's withdrawal. The school was not fully enrolled and was running at a loss when the parents signed the contract. As the clause was a valid liquidated damages provision, rather than an illegal penalty, the parents had to honor it. *Turner v. Atlanta Girls School*, 288 Ga.App. 115, 653 S.E.2d 380 (Ga. Ct. App. 2007).

D. Discipline, Suspension and Expulsion

Pennsylvania has a "deference rule" preventing court review of a religious organization's internal decisions about discipline, faith or ecclesiastical rules. Similarly, Louisiana courts can only overrule private school disciplinary decisions that are arbitrary or capricious.

◆ An African-American senior at a Catholic school in Louisiana created several Facebook accounts and made mocking references about a bishop – as well as profane and mocking comments about her class, the school and certain teachers and administrators. The activity on Facebook violated several of the school's handbook provisions. Other students also joined the sites and commented on the postings. After administrators discovered the Facebook accounts, they disciplined the students involved. As the creator and administrator of the accounts, the student received a nine-day suspension. She sued the school for race discrimination under Section 1981, but the Fifth Circuit ruled that there was no violation of Section 1981. **The student got the longest suspension because she committed the most serious offense.** *Jegart v. Roman Catholic Church of the Diocese of Houma-Thibodaux*, 384 Fed.Appx. 398 (5th Cir. 2010).

◆ A California Lutheran high school teacher learned from a student that two female students had an ongoing homosexual relationship. After the teacher viewed a number of student MySpace pages, she believed the account and reported it to the school's principal. He expelled the female students on the ground that they had a homosexual relationship in violation of the school's Christian conduct rule. The students sued the school and principal for discrimination based on sexual orientation, in violation of the California Unruh Civil Rights Act. The court held for the school, ruling that it was not a "business enterprise" subject to the Unruh Act. The Court of Appeal of California found no error in the judgment. **Lutherans believed that homosexuality was a sin, and the school's policy was to refuse admission to homosexual students.** The Christian conduct rule permitted expulsion for "immoral or scandalous conduct," whether on or off campus. This would include homosexual conduct. *Doe v. California Lutheran High School Ass'n*, 170 Cal.App.4th 828, 88 Cal.Rptr.3d 475 (Cal. Ct. App. 2009).

◆   A Kansas private middle school principal wrote a letter to parents that formalized an English-only policy, citing name-calling, lack of inclusion, put-downs and bullying as grounds for discipline. Her letter required English to be spoken at school at all times. Three sixth-grade students and their parents claimed the English-only rule discriminated against them on the basis of race or national origin. Each of the families spoke English as their primary language. After the diocese that operated the school affirmed the policy, a student refused to sign a policy-related document. He left school, claiming he was expelled. His family and two others sued under Title VI of the Civil Rights Act of 1964. The families had to show that the students were members of a protected class who suffered adverse action and were treated less favorably than similarly situated students. According to the school, there was no "adverse action" here because there is no right to speak a foreign language at a private Catholic school, and each of the students spoke English as their first language. The court found that **English-only rules as applied to bilingual speakers are generally not discriminatory.** The English-only policy in this case resembled a private school rule mandating uniforms. Just as schools could require uniforms, they could dictate the language spoken when based on an appropriate reason. However, a hostile environment claim could proceed, based on the assertion that staff watched the Spanish speakers more closely than other students. *Silva v. St. Anne Catholic School*, 595 F.Supp.2d 1171 (D. Kan. 2009).

◆   Seventh-grade boys at a Pennsylvania Catholic school became fascinated by gangs and knives after their teacher had them read a book describing gang violence. One student admitted bringing a miniature Swiss Army knife to school and was expelled. The school sent a letter to other parents informing them that an unnamed student had been expelled for bringing a penknife to school. The student's parents sued the principal, pastor, school and archdiocese. They claimed their son had brought a small personal manicure set to school – not a knife. The case reached the Pennsylvania Supreme Court, which noted that **the state's "deference rule" prevents court review of a religious organization's internal decisions about discipline, faith or ecclesiastical rules.** However, the deference rule should not apply at the initial stages of a lawsuit for defamation and infliction of emotional distress. Disputes concerning questions of civil law do not require deference to religious doctrine and may be resolved based on neutral principles. The court allowed the defamation and infliction of emotional distress claims to proceed. *Connor v. Archdiocese of Philadelphia*, 601 Pa. 577, 975 A.2d 1084 (Pa. 2009).

◆   A Louisiana Catholic high school senior played on the varsity basketball team. He was placed on probation for plagiarism after his teacher noticed his paper on "Pride and Prejudice" was virtually identical to papers submitted by 13 others in the class. The student handbook stated that plagiarism was a "Class C" offense calling for a one-day suspension or detention plus a nine-week probation. Dishonesty was a "Class D" offense, requiring a full year of probation. While on probation, students could not participate in varsity sports. Twelve students admitted plagiarizing from a website, but the student didn't. The principal placed him on "special disciplinary probation" for the rest of the school year for dishonesty. When the student's father sued the school for an order to allow his son to play on the basketball team, the Court of Appeal of Louisiana found that the school's handbook vested disciplinary decisions with the principal. **Louisiana courts can only overrule private school disciplinary decisions that are arbitrary or capricious.** The decision in this case was neither. A year-long probation was within the principal's discretion. *Lawrence v. St. Augustine High School*, 955 So.2d 183 (La. Ct. App. 2007).

◆ Four 14-year-old Alabama private school girls played strip poker at a party in a private home. After leaving, they communicated electronically with boys who had been at the party. The boys convinced them to photograph themselves in the nude and email them the pictures. The boys promised that they would delete the pictures after viewing them. Instead, they circulated the photos to others. Copies were distributed throughout the school and an explicit photo was set as the wallpaper on a computer in a sixth-grade computer lab, leading to a shutdown of the system. The school's headmaster expelled the girls and the boy who had taken responsibility for distributing the photos.

The girls sued the school, headmaster and the school board chair for breach of contract, negligence, invasion of privacy and related claims. The case reached the Supreme Court of Alabama, which rejected the students' claims that the school breached the enrollment contract by failing to provide them with due process during the investigation. The headmaster met with the parents, informed them of the situation, showed them the photos, and gave them a chance to respond. **Each of the students and their parents had signed a pledge in which they promised to abide by the student handbook,** and the handbook expressly provided that "[o]ff-campus behavior which is illicit, immoral, illegal and/or which reflects adversely on [the school] subjects the student to immediate expulsion." The school did not breach the enrollment contract. *S.B. v. St. James School*, 959 So.2d 72 (Ala. 2006).

E. Students with Disabilities

Private institutions must comply with laws requiring the accommodation of students with disabilities, such as the Americans with Disabilities Act (ADA). Section 504 of the Rehabilitation Act applies to any institution that receives federal funding, which brings some private schools within its scope. Students with disabilities must be reasonably accommodated, but only to the extent that it does not impose an undue hardship on the school. But the Individuals with Disabilities Education Act (IDEA) does not apply to private schools, as they are not included in the definition of "local educational agencies" under the IDEA.

◆ A Maryland private school student with disabilities was ineligible for IDEA services. Although a school district declared him eligible under Section 504, the district advised his parents that it could not provide Section 504 services unless he enrolled in a public school. Since Maryland law did not permit simultaneous dual enrollment in a public and private school, the district's position would have forced the student to withdraw from his Yeshiva to receive the services. After an administrative challenge, a federal court upheld the district's decision. The case then reached the U.S. Court of Appeals, Fourth Circuit, which noted federal guidance under Section 504 declared that a school district was not obligated to provide educational services to private school students placed on the basis of parental choice. A federal regulation declared that no parentally placed private school student with a disability had an individual right to receive some or all of the special education and related services that would be provided at a public school. Section 504's remedial purpose did not extend as far as the parents claimed. For this reason, the court held **Section 504 and its regulations did not require public schools to provide access to eligible students who opted out of their programs by enrolling in private schools**. *D.L. v. Baltimore City Board of School Commissioners*, 706 F.3d 256 (4th Cir. 2013).

◆   The parents of a New Jersey student with autism and other disorders placed him in a private school for grade five after becoming dissatisfied with his IEP. The district denied tuition reimbursement. The following year, the parents sought an evaluation and IEP meeting, but the district claimed that the student had to re-enroll in the district to be served by it. The parents kept the student in the private school and filed for due process, seeking tuition reimbursement. An administrative law judge and a federal court ruled that the district had offered a FAPE for the first year the student attended the private school. However, **the court rejected the district's claim that it did not have to reevaluate the student or offer an IEP because he was not enrolled in a district school**. The parents were entitled to tuition reimbursement for the time period after the district failed to reevaluate the student. *Moorestown Township Board of Educ. v. S.D.*, 811 F.Supp.2d 1057 (D.N.J. 2011).

◆   A New York court held a private school had no duty to hold a manifestation hearing prior to expelling a disabled student with an individualized education plan. After the private school expelled the student, his parents obtained a state court order holding this action could not be taken prior to a manifestation determination hearing. The school appealed to a state appellate division court, which noted that the parents failed to exhaust their administrative remedies under the state education law. Even if the parents had exhausted administrative remedies, they still would not be entitled to relief. **The education law places the burden on public schools to provide special education services, and not upon non-public schools**. The lower court decision was reversed. *In re Pelose*, 885 N.Y.S.2d 816 (N.Y. App. Div. 2009).

◆   A private school contracted with a Virginia school district to provide educational services for an autistic student. The contract allowed either party to terminate the agreement upon 30 days' notice. The school could also terminate the contract if the student committed a serious incident. When the school sought to discharge the student over safety concerns, his parents objected and requested a due process hearing. A hearing officer ordered the school to comply with the stay-put provision of the Individuals with Disabilities Education Act (IDEA), finding that **its contract with the district required it to comply with the IDEA**. The school sued the school district to challenge the order and then reached a settlement with the district releasing it from the contract. The federal court then refused to intervene in the dispute, leaving the due process hearing over the decision to expel the student to the hearing officer. *Virginia Institute of Autism v. Virginia Dep't of Educ.*, 537 F.Supp.2d 817 (E.D. Va. 2008).

◆   The mother of a New Hampshire wheelchair-bound student claimed that his school district failed to follow his IEP and erroneously decertified him from eligibility for special education. She filed a complaint with the state department of education. After an administrative ruling against her, she placed her son in a private school outside the district. When she sued the school district under the IDEA and Section 504, a federal court held that **most of her claims failed because the private school was outside the district and she did not intend to return her son to district schools**. Her tuition reimbursement claim under the IDEA remained viable, but her claims against individual employees under Section 504 failed. *J.P.E.H. v. Hooksett School Dist.*, No. 07-CV-276-SM, 2008 WL 4681925 (D.N.H. 10/22/08).

Subsequently, the court determined that tuition reimbursement was not in order because the student's classroom performance demonstrated that he was no longer qualified as a child with a disability under the IDEA. *J.P.E.H. v. Hooksett School Dist.*, No. 07-CV-276-SM, 2009 WL 1883885 (D.N.H. 6/30/09).

◆   The Third Circuit decided that more evidence was needed to establish if a private school with a strong Quaker affiliation fell within the ADA's religious exemption to lawsuits. The parents of a student with Attention Deficit Disorder and other learning disabilities claimed the school's staff did not give him the help he needed and tried to pressure him into leaving school through a campaign of public humiliation and improper physical discipline. They sued the school in a federal court, claiming the school subjected him to a discriminatory environment and failed to accommodate his disabilities. The court held that the school could not be sued under the ADA because it was a religious organization. The Third Circuit reversed and remanded the case to the lower court for further consideration. **The ADA exemption applied if the school was a religious organization or under the control of one.** As the only evidence presented was an affidavit by the school's headmaster, the parents should have the chance to gather more information to determine if the school was a "religious organization." *Doe v. Abington Friends School*, 480 F.3d 252 (3d Cir. 2007).

◆   A private school student in Michigan had a brain tumor that was in remission. Because of his problems walking, his mother requested a physical therapy needs evaluation from the school district. The district found that he did not need additional physical therapy. The mother then asked for an individual educational evaluation at the district's expense. When the district refused, a lawsuit resulted. The Michigan Court of Appeals held that state law required special education for "every handicapped person." Further, **nothing in state law limited individual educational evaluations to public school students.** The district had to pay for the evaluation. *Michigan Dep't of Educ. v. Grosse Pointe Public Schools*, 701 N.W.2d 195 (Mich. Ct. App. 2005).

IV. PUBLIC AND PRIVATE SCHOOL COOPERATION

Cooperation between public and private schools must avoid the appearance of government approval of religion and must not constitute government aid to, or excessive entanglement with, religious organizations.

A. Dual Enrollment

◆ An Illinois student tested above grade level at a private school. His mother asked the superintendent of their school district for permission to enroll him in an Algebra II or geometry class in district schools as he entered grade eight. The private school principal made a request to place the student in a public school math class the next year. The superintendent contacted the principal and the independent study teacher, seeking the student's grades, homework, quizzes, tests and scores. The superintendent allowed the student to enroll in district schools on a part-time basis, but placed him in an Honors Algebra I class. The student instead enrolled in an Algebra II course at a local community college while remaining in eighth grade in his private school. The family sued the district and superintendent for due process and equal protection violations. The court noted that an Illinois law permitted private school students to attend public school part time. Here, the superintendent conferred with private school staff and reasonably determined that the student's proper placement was in Honors Algebra I. **State law did not create a protected property interest to attend a student's class of choice.** The court held for the district and superintendent. *Hassberger v. Board of Educ., Cent. Community Unit School Dist. 301*, No. 00 C 7873, 2003 WL 22697481 (N.D. Ill. 2003).

◆ Many Indiana local educational agencies and private schools employed dual-enrollment agreements under which the agencies provided secular instruction to private school students at public schools. Public funds were also used to provide computer and Internet services to private schools, including those with religious affiliations. A group of taxpayers opposed the dual-enrollment process as a public subsidy of religious schools. They sued for violations of Article 1, Section 6 of the Indiana Constitution. A court held that the dual-enrollment process did not violate the state constitution. The Supreme Court of Indiana affirmed. **The dual-enrollment programs did not result in the payment of public funds directly to religious institutions,** and any cost saving realized by parochial schools was relatively minor and incidental. The programs did not confer substantial benefits on religious institutions or directly fund religious activity. *Embry v. O'Bannon*, 798 N.E.2d 157 (Ind. 2003).

B. Textbook Loans and Other Materials

The provision of textbooks by the state to private and parochial school students is permissible under the First Amendment. In Cochran v. Louisiana State Board of Educ., *281 U.S. 370 (1930), the U.S. Supreme Court upheld a state law that authorized the purchasing and supplying of textbooks to all schoolchildren, including parochial schoolchildren, on the basis of what is now called the "child benefit" doctrine. The Court held that the textbook loan statute was constitutional because the legislature's purpose in enacting the statute was to benefit children and their parents, not religious schools.*

♦ A group of Louisiana citizens sued the Jefferson Parish School Board in 1985 for violating the First Amendment, alleging that the board improperly provided Chapter Two funds to parochial schools to acquire library materials and media equipment. The group asserted that expenditures for books, computers, software and other audiovisual equipment violated the Establishment Clause. A federal court agreed, granting pretrial judgment to the group because the funding failed the test from *Lemon v. Kurtzman*, 403 U.S. 602 (1971). The court held that the loan of materials to sectarian schools constituted direct government aid under *Meek v. Pittenger*, 421 U.S. 349 (1975) and *Wolman v. Walter*, 433 U.S. 229 (1977). Two years later, the court reversed itself, citing the intervening *Zobrest v. Catalina Foothills School Dist.*, 509 U.S. 1 (1993), decision. The citizens appealed to the Fifth Circuit, which held that the Chapter Two grants were unconstitutional under *Meek* and *Wolman*.

The U.S. Supreme Court then stated that there was no basis for finding the board's use of Chapter Two funds advanced religion. Use of Chapter Two funds by private schools did not result in government indoctrination because eligibility was determined on a neutral basis and through private choices by parents. **Chapter Two had no impermissible content and did not define its recipients by reference to religion.** A broad array of schools was eligible for assistance without regard to religious affiliation. Students who attended schools receiving Chapter Two funds were the ultimate beneficiaries of the assistance. The Court upheld the board's use of Chapter Two funding and held that the parish did not need to exclude sectarian schools from its program. *Mitchell v. Helms*, 530 U.S. 793, 120 S.Ct. 2530, 147 L.Ed.2d 660 (2000).

♦ The U.S. Supreme Court reaffirmed the validity of the child benefit doctrine in a case involving a New York textbook loan statute. This statute required local school districts to lend textbooks free of charge to all children in grades seven through twelve. Parochial school students were included. The Court observed that the textbooks loaned to parochial schoolchildren were the same nonreligious textbooks used in the public schools. **The loaning of textbooks was permissible because the parochial school students used them for secular study.** The state of New York was merely providing a secular benefit to all schoolchildren. *Board of Educ. v. Allen*, 392 U.S. 236, 88 S.Ct. 1923, 20 L.Ed.2d 1060 (1968).

♦ The Supreme Court held that **private schools with racially discriminatory admissions policies may not benefit from textbook loan programs**. The state may not give assistance to acts of racial discrimination. Textbooks are "a basic educational tool," said the Court, and to permit racially discriminatory private schools to benefit from state textbook loans would be to allow the state to accomplish indirectly what it could not accomplish directly: a state-funded racially segregated school system. *Norwood v. Harrison*, 413 U.S. 455, 93 S.Ct. 2804, 37 L.Ed.2d 723 (1973).

C. Transportation

The use of state funds to reimburse private schools for transportation for field trips was declared unconstitutional by the U.S. Supreme Court in Wolman v. Walter, *433 U.S. 229 (1977). There was no way public officials could monitor the field trips to assure that they had a secular purpose. Even if monitoring by the state was feasible, the monitoring would be so extensive that the state would become entangled in religion to an impermissible degree.*

◆   A group of Illinois parochial school students objected to their local school district's decision to discontinue their bus transportation on days that district schools were not open. A state court held Illinois law did not require the district to provide transportation services in excess of what it provided its own students. The families appealed to the Appellate Court of Illinois. It found the legislative intent of relevant school code sections was that private school students enjoy transportation "only on the same basis on which it is provided to public school students." Like the lower court, the appellate court found **the school code's purposes included minimizing costs to public schools, without interfering with their convenience or efficiency**. Proof of the legislative intent was found in a code provision permitting school districts to establish separate routes for nonpublic school students, but only if the operation of such routes was more economical and more efficient. In affirming the judgment, the court held **district school buses did not have to "go out of their way to transport nonpublic school students."** *C.E. v. Board of Educ. of East St. Louis School Dist. No. 189*, 970 N.E.2d 1287 (Ill. App. Ct. 2012).

◆   For about 10 years, an Indiana school district offered free bus transportation to students attending two schools operated by the Archdiocese of Indianapolis. Private school students who lived along regular bus routes rode them to a public school site. From there, the district offered free shuttle buses to the private schools. No contract governed the shuttle arrangement. But in 2009, the district's board voted to assess a fee for the shuttle bus service due to increased daily operation costs. The Archdiocese refused to sign service contracts that would have cost it $4,922 per year, and it sued the district. The board then voted to terminate the shuttle bus service even though the current school year was not over. Parents of students at the private schools filed a new action. The case reached the state court of appeals, which noted that state law required school districts to provide transportation to private school students who live along a regular public school bus route. The statute authorized the district to drop off private school students either at their school or at "the point on the regular route that is nearest or most easily accessible to the nonpublic school." **The law did not require the district to deliver the nonpublic students to the nonpublic schools.** *Roman Catholic Archdiocese of Indianapolis v. Metro School Dist. of Lawrence Township*, 945 N.E.2d 757 (Ind. Ct. App. 2011).

◆   South Dakota school district buses picked up Lutheran elementary school students who lived along its bus routes until the state attorney general suggested that transporting private school students might violate the South Dakota

Constitution. The state legislature then enacted a new law expressly allowing school districts to provide transportation for private school students, if this did not cost additional public funds. Prior to the reinstatement of busing, parents of students who attended the private school sued the school district for constitutional violations. The case reached the U.S. Court of Appeals, Eighth Circuit, which explained that the parents lacked standing to sue because they "failed to take even the simple step of requesting that the School District resume busing." In fact, the district had advocated for the legislation to allow busing. *Pucket v. Hot Springs School Dist. No. 23-2*, 526 F.3d 1151 (8th Cir. 2008).

◆ Transportation may be provided to parochial school students without violating the First Amendment under a 1947 U.S. Supreme Court case. The case involved a New Jersey law that allowed reimbursement to parents of children attending nonprofit religious schools for costs incurred by the children in using public transportation to travel to and from school. The law's purpose was to provide transportation expenses for all schoolchildren regardless of where they attended school, as long as the school was nonprofit. The Court analogized free transportation to other state benefits such as police and fire protection, connections for sewage disposal, and public roads and sidewalks, which also benefited parochial schoolchildren. **It was not the purpose of the First Amendment to cut off religious institutions from all government benefits.** Rather, the state was only required to be neutral toward religion. *Everson v. Board of Educ.*, 330 U.S. 1, 67 S.Ct. 504, 91 L.Ed. 711 (1947).

D. Personnel Sharing and Outsourcing

◆ **A Tennessee education board voted to eliminate an alternative school and the jobs of three teachers** – one of whom also served as the principal. Two weeks later, it voted to contract with a religious school to provide public alternative school services for the next school year. The teachers sued for constitutional rights violations. The case reached the Sixth Circuit, which held that only two of the teachers could continue the lawsuit. They were resident taxpayers who could pursue an Establishment Clause claim. *Smith v. Jefferson County Board of School Commissioners*, 641 F.3d 197 (6th Cir. 2011). A full summary of the case appears in Chapter Four, Section IV.

◆ Title I of the Elementary and Secondary Education Act of 1965 provides federal funding through the states to local educational agencies for remedial education, guidance and job counseling to at-risk students and students residing in low-income areas. Title I requires that funding be made available for all eligible students, including those attending private schools. Local agencies retain control over Title I funds and materials. The New York City Board of Education attempted to implement Title I programs at parochial schools by allowing public employees to instruct students on private school grounds during school hours. The case reached the U.S. Supreme Court, which held that this violated the Establishment Clause in *Aguilar v. Felton*, 473 U.S. 402 (1985).

A federal court then ordered the city board to refrain from using Title I funds for any plan or program under which public school teachers and counselors appeared on sectarian school grounds. Local education boards modified their Title I programs by moving classes to remote sites including mobile instructional units parked near sectarian schools. A new group of parents and parochial school students sought relief from the permanent order. The case again reached the U.S. Supreme Court, which held that it would no longer presume that the presence of a public school teacher on parochial school grounds creates an unconstitutional symbolic union between church and state. The provision of Title I services at parochial schools resembled the provision of a sign-language interpreter under the Individuals with Disabilities Education Act. **New York City's Title I program was constitutionally permissible** since it did not result in government indoctrination, define funding recipients by reference to religion or create excessive entanglement between state officials and religious schools. *Agostini v. Felton*, 521 U.S. 203, 117 S.Ct. 1997, 138 L.Ed.2d 391 (1997).

◆ In *Lemon v. Kurtzman*, the U.S. Supreme Court invalidated Rhode Island and Pennsylvania statutes that provided state money to finance the operation of parochial schools. It applied a three-part test, which remains in use by the courts today. First, the statute must have a secular legislative purpose. Second, its principal or primary effect must be one that neither advances nor inhibits religion. Last, the statute must not foster an excessive government entanglement with religion. **The programs excessively entangled the state with religion** because of the highly religious nature of the Roman Catholic parochial schools that were its primary beneficiaries. Consequently, the programs violated the First Amendment. *Lemon v. Kurtzman*, 403 U.S. 602, 91 S.Ct. 2105, 29 L.Ed.2d 745 (1971).

E. School Facilities and Property

◆ A Georgia school board authorized the lease of classroom space at the Buckhead Baptist Church to create a kindergarten annex. The lease required the school system to rent space from the church for over five years and pay for renovations and improvements on church property that would be credited against rent due. A citizen claimed the lease agreement violated the Establishment Clause of the Georgia Constitution and sued the school system to halt payments to the church. A court ruled for the school system.

The Georgia Supreme Court explained that the state constitution's Establishment Clause prevented the state and its political subdivisions from owning, controlling or giving monetary aid to a church or religious institution. However, this did not mean that a state political subdivision could not "enter into an arms-length commercial agreement with a sectarian institution to accomplish a non-sectarian purpose." Here, the school system had simply leased space from the church to run a public kindergarten in a non-sectarian environment. **Lease payments did not foster the education of students in a sectarian school and was not state monetary aid to the church.** As the lease agreement did not violate the Georgia Constitution, the court affirmed the judgment for the school system. *Taetle v. Atlanta Independent School System*, 280 Ga. 137, 625 S.E.2d 770 (Ga. 2006).

◆   The Milwaukee Parental Choice Program was created to subsidize private education for underprivileged students in Milwaukee. A Catholic High School located primarily in St. Francis, but with 20% of its school grounds, including green space, a parking lot, driveway and track area located in Milwaukee, petitioned the state superintendent of public instruction for an order declaring it eligible to participate in the choice program. This request was denied. In the lawsuit that followed, the Court of Appeals of Wisconsin noted that **the statute plainly indicated that the school was not eligible to participate in the program**. The title of the statute was "Milwaukee parental choice program." Had the legislature intended for schools with buildings not located in the city to participate in the program, it would not have required them to submit copies of their certificates of occupancy "issued by the city." Under the school's argument, "any school, anywhere can become a Choice school by buying a small plot in the City of Milwaukee." Without the required certificate of occupancy from the city of Milwaukee, the school was ineligible for the program. *Thomas More High School v. Burmaster*, 704 N.W.2d 349 (Wis. Ct. App. 2005). The Supreme Court of Wisconsin denied further review.

◆   An Iowa parochial school held a fundraiser for its baseball and softball teams. Individuals and businesses purchased 37 boosters signs that were hung from the outfield fences of school athletic fields. The Iowa Department of Transportation (IDOT) determined that the signs violated a state law prohibiting billboard advertising within 660 feet of a state highway. The school challenged an IDOT directive to remove the signs, claiming they were not visible from the highway and that IDOT was infringing on commercial speech in violation of the First Amendment. The Iowa Supreme Court held that the signs clearly violated the statute, as they were visible from the highway. **The statute regulated signs based on their location, not their content.** Here, the statute did not impermissibly restrict the school's speech rights. IDOT had a compelling state interest in traffic safety and ensuring an aesthetic environment. The statute only prohibited the booster signs from being placed where they were visible from the highway. The school could still place them elsewhere on its property. *Immaculate Conception Corp. and Don Bosco High School v. Iowa Dep't of Transportation*, 656 N.W.2d 513 (Iowa 2003).

◆   Under a Montgomery County, Maryland, zoning ordinance, all businesses and organizations must obtain a special exception in order to build a non-residential structure on land designated for residential use. The county appeals board grants petitions for special exceptions only after determining, through a public hearing, that the new building will not disrupt the surrounding community. The ordinance exempts lots owned or leased by religious organizations from having to obtain a special exception. A federal court examined the constitutionality of the exemption after residential neighbors of the Connelly School of the Holy Child, a parochial school, objected to the school's construction of a new building. The court found the exemption unconstitutional. The Connelly School appealed to the Fourth Circuit.

   The court of appeals reversed, holding that **the exemption had the secular purpose of allowing the county to prevent government interference with** the religious mission of various organizations and avoided creating a forum during special exception hearings in which anti-religious views might be expressed. The exemption neither advanced nor inhibited religion. The county merely relieved religious schools from the burden of applying for a special exception. Any advancement of religion that followed would be the result of the religious schools' own acts in light of the exemption. Finally, the exemption did not foster an excessive entanglement with religion. *Renzi v. Connelly School of the Holy Child Inc.*, 224 F.3d 283 (4th Cir. 2000).

F. Release Time Programs

◆   South Carolina parents objected to a school district policy that permitted students to earn credit for off-campus, released time religious instruction. The policy was created under the state Released Time Credit Act. This act allows school districts to award high school students up to two academic credits for completing religious classes during released time. In a three-year period, only 20 of the school district's 1,500 students participated in a released time course credit program. A federal court rejected the parents' Establishment Clause challenge. On appeal, the U.S. Court of Appeals, Fourth Circuit, noted an off-campus released time program was upheld in *Zorach v. Clauson*, this chapter. In affirming the judgment, the Fourth Circuit held the school district's policy complied with the Establishment Clause. In the court's opinion, **public schools have broad but not unlimited discretion to release students for off-campus religious instruction**. In fact, the court held a failure to accommodate the religious desires of students and parents in this case could result in a religiously hostile environment that would violate the Constitution. *Moss v. Spartanburg County School Dist. Seven*, 683 F.3d 599 (4th Cir. 2012).

◆   **An Illinois program allowed public school students to receive religious instruction in their public schools.** Although religious groups supplied the religious education teachers at no cost to school districts, the superintendent of schools exercised supervisory powers over them. A taxpayer sued a local school board, claiming the release time program violated the Establishment Clause. The U.S. Supreme Court agreed. "This is beyond all question a utilization of the tax-established and tax-supported public school system to aid religious groups," said the Court. "[T]he First Amendment has erected a wall between Church and State which must be kept high and impregnable." *McCollum v. Board of Educ.*, 333 U.S. 203, 68 S.Ct. 461, 92 L.Ed. 649 (1948).

◆   Four years later, the Supreme Court upheld a different kind of release time program. In this New York program, students could be released from public school classes during the school day for a few hours to attend religious education classes. Unlike the program in the *McCollum* case, students in the New York release time program received their religious instruction off the public school grounds. Church officials made out weekly attendance reports and sent the reports to public school officials, who then checked to assure that the released students had actually reported for their off-school-grounds religious instruction. The Court approved the New York program largely because the religious instruction took place off school grounds. **There was no religious indoctrination taking place in the public school buildings nor was there any expenditure of public funds on behalf of religious training.** Also, there was no evidence of any subtle or overt coercion exerted by any public school officials to induce students to attend the religious classes. The public schools were merely accommodating religion, not aiding it. The Supreme Court declined to invalidate the New York release time program, saying, "We cannot read into the Bill of Rights such a philosophy of hostility to religion." *Zorach v. Clauson*, 343 U.S. 306, 72 S.Ct. 679, 96 L.Ed. 954 (1952).

V. STUDENT FINANCIAL ASSISTANCE

To be constitutional, government financial assistance for religious school students must primarily benefit the students, not their schools. Federal funding of programs and activities requires compliance with federal statutes such as Title VI, Title IX, the Rehabilitation Act, the Americans with Disabilities Act and the Age Discrimination in Employment Act. Students receiving federal grants will be deemed to be receiving assistance for federal law purposes. For more cases involving school voucher programs, please see Chapter Four, Section IV.

◆   **Oklahoma's Supreme Court held a pair of school districts had no legal standing to challenge state legislation creating a scholarship program for students with disabilities in the state.** Although the districts claimed the legislation violated several provisions of the state constitution, the court held that school districts were "merely the Legislature's vehicle" for the provision of public education. Program funds were deemed part of the legislature's general grant. As school districts were not charged with the duty to provide public education, the court held the legislative decision to withhold some funds from them for the program did not violate any protected interest. The school districts could not pursue the case. *Independent School Dist. No. 5 of Tulsa County, Oklahoma v. Spry*, 292 P.3d 19 (Okla. 2012).

◆   An Arizona law offered students with disabilities up to $5,000 for tuition and fees to attend private schools. Objectors to the program sued state officials, asserting constitutional violations. The case reached the state supreme court, which noted that Arizona Constitution Article 9, Section 10, the "Aid Clause," was "aimed at placing restrictions on the disbursement of public funds to specified institutions, both religious and secular." The court distinguished the program from a state tax credit for contributions to school tuition organizations and held **the scholarships provided aid to private schools in violation of the Aid Clause**. *Cain v. Horne*, 220 Ariz. 77, 202 P.3d 1178 (Ariz. 2009).

◆   A 67-year-old disabled Washington man failed to repay federally reinsured student loans he incurred between 1984 and 1989 under the Guaranteed Student Loan Program. The loans were reassigned to the Department of Education, which certified the debt to the U.S. Department of Treasury through the Treasury Offset Program. The U.S. government began withholding part of the man's Social Security benefits to offset his debt, part of which was more than 10 years overdue. He sued, alleging that the offset was barred by a 10-year statute of limitations of the 1982 Debt Collection Act. The court dismissed the case, and appeal reached the U.S. Supreme Court. The Court explained that **the Higher Education Technical Amendments of 1991 "sweepingly eliminated time limitations as to certain loans."** This included student loans. The Debt Collection Improvement Act of 1996 clarified that, notwithstanding any other law, all payments due under the Social Security Act were subject to offset. Moreover, the Amendments removed the 10-year limit that would otherwise bar an offset of Social Security benefits. The Court affirmed the judgment for the U.S. government. *Lockhart v. U.S.*, 546 U.S. 142, 126 S.Ct. 699, 163 L.Ed.2d 557 (2005).

◆ Washington law created a scholarship that made state funds available to qualified students for education-related costs. A student who received a scholarship enrolled as a double major in pastoral ministries and business at a private Christian college. The college director of financial aid advised him that he could not use the scholarship to pursue a devotional theology degree. When the student sued, the U.S. Supreme Court, held that the Constitution permitted states to deny funding to students pursuing devotional theology degrees. Here, **the training of ministers was essentially a religious endeavor that could be treated differently than training for other callings**. There was no evidence of any state hostility toward religion. Only students seeking a theology degree were denied scholarships. Nothing in the history or text of the Washington Constitution or the program suggested anti-religious bias. *Locke v. Davey*, 540 U.S. 712, 124 S.Ct. 1307, 158 L.Ed.2d 1 (2004).

◆ The parents of three Georgia private school students sued the state, the Board of Education and others for the enforcement of the state Tuition Grant Act, which provided for direct grants of money, under specified conditions, to the parents of students attending grades K-12 in nonsectarian private schools. The parents alleged that they were denied these grants which, in turn, denied them the equal protection of the law since students in pre-kindergarten and post-twelfth grade programs at private schools had state funds available to them. The Supreme Court of Georgia noted that the two groups were not similarly situated. Children in K-12 had a constitutional right to an education at state expense and were required to attend school. However, the group of children in pre-kindergarten and post-twelfth grade had no constitutional right to education and were not required to be enrolled in educational programs. **The disparate entitlements and obligations of the two groups meant that the parents were not entitled to relief.** *Lowe v. State of Georgia*, 482 S.E.2d 344 (Ga. 1997).

◆ A private, not-for-profit technical school in Indiana participated in the Guaranteed Student Loan (GSL) program authorized by Title IV of the Higher Education Act. The program required the school to make refunds to the lender if a student withdrew from school during a term. If the school failed to refund loans to the lender, the student would be liable for the full amount of the loan. The treasurer of the school conferred with the school's owners and initiated a practice of not making GSL refunds. As a result, the school owed $139,649 in refunds. After the school lost its accreditation, a federal grand jury indicted the treasurer for "knowingly and willfully misapplying" federally insured student loan funds in violation of 20 U.S.C. § 1097(a). A federal court dismissed the indictment because it lacked an allegation that the treasurer intended to injure or defraud the United States. The U.S. Supreme Court then held that Section 1097(a) did not require the specific intent to injure or defraud. **If the government can prove that the defendant misapplied Title IV funds knowingly and willfully, that is sufficient to show a violation of Section 1097(a).** The treasurer could be prosecuted. *Bates v. U.S.*, 522 U.S. 23, 118 S.Ct. 285, 139 L.Ed.2d 215 (1997).

◆ A blind student sought vocational services under a Washington law making visually impaired persons eligible for educational assistance. But as the student attended a Christian college, the state commission for the blind denied the request. The state supreme court upheld the decision on First Amendment grounds. But the U.S. Supreme Court noted that the commission paid money directly to students, who could then attend the schools of their choice. **The fact that this student chose a religious college did not constitute state support of religion.** The Court held the First Amendment was not offended. *Witters v. Washington Dep't of Services for the Blind*, 474 U.S. 481, 106 S.Ct. 748, 88 L.Ed.2d 846 (1986).

The case then returned to the Washington Supreme Court. It held that **vocational assistance funds for religious education violated the state constitution**. The state constitution was far stricter in its prohibition on the expenditure of public funds for religious instruction than the U.S. Constitution. *Witters v. State Comm'n for the Blind*, 771 P.2d 1119 (Wash. 1989).

◆ The U.S. Supreme Court upheld a Minnesota program that involved tax deductions for parents of public and private schoolchildren. In upholding the program, the Court held that the state had a legitimate interest in assuring that all its citizens were well educated. Also, the tax deductions in question were only a few among many other deductions such as those for medical expenses or charitable contributions. Unlike the program in the *Nyquist* case, **the Minnesota program was part of a bona fide income tax deduction system available to parents of all schoolchildren**. The Court held that the First Amendment was not offended by the Minnesota tax deduction program. *Mueller v. Allen*, 463 U.S. 388, 103 S.Ct. 3062, 77 L.Ed.2d 721 (1983).

◆ The U.S. Supreme Court invalidated a New York program that provided $50-$100 in direct money grants to low income parents with children in private schools and authorized income tax credits of up to $1,000 for parents with children in private schools. **The program had the primary effect of advancing religion** and thus was constitutionally invalid. The Court characterized the tax credits as akin to tuition grants and observed that they were really cash giveaways by the state for religious schools. *Committee for Public Educ. & Religious Liberty v. Nyquist*, 413 U.S. 756, 93 S.Ct. 2955, 37 L.Ed.2d 948 (1973).

APPENDIX A

United States Constitution

[Provisions of Interest to Educators]

ARTICLE I

Section 1. All legislative Powers herein granted shall be vested in a Congress of the United States, which shall consist of a Senate and House of Representatives.

* * *

Section 8. The Congress shall have Power To lay and collect Taxes, Duties, Imposts and Excises, to pay the Debts and provide for the common Defence and general Welfare of the United States; but all Duties, Imposts and Excises shall be uniform throughout the United States:

To borrow money on the credit of the United States;

To regulate Commerce with foreign Nations, and among the several States, and with the Indian Tribes;

To establish an uniform Rule of Naturalization, and uniform Laws on the subject of Bankruptcies throughout the United States;

* * *

To promote the Progress of Science and useful Arts, by securing for limited Times to Authors and Inventors the exclusive Right to their respective Writings and Discoveries;

* * *

To make all Laws which shall be necessary and proper for carrying into Execution for the foregoing Powers, and all other Powers vested by this Constitution in the Government of the United States, or in any Department or Office thereof.

* * *

Section 9. * * * No Bill of Attainder or ex post facto Law shall be passed.

Section 10. No State shall * * * pass any Bill of Attainder, ex post facto Law, or Law impairing the Obligation of Contracts, or grant any Title of Nobility.

* * *

ARTICLE II

Section 1. The executive Power shall be vested in a President of the United States of America.

* * *

ARTICLE III

Section 1. The judicial Power of the United States, shall be vested in one Supreme Court, and in such inferior Courts as the Congress may from time to time ordain and establish. The Judges, both of the supreme and inferior courts, shall hold their Offices during good Behaviour, and shall, at stated Times, receive for their Services a Compensation, which shall not be diminished during their Continuance in Office.

Section 2. The judicial Power shall extend to all Cases, in Law and Equity, arising under this Constitution, the Laws of the United States, and Treaties made, or which shall be made; under their Authority; to all Cases affecting Ambassadors, other public Ministers and Consuls; to all Cases of admiralty and maritime Jurisdiction, to Controversies to which the United States shall be a party to Controversies between two or more States; between a State and Citizens of another State; between Citizens of different States; between Citizens of the same State claiming Lands under the Grants of different States, and between a State, or the Citizens thereof, and foreign States, Citizens or Subjects.

* * *

ARTICLE IV

Section 1. Full Faith and Credit shall be given in each State to the public Acts, Records and judicial Proceedings of every other State.* * *

Section 2. The Citizens of each State shall be entitled to all Privileges and Immunities of Citizens in the several States.

* * *

Section 4. The United States shall guarantee to every State in this Union a Republican Form of Government, and shall protect each of them against Invasion; and on Application of the Legislature, or of the Executive (when the Legislature cannot be convened) against domestic Violence.

ARTICLE V

The Congress, whenever two thirds of both Houses shall deem it necessary, shall propose Amendments to this Constitution, or, on the Application of the Legislatures of two thirds of the several States, shall call a Convention for proposing Amendments, which, in either Case, shall be valid to all Intents and Purposes, as part of this Constitution, when ratified by the Legislatures of three fourths of the several States, or by Conventions in three fourths thereof, as the one or the other Mode of Ratification may be proposed by the Congress; Provided that no Amendment which may be made prior to the Year One thousand eight hundred and eight shall in any Manner affect the first and fourth Clauses in the Ninth Section of the first Article; and that no State, without its Consent, shall be deprived of its equal Suffrage in the Senate.

ARTICLE VI

* * *

This Constitution, and the Laws of the United States which shall be made in Pursuance thereof; and all Treaties made, or which shall be made, under the Authority of the United States, shall be the Supreme Law of the Land; and the Judges in every State shall be bound thereby, any Thing in the Constitution or Laws of any State to the Contrary notwithstanding.

The Senators and Representatives before mentioned, and the Members of the several State Legislatures, and all executive and judicial Officers, both of the United States and of the several States, shall be bound by Oath or Affirmation, to support this Constitution; but no religious Test shall ever be required as a Qualification to any Office or public Trust under the United States.

* * *

AMENDMENT I

Congress shall make no law respecting an establishment of religion, or prohibiting the free exercise thereof; or abridging the freedom of speech, or of the press; or the right of the people peaceably to assemble, and to petition the Government for a redress of grievances.

* * *

AMENDMENT IV

The right of the people to be secure in their persons, houses, papers, and effects, against unreasonable searches and seizures, shall not be violated, and no Warrants shall issue, but upon probable cause, supported by Oath or affirmation, and particularly describing the place to be searched, and the persons or things to be seized.

AMENDMENT V

No person shall be held to answer for a capital, or otherwise infamous crime, unless on a presentment or indictment of a Grand Jury, except in cases arising in the land or naval forces, or in the Militia, when in actual service in time of War or public danger; nor shall any person be subject for the same offence to be twice put in jeopardy of life or limb; nor shall be compelled in any criminal case to be a witness against himself, nor be deprived of life, liberty, or property, without due process of law; nor shall private property be taken for public use, without just compensation.

AMENDMENT VI

In all criminal prosecutions, the accused shall enjoy the right to a speedy and public trial, by an impartial jury of the State and district wherein the crime shall have been committed, which district shall have been previously ascertained by law, and to be informed of the nature and cause of the accusation; to be confronted with the witnesses against him; to have compulsory process for obtaining witnesses in his favor, and to have the Assistance of Counsel for his defense.

AMENDMENT VII

In Suits at common law, where the value in controversy shall exceed twenty dollars, the right of trial by jury shall be preserved, and no fact tried by jury, shall be otherwise re-examined in any Court of the United States, than according to the rules of the common law.

AMENDMENT VIII

Excessive bail shall not be required, nor excessive fines imposed, nor cruel and unusual punishments inflicted.

AMENDMENT IX

The enumeration in the Constitution, of certain rights, shall not be construed to deny or disparage others retained by the people.

AMENDMENT X

The powers not delegated to the United States by the Constitution, nor prohibited by it to the States, are reserved to the States respectively, or to the people.

AMENDMENT XI

The Judicial power of the United States shall not be construed to extend to any suit in law or equity, commenced or prosecuted against one of the United States by Citizens of another State, or by Citizens or Subjects of any Foreign State.

* * *

AMENDMENT XIII

Section 1. Neither slavery nor involuntary servitude, except as a punishment for crime whereof the party shall have been duly convicted, shall exist within the United States, or any place subject to their jurisdiction.

Section 2. Congress shall have power to enforce this article by appropriate legislation.

AMENDMENT XIV

Section 1. All persons born or naturalized in the United States, and subject to the jurisdiction thereof, are citizens of the United States and of the State wherein they reside. No State shall make or enforce any law which shall abridge the privileges or immunities of citizens of the United States; nor shall any State deprive any person of life, liberty, or property, without due process of law; nor deny to any person within its jurisdiction the equal protection of the laws.

* * *

Section 5. The Congress shall have power to enforce, by appropriate legislation, the provisions of this article.

APPENDIX B

Subject Matter Table of
Education Cases Decided by the
United States Supreme Court

Note: Please see the Table of Cases (located at the front of this volume) for Supreme Court cases reported in this volume.

Academic Freedom
> *U.S. v. American Library Ass'n, Inc.*, 539 U.S. 194, 123 S.Ct. 2297, 156 L.Ed.2d 221 (2003).
> *Univ. of Pennsylvania v. EEOC*, 493 U.S. 182, 110 S.Ct. 577, 107 L.Ed.2d 571 (1990).
> *Epperson v. Arkansas*, 393 U.S. 97, 89 S.Ct. 266, 21 L.Ed.2d 228 (1968).
> Meyer v. Nebraska, 262 U.S. 390, 43 S.Ct. 625, 67 L.Ed.2d 1042 (1923).

Aliens
> *Toll v. Moreno*, 458 U.S. 1, 102 S.Ct. 2977, 73 L.Ed.2d 563 (1982).
> *Plyler v. Doe*, 457 U.S. 202, 102 S.Ct. 2382, 72 L.Ed.2d 786 (1982).
> *Ambach v. Norwick*, 441 U.S. 68, 99 S.Ct. 1589, 60 L.Ed.2d 49 (1979).
> *Vlandis v. Kline*, 412 U.S. 441, 93 S.Ct. 2230, 37 L.Ed.2d 63 (1973).

Collective Bargaining
> *Chicago Teachers Union v. Hudson*, 475 U.S. 292, 106 S.Ct. 1066, 89 L.Ed.2d 232 (1986).
> *Minnesota State Board for Community Colleges v. Knight*, 465 U.S. 271, 104 S.Ct. 1058, 79 L.Ed.2d 299 (1984).
> *Perry Educ. Ass'n v. Perry Local Educators'Ass'n*, 460 U.S. 37, 103 S.Ct. 948, 74 L.Ed.2d 794 (1983).
> *City of Madison Joint School Dist. v. WERC*, 429 U.S. 167, 97 S.Ct. 421, 50 L.Ed.2d 376 (1976).

Compulsory Attendance
> *Wisconsin v. Yoder*, 406 U.S. 205, 92 S.Ct. 526, 32 L.Ed.2d 15 (1972).
> *Pierce v. Society of Sisters*, 268 U.S. 510, 45 S.Ct. 571, 69 L.Ed. 1070 (1925).

Continuing Education
> *Austin ISD v. U.S.*, 443 U.S. 915, 99 S.Ct. 3106, 61 L.Ed.2d 879 (1979).
> *Harrah ISD v. Martin*, 440 U.S. 194, 99 S.Ct. 1062, 59 L.Ed.2d 248 (1979).

Corporal Punishment
> *Ingraham v. Wright*, 430 U.S. 651, 97 S.Ct. 1401, 51 L.Ed.2d 711 (1977).

Desegregation
> *Missouri v. Jenkins*, 515 U.S. 70, 115 S. Ct. 2038, 132 L.Ed.2d 63 (1995).

U.S. v. Fordice, 505 U.S. 717, 112 S.Ct. 2727, 120 L.Ed.2d 575 (1992).

Freeman v. Pitts, 503 U.S. 467, 112 S.Ct. 1430, 118 L.Ed.2d 108 (1992).

Board of Educ. of Oklahoma City Public Schools v. Dowell, 498 U.S. 237, 111 S.Ct. 630, 112 L.Ed.2d 715 (1991).

Missouri v. Jenkins, 495 U.S. 33, 110 S.Ct. 1651, 109 L.Ed.2d 31 (1990).

Crawford v. Board of Educ., 458 U.S. 527, 102 S.Ct. 3211, 73 L.Ed.2d 948 (1982).

Washington v. Seattle School Dist. No. 1, 458 U.S. 457, 102 S.Ct. 3187, 73 L.Ed.2d 896 (1982).

Board of Educ. v. Superior Court, 448 U.S. 1343, 101 S.Ct. 21, 65 L.Ed.2d 1166 (1980).

Columbus Board of Educ. v. Penick, 443 U.S. 449, 99 S.Ct. 2941, 61 L.Ed.2d 666 (1979).

Bustop v. Board of Educ., 439 U.S. 1380, 99 S.Ct. 40, 58 L.Ed.2d 88 (1978).

Vetterli v. U.S. Dist. Court, 435 U.S. 1304, 98 S.Ct. 1219, 55 L.Ed.2d 751 (1978).

Dayton Board of Educ. v. Brinkman, 433 U.S. 406, 97 S.Ct. 2766, 53 L.Ed.2d 851 (1977).

Milliken v. Bradley, 433 U.S. 267, 97 S.Ct. 2749, 53 L.Ed.2d 745 (1977).

Pasadena City Board of Educ. v. Spangler, 427 U.S. 424, 96 S.Ct. 2697, 49 L.Ed.2d 599 (1976).

Milliken v. Bradley, 418 U.S. 717, 94 S.Ct. 311, 41 L.Ed.2d 1069 (1974).

Bradley v. School Board of City of Richmond, 416 U.S. 696, 94 S.Ct. 2006, 40 L.Ed.2d 476 (1974).

Keyes v. School Dist. No. 1, 413 U.S. 189, 93 S.Ct. 2686, 37 L.Ed.2d 548 (1973).

Drummond v. Acree, 409 U.S. 1228, 93 S.Ct. 18, 34 L.Ed.2d 33 (1972).

U.S. v. Scotland Neck City Board of Educ., 407 U.S. 484, 92 S.Ct. 2214, 33 L.Ed.2d 75 (1972).

Wright v. Council of City of Emporia, 407 U.S. 451, 92 S.Ct. 2196, 33 L.Ed.2d 51 (1972).

Winston-Salem/Forsyth County Board of Educ. v. Scott, 404 U.S. 1221, 92 S.Ct. 1236, 31 L.Ed.2d 441 (1971).

Dandridge v. Jefferson Parish School Board, 404 U.S. 1219, 92 S.Ct. 18, 30 L.Ed.2d 23 (1971).

Guey Heung Lee v. Johnson, 404 U.S. 1215, 92 S.Ct. 14, 30 L.Ed.2d 19 (1971).

North Carolina State Board of Educ. v. Swann, 402 U.S. 43, 91 S.Ct. 1284, 28 L.Ed.2d 586 (1971).

McDaniel v. Barresi, 402 U.S. 39, 91 S.Ct. 1287, 28 L.Ed.2d 582 (1971).

Davis v. Board of School Commissioners, 402 U.S. 33, 91 S.Ct. 1289, 28 L.Ed.2d 577 (1971).

Swann v. Charlotte-Mecklenburg Board of Educ., 402 U.S. 1, 91 S.Ct. 1267, 28 L.Ed.2d 554 (1971).

Northcross v. Board of Educ., 397 U.S. 232, 90 S.Ct. 891, 25 L.Ed.2d 246 (1970).

Carter v. West Feliciena Parish School Board, 396 U.S. 290, 90 S.Ct. 608, 24 L.Ed.2d 477 (1970).

Dowell v. Board of Educ., 396 U.S. 269, 90 S.Ct. 415, 24 L.Ed.2d 414 (1969).

Alexander v. Holmes County Board of Educ., 396 U.S. 19, 90 S.Ct. 29, 24 L.Ed.2d 19 (1969).

U.S. v. Montgomery County Board of Educ., 395 U.S. 225, 89 S.Ct. 1670, 23 L.Ed.2d 263 (1969).

Monroe v. Board of Commissioners, 391 U.S. 450, 88 S.Ct. 1700, 20 L.Ed.2d 733 (1968).

Raney v. Board of Educ., 391 U.S. 443, 88 S.Ct. 1697, 20 L.Ed.2d 727 (1968).

Green v. New Kent County School Board, 391 U.S. 430, 88 S.Ct. 1689, 20 L.Ed.2d 716 (1968).

Rogers v. Paul, 382 U.S. 198, 86 S.Ct. 358, 15 L.Ed.2d 265 (1965).

Bradley v. School Board, 382 U.S. 103, 86 S.Ct. 224, 15 L.Ed.2d 187 (1965).

Griffin v. County School Board, 377 U.S. 218, 84 S.Ct. 1226, 12 L.Ed.2d 256 (1964).

Goss v. Board of Educ., 373 U.S. 683, 83 S.Ct. 1405, 10 L.Ed.2d 632 (1963).

U.S. v. State of Louisiana, 364 U.S. 500, 81 S.Ct. 260, 5 L.Ed.2d 245 (1960).

Cooper v. Aaron, 358 U.S. 1, 78 S.Ct. 1401, 3 L.Ed.2d 5 (1958).

Brown v. Board of Educ. (II), 349 U.S. 294, 75 S.Ct. 753, 99 L.Ed. 1083 (1955).

Bolling v. Sharpe, 347 U.S. 497, 74 S.Ct. 693, 98 L.Ed. 884 (1954).

Brown v. Board of Educ. (I), 347 U.S. 483, 74 S.Ct. 686, 98 L.Ed. 873 (1954).

Disabled Students

Forest Grove School Dist. v. T.A., 129 S.Ct. 2484 (U.S. 2009).

Winkleman v. Parma City School Dist., 127 S.Ct. 1994 (U.S. 2007).

Arlington Cent. School Dist. Board of Educ. v. Murphy, 548 U.S. 291, 126 S.Ct. 2455, 165 L.Ed.2d 526 (2006).

Schaffer v. Weast, 546 U.S. 49, 126 S.Ct. 528, 163 L.Ed.2d 387 (2005).

Cedar Rapids Community School Dist. v. Garret F. by Charlene F., 526 U.S. 66, 119 S.Ct. 992, 143 L.Ed.2d 154 (1999).

Lane v. Pena, 518 U.S. 187, 116 S.Ct. 2092, 135 L.Ed.2d 486 (1996).

Florence County School Dist. v. Carter, 510 U.S. 7, 114 S.Ct. 361, 126 L.Ed.2d 284 (1993).

Zobrest v. Catalina Foothills School Dist., 509 U.S. 1, 113 S.Ct. 2462, 125 L.Ed.2d 1 (1993).

Dellmuth v. Muth, 491 U.S. 223, 109 S.Ct. 2397, 105 L.Ed.2d 181 (1989).

Honig v. Doe, 484 U.S. 305, 108 S.Ct. 592, 98 L.Ed.2d 686 (1988).

Honig v. Students of California School for the Blind, 471 U.S. 148, 105 S.Ct. 1820, 85 L.Ed.2d 114 (1985).

Burlington School Committee v. Dep't of Educ., 471 U.S. 359, 105 S.Ct. 1996, 85 L.Ed.2d 385 (1985).

Smith v. Robinson, 468 U.S. 992, 104 S.Ct. 3457, 82 L.Ed.2d 746 (1984).

Irving Independent School Dist. v. Tatro, 468 U.S. 883, 104 S.Ct. 3371, 82 L.Ed.2d 664 (1984).

Board of Educ. v. Rowley, 458 U.S. 176, 102 S.Ct. 3034, 73 L.Ed.2d 690 (1982).

Univ. of Texas v. Camenisch, 451 U.S. 390, 101 S.Ct. 1830, 68 L.Ed.2d 175 (1981).

Southeastern Community College v. Davis, 442 U.S. 397, 99 S.Ct. 2361, 60 L.Ed.2d 980 (1979).

Discrimination Generally

Crawford v. Metropolitan Government of Nashville and Davidson County, Tennessee, 129 S.Ct. 846 (U.S. 2009).

Engquist v. Oregon Dep't of Agriculture, 128 S.Ct. 2146 (U.S. 2008).

Kentucky Retirement Systems v. Equal Employment Opportunity Comm'n, 128 S.Ct. 2361 (U.S. 2008).

Smith v. City of Jackson, 544 U.S. 228, 125 S.Ct. 1536, 161 L.Ed.2d 410 (2005).

Lapides v. Board of Regents of Univ. System of Georgia, 535 U.S. 613, 122 S.Ct. 1640, 152 L.Ed.2d 806 (2002).

Toyota Motor Manufacturing, Ky., Inc. v. Williams, 534 U.S. 184, 122 S.Ct. 681, 151 L.Ed.2d 615 (2002).

Reeves v. Sanderson Plumbing Products, 530 U.S. 133, 120 S.Ct. 2097, 147 L.Ed.2d 15 (2000).

Kimel v. Florida Board of Regents, 528 U.S. 62, 120 S.Ct. 631, 145 L.Ed.2d 522 (2000).

Murphy v. United Parcel Service, Inc., 527 U.S. 516, 119 S.Ct. 2133, 144 L.Ed.2d 484 (1999).

Sutton v. United Airlines, Inc., 527 U.S. 471, 119 S.Ct. 2139, 144 L.Ed.2d 450 (1999).

Bragdon v. Abbott, 524 U.S. 624, 118 S.Ct. 2196, 141 L.Ed.2d 540 (1998).

U.S. v. Virginia, 518 U.S. 515, 116 S.Ct. 2264, 135 L.Ed.2d 735 (1996).

Jett v. Dallas Independent School Dist., 491 U.S. 701, 109 S.Ct. 2702, 105 L.Ed.2d 598 (1989).

Carnegie-Mellon Univ. v. Cohill, 484 U.S. 343, 108 S.Ct. 614, 98 L.Ed.2d 720 (1988).

School Board of Nassau County v. Arline, 480 U.S. 273, 107 S.Ct. 1123, 94 L.Ed.2d 307 (1987).

Monell v. Dep't of Social Services, 436 U.S. 658, 98 S.Ct. 2018, 56 L.Ed.2d 611 (1978).

Hazelwood School Dist. v. U.S., 433 U.S. 299, 97 S.Ct. 2736, 53 L.Ed.2d 768 (1977).

DeFunis v. Odegaard, 416 U.S. 312, 94 S.Ct. 1704, 40 L.Ed.2d 164 (1974).

Due Process

Gilbert v. Homar, 520 U.S. 924, 117 S.Ct. 1807, 138 L.Ed.2d 120 (1997).

Univ. of Tennessee v. Elliot, 478 U.S. 788, 106 S.Ct. 3220, 92 L.Ed.2d 635 (1986).

Memphis Community School Dist. v. Stachura, 477 U.S. 299, 106 S.Ct. 2537, 91 L.Ed.2d 249 (1986).

Cleveland Board of Educ. v. Loudermill, 470 U.S. 532, 105 S.Ct. 1487, 84 L.Ed.2d 494 (1985).

Perry v. Sindermann, 408 U.S. 593, 92 S.Ct. 2694, 33 L.Ed.2d 570 (1972).

Board of Regents v. Roth, 408 U.S. 564, 92 S.Ct. 2701, 33 L.Ed.2d 548 (1972).

Elections

Reno v. Bossier Parish School Board, 528 U.S. 320, 120 S.Ct. 866, 145 L.Ed.2d 845 (2000).

Texas v. U.S., 523 U.S. 296, 118 S.Ct. 1257, 140 L.Ed.2d 406 (1998).

Reno v. Bossier Parish School Board, 520 U.S. 471, 117 S.Ct. 1491, 137 L.Ed.2d 730 (1997).

Dougherty County Board of Educ. v. White, 439 U.S. 32, 99 S.Ct. 368, 58 L.Ed.2d 269 (1978).

Mayor of Philadelphia v. Educ. Equality League, 415 U.S. 605, 94 S.Ct. 1323, 39 L.Ed.2d 630 (1974).

Kramer v. Union Free School Dist. No. 15, 395 U.S. 621, 89 S.Ct. 1886, 23 L.Ed.2d 583 (1969).

Sailors v. Board of Educ., 387 U.S. 105, 87 S.Ct. 1549, 18 L.Ed.2d 650 (1967).

Federal Aid

Lockhart v. U.S., 546 U.S. 142, 126 S.Ct. 699, 163 L.Ed.2d 557 (2005).

Traynor v. Turnage, 485 U.S. 535, 108 S.Ct. 1372, 99 L.Ed.2d 618 (1988).

Selective Service System v. MPIRG, 468 U.S. 841, 104 S.Ct. 3348, 82 L.Ed.2d 632 (1984).

Bell v. New Jersey and Pennsylvania, 461 U.S. 773, 103 S.Ct. 2187, 76 L.Ed.2d 312 (1984).

Valley Forge Christian College v. Americans United for Separation of Church and State, 454 U.S. 464, 102 S.Ct. 752, 70 L.Ed.2d 700 (1982).

Board of Educ. v. Harris, 444 U.S. 130, 100 S.Ct. 363, 62 L.Ed.2d 275 (1979).

Wheeler v. Barrera, 417 U.S. 402, 94 S.Ct. 2274, 41 L.Ed.2d 159 (1974).

Tilton v. Richardson, 403 U.S. 672, 91 S.Ct. 2091, 29 L.Ed.2d 790 (1971).

Financing

Hibbs v. Winn, 542 U.S. 88, 124 S.Ct. 2276, 159 L.Ed.2d 172 (2004).

Locke v. Davey, 540 U.S. 807, 124 S.Ct. 1307, 158 L.Ed.2d 1 (2004).

Camps Newfound/Owatonna, Inc. v. Town of Harrison, Me., 520 U.S. 564, 117 S.Ct. 1590, 137 L.Ed.2d 852 (1997).

Papasan v. Allain, 478 U.S. 265, 106 S.Ct. 2932, 92 L.Ed.2d 209 (1986).

Bennett v. New Jersey, 470 U.S. 632, 105 S.Ct. 1555, 84 L.Ed.2d 572 (1985).

Bennett v. Kentucky Dep't of Educ., 470 U.S. 656, 105 S.Ct. 1544, 84 L.Ed.2d 590 (1985).

Lawrence County v. Lead-Deadwood School Dist. No. 40-1, 469 U.S. 256, 105 S.Ct. 695, 83 L.Ed.2d 635 (1985).

Grove City College v. Bell, 465 U.S. 555, 104 S.Ct. 1211, 79 L.Ed.2d 516 (1984).

San Antonio v. Rodriguez, 411 U.S. 1, 93 S.Ct. 1278, 36 L.Ed.2d 16 (1973).

Freedom of Religion (see also Religious Activities)

Edwards v. Aguillard, 482 U.S. 578, 107 S.Ct. 2573, 96 L.Ed.2d 510 (1987).

Ansonia Board of Educ. v. Philbrook, 499 U.S. 60, 107 S.Ct. 367, 93 L.Ed.2d 305 (1986).

Freedom of Speech

Johnson v. Poway Unified School Dist., 132 S.Ct. 1807 (U.S. 2012).

Policastro v. Tenafly Board of Educ., 132 S.Ct. 1546 (U.S. 2012).

Pleasant Grove City, Utah v. Summum, 129 S.Ct. 1125 (U.S. 2009).

Morse v. Frederick, 127 S.Ct. 2618 (U.S. 2007).

Garcetti v. Ceballos, 547 U.S. 410, 126 S.Ct. 1951, 164 L.Ed.2d 689 (2006).

Rumsfeld v. Forum for Academic and Institutional Rights, 547 U.S. 47 (2006).

Board of Regents of Univ. of Wisconsin System v. Southworth, 529 U.S. 217, 120 S.Ct. 1346, 146 L.Ed.2d 193 (2000).

Rosenberger v. Univ. of Virginia, 515 U.S. 819, 115 S.Ct. 2510, 132 L.Ed.2d 700 (1995).

Board of Educ. of Westside Community School v. Mergens, 496 U.S. 226, 110 S.Ct. 2356, 110 L.Ed.2d 191 (1990).

Board of Trustees of the State Univ. of New York v. Fox, 492 U.S. 469, 109 S.Ct. 3028, 106 L.Ed.2d 388 (1989).

Hazelwood School Dist. v. Kuhlmeier, 484 U.S. 261, 108 S.Ct. 562, 98 L.Ed.2d 592 (1988).

Bethel School Dist. v. Fraser, 478 U.S. 675, 106 S.Ct. 3159, 92 L.Ed.2d 549 (1986).

Board of Educ. v. Pico, 457 U.S. 853, 102 S.Ct. 2799, 73 L.Ed.2d 435 (1982).

Givhan v. Western Line Consolidated School Dist., 439 U.S. 410, 99 S.Ct. 693, 58 L.Ed.2d 619 (1979).

Mt. Healthy City School v. Doyle, 429 U.S. 274, 97 S.Ct. 568, 50 L.Ed.2d 471 (1977).

Papish v. Board of Curators, 410 U.S. 667, 93 S.Ct. 1197, 35 L.Ed.2d 618 (1973).

Grayned v. City of Rockford, 408 U.S. 104, 92 S.Ct. 2294, 33 L.Ed.2d 222 (1972).

Police Dep't v. Mosley, 408 U.S. 92, 92 S.Ct. 2286, 33 L.Ed.2d 212 (1972).

Tinker v. Des Moines, 393 U.S. 503, 89 S.Ct. 733, 21 L.Ed.2d 733 (1969).

Pickering v. Board of Educ., 391 U.S. 563, 88 S.Ct. 1731, 20 L.Ed.2d 811 (1968).

Keyishian v. Board of Regents, 385 U.S. 589, 87 S.Ct. 675, 17 L.Ed.2d 629 (1967).

Adler v. Board of Educ., 342 U.S. 485, 72 S.Ct. 380, 96 L.Ed. 517 (1952).

Labor Relations

Ysursa v. Pocatello Educ. Ass'n, 129 S.Ct. 1093 (U.S. 2009).

Davenport v. Washington Educ. Ass'n, 127 S.Ct. 2372 (U.S. 2007).

Christensen v. Harris County, 529 U.S. 576, 120 S.Ct. 1655, 146 L.Ed.2d 621 (2000).

Cent. State Univ. v. American Ass'n of Univ. Professors, Cent. State Univ. Chapter, 526 U.S. 124, 119 S.Ct. 1162, 143 L.Ed.2d 227 (1999).

Lehnert v. Ferris Faculty Ass'n, 500 U.S. 507, 111 S.Ct. 1950, 114 L.Ed.2d 572 (1991).

Fort Stewart Schools v. Federal Labor Relations Authority, 495 U.S. 641, 110 S.Ct. 2043, 109 L.Ed.2d 659 (1990).

Minnesota State Board for Community Colleges v. Knight, 465 U.S. 271, 104 S.Ct. 1058, 79 L.Ed.2d 299 (1984).

NLRB v. Yeshiva Univ., 444 U.S. 672, 100 S.Ct. 856, 63 L.Ed.2d 115 (1980).

NLRB v. Catholic Bishop of Chicago, 440 U.S. 490, 99 S.Ct. 1313, 59 L.Ed.2d 533 (1979).

Abood v. Detroit Board of Educ., 431 U.S. 209, 97 S.Ct. 1782, 52 L.Ed.2d 261 (1977).

Loyalty Oaths

Connell v. Higgenbotham, 403 U.S. 207, 91 S.Ct. 1772, 29 L.Ed.2d 418 (1971).

Whitehill v. Elkins, 389 U.S. 54, 88 S.Ct. 184, 19 L.Ed.2d 228 (1967).

Elfbrandt v. Russell, 384 U.S. 11, 86 S.Ct. 1238, 16 L.Ed.2d 321 (1966).

Baggett v. Bullitt, 377 U.S. 360, 84 S.Ct. 1316, 12 L.Ed.2d 377 (1964).

Cramp v. Board of Educ., 368 U.S. 278, 82 S.Ct. 275, 7 L.Ed.2d 285 (1961).

Slochower v. Board of Higher Educ., 350 U.S. 551, 76 S.Ct. 637, 100 L.Ed. 692 (1956).

Maternity Leave

Richmond Unified School Dist. v. Berg, 434 U.S. 158, 98 S.Ct. 623, 54 L.Ed.2d 375 (1977).

Cleveland Board of Educ. v. La Fleur, 414 U.S. 632, 94 S.Ct. 791, 39 L.Ed.2d 52 (1974).

Cohen v. Chesterfield, 414 U.S. 632, 94 S.Ct. 791, 39 L.Ed.2d 52 (1974).

Private Schools

Hosanna-Tabor Evangelical Lutheran Church and School v. E.E.O.C., 132 S.Ct. 694, 181 L.Ed.2d 650 (U.S. 2012).

Arizona Christian School Tuition Organization v. Winn, 131 S.Ct. 1436, 179 L.Ed.2d 523 (U.S. 2011).

Zelman v. Simmons-Harris, 536 U.S. 639, 122 S.Ct. 2460, 153 L.Ed.2d 604 (2002).

Brentwood Academy v. Tennessee Secondary School Athletic Ass'n, 531 U.S. 288, 121 S.Ct. 924, 148 L.Ed.2d 807 (2001).

Mitchell v. Helms, 530 U.S. 793, 120 S.Ct. 2530, 147 L.Ed.2d 660 (2000).

Bates v. U.S., 522 U.S. 23, 118 S.Ct. 285, 139 L.Ed.2d 215 (1997).

Agostini v. Felton, 521 U.S. 203, 117 S.Ct. 1997, 138 L.Ed.2d 391 (1997).

Farrar v. Hobby, 506 U.S. 103, 113 S.Ct. 566, 121 L.Ed.2d 494 (1992).

Corporation of the Presiding Bishop of the Church of Jesus Christ of Latter-Day Saints v. Amos, 483 U.S. 327, 107 S.Ct. 2862, 97 L.Ed.2d 273 (1987).

St. Francis College v. Al-Khazraji, 481 U.S. 604, 107 S.Ct. 2022, 97 L.Ed.2d 749 (1987).

Witters v. Washington Dep't of Services for the Blind, 474 U.S. 481, 106 S.Ct. 748, 88 L.Ed.2d 846 (1986).

Aguilar v. Felton, 473 U.S. 402, 105 S.Ct. 3232, 87 L.Ed.2d 290 (1985).

Grand Rapids School Dist. v. Ball, 473 U.S. 373, 105 S.Ct. 3216, 87 L.Ed.2d 267 (1985).

Grove City College v. Bell, 465 U.S. 555, 104 S.Ct. 1211, 79 L.Ed.2d 516 (1984).

Mueller v. Allen, 463 U.S. 388, 103 S.Ct. 3062, 77 L.Ed.2d 721 (1983).

Bob Jones Univ. v. United States, 461 U.S. 574, 103 S. Ct. 2017, 76 L.Ed.2d 157 (1983).

Valley Forge Christian College v. Americans United for Separation of Church and State, 454 U.S. 464, 102 S.Ct. 752, 70 L.Ed.2d 700 (1982).

St. Martin Evangelical Lutheran Church v. South Dakota, 451 U.S. 772, 101 S.Ct. 2142, 68 L.Ed.2d 612 (1981).

Committee v. Regan, 444 U.S. 646, 100 S.Ct. 840, 63 L.Ed.2d 94 (1980).

NLRB v. Catholic Bishop of Chicago, 440 U.S. 490, 99 S.Ct. 1313, 59 L.Ed.2d 533 (1979).

Racial Discrimination

Religious Activities in Public Schools

Christian Legal Society Chapter of the Univ. of California, Hastings College of Law v. Martinez, 130 S.Ct. 2971 (U.S. 2010).

Elk Grove Unified School Dist. v. Newdow, 542 U.S. 961, 124 S.Ct. 2301, 159 L.Ed.2d 851 (2004).

Santa Fe Independent School Dist. v. Doe, 530 U.S. 290, 120 S.Ct. 2266, 147 L.Ed.2d 295 (2000).

Board of Educ. of Kiryas Joel Village v. Grumet, 512 U.S. 687, 114 S.Ct. 2481, 129 L.Ed.2d 546 (1994).

Lamb's Chapel v. Center Moriches Union Free School Dist., 508 U.S. 384, 113 S.Ct. 2141, 124 L.Ed.2d 352 (1993).

Lee v. Weisman, 505 U.S. 577, 112 S.Ct. 2649, 120 L.Ed.2d 467 (1992).

Karcher v. May, 484 U.S. 72, 108 S.Ct. 388, 98 L.Ed.2d 327 (1987).

Bender v. Williamsport Area School Dist., 475 U.S. 534, 106 S.Ct. 1326, 89 L.Ed.2d 501 (1986).

Wallace v. Jaffree, 472 U.S. 38, 105 S.Ct. 2479, 96 L.Ed.2d 29 (1985).

Widmar v. Vincent, 454 U.S. 263, 102 S.Ct. 269, 70 L.Ed.2d 400 (1981).

Stone v. Graham, 449 U.S. 39, 101 S.Ct. 192, 66 L.Ed.2d 199 (1980).

Epperson v. Arkansas, 393 U.S. 97, 89 S.Ct. 266, 21 L.Ed.2d 228 (1968).

Chamberlin v. Dade County Board of Public Instruction, 377 U.S. 402, 84 S.Ct. 1272, 12 L.Ed.2d 407 (1964).

Abington School Dist. v. Schempp, 374 U.S. 203, 83 S.Ct. 1560, 10 L.Ed.2d 844 (1963).

Engel v. Vitale, 370 U.S. 421, 82 S.Ct. 1261, 8 L.Ed.2d 601 (1962).

McCollum v. Board of Educ., 333 U.S. 203, 68 S.Ct. 461, 92 L.Ed. 649 (1948).

West Virginia Board of Educ. v. Barnette, 319 U.S. 624, 63 S.Ct. 1178, 87 L.Ed. 1628 (1943).

Residency

Martinez v. Bynum, 461 U.S. 321, 103 S.Ct. 1838, 75 L.Ed.2d 879 (1983).

Elgins v. Moreno, 435 U.S. 647, 98 S.Ct. 1338, 55 L.Ed.2d 614 (1978).

School Liability

J.D.B. v. North Carolina, 131 S.Ct. 2394, 180 L.Ed.2d 310 (U.S. 2011).

Camreta v. Greene, 131 S.Ct. 2020, 179 L.Ed.2d 1118 (U.S. 2011).

Chavez v. Martinez, 538 U.S. 760, 123 S.Ct. 1994, 155 L.Ed.2d 984 (2003).

Owasso Independent School Dist. No. I-011 v. Falvo, 534 U.S. 426, 122 S.Ct. 934, 151 L.Ed.2d 896 (2002).

Clark County School Dist. v. Breeden, 532 U.S. 268, 121 S.Ct. 1508, 149 L.Ed.2d 509 (2001).

Gebser v. Lago Vista Independent School Dist., 524 U.S. 274, 118 S.Ct. 1989, 141 L.Ed.2d 277 (1998).

Regents of Univ. of California v. Doe, 519 U.S. 337, 117 S.Ct. 900, 137 L.Ed.2d 55 (1997).

Bradford Area School Dist. v. Stoneking, 489 U.S. 1062, 109 S.Ct. 1333, 103 L.Ed.2d 804 (1989).

Smith v. Sowers, 490 U.S. 1002, 109 S.Ct. 1634, 104 L.Ed.2d 150 (1989).

Deshaney v. Winnebago County DSS, 489 U.S. 189, 109 S.Ct. 998, 103 L.Ed.2d 249 (1989).

Sex Discrimination

Burlington Northern & Santa Fe Railway Co. v. White, 548 U.S. 53, 126 S.Ct. 2405, 165 L.Ed.2d 345 (2006).

Michigan High School Athletic Ass'n v. Communities for Equity, 544 U.S. 1012, 161 L.Ed.2d 845 (2005).

Davis v. Monroe County Board of Educ., 526 U.S. 629, 119 S.Ct. 1661, 143 L.Ed.2d 839 (1999).

National Collegiate Athletic Ass'n v. Smith, 525 U.S. 84, 119 S.Ct. 924, 142 L.Ed.2d 929 (1999).

Burlington Industries, Inc. v. Ellerth, 524 U.S. 742, 118 S.Ct. 2257, 141 L.Ed.2d 633 (1998).

Faragher v. City of Boca Raton, 524 U.S. 775, 118 S.Ct. 2275, 141 L.Ed.2d 662 (1998).

Oncale v. Sundowner Offshore Offshore Services, Inc., 523 U.S. 75, 118 S.Ct. 998, 140 L.Ed.2d 201 (1998).

Franklin v. Gwinnett County Public Schools, 503 U.S. 60, 112 S.Ct. 1028, 117 L.Ed.2d 208 (1992).

Ohio Civil Rights Comm'n v. Dayton Christian Schools, 477 U.S. 619, 106 S.Ct. 2718, 91 L.Ed.2d 512 (1986).

Mississippi Univ. for Women v. Hogan, 458 U.S. 718, 102 S.Ct. 3331, 73 L.Ed.2d 1090 (1982).

Rendell-Baker v. Kohn, 457 U.S. 830, 102 S.Ct. 2764, 73 L.Ed.2d 418 (1982).

Cannon v. Univ. of Chicago, 441 U.S. 677, 99 S.Ct. 1946, 60 L.Ed.2d 560 (1979).

Board of Trustees v. Sweeney, 439 U.S. 24, 99 S.Ct. 295, 58 L.Ed.2d 216 (1978).

Striking Teachers

Hortonville Joint School Dist. v. Hortonville Educ. Ass'n, 426 U.S. 482, 96 S.Ct. 2308, 49 L.Ed.2d 1 (1976).

Student Searches

Ryburn v. Huff, 132 S.Ct. 987 (U.S. 2012).

Board of Educ. of Independent School Dist. 92 of Pottawatomie County v. Earls, 536 U.S. 822, 122 S.Ct. 2559, 153 L.Ed.2d 735 (2002).

Vernonia School Dist. 47J v. Acton, 515 U.S. 646, 115 S. Ct. 2386, 132 L.Ed.2d 564 (1995).

New Jersey v. T.L.O., 469 U.S. 325, 105 S.Ct. 733, 83 L.Ed.2d 720 (1985).

Student Suspensions

Regents v. Ewing, 474 U.S. 214, 106 S.Ct. 507, 88 L.Ed.2d 523 (1985).

Board of Educ. v. McCluskey, 458 U.S. 966, 103 S.Ct. 3469, 73 L.Ed.2d 1273 (1982).

Carey v. Piphus, 435 U.S. 247, 98 S.Ct. 1042, 55 L.Ed.2d 252 (1978).

Board of Curators v. Horowitz, 435 U.S. 78, 98 S.Ct. 948, 55 L.Ed.2d 124 (1978).

Wood v. Strickland, 420 U.S. 308, 95 S.Ct. 992, 43 L.Ed.2d 214 (1975).

Goss v. Lopez, 419 U.S. 565, 95 S.Ct. 729, 42 L.Ed.2d 725 (1975).

Teacher Termination

Patsy v. Board of Regents, 457 U.S. 496, 102 S.Ct. 2557, 73 L.Ed.2d 172 (1982).

Chardon v. Fernandez, 454 U.S. 6, 102 S.Ct. 28, 70 L.Ed.2d 6 (1981).

Delaware State College v. Ricks, 449 U.S. 250, 101 S.Ct. 498, 66 L.Ed.2d 431 (1980).

Beilan v. Board of Public Educ., 357 U.S. 399, 78 S.Ct. 1317, 2 L.Ed.2d 1414 (1958).

Textbooks

Norwood v. Harrison, 413 U.S. 455, 93 S.Ct. 2804, 37 L.Ed.2d 723 (1973).

Board of Educ. v. Allen, 392 U.S. 236, 88 S.Ct. 1923, 20 L.Ed.2d 1060 (1968).

Cochran v. Louisiana State Board of Educ., 281 U.S. 370, 50 S.Ct. 335, 74 L.Ed.2d 1929 (1930).

Transportation Fees

Kadrmas v. Dickinson Public Schools, 487 U.S. 450, 108 S.Ct. 2481, 101 L.Ed.2d 399 (1988).

Use of School Facilities

Good News Club v. Milford Cent. School, 533 U.S. 98, 121 S.Ct. 2093, 150 L.Ed.2d 151 (2000).

Ellis v. Dixon, 349 U.S. 458, 75 S.Ct. 859, 99 L.Ed. 1231 (1955).

Weapons Control

U.S. v. Lopez, 514 U.S. 549, 115 S. Ct. 1624, 131 L.Ed.2d 626 (1995).

THE JUDICIAL SYSTEM

In order to allow you to determine the relative importance of a judicial decision, the cases included in *2014 Deskbook Encyclopedia of American School Law* identify the particular court from which a decision has been issued. For example, a case decided by a state supreme court generally will be of greater significance than a state circuit court case. Hence a basic knowledge of the structure of our judicial system is important to an understanding of school law.

Almost all the reports in this volume are taken from appellate court decisions. Although most education law decisions occur at trial court and administrative levels, appellate court decisions have the effect of binding lower courts and administrators so that appellate court decisions have the effect of law within their court systems.

State and federal court systems generally function independently of each other. Each court system applies its own law according to statutes and the determinations of its highest court. However, judges at all levels often consider opinions from other court systems to settle issues which are new or arise under unique fact situations. Similarly, lawyers look at the opinions of many courts to locate authority which supports their clients' cases.

Once a lawsuit is filed in a particular court system, that system retains the matter until its conclusion. Unsuccessful parties at the administrative or trial court level generally have the right to appeal unfavorable determinations of law to appellate courts within the system. When federal law issues or constitutional grounds are present, lawsuits may be appropriately filed in the federal court system. In those cases, the lawsuit is filed initially in the federal district court for that area.

On rare occasions, the U.S. Supreme Court considers appeals from the highest courts of the states if a distinct federal question exists and at least four justices agree on the question's importance. The federal courts occasionally send cases to state courts for application of state law. These situations are infrequent and, in general, the state and federal court systems should be considered separate from each other.

The most common system, used by nearly all states and also the federal judiciary, is as follows: a legal action is commenced in district court (sometimes called trial court, county court, common pleas court or superior court) where a decision is initially reached. The case may then be appealed to the court of appeals (or appellate court), and in turn this decision may be appealed to the supreme court.

Several states, however, do not have a court of appeals; lower court decisions are appealed directly to the state's supreme court. Additionally, some states have labeled their courts in a nonstandard fashion.

In Maryland, the highest state court is called the Court of Appeals. In the state of New York, the trial court is called the Supreme Court. Decisions of this court may be appealed to the Supreme Court, Appellate Division. The highest court in New York is the Court of Appeals. Pennsylvania has perhaps the most complex court system. The lowest state court is the Court of Common Pleas. Depending on the circumstances of the case, appeals may be taken to either the Commonwealth Court or the Superior Court. In certain instances the Commonwealth Court functions as a trial court as well as an appellate court. The Superior Court, however, is strictly an intermediate appellate court. The highest court in Pennsylvania is the Supreme Court.

While supreme court decisions are generally regarded as the last word in legal matters, it is important to remember that trial and appeals court decisions also create important legal precedents. For the hierarchy of typical state and federal court systems, please see the diagram below.

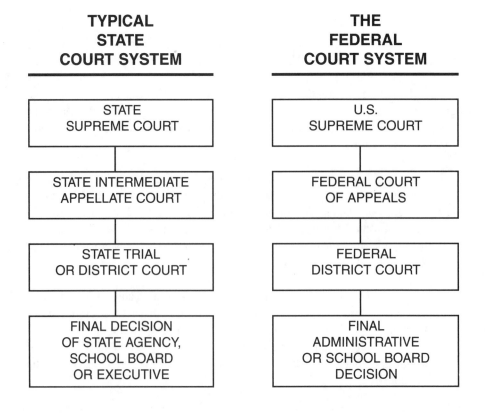

TYPICAL STATE COURT SYSTEM	THE FEDERAL COURT SYSTEM
STATE SUPREME COURT	U.S. SUPREME COURT
STATE INTERMEDIATE APPELLATE COURT	FEDERAL COURT OF APPEALS
STATE TRIAL OR DISTRICT COURT	FEDERAL DISTRICT COURT
FINAL DECISION OF STATE AGENCY, SCHOOL BOARD OR EXECUTIVE	FINAL ADMINISTRATIVE OR SCHOOL BOARD DECISION

Federal courts of appeals hear appeals from the district courts which are located in their circuits. Below is a list of states matched to the federal circuits in which they are located.

First Circuit	— Maine, Massachusetts, New Hampshire, Puerto Rico, Rhode Island
Second Circuit	— Connecticut, New York, Vermont
Third Circuit	— Delaware, New Jersey, Pennsylvania, Virgin Islands
Fourth Circuit	— Maryland, North Carolina, South Carolina, Virginia, West Virginia
Fifth Circuit	— Louisiana, Mississippi, Texas
Sixth Circuit	— Ohio, Kentucky, Michigan, Tennessee
Seventh Circuit	— Illinois, Indiana, Wisconsin
Eighth Circuit	— Arkansas, Iowa, Minnesota, Missouri, Nebraska, North Dakota, South Dakota
Ninth Circuit	— Alaska, Arizona, California, Guam, Hawaii, Idaho, Montana, Nevada, Northern Mariana Islands, Oregon, Washington
Tenth Circuit	— Colorado, Kansas, Oklahoma, New Mexico, Utah, Wyoming
Eleventh Circuit	— Alabama, Florida, Georgia
District of Columbia Circuit	— Hears cases from the U.S. District Court for the District of Columbia
Federal Circuit Appeals	— Sitting in Washington, D.C., the U.S. Court of Federal Circuit, hears patent and trade appeals and certain appeals on claims brought against the federal government and its agencies

HOW TO READ A CASE CITATION

Generally, court decisions can be located in case reporters at law school or governmental law libraries. Some cases can also be located on the Internet through legal websites or official court websites.

Each case summary contains the citation, or legal reference, to the full text of the case. The diagram below illustrates how to read a case citation.

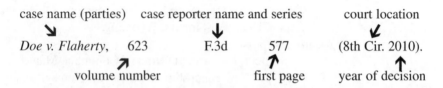

Some cases may have two or three reporter names such as U.S. Supreme Court cases and cases reported in regional case reporters as well as state case reporters. For example, a U.S. Supreme Court case usually contains three case reporter citations.

first reporter   third reporter

Gratz v. Bollinger, 539 U.S. 244, 123 S.Ct. 2411, 156 L.Ed.2d 257 (2003).

second reporter

The citations are still read in the same manner as if only one citation has been listed.

Occasionally, a case may contain a citation which does not reference a case reporter. For example, a citation may contain a reference such as:

case name   year of decision   first page   year of decision

Saxon v. Chapman, No. 266077, 2006 WL 1237036 (Mich. Ct. App. 2006).

court file number   WESTLAW[1]   court location

The court file number indicates the specific number assigned to a case by the particular court system deciding the case. In our example, the Michigan Court of Appeals has assigned the case of *Saxon v. Chapman* the case number of

---

[1]WESTLAW® is a computerized database of court cases available for a fee.

"No. 266077" which will serve as the reference number for the case and any matter relating to the case. Locating a case on the Internet generally requires either the case name and date of the decision, and/or the court file number.

Below, we have listed the full names of the regional reporters. As mentioned previously, many states have individual state reporters. The names of those reporters may be obtained from a reference law librarian.

P.   **Pacific Reporter**
Alaska, Arizona, California, Colorado, Hawaii, Idaho, Kansas, Montana, Nevada, New Mexico, Oklahoma, Oregon, Utah, Washington, Wyoming

A.   **Atlantic Reporter**
Connecticut, Delaware, District of Columbia, Maine, Maryland, New Hampshire, New Jersey, Pennsylvania, Rhode Island, Vermont

N.E.   **Northeastern Reporter**
Illinois, Indiana, Massachusetts, New York, Ohio

N.W.   **Northwestern Reporter**
Iowa, Michigan, Minnesota, Nebraska, North Dakota, South Dakota, Wisconsin

So.   **Southern Reporter**
Alabama, Florida, Louisiana, Mississippi

S.E.   **Southeastern Reporter**
Georgia, North Carolina, South Carolina, Virginia, West Virginia

S.W.   **Southwestern Reporter**
Arkansas, Kentucky, Missouri, Tennessee, Texas

F.   **Federal Reporter**
The thirteen federal judicial circuits courts of appeals decisions.

F.Supp.   **Federal Supplement**
The thirteen federal judicial circuits district court decisions. *See, The Judicial System, p. 615* for specific state circuits.

Fed.Appx.   **Federal Appendix**
Contains unpublished decisions of the U.S. Circuit Courts of Appeal.

U.S.   **United States Reports**
S.Ct.   **Supreme Court Reporter** > U.S. Supreme Court Decisions
L.Ed.   **Lawyers' Edition**

GLOSSARY

Age Discrimination in Employment Act (ADEA) - The ADEA, 29 U.S.C. § 621 *et seq.*, is part of the Fair Labor Standards Act. It prohibits discrimination against persons who are at least 40 years old, and applies to employers that have 20 or more employees and that affect interstate commerce.

Americans with Disabilities Act (ADA) - The ADA, 42 U.S.C. § 12101 *et seq.*, went into effect on July 26, 1992. Among other things, it prohibits discrimination against a qualified individual with a disability because of that person's disability with respect to job application procedures, the hiring, advancement or discharge of employees, employee compensation, job training, and other terms, conditions and privileges of employment.

Bona fide - Latin term meaning "good faith." Generally used to note a party's lack of bad intent or fraudulent purpose.

Class Action Suit - Federal Rule of Civil Procedure 23 allows members of a class to sue as representatives on behalf of the whole class provided that the class is so large that joinder of all parties is impractical, there are questions of law or fact common to the class, the claims or defenses of the representatives are typical of the claims or defenses of the class, and the representative parties will adequately protect the interests of the class. In addition, there must be some danger of inconsistent verdicts or adjudications if the class action were prosecuted as separate actions. Most states also allow class actions under the same or similar circumstances.

Collateral Estoppel - Also known as issue preclusion. The idea that once an issue has been litigated, it may not be re-tried. Similar to the doctrine of *Res Judicata* (see below).

Due Process Clause - The clauses of the Fifth and Fourteenth Amendments to the Constitution which guarantee the citizens of the United States "due process of law" (see below). The Fifth Amendment's Due Process Clause applies to the federal government, and the Fourteenth Amendment's Due Process Clause applies to the states.

Due Process of Law - The idea of "fair play" in the government's application of law to its citizens, guaranteed by the Fifth and Fourteenth Amendments. Substantive due process is just plain *fairness*, and procedural due process is accorded when the government utilizes adequate procedural safeguards for the protection of an individual's liberty or property interests.

Education for All Handicapped Children Act (EAHCA) - [see Individuals with Disabilities Education Act (IDEA).]

Education of the Handicapped Act (EHA) - [see Individuals with Disabilities Education Act (IDEA).]

Employee Retirement Income Security Act (ERISA) - Federal legislation which sets uniform standards for employee pension benefit plans and employee welfare benefit plans. It is codified at 29 U.S.C. § 1001 *et seq.*

Enjoin - (see Injunction).

Equal Pay Act - Federal legislation which is part of the Fair Labor Standards Act. It applies to wage discrimination which is based on gender. For race discrimination, employees paid unequally must utilize Title VII or 42 U.S.C. § 1981. Unlike many labor statutes, there is no minimum number of employees necessary to invoke the act's protection.

Equal Protection Clause - The clause of the Fourteenth Amendment which prohibits a state from denying any person within its jurisdiction equal protection of its laws. Also, the Due Process Clause of the Fifth Amendment which pertains to the federal government. This has been interpreted by the Supreme Court to grant equal protection even though there is no explicit grant in the Constitution.

Establishment Clause - The clause of the First Amendment which prohibits Congress from making "any law respecting an establishment of religion." This clause has been interpreted as creating a "wall of separation" between church and state. The test frequently used to determine whether government action violates the Establishment Clause, referred to as the *Lemon* test, asks whether the action has a secular purpose, whether its primary effect promotes or inhibits religion, and whether it requires excessive entanglement between church and state.

Fair Labor Standards Act (FLSA) - Federal legislation which mandates the payment of minimum wages and overtime compensation to covered employees. The overtime provisions require employers to pay at least time-and-one-half to employees who work more than 40 hours per week.

Federal Tort Claims Act - Federal legislation which determines the circumstances under which the United States waives its sovereign immunity (see below) and agrees to be sued in court for money damages. The government retains its immunity in cases of intentional torts committed by its employees or agents, and where the tort is the result of a "discretionary function" of a federal employee or agency. Many states have similar acts.

42 U.S.C. §§ 1981, 1983 - Section 1983 of the federal Civil Rights Act prohibits any person acting under color of state law from depriving any other person of rights protected by the Constitution or by federal laws. A vast majority of lawsuits claiming constitutional violations are brought under Section 1983. Section 1981 provides that all persons enjoy the same right to make and enforce contracts as "white citizens." Section 1981 applies to employment contracts. Further, unlike Section 1983, Section 1981 applies even to private actors. It is not limited to those acting under color of state law. These sections do not apply to the federal government, though the government may be sued directly under the Constitution for any violations.

Free Exercise Clause - The clause of the First Amendment which prohibits Congress from interfering with citizens' rights to the free exercise of their religion. Through the Fourteenth Amendment, it has also been made applicable to the states and their sub-entities. The Supreme Court has held that laws of general applicability which have an incidental effect on persons' free exercise rights are not violative of the Free Exercise Clause.

Handicapped Children's Protection Act (HPCA) - (see also Individuals with Disabilities Education Act (IDEA).) The HPCA, enacted as an amendment to the EHA, provides for the payment of attorneys' fees to a prevailing parent or guardian in a lawsuit brought under the EHA (and the IDEA).

Hearing Officer - Also known as an administrative law judge. The hearing officer decides disputes that arise *at the administrative level*, and has the power to administer oaths, take testimony, rule on evidentiary questions, and make determinations of fact.

Incorporation Doctrine - By its own terms, the Bill of Rights applies only to the federal government. The Incorporation Doctrine states that the Fourteenth Amendment makes the Bill of Rights applicable to the states.

Individualized Educational Program (IEP) - The IEP is designed to give children with disabilities a free, appropriate education. It is updated annually, with the participation of the child's parents or guardian.

Individuals with Disabilities Education Act (IDEA) - Also known as the Education of the Handicapped Act (EHA), the Education for All Handicapped Children Act (EAHCA), and the Handicapped Children's Protection Act (HPCA). Originally enacted as the EHA, the IDEA is the federal legislation which provides for the free, appropriate education of all children with disabilities.

Injunction - An equitable remedy (see Remedies) wherein a court orders a party to do or refrain from doing some particular action.

Jurisdiction - The power of a court to determine cases and controversies. The Supreme Court's jurisdiction extends to cases arising under the Constitution and under federal law. Federal courts have the power to hear cases where there is diversity of citizenship or where a federal question is involved.

Mainstreaming - Part of what is required for a free appropriate education is that each child with a disability be educated in the "least restrictive environment." To the extent that disabled children are educated with nondisabled children in regular education classes, those children are being mainstreamed.

National Labor Relations Act (NLRA) - Federal legislation which guarantees to employees the right to form and participate in labor organizations. It prohibits employers from interfering with employees in the exercise of their rights under the NLRA.

Negligence per se - Negligence on its face. Usually, the violation of an ordinance or statute will be treated as negligence per se because no careful person would have been guilty of it.

Occupational Safety and Health Act - Federal legislation which requires employers to provide a safe workplace. Employers have both general and specific duties under the act. The general duty is to provide a workplace which is free from recognized hazards that are likely to result in serious physical harm. The specific duty is to conform to the health and safety standards promulgated by the Secretary of Labor.

Overbroad - A government action is overbroad if, in an attempt to alleviate a specific evil, it impermissibly prohibits or chills a protected action. For example, attempting to deal with street litter by prohibiting the distribution of leaflets or handbills.

Placement - A special education student's placement must be appropriate (as well as responsive to the particular child's needs). Under the IDEA's "stay-put" provision, school officials may not remove a special education child from his or her "then current placement" over the parents' objections until the completion of administrative or judicial review proceedings.

Preemption Doctrine - Doctrine which states that when federal and state law attempt to regulate the same subject matter, federal law prevents the state law from operating. Based on the Supremacy Clause of Article VI, Clause 2, of the Constitution.

Prior Restraint - Restraining a publication before it is distributed. In general, constitutional law doctrine prohibits government from exercising prior restraint.

Rehabilitation Act - Section 504 of the Rehabilitation Act prohibits employers who receive federal financial assistance from discriminating against otherwise qualified individuals with handicaps solely because of their handicaps. An otherwise qualified individual is one who can perform the "essential functions" of the job with "reasonable accomodation."

Related Services - As part of the free, appropriate education due to children with disabilities, school districts may have to provide related services such as transportation, physical and occupational therapy, and medical services which are for diagnostic or evaluative purposes relating to education.

Remand - The act of an appellate court in returning a case to the court from which it came for further action.

Remedies - There are two general categories of remedies, or relief: legal remedies, which consist of money damages, and equitable remedies, which consist of a court mandate that a specific action be prohibited or required. For example, a claim for compensatory and punitive damages seeks a legal remedy; a claim for an injunction seeks an equitable remedy. Equitable remedies are generally unavailable unless legal remedies are inadequate to address the harm.

Res Judicata - The judicial notion that a claim or action may not be tried twice or re-litigated, or that all causes of action arising out of the same set of operative facts should be tried at one time. Also known as claim preclusion.

Section 1981 & Section 1983 - (see 42 U.S.C. §§ 1981, 1983).

Sovereign Immunity - The idea that the government cannot be sued without its consent. It stems from the English notion that the "King could do no wrong." This immunity from suit has been abrogated in most states and by the federal government through legislative acts known as "tort claims acts."

Standing - The judicial doctrine which states that in order to maintain a lawsuit a party must have some real interest at stake in the outcome of the trial.

Statute of Limitations - A statute of limitation provides the time period in which a specific cause of action may be brought.

Summary Judgment - Also referred to as pretrial judgment. Similar to a dismissal. Where there is no genuine issue as to any material fact and all that remains is a question of law, a judge can rule in favor of one party or the other. In general, summary judgment is used to dispose of claims which do not support a legally recognized claim.

Supremacy Clause - Clause in Article VI of the Constitution which states that federal legislation is the supreme law of the land. This clause is used to support the Preemption Doctrine (see above).

Title IX, Education Admendments of 1972 - A federal law that prohibits sex discrimination and exclusion from participation in any educational program on the basis of sex by any program or activity receiving federal funding.

Title VII, Civil Rights Act of 1964 (Title VII) - Title VII prohibits discrimination in employment based upon race, color, sex, national origin, or religion. It applies to any employer having fifteen or more employees. Under Title VII, where an employer intentionally discriminates, employees may obtain money damages unless the claim is for race discrimination. For those claims, monetary relief is available under 42 U.S.C. § 1981.

U.S. Equal Employment Opportunity Commission (EEOC) - The EEOC is the government entity which is empowered to enforce Title VII (see above) through investigation and/or lawsuits. Private individuals alleging discrimination must pursue administrative remedies within the EEOC before they are allowed to file suit under Title VII.

Vacate - The act of annulling the judgment of a court either by an appellate court or by the court itself. The Supreme Court will generally vacate a lower court's judgment without deciding the case itself, and remand the case to the lower court for further consideration in light of some recent controlling decision.

Void-for-Vagueness Doctrine - A judicial doctrine based on the Fourteenth Amendment's Due Process Clause. In order for a law which regulates speech, or any criminal statute, to pass muster under the doctrine, the law must make clear what actions are prohibited or made criminal. Under the principles of the Due Process Clause, people of average intelligence should not have to guess at the meaning of a law.

Writ of Certiorari - The device used by the Supreme Court to transfer cases from the appellate court's docket to its own. Since the Supreme Court's appellate jurisdiction is largely discretionary, it need only issue such a writ when it desires to rule in the case.